The Horned Whale
or
An Morvil Kornek

Jeremy Schanche

The Invertebrate Press

First published in ebook form by The Invertebrate Press, 2016.

This paperback edition published by The Invertebrate Press, 2024.

Copyright © Jeremy Schanche, 2016, 2024.

All rights reserved by the author.

ISBN: 978-0-9934909-0-3

The Janetta Stone was originally published in serial form in The Limpet, 2009 – 2011. The Limpet can be found at savetheholyheadland.blogspot.com

The Kramvil was originally published in serial form as The Journal of Elias Gillpington, in The Caterpillar, 2011 – 2015. The magazine has also featured several of the poems found in this book. The Caterpillar (and The Caterpillar Dub) can be found at yecaterpillar.blogspot.com

All editions mentioned, including those available at the above blogs, are covered by this copyright notice and may not be reproduced for financial gain, in any form whatsoever without the written permission of the author.

All illustrations are the work of the author and are subject to these same copyright protections.

Contents

THE JANETTA STONE   9

THE KRAMVIL   61

POEMS   405

GHOST-HULK OF A PHANTOM   425

GERLYVRYNN KERNOUAC / CORNISH

GLOSSARY   511

INTERNATIONAL GLOSSARY   515

to the people

THE JANETTA STONE

Chapter One

A fog had swept in from the sea bringing fresh, damp air and the smell of the ocean. I wandered through this briny air all along the promenade, lost in thoughts of the sea and underwater fish types.

It was good to be outside. I'd found the office a bit limited and constricting lately. 'The Limpet' was one of those local papers that was small, old-fashioned and fiercely independent – much like its editor, Brennigenn Pennskrifer. It's not that I didn't like the old geezer, it's just that his concept of 'editorial parameters' was just a wee bit narrower than mine. I wanted to expose local government corruption, police brutality, custody deaths, the Chinese slave labour camps that flood the West with cheap goods… issues that *mattered*. Brennigenn always listened sympathetically and agreed that the world was a terrible place but that *our* job was to report only the events that occurred locally, in the far-flung western tip of Britain's toe, whether they be dog-shows, cricket-matches or pasty-suppers.

Besides, we did get an interesting story once in a while, like the case of 'Old Janner', a self-styled, latter-day prospector and tinner who had just announced his claim to the mineral rights of Battery Rocks. This would have been passed over as mere eccentricity but for one thing. The multinational Royale Group had recently unveiled their extremely controversial plan to build a massive hotel and apartment complex *right on the beach* at Battery Rocks. This had annoyed a lot of people. Admittedly it was a small and insignificant beach, surrounded by rocky outcrops and largely overlooked. But it had a certain wild beauty to it, as a playground for snakelockses and seals – and to destroy a Cornish beach in the name of attracting tourists seemed a pretty crass idea to most people in the town, so the sudden emergence of Old Janner as the 'rightful claimant' of the area caused a smile to ripple through the town.

The whole business had a slightly abstract quality about it that was mystifying and archaic. Our medieval Cornish legal system was still alive in the twenty first century and it seemed that this 'Janner' character was using Stannary law to assert his rights. Sounded like a good Local Interest story – just the kind of thing old Pennskrifer liked.

A wave burst over the prom and spattered puddles of frothy brine at my feet. Gulls were skrawking and the light was failing – I decided to head back to the office. Climbing the stairs to the fifth floor I heard the incessant ringing of a telephone. The light was murky and greenish coming through the skylights. I looked into my desk. There was a paper bag with half a saffron bun in it – stale. I put some coffee on to reheat. Just then the rain started in earnest – a fog had swept in from the sea. The room felt like an aquarium – the light was thick and gelatinous. I noticed ticker-tape spilling onto the floor. I checked the teleprinter and found the following wire…

    To: Pat Vulgata
    Re: Battery Rocks
Get yourself down there tonight at 7.00 to meet 'old Janner' – he's agreed to talk to us. Good luck! Brennigenn

Hhhmmmm… I mused – good old Brennigenn, laconic as ever. I liked the idea of meeting this old miner though, I was curious to see what lay below his talk of tin and copper and seams of mineral wealth. I feasted on stale bun rehydrated with coffee and headed down to Battery Rocks.

I found Old Janner waiting on the rocks, standing gaunt as a jynnji against the darkling sky – he was staring out to sea. A barrel of strength in his overcoat, he exuded a glow of health. His age was indeterminate, his face rounded and open. We greeted each other and I started to ask him a few questions.

"So, I understand that you've claimed this area of beach and rocks for your mineral ventures, is that right Janner?"

"That's right Pat, rocks and beach, and an area of sea-bed too. It was when I was walking on the beach down there, found some fine pieces of cassiterite I did – that's tin-ore, that is – and I thought to meself 'J, here's my chance'. I 'bounded' the area and wrote a letter to Truro, all legal and proper, telling the Stannary authorities that I was registering a claim and I intended to start work directly."

"And how do you 'bound' an area of sea-bed?" I asked him.

"Ah well, that was easy! I just went out in me little boat and dropped a few rocks overboard at the two seaward corners of my bounds. Marking the corners with stones – that's what we was doing long before the Black Prince come along and wrote it up into a law-code. Some of these old traditions, see, they lie at the very *roots* of mining."

"You must have looked into all this in some depth…"

"Well, it's a deep subject, i'n'it? Deep as Dolcoath! Ha ha." Old Janner seemed to be rooted in the rocks and earth and his laugh came from deep inside him, like the mineral, booming voice of the earth.

"And have you had experience of mining before now?"

"Oh yes, I've had some experience here and there." He gazed off into the misty distance. "In the old days, we used to say 'when it's not farming time it's mining time'. Most people would have their own little patch of land, and when all the planting was done we'd go back to the 'bal' or the stream-workings till it was harvest time. It's a good land to work. What more could 'e want? Beautiful blue sky above, an ocean that rolls at our feet and a good bit of pasture-land and what have you. Underneath the land lies wealth, if you can find it and dig it out – tin, copper, lead, wolframite, gold…. Oh yes… many a day I've spent down there Pat, it's another world, I can tell 'e! You know sometimes I'd be working a level on my own. I'd stop to eat me kroust – we usually blew out the candles at kroust to save wax. All alone – just me and whatever wallows in the tewlwolow. Sometimes I thought I could hear the tapping of a little pick, like a spriggan working away in the gloomy half-light. You know, sometimes you're working away and the candle gutters and spits, it goes quiet, you can hear the sea booming and something like, it's a funny thing to try to put into words, but anyway, it's like a feeling that the rock all around you feels like a good place, that's the only way I can put 'n, it feels right to be working away there, where the old ones worked before, inside the land. 'Cause you know Pat, land ain't just something on a piece of paper, or a word in a book. It's one thing to walk across it, on a sunny, rainy or windy day, but to be *inside* the land, the granite that supports the land – that's a deep feeling, my friend. After so long underground it becomes another home for you and you're happy there. Not that mining's one long picnic, I can tell 'e!" A shadow flickered over his face, as if he was recalling some past sorrow.

"It must be a tough life," I agreed, feeling like I was stating the obvious.

"You get used to it – it's a living and anyway, it keeps the rain off your head. Look, we didn't use to *make* money so much as dig it up, you see. Mineral *is* money. Our word *moenek* means mineral. Everything's just what people agree it is, mostly. People always wanted our tin so we always dug it up and sold it to 'em. Then, after so, so long, something caved in, the market subsided and our ancient industry just frizzled out like a spent candle on a winter's night. Well, that was a terrible shock to we, I can tell 'e, it was hard for us to understand, still is. Anyway, contrary to what most people think, mining never really died – it just went underground. Not buried, more like withdrawn into itself like the sap of a tree in winter, waiting for the spring to bloom, and bloom it will. You must surely have wandered alone across the high moors under a hunter's moon, following ancient trackways and recalling ancient memories as the world slumbers and the wind shrieks around your ears like a seething hellion spending its last vain breath in an eldritch wail of despair. Have you never seen lights around the old stacks and engine houses then, strange lights, and heard the song of pick and shovel a-tappin' and a-scrapin' away for all the devil, eh? Come on boy! Don't bother denying it, we all have. So yes, mining is tough, but losing it was tougher. The spirit flickers, it might wane but it will not die out. It lives on unseen, as spirits do, of course."

"Well, the spirit certainly seems to live on in *you,* Janner," I smiled. He was gazing out to sea again, darkness was falling all around us.

"Well," said Janner, "anyone who wants to get a taste of the miner's life should take an underground tour – there's still a couple of old mines here in Cornwall that are open to the public. You pay your ten bob and they lead you all round the adits and round about. You can see where the old-time miners, men and boys laboured away for generations, hundreds of years of history, right there in the rocks!"

"Sounds well worth a visit."

"Like visiting mines, do 'e?" asked Janner suddenly with a little glint in his eye. "Well, step this way Pat, and I'll show 'e round mine!"

We walked over the rocks and down onto a strip of shingle. After glancing around furtively once or twice, he produced from his pocket a tiny wicker-work basket crudely covered in leather. He let me examine it for a couple of seconds, then, much to my surprise he flung it into the water.

"Will you look at the state of the *wall?*" he suddenly shouted with such violence that I spun round, alarmed – and found myself examining the neglected pointing of the pier. "Come on boy." Now he was striding towards the water's edge; I followed and was stunned to see floating a couple of feet away from us, a coracle that exactly resembled the little basket. My mind was racing now and I suddenly realised that my heart was beating very fast. "Don't worry skipper," said Janner, divining my mind, and something about the flavour of his broad grin assured me that I really didn't have to worry. I thought to myself wryly that I needed to get out of the office more often and have the odd adventure before middle-age condemned me to some grey hell of dullhood. Get away from the ridiculous clicking of the 'Go-Getter' Gestetner machine that reeks of purple ink; the 'wire' machine that seems to flicker inside its bakelite casing with rogue flashes of miniature lightning and of course, that preposterously raucous and irregular photocopier. Anyway, like I said, it was time for an out of office experience….. I really was day-dreaming again. Janner guided me patiently towards the little boat and we embarked without getting too wet, which surprised me. If I'd tried to do it on my own, I'd have probably fallen in.

With ease, the Captain of this funny vessel paddled towards the open sea. "You weren't kidding about claiming a bit of sea, then?" I ventured. Janner chuckled quietly. Then, clearing his throat, he seemed to take on the air of a museum guide showing wide-eyed children the skeleton of a megatherium. "This is the rannvor," he announced. "I used to do a lot of diving round here in the old days." The sea was glossy black slopping at the gunwales of our Celtic saint-basket. Glinting and reflecting were gleams of running silver light, flashing and flowing together in universal flux. A sense of quiet happiness descended and the atmosphere felt charged with a calm sparkling vibrancy. Black sea-water under the twinkling stars, vague patches of deeper blue in the murk. Were we really just a few yards from Penzance? Suddenly the shore I'd just left and the world it borders and everything that goes with it seemed ineffably remote like the half-recalled dream of a sunny morning in childhood, the falling of a single beech leaf.

"Now, let's have a little light on things" – and Janner was striking a match and lighting a stub of candle. He produced two hats of compressed felt, with lumps of clay on the brims. "Here, like this," he said, sticking a candle into one of the lumps of clay and putting on the strange headgear. I did likewise. "Nice bit of stars tonight though?" he said as he flicked the burning match into the black sea. It flew through the air leaving a miniature trail of smoke like a stricken Messerschmidt. I looked up at the firmament. Wondrys, truly wondrous. The stars were swimming along with the glinting mackerels and skates below. I looked down. I didn't remember seeing a little wooden pontoon rising out of the dark water before... Not much bigger than a kitchen table, fashioned of battered sea-timbers, a trap door in the centre. We tethered up the boat and stepped aboard the weird island.

For just a moment, when my foot I did place on the old oaken deck, I thought I could hear the sound of singing, distant singing. The impression was very brief, yet quite vivid. I had a sense of the presence of many singers, strong young singers and old ones, working together in the yellow candle-light a long time ago. The voices were pure and totally natural – sometimes lapsing into what seemed like a few bars of call and response before soaring off into layers of hearty and cheerful harmony that seemed to shine like an underground light. "Easy now, 's a bit slynk, y' know." My foot was sliding on the deck, but Jan caught my arm. "Sorry, squire, guess me mind was wandering," I apologized. He didn't seem to mind, but simply fumbled in his pocket and produced a large metallic key. Then I noticed that the trap door was secured by a large padlock that was countersunk into the surface. This seemed to be wrought from the same stuff as the key – top grade Cornish tin… Janner opened the padlock and went to lift the trap. "Here, give us a hand, will you?"

Chapter Two

"Wait a minute" said Janner, suddenly changing his mind. He paused, then pointed at the sparkling moonlight glittering on the dark waves. "Do you see that?" he asked. "Yes." "Do you know what it is?" "What do you mean, Janner?" He didn't take his eyes off the water, but slowly pointed again – "Do you know what it is?" he asked again, in what seemed like exactly the same tone. "No," I said. He paused again. The sound of sploshing waves sounded rather nice and although it was an odd place to be at night it did have a certain wild beauty and peacefulness about it. The odd question he had asked had faded from my mind and I was quite happily absorbed in watching the dark little mountainous waves dancing and breaking and dancing anew. I'd never really looked up close at the surface of the sea at night before I s'pose, and suddenly I realised that I'd been missing out on something kind of beautiful, in a wild and vaguely unsafe sort of way.

"Come on greenhorn!" he guffawed loudly and I started chuckling and the mystery fizzled into laughter. After a moment we both looked towards the great ring of tin at the centre of the old wooden trap-door. "Here, give us a hand will you?"

Our combined efforts soon had the trap-door up and I followed my companion into the pit. It was only the effects of cold that had me shivering, my wet clothes clung to me with a nauseating embrace and I confess it an effort to control the shudders that threatened to overwhelm my frame. The iron ladder to which I clung offered no scintilla of warmth to my magpie hands as we descended. I recall an impression of damp walls of granite, rusty looking and composed of many textures – the next thing I knew we had reached the floor of the initial shaft and I now followed Janner along a tunnel – I cannot say in what direction it led, but it continued straight for a couple of minutes, always through unpropped granite, and soon we were standing in front of a low wooden door. Janner produced another key and we stepped in.

I almost laughed aloud in surprise to see the comfortable chamber that had been hewn from the rock – a subterranean dwelling of style. It was rounded, without corners, and seemed to recede into the distance. Jan lit various candles and a clearer picture emerged. I immediately noticed bookshelves, a large collection of tools, ropes, all manner of gear, numerous sea-trunks and a small galley area. Some archaic portraits of mining ancestor types graced the walls. "Right, let's get you kitted up then" said Jan and threw down on the table a set of mining clothes, a hunk of bread and some cheese. "I'll be back in a minute when I've got the beam-engine going." The door closed. I looked around in amazement. In the ceiling was a small extraction shaft for the stale air – this place was immaculate! I donned the miner's garb and attacked the victuals. *This was more like it! No more splashing around in the ocean of everyday boredom, darkness and confusion.* Mining seemed to offer a release from so much of what was wrong up above. But mining for what? And to where? The centre of the Earth? Or the very bowels of Hell? OK – take a deep breath, get used to the novel situation, don't let it go to the head... My scattered musings were interrupted by the intrusion of a vague thumping, chugging noise, more felt than heard. The old man must have that *beam-engine* of his going. It must do a pretty good job, to stop this whole place being flooded by the sea – wait a minute though, it wasn't even running till we got here... this struck me as odd. The door opened and Jan ducked through. "There's much to explain to 'e Pat, but we'll do it as we go along." That seemed fair enough. We ate together in silence for a while and Janner made some coffee. "Ever been underground before, Pat?" asked my companion. "Only if you count the tube," I replied with a smile. "Hmmm, that's like a kind of goldmine I suppose – for the ticket-company!" quipped the old one.

After these refreshments we left the Kroust Hut, as Jan seemed to call it, and he led the way along what he called the Top Adit, another monument to some very strong men, whose pigells and visgeys had gnawed their relentless way through this rock like a philosopher chewing through the flimsy arguments of a bunch of sophists. Here and there were little niches in the rock wall, some held old candle stumps and were bearded with ancient wax drippings. There was a lingering smell. A bit like earth, a bit like rock, somewhat damp and very subtly stale, though without offending the nostrils – something like the smell of a stone when you dig it up. I was to become very familiar with this ambient osmosis in the time to come, the time that I had just entered, unbeknowingly, when I walked out of that stuffy old office and decided to see just what this crazy old geezer was up to. I'm so glad I made that choice. How was I to guess what wonders would lie awaiting beneath the overburthen of daily dust and quotidian clods; what mysteries lurked under the crust, the patina of the Earth. All my life I'd lived 'topside' like a man asleep, never once thinking about what *was* the ground that supported my questing restless feet. And now, because I had gone for the adventurous option and decided that rather than rejecting him as a colourful but perhaps time-wasting fool; because I had approached Mr Janner with an open mind, he was now giving me the incredible privilege of a tour round his subterrain.

I was glad to be warm again and enlivened by the food. My attention was on the rock walls around me, their changing faces, all the hues and grades of granite were gradually being unearthed and revealed to me. In fact, there was something quite hypnotic about walking along this old adit of his, like motorway driving, part of your mind switches off, and another part can switch on. Janner's footsteps kept up a rhythmic and unvaried pulse ahead of me, our twin candles guttering and flickering and emanating magic paintings from their kysten liwyow skeusek (their shadowy box of paints.)

I was definitely settling into the experience and starting to feel at home. This took me back to a remark the old man had made earlier, something about being safe inside the rocks. I felt like I was starting to get it, even though I was conscious of being a novice, a novelty-taster, compared to one who had worked long and dangerous years down here. Still, I felt more than content; I was excited, *enthusiastic* for the journey to the centre of the mine. It did start to occur to me that we'd been walking for a good few minutes now, we must have covered several hundred yards, how long had he been working at this place? Was it just him – had he had help? Were these workings ancient or modern? Nothing seemed clear. Anyway, on reflection I decided not to worry about it – hadn't Mr J said that he'd explain things in due course? I felt that I would trust to his words. So far he had certainly not let me down in any way. Besides, curiosity was the far strongest force at work, and this, combining with the sheer joy of adventure – rare food for a small-time West Country journalist such as I – was enough to make me grin like the Cheshire Cat.

Finally, after several more minutes of speculative trudging along the adit, Janner broke the silence. "Now I do have a promise from my friend Mr Treviddick to help sort out the tren for me, but he had to rush up to London where some gentlemen up there wanted him to burrow a road-way under their River Thames for 'em. 'Course he couldn't afford to turn down a chance like that so 'e's off to Blighty to strike it rich by mining out a few English pockets HA HA HA ha ha!" "What, so this pal of yours, is he working on the Docklands project or something like that?" I asked. "Some such grand scheme" said Jan, perhaps slightly disapproving of tunnelling that was not aimed at tin. "Anyway, Ricky's got an 'andsome design for a new engine for the tren, but till he gets back to *our* country, we'll just have to make do with this…" and as he finished speaking we arrived at the start of a metalled railway track, only a couple of feet wide. Sitting on the track was a bizarre vehicle wrought from dark iron and tarred wood with brass bolts. The front was just an open wooden box with a couple of old crates serving as seats, this section was followed by a large enclosed box, and behind that was one of those V-shaped ore-car things that tip up. I noticed a small deposit of extremely fine grade tin-ore lining the mineral ore-car, and some glittering bits of crystal collected in the front of the truck-thing. "You said you liked tube trains I believe, Mr Vulgata?" said Jan with a twinkle in his eye as he made an ushering gesture with his hand towards the extraordinary ersatz Hadean chariot. "What makes it go, Jan?" I couldn't help asking. "Well, OK, first, you and me start pushing until we're up to a good run; then we jump on, and, that's it!" I must not have looked too thrilled. He frowned for a second then burst out laughing once more, in which I joined again. Then we pushed that crate of preposterous Orphic propulsion out of its inertia until its iron wheels were clicking over the rails with a regular ticking.

It wasn't actually going *that* fast when Janner said "OK, watch what I do, then copy," and breaking into a little sprint he drew alongside the front of the tren and jumped in. I did likewise. He reserved the forward seat for me – as the *skrifer* I was there to observe and record and now I was in a supreme position to do both.

There must have been a very slight decline to the angle of the floor, because no sooner had we got on board than the little tren started to gather momentum.

I must have dozed off, it had been quite an eventful evening, what with the coracle and going underground and everything. On a normal evening I'd probably be nodding off by now, with some early Duke Ellington and some endless Russian novel I was always trying to read, but it always had the unfortunate effect of putting me out. Anyway, you know how a train journey can make you sleepy… I was in the hypnagogic trance, flitting like a swallow in the rare aether that separates sleepfulness from wakefulness. A rich broth of imagery betided my mind and left a telling flotsam. I recall seeing Aethiopians hollowing out Coptic temples. Inspired by their faith, they worked down into the rocks, the cool deep bedrock of Africa. They sculpted altars and holy images and forms. Other temples opened up – Hindu masterpieces of mystery initiation and yogic white heat – Petra seemed very familiar to me, I was right up in one of

the high galleries, looking down on the street below, full
of life, people and camels passing, shouts and laughter and
donkeys braying – a thriving city in the rock. The mesas of
the American Southwest gave way to an indescribably ancient
city now swallowed by the Sea of Japan. The catacombs of
Rome seemed to connect to the silver mines of Laurium and
the quarries of Syracuse. Then I seemed to dream of a vast
tube-system, linking the London Underground with the New
York Subway, Paris Metro, and all the other metropolitans and
centrals all over this earth. Then I awoke and we were still
trundling forward in Janner's old tren under the rannvor, that
dark and glistening sea that swelled and swirled around the
weird wooden island just off Battery Rocks – the pit-head of
this most extraordinary bal.

Janner was humming a little air to himself, the tren
seemed to be slowing down. "Now, let's have a little look
down here, shall we?" says he, just as the tren pulled up
to a halt. We stepped out of the curious vehicle and started
walking up a side tunnel. There was no rail going along this
bit of tunnel and it was a bit narrower and lower than the
previous one. The walls too, seemed to have been hewed out
much more crudely and irregularly. Then I was amazed to
see a strange image of a horse, daubed onto the rock wall.
I was about to comment on this, but at that moment Jan
pointed forward and I noticed a curious light, well, at least,
a light, coming from ahead of us. We walked on. The light
grew gradually brighter, warmer and *what was that sound?* I
thought I heard a tapping, ringing noise in the distance – are
there some *other* miners down here? Then we were out of the
tunnel and back in the daylight, the terra firma, the world of
sunshine and clouds and breezes blowing across green fields
that run down to the sea.

Before I could begin to speculate on how we had got
there, I noticed a group of people in the distance, huddled
around a fire, and again that tapping noise. "Don't worry,"
says Janner, and we strode towards the strange group. We
walked down a wooded incline into a lovely valley. There
were a couple of very rough looking huts on the flat land
of the valley bottom and everyone seemed to be watching a

tail of smoke emerging from some kind of earth oven. Then I noticed the hammering – actually it stopped when *they* noticed *us*.

For a couple of seconds I confess to feeling a little nervous – but then such a shout of joy went up as they seemed to recognize Janner, that any forebodings instantly evaporated. There was a lot of embracing and babble in a strange language and general excitement. Then they showed us how they broke up the ore with their hammers, they kept pointing at the little stream, indicating it as their ore-source. Next they showed how the crushed ore was put into clay molds and pushed into the earthen furnace with a pole. Finally they took us to one of the huts and showed us some axe-heads, sickle blades and spear points they'd fashioned for themselves, as well as a quantity of big irregular-shaped ingots that seemed to be their 'savings' perhaps, or goods to be traded with some other group. Considering these people were barefoot and dressed in skins, they certainly seemed to be catching up with the technological side of life. I could have *sworn* one of them looked a tiny bit like Janner… anyway, they made us most welcome and luckily weren't offended when I declined their food, just burst out laughing. They seemed so *innocent* and friendly, despite the nascent armaments factory they had going. Theirs was a *very* direct and open way of communicating, devoid of the usual layers of false sophistication and distrust inherent in most 'civilized' conversation. I could understand their mumbo-jumbo now, and it was starting to *make sense!*

Sadly we had to leave almost as soon as we'd got there, they escorted us back up to the cave mouth – I couldn't help noticing another curious painting above the cave – another horse, only this one was sporting a *wheel* under each hoof… hmmmm. With much laughter and shouting the wild folk bade us their goodbyes and old Janner and I set off down the tunnel again, past the other horse and back to the main adit where our Orphic Victorian chariot lurked locomotive.

Chapter Three

My companion ushered me towards the unworldly vehicle once again and we boarded in silence. The only sound was a faraway gentle dripping, drops of water falling onto granite in dark cavernous obscurity, dripping. The faint, stale, earthy smell of the rocks filled the atmosphere. We trundled slowly forth, to who knows where. Monotonous walls of damp granite flickering in the light of our candles, yard after yard, minute after long subterranean minute. The hardness of the granite was unrelieved by any softening influence, as you usually experience in the upper world, the world we'd left behind. No trees, no gorse or bracken-clad hills rippling in the wind. No rolling seas, no skies, no blue.

"Time for a bit of kroust, eh?" Mr Janner's remark brought me out of my reverie and I looked back to see that he was opening a small wooden hatchway in the boxlike middle section of the tren. After reaching inside he produced two large pasties and passed one to me. It was hot. I looked at him in amazement, but he merely took a large bite out of his pasty with a look of joyful concentration in his twinkling eyes. I followed his example. The pie was more tasty than I can possibly describe. From the first bite of crust it kept getting tastier until in was gone and, not realizing how hungry I'd become, I was now pleasantly full. The kroust had seemed to contain all the goodness of the country, the wheat of the crust had taken me back to the sunny fields near Zennor where the stooks of corn had dried in the wind and summer sun as the downvor ocean rolled in inky writhing energy-display at the foot of the cliffs. I thought I heard larks singing and bees buzzing drowsily as butterflies whirled by in flickers of flight. A lizard played in the sunshine of the granite wall and the distant tolling of the church bell was punctuated by the clattering hooves of a pony. "You know Janner, that has got to be the nicest pasty I've ever had," I told him. He passed me a mug of hot tea. "It's always best when you use you own ingredients," he replied. "One day I'll have to show you my place up at Chyannor, got a nice little losowegi, little veg-garden up there." "That would be great – but I wondered, when you're down here for long periods, don't you ever miss the upper world, you know, the sky and everything?" "Hang on," he replied mysteriously, and once again he was searching around in that *box* of his. This time he produced a Davy Safety Lamp, lit it and handed it to me. He showed me how it fixed onto the front of the tren. "Now, let me show you something," he said.

The tren rumbled on at a gentle speed. The adit seemed to open out now as if we were going through a cavern of some kind. The walls were increasingly coated with an unearthly green moss, that seemed to glow slightly with its own preternatural luminosity. There were great rounded boulders heaped up in the cavern, all coated with the iridescent carpet of golden green, resembling ranges of tiny green rolling hills. "Now," said Janner, "there's some green hills to keep you going for a while!" I couldn't help laughing. The track snaked around all these velvety green boulders – a miniature landscape! After a while, the cavern walls seemed to open out even more, and to take on a darker, more violet bluish hue. "And there's a nice blue sky for you" said Janner. The cobalt blue was startlingly refreshing to the eye and did actually remind me of a summer sky in the heat of noon. As we travelled on, the 'sky' of blue rock darkened into black. Tiny crystals of quartz now started occurring in the upper reaches of the cavern – stars to glitter in our rocky underground sky. The microcosmic illusion was completed by a small rivulet running alongside the tracks like a slow-worm and reflecting the glittering 'stars' on its shiny skin. I caught his eye and laughed with delight – this place really had everything!

Janner's face became serious. "How are you with depths?" he asked. "Depths?" I echoed, but as curiosity tried to frame the question that was welling up in my mind, it suddenly became clear what he meant by 'depths'. The cavern opened out – in all directions, including down! The rails seemed to be suspended in space by a flimsy superstructure of spars, runners and tubular poles, teetering out into an abyss, as the floor fell away into a gaping void. The little rivulet suddenly became a miniature Niagara as it leapt down the staggering rock-face in silver splashing tongues, disappearing into the gloom below. The walls receded to left and right, and the roof rose above; our flickering lights could not reach a surface to illuminate and for a while we rushed onwards in a great empty dark space, dizzyingly vast. We seemed to be picking up speed all of a sudden too. I started to get glimpses of the cave's floor, far far below us. Large pools of water seemed to shimmer down there, but quickly the vehicle passed on. I would be glad when we were back in a normal tunnel again, I wasn't happy on this 'bridge of hairs'. Our truck was going so fast it was starting to vibrate, and the structure supporting the tracks was rattling and clacking back. The Davy lamp was blazing up in the stream of oxygen and the wind was rushing in our ears. The place seemed to be more and more filled with light – the walls were closing back in again and the gulph below us was being filled with rising boulders – terra firma at last! A few more moments and everything seemed back to 'normal' and we were back in the regular adit. Janner laughed and clapped me on the shoulder – I laughed with relief.

The next moment we were in a moderate sized cavern, or chamber, surrounded by the activity of men and machines, operations were in progress. Now the singing welled up as the miners harmonized on an old song. Then I noticed the 'mills', wooden chutes that spewed out streams of ore into the waiting trucks, each pushed away by a miner. Others were swinging hammers at spikes and chewing into the seam wherever they found it. There was sawing too, as a team of carpenters cut wood to various sizes. All the miners seemed to favour an archaic look, with drooping moustaches and hobnail boots. They shared our unworldly headgear of felt hat-caps, with the lump of clay stuck on the brim, to hold the candles. The ore-trucks were being emptied into the cage of a herculean skip and hoisted aloft. A bell was rung and the burden went soaring up, followed by the high-pitched whirring of the winding gear. The men would return the empty trucks, or 'trams' to the face and the whole operation would start another round. Picks eked out the mineral, grain by grain. Long handled shovels threw it into the cars. The work-song seemed to keep stopping and starting. Then our tren came to a halt and several of the miners recognized Janner and called out and waved to him. They clustered round our vehicle and it seemed that we were all shaking hands at the same time, and Janner was introducing me to the gang.

"How are 'e getting on Davy?" asked Janner of an old miner with sideburns and a barrel chest. "We've found a beauty of a lode, and we're digging like there was no tomorrow. Keeps getting wider as we go. The whole village is starting to prosper!" "Glad to hear it, boy!"

Janner produced a tall earthenware jar of ale and a large loaf of bread and some other provisions and placed them on a flat stone by the side of the tracks. The miners were pleased with the offering and threw shovelfuls of glittering mineral into the ore-compartment of our tren. We said our goodbyes and the miners pushed the tren back into motion. Our course lay in front of us. We must follow these tracks of steel through the growanek wonderland under the ground, under the sea, the dark, glittering rannvor.

Chapter Four

We seemed to have been in the underworld for an eternity. Boring along inside the rocky skin of the Earth like a death-watch beetle in an oak panel… It seemed like an incredibly long time since I'd walked down the stairs of the Invertebrate Press Office, back in Penzance, eager to set out on this assignment with the enigmatic mineralist of Battery Rocks. Anyway, all that was a long time ago now, and I seemed to be starting to get 'tunnel-fever' from being underground too long. The diet of tea and pasties was OK and certainly Mr Janner could not have been kinder, I could hardly imagine a more pleasant companion, yet I felt a slight yearning for the upper world.

"Now, if you go to Helston, you'll notice that Wendron Street runs down into Coinagehall Street – why do you think that is?" asked Janner out of the blue, as the little tren clattered along its cold steel rails. I had to admit I did not know the answer to this riddle. "Well," said the old one, "Wendron is the tin country, you see, and Helston is the coinage town. Now, in Cornish, *moenek* means mineral, and this is where the English get their word *money* from, and no doubt *mint* too. So, back in the old days, our mineral wealth, our tin, was taken from Wendron down to Helston, via Wendron Street, to the Coinage Hall street, where we made a *mint* and 'coined it in', as they say. *Mineral, mining, money*, they all mean the same thing you see, well at least round here they do," said Janner with a sweep of his hand. Although he gesticulated at bare rock walls, I felt that he was speaking for Cornwall as a whole.

"I hear Wendron has quite an ancient history of mining," I said. "Older than you'd think, old chap," replied Janner with a twinkle in his eye. "There's a mention of a mine down Wendron way in an old paper from 1856, which talks about 'Old Man's Workings'. It talks of a certain Wheal Roots, and describes it as "an ancient tin mine," and that was in 1856!" Something about that name, 'Wheal Roots' struck a deep chord within me – I don't know why, sometimes you just feel a strong reaction to something you encounter, and that name seemed to stir my imagination in a way I could neither fathom nor explain, yet it sent a thrill through me like a half-forgotten dream.

"We'll be there soon, at Wheal Roots," announced Janner calmly. "But I thought...." my voice trailed off into nothing. I was mystified. "You mean we're nearly at *Wendron?*" I asked in astonishment. "Oh yes," he replied with a smile, "nearly back to the Roots!"

I had somehow assumed we were still in the West Country, in Penwith, in some outlying section of Janner's Mine at Battery Rocks. I had no idea we had travelled all these subterranean miles, but Old Janner seemed to take it all as perfectly normal, all this tube-training around under Cornwall's hills and fields in our crazy little mineral chariot. Arne Sacknussen would have been right at home with me and the old one on this Central Line to Cornwall's mineral treasury.

The Davy lamp cast a flickering white glow on the granite walls and occasional timber stulls, as the Cornish miners call their props when they have occasion to use them.

The experience of spending so much time *inside* the earth seemed to lend me a curious strength and give a sharpness to reality. Hanging out on the *surface* of the earth all the time tends to make you forget the titanic realms below your feet. People travelling in ships at sea don't usually spend too much time contemplating the oceanic depths beneath them, but they are there none the less. When you travel by road or across country in Cornwall, you are constantly passing over deep subterranean passages, countless miles of dark, flooded, abandoned mine workings lurk beneath your wheels as you zoom along the surface. How often do people remember the generations of men and boys who worked so hard down there, for so little reward? From what Janner had shown me so far, it seemed that a lot of these workings had never been completely abandoned, and there seemed to be some twilight miners, moonlighters and bootleggers, who either made periodic forays underground, or else had simply moved down there hundreds of years ago, and never come back up – it seemed hardly possible, but then I was learning not to rush too quickly into concepts of what might or might not be possible in a world such as this.

There seemed to be a pounding of hammers coming from far above, as if there was a gang working a stope, or perhaps we were passing underneath some gigantic forge. After a while we passed a series of sumps, where strange wooden pipes were drawing the water upwards to some kind of pumping system. There was a clanking noise of chains coming from above, and the slurping and sloshing noises of water in motion. "Got to keep the Cober out, boy!" said Janner. The Cober, I seemed to recall, was the river that wound through that part of the country, taking its name from the Cornish word for copper.

"Right then, old chap, how about a breath of fresh air?" quoth my companion. "Air, did you say, air, Janner – as in breezes and clouds, are you talking about *up there?*" Janner just smiled and lolled back his head, his eyes pointing upwards with a deal more eloquence than a forefinger could have achieved. Jan took his pick and held it over the side of the tren with both hands. A cloud of sparks flew up with a grinding noise and soon we were at an unaccustomed halt. The stillness and quiet were pregnant and loaded. The sense of possibility oozed out of the rock walls, roof and floor that formed our world. A drip, drip, dripping soon met the ear, and then, in the distance the rattle and clunk of the primitive Cober-Extractor. Janner rummaged in the box-compartment of our unlikely chariot and seemed to be packing provisions – I glimpsed the ubiquitous pasties, and the old stoneware tea-bottle, as well as some other small objects that I could not make out properly. We set off on foot. After speeding along on wheels for so long, it felt good to move my legs, and also I could now examine the walls of the adit a little more thoroughly. I was amazed to observe that the surfaces were totally covered in pick-marks, telling me that this section of the *Minotaurean* realm was chipped out by hand. "Oh yes," said the old one, divining my mind once more, "our work was a lot harder before Tommy, I mean, before Mr Epsley brought in the black powder." "When was that then, Jan?" I asked. "Oh, let's see now, that'd be the mid-summer of '89." I must have looked at him very quizzically – I always got that strange, dislocated feeling that he was back there in history, like he had a personal connection with the past. "What, 1889, or…" my voice trailed off into the uncertainty that was flooding into my chest. "No Pat, that would be in the year of our Lord 1689, the year after our good bishop was put in the tower. There was a notion going about that we'd use it to help ease the king's door open, but it didn't come to that in the end."

A squeaking noise from above stole my attention, and I looked up to see that we were under a shaft and that a crude basket was descending towards us, the squeak evidently coming from the whim far above. The old tinner gestured theatrically towards the crumpled basket at our feet, and like Victorian balloonists we climbed in and rose. The basket started spinning dizzyingly round and round, turning our balloon ride into a fairground experience. At one point I stupidly looked down – seeing the tren look small enough to put in my pocket did not do much to make me feel secure. The next moment though we had risen up through a trap door and grimy strong hands were grabbing the rope and swinging us onto a sturdy platform of hewn timber.

"How are ye, Mr Janner, and who's the gentleman with ye? But first, let's take a morsel!" The unbroken voice came from a lad of twelve or thirteen years, he seemed to be the leader of several others, by dint of being the oldest. His arms were well developed by labour though his face spoke of childhood and an innocent heartiness. "Bless you Joseph, I am well. This is Mr Vulgata, we'll call him Patrick, he works for one of them fancy newspapers out West. He's come to have the 'grand tour' of our world, ain't you Pat?" They looked at each other, then at me, and for some reason, we all started laughing.

A few moments later, as we wiped the crazy tears of humour from our various blinking eyes, we sat together and broke the ceremonial crusts. One particularly ragged boy hesitated for the briefest moment, but he was literally shoved forward into the circle of feasting stennors. "Come on Eddy-Boy, have you forgotten 'All for One and One for All?'" It seemed these fellas had their own home-made social security system going and by the time Eddy had taken his place in the circle there was a very generous pile of food in front of him; in fact, he soon had more than any of the others! "And there's a crumb to take home for your kin," said Janner, placing two extremely large 'plate-hanger' pasties, a pound of cheddar and a bottle of cream in front of the ragged Eddy-Boy. "We all give what we can, see?" explained another young subterranean. "Old Ed's got a nose for tin, see? We reckon his eyes can burrow through granite like a cannonball through snow and see the seams hiding inside. You never fail us, do you Eddy-lad?" Eddy murmured some incomprehensible syllables through his pasty-mouth and the laughter started up again.

"I saw a newspaper once, it showed King George coming back from the wars a-France." The food had loosened everyone's tongues and set their shrewd minds at work. "What's the name of your newspaper, Mr Patrick?" asked one. "Oh, it's, er, The Limpet." I felt vaguely embarrassed to be merely digging out words and stories while these guys were dealing with much tougher material. "Limpets? We d' boil 'em up with calf-tongues and cream for broth," said one. "I heered that in 'zance they d' go a-merry-making and throw the old krogens against the gentlefolks' doors!" offered another. "Well, you know boys," said I, "a lot of doors in Penzance slam shut tight when they see *this* Limpet coming!" This time the laughter was unstoppable and it rang through the levels like fire in a chimney.

Soon the young miners trooped off along another tunnel, after many 'Fare ye wells' and 'God be with 'e's'. Jan and I took our own way along yet another passage, this one considerably narrower than any I had yet seen; it led to another wooden platform, at the bottom of another shaft. Protruding up from this platform was a great angled beam, near on two foot square, but angled acutely up a-tilt. Janner grabbed a line running along-side this mighty old beam and gave it a tug. A bell sounded dimly from far above, and the beam dipped down, only to rise again. "Jump on!" he said, and leapt onto a tiny plank that was set into the beam. I followed him onto a lower plank and soon we were soaring gracefully upwards, through a floor above. "Jump off!" he commanded. By this time I was feeling a long way from the Press Office, and had learned to trust instantly to Janner when he spoke with seriousness. Standing on that second platform, we watched the crude lifting engine descend again. As it rose back up, we simply stepped back on and rose up another level. "What do you call this thing?" I asked Jan. "Man-Engine," he replied. I lost counting after about twenty-eight such junctions – these mines go deeper than you think! At last we reached the top of the man-engine and met its keeper - a moustachioed gaffer wearing a Sou'-Wester that sported a flickering stub of candle packed into the now familiar blob of clay, and tall sea-boots that spoke of another life. "Mornin' Mr J, how are e' farin'?" His face cracked into the familiar grin that all these fellas seemed to put on with such ease. "Hallo Mr Morgan, not too close to the wind, I'll venture!" replied my guide with warmth. "I trust your voyage up the pole was to your liking, sir" twinkled the old fella. Our laughter was drowned out by the sound of a stream of atal hitting the floor, echoing down some distant level in this Cretan wonderland of ours. "Long as we all net a profit!" quipped Mr Morgan as he pulled out a clay pipe and a tiny paper twist of rough black baccy. "Touch pipe?" he asked. We both declined, Janner because it was 'not his way', and me because I didn't want to puke my guts up in front of the guys. I've never been the macho type, and it's always good to try and keep your dignity… "I trust Mary is well" asked J. "Back to her girlish health, thanks be to The Lord – and our good Wendron Parish fresh air…" "Glad to hear it Morgowles," said Jan – this was really too much and the two of them laughed like a pair of jellies. "Morgan, you look smugger than an earl, a right smug earl!" said Jan, and we were off down another level – or rather, along it, I should say.

Sometimes, when you look back, things are not so clear. Think of those warm hazy childhood impressions, those distant things of the self, those – were they dreams? Are they memories? What's a memory? Sometimes you catch yourself musing, imagining, or lost in capricious Zephyr's breath, floating in mind's rich and tasty soup.

I recall stopping to put a new candle on me hat-cap, I think Mr J had walked on a few paces. I do clearly remember being thrilled to see a great wall of sparkling crystal in front of me, and stopping to examine it closer. The logical explanation is that I either swooned for some reason or other; *or,* well, I'm not sure what really. Anyway, I was looking over the surface of the crystalline wall, then I was checking-out individual crystals with greater curiosity. I was musing that I'd entered into a fantastical world and was being curiously influenced by its characters. It was as if I was having a moment's objective distant and detached view of the whole situation. I felt like a modern, 'logical-scientific' type, an *empiricist* for God's sake! What in the Jimminy was I doing in *this* deeply weird scenario? Suddenly the fundamental *strangeness* of it all seemed to flood into my realisation and overwhelm my mind. I couldn't stop laughing, but this time it was not the comradely laugh I'd so recently shared with these twilight miners, but rather the hilarity of a mind suddenly aware of its joyful awakeness.

And then, gradually the mirth turned to a sombre tranquillity as I was drawn in by the beauty of the glittering crystals before me. My eyes were entranced by what they beheld. Looking deeper and ever deeper, I seemed to pass *through* the translucent shining wall, and into – beyond.

Then I saw many things. I saw a trireme moored in a lake. I saw a train of ponies plodding onwards through fog and misty rain, over the high moors of Kernow. Guided by a couple of hooded figures with long poles, they forwarded a burthen of cassiterite, the raw rock from which the tin is processed. I saw some wild and savage people wading in the Cober, which flowed through the bottom of a deep wooded valley. They were scooping up trout from a wickerwork trap in the deepest part of the river's stream, overhung with dripping willows and damp ferns. One of the wild-haired folk dived under the water and came up holding a black rock. A blue-black rock that glittered. He held it up to the sun and they all let out a wild cry of joy. Then I was in some other, some far-off land, a land of warmth and sun. Pine trees and loud insects singing. A boy and a girl, different, a different race. They were playing with toys, toys not like the ones we have now. The girl had a doll, but fashioned of terracotta and wrapped in archaic garb, rounded and fat like a Russian doll. The boy had a horse, angular and thin, stylized; kind of Mycenaean or maybe Minoan. The horse was not ordinary though, its hooves had wheels, large, spoked wheels. Then I was back in Cornwall, in fact I was near Ictys, Myctis, St.Michael's Mount. But of course the forest was still there, just like you've heard about, and in the distance I could see the Pen Sans with its little Chapel, its fisherfolk, and its cluster of smoky huts and little dwellings. In a small glade near to Myctis was a large gathering of people. Some were obviously holiday-makers, or visitors of some kind, as they had much darker skins and spoke with very strange accents. Their dress was markedly different too – woven textiles in geometric patterns, sandals of skilfully worked leather, and all of them festooned in bronze clasps and brooches. That's something they seemed to have in common, for the Kernish people there were also wearing bronze ornaments and pins in their hair, but their clothes were rougher and more rustic. Quite a few of them were clad in cattle-skins, with the long hair still on them matted and raw. Then I seemed to see a man in black, black waistcoat and trousers, and gold watch-chain across his breast. He was trundling along a wooden wheel-barrow, a pipe jutting out of his teeth. His barrow, with its creaking wooden wheel, carried the crumpled and broken body of a miner, moaning softly. He advanced down an evening street, small and muddy. He knocked at a door. It opened. A woman, frozen horrified on her doorstep before the cry welled up in her and broke through the streets. The sparkle of tiny cassiterite crystals, some black, some so clear and shining and I was back in that clearing again, glancing up at the Mount, to see no castle there. There was rather a different structure, smaller, yet more noble. Looking down, I saw one of the foreigners or traders was scratching something in the sand. Shapes – triangles… geometry! He seemed to be giving a demonstration of some intellectual point to a group of intently watching locals. Some of the Cornish tribesmen and women were scratching things onto little tablets of fresh clay with little styli. This activity took place a little way away from where the tin was actually being bartered. A rudimentary harp was passed back and forth between a local and a Greek, or whatever those sea-travellers were, and songs of many hues and tones were brought to life. This soon replaced the angular studies as the main feature of interest between the beech and alder trees. "Bardhonieth" said one. "Muzikee" said the other. They bowed heads to each other, and then seemed to want to try and say each others words, which led to more laughter and banter.

The clink of metal took my ear and I strolled through the trees to see that the stannary business was in full swing. The holiday-makers had amphorae of dark wine and olives in oil and some carved pieces of white and creamy marble. These were spread out on rich cloths of beautiful design. The Kornewek had food, lots of food, some fine jewellery and woven cloaks, and of course the tin, the great magnet that brings them all here.

This time though the tin was worked and smelted into

ingots of various sizes, again the familiar knuckle shapes. The trading seemed to be highly ritualized and formalized at one minute, then again a spontaneous play with many handclaps, and ingots slammed down with abandon the next.

More crystals swam before me and now I saw the land of the foreigners – a workshop or factory of some kind. A couple of workmen, more plainly dressed than the traders, but with similar features and the same dark hair; they were chipping away at a mold with hammers. The mold came away bit by bit to reveal, gradually, a life-sized human figure of startling beauty, a young warrior, or rather, a charioteer, whose face shone with life and wisdom. A stunning masterpiece worthy of the highest temple. The master rushed out from an adjoining shack, caught sight of the charioteer and stopped dead in his tracks, tears welling in his eyes. In the corner of the yard were various heaps of raw materials, ores, piles of fire-wood, heavy tools and an old shield. Water was held in several amphorae, one of which could have concealed a large man. Next to the great jar was a neat stack of ingots, astralogoi – knuckles of Cornish tin.

Then I felt a hand on my shoulder, shaking me. "Up you get, Pat" – it was Janner come back to find me. I was lying on the floor of the level, grit stuck to my forehead. As I brushed if off it glittered crystal. "You alright boy?" I rubbed my head again, my felt hat-cap lay next to me, the candle extinguished. "Yeah, I think so," I answered the old one, "musta hit me head…. thoughtless of me." "We all do it sooner or later," said Jan. "Reckon you got off lightly – you'll live! In situations like this there's only one thing to do." Janner reached inside his coat and produced a couple of pasties and equilibrium was soon restored. "I seem to remember promising you a breath of air, that should clear your head." My guide motioned me to my feet and we started to walking. More damp, streaked wall of granite, sometimes rusty looking, sometimes grey; less crystalline than before and always that earthy smell. With candles re-lit and firmly stuck in their clay lumps on our headgear, the shadows danced and reared over us. I made a conscious effort to concentrate and avoid any more accidents – I'd had enough blows to the head for one day, besides, I wanted to retain my clarity so I could write up my notes later for the paper. The paper! That little attic office back in Penzance seemed very far away now, not so much in mileage, but in experience. A voyage up the Congo could hardly have taken me to a more different world than the one Janner was showing me. I still had my notepad and a couple of pens stashed in my hatband – I'd managed to jot down some of the main points as we went along and would expand on these whenever I got the chance. I was beginning to wonder what the editor would make of my report – old Pennskrifer was pretty hard-boiled, and, let's face it, this stuff was going to read more like a phantasy than straight reportage – maybe he'd split the difference and put it in as a 'think-piece', that's probably what he'd do…. Let's face it, for all its devotion to accuracy and realism, the old 'Limpet' had pretty wide editorial parameters! My musings were brought to an end by an unfamiliar sensation – I could have sworn I felt a breath of *wind*… and then the presence of a couple of cobwebs told me we could not be far from the surface – you don't get those fellas below a couple of fathoms. Curiously, the idea of leaving the Minotaurean realm for the mundane one left me with a wistful nostalgia. I felt as if I was leaving all those characters behind me, all those archaic stennors, those unseen heroic breakers of rocks and the ground underground. Still, a change of scene is always interesting. But could the overworld compete with what I'd seen for sheer grandeur, mystery and adventure? I think Old Janner was slowly turning me into a troglodyte.

Emerging into the overworld was no disappointment. I'd forgotten the tenderness of the soft Cornish air, the grey light of a misty day, the sighing and soughing of leaves and the lonesome crawk of the solitary raven – I'd forgotten the lush living joys of the World that nurtured me and I'd forgotten the damp breath of drizzle on my face. One minute we were trudging along the adit-level, and the next we were emerging into the beyond, the above. The light of the overworld penetrated for a few yards into the mouth of the adit – I remember it had seemed to blaze so bright, but it was only the contrast, only the adjusting of the eyeballs to a once-familiar realm of radiance. Actually the day was overcast and the creaking of the great elms that greeted us in the rolling wind seemed to promise impending rain. It felt like late afternoon, dark birds circled overhead and there was moisture in the air. We brushed through the overhanging ferns damply and kicked aside the branches of gorse that had accumulated to clog the mouth of the old adit. It had a curiously abandoned air when looked at from outside.

Without a backward glance, Janner led on. We scrambled down a little slope and soon picked up a cart-track. "This is the Cober valley" said he as we passed thickets of dripping goat-willows and dense marshy lairs. The whole place had a most wild aspect to it, we could have been a long way from any civilization. You could actually see the mist, the droplets wafting around the air and tracing whirling forms before dissolving into ever-new patterns. The smells of the country were a great joy to me. Even in this damp marshy spot there were so many different flavours of nature, everything seemed so fresh, wild and pure. The willows were crusted and bearded with lichens and at their feet grew spiky swamp-grass and occasional tufts of eyles or sundews, those exotic carnivores that digest insects for a living. I thought of Edgar Allen Poe – he would have felt right at home here.

We followed a curving track uphill and soon an ancient church-tower loomed ahead out of the mist, flanked by a few cottages, some slated, some thatched. The council had been pretty slack about keeping up the roads around here, not a trace of tarmac to be seen! In fact, not even any signposts, just a granite milestone pointing the way to Helston, 2 ¼ miles. A gaggle of ragged urchins clattered along the cobbles, the laughing leader spinning a hoop with a little stick. The next moment they came pouring back, chasing a large white clacking goose and shrieking with laughter. The distant cow-call of a farm-hand was answered by a lowing of cattle. Hooves could be heard on a hidden winding lane, overhung with dripping foliage. Crows swirled cawing. A large fly buzzed loudly droning past my ear. Had time stood still, or merely melted away to reveal its honeycomb core? Weak spears of sunshine split pastel prisms through ripped pages of mist.

"Come! I'd like you to meet my aunt" said Janner, grasping me by the arm and leading me towards one of the archaic abodes lining the horse-hobbling road. Beams leaned at crazy angles. The window-glass was murky grey green and mottled, great broken bubbles crowned its panes. A babbling horde of hens emerged out of the yarji in a clucking convulsion. Pecking and clucking and looking for worms and scraps, they scurried out and scattered at our approach. A lazy hound opened one eye, glanced at us, scratched its ribs and fell back to slumber. This really was the most extraordinary place! Janner raised his fist to knock on the ill-fitting wooden door, but before his knuckles could knock the door creaked open, revealing the quizzical features of a time-blasted crone. Her once-young face was creased and re-creased into a map of life's journey. Grey locks burst from under a bonnet of worsted wool. A shriek of delight burst from her lips as she recognized her kin. "Why it's young master Jan of Chyannor!" she exclaimed in evident delight. "Yes aunt, it's me alright, and this is a good friend of mine, Mr Patrick Vulgata of Penzance!" "Come in, come in!" said the dame. "There's pies in the range and a good strong kettle of tay for us! Why this *is* a surprise! But how ever did you get here, all the way from the West Country?" "Oh, that was easy," Janner said catching my eye, "we just got the tube! Patrick, me boy, I'd like you to meet my aunt Dorothy." The crone held out a brown, work-worn parchment hand. "It's a great pleasure to meet you, aunt Dorothy," said I, and with that she ushered us over the granite threshold and into the cot.

Soon we were seated in front of the fire of turfs and gorse as the old lady fussed back and forth to the range and prepared the tea. "After we've wet our whistles we'll have those tatty-pies and spinach, but first let's have a look at that head of yourn." She took my head between the parchment hands and examined the wound. "You won't be needing this anymore" she said mysteriously as she retrieved a tiny piece of quartz crystal from the dried blood on my forehead and cast it into the fire where it fizzed and gave off a blaze of blueish light. "I expect you've already seen plenty down young Jan's pit." She looked me in the eye. Hers were eyes that were lit with the spark of intelligence and a deep understanding, a knowledge that comes not from books and fine theories, but rather from a long life on the land, gathering eggs, delivering calves and babies, turning the spinning wheel of the seasons time and again. She had no doubt seen a lot. "I'll dress that for you after we've eaten," and with that she ushered us to the table and we shared the meal together. An old brass lamp shone above the table, and as darkness gathered, rain started to spat against the windows. A horse neighed in a neighbouring paddock and a calm fell upon the village. I felt a profound drowsiness weighing upon my limbs – the old lady produced some jars of herbs and powdered roots and started to mix the medicine. She applied the paste to my temples. "You'd better take care when you're a-ramblin' round under the earth with that wild relation of mine" she said with a twinkle in her eye. "Many have come to good down there, and not a few come to grief too." I remembered the image of the young wife opening her cottage door to see the broken body of a miner in a wooden barrow, probably not an uncommon occurrence around here. "I reckon I'm pretty safe with Mr Janner," said I, "he seems to know the ropes." "He knows his trade well," said she with sincerity. "Now, how is that wound o' yourn coming along?" My head felt at ease, only the drowsiness was pulling me down. "It's a lot better, thanks to you aunt Dorothy" I said. "Good! Now, you must get some rest while this lad and I talk of the West Country and our kin. Take this candle and follow the stairs up to the right and God keep you safe through the night." Soon I was falling into a profound slumber, like sinking into a vat of feathers on a sunny afternoon.

    I'm sure my sleep was full of luminous bright dreams but on awakening I could recall none of them. The chirping of a thousand songbirds drove away the vapours of the night and the bright sunshine hurled its javelins through the tiny windows into the room. When I got downstairs Jan and Dorothy were just griddling some bannocks and brewing more tea. "I'm afraid Wendron can't quite match the delicacies of a fine city like Penzance," chirped the crone, "but we pride ourselves on never letting a guest go hungry!" "Why really Mrs Dorothy, you've been most kind and I shall certainly never forget the fine welcome you've given me," I said. Smiling, she refilled the tay-kettle. "And I gather that wild nephew of mine has more adventures planned for ye this morning!" We both turned and looked at Janner who was feeding twigs into the range. "Er, yes, boys will be boys y' know! But first, Aunt, we'll chop you a good load of logs and dig up some turnips for you. Then, when we've finished the chores, I'll take Mr Patrick here back down to Trenear; there's something I wish to show him there."

After a couple of hours work around the farmstead we took our leave of the old dame with many blessings for the folks in the West Country and many 'come back soons' and strode out for Trenear and Wheal Roots.

The morning seemed so fresh and new and a combination of old Aunt Dorothy's herbal poultice and the good sleep I'd enjoyed seemed to recharge me for new meanderings through Janner's beloved land of adventure. "No need to stick to the high road," says Janner, "we'll go through the fields." And with that we climbed a stile and headed into the rich pasturage. Glinting dew-drops caught the light of the late-morning sun like little jewels, showing all colours. Caterpillars crept along the herbage and wild flowers showed their fragile trumpets. The breeze caused the ashes and elms to whisper strange secrets to each other and skylarks laughed back to the wind, skitting through the clouds and turning tails to the lumpen ploughed fields of the Earth. As fine a day as any. Bees idled at their pollen duties, preferring to enjoy a chat in the balmy sun. Cloudscapes blurred and melted softly together, light blue, shade upon shade, ever transforming and evaporating into the arc above. Glinting beetles scuttled below, busy with insectivorous tasks exquisite and unnamed unto man. Leafs fluttered around. Rabbits scooted off in a big hurry back to their burrows and the screeing cry of the buzzard pierced the upper air as the old hawk spun circles of crystal air, ever searchful for meat morsels a-scurry below. The braying of an old donkey rolled through the morning air, toiling and tolling away on a summer's day. Drowsily a dragonfly buzzed, little crystal dinosaur, glinting and whirling diaphanous. The next field was much the same really, only being more sheltered by trees, the dew had been slower to dry, and it lined the carpet of gossamer like ten thousand miniature strings of pearls or diamonds waiting for little eyes to behold them. Reaching the end of this wonderful field, we took up a winding track that led downwards between hedges bursting with cow-parsley and rich, swampy vegetation. The emerald weeds towered over us and the path narrowed into a marshy and little-used path. More dragonflies appeared, buzzing and swarming around. Soon we were back in the thicket of goat-willows and sundews, pools of standing water swarmed with waterboatmen and other long-legged aquatic beetles. Methane painted rainbows of metallic hues on the pools of swamp-slime. Teeming with life under the sun, this place cannot have changed a bit in fifty thousand years. I had never felt more content. My companion had maintained a sober silence for some time, I think he too was affected by the strange primal beauty of the scene. At length we came to a primitive bridge over the Cober, a simple trunk of an alder tree that had been hewed flat on top by an adze. As we crossed the river, I glanced down into its swirling depths, through a yard of cool water to the sands and gravel below. The water looked so beautifully cool and clean, so tempting to jump right in and feel it washing over me. Minnows darted within and I saw three or four speckled trout glide like Zeppelins through the cool resplendent aqueous flow. I never wanted to see my office again. I was enthralled by the wild perfection of this original hidden swampland – how lucky I was to have taken this assignment and been shown these marvellous things – what a great guide and companion was Mr Janner – how could I ever repay him for all the things he had shown me?

We journeyed on through this atavistic realm, lost in blissful reverie. Swamp irises, skunk-cabbages, pools of duckweed like village-greens unfolded and ever the lichenous willows. What extraordinary peasants traversed this track as their quotidian highway? What noble roughshod feet tramped this trembling track through quaking bog and rotten log? What fair fortune brought my wandering feet to such a pass?

What squadrons of emerald frogs lived out their gleeful days under this secret canopy? What eloquent piping was heard here at night, under a gibbous and kwllkyn misty moon?

And what unearthly lights globular floated above these bogs and bayous under the shimmering glimmering sparkling stars of a fresh heaven? Who will ever know! The piping of marsh-beasts, the writhing of blood-worms, and the pronouncements of the scholastic heron – these were the truths of this place and I leave it to them to speak for it. As for me, I was honoured to be taken into such a realm and nestled in the breast of nature. To leave off from the highways of man's incessant stressing chatter, vain dreams and worries – I was grateful to be shown the wild kingdom in all its obscure and occult glory. Life was rich and infinitely dynamic and I was like a child on the first day of spring, laughing at the sheer profusion and explosive beauty of the World.

Light streamed in as the trees opened out to reveal a small meadow surrounded by elms. A buzzard that was basking in its centre languidly took wing and soared aloft into the sky. After the closeness of the swampland, this little green meadow felt like a miniature prairie kingdom. The long grass was still wet with glistening dew. The sun was rising now and so was the ground. We wandered on – Janner always seemed to know which way to go – and we followed a path through the field and up a gentle hill.

We ascended the wooded slope. "This is Gwyd Skeusek – the shadowy wood," said Jan. "Mostly elowenn ha skawennow-gwragh – the light can play tricks on your eyes here," he added mysteriously. It wasn't a particularly dark wood, but the branches of the elms and elders swayed in the breeze, creating a pattern of flickering light and shadow, like a natural stroboscope. The ubiquitous crows circled cawing overhead. Large granite outcrops protruded through the ground at intervals and moss and ferns softened the effect. I noticed Janner had been pretty quiet this morning, seeming sunk in thought's depths – why not? I saw no reason to question him, or break his reverie. As we climbed higher I caught the sound of muffled distant voices and percussive noises as of work.

As we rounded the shoulder of the hill, a strange sight greeted our eyes. In a spacious clearing stood a large, rounded stone, larger than a good-sized table. Swarming around and on top of the stone were more of those ancient tribesmen I had seemed to see before in my visions underground. Again they were of two different tribes, different races with distinctive costumes. The more numerous group were dressed mainly in skins and had matted hair. The others had a Mediterranean look about them and wore robes of some kind of flax or cotton-like material. I rubbed my forehead in disbelief, trying to take in what my eyes were showing me. My skin felt very smooth, must be the after-effects of old Auntie's poultice. As before, the people were not threatening and after a brief moment of mutual inspection the atmosphere seemed to relax and a pair of wild-looking children ran up to Janner and grasped his hands, leading him forward – I followed, fascinated at the scene before me. There was a hiving buzz of activity. People were scrambling over the monumental rock, and swarming all around it. Some were bringing wicker baskets full of stones of various sizes. These were being passed up to the people on top of the great stone who poured them into a series of bowl-shaped hollows, there must have been nearly twenty such mortar-holes. The wild folk then pounded the rock-filled hollows with large, pear-shaped rocks, like primitive pestles. They seemed to be crushing and grinding the smaller rocks into a gravel. I heard one of the Minoan types say the word 'kassiteros' – then I understood what was going on – it was cassiterite, tin-ore! Amazing how they could understand each other's language, though they were obviously from totally different cultures. But of course, how could they trade and interact without some form of mutual linguistic comprehension? My mind was racing, trying to fathom and grasp the scene before me. I remember actually rubbing my eyes in joyful amazed disbelief once or twice – and each time I did, I remembered the poultice, the bang on the head with the crystals and all the other strange and wonderful sights that I'd taken in over the last few days.

The people on top of the monumental grinding stone were passing the finely ground ore back down to those who waited below, and these took it to a little furnace very much like the one I'd seen before, when we met the 'tribe of the wheeled horse' all that time ago. Heaped next to the little furnace of rocks and clay were more of the astralogoi. Some of the wild looking youths were showing off by lifting them repeatedly over their heads; counting onen, deu, try, peswar, pymp, whegh, seyth, eth, naw, dek, unnek, deudhek, tredhek… One of the Achaeans was echoing the count in his own tongue – enna, dio, tria, tessera, pente, exi, efta, okto, enaya, dekka, endekka, dodekka, dekkatria… this produced much laughter. Next to them a serious looking 'wild-man', a Kernow, was making marks on a clay tablet. One of the Kernewes devised a great joke. Grabbing the cattle-skin cloaks off the backs of a couple of children, she started wrapping them around her legs in imitation of our trousers. This got everybody laughing outrageously and she repeated the pantomime several times. I suppose our mining suits must have looked as odd to them as their kilts and cloaks did to us. One of the children showed some curiosity about our headgear so Janner decided to give them a surprise. He took off his hat and placed it on his knee, to more laughter. Then, after holding up his hand as a sign, he produced flint and steel and lit his candle. Amazement was complete when he placed the illuminated hat-cap back on his head. The effect was outrageous – first a stunned silence, then a general hubbub of excitement. To enhance the effect I followed suit and lit up my own hat-candle. After the excitement had subsided a little I noticed two figures approaching. It was the Kernow 'skrifer', the scribe, accompanied by one of the Achaeans; their faces exuded a spontaneous nobility. The Cornish one nodded to Janner, who turned and pointed to me saying "skrifer". The two men met my gaze, as if searching my soul. "Come on," said Janner, "I think you'll find this pretty interesting Pat."

Chapter Five

We walked over to the great stone and round behind it where there was a hole in the ground. The two skrifers led the way and we descended some steps down, down into the subterrain, that realm that had become like a second world to me. The passage seemed to curl round to the right, following the contours of the great monumental rock where the tin was still being ground above. This stone was obviously like an ice-berg – nine tenths of it seemed to lie beneath the surface. Perhaps that is why I had heard it referred to as a Karrek Sans – a Holy Stone, joining the overworld with the underworld. The Kernewek and Achaean skrifers lit resinous pine-twigs from our hat-candles and by their combined light we could see some curious markings hewn into the side of the mighty granite boulder. At first there were just some fairly primitive looking pictographs – a rounded woman figure, some deer, the sun and stars, men with bows and arrows, some cattle, trees, a woman giving birth, a man with antlers and a fire. Then, as we followed the downward spiralling tunnel, it was as if I could see the genesis of language, of writing; from the first crude scratching, to some kind of evolving rudimentary form of alphabetic representation.

Next to the pictogram for *sun* were the Greek characters ἤλιος. The Hellenic scribe pointed and said "Ylios". Underneath were some obscure marks of a strange alphabet. The Kernewek scribe pointed to them and said "Howl". They looked at Janner. He pointed to the pictogram and said "Sun". Next the Achaean pointed to an eclisiastical-looking pictogram of a temple. The script below said ἐκκλησία. "Ekklisia" said the Greek. "Eglos" answered the Keltek skrifer indicating the word in his own script. "Church" said Janner – the word sounded odd. "Sowsnek" explained Janner, catching my eye, "you know, Saxonage". We followed the strange linguistic fougou as it spiralled into the dark Cornish earth, feeling its way round the vast rounded rock that seemed to be a cultural touch-stone, a key to so much human culture. Janner demonstrated a remarkably scholastic grasp of ancient Greek for an old Cornish miner; but then I've always found it dangerous to pigeon-hole people according to notions of class and background. He conversed with the Cornish and Achaean scribes with apparent ease. I struggled to keep up, but was rather out of my depth. Jan kindly interpreted for me, as we examined the ongoing series of glyphs and syllables etched into the side of that mighty hunk of granite. Luckily I had remembered the advice of my first editor back in the days when I worked for the Goonhilly Daily Gleaner – always keep pen and paper secreted within your hat! A good reporter must always have the wherewithal to take notes!

I was amazed to discover that our English word for *dream* is *oneiro* in Greek and *hunros* in Kernewek. The Greek *techne*, meaning fine or skilled, gives the Cornish *tekka*, lovely, and our English equivalent *technique*. The English *hour*, and Cornish *eur* come from the Greek *ora*, which in turn is from the Egyptian god of light, *Horus!* Hence also our word *aura*. Perhaps our *sunset* comes from the Egyptian god of darkness, Sett. Sunset in Kernewek is *howlsedhes*. The Mediterranean people came to Kernow because it was the tin territory. For them it was the *tenekes sterea* – in Kernewek *sten tir*. Word-order may differ but the sense shines through consistently. The others smiled at my frantic scribbling and note-taking – their superior memories seemed to be all the recording gear they needed. They'd left their clay tablets and styli up above. Some of the carved letters were caked with slimy mud. The Achaean skrifer swept them clean with his fingers, saying "skoupeezo" – I sweep. The Cornish skrifer looked at his dirty fingers and said "skubyon" – sweepings. Janner pointed out that while *gofalu* is Welsh for *mind*, *kefali* is Greek for *head*. By this time, my *kefali* was starting to spin a bit with all this unaccustomed intellectual work – just at the right moment the Greek scribe produced some curious pasties. Flaky pastry with an olive and white goats cheese filling – delicious! Then the Achaean produced a miniature amphora of curious drink. Janner took a sip and recognized it as gwin pinenn or pine-wine – the finest retsina I had tasted since I wandered on Olymbos, all those years ago.

We sat together, Cornish and Greek, in mutual fascination. The Achaean scribe leaned towards Janner with an inquisitive gesture – "Poios?" "He's asking *who* I am," Janner explained to me. "Janner," said the old miner, tapping his chest. Then he asked the same question in Cornish – "Pyw?" "Yianni" – replied the Greek with a smile – it seems they had the same name! This called for another libation or two. It soon developed into a game of Chinese whispers, with the Achaean and Keltek scribes comparing words, which Janner rendered into plain Anglikos, Sowsnek, Sassanach, Saxonage, English. The pine-wine was offered generously and Yianni was telling the original shaggy dog story. He was saying something about how if you got too metho – medhow – drunk – you will feel like a kyon – ky – dog, avrion – a-vorow – tomorrow and for olos – oll – all the meis – mis – month!

The time to say goodbye had come, and after fond wishes had been exchanged Janner and I set off down the level. Soon the familiar distant clanking noise returned; the old rag-and-chain pumping system for keeping the waters of the Cober out of Wheal Roots. Jan had told me that in days of yore, the river-valley had been much deeper, but it had gradually silted up. Possibly this was a result of substantial mining activity going on just up the valley towards Porkellis. Or maybe just thousands of tons of top-soil being washed down into a glacial valley? The quality of blue cassiterite was certainly very high. The lodes were also remarkably near the surface here at Wheal Roots, which was an obvious advantage. Come to think of it, it was only the invention of efficient steam-powered pumps which had opened up the possibility of mining to any great depth. "I hope these skeulyow, these ladders are still alright." I noticed a slight look of concern cross Janner's brow. The level we were following had led to an opening in the floor, about eight feet across with a ladder descending down what looked like a long way. I followed Janner over the edge and into the pit.

The ladders looked like they'd seen better days – perhaps the days of King George….. they were pinned to the granite walls of the shaft with wooden pegs. Luckily I had the presence of mind to just look at my hands gripping the rungs, and not to risk a curious look down. Better not to know how deep the drop might be. Better to just concentrate on climbing skilfully and not making a slip. We lowered ourselves rung by rung through a gigantic stope – a cavern hollowed out where the lode has been followed and extracted. There were some very aged looking wooden platforms where men had stood high up under the hanging-wall, as they called it, and fed the ore down to the trams below. But this was not the level that we wanted, and we were soon climbing through the floor and down again. There was water dripping, sometimes splashing us with icy drops. Janner's hat-candle projected my shadow against the walls of the shaft, turning me into a flickering giant, gliding over the archaic granite wall.

The shaft angled out at about 45 degrees and we slithered and slipped along, making many twists and turns. By this circuitous and labyrinthine route we arrived at last back at our faithful 'tren'. I was wondering how we would get the vehicle pointed back to Penzance, but Janner opened a small door in the box part of the tren and started turning a handle. A built-in jack underneath the middle of the tren soon raised it up and with a little push from the two of us, we spun the vehicle around. "Well Pat – let's give 'er a push and head back to the West Country." We turned our backs to West Saxony, or Wessex, as some call it, and were soon trundling back to the 'Shining Land', West Penwith. It was a long time since I'd heard the mordros booming surf and squinted at the dazzling rolling sea, stifek with squids rolling and jelloid smugairles squirming as cuttles cluster round and splintered waves splatter and shatter on sandy ground. A long time gone since I'd snaked my way through one of Penzance's notorious 'pease-pudding' fogs, those yellowish green vapours that descend on the town, casting a veil of mystery and dark wonder over the lichen-crusted granite of that eldritch and decaying sea-port. I wondered about my colleagues at the Invertebrate Press Office – what did they think had happened to me? Shame I couldn't wire them. In my mind's eye I saw great waves breaking over the prom, soaking committees of town-planners and corrupt concrete-merchants.

Like the wizard of Pengersick, I felt that I had a special eye that could see far-off and hidden things – I'd probably been underground too long – must keep a clear head. "Try this" said the Old One, handing me another of his enigmatic supply of hot pasties. This time he excelled himself – veg vindaloo! How did he always anticipate my wishes like that?

"There's more to the pasty than meets the eye" chuckled Janner as he handed me a mug of hot tea...

I might have drifted, lulled into sopor by the repetitive clacking of the train's steel wheels on the metallic tracking. I glimpsed more in that universal series – that tumultuous conglomeration of tunnels, adits, levels, winzes, catacombs and fougou-flumes. There was a Moscow underground railway platform, transformed into a war-time dormitory – packed with slumbering and dozing people sheltering from the German's incendiary blitz; there was a scene in the Inuit ice-tunnels of the cyclonic Aleutian Islands, replete with walrus tusk talismans and walfisch-oil lanthorn lights glimmering. A speleological tour of some of the great guano bat-dropping caves of Borneo leached into a scene from an Albanian lignite mine where dirty sulphurous brown coal is gnawed out by swarthy troglodyte-men driving dodgems underground. The braying of a mule in a Californian gold working, as it hauled its burthen of dirt towards the whim. The Viet Cong tunnels of Indochina morphed into the vast curve of a Swiss particle accelerator, luckily not operational. Then more familiar sights arose – trams full of Cornish copper ore being pushed along by sinuous men with moustaches, candles on their felt hat-caps. I seemed to see the walls of granite running like hot liquid in its original molten state. Matter in flux, stone liquified. Is this how worlds are born? Is this when gross matter runs like honey, seething with potentiality? Was it once like this for *our* World? Our ancient unconscious World – is it running aflux, a flow of universal possibility? Is it offering life, fresh, anew, ever-new?

I awoke from these strange vivid images and impressions to be greeted with the now-familiar sight of the granite walls rolling by with monotonous predictability. Sometimes the walls were stained with streaks of red, sometimes veins of dark rock decorated the passing walls – always the dank odour of dark, cavernous rock as we beetled along in the skin of the Earth. At one point I heard the distant sound of singing again – the bright shining harmonies and strong call and response – I think it was a chapel hymn. This was mixed with the metallic tapping of crow-bars, picks and hammers and the primal rumble of rock atal and rubble rolling down the chutes into the mineral trams. Occasionally we heard the muffled roar of a blast – I think Janner said we were under the region of Tregonning and Godolphin – a particularly rich skovenn or tin-ground.

"So, Janner," I asked him, "how did you get into this mining game then?" "Well", he says, looking around him at the granite rushing by, illuminated by the flickering Davy lamp, "back awhile I was thinking of going into the veg business, y'know, with me losowegi and all – you know, me garden up at Chyannor." "Well, it certainly produces some tasty food, I'll vouch for that!" I answered, gulping down the last bite of home-made pasti. "Good earth, a warm sun and plenty of fresh Cornish rain…" laughed Jan. "Thought I might plant up loads of spuds and maybe open meself a nice little chip-shop! But anyway, I looked into it and by the time we'd fed ourselves and all, there wasn't much to sell really. So, about the same time," he was always a bit vague about time, so I didn't press him with questions… "this cousin of mine got a job up at Wheal Fortune and said he could get me in there too. Well, I had a little think about it, and I thought to myself *'J – here's my chance!* It just seemed like *me!* Like the perfect thing for me… 'course lots of me family in the past had worked in the pol – the mines, and working up top too, so it seemed like a good job for a Cornish lad." "I see what you mean, Jan," I replied. "It's been amazing for me, seeing your world, your realm. You know, my normal work is usually pretty straightforward – reporting on local dog shows, interviewing life-saving dogs on Cornish beaches, writing the weekly column on local pasti-supper evenings at The Friends of the Cornish Pasti Society or the Penzance Village Green Preservation Society, ya know the kind of thing." "Ripping stuff indeed" rejoined Janner, "but don't you ever get sent out to report on *murders* and crimes and such?" "Well, ya know Janner, it's a bit more complicated when the murderers are wearing uniforms – I do do some Human Rights reporting, it's er, rather specialized work, letter writing mostly, punching away at the old jynn-skrifa, the telex and wire machines – ink all over the place and rattling keyboards, but, ya know, it's work that needs doing… It's not always local stuff, but it deals with crime alright-" "Damn right!" blurted Jan in a rare moment of ebullience "without Human Rights we might as well be beasts, herded around, fleeced and slaughtered like cattle!" I glanced up at this point, to see the level had opened right up and the rock-ceiling stood high above. Some blackened old timbers lurched up into the gloomy space above our heads. They were crusted with white mould and looked like they could collapse and disintegrate at any minute, crushing us with their rotten weight. The way their dark and sinister frame loomed over us at that moment seemed to embody the evil that Janner had referred to – the vile malice that can turn people's hearts to paths of evil, paths of ill to humanity. The moment passed and the tunnel seemed to become smaller and more friendly again, but the impression lingered in my mind and quickened my resolve to return to the ongoing struggle against the rising tide of conformity, tyranny and oppression. Fascinating as this subterranean mission had been, I seemed to remember that there were other things to do up there, above ground, in that other and everyday world. So much life and possibility seemed to wait up there for me – my girlfriend, Ella, back in the Shining Land, she'd be wondering when I'd be emerging from this land of Orpheus. My colleagues above in the bracken sunlit land, they'd be wanting me back from the country of Morpheus.

"So, what did you think of the Janetta Stone then?" asked the old one, but before my reeling mind could formulate a reply, he pulled a scrap of parchment from his pocket. "Here's another word we got from them old Greeks – *Bywnans* – our Cornish word for *Life*. It's from the Greek *Bios! – Life!* Oh yes, they got around, those Greeks" said Jan, "but then, so did we Cornish…" he chuckled his infectious laugh and I soon found myself joining in with his free-style mirth. I thought of the Cornish miners who had scattered across the World, to South Australia, Africa, Mexico, Peru, Minnesota and California – 'wherever there was a hole in the ground… you could be sure to find a Janner at the bottom of it, digging away like blue blazes…' In the American States, you could still find places that sold 'Genuine Cornish Pasties',

but they were strange, small, round, flaky pies, served with
noxious fizzy drinks and side orders of fries….. a kind of
continental de-evolution… oh well, perhaps they were better
than having no pasti at all….. I followed these musings, as
we trundled along through this 'Cretan maze' and a warm
sense of well-being crept over me, as in a youthful reverie on
a bright summer's day in the morning. My eye rested on the
small collection of glittering crystals at our feet in the front
part of our mineral chariot. How they glistened and glinted,
what delicate and enchanting hues, sparkles and scintilla they
emitted… What titanic forces of the newly-forming planet had
birthed these gems of pure translucence? And how curious
that they should lurk countless aeons, hidden from the sun's
howlyek glinting rays of warmth before finally being scooped
up by Old Janner and his unorthodox Orphean chariot! That
friend he had mentioned, that Treviddick fella certainly did a
good job – I wondered if he was one of the Cornish Men of
Steam… Though the front compartment was basic in design it
served us well enough. The middle, the 'box' section seemed
to be an ever-fruiting cornucopia of good things and the
V-tram at the back was ideally suited to the motivation and
raison d'etre of the whole expedition – the collection of fine
Cornish minerals, namely the excellent and far-famed deep
blue kassiteros, the tin-ore!

Chapter Six

Tin. Tin of Cornwall. Sten Kernewek. Fine stuff. Black
tin, white tin – crude, smelted or worked. Coating a billion
cans of beans, or blended into the bronze form of a Hellenic
masterpiece. To say that tin had made the Cornish who we
are would not be an empty figure of speech. Tin had been the
magnetizer, the lode-stone, the touch-stone that had drawn
wave after wave of invaders, long before the Keltic culture
had evolved and become dominant. Each successful incursion
of tin-prospectors from overseas had mixed their genes in the
Cornish gene-pol and helped to shape the people of today.
This process had spun out four thousand years and more, all
accompanied by the tap – tap – tapping of pick against stern

granite, and the close comradeship of the men who went underground to seek their bread.

Such musings flickered through my psyche as our ludicrous Orphic vehicle clatter-rattled its way back to old Pensanse. What a long, strange trope it's been. Still, life in this world is a pageant, so why not expect ye signs and wonders? Must it all be so prosaic as the modern culture, the cults of celebrity, media, consumerism, violence and technology? My whole time underground had constantly challenged my sleeping perception of what life could be – how it could be.

Some minutes back Janner had passed me a mug of tea and told me we only had a couple of miles to go before we were back at the Battery – even at our gentle pace a couple of subterranean miles would soon be achieved. I couldn't help wondering what I'd find when we got there. It had felt like a long time being 'shown around a bit of the old pol' by Jan, and although we couldn't have been gone all that long, events were moving pretty quickly up at grass.

Nothing particularly out of the ordinary happened on the final leg of our journey. There was just one point when we went past a side-tunnel, or level, when I glimpsed the faint glimmer of yellow candle-light flickering down to us and I distinctly heard a tiny snatch of music, the music of voices lifted in soaring harmonies, hearty and strong. It was just a little glimpse of the past, like you get sometimes.

The tren clattered on. Janner started to hum a little tune that sounded a bit like a mangled version of 'Trelawny' – the old one seemed to be in good spirits. "Not long now Pat – I 'spect you'll be glad to get back to that desk of yours… and your young lady, no doubt." "That's right Janner, if she'll forgive me for going underground for several days and not phoning – I've got a good excuse though – the signal's *terrible* down here." Janner smiled, "Yes, word of mouth seems to work best down here."

The thought of the Invertebrate Press Office seemed pretty prosaic after all these subterranean adventures, but I s'pose the West Country must be kept informed about what's happening in the World – and under it…. Streaks of rusty mineral deposit ran down the walls intermittently and the smell of damp granite seemed to intensify. The clattering wheels drowned out the soft steady dripping of water that you always find in mines. The occasional seam of quartz crystal glittered in brief glory as we trundled past, the light of the Davy lamp casting its radiance against the stony meynek walls.

The endless view of damp, dark granite walls had been flowing through my vision for so long, that when the tren gradually slowed down and came to rest, the stone walls of the old mine seemed immeasurably more solid and unyielding. "Well, here we are then Pat" said Jan. We had reached the end – or rather, the beginning of the track. We gathered up a few supplies from the 'box' section of the unlikely vehicle and set off on foot, Janner bearing the Davy lamp and we also lit our hat-caps, which seemed to lend the occasion a vividly ceremonial air. Soon Janner opened a small wooden door in the side of the level and we stepped into the 'jynnji' or engine-house. This contained an object of much pride and fascination for my subterranean companion – the jynn-keber or Cornish beam engine. It squatted like a vast grass-hopper, clicking and twitching in rhythmic precision. I felt like a boy viewing a Victorian traction engine! I must admit to being thrilled when Jan asked me to "chuck a couple of shovels of coal in, while I do the oil." He adjusted a couple of dials and we stood a moment watching the mesmeric pulse of the archaic mechanism. Then we followed the old adit, as we jestingly called it, and soon arrived back at the ante-chamber or kroust-hut. I changed back into my street clothes but Janner told me to keep the miner's toggery – he said I'd earned it. I cast my eye over the portraits of 19th century Mine Captains and stout-hearted stennors. Coils of rope hung from pegs, and various drills, barrows, tackles and chests of tools and gear lined the growanek floor. I'd certainly seen a lot since I last sat in this room with the old one at the very outset of our labyrinthine odyssey.

"I really want to thank you Janner. You've shown me so much, such a world as most people never even get a glimpse of – a different world. Thank you so much." "The pleasure was mine too, Pat. I'm always glad when someone shows an interest in the old bal – gives me a good excuse to get back to the place I love!" We laughed again. Our trip had been punctuated by a lot of laughter since the beginning.

Soon our grasping hands gripped the cold iron rungs of the ladder, and with a strong mixture of enthusiasm to see the upper world again and regret at coming to the conclusion of our adventure, we steadily ascended. Just as Janner was about to push upwards on the trap door above us, I had a sudden horrific thought – what if they've started constructing that ridiculous *development* that's been causing such vile dread in Penzance Church Town? I imagined landing-craft delivering a squad of bulldozers and concrete-pourers to the cove. I sensed Janner would have had an absolute *gyp-fit* if anyone had jumped his claim. These old Cornish geezers can be right easy-going and good-humoured most of the time, but it's not wise to cross them. All these thoughts rushed through my brain in a second and the next moment I felt the in-rush of cool air, briny air, as Jan lifted the lid and we climbed out onto the pontoon. Again it was a moonlit night, the moon was almost full, and its silvery light danced and squiggled on the restless waters, the black waters of the night. The mordros whispering surf was at play and splashed rhythmically at the oaken structure on which we perched. Janner locked up the precious bal while I gazed in happy abstraction, my eyes scanning the open sea towards the Lizard. The glimmering moon-blaze was a most wonderful sight, especially when observed from sea-level. A vast band of the sea was shining and sparkling with the moonlight. Aglow, golow, aglowin'. After so long in all those narrow tunnels, the sense of expansion was euphoric as my eyes swept the vast open vistas around me. The lights of Porthleven and the twinkling lighthouse on the end of the dark Lizard peninsula. The sea litten with dancing light to the horizon, like a magical path you could walk to another realm. Then the friendly lights of New Lynsmouth. The jazz-age art deco cake that is Jubilee Pool, shining in the moonlight like an alabaster palace in a thunderstorm. The dark hulking Battery Rocks, spreading out under a low tide, the island transformed into a Cornish hill, with its secret lagoon. The war memorial, great Egyptian obelisk pointing off towards a distant galaxy where…

And the little beach, all looked intact there. The old parade ground, the triangle, still looking good. The pier snaking along, its solid granite blockwork standing bold against the waves. All looked as it should, only better. More enticing than usual as the moon's gloss glow shone in show of sight. "Are you ready to take the Sea-Link?" asked Janner. I followed his gaze to the coracle that was tied to the weird island on which we found ourselves. I smiled as I remembered our last little voyage. We jumped in without a splash and soon were plying our way back to Janner's skovenn.

The waves were like black glass. The dancing light on the water scintillated and swam before us and the fresh smell of brine was a balm.

A fog had swept in from the sea in the afternoon bringing fresh damp air and the smell of the ocean. The mordros lapping waves were glistening black and breaking white against the little beach ahead. For all its humbleness, the little cove had a charm all of its own that night, and I felt strangely moved to be once more back in familiar and homely surroundings. As we hit the beach a flock of the little purple sandpipers took off wheeling together in a flash of white, heading out to sea before sweeping round and alighting on some of the rocks under the old pier. I looked around. Of the coracle there was not a sign. "Come on," said Janner, and we strode crunching along the beach towards Battery Rocks.

Things seemed a little dreamlike and unreal after so long in the rocky realm, the realm that everyday folks don't see or know about. I thought of all the characters I'd met on our adventure – who would have ever guessed that so many twilight miners still toiled away down there in the tewlwolow hollow? We stepped up onto a rock encrusted with barnacles; one of the bony ramparts of this beautiful and tiny outcrop of limpets and winkles. I thought I caught sight of a snakelocks swirling in a pool in the rocks. Then the moon peeped out from behind a scudding cloud and threw its gleaming face into the water of the rock-pool. I thought of all the tiny life within that one tiny pool, all those tender and miniature souls slithering, growing, mating, hanging on in their fresh homes against the blasts of Atlantic weather and swell, clinging to the bedrock of a phenomenal life, before finally letting go and reuniting with the great ocean. All this *life*. All these little entities so like us all with their living, their will, their striving and their partial seeing. I shuddered at the strangeness of life. "Come on boba!" said Jan, guiding me over the slippery rocks. There was a way of walking where your foot always slid into the contours of the stone, or found purchase against the barnacle crop. This way you could walk with sure footing and be at home in such a place – even in darkness, wind and rain.

We soon made it up to the obelisk and the concrete path. The tame world. The world shaped by man, subdued and all too often made ugly, made less. "I see your work-mates have been busy whilst you and I have been off on our jaunt," said the old one, pointing to the copy of The Limpet that had been crudely taped to the sea-wall, up by the telescope. BATTERY ROCKS SAVED – ROYALE GROUP BOSSES FACING MAJOR FRAUD INVESTIGATION! screamed the bold headline in cheap ink. "What?" I was stunned. "Now you're free to get back to the bal!" said Jan with a glint of eye, before shaking my hand. "I can't believe it Jan," said I "it's been so long, I can hardly believe it.." I was, for once, at a loss for words. "Yep! And you can believe there'll be some pissed-off masons in this town – and in Truro!" he replied.

We leaned over the sea wall and surveyed the cove again. The same yet different. Like a reprieved prisoner, a prodigal returner. More intensely there for having been in such jeopardy. I thought of the millions of pounds that had been wasted trying to push that ridiculous scheme through and all the food and medicine that that money could have bought. I thought of the sulky air of belligerence and bickering that had clouded the town's psyche with its strife, rumour and accusations. Then I thought of the people getting their way and sense and reason prevailing against corruption, insider trading and divisive political manoeuvring. The sheer amount of people's energy that had been poured into the controversy over this little slice of wilderness. Mainly though I thought about the wild and watery creatures who dwell and roam around the dark rocks and swirling sea. All those shellfish, starfish and even seals, going about their lives, blissfully unaware of the conceptual dreams of Humanity taking place just a few feet away, on the *land*, the Human Realm.

"I'll be off now Pat," said Janner. "It's a few miles I've got to travel to get back to the West Country, you know, back to Chyannor." "OK Jan, I'll write up the piece on y' mine and send a copy up to your place for your final approval and edit." "No, don't do that" said he, "you bring the thing yourself, then I can introduce you to the missus and show you our place!" "You've got a deal, Jan, and thanks again for showing me round the old bal!" He patted me on the arm and strode away down the prom, merging quickly into the drifting fog of the night. I turned my heels for home and my girl. The old town was dripping in Cornish night-fog – the densest kind. The lamps gleamed yellow, their faint glimmer falling on old St.Anthony's and casting a warm light around it. The heart of the old town slumbered, awaiting its awakening.

THE KRAMVIL

Chapter 1

Whilst it paineth me greatly to put pen to paper, I feel it my bounden duty to do so, if for no other reason than to serve a clarion call of warning to my brethren, compatriots and fellow worldlings. Indeed it would be most remiss of me if I were to shirk the clear moral task of informing my cohabitors and orbic kin of the great perille that looms darkly over the innocence of their sleeping lives, dreaming fast, as they do, in the rustic hundreds of the Great Shyre of West Kirnowe.

I ask not for your belief, neither your indulgence – I ask only that you weigh my words each by each, and weigh them well – for what I have to relate is a thynge both singular and perplexing; a thynge meant not for the chubby ears of a succulent and well-tempered Humanity.

On the shady and misty evening of January the 11th, 1911, I'd tottered down the ancient and lichenous alley, as of yore, for to buy a flask of butter-milk from the pantiled merchant-house down by the sea-slopping flatfish harbour in that gabled and time-honoured towne of New Lynsmouth, skittering rain spattering my mottled flaxen cloak as the freshe wind stirred the darkened swirling waves of a black and deep-swirling sea-mor.

Ahh but who are we to choose our fates, upon this blue-green cloudy world, this honeysuckle marbled glistening globe of aery orbs and bronzen gods? So let lute and lyre sound and winged feet trip light upon this flickering stage; for fast falls the curtain upon our dance...

Having at length traced my twisting way back through the guttural and labyrinthine alley-ways of the centuried and crumbling sea-port, I stumbled exhausted through the portal of my own humble cotting and swooned upon the Damascus divan. Aslumber I stirred not, yet still I became conscious of being awalk down the dusty roads of summer in a far-famed realm a-foreign. Forging forth through fields of copper shivering leaves and tremulous buds, the horizon shimmering in nostalgic sepia heat-haze, I loomed sunwards over dry dusty hills of summer. I voyaged undreampt depths of rural idyll and trod the clods of ox-ploughed fields rolling

and tumbling to seas dark and twinkling, my shoes mere
shillings spilling shear silver trails o'er dewy railroad rails
as dark boats sailed. I lurched, and swaying drifted forth,
alive, aloose and aloom. Tracks of trees marked my route
scattering forth shoots and ground-swelling roots of flavoured
woods. Cinnamon breezes blew, played and fluttered, bringing
mutterings from the glittering black seas upon which zephyr
played and zographos prayed. Stretching out my sun-drenched
hand to grasp the sky in raptured amazing gasp I caught at
cotton clouds, vaporous shrouds that flittered and skittered
through the lightning brittle sky, unravelling into breath. Such
were the chimeras that vaulted like viridian grasshoppers
through the rustling corncrakes of my drowsy top as I lay
aslumber drifting. And when I awoke, it was to a knowledge
of a thing vast, dizzying and beyond. Again I wandered those
time-pocked lanes of that West Country seaboard towne,
dripping with myre, fog and rain – always the spattering
shattering rain that swirled in from western deeps. The rotting
dwellings lurched and leaned over lanes greened with mossy
stones trod once by bright-buckled shoes. The black beams
of a half-timbered heap leaped up out of the gloom – a light
glimmered in a room, yellow, sputtering of tallow and crone's
monotonous muttering. Carriages rattled away down the
cobbled distance bearing nobles away as humble fisher-folk
hauled half-caulked and archaic barques up slips, keel-alleys
and slime-dripping slopes. At the crazed conjunction of Iron-
Foundary Way and Orchard Street lurked the eldritch dwelling
on gambrelled peaks and misty grey-green bubbled panes of
leaded glass. It was there dwelled the scholar, that paragon of
obscure research and terrible forbidden lore who was to cast
such a shadow on the towne with the influence that emanated
forth from that centuried and worm-ridden house that tottered
above the ditch on that terrible corner, deep in the heart of
the ancient ghetto that crawled down the hill towards the fell
and foul taverns of the towne. And yet, on first espial, the
house was not so very terrible to behold. Its aspect even held
a certain faded majesty, as if it were dreaming away its latter
days, musing upon the bygone eras, the harvests of forgotten
golden corn, of many a net-load of silver sparkling pilchards

hauled aboard and brought safely back to shore in days gone to yore. Slumbering and drowsing on its medieval plot, bristling with nettles and weeds, aprey to howling moggies and scuttling slitherers, it shivered out many a frosty winter's day, waiting philosophically and most stoically for the kindness of the sun's rays to give forth the generous splendour of warmth, like an old man seeking to warm his bones before a bright hearth-blaze in a good inn of cheer and humour. Yes, dear reader, the old house seemed benignant enough to begin, but t'was not to remain so for long.

Chapter 2

Forgive me, if you will, dear reader, for once again troubling your peaceable and well-earned rest with the unsavoury and distasteful jottings of a fever-ridden and much maladjusted psyche; but I would crave your attention once more, whilst I continue to set forth my half-unbelievable tale of jittering, skittering vileness... Twas at that blasted corner, that unlovely meeting of Iron-Foundary Way and Orchard Street, in the Olde Quarter of New Lynsmouth that I stumbled upon a quaint sight in this towne of unlettered, shuffling half-things – for it was there that I beheld a trestle tumbling with good tomes and periodicals, being offered up for sale... Being a somewhat pale and bookish individual myself, I halted in my clattering tracks, agog and agape at the sight I beheld. What good fortune, thought I, what great good fortune to discover a seller of learned volumes in this benighted and doom-splattered village, this pile of vile domiciles, dreaming awhile in eternity's smile... The volumes I espied beneath the guttering gas-lamp were indeed an oddly assorted bunch of quaint bed-fellows. There were pamphlets on Bicycling in the Lake District; The Mixing and Application of French Polish on Fine Mahogany Furnishings; Raise Fowls in your Backyard; Arabic in a Week; Why Keep Bees, by A.P.R. East; various novellas of a romantic nature; some dull-looking autobiographies by people of minor fame; a couple of volumes of the Cowboy Adventure Annual from the eighties – very dog-eaten and tatty; a much scribbled-on copy of the Communist Manifesto; a folio of sheet-music – works by Corelli, Gesualdo, Paganini and both Scarlatti's; a work on the maintenance of marine engines; A copy of Penbourough's Great Medieval Sepulchres of Middle Europe – so coated in grime as to render it illegible; a couple of volumes of Dickens from the Shilling Classics series – I think it was Dombey and Son, and Bleak House; this last I picked up to examine. I'd always liked the title 'Bleak House' and smiled to myself as I cast a wry gaze over the most verily bleak edifice before me, the book-seller's own crumbling and time-battered dwelling... The volume was missing the last few pages however, so I returned it to the groaning trestle to nestle with its ill-assorted fellows. My attention was arrested by the sound of tapping and scraping as a blind-man slowly made his way up the meandering alley. Though I maintained a withdrawn silence, he perceived me yet and thrust out a rust-pocked tin mug – "Alms, brother, alms, if ye will!" I dropped a couple of shillings and a flurry of pennies into his venerable vessel, wishing to continue my perusal, yet somehow this figure demanded my attention and as my gaze fell fully upon him, I took in a figure in battered canvas cape, hooded, huddled and bundled up against the chilly damp. The boots of his feet were wrought of an archaic cast and coated in black mud from rustic ramblings. His breeches that had once been scarlet were now faded to the hue of stale claret, his ruff a scruffy scraggy thing of baccy-stained dust, his visage hewn from pewter set bold against the sky, white cloud in his eye. His bony hand shot out of his shallow silk sleeve and gripped my shivering wrist – "Mind what ye be a studyin' of!" sayeth the old sightless one. "What do you mean man – tell me what you're getting at!" I exclaimed in annoyance – hadn't I already paid him well? Why this cryptic pronouncement from one so battered and bold? "I'll say no more," sayeth he, and tottered away on his old silken pins. 'Scuttling wretch!' thought I, but said nothing; truth was, the old one had shaken me from out of my pleasant reverie and cast his gloomy shadow over my harmless perusal of this unwanted street-corner library. What need I for another shadow in this veritable play of shades? Ah well, the old rogue's probably half addled from grog, likely he's long been a-swilling down at The Marlin Tavern down yonder way… I'll not let the old fool darken my day, back to the books, perhaps I'll find a treasure yet… Leafing through the quotidian and the mundane I gradually blundered into the exotic, the profound, the un-dreampt-of. A Treatise on Javanese Animism by A.E.Hunderlich! I'd been after that egg for many a year! Then there was Cults of the Solomon Islands by Professor Charleston; a worm-riddled but intact copy of Cotton Mather's The Wonders of the Invisible World – a first edition from October 1692! Shaking with excitement I continued… Manoral Life in Olde Pengersick by James

Wattleby! An absolute classic and as rare as reindeer's breath in the Serengeti! And there, casually lying there on that drab street-corner book-stand was an original copy of Jones' Greek-English Lexicon from 1825! My luck was surely in – I cast a furtive glance around me, jealously hoping that the alleys were not suddenly seething with eager and hunger-maddened bibliophiles like myself – a fight might ensue if a fellow book-worm were to set his jaundiced and squinting peepers on this heap of glittering treasure! But no, the byways were devoid of human society – I had the place to myself and I was *happy,* most happy; revelling in that rare joy that only a rabid lexicographer such as I could know. Deep did I drink as my yearning digits furrowed through the bizarreries exhibited there, under the guttering gaslight and fogbowed gloom... Works by the great Indian Masters emerged from between the gardening manuals and tomes on the pickling of herrings and codfish. A Victorian edition of The Teachings of Nagarjuna – forming part of a series with similar collections of Shantideva, Tilopa and Naropa! I didn't even know half of these things were in print! On the Nature of the Universe by the great Lucretius and The Letters of Pliny the Younger! Even How to Fly by Claude Graham-White, that intrepid pioneer aviator who had not long ago flown his canvas and wooden biplane from Poniou Farm, out Gulval way, swooping over the shrine of Saint Wolvela and startling the goodly burghers of Pensanskrit church-town by winging his windswept way over Caunseway Head, Market Jew and Voundervour Lane. This excellent manual went to great lengths to warn the would-be airman of the dangers of stalling in a pusher biplane, such as the Farman Longhorn or Sopwith Bat Boat.... Invaluable for the polymath with aeronautical pretensions.... And there, next to it was a leather-bound copy of The Nile, from Delta to Desert and Beyond by Lieutenant Worthing, D.S.O. *The* textbook for Nilologists everywhere! Trout Fishing in Northern California by Van Der Vliet! Ah, could it be? Yes! The Last Days of a Philosopher by Sir Humphry Davy! My joy was complete, as I had long sought this noble work. Just then my blissful reverie was broken by the cracked and rasping tones of a voice, a voice both human and ethereal, issuing from the now opened portal of the sagging and gambrelled edifice before my blinking eyes. "You'll be needing this, my good fellow" said the man, passing me a large cardboard box to contain my treasures. I glanced up at my interlocutor, an aged gentleman, a decayed and noble gentleman... His cataracted eyes gleamed white through gold-rimmed lunettes, his coat was of an archaic cut, as was everything else about his aged yet graceful figure. "B-but the *price?"* I mumbled, "what price do ye ask for such, such treasures as I have here?" I indicated the towering pile of rare, precious, *priceless* volumes I had selected, with a hand whose tremulations, I'll own, I could scarce control nor inhibit. "The *price?* The *price,* y' say?" asked the aged one. "My vision is fading like the falling of night; scholarship is waning in this mechanistic age and I am happy foremost that the editions go to one whom may best benefit from them." He glanced at my intended purchase. "A guinea the lot!" My head reeled. "But sir, I cannot-" "You cannot rob an old man, is that what ye mean?" He shot back. "I well know their value, young fellow, and I'll take a guinea or nothing!" Seeing his intent, and that argumentation was futile, I drew out a ten-bob note, a crown and six shillings and tipped it into the gnarled claw of the antique gentleman. "There is one thing" he said, as the penultimate coin jingled against its fellows in his yellowed palm. "I'd count it as a great service if ye'd come and read to me a little some day – my eyes are so weak now y' see?" "I'd consider it a great honour to aid a scholar such as yourself" I replied, "I, I-" but the door had closed and the old one was gone inside... My head, as I say, was still a-spinning and a-reeling from the great excitement of this most fortunate encounter. Packing my newfound treasures into their humble casement of fragile card, I turned on my heel and found my way back through those *Cretan* and most labyrinthine alleys, back to my tumbling cotting – whence my trembling hand could scarce fit key to lock, then lighting some stubs of tallow candle and setting them upon divers jars for luminence, I reclined on the rococo divan to gaze at my wonderful new acquisitions, without so much as brewing a jar of tay...

Chapter 3

I drank a deep draught of obscure, arcane and subtle learning, feasting my arid soul on the sweet and heady fumes of a cup that in very truth ran spilling o'er with jewel-like sparkles of joyous illumination. I fell, swooning into a trench of warm slumber upon my time-faded Turkey divan – my mind in dream span. I soared awake, refreshed and amazed by the clarity and phosphorescent nature of my plunge into Lethe's sweet waters. I awoke feeling in need of moistures and soon had the old copper kettle singing on the range for to brew-up my tay.

 Supping up my accustomed brewage I hydrated my mortal cells and decided to wrench myself momentarily away from the wonderful vortex of fascination that the newly-bought books were exerting most strongly upon my minde. I would take the airs of the evening, foggy and drizzly though it be – I would perambulate forth amongst my beloved labyrinthos of squirming thoroughfares and beetling boulevards. I would let my boots take me where they would – sometimes it is good to wander without purpose, open to life's display of energy, beings, phenomena, drama, drops of rain and beams of watery sun. I soon closed my front-door and set forth from out of the rotting gambrels and sagging tiles that festooned the foetid roof of my engabled gaff.

 Boom-shaka-laka-laka-Boom! The sea roared and surged, breaking with wild and unbridled violence against the mighty stone bulwarks of the ancient haven, the shelter of caravelles, clippers, kipper-smoker's canoes and bream-bursting beamers. Black clouds swirled around the gibbous moon like troops of vile and malignant bats bent on battering and bantering in bleak bushels of bosch. I turned my boot-heels abruptly at the Ope, meaning to strike out for the High Road, a tune still on my lips; when the vulgar rasping of a motor-car sent me back into the fragile ghetto district, recoiling from the automated intrusion. I followed my feet I know not where. Like the meanderings of the river of Ilium I wound and wended my way past Wednesday… The first few drops of rain had spattered against my overcoat and were soon

followed by so many more. Thinking to elude the deluge I
deludedly knocked at a faded green door under the sputtering
light of a gas-lantern that swung creaking in the swelling
breeze. Seeking not to intrude I knocked again and the door
swung open… No Human hand or countenance greeted me
within. The door had merely opened under its own volition,
I being an involuntary visitor to what lay within. I found
myself in a large open space, a space of light, of greenness,
of herbage and foliage, of leaf, flower and bower – in short,
I was in a garden. A garden not ordinary. A garden lumed by
a warm and shining sun. A garden drowsy with the droning
of ten thousand wing of bees. A garden enchanted and
luxuriating in the beauteous sight of many countless varieties
and examples of every known, and many unknown, kindes
of flowers. Suche realm as this was a great and bounteous
thing for my soul to behold. Such an thynge as thys doth pour
balm upon my spirit. Thus, my brothers and sisters, do I share
with ye the tale, just as it was, and just as it happened to me,
Elias Gillpington, in this very towne of New Lynsmouth.
Botheration was unknown in that sweet pleasance, and,
most curiously, the sun now shone out its friendly rays
of welcoming warmth, e'en though the night had yet just
been upon my heels, with night-bats a-flutter and rooms all
a-shutter. No matter! What mattered was the joy of now, not
the tedious ciphering of how it came thus! And so upon those
blessed paths I walked and set my foot forth. Winding, turning
about and following those happy paths was rapture's reward
re-wrought. I can scarce name but a handful of the flowery
blooms that seemed heaped up in that realm of content, for
my botanical knowledge is sadly scanty and slim. I can only
liken the experience to walking into a wonderful painting,
guided by the Nine Muses of Ellas. Every hue and tint was
represented amongst the rich profusion, the cornucopia of
anthers, stamens, petals and stems. A waft of pollen golden
was pulling at my nose and goading my gaze to where the
crocus grows. Peeling petals strewed the speckled and dew-
drenched pathway, past rosemary, jasmine and oriental statues
of luminous cool jade. Groves of leafy soft verdure waved in
the gentlest breeze, bees droning in their honey-zone weaved

their trail of luminous buzz. Cool green pools, ponds and pols pulled the gaze to waters glazed with glittering ripples and duck-weed dappling in the drowsing sleepy sun. A summer afternoon, the fresh cool tang of morning. Dynasties of monasteries in millennial slumber drifting could shew no finer bower than this. Tinkling waters plashed in the ponds where sleepy dace and trouts hid snouts and masques were played out by shy romancers replete with requisite appliqué replica ruses. Rushes whispered and rattled as chaffinches chattered and robins warbled. Perfumed scents drifted on warm soporific airs, erasing cares and ruffling hairs. Lupins loomed large, lunging forth lustily as all manner of blooms, bells, spikes and clusters clamoured like camels at a desert-fair. Of this beauty I drunk deeply as of a cool well. Glossy green leaves of shrubs interspersed the banks of blooms, breaking them into a series of surprises. Twisting paths held forth new treats at each twist and turn. A tinkling lyre issued from an unseen source, completing the idyll. The droning bees. The sleepy warm sun. The colours of many flowers. The freshness and cleanliness of the air. The quietude – the great quietude of the place was alluring, satisfying and fair. I had no idea such storied and ancient bowers and realms of beauty still existed, just around the corner from my own dwelling. All the time this place had been so close, hidden, waiting.

Fronds of green ivy dangled over the sunlit red tiles atop the wall, harbouring a great many wrens, which swarmed out at intervals, chirping merrily and loudly, whilst blackbirds set up a fine, sweet song in the boughs of various blossoming fruit trees. From time to time an overhead whirring would tell the presence of a cloud of starlings, flowing and rushing together through lambent air, so many druids a-wing. The ivy berries with their golden dust seemed to give out an intoxicating smell and the sun above was lulling me. Around the various ponds and rivulets, dragon-flies droned, they glittered as jewels and flashing passed my sight. Twinkles of prismatic light played and danced, shimmering on the waters. The warm sun played down mercifully around, painting a pleasing glow on the old wall at my side, animating the scene and giving it life. Looking at the ancient and crumbling plaster all litten up as of eld set my minde reminiscing and recalling a former state of warm contentment, slumberous ease. The place around me drowsed. I was carried forth by my feet's forward lurch and loom, thinking not where I would wind my way to. A pair of butterflies spiralled up past an outburst of lupins and circled tremulously in the warm and fragrant air. One of the butterflies brushed my face with its wing, and at the same time I found myself opening the door and stepping out of the garden.

There was a jolting crack of lightning which flashed and shone in the alley, and thunder rumbled deep in the far hills of a bleak and rain-lashed winter night. Spatters of rain dotting my surcoat again, followed by the onset of a great downpour – I turned and struggled back up the ill-litten alley, fighting a fierce wind that howled through the rolling night, pouring in off the sea, the deep black sea of such untold depths. The sea that bred that wind was dark, rolling, black and cold, so vast and wild. Its chilled and saline breath gripped me. I stumbled towards my own branch of the labyrinthos and the safety of my tumbling cottage on cobbled corner crouched. A final great blast from the swirling black ocean had me reeling as I rounded the triangular corner of the thoroughfare and threaded my way between sagging gambrelled houses, their green-glass windows glimmering with candles in the rooms burning. As I stood in front of my own domicile unlocking the front-door, it struck me that the whole conjunction of events had been as singular as it was perplexing…

Chapter 4

As angular as it was reflecting, rapture's fractured and shattered circus deflected memories of looking-glass perception. Rain ran trickling and splashing into gleaming moonlit pools captured in flat angles of sagging gambrels. Leaden green glass twinkled and rattled in the rainy clouds of niwl night-air; aether swirled.

Masts, blocks and rigging creaked and croaked in the arboure, hulls quivering, riding at anchor as tethered nags will gallop and loom. The sea came in waves. Spray, a lattice on the beach; lace on dulse and kelp. Sea-lettuce branches loose in the mordros booming surfroar. A brine full of herrings, a cold mackerel soup flapping, a water-mess trembling and trying to take to lande. Old luggers rattling, slats ran salty as Aeolian blasts blew slates off the crouching huddled hovels round the harbour, along the Strand, to the Marlin Tavern and the old bridge.

As raging gouts of tar hailed down around the pierhead and fisherfolk flew for shelter and warmth from the tempest and hats were hurled aloft afloat on swirling aethers I crossed the three-cornered threshold and stepped within my domicile.

Kindling a guttering tallow candle I surveyed the sight of eyes before me. My questing eye fell upon the carton of volumes afloor.

Eschewing brew I forthwith decided to embark on a voyage on the verge of immersion in learning's printed prologue version. On the brocade couch once more enslouched ensleuthed on nature's trail, sparkling under a full head of sail. Down to New Lynnsmouth Harbour to embark on a crabbing boat for the far Solomon Islands, where under tropic suns, shaded by bursting foliage and luxuriant fruitage, there to observe and catalogue the ritual life of the indigenous tribespeople. First to follow the trail of swirling foam across Atlantic and Pacific waters 'fore hauling up at last on a beach of fine white sand, where old leathery turtles bury their eggs in the spring. Flickering rippling waters clear under a sky of darkest bright-blue. And then to the hinterland. First contact with the wild-men… The book slipped from between my clutching fumbling fingers as the intoxicating words lit my minde's eye with bright pictures.

I was in a glade in a forested mountain, sitting with yogis in a time distant past like yesterday. The teachings entered my minde-stream and worked like medicine on me. These Eastern wise men had peered deep into the mysteries and become enstrengthened through their constant and determined looking in. A subtle breeze played around the glade and the fragrance of flowers drifted along. Clouds journeyed through the clear blue above, constantly revealing the splendour of the sun.

Glistening sunbeams in the twinkling dew of the grassy

field – Poniou Field, near St.Wolvela's Church-Towne. A crowd had bought their tickets at the china-shop in town and come along to see the intrepid Mr Graham-White take off in his heavier-than-air machine and perform a series of swoops and turns. The dewy grass blurred with the speed of the tiny pusher motor and the two-winged bat thing chugged along so merrily through the bottom-meadow that it did actually take wing and soar aloft! The audience literally gasped, before breaking into a rousing cheer. High above, Claude could not really hear it above the roar of the internal-combustion beast that was pushing his aerofoils through the aether and the singing of the bracing-wires.

Pushing against the great river's flow, the keel of the dhow sliced gracefully through the sparkling waters of the venerable Nile. The members of Queen Victoria's Botanical Collecting Society were dispersed around the deck at their leisure. A drowsy lassitude set in as the sand-blasted desert air weighed down on the over-dressed Europeans. Moustache-wax was melting and it was curious to imagine that at that very moment, most of England was being blasted by storms of wind and heavy rain. Professor Crantock had been debating with Lieutenant Worthing on the recognition and classification of various irises by the configuration of their stamens. Dr Barberry was writing a letter home to his sweetheart and intended, the vicar's daughter. The trip up-river would take four to five weeks and should reveal some new insights into the various scientific fields of the men on board.

The Javanese autochthonous priest has many functions, ranging from psychopomp, to village druggist, to psychologist, to curer of chickens and goats. He is credited by the villagers and those of his flock, with having the power to leave the everyday world and go into the realm of the departed ancestors – there to roam about more or less at will, locating spirits and learning the lessons of the beyond. One particularly memorable ceremony that I witnessed during my time in the foothills involved the participants staying up for three nights, covering themselves in ashes, singing an interminable song in tremulous voice and appearing to rise off the ground by a foot or so during the moonlit climax to this outlandish sabbath. Again my lobstering fingers clutched at the faded volume, again it slipped to the floor with a resound as I seemed to swoon upon the patchwork quilted sofa and my minde whirled with imagery so rich and dripping with various magical glimpses of worlds unimagined that lo the night was ere long dawning into the light; the green, briny light of a dripping dawn over New Lynnsmouth.

Chapter 5

Aye, green and briny, dripping like a lobster, the light rolled greyly over a fog-bound and forgotten porth on the South Western seaboard of Kirnowe – the ill-starred and fate-blasted New Lynsmouth. Rain spattering the globulous green window-glasses in trellis and tattered curtains that flapped and flapped in the sighing swelling breeze that swept the streets and alleys of old. Dawn squirmed in like an eel, uncoiling an oily and ashen semblance of luminescence.

I wound up the phonograph to listen to my favourite album – A Pepper at the Gates of Edawn – and settled back to relax and uncoil my well-oiled minde; enriched by literature's flitting pictures. Must have drifted into slumber, like a log drifting downstream to the lumber-mill; where stillness ripples not the rill and singeth not the whippoorwill. Rivulets of rippling running sparkling mercury fluttered and seethed, soothingly soughing into my fertile and palpably gnosient psyche. Dream's vapours fogged the mirror of my minde, misting it over with mysteries and inexplicable phenomenal arisings. I seemed to be in the alley, Iron-Foundary Way, walking slowly on liquid feet towards that hoary tavern, the Marlin, but, as is the way of the Dream, the alley changed its nature and became a railway-carriage. The carriage clacked on clicking tracks, lulling me into slumberous ease. Trees sailed by my window, I had a compartment to myself. It was autumn. Leaves were yellow and heavy to drop from dripping twigs. Mould, truffles and wildboar's breath scented the damp, still air. Blazes of red and orange fungi poked out from the twisting whirling roots of ancient trees. Chestnuts thudded to the ground, bouncing and rolling. Crows flappered inky wings acroak. Charcoal-burners tramped through pockets of dense, dripping woodland. The land opened out, an endless vista of fields, potatoes and golden wheat. Hamlets hovered in patches of glistening silver lands. Subtle misty niwl rain and drizzle floated by gently in puffs, clouds and quilts. Rippling rain dancing by.

These sidereal apparitions faded – as things of the night must do – and my sight was suffused with a gentle blur of light. Like a golden harvest being poured into a ritual basket, the morning sun flooded and flowed into my chamber. The harvest reaper swung his silver sickle and garnered the grains of the Earth's gains. Rich and rusty red the light leaked and seeped in through the bubble green glass casement bay-windows and onto the patchwork settee that served as my resting place. In short, I opened my eyes to another day.

My attention was arrested by the sight of the pile of books that had emerged from their cardboard box and spilled onto the floor next to the rococo divan on which I rested. Dizzying visions of the night's reading came back to minde and with them the realisation that I should honour my promise and go and read to the old scholar, the one who had sold me the books...

I soon found myself afoot down the coiling clutter of alleys and cobbled quiet byways. The district was sleepily enjoying a balmy warm day and geraniums and rambling roses in front of the crabbing cottages brightened the scene. Bees buzzed slowly amongst the potted herbs, gleaning their precious nectar. Sun-soaked cobbles bobbed in a sea of light. Turning my wandering feet around the crazy curled corner I advanced towards the sloping pile, the rotting and gambrelled edifice which the old one called home. It sagged and swayed before me, pitching aslant in its weed-sprouting lot. The archaic manse was dignified by a 'moat', in truth a simple ditch of a foot or so deep by as wide and was bridged by a slate slab that led to the lair of the reclusive denizen within its crumbling and time-bespattered walls.

An air of dereliction had long ago settled on the place, though it had obviously once been a sturdy and handsome home in times of yore. The curtains were ripped to shreds and bore the weight of many a cobweb. These tattered rags were supplemented by stout oaken shutters, which, true to their name, were usually to be seen shut.

Chapter 6

Thus is was that I found myself crossing the 'moat' and approaching the door to the house of that most extraordinary, singular and scintillating fellow, the learned and esteemed bibliophile who dwelt in that *Cretan* labyrinthos that comprises the Old Quarter of New Lynsmouth. 'Twas dripping in anticipation that I steadied my steps at his station in life's manifold manifestation. The shuttered rooms loomed before me, constituting the former premises of Brown, Jenkin and Co., Chandlers and Cod-Brokers to the Trayde. The sagging, guano-encrusted edifice 'pon which my glaucous orbs did fixe was once battered by the photons rainbows niwl mist blizzards and sea-fog turns of chance of ages past streaming of a million screaming skrawks, swirling buzzard-hawks clocks molecules sunbeams and the spattering salt spray of an untamed ocean of times winged nothing. The lichenous walls dripped rime, moss, stonecrops, sedi, lycanthropic foxhair ferns sprouted a-spew across the lintels and outer decorative cornice work was neath thyme's grained eye stained.

The door was of stout Chilean simian pine plank and the knocker, fashioned out of bronze-work, was in the form of an anchor, harking back to hanker for the briny wet nautical seagoing past of the ill-famed former freemen, Brown, Jenkin and companie. Aye! 'Twas fyshe that made this towne, right enough, and no man will deny it, blast ye! Why, if it weren't for the flockles of flecking silver fellows there'd be no cluster of cottages on this Cornish cove and no clatter of donkey's and oxen's hooves on Kyvounder Hill, beetling up with loads of provender for the West Countrie beyond.

The anchor on the pine plank door was just another token of sea-going broken barks neath neep moons, rising tides and jellyfish bloom clusters mustering mullet with lanthorn and lump-hammer. Skeining for shoals of lumpsucker, succulent hosts of Cornish Suckers, Haddock, Hake and Shinnegan's Blake. Back in the Marlin after many a moonshine voyage playing euchre, pochre and beggar me neighbre – shifty salts cheating, trying to pull the old win again's fake.

I seemed to hasten to hesitate afore the door as old New Lynsmouth cast its spell over me once again like a creeping niwl kommolek cloud that seeps into ya evening bringing softening mists that hold spirits mysterious and voices ringing from the past. Great herring gulls! How the minde wanders down dappled streetings and chance passings on meandering rivers of cobblestoned corners quaint mewses and opes opening onto rows of creaking cottages, thatched, tiled, pantiled and chimney pots smoking in the autumn wind, crows clack and flapping by. I put my hand upon the ancient door-knocker and lifted the outré objet with my gnarled palsied claw. A flight of gulls skrawlled overhead spattering their snowy guano over the alleyways and the front of the eld manse afore me. Pesky feathery things- just missed my coat! Was that a darkening cloud above me? The air seemed ripplingly chillier than afore- was it the mere caprice of a fanciful mynde? The bronze anchor struck upon its sounding plate with a stentorian resounding report. The bubble green grey glaucous panes of crude glass in the time-blasted windows evinced no clew as to the existence of the denizen alurk within. A few drops of a heavy grey oily rain came spattering down, running tear-like down the window-panes. I drew my coat more tightly around my shoulders and waited grimly before the grime-enrichened habitation upon which it was my fated fortune to caste the sight of my globulous eyes.

I did not have to wait long, for soon I heard the drawing back of a large and heavy bolt and the creaking of the august portal upon its sagging and corroded hynges. A waft of bookish dust and parchment-vapour greeted my nostrilii as the portal departed from its post and the latch was loosened at last. The handle spun on its shaft and unjammed itself open. Eldritch was the paragon of obscure research who lurched forth from within that tottering and gambrel-rotting pyle. "Who be ye?" rasped the eld one. "It is I, your neighbour to whom you sold the volumes" quoth I, and with that I was ushered into the house. "Weather's brewin' up" saith the elder as rain did fall unushered beyond the shutters. "Lurked ye long on the threshold?" "Oh no, I only just got here." "Aye, well, tay's a brewin" and with that the ancient scholar turned and wandered into the kitchen to see to the preparations, giving me a chance to glance round the room as through a pair of dark glasses the kommolek rattling clouds of moisturous vapour did clothe and coat the sky in darkening and sombre rags of ragged wrath. The voluminous volumes and velums of a lofty and laudable library greeted my conscious quivering gaze. The scope and range of his erudition was embodied here in this veritable constellation of study's riches, this treasury of culture's quotidian gleanings. A bizarre collection of antiques and curios also greeted the relishing spirit of aesthetically inquisitive inward intelligence. Fine oriental artefacts bestowed calm and subtle refinement and upliftment to the sparkling spirit. Jade figures adorned niches and vases from old China shewed scenes of that glorious country. Mandarins walked over bridges over lily ponds under weeping willows and stylized clouds drifted silently by. Lapsang tea gently scented the air in which song birds rilled and trilled and jade maidens enrobed in silks smiled wisely under the full moon. Camels in great herds played over the vast desert upland hinterland regions of Mongolia, stampeding as quasi-quadrupeds cantered ominously close to crushing and quashing pedestrian punters and seasick sampan sailors with Javanese whalers. Another such vase depicted in blue and white the solitary joys of the hermetic life of a mountain-dwelling sage, ceasing to engage with the world of dust, seeking the thread of nature's way. Peaks of crazy cragged looming mountains, washed with falling torrents of glistening water splashing and playing over rocky cataracts. Pines cling, swallows sing, mists swirl with subtlety as humble and hardy sages gaze in contemplative living joy, drinking in the view as the sun competes with the mist in the contest between the swirling harmonious elements. Yet another vase shewed the curling slow and lazy Pearl River as it wound through the rainy southlands, carrying sampans on swollen torrents of mercury grey rain, through grain-fields – corn, rice, water-chicken. Straw-hats, peasants, barefoot, carry baskets slung from poles, lurching along with wobbling walk. Parcels of steamed vegetables and rice dumpling balls. Sauces and pastes, piquant spicy and glutinous tastes all rolled up in bamboo-leaf parcels, going to market. Now the Emperor's palace – the Ming, the Quing, the Ching. Pagodas, parks, ponds and tinkling temple-bells. The 'Old Man of the Tower of the Sea-Beast's Lair', a moonlit pagoda of tranquil study, with cool wine in moonlight. The Tower of Contentment. Lotus blossom lanterns. Chop-sticks glint by lamplight. There is poetry, conversation, the appreciation of flowers and the enchanting tinkling of a lute. The cranes are flying over the lake and the fisherman is safe in his hut before the rains fall, ushered in by a rippling breeze ruffling the trees.

The man obviously had a fine taste in ceramics as well as book-learning. The fading aquatints and rich works in oils that hung upon the walls of the chamber enhanced the air of culture, depth and a wide worldly experience; depicting as they did such scenes as classical Greece had to shew. There were various works shewing scenes of Russia's glittering onion-domes, ships blasted by vast storms on the ocean and panoramas of snowy mountain clarity.

Hearing the shuffling of ancient feet upon the faded Persian carpet, I turned to see the figure of my neighbour approaching with a tray of tay. He bade me be seated and we took our tay and began to talk as the rain rattled the windows and darkened the sky still further an ominous hue. His cataracts flashed as the words rasped forth in a stream of conch-house-ness, anchored in the illumination of ten thousand candle-power. Drawing air, his wizened wizard's wind-gizzard gave forth froth of formless former days, formally hiding in frozen formaldehydeparkcorners of the speaker's minde. No tie-burn nicked nor nettled his neck as flecks of fluvium specked his ruffed russet crested grebe foliage a-feather - - - perhaps I exaggerate; but he certainly could talk up some. Serpentine slithering in a manner born of speaking the high glossary was finished yet ere begun as Bedouin hubbubs span and spun puns and spoonerisms as we spooned up the tea and current of fair buns. Dropping

no crumbs we exclaimed on this and that and rattled our
clacking jaws agape in chat – magpies laughed to see us chat
at that. Lunettes loomed large on aquiline beak as twinkled
the eyes the eld did speak. And though we passed not upon
the stair, yea though we talked of was and when as though we
wasn't there. The eld had trav-elled wide and far a-foreign,
steering his hoary herring-bark by glittering star-spangled
skies. Lit by the Great Golowji of Alexandria he had delven
deep as Dolcoath into the labyrinthine libraries, juddering
glossaries, flashing biblioteques, archetypal archives of the
architrave and adamantine ambulatory prop-up kiosks of
periodical perusal-learning, the booths of one-book public
libraries and laboratories (summing up the politics) and
gleaning a great grasp on the slate hasp of knowledge's last
gasp, down to the dregs of the cup of the tribe of the land
of the skies of the mountain-cloud-whippoorwill airs of
night. Yeah, old whippoorwill barking and warbling down
an old lost highway- weep not for me, said they. Tropical
nights and fruitbats shaded the studied, centuried and storied
wanderings of the encatarracted eld. And rich held the hand
of gold doth learning boldly go split to infinity's toe-hold?
Seeking ever more subtle and accurate acumen of clear,
krystallon understanding; comprehension; didactic pterodactyl
dionysiac melodramatic grammatic pedantic theatrics,
ceramics, beer-tricks, train-tracks and hairline cracks. Such
subjects should serve to sunder sundry solipsisms should such
suddenly slither slothlike to. In younger days far off twilight
in twinkling minde's eye he had papered his chamber with
the randomscattered fragments of twenty-seven dictionaries,
finely chopped and stirred in with a bucket of paste. Varnish
completed the glossolalia and his young sparkling jelly-eyes
of tender vision were free at liberty be to so be and thus to
touch and suss and see frankly and fairly the language he so
earnestly thought he sought. Stillness too. And clarity from
eastern fragrance lotus blossom as dew drop of free original
clarity rose naturally in student's minde. O'er many top picks
of subjective collective did his intelligect intentionally collect
lectures of learning for later inspection. Taking practicality
into the equation, his field-studies were exhausting and

astronomically sky-grazing the star gazing ratio ration-book
say pie are squared! The classics, geomancy, geometry, poetry,
Al G.Bra, Hessiod, Hassidic hermetics, phonetics, dialectics,
poetics, rhetoric, clay tablets and herms. Without pause he
had absorbed the Middle Kingdom, I Ching, Mesopotamia
and the cargo cults of the Autumn Islands. Anthropology.
The Yogas. Aeronautics. Zinc. Automatic writing, dAdAiSm,
phonograph rolls, papyri and porphyry portcullises from
Portugal to Porkellis. Relishing jelly's molecular structure
and substantiality, he had poured over volumes of chemistry
and micro-rhyzomic mycology. He had even, as a youth,
tried his hand at forging poetry, and filled glowing notebooks
with molten word-coinage, battered out on the anvil and
village green, green as willows wind up the hill. Carrying his
voluminous buksack up Nancarrow Hill to cherish cherries
from orchards by the punnet. Pianism primed his sorcine
pumice and the ragas, Greek modes and Arabic intervals
were all scanned by his once sharp hearing-ears, glimpsed
by his conscious jelly-eyes. Info in, and cross-referencing
and floating to feel the spontaneous *free* moment, thus had he
piscine swam and dived drenching and almost quenching the
liquid flow of lightning conscious understanding as blazed the
light. And a light once blazed will e'er echo anon and on to
another noon of knowing.

Chapter 7

I must have nodded off whilst waiting for the old geezer to
bring the tea. A stalactite of drool bedangled from the corner
of my lower lip, down the angle of my chiselled chin, and
onto the collar of my coat – what embarrassment! I swiftly
wiped it up with a swivelling side-swipe and feigning a
veneer of alertness sat bolt upright on the time-blasted
Chippendale chaise-longue; my face composed into a grim
rictus of living, writhing, pullulating awareness. Great
Herrings! It would never do to let the old codger think I was
bored shirtless, veritably and virtually brain-bogglingly bored
out of my tiny minde! Not that I was; I had merely succumbed
to the soporific and drowsy vapours of a grey mid-day of dog-

day doom-blasting shuddering equilibrium of eternal brown crackling leaves, shreds, shards and schrapps of newspaper newsprint, juddering junkets, jackanapes, jackarandas, Jaculus jaculi, jive jam-jar jitterbugs, neon-pulse angles, feline heliotrope re-shuffles, re-calibrated de-hulling harrow-drills, half-remembered advertising slogans for Everbrite Soapflakes, snatches of dialogue from obscure silent movies, impenetrable facial expressions glimpsed from the visages of men in '40's illustrative combination suits, painted in brown ink – scowling purposefully towards non-existent unreal future scenarios of glib housing-schemes of concrete and cracked snapjacks ablaze in the sunshine splendid radiance of 60's council estate middle British England, discus distractions dithering dilate in dissolute disc-winged distinguished, dystopian descriptive dither-dodder. Yeah, you can see why I slipped and slithered in sidereal slobbering saliva-shunting joyfully sideways aslew in gelatinous new blue goo, can't you?

The eld richly approached approximately my personal proximity and *a claw shot forth,* extending friendship's free-form flow of far-fetched fingers – "Taxon's the name," sputtered he raspingly, "Lazarus Taxon." "Gillpington," said I, "Elias Gillpington." We clutched claws in a hearty hand-clasp and I sussed his soul to be good.

Bleary the fishe were the eyes that peeped popping from lunettes as slow the sea oily slopped abroad the sloping shore, kelp flung far forth in its wake and seals bobbing the minimountainous waves. Taxon, that bird-lime encrusted and garrulous old gaffer ushered me with an extended index digitus to an ante-chamber in his lugubrious manse, his tumbling and trembling, red-tiled mansion amongst the twisting time-alleys of New Lynsmouth. The archaic room into which we emerged had been converted into what resembled some kind of scientific experimentorium, or laboratory. The lofty chamber was leafed and roofed in glass of a glint greenish, bottle, that is to say. The sun loomed down through this wonderful tinted carapace, suffusing the *laboratory* with a subtle and restful hue. A profusion of apparati occupied the mahogany work-tables, some of it electrical in nature, some clearly mechanical in an autokinetic sense; some pertaining to other, somewhat more *outré* branches of 'science.' Racks of tubes and phials of most curious liquids and suchlike lined the walls, between illustrations of skeletal diagrams, musculature ligature, leguminous entities and the algebra of algae, amongst others. Old Lazarus was like a quaint bird of the sea come home to roost in a fine and feathered nest, a restful caress of culture to clash clatter his brains and stir the ocean of his vast and soaring soul. Many and much were his wide and broad fields of learning gleaned and learned by him, as oft I've hinted in soft tints afore. There were sketches pinned to the white-alabaster plaster wall that seemed to suggest ornithopters aflap and afall well enthralled by gravity's grawl. Some extremely large Elephant-Horned Beetles had been carefully preserved and glued to faded cardboard quadrant quintets, gleaming with an unearthly blue sheen haze. Retorts and beakers of turquoise blue and green encrystallyzed scintillating fragments glittered with twinkling merriment in the now warm and pleasant shining of the sun into this grotto of wonderments, this very forge and factory of empirical expedient exegesis and all things best not ovoided. The brass fittings and the hinges and handles of the many small specimen cabinets gleamed with an aquatic ship-shape glimmer and the dark violet velvet drapes luxuriated in the basking warmth of the sunlight of the day. Instruments of obscure and technical leanings were scattered about this realm, as if they had recently been in use. "Perhaps, my dear Gillpington," uttered the rasping croak of the eld, "rather than merely *read* of science, you would care to *participate* and help me out a little with a matter I've been turning my attention to…" I rapidly assented, being very much in awe of the clear and high-flying intellect of the elder elect intelligent gentlefellow. I followed his glassy lunar gaze and the rays of his eyes lit upon a covered object upon the work-table before us. I had not noticed it before, curious, as it now seemed to dominate the table. It was wrapped in a Mexican cattle-cloth of deepest dark cactus green, brocaded with a border parade pattern of golden yellow and orange upon the hue. The gnarled, leathery, yellowish and time-honoured claw of the goodly and gregarious Taxon gripped the Mexican cattle cloth and whisked it sharply away, sending little sparkling constellations of dust into the dancing photon sunbeam air. My eyes fell full upon an object, a bulgeous foot-high bone-toned spheroid, to wit, an egg. An ivory-fissured, slightly flattened, slate-speckled and massy egg, sitting so quietly there on the table.

Chapter 8

An appalling silence thundered throughout the house. Globose snails of rain snaked and slithered down the cracked green-grey glas panes of the Botany Bay window. Somewhere far off an eel shrieked. The chronometer tocked with woody-bronzed abandon, a shudder in eternity. The lonesome and melancholy crying of the gulls resounded in the air above, almost human in its plaintive mewing in the watery and damp drenched vapours of the salted breezes of New Lynsmouth.

Horn hollow blow, worldbowl, blown – Blow now, blow near, blow north, blow news. Sea shell, bullhorn, sea's east blast, blow tidings fast down the old submerged and sunken road to New Lynsmouth towne. Don't fail to follow the hollow shingle's jangled murmuring muse. Sound hard the bugling bullhorn's blast and tell us what has passed?

A great wind came in from the sea that night; a rare and raging wind to worry the townesfolke and rob them of their star-scattered sleepe. The ocean groaned and surged, splashing its fishy waters abroad and afar, rolling great boulders along the deep sea bed. Howling shreds of blasting battering breeze attacked the straggling trees, moaning their tawny boughs. Rain bullets were hurled at the windows of my lurching tenement and the chimney howled in the tempest. Rooks raked and strafed the shattered oily clouds flapping frenzy. Telegraph wires shrieked with the beaks of banshees and a great roaring was heard to rend the ears of the old towne. Slates slackened flew reeling from roofs uprooted spin - hurling to the ground shattering in shock. Cats scurried for cover from lugubrious nettled lots. Windows rattled in the Old Quarter and sleep was ransomed off to the gods of storm.

My minde turned upon the events of the day. Old Mr Taxon had made a most favourable impression on me, his delicate selection of subjects to study, like a great bee, supping up and storing rich nectars of the sweetfruitment. Nozzling proboscises in pollen ponds and cuttlefishpools awash ye shippe of fools! His library shewed exotic and refined taste, his company was convivial and illuminating. In short, he was a most fascinating and revered neighbour. And then there was his interest in science- his laboratory- his *GIANT EGG!* Oh, it was probably nothing, but, *what the deuce was the species of that outsized ovoid?* This question seized possession of my minde for some time, as the swirling black storm outside raged rattled and ranted in zephyr gusts it glutted its buffering blasts. My scant scientific training was enough to tell me that that *thing,* whatever it was, was *no mammal's egg!* So what in the Jimminy was it then? A *fish?* A fledgling flap-feathered leathery fledgling owl-wool beakster thing? A lizard, snake or eggfish? Some prehistoric Pre-Devonian dinosaur prehensile jibbering thing? Or some vile molten beast, barely able to hack and attack – its clotted claws clutching and hacking at humans? No! I thrust these turmoils from out my broiling brains and would not let them haunt my soul with their appalling hints and devastatingly ghastly apparitions. I decided to calm my sparkling nervous system with some subtle draughts of music and arose to prepare the Victrola and listen to an album of Cod-Eye. I followed this up with Vullgar's Cello Concerto, and my sinews were soon truly soothed. I decided that Old Mr Taxon was a worthy man of letters and learning, and that any experiments he conducted could only be for the good of Humanity.

The storm seemed to settle a little, spending its spewing waves of spume flecked whale-ways and narwhal alleys. And though the wind still prowled the streets and fields, and though the rain still scatted down upon the slates and the glass window-panes, still I fell into a steady slumber, lulled by the raucous soaring cries of the gulls.

And yet though I sleapt, I rested not, but was rather pursued down interminable ghastly boulevards of marble sepulchres, vile and unwholesome to the naked eye, or the sleeper's dream-vapoured swim through great and deep ponds of ideas and understanding. I seemed to be cast into the great unfathomably vast gulphs between time's very abysses! Such a conceit was a most wearisome and troublesome thing upon my nerves, and a subtle, misty sense of unease seeped in like a breath of fog, that creeps into a room at night, through an open window, bringing a chilling, cooling effect. This exhausting series of visions of the yawning kosmos had seemingly been accompanied by a strange, deeply strange form of music, more akin to the piping and insane fluting of that cult of the unspeakable and most unutterable denizens of some extremely deep and slitherous pits indeed. This piping, bleating and almost bovine braying, generously mixed with the skrawking of ten thousand sea-birds, and the flapping of some flounders, flatfish and cuttle-pool-fish upon the black waters of the breakwater under the greenish and chubby moon; this was the unholy and unpretty symphony that serenaded my feverish and desolate sojourn in the aery realm of ye sleepe and ye dreams. Ancient rites had, I fear, been enacted; long-forgotten presences hailed and summoned from grim sleep. A series of drunken and insane geometrical patterns seemed to point a grizzled digit towards something so *ghastly,* so devastatingly foul and *eldritch,* so very unspeakably inhuman, so utterly *vile* as to wrench out the very pit of my already retching stomach and hurl it, yelping, into the *pit!*

    I rose with the weak and watery sun, and prepared myself a strong brew of coffee, determined to rid my minde of the last shreds and shrouds of unwholesome dream-vapours, and, thus refreshed and recharged, to turn my minde resolutely towards science and the pursuit of *knowledge.* If old Mr Taxon can continue to pursue his enquiries into the physical world at his age, then surely a comparatively young fella like me should be throwing myself into the Great Quest for Learning, and all that sort of thing… Reasoning thus, I decided to engage in some preliminary study, before calling on the elderly scholar, and selected some volumes from the shelf. Ah yes, how good it was to fix the minde on study, to put aside the night's fevered and frenetic phantasies and sharpen the arrow of intellect. My efforts were successful, or at least they were, that is, until I glanced down at my note-book and saw that I had absent-mindedly scribbled some rather outré patterns and diagrams, the nature and configuration of which, I can only say, had a most powerful effect of depressing and disturbing my spirits once more. The unfamiliar patterns seemed to take me back to the strange series of dreams from the night before, with their half-veiled hints at semi-hidden gateways to whole other dimensions and realms, far beyond the boundaries of the one we know now... They were not without a certain intricacy and refined style, only it was just not *human*. I strove again to put such ill-founded and unhealthy thoughts behind me, and once again returned to my scientific journals, brushing up on various topics such as aeronautics, automata, the uses of magnetism, some alphabets and scripts, linguistic glyphic elipticles, a smattering of lepidoptery, and such like matters.

A knock at the door wrenched my attention away from the tottering heap of volumes both musty and glossy, the lexicons, theses and glossaries written in squid-ink. I soon found myself looking into the round, rotund and jocular visage of Mr Paul Hill, Gentle-Squire. He was dressed impeccably, as is his way, in wing-collar, tweed-suit and burnished brogues. An ostentatious carnation decorated his buttonhole. His face was lit with enthusiasm. "Ah, Gillpington," said he, "glad I caught you in, thought I'd pay me regards, see how you were, that sort of thing – how the devil are you?" "I'm fine, Paul, come on in and tell me all the news." We were soon seated by the fire, deep in conversation, when a second knock at the door announced the arrival of Mr Jack Lane, Esquire and Gentlefolke. "I see you're already harbouring one reprobate!" quipped Jack as he caught sight of Paul toasting a tea-cake in the fire on a long brass toasting-fork. "Ah, Mr Lane," said Paul, "and how is the bewitching Miss Place these days?" Jack Lane's courtship of the fiery Miss Florence Place was a topic of seemingly inexhaustible humour to the friends, though in truth we were all fond of her. "She's calmer this week. Last night I took her out for Squid in the Basket at the Tallcorne Inn. An enchanting experience altogether!" Laughs all round greeted this announcement. Jack was known for his roguish and sometimes cynical sense of humour. Lankier and slightly older than Paul and I, he had a slightly lupine or foxy air about him. His clothes were informal, bordering on tatty. "Elias, you started telling me about that old scientist fella you met," hinted Paul. "Well, yes. He's very ancient, a scholar, vast library, he sold me some books and I'm going to help him out with some of his scientific work, could be a great learning-opportunity to work with a man like that." "Yes, but what sort of projects is he working on?" asked Jack with a quizzically raised eyebrow. I thought it best not to mention the egg, not sure why, just a presentiment that it would be better thus. "Well, you know, he's a bit of an all-rounder, hasn't actually gone into details about the nature of the experiments yet," I answered. "You want to be a bit careful," put in Jack, "he's probably working on reanimating zombies or building some kind of damned fanatical monster!" "Could be just about anything really," I retorted, side-stepping his jocular remarks, "he's quite interested in heavier-than-air machines, amongst other things, seems to have a fondness for the humble *ornithopter...*" "You *don't* say!" blurted Mr Lane, with a twitch of the moustache – "Just you be careful Elias!"

    His half-serious, half jesting remarks echoed around my minde after the friends had left, and I returned briefly to my studies with a sober cast of mood. I found my glassy and globulous eye falling flat once again upon my notebook, particularly upon that page on which I had absently originated such a curious and perplexing set of sketches. I felt again the rising of that nausea that had previously gripped my viscera and cast its velvet drape of shadow over the sunlight of my day. Gagging at the stench of a fetid and ghastly alienage, my temples spun and pulsed, appalled and utterly devastated by the pullulating immensities that gaped and gagged, gasping and leering their unspeakably unpleasant fetor into my furrowed and horrified face. My table and chair, and I with them, seemed to drop through the floor into an unfathomable gulch of gull-crunching absurd vermilion sulphur ruffling sullied squalls in spacetime. Infinities of crystal perpendicular pulse-emanating galactic matter swirling dark in vortexes of sci-fi green. Immeasurable caverns dark and dripping and populated with baboon armies of gibbering slobbering halflings, howling in the darkness of very doom. Worlds seemed to spin and slip away, hurtling and whirling into the vast pool of space, only to be replaced by more and ever more. The interdimensional dislocation left me feeling weary – I resolved to fight off the spell of dizziness and feverishness and not let it take me over. I would put such unwholesome pictures as I had seen out of my thoughts. Again I dove into my studies, and lost myself for an hour in the world of ideas. I wanted to rekindle that curiosity of the intellect that seeks and thirsteth after knowledge and understanding. That little light that shines its little glow upon the things of this World, the things of life. In short, I wanted to brush-up my overall scientific methodology and make myself a worthy assistant for the research of one Taxon – *Lazarus* Taxon Esquire, the most eminent scholar in all of New Lynsmouth.....

After taking a little morsel and a cup of hot tea, I found myself locking my door and setting out once again into that bizarre and beetling warren of crumbling and half-unforgotten alleyways and side streets that constitutes the Old Quarter of our goode towne. Leaves were spiralling in the sunlight-air and the blue dancing photons lit the firmament with a warm and spacious freshness. The trees sighed and swirled. Clouds of endless configuration and form floated formlessly above an empty sky. The World seemed hushed and poised, alert and focused under the friendly sun. Leaves swayed and danced gently on the trees that overhung the twisting maze of alleys. Ants scurried over little piles of dust at the edges of houses as cats drowsed and dreamed away their sunny day's time on cobbled corners and various nooks. A ragged crew of crows flew crowing and crawing in jagged flow, slowly over, they flew over the view. Beaks brazen of horn and feathers glinting with hidden tints of green and blue amongst the metallic black of sheen. Eyes glazed jellied and aware, so sharp, scanning the cold ground for any scrap of thing to eat. Creaking wings, gaunt feet and a robe so black for your garb. Crawking they wheeled and departed. The sun on the alley walls, picking out the detail of old plaster, crumbling earthen mortar with glittering quartz crystals studded in – all this picking up the sun, the warming orange sun that made everything welcoming and friendly. The ancient marked plaster of walls washing away with autumn storms, walls that have stood time's testing taste and wasted not away. The tiles, the familiar redbrick timeworn tiles that topped the walls. The glossy green ivy that sprawls and crawls over the crumbling ancient and sunny walls. The wonderful rich smell of the ivy, the drone of the bees that feast upon the ivy-berries. Songbirds chirruped from behind a garden wall, the wind sighed gently over the day.

Merrily the sun danced dazzling on the sea, glimpsed glinting through a glazed gateway. Scintilla flotillas flicked flecks of shimmering sparks on a rolling main; a heaving turning ocean of sighing waves ever a-dance upon the bed of the sea. Rococo rivulets running together in tributaries runnels and gunwales. Ten thousand flounders lurked below the shivering meniscus, composed of shimmering ripples and silvery rills. Glaucous raucous skrawking gulls spun and whirled o'er waves of spume on white wings, hacking beaks clacking. Still the scintilla shivered on the sea's silvery mirror. Mere man's glimpsing jelly-eye the fleshy organ-object of direct perception consciously consuming waves of light-projection. I walked on and the glimpse was gone. My phasing footfalls resonated off the alley's walls. Passing the well where women are wont to draw a pitcher of water, I paused poised in prized perfect perusal. Nobody here. Nobody near. Footsteps few fell faltering far. Clatter hoof-heels hopping nocturnal like a nonplussed nightjar. The coast seemed clear of clustering crowds, on nimble toes I breathed aloud. Behind the bulging of a bay-window the sawing of a string quartet soared aloft above the Old Quarter. Quaintly off-quay tumbled skeins of melody and countermelody, like coils of oily rope unravelling, like meat-heads meeting on fleeting masthead mastodon flotillas. Great Thoughts will be thunk thusforth. Run rind or run risk, run wind or run whisk.

A shrill clucking rent the village air and I turned to see a very elderly hen pecking and scratching and lifting its feet around the edge of the 'moat' of the Taxon residence.

The curious old bird seemed to bear a strange resemblance to the eld scholar, with its splay-feet, ruffled and threadbare plumage, and its skin like savoy-cabbage. This old fowl and her fellows spent their days rooting around the nettles, rank weeds and stunted hawthorns that surrounded the aforementioned domicile like a miniaturized jungle surrounding a great mountain. Their eldritch squawking would oftentimes rent the misty night-air of the Old Quarter, when spooked in their dinosaur-dreams, they would flap and flutter into a raucous and rattling din. Clucking and collecting corn on sunny summer morns they crowed, shaking their rattling beaks, beady eyes staring, ever-vigilant for crumbs, crusts and sundries.

A stout rap at the door soon summoned the goodly Mr Taxon from within his lair, and this time, without further ado, he conducted me straight into the laboratory. The place had been given a bit of a tidy-up and everything was in order, organized for organic chemistry or glyptographic research. All had an air of *readiness*. The mahogany gleamed with tropic oils and glass shone pristine on the shelves. Mr Lazarus Taxon extended an osseous hand towards the central work-bench, on which was the egg, covered, once again, by the Mexican cattle cloth. "I obtained it from a fellow antiquary" the olden one explained, "an old salt who deals in exotic curiosities, Vagahorn is his name, I got it from him. It was part of a job-lot, included some old manuscripts and texts from overseas that I had an eye for, but he insisted I take the *egg* too. I don't minde a-tellin' ye I didn't have much use for it at first. Then my ongoing studies led me to the obscure realm of *magneto-animation,* and it is within that realm of science that I pursue my particular specialization." Taxon seemed to wax more serious as his minde focused in on his branch of science. "So the old egg stood in a corner of my library as an ornament, for some years; one particularly lean year when famine stalked the wind, I was considering making an enormous omelette out of it, to feed half the neighbourhood, but the village survived and so did the egg." It was on the tip of my tongue to ask the old one about the species of the cyclopean ovule, but I thought it best to let him get to that point in his own singular time and fashion. There he stood before me, a figure of faded glory. The moths and lichens of time and bird-lime had worn their mark upon his antique countenance and stooped his once-bold shoulders. The cut of the coat, the lay of the moat, all spoke of an earlier time, a grandpaternal time, a time of yesterdays, shadows and dappled light, sepia. The shape of his shoes, so like a pair of sailing-luggers about to ensail for the Grand Banks of fine Newfoundland cod, braving the salt sea splash and the starfishes sting. Sailing in a bioluminescent sea-snail flotilla of whirling squids, squirts and various marine molluscs. His birdlike eyes glittered and twinkled with the light of intelligence. His face was as if made of parchment, as if sewn together with scraps of the Dead Sea Scrolls. If you could somehow have joined up all the lines, crow's feet and wrinkles on his face they would have reached half way to Buryan. Not only his appearance and dress seemed distinctly anachronistic, but his speech was peppered with archaisms and allusions to things past. Lazarus Taxon went on to tell me something of his researches into the topic of magneto-animation, but I confess that despite his best efforts to elucidate the matter, I did not fully comprehend the meaning of the old one. But the long and short of it was that he wanted to do an experiment on the egg and I was to be his Lab Assistant.

    The first thing he wanted me to do was to bathe the egg in a special solution of mineral salts that he had compounded. This, he explained, would increase the receptivity of the calcareous shell to the influence of the magnetic rays he intended to focus on it. While I proceeded to gently swab the egg in the bluish-grey solution, Lazarus pored over his notes in his various and bursting note-books, adding occasional foot-notes to the notes he'd already taken. After this we spent a considerable time polishing and arranging a series of mirrors and lenses around the lab. These were large and circular in design, about two feet wide and cast in the finest quality glass. Having set this gleaming array of orbic apparati in position, Mr Taxon adjusted some dials on his magnetizing machine and taped a couple of copper wires that trailed out of the machine to the opposite ends of the egg. "We shall start the process very gradually" explained Lazarus, "so as to mimic what the Chinese sages call the *Chi* effect." I had read something of China's reclusive men of the Tao, and how they tend to believe in subtle currents of energy or life-force, and how these can be 'cultivated'. It seemed that the Cretaceous Mr Lazarus Taxon was selecting the fruit of the searches through various of his many beloved branches of the hallowed Tree of Knowledge and combining them in his latest experiment. At that moment the cloud that had obscured the sun was sent on its way by the zephyr winds, and the radiance of the sun came into sharp focus, through the large windows and skylights of the laboratory, through the lenses and mirrors and onto the surface of the egg. The shell seemed to glow with an inner, bronzy lustre, as if kindling a fire deep within. The old one made some adjustments to the series of optical enhancers, explaining to me as he did so that it was important not to overheat the egg, just to gently warm it. He also intimated that the influence of lunar light by night would help 'bring on' the egg. He then flicked a switch on the magnetizer, and a barley audible low-pitched hum throbbed and pulsed slowly through the air. Having seen that everything was in order, we retired to the library for a refreshing pot of tay and some grilled muffins and chestnuts.

Having taken my leave of the decayed gentlefellow I decided to air my toes with a saunter along the bustling quays and jetties of the pulsing and ululating seaport towne of New Lynsmouth. The crumbling warves lurching on leaning and staggering beams threw a dull ray of familiarity and comfort through the grey drizzle of my late afternoon perambulation. Dull greasy yellow lights shone dimly through the dense and lumpy niwl mizzle mist, their rays filtering dimly as they fumbled for objects on which to rest. Flurries and squalls of guttural and shrill laughter wafted forth from the inglorious taverns that clustered around the rotting water-side, like so many nests of cackling crows. The fish-market itself was almost deserted – a few disgruntled mongers and hawkers still displayed their wares on teetering and worm-eaten barrows and push-carts. A fitful few flabby flounders flung discontentedly on boards of slippery elm. Dull rainbow sheens glimmered on the backs of flatfish flung forlornly on the monger's carts. All was penumbra. Dulth hung the shady glim of atmospheric whirling fog. Pierced and galvanized by the dim rays of a gibbous moon, the murk hung massy and leaden, oozing from courtyards, dank footways and sagging shedments. Gelatinous indeed was the provender proffered in that accursed market. One would think that all the good and normal fishe had been sent to London Church Towne on the express locomotive, leaving only the freakish and novel, the eldritch and unclassifiable offerings of the swirling black ocean. That great salty element that lapped at and delineated the rot-infested port, that great swirling green swooshing salt sea that had given a sort of living to the goodly folk hereabouts, that prime brine element now sulked and swelled, slurping at the piers and pillars of the ancient and barnacle-encrusted wharf-district, threatening to spit up secrets best buried in its impenetrable fathoms. The very *atmosphere* seemed charged up and pregnant with a dull and crushing dread. Was it only my overwrought imagination? Was I the *only one* who sensed the presence of *evil,* far off now, yes, but creeping incrementally closer by the hour? Perhaps I had been working rather too hard of late, putting in too many late-night sessions with lantern and tomes, poring over my texts, notes and parchments; my head filled with the nouveau-magnetic theories of my new-found neighbourly bibliophile. A solitary auk hurled its dark form against the churning sky, barking in melancholy protest at the black night falling. A steady drizzle descended, softening and obscuring the sharp edges of the granite fish-cellars and warehouses that lined the lugubrious seafront. A line of creaking wych-elms lined the sky, striding the hill up behind the fish-port. Ivy-clad, idhyowek they loomed dark against the darkling sky, sighing and moaning in the sagging wind, dark, so dark and damp. Rooks rattled and raided the dwellings, causing swelling cursings to course forth. Black birds of blasted doom! Cackling they mocked human endeavour and honour, pecking and clawing at man's good works. Sneering beaks flashed in the gathering gloomness. Feathers green-black, blue-black, claws clutching at barnyard straws, they teemed, wheeled and hurtled down among the yards and tenements of the town. Gaslight sputtered, flickered and shone weakly from the standard lamps, weak and dilute like adulterated ale, failing to penetrate the glaucous and greedy gloom of the falling of the eve. A doleful drear seared the souls of all who slunk the alley's murk.

I soon made my way home and lit lanterns. I kindled a fire in the grate and prepared a meal. Mustn't let science drain me too much, I thought, a relaxing evening away from the rigours of study would only do me good. I fell early into a deep slumber, but was disturbed by dreams that seemed to be based on the configuration of those unearthly sketches or *diagrams* I seemed to have produced in my notebook by a process of automatic writing. I seemed to be struggling to keep a great door closed, and on the other side of the door was some great force, I know not what, but it kept pressing and pushing against the door with all its might, and I knew that I had to protect the door and not let the thing pass. Such apparitions reduced my sleeping hours to a sinister torment and I awoke, feeling little-rested, to the dull grey of a day of steady drizzle falling. Doubts plagued my minde – what if it was somehow not right to hatch that egg, that *thing!* What if the old man was really mad, and was dabbling with unknown forces? No! I must firmly dismiss such tremulous doubts and meanderings from my minde! Taxon is a man of high learning, his purpose must be lofty and his technique subtle. I steadied my nerves with a cup of strong tea and resolved to continue my association with the learned elder and his quest into the mysteries of magneto-animation. We could be on the very verge of a great scientific discovery, after all – who knows *what* great benefit we could be just about to confer upon Humanity? Only time could tell, and tell it soon would.

And yet the rain it raineth every day and with every damned miserable droplet of the stuff my soul seemed soaked and weighed down, as an ox floundering in a great mire, and my burden seemed to increase and a darkness came stealing over me, making me giddy with the yawning gape of the abyss. My reeling senses foundered and fumbled, fluttering with dread anticipation. I found it hard to shake this feeling of devastation and ghastliness from the folds of my heart. Truly a raven somewhere tore and clawed at the pages of the book of my destiny, in a lonely ruined tower, entwined with a rich and luxuriant growth of ivy, as the last rays of the sun ripped ragged through the dark cloaks of cloud and an ill night-wind stirred. Surely some black bird of doom and despair was pecking and mocking at my humble human fate, as it spun circling between the stars and their vast, dizzying gulphs. Surely the fell shadow of a pair of dark and ragged wings sailed o'er me, blotting out the healthy sunlight and joyous freshness of my spring morning – surely the harsh sneering croak of this unlovely fowl filled my ears to overflowing and drowned out the gentle song of the songbirds that should rightly have soothed my ears and nerves with their melodious outpourings.

And then it was that I espied my notebook, that I had left next to my place of slumber. A desperate and frenzied hand had festooned the yellowing pages with a truly bizarre and monstrous set of scripts, glyphs, diagrams and angular projections. The beastly alienage of the workmanship was unfamiliar to me, despite many long hours spent poring over the most arcane and outré side-shoots of the tree of knowledge. The ghastly *otherness* of these fetid inscriptions left me gasping and spinning in nauseous waves of antiperistaltic revulsion – how *could* they be the work of my own hand? Yet how *could* they be any other? This vile dilemma veiled my dial with dire inclemency. Those beastly and hideous scrawlings spoke of all that should not be spoken of. And yet, what *were* they? A mere abstraction of lines, planes and unknowable symbols – so what threat could they reasonably pose to me? I grappled with my logic to overcome the irrational revulsion that threatened to grip and possess my soul and minde. Perhaps the scribblings represented nothing more than the senseless yet systematic outpourings of an over-worked psyche? Then why their powerful grip on me, why their dread influence? I could find no satisfactory answers to such unquiet riddles as these, and realised that I might simply have to endure them for the time being.

I decided to take a constitutional stroll down to the

end of New Lynsmouth's jutting North Pier. The morning was bright and fresh, the sun a rich chewy yolk of warmth. A neighbour greeted me, hanging out the washing on a line slung along the side of her house and propped up with a pole. Gardens were scarce in the Old Quarter and the streets themselves served for many a domestic purpose. Old ladies plodded along with baskets of groceries or creels of fish. A carpenter whistled as he sawed the end off a plank. Even the fish-market seemed bright and cheery. Stalls of sea-urchins, samphire, carrageen, cockles, whelks, wrack, puffins, conger-eels, mor-sarfs – sea-serpents, black lobsters, little bunches of eel-grass and punnets of squid were offered for sale, alongside stalls sagging under the weight of opalescent sea-snails, auk's eggs, tubs of glistening sea-jellies and bunches of moray-eels, all tied up with straw. Trade was bustling and the mood seemed hearty, fresh and sunny. I left the market behind and carried on down the pier. A small fleet of luggers had just put in to harbour and the men were busy with coiling ropes and hoisting baskets of pilchards and other fare onto the quay-side. The work-a-day bustle of the place was a fine tonic for clearing my minde and refocusing on the quotidian and safely predictable rhythm of life, as pursued by so many good folk.

    I reached the end of the pier and looked across the gaps to where the red and white striped lighthouse radiated safety to all. Glancing back at New Lynsmouth I noticed a funereal veil of fog was creeping over the surrounding hills, consuming and obscuring the amphitheatre of the port, nibbling away and erasing the streets and buildings one by one. A slight but distinct chill was stealing into the air. Looking over the bay, beyond the isle of Myctis to Tremarazephron, half the village stood out in bright but slightly muted sunshine, cutting a weird contrast to the rest of the darkling scene of land, sky and sea.

    Myriad droplets dancing suspended in the aery miles of spinning space across the sea-bay, from here to the Lizard. Port Levi was painted its typical sunny gold-copper lustre, standing out like a gleaming pin-point jewel on the apex of a wasp's hive, darkly brilliant. The slate bronze mist overarched and defined the scene, by wrapping the panorama in its lustrous woolly cloak. Stillness hung in the air and the atmosphere thickened – glints of light were reflected dancing and squirming on the darkening waters. The sky seemed mosaiced of albumen, shellac, chalk and nitrogen, an obscuring ovoid dome. The changing flickering nature of the scene held me spellbound for some moments, blissfully swimming in quiet and rapturous reverie. The unusual light caused by the great concatenation and congruence of rain-clouds and sunlight, of fog, mist, wind and light reflected and bounced off the water all congealed and contributed to the charged and unique morning. Then curiosity awoke again, and the compass needle of my quickening and searching thirsty minde swung directly towards the corner of Orchard Street and Iron-Foundary Way. I turned on my heels and, translating this insubstantial thought into physical motion, I headed back down the pier towards the Old Quarter. The sea slopped and slewed around the pillars of the jetty as I crossed the road and passed by the old pantiled merchant-house that never seemed to tire of trade; down the alley between the Marlin and the Porpoise taverns, stepping deftly over puddles of spilled ale and worse, and foot-soling it along, I ascended Iron-Foundary Way through a cloud of hot chop suey fumes issuing forth from the sizzling grill of the Hong Kong Garden. These tasteful oriental odours gave way to the sickly-sweet blet of rotting brown apples that had fallen from an overhanging tree. On the other side, on my left, wasn't that the old garden where............... but a vague confusion floated in my minde, the door in the wall was sealed with a rusty and ancient padlock, and the door itself was choked with a rank growth of weeds and ivy – it obviously hadn't been opened in many a long year................. I shuddered and carried on walking.

Phasing, my footfalls fell thudding on the cobbles of the alley. I passed the old well on the corner, where the villagers filled pitchers of water. There across from me, across the junction of the alleys, lay that ill-kempt manse, that brooding and beetling building, dwelling of that goodly man of science, Mr Lazarus Taxon.

Nettles rattled in front of the lurching and decadent structure upon which my eye fell. Towering up on the corner, the grim and rotting gambrels of the aged abode sagged and tottered as if drunk on smuggled cognac. The weed-sprouting yard yawned wide a yard away – I waded towards it. The elder's Chilean pine simian plankwood door loomed forth before me; the knocker fashioned like a little bronze anchor from the days of Brown, Jenkin and Co.. I raptly announced my presence to the eld who held the door ajar and bade me step within.

Chapter 9

Ah, within now, within those walls. The walls that had sheltered the various archaic denizens in former days of yore now yawned forth to enclose me as I meandered into the lurching manse of my scientifically-minded colleague. What fascination I drew from gazing upon that parchment-like face, and how instantly I could divine from it that something was *afoot.*

"Elias," said he, "let us postpone our customary refreshment until we have repaired to the laboratory together – I believe things are starting to happen!" I assented with enthusiasm and we found ourselves in that leaden-glazed lab of greenish and grey glass, so subaquatic in its feel. Some heavy drops of rain were just starting to spatter the panes, running down like the tears of a large-eyed tragedian.

I'll never forget the poignancy and timeless eloquence of that scene – the sky darkening with the afternoon's rain, the stirring of the wind above, the calm orderliness of the laboratory, all as if lit by the eager face of the aged investigator, Lazarus Taxon.

The centre of that glowing and mellow scene was the workbench upon which stood the egg with its attendant electrical connections and monitoring instruments and apparatus. Great ovoid lurking hulk, its bulk pulsing and illuminated with a green-is-bluish hue. The egg had *changed,* had enhanced and expanded itself, as if straining at its own shell, bursting with inner life. Emanating a vigorous vitality it seemed to subtly pulse, as if putting forth energy gradually.

As I let my lead-glazed gaze glance over the ovoid

scene before which I'd seemed to see, seeing with seen and seeing eyes, that is, a scene of scintillating prescience, as if glimpsed in the glazen depths of a cool deep glass interior mirror – a looking glass. And glancing thus and glancing deep, did I by inches creep into glimpses of eldritch tales of unutterable alienage. A ghastly yet formless foreboding slithered and writhed around my nervous system, as writheth a serpent or some foul thyng of ye night. Shivering, I could not yet detach myself from the phantasmagoria before which, ere long, I stood rooted, contemplating the haggard and blighted blossoms of doom itself. I saw people, people running, running down alleys, alleys of twisted cobbles and clack-heels careering down side-streets, spilling pails and overturning stalls in their desperate and frenzied flight from – from what? I think I glimpsed a dark and ominous shadow soaring overhead as the ivy-clad trees' grasping fingers waved on the windy hill's horizon-line. I could not be sure, minde, but I think there was a dark, shadowy thing. Again, I associate these flickering, chimeric, cinematographic, magic-lantern pictures with a persistent hissing or phizzing noise, as of the seething of great terrible vats of steaming broth. I must have fallen into a brief state of stupor. My thoughts were strewn about and stewed in grim apprehension of an impending, approaching… what? Something I could name not, yet from which I shrank back as a fish from the net shrinketh. I gleaned some hint of a dread of a most reptilian and reprehensible character. A sarfek and nameless monster lurking on the bed of the sea, stirring slowly from a chasm of aeons of unconscious eternities. A beast most fell must fall best east but most of all must fall when fell full foul. Such delirious ramblings and witterings raced through my straining and tremulous brain as I reeled back to consciousness, grasping the side of the work-bench for support and rubbing my eyes to blink back at the room, the *laboratory,* and Lazarus.

    The old one had not noticed my temporary aberration, which, it seemed, had lasted but a couple of seconds, and was still busily studying his egg. He gazed at it through a special optical eye-piece, squinting and blinking, winking and blinking and staring at it. Over and over his eye fell falling on the ovoid. His glazed and glaucous pupils seemed to bore right through the shell and to peer within. *What did he see?*

Spinning round suddenly "look!" he rasped, and pointed his osseous and dexterous digit to the great egg. A crack had appeared, not large, but undeniably the shell had started to crack and there would be no putting it back together again.

"It is time to discontinue the galvanic treatment," announced Mr Taxon, and thus we disconnected the voltaic wire attachments from the classical ivory surface of the great egg.

With loathly and utterly ghastly fascination we observed the obverse of the ovoid pod juddering as it rent, tore, split and cracked itself asunder, and a *form,* appeared, emerging in sickly writhing motion before our dread-filled eyes. A head, a sharp and grotesquely reptilian head broke through the brittle ivory carapace of the egg, eyes of green stared unblinkingly above tiny nostrils. A tongue of black flickered back and forth. The head glanced and moved around, alert and aware. The neck came next. It didn't stop until the creature had slithered all the way out of its egg, for the creature was a tiny serpent and serpents are all neck! This scaled-down sarf was about a foot in length and of a hue that seemed to alternate between olive-green, deep blue and black. Lazarus grasped the beast immediately behind the head and I got a glass tank from the shelf and we soon had the reptile-thing safely corralled, a small dish of insects providing the ghastly nourishment. I must confess that during these dramatic moments I was not unshaken by what I was witnessing. The sudden appearance of the snake-thing was indeed a profoundly hellish and eldritch event. Some might have said it would have been better for the towne of New Lynsmouth had that outlandish egg not hatched at all – rather that it be thoroughly addled, scrambled, churned and burned by churlish omelette-hurlers.

I tried to dismiss my forebodings and share in Mr Taxon's evident jubilation at the success of the experiment. After all, we had succeeded in incubating the mysterious egg, by means of galvanic mesmerism, magnetic pulse-waves and the application of a chemical salt solution. Our work had produced the most desirable result, and furthermore, the entity was securely lodged in its new environment – if it proved to get too big, we could always take it to a zoo or something, couldn't we?

After many congratulations and a promise to look in upon the morn, I took my leave of the aged one and stepped my foot into the spinning maze of alleys and byways that threads its silvery-grey net around the goodly, if decayed seaport of New Lynsmouth. A fog had newly come in from the swirling briny ocean and the lights were muted by its feathery blanket. The newly-gone niwlgorn fog-horns honking from lurching piers in the old fishing-harbour were tempered by tremulous droplets off tremendous tenement's rotting roofs.

The night was thickening, the mists were swirling deeper now and mystery was afoot. I could only turn my heels and let them go which way they would, trusting to the pull and sway of the World. The vapours of the night were rich food for my pulsing temples, my racing minde. All that I had seen just now, back at the house, the Taxon place, danced and swirled before my minde's inner eye. The familiar doubts that had nagged me about this whole business now welled up anew in my breast as I contemplated the zoologically dubious and potentially downright dangerous nature of the project upon which I had now, so impetuously, embarked. The district in which I now found myself did not help in any way to lift this dread and sinking ennui, this veritable foreboding that slowly took possession of my soul. The area had a run-down and pinched quality to it, lacking the usual charm and character of the old back-streets. The ill-kempt and sagging fish-lofts and cellars gave out a chill, dank air, as of hardship and grimness. A sign ahead indicated the way to *'Ynkleudhva'* – which, in the atavistic linguistic of this shyre, is the word for 'cemetery'. I turned the other way and wandered towards what I thought should be the coast of the high-running sea, seeking solace in the briny roaring deeps, thereby to stroll and take thought and air. But wander as I would, I kept somehow returning my clack-heels to that district of cabbage-soup and howling dogs. And in my minde I reflected on the events that were gathering around me, around Lazarus Taxon and around the aery and archaic towne of New Lynsmouth.

A faint ethereal sense of amazement at the hatching of the mussy ovule was increasingly eclipsed by the thought of the *development* of the animal. When I thought of that creature back at the laboratory, my feelings were now not unmixed with a hint of nausea. I felt that I had agreed to help Mr Taxon, that I was a party to whatever adventure we had embarked upon, and that somehow I had to see this business through. After all, it was only a minor scientific experiment – merely one with an unexpectedly fecund and fruitful result. Perhaps I was making too much of all this after all; perhaps the old scholar would like a nice *pet snake* to keep him company in his old age! Also, Mr Taxon seemed to exude the erudite air of an experienced man of science, which allayed my own confidence regarding our venture. Still there came unbidden, stealing over me like a ghastly shadow, the minde-churning and headlong rush into the unutterable, hideous and lugubrious vortex of spinning stark nightmarish desolation. A howling and grinding despair of fathomless obscurity, punctuated by the tormented and deranged gibberish of a thousand vile ghouls.

Chapter 10

Mordros murmuring was filling full my ears with the lurch, break and wash of the ever-restless ocean. I could hear it getting a little louder and swelling fuller as my cobble-clacking boot-heels ate up the yards and fathoms of the alleyways' maze, the sprawl of trawlermen's cawls and cabbage-garden cottages up the lee-side of landward-ho. Here had I thus meandered, seeking to exclude myself from the dreary and shadowy district of the 'Ynkleudhva'

Rounding a corner's square rightangular turn, I was washed in the swell of a fresh sou'westerly wind, rolling in from the howling and high-running sea. The swirling mists and niwlek foggy dew-drop furls of New Lynsmouth now blended like teas with those niwllaw drizzle-rills of the oceans deep and mighty main. Seven seas swirled together, slewing starfish and sea-urchin lurching as one, in crazy pympbys dance. Exoskeletal carapaced remains rattled and battled it out together in Davy Jones' Lock-Up. Froth furled and played atop the swaying briny mass, gelatinous it writhed upon the shore, the morrab and the keynvor. The great cummulic clouds, those dank and dripping niwllaw vapours of the night rolling off the looming land seemed to merge and mingle with those that danced upon the deep.

Strolling thus at leisure next to the sea could I let roll my thoughts and feel more at ease in my minde to cogitate and contemplate the incredible developments of this day. But though the freshness of the scene granted relief, the dense and brooding hills of granite that loomed over the area, those weird and doom-blasted hills exerted their familiar pull and pall of gloom. Mockingly the ancient hills leered out from between the patched and ragged flaps of kommolek ethereal cloud-blankets, flapping, flaunting and flying in the face of all that faced north. The rapid spread of their dread ennui left me aghast, embittered and reeling. Hunching my cloth-collared coat I turned my shoulders towards the sea again.

My thoughts returned tumbling to the play of events, the emergence of the creature, the snake-thing, whatever it wąż. In what remote and tremulous branch of the Animal Kingdom did the thing hold office? Llithro slither! Pesky lurking fearful spawn of palaeological time-poached egg! And now I was saddled with the tiresome task of assisting the aged one with caring for the *hissing one,* the, shall we say, the *subject of our experiment!*

Seething with a swelling sense of anguis, both vicarious and viperous, I saw the slithering sarf, the snake itself, in minde's mirror cast, as in a glass glimpsed. Serpiente swirled the sea, crashing white foam on the winding shore, breaking. Clippers rode at anchor, carrying cargo of turpentine, wine and coals. Shoals of shellfish slithered in rivulets abreast of the seabed's shore. The snake! The snake! How long had it lain, coiled in that ovoid carapace of golden-ivory virginal Parthenon pure alabasater albumen? The krogen, the shell that shielded it for how long and where? Buried in the silk-road windy waste-deserts of old Cathay perhaps, what with the aged one's passion for *sinology*… Minde ye, minde, his kaleidoscopic and much-cultured minde swept broadly over so many topics, realms, regions and tropics, that the egg could have originated from just about any torrid or arid zone of this Earth, from Easter Island to Arizona.

It did me irreparable good to brood on the breed of the serpentine birth. Sliding round that tank, it was; gobbling up grasshoppers and god-knows-what. A petty behemoth of micro-gigantic proportions. Rearing its ugly pointed little head in the humble hive that once housed the renowned premises of Messers Brown, Jenkin and Co., refiners and merchants of fine and marvellous morvil whale-oil, by the gallon or the hogshead... How times change. Now ranged the sarf, serpentine writhing in the laboratory of Lazarus, looping, coiling and winding its way around its glassy domicile.

As I turned from the seething shore of the high-running sea to trace my way back to my own humble cotting, it dawned upon my already somewhat overwrought minde that there was something, in an irrational yet singularly compelling fashion, something in the aspect of the snake-thing that took me back to those sombre and eldritch *automatic drawings and outrageously alien diagrams* that I had recently produced in a dream-vapoured sopor. This thought, mingling as it did with the glimpses of those fell and ill-starred leering hills through the mist, contrived to cultivate a jolt of arch horror through the gargantuan depths of my timeless breast.

Seeking rest suddenly swept thither by weary waves of leaden drift, I relentlessly pressed on, leaving the heaving shore and snaking through the alleyways and ill-lit cobbled by-ways of old New Lynsmouth towne. Fyshe-scales glittered shimmering on the causne and from lanthorns eld rays of light mantled manta mana of piscine dishes according to the wishes of the simple fisher-folk who coiled the ropes and toiled the boiling boats on seas slick, rearing and roaring like horse-bears of the rolling night. Goodly folk, aye, but don't cross them minde, not if ye've an eye to your future... And hell help the hell-hound who hikes the price of hake whilst on the make at market, mark me well!

Slumber lay a heavy quilted blanket over the drowsy

port as chimneys gave forth fumes last gasp of evenings
ash-log fires or furze in ranges blackened and gleaming.
Pasties and pies steaming no longer, last crumbs scoffed and
scones quaffed with relish quick. Blooming, rolling round
clouds kommolek loomed ahead, overhead, heading my
way. Sagging clouds shattered as rain ripped and spattered
on glass-patter-panes where guttering candles waned and
lanthorn's glimmers claimed the last of their thane-hood.

Finding at last my own twisting street I aimed my
rambling feet and sailed into port. Thoughtfully I found my
key and unsealed the portal to my tottering manse. Stepping
forth, within at last, the snug familiarity of my own humble
dwelling-place. Tay was soon bubbling on the stove and I
could recline at ease, letting reverie's breezes blow o'er me
whence they would. After taking my morsel of toast and
cheese I stretched out on the time-winnowed divan of rich
lime-green and cream silken brocade.

I fell rapidly, spinning and whirling, turning and turning,
slipping, sliding and falling into an unfathomable abyss of
profound, leaden sopor – a torpor so richly intense that soon
the webs of dream were furled round my limbs like so many
silken threads, strung with glittering jewels of dew-drops. My
limbs loosened and lolled as my spirit flew through the gallery
of endless imagery.

Thus spun the night-thoughts of a night-gaunt, haunted
and hunted by heinous and harrowing herring-bone horrors.
I seemed to be running down alleys of angular singularity.
Spinning and losing my equilibrium and clarity. After me
lurches some doom-spawned slithering *thing* – some vaguely
familiar and horribly half-enfleshed manifestation of minde's
wild projection. Alleys leaned, leered, veered and tailed off
into misty nothing. Cobbles echoed to pattering footsteps
and rain rattled panes of leaden-grey-green glass, dim
glowingly lit yellow from tallow lights within. Finally freeing
my frenzied feet from the labyrinthine twists of old New
Lynsmouth and her incessant blanket of mist, I found myself,
adrift in dream's vapours, afoot in those hills, those very
weird hills that loom above our towne, at angles suggestive of
some unfathomable and ghastly cosmic mystery. Those barren

and blasted grey hills, burnt black, scarred green with yellow gorse, barren, dry, hard hills of granite, ancient and crusted in lichen. These undulations of the topography harboured the last vestige of the autochthonous peoples of the region. In many a crumbling and frankly rotting farmhouse in these very hills, slept secrets deep of past ages of dread and glory, of enchantments and other things. Baked grey clay cracked in splintered sagebrush empty plains. Pools of dark water on moors of windswept heather and gorse. The aspect of some of these farms was truly terrible to behold, and I wondered, shudderingly, what form of horned beast bellowed thus forth from the crazily-leaning cracked granite barn – thunderstruck and lichen-dusted, orange bloom of time's mellow roof-top crown upon the top. Taking shelter among the twisted hills in storms of shattering rain. Night-thoughts, dark and drear, rattling lead-glass window-panes. Swooping dark storm-birds, birds of the night and the dark cloud flapping. Riding the rain in waves. Crows flying in from the East. Feathers outstretched, arching over the brood of granite hills, the land of the elders, rich in secrets and fabled wondrys things.

Puritan creeds clung on in this territory, the dour and the sombre outlook of these austere and atavistic villagers and rustics was cast in their features in the form of a perpetual frown, or scowl of narrow and ignorant suspicion towards one and all. It was in regions such as these, that I dreamily wandered, pursued by unease, and the gibbering and ghastly verbiage of a thousand shrivelled and reptilian tongues. Much was here whispered in hushed and guarded tones, but little was spoken outright. That which was hinted at was dark, foul and inconceivably ancient – a slumbering nemesis rippling in the undertow of an oceanic and unutterably ghastly vortex of pullulating revulsion. These blasted heaths and time-battered crone-cottages could harbour naught but ill; naught but that which should not be. And what white beasts lurked in the depths of their wells, these fourteen hundred years gone? What scuttling mutterers curled beneath their musty ricks of old hay, decaying in the sun these hundred balmy summers gone? What gangling, dog-faced abominations prowled the lanes and meadows at night, roaring for blind oblivion? Answer me that, with your fine city ways, and your fancy clothes oh so neat! What eels reeled in your streams, beneath the water-cress so dark and cold – what *eels* I say! And *bats, bats I say* – why man, bats like *monoplanes* roamed those sultry nights upon the hal, the hilly moor so high. What withered nags ride stag o'er blasted moor at night, clattering hooves a-spark on rabmen bridleways and paths of crystal twinkling quartz, forewarning benighted country folk of dark death and impending doom. Spiders and small, fell, foul things cowered under elder twigs and jelly-ear sprigs, as moss abides in dankness. Prattling chuckling voices welled forth from pools and streams, casting their archaic and immemorial enchantments on those unwary and simple-minded souls who paused to drink unawares. The very cattle and hogs of this region seemed somehow *shrunken,* huddled and withdrawn into themselves, as if no living thing could prosper on such an accursed and ill-fated plateau. And over it all loomed those *hills*. Those sheer and twisting conical pyramidal hills. Leering and a-waiting. Waiting and a-watching. Those hills so like the spines of a sleeping leviathan, an ailing behemoth elder, sojourning neath slumb'ring summits and wind whistling carns and cairns. Humped and hunched like morvil aquatic sea-beast whales ran the hills, outrunning gales and scattered squalls of shattering hail and blizzard. Ill-fated hills. Rank sour rivulets running and splashing in rills, trickling through those dour and grim-faced hills. Twisted cones, curling upwards in geometric vast immensities. Insensible to human feelings or the warmth of a feeble human heart – you HILLS! Curse your bleak unwelcomehood, spurning and a-mocking of my greenhornhood. Blasted and shattered hills, heaps of pestilence and all that ails, bewails a futile fate, feebly flickering a greenish hate. Oh you hills that rise up rocking like black oceanic waves, must ye mock? Must ye sneer on human warmth? Must ye spit on our precious and brief dreams? Ye heartless and granite outcrops of cold and bitter rock, have you no shelter for shivering mankind and his bedraggled beasts, his cattle and his swine? You bleak and harrowed hills of grief, I see now why your central plateau is so sparsely peopled with the archaic and autochthonous folk of yore! I see now how you drove them, trickle by trickle you drove them and you pushed them towards your perimeters, to the 'low-lands', to the coast of the high-running sea, the black and slopping sea, and e'en unto that primal and most terrible village of New Lynsmouth, there to await a harsh fate more terrible yet than all you can threaten with your dark and hulking *hills*.

And so I wandered in this region, slipping away in slumber as my soul swooned and soared. Plundering the orchard of night's aery vapour, my thoughts I did nightly outpour, thus venting psyche's meandering psychotropisms. Gathering rich fruit of symbolic trees I grazed, chewed and browsed, feasting well on aether's cloudy airs – dew running down succulent pears.

Later though, as the night's gloom drew on to fullness, my dreaming imagery became more restless and more concerned with the geometry of the hills and the plateau – and the encrypted meanings and significances of that geometric pattern. That dread pattern that I now recognized and correlated as that which I'd scribbled before when asleep, giving rise to the curiously singular collection of 'automatic writings', or, more specifically, 'automatic geometry!' The churning wave of nausea that these half-hinted correlations aroused within my breast was enough to shatter the film of sleep, and hurl me rudely back to wakefulness, to greet a grey New Lynsmouth dawn.

I lit the lanthorn and my gaze fell upon the heap of books that I had so recently purchased from Mr Taxon. They had lain untouched for some days now; the intensity of the scientific work seemed to somehow take all my strength, leaving little enthusiasm for study and research. Still, they were a great investment, the books, and as soon as my leisure-time was sensibly scheduled again and all these experiments were behind us, then, no doubt, I would immerse myself properly in my studies once again. Meantime I had to conserve my powers, such as they were, to be of service to the eld scholar, and help see this dubious project through!

I took some tay and toast and gradually started to feel a little more human again. Musing a moment on the situation before me, I decided to waste no further time, but to pop straight down to Lazarus's place and see how things were getting on down at the lab…

I must admit, I did harbour some foreboding at the idea of the potential of the snake-thing to grow a lot bigger than it already was. I think this fear was already gnawing and teasing at the corners of my consciousness, and was probably what had caused me to have such a poor night's sleep, haunted as it was by those unrelishable and distempered dream/phantasms, centring on a grim and terrible range of bleak, granite hills.

Having extinguished the lanthorn and put away the remains of the loaf, I locked my door and set off down the Ox-Road to see the elder scientist and his, er, *companion*…

'Twixt tottering walls ivy-clad towers teetered tall, rooks rocking their raucous calls. Mellow sun and golden – speckled rain a-spattered – wind stir a rush, a howl. Clouds scud and scutter, mackerel shoals, coals, crones, crawls, cat-calls and bradawls. Shells shimmy, dull, tortoise-shell brown, speckled. The sky's flickering dance of cloud and sun, brightness and shadow weaved its whimsical spell over me and though I'd slept ill at ease, yet the day seemed fresh and full of promise. The old fishwives were hanging washing in cobbled back-streets as hooves of donkey-carts clattered by, hawking stoneware pitchers of farmyard milk, and eggs done up in twists of straw. Dogs yelped and alley-cats scampered and played.

I knocked firmly on Lazarus Taxon's door and was soon admitted into his curious domicile. I found Mr Taxon that day in a state of some excitement, and, as before, he was eager to proceed straight to the laboratory to shew me the latest developments. "Do follow me, Elias, and we will examine the creature…" His voice almost shook with emotion – was it *pride,* or perhaps even an awed humility. Either way, the elden one was clearly moved by the success of his project to galvanize the egg – that much was clear.

I'll own I was somewhat aghast at the *size* of the thing – for surely it was fifty per cent bigger than when I had seen it just last night! Lazarus had obviously observed the development too, and was eager to get my appraisal of it

"Well Lazarus" said I, "our little beauty seems to be growing up fast! Is it still enjoying a hearty meal?" "Oh yes Elias, it eats like a horse. I've had to fetch it all kinds of titbits from the larder; why, I've precious little left for my own meal!"

The beast was writhing and uncoiling, slowly, lazily, as if contented with the bill of fare and happy to drowse and recline. It seemed a strong creature, as if just growing into its strength; flexing its musculature. But not only was the creature bigger and thicker and generally more hefty looking, but it had also subtly changed shape. A little way down from the head, and again down towards the tail, there seemed to be small irregular bulges, reminding me of pictures of pythons that had swallowed donkeys and oxen. Sometimes, as the creature awoke more and became more lively in its motions, it seemed to switch between its familiar serpentine and sarfek writhings; and a singular form of locomotion in which it seemed to use the bulging areas as a means of propulsion and move rather more as a caterpillar would move. This cast a very odd aspect and Taxon and I both noted it with some interest.

Having weighed the creature and made approximate measurements of it – it was around one foot eight inches in length – we replaced the reptile in a larger glass tank with the hope that it would feel more at home there. Having replenished its food dish with some scraps of meat, we repaired to Mr Taxon's reading-room and took tay.

Through the bubble-glass window the tinkling strains of a harpsichord drifted in with a hint of sea-mist. The lobster-pot windows twinkled with mellow tallow light, orange/ yellow and warm. The damp afternoon was grey, leaden and luminous. The fragrance of jasmine tea scented the still and lucid air.

Through the glutinous green glass of the arch-gable window I, through the orb of my eye, could espye the lichenous and dream-clouded towne around me, it's amphitheatrical bowl dissipating and disappearing into the vaporous blanket of foggy mist that swelled and slopped in over the plateau, drifting in from over the rolling black sea, the rollicking mor, and over those weird, squat and brooding hills of West Kirnowe. This effect of the mist-cloud lent an air of unreality to the towne, seeming to suggest that the lower district was relatively solid and real, whereas the higher cottages, straddling the steeply inclined hill were gradually less solid, and more ephemeral, until, reaching the top of Guava Hill, there seemed to abide a mere faery-village, a half-dreampt apparition, a chimerical eidolon.

In my minde I could fly back two or three thousand years and imagine the whole hillside void of population, a mature forest straggling the trackless slopes, tree-tops melting and dissolving into just such a mist as today softens and washes out the sharp defining outlines of the village. I could well imagine that the first dwellings had simply crystallized out of the mist, like stalactites in a cave, or dewdrops on a cobweb. In the same way, I could well imagine that the first people around here had simply risen up out of the earth, like bracken, and detaching themselves from their root, had wandered off and found refuge between boulders of granite, subsisting largely on a diet of fish, caught upon the 'Misty Lake' or 'Niwl Lynn'. Returning home from sea, these early pyskadors might have headed back to the fog-bank, or 'Niwlenn.' On fine days they might have gone ashore and lost themselves in meadows of a grass of the darkest green, a green that is seldom seen in this age. They would have wandered ancient tin-lanes across the hinterland, under the snowy blackthorn blossom, fringed with wild snowdrops, drinking from twisting shimmering streams of clear water. All these elder generations, swarming and teeming with life, now passed before, but not forgetting to beget the present brooding breed, stalwart stallions of a champion steed. And passed and gone is the age of enchantment and drolls, and the age of the fireside tale, the wayfarer at the lonely country inn, with tales of far-away lands and strange goings-on between folk and half-folk. How the millennia and centuries had drifted and dreamed away, like reflected forms in a burnished copper kettle, passing and vanishing; passing and vanishing, like clouds, like steam, like breath. And now we had arrived at the Scientific Age, the age of Rationality, of Discovery and Advancement. The dank and heavy vapours of ignorance were being scorched and burned away by the searing Light of Knowledge – the Spirit of Enquiry was issuing a challenge to the bogey-men of fable and myth, and finding the bogey-men a little slow to answer. And what with heavier-than-air flight and wireless telegraphy and everything, surely a reasonable age was being ushered in, was smoothing out the rough ground we had inherited from our woolly ancestors and laying the cool marble foundations for a glittering palace of culture and applied science. And the men, and indeed women of this age, this new epoch, could take a small measure of pride in this great collective achievement. Scientists leading a faltering Humanity forward, compassionately holding the hand of Man, and guiding the species onwards and upwards to our great unrealised destiny.

And here was I, with my rigorous training, contributing to this great process by helping an eccentric and solitary old man to hatch god-knows-what out of an obscure and dubious *egg!* Great God, I hope I was doing the right thing!

Chapter 11

Yes, as I say, Gillpington's the name, that's *Elias* Gillpington – G-I-L-L-P-I-N-G-T-O-N. Amateur scientist, scholar and denizen of fair New Lynsmouth. My minde had been much preoccupied of late with the matter of the *experiment* conducted by my earnest and wise neighbour. More came from this association than I would have dared to imagine, dared to think, dared to dream, to suss, to guess, to glean, to have seen, to have been – yes to have been, I say, a being of spleen, devoid of ennui and inured to the void.

Unrelishable indeed was my position, as regards the *thynge,* the *entity,* the *being,* the *beast* that we had brought forth into the green glass leaden light of a Kernish day. I'll own my thoughts revolved around that *creature* with increasing regularity, as if orbiting a small dark planet of great magnetic energy. This untrodden avenue of discovery was a strange and eldritch highway indeed, unrelishable to all but the most fervent and immutable madcaps. Investigation into the natural world was not for those unstout of heart, for those liverish and gutless wunderkind who balked at the sight of a gleaming scalpel, lunging to escape the hallowed laboratories of the noble pioneers of knowledge's far frontier.

Such thoughts as these mulled, milled and mulched into mush in my mynde. Or rather in my minde's imaginary eye of seeing. So seeing thus I sought sleeps slumberous repose and rested out the night ere I arose. Dreams swirled their mystic vapours once again- outré geometry once more etched its curious and disturbing sketch - hills, hills were in it, but I knew them not. Nay, they were a gross and ghastly parody of these ill-haunted local hills of ours that so blast and curse at ones life, mocking and leering their unlovely and fog-bitten peaks in eras geological.

I was hurled from these flimsy nocturnal reveries by a loud rapping at my door. Upon opening it I was greeted by the sight of a wild-eyed urchin, apparently in a state of some excitement. "Be you Mr Grillpington sir?" "Yes, I'm Gillpington – what is it?" I enquired. In a quavering voice the bairn replied "it's Mr Taxon what sent me sir, 'e says you're to pop round to 'is 'ouse right away sir, 'e was most partic'lar about the 'right away' bit an' all." I thanked the waif and sent him away with a florin.

Hastily grabbing a hunk of bread I headed out of the door and wove my way through the teeming alleys and backstreets of the towne, wondering with all alacrity what could have caused the old one to send for me with such evident urgency. Bolting round a corner, I nearly bumped into a lurking figure in the fog. There was something chillingly familiar about the antique hulk that loomed before me. I'd seen those mud-bespattered boots, pale-claret breeches, that battered canvas cape and that absurdly misplaced ruff before – why, it was the blind man, the one who'd warned me gauntly and obliquely before.

"And how goes the *science,* young sir?" quoth the sightless wretch in a mocking, rasping croak. "How did you know it was me?" I blurted out, unsettled by his uncanny perception of my person. "It's the boots – I know 'em all by the sound of their boots, you see." My exclamation of wonderment was drowned out by the booming of a ship's foghorn. "Oh yes," he rambled on intemperately, "I've got you all by the sound of your boots! Ha ha ha!" There was something in his tone that I did not like one little bit. My nerves, I'll own, had been stretched to extreme degrees of tension recently and I seemed to have traded the calm, balanced life of self-cultivation for a hectic and unpredictable sleigh-ride to the very Halls of Hades. "Away now man" I muttered through clenched teeth, but his osseous claw gripped suddenly at my arm and he hissed quietly into my ear – "Don't you worry now Mister, I'll say nothing, *nothing at all...!*" and with that he slithered off, tapping and scraping and cackling down the dream-drenched alley, vaporous, fog-bowed and soon disappearing.

A shadow seemed to fall over New Lynsmouth at about this point. A turbulent wind began to blow through our lives, and who knows whither it shall blow us? These goodly and honest folk didn't need to be troubled by the *sinister,* the *outré,* the ghastly and unloveable. They didn't want their humble and hard-working lives to be blasted and shattered by a bane beyond human imagining. Why would they? Why would anyone want to suffer the dread shadow that befell our upright and trusty towne? Why would anyone in their right minde want to endure the torments that struck and hacked at our heart like some unspeakable ghastly, reeking, roaring, gnashing vile beast; oh vile, vile beast!

With such cheerful thoughts as these for company I soon found myself, breathless and with pounding heart, outside the noble residence of ye good scholar and elder man of science. The rank patch of lank nettles, the old chicken that always reminded me of Mr Taxon himself – the rotting archaic gambrels of the lurching domicile, spattered in guano and time's lichenous crusts, the shutters shut and curtains cobwebbed– all was the same... My knock upon the Chilean pine plank door was instantly responded to by Lazarus Taxon, who threw the door open with eager, bony hand, and ushered me in. I could see that the elder was in a state of some excitement. "I'm obliged to you for coming round so early Elias, but I thought you should see... well... look!" We were by then in the laboratory, approaching the glass-case wherein lurked the snake – only what met our eyes could hardly be still called by the name of snake.

The two pairs of protuberance that had been observed the previous day, upon which the creature had started to execute a rudimentary shuffle; these were now extending from the body in the form of proto-limbs! Great Cod! It was like watching evolution unfold before your eyes in the course of days rather than scores of millennia! The creature was dragging its body forwards on its new-found feet, back and forth across its tank! The persistence with which it pursued this singular form of locomotion was again noted and nodded over by both Taxon and I. Furthermore it did not escape our notice that our *little one* had overnight accumulated five inches of length and was now two feet and one inch long… The serpent was indeed taking on a more *saurian* appearance – the body between the two pairs of stubby 'proto-limbs' was thickening, as if developing more sophisticated internal organs. The 'tail' was now becoming more distinct and differentiated – taking on an apparent balancing function during attempts at locomotion. The neck was also thickening somewhat- a ghastly suggestion of *lizard* was stamping its influence onto the creature.

Mr Taxon was most excited by these new developments and we discussed them at length and with enthusiasm. We felt, dare I say it, rather like explorers setting foot on some great, uncharted continent that had somehow escaped the notice of the world. And like explorers blindly walking into a wilderness, we steered our destiny towards danger, towards darkness, towards doom.

It was agreed that I would leave Mr Taxon to write up his notes and further observe the creature, whilst I went and procured some meats and viands for to feed the beast. The pantiled merchant-house brought forth the fodder and a hasty transaction was completed. Carrying the gross bundle of unspeakable foodstuffs on one arm, I turned my clattering footwear towards the Old Quarter, a steady drizzle was niwly falling faintly, as it drifted in from the mullet-soughing and black-slopping sea, the briny deep of starfish and wondrous gazing haddocks. But this was nothing to me as I bestrode the archaic Keltek alley, my thoughts full of the evolution of certain *entities…!*

"What you got there Ellas?" a shrill voice rang out beside me. Turning, I beheld the gaudy visage of that local vulgarian, Scarlet McAwe- seemingly she'd just left the Marlin tavern after one too many goblets of grog. "Er, just some food for my friend's pet" I blustered, determined to conceal all, and nonchalantly resenting the intrusion. "Oh yea," she giggled inanely, "what kind of pet is it then?" "Erm, it's a" (think fast) "it a *rabbit* actually." At this her mirth burst forth unbridled as she poked at my parcel of provisions. "Carnivorous is 'e?" She'd yanked back the sack-cloth covering and revealed a large bone, a bundle of meats and a chicken. "I never heard o' no flesh-eating rabbit before!" She shrieked with laughter. My minde spun in a nauseous whirl of annoyance, worry, foreboding and a deep deep wish to be left alone. I could hardly reveal the true nature of the one that I was feeding, yet to even appear evasive would in itself further arouse suspicion. You know how people *do* like to gossip and talk on in these quiet little towns and villages of ours, don't you. Oh yes, they love to talk, and I could hardly have them all talking about how Messers. Gillpington and Taxon were raising unholy snake-things in a great glass tank in the old man's laboratory – it just wouldn't go down too well with these good, honest, God-fearing fisherfolk, these humble cottagers and rustic, besmocked shepherd-types, no, not at all well… "Um, he's got a dog as well" I muttered, turning crimson, for it was against my principles to tell a lie, however insignificant. Little could I foresee how many more of my precious 'principles' would soon be burnt as offerings on the Moloch-altar of science. Scarlet screeched with squawking laughter and tottered off to her notorious rookery, gibbering some incomprehensible clack as she left. I heaved a sigh of relief and trod forth to the doom-blasted corner of Orchard Street and Iron-Foundary Way, where lurked the eldritch dwelling of one Lazarus Taxon, man of learning.

The elder greeted me cordially and ushered me in. "Bring the vittles, Elias, if ye would, I think our wee friend is a trifle peckish!" He laughed a strange knowing, nervous little laugh and we entered the lab. Light leached down now through leaden green-glass window-panes as a light coastal rain spattered and pattered once more onto the glass. The intense stillness of the scene was broken only by a noise – a repeating percussive sort of noise. It was the sound made by *the tail of the creature hitting against the glass!* Great Herrings! The lavish beast had grown even in the short time I'd taken to go and get its food! Was there no keeping apace of this flagrant increasement? Its girth had swelled, it must have added another five or six inches to its length, and the *limbs…!* These truly were 'proto-limbs' no more, but rather style them 'protean-limbs' for they had undergone a very transformation, and the rudimentary, proto-vestigal original limbs had developed into fully articulated scaly legs, with knee-joints and clawed-toes – fat, green, reptilian legs! The animal was – shall we say – swaggering on these novel appendages like a buckaroo bronco on a rodeo-yodel hoedown. Its earlier, crude attempts at self-propulsion had been replaced by the natural gait of a species of creature that was confident as a quadruped, its head resembling that of an iguana, perhaps, or a rare kind of desert-dwelling skink.

At this point an incident occurred that was to give insight into the hindsight of the matter aforementioned above. While Lazarus and I were marvelling over the creature's greatly accelerated rate of cellular growth and advancement, I had balanced the parcel of meat-stuffs in its sack-cloth bundle on the edge of the glass tank. A sudden lunge from the tank's inmate rent the parcel open, causing the chicken to fall into the tank. What pandeamoneum did we witness then? Our fascinated eyes of horrific observance soon saw the sight of the beast rapaciously ripping into the chicken like an enraged velociraptor let loose in a helicopter hen-house. In less than a minute the mere skeleton of the fowl was all that reminded. But it didn't remain because it too was soon gnawed and crunched and chewed away to nothing.

"We must *contain* the creature!" exclaimed Lazarus with an air of some alarm. It was easy to see that at its current rate of growth, it would soon step out of its tank and- "Yes, but *how?"* I wondered aloud unclear. It was becoming apparent that the creature was exerting an almost magnetic fascination over us, and it was indeed hard to stop looking at the prodigious animal that it was; the changeling. Its back seemed to glitter in scales iridescent and remembering a reverie dreampt of many past years sleapt. Its noble archaic ancient head, a swivelling looming blunt cliff of a head. The eye, a glaucous glass watery globe ponderously gloating, watching, knowing, seeing, blinking a see-through lid, pupil a mere slit. Bulging orbs scanning atavistically for evolutionary edge. Conical eye, many sided and stepped like an Aztec pyramid or Toll-tccnology. Pupil glazed and gazing long. Gazing long into space. Glazed as a fly goes by, unfazed. The tongue a great, black ball-club - ready to extend and grab. Chameleon-coat, the dandy-lizard, dapper Silurian fellow off to the opera in your tall hat and glasses, your galoshes over your arm. A lizard in sheep's clothing - that's what *you* are! Its green flesh, fine though it be, was not of our flesh. Its chlorophyll-pigment scales gleamed cactus-viridian as the sun reached the meridian. Its vigour, its vivacity, its vitality – all these drew the mynde into the creature's orbit and kept it there. But this was an orbit about to explode and throw out a hundred thousand scintilla, scattered, shimmering, across the dark glass of the night.

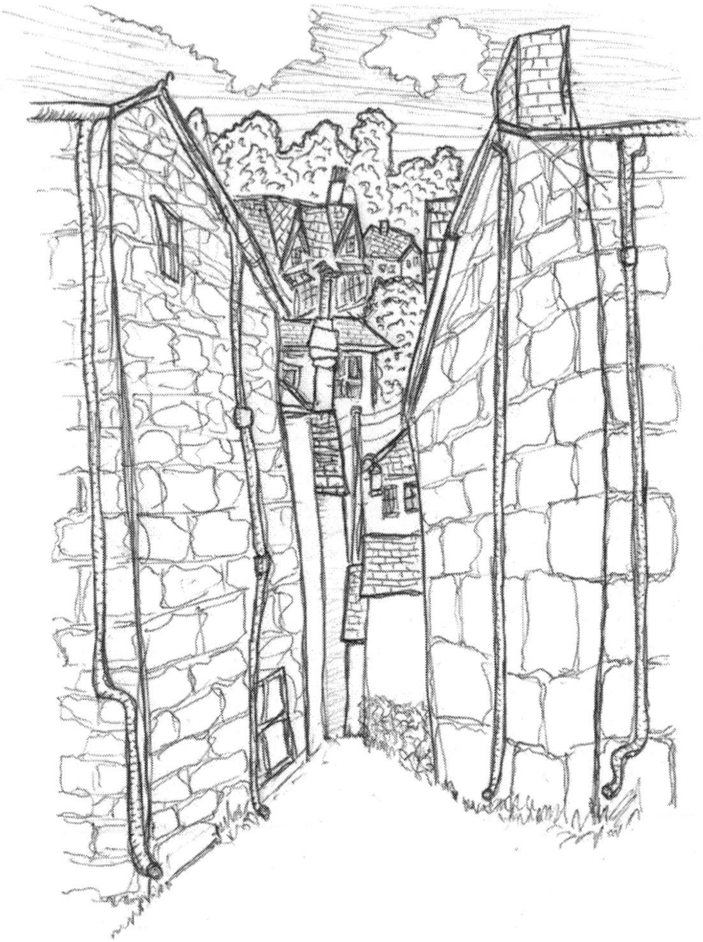

Chapter 12

Twisting and tumbling, the mountainous black rills of Atlantic swirl roll against the pre-Devonian hulk of West Kirnowe; battering and pounding the Shyre with universal fury. Monstrous morvil hulks broadsiding the keel of Kirnowe's blasted bark. Sea so vast, shyre so small – a speck in the oceanic. Speckled granite in titanic hunks, from the Lizard to the Lands End sulks, lurks and looms leering aloft.

And stratified into this rock-ridden claw were metamorphosed many lives, writhing lives of myriad beings; atavisms and revisitations; enfolded in the magma, bombarded with gamma and lambda rays, bathed, swayed and blazing in stellar brilliance, a-sparkle in splintered sunlight. Orange light, Atlantic light on gorse, on bracken, on moss and dripping fern. Grey light, coming through clouds of woolly moisture, nautical fog, atmosphere dense.

Marine-iguanas must have swarmed and swam here on igneous rocky shores, licking the archaic algae with their black-tongues. Lapping mor ashore the sea-swirl laps at wracked rocks and krogens lost –tiny outcrops of limpets and winkles. And how the fresh spring breezes caress the soft land; and how the warm orange light of eve falls on the fallen leaves of orchard and lane. Yes, a good land - till the shadow fell, and fell falls the veil full fast.

By Crikey! This saurian atavism was electrifying our lives, like the blistering unearthly glow of St.Elmo's Fire a-flickering up the mizzen mast in a wild sou'-westerly wi' an 'undred hounds o' Hell yapping and a-snapping at y'r heels, I say! The glimmering blue fire, dancing and a-glowing and a-rattling the lanyards. The calling of the whippoorwills outside was reaching an inordinate intensity. Great crossbilled bee-eaters that they were! A shrillin' and a trillin' for all their little feathery hearts and wing-flying souls. Hatching that beast had been like bringing cauls to Newcastle and casting the clout to play May out. Unleashing this kramvil ephemeron upon a Worlde grown weary of wonders and spectacles would indeed be a species of dementia praecox; a fevered, foetid, false and futile faux pas. Yet birthed the Beast we had, aye, that we had, and now we hadst to raise the critter. Glaw-spattered maw of murk! The *Reptyle,* the *Kramvil,* it was swelling and bloating out to extend its dimensions, quadrilaterally trapezoid it looms and waxeth. Like a tapestry woven of gossamer notions, my minde flickered with thoughts and images reptilian and ghastly. Filaments leach laterally, [exuding blue luminosity.]

Mr Taxon and I worked into the long juddering night with hammer and nails intent on the most urgent task of securing said entity within some kind of ad hoc corral, at least for the immediate present, for, growing as it was, I hardly relished the prospect of speculative enquiry as to the future dimensions of our creature.

At last the ghastly Kramvil was all walled in and pent up within its pen. I bade a tremulous 'goodnight' to an ashen and harrowed Taxon and stepped out into the alley.

As I walked down by Eldritch Gardens, and all along the Creeping Lane I slunk and crept; I turned my feet upon the wandering paths and byways and there I mused while others gently slept.

Once in a blue moon, what you thought was a white elephant turns out to be a red herring. This whole *reptile* business was taking its toll on the booth of us, goodly Taxon and Self. Nothing like a wandering walk to calm the enfevered brow in times of duress. Great Herrings! Things were indeed hotting up. The pall of this foetid morbidity must ere long petrify the tenebrous liquescent feotor that welled up loathly and vile within the gaunt-haunted and shrill echoing chambers of my noctambulatory psyche an' all. Swaddled in my surcoat I took refuge from the mal aery vapours which, sweeping in from Atlantic's swells at this hour of the night, can bring on an access of the rhinoconjunctivitis. Flotillas of by-the-wind-sailors swarmed out there, dogged by some Portuguese men o' war, whose blue blood was up for the chase. That great swirling sea of exoskeletal beasts, of diatoms, fan-worms and great four-square triangular flatfish a-flop with fishy glee. Glaucous and glassy eyes unblinking through the piscine depths of the aqueous night. So much slithering brine bursting and breaking against the grim granite bone of Kirnowe, how it did endure! And here was I, Gillpington, caught in this drama, strolling this brief stage, as mortal man must play his part. And all around that great sea sloshed and that grand mor mawled the bays with mountainous seas – sands the mere by-product of seething energy mashing mass into matter. And limpets gnawed the cliffs.

And turning first my feet at last I wandered forth both free and fast, a shattered wind did stalk my trail, my soul did quake from white to pale.

The old boot-heels seemed to be a-wanderin' down through the Old Quarter of the night, past dusty plains of windmills and sun-drenched caravans; past flickering chimeras of spontaneous automata, slivers of light – gaunt fantastic shadows – hints – words – fingers pointing – voices muttering and sputtering in alleys dark and echoing – signs and significations, great fiery wheels and seals in the sky – rippling red-brick realities of a sunny Thursday afternoon in long ago sunlit city seemed to recur and resurface like so many long-forgotten memories, pictures, photographs and postcards of the past. Seemingly I tripped my feet past fairs and far-flung fakirs, Mongolian tents with pennants fluttering and great street market babbles. A-roaming these streets was to open the imagination's flow and walk the night of a daydream's waking forever. An echo in silver-mercury mirror of an image of reflected clarity. An oasis in muted limestone pinks, golds, mellow soft tones of honeyed stone, sun, always sun. A distant voice, rippling the surface of a dream. Rain falling in a pond in the woods, splash! The ripples radiate outwards and merge through each other ceaselessly. Thoughts and ripples outward flow and I found my feet still a-wanderin' on… damp airs of the breeze, sea breeze scudding in, fresh. Salt-cod drying in the smoke-houses, lofts and cellars of this watery quarter of towne. Salts in sou'westers saunter by slowly. Almost pinniped, their piscine boots slosh, wallow and swagger down The Strand, crunching sea-urchin carapaces into sand. And the tide, great planetary meniscus that it was, ever-slopping and slewing its juice, its aqueous brine and starfish soup into our lives, into our blood. Breeding in us a sympathy with those things that swirled in the depths of that same sea that washed our cliffs and coves, pens and porths. Running high the rannvor rolled in rhythmic eternity, singing its song to the cosmos. And in rain-washed and lichen-encrusted New Lynsmouth, many a head sunk deep in many a pillow and dreams aplenty were spun throughout the night by many a dreamy and drowsy head. An army of pyjama'd slumbering somnambulists shuffled through the streets of the Old Quarter, down along the quay, past Vagahorn's Emporium – oh most eldritch and grime-bespattered of all emporia! – and down along the taverns where the fisherfolk flock to flaked-cod blocks and salmon fear to tread. For there the salt sea is replaced by rivers and cataracts of ale, porter, stout and grog, rum, hooch and swill. My studies normally prevented me from supping up my hours in taverns, for it was the cup of knowledge alone that could slake a thirst such as mine. On that night however, I chanced to run across Jack Lane and his girl Florence, and they absolutely insisted that I accompany them to the Marlin tavern, to take refreshment with them and pass the time together. I could find no excuse that would satisfy my friends, and so, outnumbered and outvoted, I found myself crossing the threshold of that goodly and notorious house.

Looking at that evening in my minde's eye is like looking down a long hallway, through a series of glasses of water arranged in a line on the floor. Each glass contains water of a slightly murkier nature than the last. Glasses clink and voices rise through a whirling swirling hubbub. E'en as the door creaked open we were met with a wave of ale-vapour and the fug of two dozen pipes a-smoulder. Swirling laughter broke and bounced and roared around the room, a room of dark and blackened wood, of a nautical and archaic cast, of camphor hue and mahogany glister, a room that rocked with drinking, a room of swilling salts pullulating with hops and malts. Great slithering sea-snails, the place was awash with whalers, cod-brokers, tar-coilers, net-painters, water-splitters, fish-mongers, gill-netters, long-liners, ling-danglers, sou'westers, nor'nor'easterlies – neither gnawing feastily nor neighing knowingly! This fulsome formative human flotsam massed humanity aquaticus floating and floundering into the alehouse, fins newly-grown with which to swim in ale's glassy-eyed oceanic moisture-mix. Ahh, but all that slithers is not mould, my friend, mark me well... The 'clink' of glasses punctuated every thought, every remark and outburst of laughter of gruff, guttural voice raised in emphasis of some obscure point of narrative's golden shimmering flow. "What'll you have, Elias?" asked Jack, an inquisitive eyebrow arched archly in my direction. "You look like you could do with a spot of something to pick you up – been poring over those books of yours again I s'pose?" His look of exaggerated concern struck me as absurdly funny and I couldn't repress a chuckle. "Thanks Jack – I'll take a small glass of light ale." "And my good lady Florence? The usual goblet of claret deluxe?" It was Florence's turn to turn an ironic glance at Jack. "Thank you Jack, you know me well" she smiled. "Right, so a deluxe for the lady and a light glass of small ale for ye gentle-squire," muttered Jack, as he blended into the thronging crowd that surged against the bar like the swelling tide of Atlantic's main.

Outside the wind seemed to be rising. A raindrop burst upon the glaucous greenish window pane and trickled down like a tear. Skrawked a gull. Gloom of light descended on the scene, a thick, gloopy afternoon's darkness that portends of rain; clouds wet with rain, ready to be wrung out and hung out to dry. Ready to throw down their watery load, their vast clusters of molecular hydrogen and oxygen. Skywater spattered and pattered against the green grey glas, shades of darkness fell – the room seethed. Glasses clinked and laughter roared, voices swirled in snippets and scraps, interwoven in a roaring tapestry mapping minde's territorial wanderings and oceanic voyages. "...followed the boat for three nights before we lost sight of it – terrible great thing e' was..." "....ah well, you know boy, when the pilchards was..." clink – clink! "Cheers boy!" "Cheers me 'an'some's!" "...two hundred and twenty five barrels of good whale-oil we lost... ...and three quarters of the crew that night..." "Just a great wall of water" "'Course, you've got to get 'em sold once you land 'em, and then there's other things..." "Get off, they're never worth that!" clink – clink! Salts wandered from table to table telling tales of travels and years spent upon the brine. These pyskadors, these matadors of mullet and floundering flatfish, monkfish, ray, cod and ling, how they loved to swim in their glasses. The great barrel-vaulted and wood-panelled bar-room with its wooden floor and arched ceiling seemed transformed into a great barrel in which all these aqueous New Lynsmouth fishmen swam and splashed happily, turning somersaults in this beery pool. As conversation grew more animated and excited, the beer was gradually stirred up to a great frothy mass, foaming and fizzing with a head like a glass of Irish stout. The draft that Jack had brought me must have taken some effect upon my over-wrought scholar's nerves, as my sensibilities were prone to curious imaginings and conceits. Not only did the bar-room seem verily to be a great hogshead of ale with the fisherfolk swimming about inside of it, but, as the rain came in and the wind slowly rose moaning and shrieking through the towne, I also formed the strange impression that the great barrel which the inn had become was now floating gently off to sea with the falling tide! This fancy played strong in my minde, as I could have sworn I felt the decks rolling beneath my feet when I went to buy another round. It was as if we had drifted out into stormy seas indeed and the old tub was pitching and rolling on the foaming breakers, and we, the happy band of drinkers, had better just stay below decks and find something to fortify our sea-legs with. Clink! "A hammerhead it was, I tell ye! A hammerhead!" "By thunder man, seven tons of pilchards and we was almost down to the gunnels." "Course, then when we saw our first ice-berg, I said 'I told you we was off course!'" "We followed that dolphin…" "What are ye having?" "What'll it be?" "Can I get you another little drink?" "…flying-fish all over the deck in the morning…" "You know Elias, my cousin Constance is coming to stay with me in a few days, I think you might like to meet her." It was Florence who spoke, though at first her words hung in the air, only to sink in a moment later when I caught a flicker of impatience run through her eyes as I sat there staring into nothingness, preoccupied with the Kramvil, and probably looking vacant and oblivious. I'd met Constance once before and had been quite taken by her. A youthful, radiant dark-eyed girl who seemed more at peace than her lovely but volatile older cousin. Constance, eh….? "Why… yes… I" - Florence gave me a quick meaningful look and Jack returned with the drinks. "So Elias, how goes it in the ornithopteral department? Are you still tinkering around with those absurdist contraptions and outlandish aeronautical plans of yours?"

Jack's words threw me into confusion once again. I could not really claim to have been exactly working on the ornithopter research lately, after all… Important as my aviation studies were to me, they had been seriously neglected since the arrival of, you know… "Well Jack, I haven't been too focused on aeronautical business just recently… I've.. hey, here's Paul!" Saved by the Hill – Mr Paul Hill, gentle-folke etc. was making his way towards our table, glass in hand. Jack's eyes narrowed into a foxy grin of recognition. "Well, if it isn't himself…." Clink – clink! And off we sailed, rolling and pitching on that beery sea, bound for who knows where and caring not a hoot. The storm swirled outside like a lubbering blubbering seafish in a tight spot, flailing and writhing, pounding on the roof a rain-drop cascade, bouncing bullets of rain off the green-grey-glass windows. Shivering rivulets of rain now ran sparkling in freshets and torrents down every cell of every bay window bulge and every tile dripped showers and sprinkles of good fresh rain. It pattered down softly and it shattered down with feral vengeance – it was out to soak rich and poor, both on ship and shore. It would piss and it would pour – the nature of rain was to rain and rain had no choice but to be the nature of rain. Guttering, spluttering and spattering it bounced out of gutters and pipes, it splashed and played and down it came, more of it. Now in waves, now in curtains, now as handfuls of six-inch nails thrown against the windows by demented howling spectres. No this was rain. Make no mistake. Water outside and ale within and spinning bleary beer-glass blues as booze sinks in, loosens, livens, leavens and levels the great and the strong, the old, the young and the rest. Still, the room surges with waves of oceanic energy and salts come and go, notwithstanding the near-tempest howling without. A gang of harpooneers at the next table have broken into a shanty with dark, sombre harmonies and poetic words of old. Their voices colour the air and bring new life to the room, raising smiles, voices, glasses and laughter. The barrel is rolling. The decks are rolling. The barrel is riding a stormy sea, and we are all inside it, sploshing along in the beer. It's a good barrel and everybody's happy. All talk of ornithopters is washed aside and drifts off unseen to waters new. The glasses clink and the windows patter and run with rain. The whaling men have settled into their corners now, some clustered around the fire, some forming another colony up around the bar. "Great blistering barnacles man, let's take another pot of ale!" roared a woolly whaling man, his eye, grey and far, reflecting a glimpse through a porthole, a glimpse of endless grey foggy seas, seas rolling, grey, whitecaps and flapping rags of fog, stretching, rolling off to dim briny horizons where the albatross soared solo round the horns of a hurricane-gale. In his other eye swam fifty thousand fish; briny denizens; frilled sharks; various species of zooplankton; sperm-whale-fish; porpoise-fish; porpoiseless-fish and general-purpose floaters. There splashed and rolled forty-thousand orders of cordata in which to store data and more data. There flourished in the glow of his gaze thirty-thousand phyla of floundering flatfish, rays, mantas, mantras, light-rays, speckled and spectacular oracular, globular, bulbous and fast fish – notwithstanding the salmon and trout. Twenty thousand excellent exoskeletal replicas relished reluctantly their feelers replete with familiar fellow-feeling. Written in his brow were the traces of ten thousand shoals of haddock, shad, great-stickleback, sea-warbler, water-bat, rustling crustacean and scuttling carapaced scurrier.

Ale splashed and sploshed in the front-bar of the Marlin that night like a running green sea splashing the decks of a barnacle-encrusted barque amid-ocean amidships, by thunder! Fragments of conversation blended like puttee with snatches of song, clinks of glass ale-pots and the rough and raucous laughter of these beer-slurping salts who clustered around this beloved bar of theirs, as flies swarm over a mushroom. Again the decks rolled and pitched, as it seemed we had set sail upon a Sargasso Sea composed of thick gloopy stout and fizzy lager, a sea of many swirling currents and eddies. Myriad lillypad diplomats spattered and splashed slapdash balderdash in bleary bladerwrack blistering blues. Clinks – cheers! Razorshells whirl tusking at sedimentary fragments below the limits of the low-tide-mark of New Lynsmouth sands, fan-worms filter sea-fish crumbs and seaweed flakes, swirling juicily so near to the stained and straining floorboards of the ill-starred Marlin Inn. Realms existing and flowing hard by each other – world of water – world of earth. Thunderous rusks and rusty hulks rotted close by in the bowels of New Lynsmouth Harbour – lobsters scurried rattling for cover. Salt swirls of oceanic fog sent quivering tendrils and tentacles to tap tantalizingly upon the window panes of the aforementioned Ale-house; linking land and aqueous branch of water-sea. My minde seemed to swirl like that sea, as if I were a by-the-wind-sailor or Portuguese-man-o'-war, following Doctor Wind across lazy Caribbean latitudes of sultry and sulphurous sun. "Same again mate?" clink – clink! "It's good to see you back out in public again, having a drink and enjoying yourself for once, old man." It was Paul who spoke, leaning towards me with the exaggerated earnestness that alcohol lends its celebrant. "It's good to be back, Paul" I replied, with similar frankness. Paul started to tell me a long and involved tale about a friend of his who had been to Manchuria on a streamer but the sea of voices swirled around me and the unfamiliar beer did its watery work on my bejangled nervous system. "Sampan overtook them…" "What are you having, pal?" "I was on my way to see Ken and Stella, up Kyvounder Hill, when I thought I'd just take a quick drop…Ha Ha Ha!" "Thirteen barrels of the silver fellas, I tell ye; thirteen barrels full." Sliogan krogens crept stealthy lurking long rocky ledges of the brine-kingdom, rock-raspers ravaging igneous and sedimentary strata – radulas resplendent. "So I says 'Don't worry Cap'n, we'll just follow that walrus home…' great blubbery bolb swam like a morvugh all the way to Morvah, we just kept his hind-flippers in sight and he did the rest… led us all the way back to the Shyre…" "Korev?" "Aye, fill up the old kruskynn, let the beer-jug overflow!" "So anyway Elias, this cousin of mine…" "Oh yes, and Nigel's coming over from Porthmouse for the house-warming party… and he's bringing Stella, the Porthmouse Stella, that is!" "Fifteen grunions in the griddle, I tell ye mon!" "Aye and a sprat for the last man, an' all!" "Why, Florence Place, I do believe you're trying to fix Elias up with that young cousin of yours…" Jack laughed his lupine chuckle and jived his long-suffering sweetheart. His roguish ways seemed only to endear him to Miss Place, her affection in him was deep and moving. "Atlantic storm swell coming in by the morning…" "Back end of a typhoon out Sumatra way, I can tell 'e…" Clink – clink! "Get 'em down ye!" "Ha Ha Ha, Cheers matey!" Clink – "Hick! Cheers all round!" "Anyway, Elias, old chap, I wanted to tell you about the, well, first of all do you have a light? Thanks, now, first of all – oh – do you have another light? Thanks, now, as I was saying – did I already say that? Anyway, never minde, where was I? Oh yes-" "Ha ha ha ha ha" Laughter lapped around Paul Hill's muddled muttered utterances and mirth flourished and blossomed anew. "Anyway Elias…" he began again, to the general good humour of the merry band of beer-slurping oddfellows, "I think the Petroleum Jynn-Keber is almost ready to assemble – I think we've finally ironed out all of the design-problems… reckon she'll do a good twelve and a half horse-power…" This caught my attention, befuddled though it was. "An internal combustion beam engine, you say Paul?" I stared at him in amazement – astounded and thunderstruck by his words. But the ocean of words swirled swaying like kelp helpless in eddying waves of gelatinous carrageen downvor deeps. "Mullet shoal." "Pint of best – and whatever you're 'avin' mate!" "Aye, the Old Quarter was awash with Pilchards in them days, nothing like now…" "Oh, you and your pilchards! I never did like the teasy little critters much meself!" "Korev! Give us Korev! Beer, man, Beer! Ha Ha HA." Our hogshead barrel was truly pitching and bouncing now like flotsam on the flatfish briny water-place, where tides run wobbling globular from Yokohama to Penwithershins and all points East of Blighty. All aboard were in for a ride round the Horn, a dipsomaniac voyage which skirted perilous close to the dread shores of Oblivion. Many a good barque lies wrecked there – Karrak ribs and spars haunt these dismal shores. Swirl the words, the mist, the fumes of wine and the sea, the heads of one and all. "It's based on Trevithick's original – with a hint of the old Gnome Rotary... ha ha!" "I can't wait to see it, Paul, I hope you'll give me a demonstration soon." Clink – clink. More loud laughter from the whalers and tumblers were clunked down on the old mahogany bar for more. Surely the room was humming harder now, as the tiller made to sail – and my face, at first just jaundiced, turned all white and greyed to pale. I was beginning to think about the wisdom of going home, to recline in peace and get away from this babble and swirl and whirl. "She likes books, almost as much as you do Elias." It was Florence taking up the thread again, spinning the great tapestry that women weave for men. She had no need to embroider the tale, as I'd already been needled by the beauty of Constance – I think I might have agreed with Florence that we would all meet up – I didn't remember the details too clearly as the hops had done their cheery work on my cerebellum and John Barleycorn once again gave credence to the theory of reincarnation. His spirit was certainly present in the good ship Marlin that night, as it rolled and pitched on an ocean of lapping liquor that claimed all hands and emptied many a pocket of many a fat and hard-earned shilling. Clink!

And in the misty mists of summer, in the hills and in the valleys, in their dreams and in their stories, in the sighing of the wind, in the soughing of the branches, in the whispering mordros of the restless rolling ocean, between the beats of a cuckoo's heart, between the ears of a stalk of green wheat, rolling in the clouds and bubbling up from the ground was -

In the Marlin the grog was doing its work and the old barrel seemed to be heaving and bouncing like a cork in a whirlpool. Even as the infernal calling of the whippoorwills outside seemed to reach fever pitch, yet still it was drowned and drenched with the bleak ragged skrawking of the hundreds of gulls wheeling and soaring and swooping above the rooves of New Lynsmouth. Their feathery forms fluttered and filled the rolling grey rags of clouds above. The lines of ivy-clad trees against the sky swayed in the wind, their creaking reached even into the bar-room. Paul was looking a little bleary, not quite his usual chipper self. His bow-tie was even slightly askew. Florence had made her excuses and departed some time ago. Jack was still cracking jokes, though he looked somewhat flushed and ruddy around the gills – almost the colour of an old fox, padding through the bracken on an October morning. Jack helped me get Paul back on his galoshes and back up the hill. The air revived him and he was soon leading a hearty chorus of "Gwennap Kammbronn 'ill Gwendoon". His thickened syrupy voice was not to the taste of all the residents of the Old Quarter, however, and a vociferous discouragement issued from more than one bedroom window, followed, on one occasion by a flying candle-stub. Such are the perils of the amateur noctambulistic music-enthusiast. After much mirth we dropped Paul back at the Hill residence and Jack and I bade our farewells and took separate lanes to our domiciles.

Mine proved slightly harder to locate than usual, as the alleys would keep snaking and twisting - doubling back on themselves and generally wandering all over the place and being most uncooperative to my home-yearning feet. I must have burned some shoe-leather in my labyrinthine twisting travels, the alleys unwinding like the thread of destiny - a path untraceable. Gambrels lurched and rotted, arches fell and columns and lintels sagged, leaned and pitched at rakish and daring angles, like dandies posing on a street corner. Forward my phasing footfalls fell few and far between and betwixt the slumbering cottages, fish-cellars and artisan's outbuildings. After an immeasurable interval, I eventually found myself facing my own door and was soon inside and stretched insensible on the rococo Ottoman imperial.

And from the pits, caverns and stopes of unconscious slumbering depths, I sunk further and yet further into the swirling and flickering visions of the night. Through chasms vast and unplumbed, great sea-vents and unspeakably eldritch Antarctic crevasses my soul dropped full into the night. Sounds assailed my ears – hissing, the clanging of gongs and drums, the surging vast force of Atlantic's main, pushing

and battering against the huddled bulk of the Shyre – the
Shyre… the hissing and roaring, the splintering of wood and
smashing of glass, the shouting and calling of agitated voices,
the rattle of boot-heels on rain-bespattered cobble-stones at
night, the melancholy booming of a far-flung fog-horn, the
soughing of the Elowek, the elm-grove Idhyowek, twined
with twisting ivy, sending out its sickly-sweet scent. Swarms
of crows took squawking to their dark feathery fingers and
flapped blackly and softly aloft. The roaring sea spluttered
and hissed and splashed around the bones of West Kirnowe
and the hissing was spattered and punctuated by the awful
skrawking of thousands of gulls, those harsh-throated wave-
hopping chasers of herrings, mullet and skate – the gulls.
Great feathered hawks of salt-mor and splattering surf-
haunted turfs of seaside pinks and red herring shoals. Soaring
crawking hard-beaked air-sailors, screaming, crying, sounding
just like human babies, then like cats, then like nothing of
this earth. Mewing, cackling and ululating, the ever-present
gulls of New Lynsmouth, like the cats of Rome, or the owls
of Athens. There was also the soft mineral sound of rain, for
it had returned redoubled, to wash the streets of our towne,
to bless and refresh and softly sprinkle – to dash, to shatter,
to unnerve, to bombard, to attack our homes and pelt our
windows, to douse and dampen our slumpen spirits, to wet,
to soak, to flood and flow. To rise in torrents and gullies,
to flow flushing through overgrown lost valleys and covets
of the hinterland woods, to run headlong into the sea, and
there to mix freely with the fishy brine, the flatfish haddock
and squid-hiding briny salt-soup slop that runs meniscal
round globular orb eternalish. Rain, yes, and more rain.
Thunder seemed to boom and worlds explode, sleep hurled
me through a thousand intricate yet ghastly worlds, echoing
with grim and fiendish gibbers from the tormented souls
of unspeakable entities beyond imagination, description or
conception. A typical night in New Lynsmouth… Apocalyptic
convulsions rent the ground and churned the sea to froth.
Smells of sulphur, burning and decay wafted nostrillian and
nosferatu in guttural feral pulses. The groans of lost ones
merged with coarse, crude shouts, threats and animalistic

grunts. Howls rent the night. Waves exploded in vertical bursts of power. Islands rose from the sea, black, basaltic, naked and stark islands- only to be covered immediately with scurrying, slithering kramvil reptilian iguana-type things, black sea-lizards, ridge-backed, frilled, black-tongued, sharp-toed, salt-sneezing giant black sea-lizards they were. Waves surged over and destroyed this ghastly vision of a saurian archipelago, rendering it null. My body seemed hacked from the harsh granite of Kirnowe and I was pinned to the Ottoman just as effectively as though a horde of fat lobsters had parked their bulging carapaces all over my slumberous form and grasped me with their various and sundry claws, pincers and extraneous appendages. My atomic weight had been multiplied by a factor of 20,000 degrees, my molecular self had reconvened into something totally other than before, and my cellular activity was suspended in a quantum loop. I felt I fell the long night through, pitching headlong, ever-down into layers of oblivious illusion that would chatter the teeth of a natterjack toad. Curious and nauseous waves of sensation also assailed my bodily form as Lethe's waters lapped upon my fevered brow. The beguiling flavour of beer and ale had been stolen away by a gritty taste of Atlantic rain, of old harbour debris, rotting starfish and such unlovely things as lurk low and loathsome. Tingles of lightning ran up and down my nervous filaments and sleep brought no rest. Boulders rolled beneath the sea and jarred the walls of my crumbling cottage, perched as it was just near the top of Keel Alley, a local slipway running down into the waters of the harbour. In my state of alement I suffered many conceits and chimeras, many a whippoorwill will-o-the-wisp. Dark hints and mutterings of a 'shadow on the towne', of phrases like 'in the coming darkness' and other things too vile and alien to recall or represent in human speech. I saw crowds, mobs of angry people, people *hunting* for something or someone in the streets and alleys of our village-towne. The sky darkened. The hills echoed shattering with the crack and rumble of thunder reverberating and rebounding around, heralding more raking curtains of heavy grey rain to drench and subdue the land. Those hills rose again to my minde's eye, morbidly familiar, they were now the hills I dreaded to see, the hills that somehow made me feel uneasy whenever they stood before my eyes, those ghastly, bitter, mocking hills. The dream seemed to recur or have an eternal quality about it. Rain, it starts with rain, gouts and blasts of hostile rain – I run, run through those hills and take shelter where I can. Later I'm in a room and I open a book and it's full of those geometric patterns! I dash it to the floor in horror, trying to cast their influence from my minde, but it's too late and their sinuous forms seem to replicate endlessly before my tight-closed eyes, taking me on some kind of journey, imparting some utterly non-human form of information to me. The sequence runs on and on and the night churned black and howling, with a great wind getting up and stirring up the sea to boom, break and burst upon the rocky bladderwrack shore. Suddenly I hear the unfamiliar roar of a motor, just momentarily – then it is gone. Lights flash. Rain shatters and crashes. Images flicker and spin... ...a barrel is spinning... clink! Oh no more drink! My tongue is a fish... a salted codfish... a smoked haddock or bloater... a well-attired flatfish flat and tired... pounding rain and nauseous geometric figures spin and merge together and resolve into the unlovely visage of the Kramvil, the leering, cold-eyed Kramvil beast that lurketh... no! I shudder and groan in my sleep, but know not the release of even a dismal wakefulness. My head spins, the room spins, the World spins and I a speck upon it. The flapping of wings, powerful wings fan my face and send a breeze through the fetid night. A squawk, a crawk, a cackle. The images slowly fade and fall away. The roaring sea retreats. The rain settles into a steady and monotonous trickle. I fell away into the deep and knew not the why or the whether until some point later when some impulse waked me.

Chapter 13

Skraaak! Skraaaaw! Cri Cri Cri Cri Skraaaaawik! The eldritch and guttural barking of *Larus marinus* pecked and prodded at my slumberous and reeling minde- "Ty goelann hager du!" *You ugly black gull!* Its unlovely and unearthly croaking, yapping cry tormented me, as the pewter-grey light filtering into the little cottage-room seemed to bombard my eyeballs with salvo after salvo of photon-assault and vindictive, demonic fury. Ah yes, of course – realisation came trickling back like beer down a table-leg – the evening in the Marlin tavern, the drinking of much ale, scraps of excited conversation – it all started to return to me like a mosaic of turquoise and coral flakes. Great herrings! I must pull myself out of this malaise, this ale-ment. I must make ready for a day of science, a day of learning and experimentation, but first, first to get this vile taste out of my mouth.....

    I threw some water over my head and drunk some down and felt a little better. As to vittles, I could face no more than the most modest morsel of bread. I made a mental note there and then to avoid such low taverns and hostelries again and to always remember that strong drink was a veritable perhorridus Phlegethon, a seething river of trouble, flowing out of the portals of Hades to inundate its unfortunate victims in a swelling tide of minde-numbing and nerve-battering ethyl spirit-juice, wreaking havoc, phreneticus nebulosus, foggy delirium, chaos and ultimate doom.

    Shaking the clinging fumes of nausea from my countenance, I departed from home and made my way through the district distinctly dizzy and light-headed, oscillating between a sickly euphoria and a grim sense of the *mal*. I dreamed my way down Ox Road and reeled past the Keel Alley and Nagdarf Place, the arches and cobbles ringing with chattering fisherfolk; snaking my way serpere like a seething serpent crawling 'long Creeping Lane. I must see Taxon. I whirled through alleys of moss and liverwort, of myrtle and podocarpus, blet on apples, mottles, speckles, spicules, spiralling gothic spires tilting, dreaming, leaning on windmills in the drowsy afternoon sun. Floating I blended into my streets and byways, my Cretan twisting paths, my fated phasing footfalls foretelling fortune's further folded future phantasms flowing forth forever freed flung flown flew few and far between them. I must gather my wits and steer my way to that bleak house that lurks, shutters shut, cobwebbed curtains fluttering in afternoon's flyblown slow breeze, the house of Taxon. Why do I always wander so, wander astray striking astral days ways and paths Pontiac and synaptic, Coptic, eclectic and scattered? Was I avoiding something? Then the thought of our beast-thing back there in the tank, in the lab, it all came crashing back into my minde like a retching wave of very vileness. A horresco shudder shook my shoulders – I glanced ahead, looking up from my reverie, and saw in front of my eyes the dread *Ynkleudhva* district. My head spun and my legs grew weak. No! I must fight this, I must get back to Mr Taxon, he needs my help – God! What have I got involved in? I must get back….. the memory of the Ynkleudhva, with its reek of cabbage-soup, its decrepit and dishevelled denizens, its rime-dripping lichenous walls, its general stench of decadence and decay, it's teeming burial-ground with the crazy, leaning headstones and crude Keltek crosses, the whole air of doom, sheer doom, as if Death dwelt here at ease, at home and well-fed.

Again I turned my back indignantly upon the rotting and fungoid gables of the Ynkleudhva and managed to make my way through mist drenched and mizzled grey back-streets, towards the Old Quarter and the crazy crossing alleys that mark the domicile of the old scholar. Nettles rattled a deep dark green and the usual lank fowls pecked morosely round the little 'moat', or glorified ditch in front of the house, once, in glory-days gone by, the proud headquarters of Brown, Jenkin and Co., Chandlers and Cod-Brokers to the Trayde!

As I approached the Chilean pine-plank door, I was filled with a strong impression of Taxon and all his erudite learning – all the many topics his lofty minde had soaked up over the years, all the research and physical experimentation he had painstakingly carried out, the vast libraries of tomes and volumes of sheer books that he had consumed – it truly was startling. A comprehensive Sinologist, Naturalist, Aerodynamicist, Palaeolithicist and pioneer of *magneto-animation*….. A man of culture, of the arts, as well as the sciences, in short, a true polymath.

Time seemed slipped suspended still as I raised my hand to lift the door-knocker. I clearly heard a whippoorwill whirl round a-wing in far-flung flight and chirp its warbling cry. A distant cart rattled by, clip-clopping the hooves of a horse. A fly droned. Seasons seemed swung, Earth turning only slowly. I knocked and I waited. Muffled footsteps approached.

The door swung slowly open and there stood Mr Lazarus Taxon, aforementioned polyglot and scientist, looking drawn and jaded. His cataract-eyes flashed at me and he rasped a greeting. "Good of you to come back, Elias, I trust that you are well, on this fine day?" "Er, Yes Lazarus," I lied, "I'm very well."

He peered into my eyes and appeared to draw his own conclusions, then, with a subtle smile of wise irony playing across his weathered old visage, he led the way to the lab. That once orderly and pristine realm of the intellect now featured an ad hoc *reptile-house,* sprawling and lurching, its hasty and desperate construction betraying a hint of the fevered sense of apprehension that had driven the work. Spars and odd bits of timber and flotsam, nailed and tacked together like an organic encrustacean. I'll own I felt, at that moment, a hideous strong repulsion to that end of the room that contained the corral of that kramvil-beast-thing, that hideous lacerta, saura, carnivorous lizard-thing in there - that, that, I didn't like to think of it and felt nausea's sickening headstrong swoon lurch my stomach in giddy head-spinning twirls, shattering shivers and cold running sweats. Probably just the ale working its way out though my system, but the sickening loathly feeling seemed to comprise my physical state, plus a rapidly increasing dread of the *hatchling.* I was really not in the mood to face that beast just now and the revulsion of it seemed to trigger memories of unquiet dreams, of brooding landscapes, rolling broken hills, isolated homesteads and shattered heath-lands. Those unlovely geometrical abstractions leered once again in front of my weary eyes, associated with all that ails and boils an eel.

I steadied myself against the glas-glossy glistening mahogany work-bench and cast my unsteady gaze above me at the great sky-lights of carapace-green-grey glass, encapsulating spicules and splinters of sky's diamond dots. I breathed in cool draughts of sea-air, trying to shake the cobwebs from my hair and calm the fevered brow. In draughts

of saline meniscus dew I drew oceanic swirling echoes of
the myriad marine realms glittering, rolling, resplendent
idylls of the water, the rolling, landless swell that laps our
Shyre and leaps upon our shore. Those brines that hide the
deep-creeping species of slitherers, flatfish, puffers, bloaters,
clingfish, lingfish, lump-suckers, flounderers, by-the-wind-
sailors, pug-fish, lamp-fish, lampreys, congas, morays,
crayfish and crustaceans all – *herrings above!* It seethed with
the pullulating numberless masses of scaly, finned, water-
beasts, all scintillating and slow… the slow, slopping sun-fish,
like a swimming head, a quirk of Nature's humour. Branches
of coral, branches of life-forms evolving and lurking and
reverting atavistic and mystically returning, Coelacanth
heading for the Ganges as whalers roar through the forties,
hoping to lasso narwhals, and maul morvughs, morvils
and stifek – walrus, whale and squid! Bivalve interlopers
vie with monovalve monoglots. Slopping brines fronds
algae foam tides squid haddock cuttlefish sea-hare melek
mussel limpet dogwhelk gwighenn periwinkle bladderwrack
snakelocks froth swirling oceanic in mid-sea in drift in swirl
bubbles churned in immense brine-praries and brit-meadow
grazing-grounds of manatee sea-cows in mid-morning
matinee cowboy movies. Oceans adrift in Atlantic's spindrift
swirling fogs, on Newfoundland's Great Cod Banks, the
flatfish multiply and sponges, sea-cucumbers and sea-squirts
ebb and drift aquatic symbiotic crinoids voiding sea-vents
where sulphur streams from volcanic magma chasms. My
minde adrift upon these seas of seven seized forth free froth
and sooth sized and saw the situation seeth slither and soar
subtly sinking stratospherically aloft aquiver. Monstrous
the maritime unseen beastiary cartilaginous, cold, and
flapping – gills gasping. *Lepadogaster purpurea* – in that
salt-mor, that rolling, duned desert of endless salt-water,
species innumerable went their watery ways, fins walking the
plankton, isopoda and chitons unraveling, nautilus flaring,
morgowlenn and molluscs looming ahead and nebuloso
clouds of kommolek stifek squid-ink now dark-obscure the
umbrel shadowed moisture, beclouding memory, fuddling
perception and wiping out what clarity there was before. This

obscuring tactic trick lures as Lethe trickles and tantalizes, tricking mariners who drift unwary on oceanic feelings of blissful mermaid dealings. Isles afar exotic sprinkled by luminous plankton iridescent aglow with tropical sparkling scintilla. And from these far-flung thoughts oceanic and monstrous clouds of squid-ink, I fought to clear my minde and open my eyes to face whatever now grew fat and full behind the wooden walls we had so hastily built for it.

"By Jehosaphat! Will ye come and see the *creature?"* Taxon was peering excitedly into the enclosure, his attention riveted within. His thin body, clad in yester-year's velvet maroon surcoat seemed magnetized, animated by the energy of curiosity.

I was sinking into a dread, an unrelishable species of horrorum ad nauseum and the spinning, spicule centre of it all was right there behind those flimsy brittle slats at the other end of the lab. A greenbottle droned. It's song modulated by a thirteenth of a semitone. I turned towards Taxon. Whatever he could see in there had utterly captured his imagination and held him still, spellbound and transfixed. I nerved myself to face the beast.

Great Hounds of the Sea! How could it have changed so much since yesterday evening? "Its metamorphic trajectory is truly astounding!" "Yes," agreed Lazarus, aglow with zealous enthusiasm, "our, shall we say, *hatchling,* has successfully accomplished countless millennia, perhaps several million years worth of evolution *in a single night!"*

It was as if the snake-lizard-thing was constantly redesigning and reinventing itself, its restless cells bursting into galactic motion. Great bulking thynge! Hulking and bulking and swelling about the chest, the puffed-out barrel-chest that was developing, protruding, proud. The limbs had differentiated – the fore-limbs were getting proportionately longer, also flatter, like ghastly morvugh walrus wings, flippers of deep-fin dorsal dives through vast arches of underwater sunlight. The hind-limbs seemed shorter now, the shins almost stick-like, with evidence of proto-webbing between the prominent triple claws of the hind-feet. The tail had dwindled to a virtual stub, but what was far more alarming was the truly odd condition of the scales. These most atavistic accoutrements had started a grotesque process of cellular elongation and were beginning to resemble a species of early and primitive quills, giving the beast a curious and perplexing resemblance to an echidna. Indeed, there was something vaguely *Antipodean* about this whole business – perhaps we had another *platypus* on our hands – some freakish quirky creature whose ways defied any Darwinian concept of how evolution might work. The *face* of the beast, it has to be said, was not pretty. The former, chameleonesque Toltec countenance had been festooned with dark and mottled bristles, whorls of quills, stark plate-scales a la Stegosaurus. And the mouth-region! It had elongated and was differentiating into a harder, more osseous structure. The bloated Kramvil changed, mottled, dark brown, light-tan, speckles of olive-green, changed, yet different, the Kramvil cast a wary eye my way. A leery, wary, chilly eye, no longer Toltec pyramid cone-ball-eye, but now glaucous, grey, watery, red-rimmed and unblinking as the Mesozoic. What name do you call something that changes so fast, every time you see it it's a different thing? Protean is what it is – like Proteus, a god of transformations, leaving behind empty form after empty form, shedding the husks and capricious carapaces of an on-going, ever-developing experiment. The modified scales took on flickering iridescent hues, like the wings of a moth in the sunlight. It had a juvenile look about it, like a sullen and chubby offspring, biding and fattening; a spoiled aristocrat, waiting for its turn to rule. A gawky, but dangerous animal.

We had devised a way to feed the hatchling through a small aperture in the top of the improvised structure, minimizing its chances of escape. When we tipped in some scraps of meat and some fish-heads and tails, along with bread-crusts and cabbage-leaves, we noticed it evinced a preference for the fish-scraps, but still gobbled the meat with relish. The diet side of the business was proving complex. Lazarus and I thought we had better not get all the Kramvil's food from the local pantiled merchant house, as we did not want to arouse suspicion amongst these gossipy and superstitious fishers – particularly after that excruciating encounter with Miss Scarlett McAwe in the alley! We decided on a strategy of visiting a variety of butchers around Penwithershins, thus spreading our presence thinly. It fell to me, as the younger man, to procure most of the meat, a task which now involved running all over the area, constantly trying to avoid casual meetings with acquaintances and friends – I was in no mood for small talk while the thynge swelled cell by cell like a great yellow *Velella velella,* bound for a hollow Valhalla.

Lazarus gave me a key to the guano-bespattered frontdoor, saying that we ought to consider the seriousness of the 'animal' situation warranted me having autonomous access to the lab, as a precautionary measure. We decided to tell any inquisitive neighbours that Mr Taxon had hired me to do a little cooking and reading and such like, while he was a little infirm. Luckily, no-one seemed at all bothered about the activities of us two scholars, tolerated and well-known 'characters' that we were. We reaffirmed our belief that secrecy was the best policy as regards our little *experiment,* and, until we could devise some sort of plan about what to do with the hatchling, then we would endeavour to protect that secrecy. There are, after all, few villages in West Kirnowe, or anywhere else for that matter, which would knowingly relish the presence of an experimental beast, unknown to science, mutating, developing, fattening and increasing at a phenomenal rate, whilst they sleep innocently in their beds at night, whilst they go about their orderly and tranquil lives, not guessing the growing menace, the coming shadow, the dark cloud that fell upon New Lynsmouth.

In the afternoon I had bicycled over to Porthmouse, scenting nebulaeic dewy roses as I punted the pedals of my diwros velocipede along past the old Mengleudh quarry at mordryk time of low-tide and rocky wracks exposed – I was off to secure provisions for the quilled-lizard, or whatever it was – the *pedrevan!* Mr Taxon had given me strict instructions to go to Scraggend and Sons, and to avoid Shillingsworth and Sons, as they always gave short measure. So having stuffed the basket with three chickens, various cuts of lamb and a fathom of sausages, I strolled over to the inner-harbour and bought some eels, flatfish etc. from the salts who were just then unloading their catch into creels to lug it ashore where the local Pordinnousers would bake most of it into Starry-Eyed-Pie, the local dish. It seemed they ate little else in that curious village-porte. The preferred ingredient was deep-sea-angler-fish, when in season, and their little masks poked out of the crust right proper 'an'some, replica as clockwork. The velocipede soon had me back in New Lynsmouth, its rosette rose-wood wheels emanating fragrance. The coastal ride had raised my spirits and I'd enjoyed a brief glimpse of sunshine, but as I returned to my own ill-starred and decaying seaport-towne, the niwl-fog, the mizzle, the damp, misty, vaporous clinging cloud of shadow seemed to settle sombre upon the scene again.

There was the guano-encrusted manse, tottering on the crazy corner of Orchard Street and Iron-Foundary Way – its richly rotting gambrels riddled with rancid blet, barnacle littered and starling-spattered hollow timbers and sagging beams leaning and lurching over the misty cobbled byways and echoing alleys beyond. That nettled plot, its scraggy, scratching chickens, strange, lean fowl, the one resembling Taxon, gaunt, with eyes that stare. I crossed the threshold and went into the house. All was quiet. I quickly deposited all the meat and fish in one of the big kitchen cupboards and walked into the laboratory. Spinning horror – lurching – gut-wrenching nausea! I fought to take it in, to comprehend the scene before me… The lab was a mess, smashed test-tubes and equipment all over the place and Lazarus was on his back, on the floor, with that vile monstrosity sitting on his chest, pinning him down, its proboscis flailing and trying to dig, to gouge at his throat, while Lazarus desperately tried to fend it off with his arms. My first thought was simply to kill it, to batter it to death, but I heard Lazarus shout out "The net! Get the net!" So I instantly grabbed the large game-net that was used for collecting substantial specimens and threw it over the vile creature. Quills quivering, it sinuously squirmed in sarfek serpentine proto-reptilian pseudo-antipodean rage. I thought its sharpened mouth-parts might rip through the net, but with some shoving from Lazarus and me, we soon had it scooped up and writhing in captivity, the very etching-image of an unlovely and unspeakably unrelishable, slithering, twisting, coiling, quilled serpent from the depths of below. Such searing Daguerreotype pinhole-images stay etched on the viridian copper-plate files of minde's memory-tablets. Shuddering, I tipped the net out and dropped the creature back into the enclosure, securing the little door and reinforcing it by nailing more spars around it to replace the section the beast had obviously managed to shatter in its escape. I turned to see how Lazarus was, and was relieved and surprised to see him standing, apparently unhurt and unflustered. "It didn't harm me – just shook me up a bit, that's all."

But it was I who seemed to shudder longer and deeper, Taxon seemed to endure.

Chapter 14

As mercury runs, so ran the days during this time of changes and quickening. The new day had dawned grey and niwl-damp, moist and clinging close. The skrawking gulls circled overhead, wheeling with what seemed unaccustomed vigour and voluminous cackling cries. Great Jehosephat! Would they never cease? Ah, to the sea I wandered to take of the airs before initiating my scientific duties for the day. Shadows fell ashore, washed and bathed in light's grey neon gleam, streaming photons luminescent. Angles leaned swaying in time's frozen dance and waves broke ever anew on shores of Keltek rannvors and mors. The fresh sea air was charged with piranhas. And here floated Irish millstones bearing crazy sandalled saints to our rocky brine-patch. And here loomed and lurked lobsters. And here wracked the sea-moss, crept the krogen, curled the eel, congregated gelatinous floaters and bloomed the aqueous richness of it. Here by sea and sand, nothing ever swims on land. Froth of foaming breakers breaks forth fuming spume and splutters apoplectic bubbles. Brine froth a saline broth.

I turned my toes towards the jetty and picked my way between the creels of fish, whelks, crabs and eels. Salts were a-mending nets with giant needles and thread of octopus-hide.

These old birds would dip the needle in squid-ink and tally up the catch by creel. Rolling afore the mast as far as the Grand Danks of Newfoundland, these whalers and longshoremen seethed at their work and netted their breams from broad-beamed barques afloat far, wide and 'an'some. A forest of masts made matchsticks of yards of trees. Canvas flapped – dark-red and resilient. Where albatross rolled his bill in the roaring forties, these New Lynsmouth salts had rounded the horn in search of flatfish and floundering mantas. Now they swayed on tar-barrels and played accordions and whistles and tottered off down to The Marlin for their regular dose of grog. The stones of the old pier seemed sunk on history's bones and galleons and archaic fore-castles rotted in these dark waters deep.

Returning to the village-towne street's cobbled twist my heart leapt to see Florence Place walking towards me with her cousin – *Constance!*

I'll own, I'd forgotten just how beautiful she was, how she had a mysterious power to - "Elias" called Florence, "how fortunate to bump into you like this! You remember my cousin Constance, don't you?" She couldn't repress a smile, and neither could I as I took Constance's hand and looking into her eyes I mumbled some greeting. Florence led us into the Golowji Tea House and ordered a pot of Lapsang Souchong and a round of muffins. No sooner had it arrived than Florence suddenly remembered some reason she had urgently to go back to her house and I was alone with Constance, falling again into her presence. Her dark eyes darted from under her dark locks – animation danced across her face. The air seemed to quiver. Words were withheld from us both as we magnetized each other.

She lifted the spell by pouring the tea and passing me a cup of it. I thanked her and we started to chat about seemingly trivial phenomena, but with a warmth that made them seem alive. She showed great interest in my studies into aeronautics and we talked of the ornithopter-principle, the low and high aspect-ratios, theory of abstract aerodynamics and the circling flight of birds over the sea.

She told me she'd been attending nursing-college and

was thinking of going on to higher-medicine.

"I want to be able to help people, Elias". That had stuck in my head. So much of the conversation seems a blur, as other forces were unwinding. "Just like with your flying machine" she continued "once you and Mr Taxon have perfected it, who knows what benefits it could bring to the world?" Her trusting faith in my scientific altruism was momentarily overshadowed when I thought of the Kramvil back there in the lab, growing at a rate of knots not known to be grown at.

"Your name could go down in history, Elias" the look she gave me left me in no doubt – I was in love with Miss Constance!

"Oh, I shouldn't think so Constance" I replied dreamily "I think the old cabbage-crate's got some evolving to do before it gets off the ground!" She looked at me again. "Elias, when it does get off the ground, will you take me flying with you?" I smiled and took her hand. "Constance – *if* it ever gets off the ground, I *promise* to take you flying with me – I would love to!" Again we fell into each other's eyes, but this time we were rudely interrupted by an urchin tugging at my sleeve. "'Ere, Mr Gillington, Mr Gill'ampton sir!" A grubby face peered into mine with an enquiring look. I recognized the lad from the alleys. "Mr Taxon sent me to ask you to come right away sir – and to get the things on this 'ere list, 'e said." I thanked him and gave him half a crown. "I'm so sorry – it's, it's the old man, he needs my help with some important details of our experiments – I'm so sorry I have to rush off like this – I hope I'll see you again whilst you're staying with Florence." "I hope so too Elias, goodbye." And the next moment I found myself in a daze, ducking furtively into the local butchers shop for nigh-on thirty bob's worth of sausages, offal-cuts, bones, chickens, fleshes and meatpots of all descriptions to feed that beast that just dragged me away from… Stoically I stashed the fleshy fare in bundled baskets and headed hot-foot, light-headed and heart a-poundin' to the mystical crossroads of Iron-Foundary Way and Orchard Street where lurched the rotting gambrels of ye aforementioned dwelling, moat peppered with nettles. Shooing clucking fowls to scram I knocked apprehensively on the old guano-encrusted Chilean pine-plank door and stood still and rooted an eternal minute as dusty curtains leered from between half-shattered shutters. From the presence of Constance, to the grim and grisly butchers, to here, the laboratory of my new-found mystical mentor, Lazarus Taxon – and all in the space of a brief few minutes. My head whirled.

Stars seemed to circle spinning above me and atoms gleamed hovering in equidistant perfection as I stood teetering on the threshold. "Come in, my dear fellow" twinkled Taxon, his eyes a-glitter with vitality. "How are you, Lazarus, I mean, after the nasty shock of yesterday, and all that?" Lazarus closed the door behind us. "I am in good health and spirits thank you Elias. My youthful studies of what the Chinese refer to as *Chi* have stood me in good stead – as have certain herbal concoctions of my own devising and application." Ever the erudite man of science, Mr Taxon impressed me continually with his startling ability to apply his knowledge from such a vast spectrum of topics, and always apply it with such consummate skill...

"I've brought the meat." I handed him a blood-stained package which he immediately stowed away in a high cupboard. "And how is our *friend* today?" I couldn't help asking. "The beast sleeps at present," replied Mr Taxon as we took our seats in the room with the Chinese prints, the books, ceramics and exotica cosmologica.

The learned and subtle atmosphere of this room had always affected me with a tendency to reverie and now, under the influence of Eros, my minde wandered back down the alleys that led to the Golowji Tea House and Constance. Mr Taxon's rasping voice startled me from my happy thoughts. "We must not let our 'pet lizard' monopolize our scientific efforts. I feel drawn to return to the aeronautical project – these are exciting times for aviation and I think some of the ideas we discussed would be worth applying to the ornithopter-plan." His words jolted my memory. "Absolutely, Lazarus; and that reminds me," I continued, "my friend Mr Hill has been working on an internal-combustion beam-engine. Calls it his 'Jynn-Keber'." I noticed Lazarus's eyes flash with searing interest behind his gold-rimmed lunettes. "I thought the motion of the beam, or keber, could be very conducive to locomotion in the ornithopter." The eld was obviously struck with the idea, grasping it instantly. "That's it Elias! If we gear down the flapping of the keber and, assuming Mr Hill's machine gives a satisfactory power to weight ratio, we install it in the airframe we'd already envisaged, as in the blueprints – we just might get off the ground!" Lazarus chuckled with enthusiasm, he seemed animated, galvanized, like a hatchling about to take wing.

We sat in that room and sketched out a plan by which we would balance both projects – the aircraft and the *other*. We decided to continue with our *observation* of the lizard-thing – measuring it and now also photographing it. Mr Taxon would develop the silver-nitrate glass plates himself, as this was another of his skills and, naturally enough, we did not want the local chemist developing them and alerting the authorities about a 'strange beast' or anything of that nature… Meanwhile, we would also start work on the construction of our flying-machine. We would utilize the old stable adjoining the laboratory and overlooking Mr Taxon's enclosed courtyard. He had already purchased most of the necessary materials – canvas from the local sail-makers and light-weight woods from some of the local boat-builders – other bits and pieces, such as bracing wire could be acquired from Vagahorn's ironmongers department right here in New Lynsmouth.

We set to work that very day and soon a skeletal fragile thing of spindles, spars and struts took to form. We both worked with feverish calm, synchronous in our assemblage of the great monocotyledon hogweed pterodactyl. Resonating in gothic beauty its batwing lineality evoked echoes of quixotic devices archaic. If Leonardo had got drunk with Count Von Zeppelin and old man Chanute, they could not have cooked up a more eldritch and chimerical machine. A dodo, a bat-skeleton, fire-fly, dragon-fly, reed-warbler, a chattering jay-bird, flying-roach or wood-pigeon aflap – a Chinese wind-up toy, spinning-top, cotton-gin, jynn-amontya, like Babbage's Calculating Engine but with wings instead of numbers on which to whirl. The old stable was now incubating a new sort of egg – a Trojan Horse of Greek proportions – a sleek scintillating basilisk-archaeopterix – a half-timbered corvid bird, thatched with taught green canvas and reeking of fresh dope. Trestles propping up the undercart as we fused it to the fuselage.

Time was drawing forth and eveningtide waxing redgolden in nostalgia's flickering hymn of pictorial-flow. Woods of trees creaked above on the Kyvounder Hill and clacking crows whirled and vied with the gulls in avine strife. Taxon and I had worked hard and made good progress, now he looked at me and without a word, I knew what was on his minde…

We cast a last glance on our skeletal bird, then, closing the stable doors, we walked across the little courtyard and into the laboratory.

Archetypal the atmosphere in this empire of empiricism – a rigour ran wild on learning's lofty masts avast in this harbour of knowledge's hideous harbinger. Deep shiny the rich mahogany work-benches flashing lignite photon's fire. The magneto-animation device had suffered a breakage to one of its supporting columns but was otherwise intact, crackling Alexandrian pseudo-bract that it were. Some of the early sketches of the ornithopteral apparatus poignantly clung like moths to the walls of summer's hay. Flutter their tiles another dust-day. My head was filled with science, love and wonder. Such days of rising young fire – of Promethean leaps into terra nova on leathery flapping wings of the great mechanistic pterodactyl. And again globular splattered the first molucular coils of silver-leaden glaw great raindrops on the glas-green-grey leaded tracery panes of the grand laboratory sky-lights as clacked the crows and a rising wind threw leaves dancing aloft. Something awaited us across the room. The casks of chemical salts stood upon their well-ordered shelves. Pipettes, scales, callipers and barometers – crucibles and bellows next to Bunsen burners and balsam of glycerine. An orange shaft of sunlight lit through and shone the scene within – a globular eye took it. Watery like the eye of an extinct fossil-thing. Secrets released from stones and the individuality of a leaf of all the globe's trees, fluttering. Constance's dark beauty – her face – so strong in my minde! The meeting! Those eyes – and now all this – the progress on the experimental airframe and the furtive trip to the butchery, to feed – to feed the *thynge!*

I felt Lazarus's hand patting me on the shoulder – had my eyes betrayed a momentary feeling of wild and eldritch shuddering dread? Of crawling, babbling chaotic horrorum horrendum and gibbering rank insanity?

"Come on old man," he said gently and I instantly regained my spleen, nerve, pluck, vigour and rigour. Besides, I was also getting increasingly anxious to know what lurked now within the rambling structure at the far end of the lab.

We advanced together, Taxon and I, stepping forward, so it seemed, towards a new day for scientific discovery like doppelgänger Odysseuses cast adrift on an archaic Achaean bark in siren seas of deep, gloopy Mavrodaphne wine.

Ah great yolk snake lizard bee bat bird fish beaked being be ye? What be ye now, beast? To what morph ye? What form have ye emptied for another? Fish feather quiver quill heather shake the moor with your heckling hackling hue and cry. Taloned dodo morphed in rodeo click clack whirlwinds down corridors of time's evolutionary progression. Shapes slink thus hither they quiver to conscious they mew maw and clack.

"Great Herrings!" I burst out "Is it an echidna, an archaeopteryx, a walrus, fruit-bat or the very Proteus?" A colloid of amazement and dread washed me through and I'll own I was close to swooning.

"It seems our little friend has been doing some growing up" observed Taxon laconically.

"Would you be so good as to fetch the viands, Elias, and I'll prepare the camera. Perhaps we can achieve some good photographic portraits of the animal."

I soon returned with the bloodied package of meat – reeking with the quotidian death of the butcher's block. Whilst Mr Taxon set up his photographic apparatus I had a chance to take a long, cool look at the *Kramvil*...

Is it a shock to be shocked when you are expecting a shock? Yes it is. It certainly is, as no speculation can approximate a reality with a mere mosaic of spectacular and prosaic prose. Standing erect on two distinctly webbed hind-claw-legs, the pedrevan creature was now over a half-fathom's worth of explosive cellular growth and hyper-accentuated development. Dizziness opened up a gaping chasm before my fumbling feet – an astronomical gulph of vast, unutterable amazement. I must have lurched forward a little and I put my hand on the makeshift cage to steady myself – but one glance at the creature's proboscis made me instinctively get my hand well away from the hatchling. The head, now elongated and tapered, was also fronted by a bulbous protruding ossification that leered a-gawk, frog-like, scissor-like and inspiring of dread. The nostrils mere air-holes in the osseous proboscis. The eyes, now yellow-rimmed, set well aside the skull, gazed slow with cold watching distance. This wedge-like head was adorned with a garish and unlovely bonnet of quills iridescent, wavering spicules of scintilla. This quilt of specialized scales covered and cascaded down the pseudo-antipodean puffed-out-pigeon chest of the beast, covering it all over, except its gaunt and stick-like rear-limbs, which now sported socks of cold and scaly skin. The ghastly webbed claws scratched and pawed at the ground whilst simultaneously the flipper-like front-limbs were being habitually flapped and extended, still trailing the unrelishable dangling quills, like a fringed buckskin buckaroo or bucca du. Where on Earth had that trader Vagahorn acquired that outlandish *egg* in the first place, I wondered? From what uncharted island had some local sea-farer traded this Magnus Ovum for a bottle of Jamaicee rum? What remote white coral sands had warmed its ancestral bones in sparkling planktonic latitudes? Perhaps it had travelled overland, traded from the heart of one of the great continental hinter-lands or steppes.

    Mr Taxon released me from my reverie by asking me to throw some bits of meat to the creature, so that he could attempt to photograph it in action. On catching sight of its food, the Kramvil hissed like a locomotive and lunged forward, tottering on its spindly legs – flippers flailing in frustration.

    I dropped a string of sausages in through the roof of the cage – the beast clutched them in its jaws and swung them around with horrible violence. Some of the sausages were splattered against the wall, smearing it with flesh – the creature pecked and gnawed and chewed away at this until all trace of it was cleared away – it then chilled my blood by throwing back its sharp little head and squawking loudly in a hollow and deeply repulsive voice. Lazarus managed to catch this moment with his camera – the stance of the beast boasting an atavistic poise. What we did not capture, however, in that time-spattered house that leaned upon the cobbled corner, was the eldritch and unrelishable *alienage* that was contained within the animal's cry. A tone so unlovely and un-warm, a quality of voice that seemed rather to scream of black cyclonic ocean waters that roar, rage and blast, breaking their watery backs on the ragged rocks of Cape Horn and the tattered and tattooed vestiges of dread Tierra del Fuego where whirling maelstroms draw unlucky mariners down to the crushing black airless weight of the deepest ocean's depths. Something in the voice of the beast seemed to howl like the pitiless tempests that scream doom to mariners all.

I continued throwing various fleshly viands into the makeshift cage and the creature continued to lunge at the food and devour it with unnatural and morbid vigour. Its mouth parts were by now stained red from congealed gouts of blood as it picked over the remaining bones, then threw back its head once more to shriek, hiss, cackle and crow, a vile, thin and ghastly noise that still echoes through my very darkest and most malevolent nightmares.

*

Such days as these blow by fluttering like leaves torn from a book on trees, spinning and twirling and playing on the winds. Rains raked the Old Quarter, making sparks of light jump up from the cobblestones. A wind had come in from the sea, brittle like the breath of ten thousand wolves, chilling and forbidding, it frowned darkly on the little land of West Kirnowe. The rain's pellets raked the green glass bubble-glass window-panes of lurching cottages and bulging hovels as they spilled out of the harbour and up the hemispherical amphitheatrical hills that rolled on up from old New Lynsmouth, up Kyvounder, all the way to Tread-Our-Toe. Something in the configuration of the Old Quarter seemed to channel and draw all the winds of the sea into itself. Being just a keel's scrape away from the harbour, that great cuttle-fish-pool that it was, the quarter seemed to draw watery vapours to itself as does a sponge. And the great Atlantic can of course summon up vast pools of airborne watery moisture and, using its convection currents, hurl them directly onto the tiled, thatched and slated rooftops of Old New Lynsmouth towne. This process had been happening with such historic regularity that, if you stood still long enough, you could actually see the moss grow! This rich and dank club-like moss crept and prowled and preyed upon all the available surfaces of all the buildings, walls and structures of this old towne of ours. It was the outbloom of the fecundity of nature's wild efcaristirion of bounteous increase and fulfilling – a creeping green richness that embodied water in all its strands and tiny clubs.

In particularly wet seasons, as we seemed to be experiencing at the time, a tenebrous strain of unwholesome black slime-mould, neither vegetable, animal nor fungi, but representing a separate Kingdom of Life would carpet the alleys, the gutters and the low places between cobblestones and drains. In dry times this hypogeal and sooty encrustation would desiccate, shrink and crack into non-linear geometric abstract patterns, resembling the cracked silt in the bed of a dry wadi. The gnarled and knotted trunks of the many old apple and pear-trees in the various orchards and farmer's meadows hereabouts were clothed and coated in festooning fistfuls of archaic lavender-grey lichen that ran wild to the north. All these creeping epiphytes collectively held countless barrels of moisture, so that even on rare sunny days there was a raw and morbid moistness pervading the Old Quarter.

The rain had started coming in before I'd left the lab and my short journey home was a grim battle against monstrous stalactites of hydrogen-dioxide and hurtling liquid icicles. Rods and spars of rain dropping down like spears in the roads. I've got to go on – road foggy but the route dry but it still heavy rain's a gonna fall. Water asplash and a-bounce – a-come back in your face and get down your neck and creep up your cuffs and wet you. A wetting rain, a fine soft wetting rain; a mizzle, a niwl-glaw, a damp hogs-jaw of a night. Puddles, pools, pols and hog-wallows soon opened up in various dog-trots, dives and doctor's door-ways. Ah, morgowles! It's a wonder the jellyfish didn't all slither up from the harbour and bloom anew in these moisture-drenched and dripping streets of ours! Pennywort, liverwort, lungwort and sphagnum were massed here, a-quiver in crevices, bouncing with rebounding and ricocheting raindrops. Yet more drops splashed in pools as mordros surf roared around the shattering shore. Thus dampened in cloak and skin, yet curiously elated in spirit, I found myself in front of my own door and went in, stooping to pick up a letter that lay within.

"Dear Elias,

I am so sorry to have to tell you that I must curtail my visit with dear cousin Florence and leave immediately. It seems that there has been some sort of a dreadful accident at one of the mines in the Parc Hellys area, and since all the local hospitals are already greatly overburdened by the epidemic of rhinoplastic conjunctivitis, the top brass are organizing us trainees to run an auxiliary field-hospital at Windrawn.

I can only hope that we girls will lose our status as 'green-horns' and rise to the occasion. I do so want to be able to really help to alleviate the suffering of those poor men.

I did so enjoy meeting you again Elias, albeit briefly. I trust that when you're tinkering with that biplane of yours, you'll remember a certain promise you once made.

Yours, Constance."

For what felt like the hundredth time that day, I was flooded with rising tides of powerful and contradictory emotions. I was saddened and disappointed at the loss of her graceful and most lovely company – but that seemed a trifle selfish when I considered the reason why she had had to leave as she did. I was shocked to imagine her, so young, noble and fresh, being confronted with the kind of horrific injuries one typically encounters in mining disasters. The idea of sweet, gentle Constance, not yet even out of college, being exposed to the crushed, broken and asphyxiated bodies of those poor tinners – my instinct was to want to protect her from such cruel sights. On reflection however, it magnified my respect for her, as a woman who would face such things because of her strong motivation to help others in distress.

Then also, if I wasn't overly deluding myself, it seemed to me that the tone of the letter betrayed a certain *affection* towards me and this thought was so warm and exhilarating, that it tended to return repeatedly to my minde.

Thus with my head buzzing with the thousands of impressions of the day, I lit the mellow tallow candle lanthorns and brewed a jar of tay to wash down the cold pasty that passed for my meal. Guttering sputtering lantern lamps that light the chill night – beaming little golowji things, glowing yellow, shining white, waxing red, fluttering, smoking black, wavering, waning lights to light the lonely night of the learned neophyte.

To try to calm my minde after the whirlpool events of this whippoorwill-wallaby of a day, I absently perused my treasured new volume of Cults of the Solomon Islands. Even this vivid and iridescent account of atavistic *kastams* and stone-age ways of life could not divert my restless thoughts from the day's events, so, with the sounds of rain glawing and pawing at the leaden glas-green windows, I extinguished the lanthorns one by one and stretched out to recline at ease upon the rococo Ottoman divan, as velvet darkness stealed into my chamber.

Sleep melted me back into its primal ore.

Our Heavier Than Air Machine is complete and stands imperious in the stable. Lazarus keeps glancing at the blueprints, then at the aircraft and shaking his head doubtfully.

I notice the fabric of the wings is covered with thousands of tiny ribbons. I glanced down to where the undercart should be, but there in its place was a very ugly pair of huge clawed feet and between them lay a vast and distended *egg* of sickening familiarity. Egg of china dome calcium cone. The ovoid magnoid quivered and cracked open – in the next instance a strange, trance-like snake had started to emerge from the cracking egg-shell.

The stable doors were flung open and there stood Constance, looking more beautiful than ever. A look of love passed between us but then the air was filled with the ghastly moans and cries of injured and dying men and Constance seemed to step outside for the briefest instant, only to return, dragging the horribly mangled body of a miner. She turned her head slowly and looked at me, her eyes gleaming with bewilderment – "You've got to help me!" she pleaded insistently and with such an intensity as to throw me to the surface of wakefulness.

The rain's torrential play upon the roof-tiles seemed to calm and soothe me as balm. Wind rustling through the ivy-choked elder trees across the isosceles triangular street corner tangent way. Nightjar's hawk-mouth honk and froghopper's folly. The wind that shook the elders, flapping *Auricula judae* jelly-ears – tough to eat, but tougher to hear with, moonbeams etching and picking out the 3-D ridges and furrows of the eldest bark. On the old dead limbs, the elder mountains – mini-ranges of jagged Rhodope peaks on barkless half-dead branches, all a-rustle and a-crack in snaking wind's pilgrimage through chunky Aztec sandstone streets of my towne. And rain scattering on glass like rice poured and thrown at batteries of snare-drums – rain-pellets – rain-bombs – rain-funnels and rain fountains – rain washes and cleans – rain gushes spats and sputters ten million globules in formation falling – rain falling unseen into a dark sea at night – rain it rollicks sploshes and slops wet around wringing drenched gutters, whilst I, Gillpington, the neophyte, lie here warm in the dry aglow.

River rising to gush, hills awash aloft as streams in spate divulge, diverge and disgorge. Gorse on the moors washed away by the roots – black peaty sediments washed downstream to grace the sea-bed and grow food for beetling legest lobsters and telooned and segmented exoskeletal tenebral scuttlers. And atop the great rolling meniscus, oceanic swell, black waves, and dark wings over the ocean. The ocean swells salt wash at rock-blasting shore. Night black roars. Gulls and forty winds cackle and shriek in flapping abandon. When do we meet the wild men? When do we unload the precious cargo by night? Shreds and pages of books float down the swollen river that drifts past Unstable-Hobbla on down to New Lynsmouth. Pages and documents were all in there. Blueprints and art-prints and Chinese brush paintings – scientific treatises and butcher's bills – manuscripts and hieroglyphs – contents of the glyptotek – swirling scrolls and hide-bound wood-block epic myths, all rolling and tumbling down the river's swollen streaming course to the sea. Aye, green and briny, and black. Vast the ocean vast. Rolling mor of sleep of dreams all flatfish under your oily skin. Roaring nightwolves of the wind unleashed and a slate-grey slate bursts upon the cobbles shattering sleep's sweet hold for some, I for one, caught, pinned like a moth twixt worlds of surging energy. Scattered fragments blasting sleep from me for it only to return in thin nauseous trickles. Ah, the pterodactyl attack of insomnia's relentless seething flow! Wheeling skrawiks mock, squawk and flock to fly before the flecking foam.

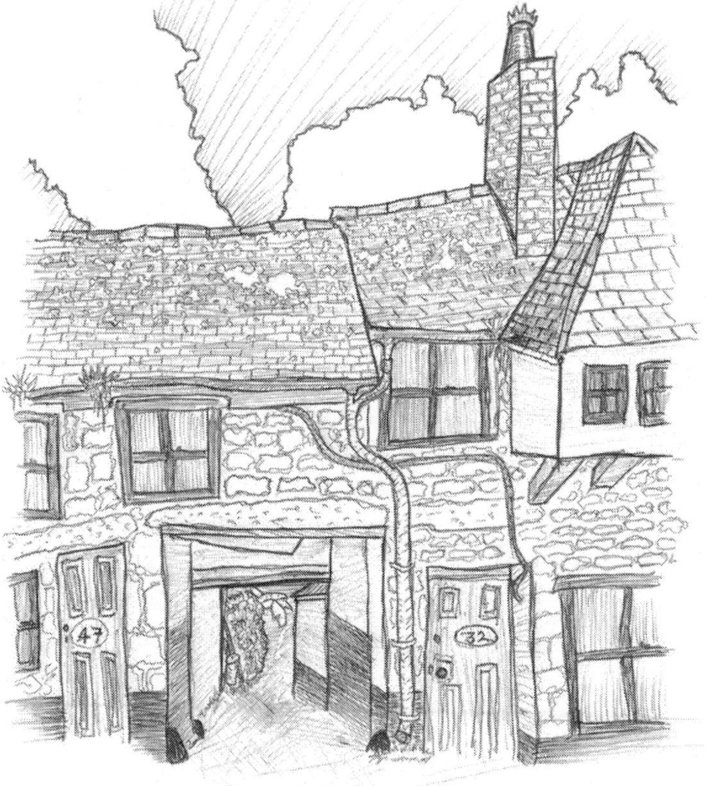
47
32

Chapter 15

Dawn's mackerel kommolek clouded blue azure crystal dome glowed fresh as night's shades and vapours fled shrieking through marble-collonaded halls of classical antiquity, back to the sepia-mercury underworld. Something in the lab. I shuddered awake, heart racing with interlacing feelings as I broke the surface and awoke to the realisation and remembrance of all that I was now involved with. Great Herrings Alive! I ought to go to Taxon's house immediately to check on the - the - whatever it was!

It was beginning to dawn in my minde around then that we ought to consider the creature's future – perhaps some municipal corporation might like to purchase it for their zoological gardens, where it could enjoy a comfortable existence... For after all, how long, realistically speaking, could a frail and elderly scholar such as Mr Taxon be expected to house and harbour a grossly mutating, belligerent, antipodean-style howling throw-back lizard-thing?

And Constance! I should reply to her letter right away, but due to the 'Kramvil' business, I thought I'd send a telegram to the field-hospital.

DEAR CONSTANCE VERY MUCH ADMIRE WHAT YOU ARE DOING. PROMISE REMEMBERED. ELIAS

Arriving imminently at the time-blasted bleak house of Taxon, as it dreamed on its medieval corner-plot, chickens scratching and cackling like micro-velociraptors around the grizzled and misshapen bushes and stunted weeds, rattling nettles, and lichenous crepuscular encrustations – I was greeted by the archaic polymath who eagerly ushered me into the house and closed and locked the stout door behind me.

"Our *reptile*-friend has evolved a little" said Taxon archly, as he led the way to the lab. Great squirming sea-beasts and shoaling sea-bass! The site to greet myne eyes was outlandish indeed – even compared to its recent, grotesque manifestations of its evolutionary 'adventure'. Our 'lizard' now stood a proud three foot six inches tall on its two clawed and spindly legs. I noticed Lazarus studying my reaction to what I beheld in that ad hoc corral. The quills had changed, branching out in fine blades along their sides; above a bulbous chest, the flippers had elongated pteradactylishly wing-warping. The red-rimmed eyes glaucously glared – the osseous proboscis had metamorphosed into what can only be described as a beak. Longer than a butcher's knife and snapping and clacking shut, the black beak became bespoke beast's bowsprit-piece piercing nostrilii. Those so called 'quills', with their absurd fluffy side-extensions bore a more than passing resemblance to the downy and immature feathers of some variety of juvenile *bird!*

At that moment I caught Lazarus's eye and we passed a meaningful look between us – eye to fleshly-jelly all-seeing eyeball. "Well, I've always wanted a budgie!" quipped the elden one, a merry twinkle in his moon-watery eye. "Incredible!" I murmured in unfolding amazement. "The sheer speed of biological development – epochs absorbed in hours – truly incredible!" My minde spun a-whirl.

It was like a great speckled chick, swaddled in its iridescent surcoat of shimmering, downy proto-plumage. A huddled brooding furtive fledgling winged-thing waiting and watching, never showing its hand. Devouring its meat with sickening tearing abandon, ripping and rending, lunging with bony beak and stabbing at the offal, bread-rolls, fish-heads and such stuffs as proved pleasing to our hatchling-fledgling protean halfling. The ghastly and unnatural cry of the thing was also getting louder and increasingly harder to tolerate when up close to the cage. Great squawking thing – lurking – tormenting – biding and seething – observing and swelling and expanding – great merciful herrings! Where will it all end?

Once again, we proceed to the old stable, taking our kroust of pasties and a pot of tay with us. We soon set to work on our experimental aeroplane. Being such a diaphanous and flimsy superstructure of spindly spars and spikes it took echoes of dragon-fly's fluting forms of fluid flights of flux. Dimetrodon-chameleon opaque snowflake fluked forked fuselage. Our 'kite' progressed rapidly and more or less satisfactorily – we both proved good at the carpentry side of aerodynamics and we were soon adding ribs and braces to rudimentary wings (movable), tail (box-kite construction), nacelle (aerial-toboggan) and a spring-loaded undercarriage made from an old pair of skis (plus tail-skid). All in all our audacious auk – our aerial-chariot – flying-carpet – heavier-than-air-machine ornithopteral apparatus was shaping-up well. The insect-bejewelled glistening silver wings extended gracefully forth, stretching for the air and its ephemeral paths. These daring wings of ours were skilfully affixed and pivoted, leaving long spars to attach to the jynn-keber to power the beast. The attaching of said engine, the creation of Mr Paul Hill Esquire, gentleman of engineering-science, should be a straightforward matter. He had a little workshop up at the old family 'house' – in fact a capacious and rambling country mansion with generous formal gardens and lands. It was up there that Paul conducted most of his mechanistic projects, wisely away from the prying eyes of the locals, who could sometimes be none too welcoming to the latest offerings of the physical sciences.

Somehow my minde orbited, gravitated towards and finally landed on the thought of that overblown hunk of poultry we had inadvertently 'generated' in the laboratory – that thing that slithered and reared up and shot from serpentine to saurian to avian in so ephemeral a handful of days... what forces stirred the inertia of that creature's cells? What initiated this explosive, high-velocity growth? Was it merely down to Mr Taxon's techniques with the mirrors, mineral salts, application of electrical-fluids, etc.? Or was it in the very molecules of that kramvil-buzzard-hawk-critter? That squawking skrawking thing! It's at it again! Lazarus shot me a glance as we heard the braying of our great speckled baby-bird, coming from the laboratory.

"I'd be worried about that cry drawing unwelcome attention to our project if it wasn't for one thing," said Lazarus. I wheeled round to glean his meaning. "Its voice blends in with the ubiquitous cries of the gulls hereabouts, because it somewhat resembles them," observed the eld, richly.

We decided to adjourn the ornithopterals and I headed down to the harbour to procure a couple of bushels of fish-scraps to feed our flapping and stirring fledgling. A bag of starfish; some eel-tails, damaged in transport; some squid arms and legs going for half a quid; a crawling creel of crustaceans, sea-brittles, crawfish scuttlers, bristlers, coelacanth scales and baleen dust of the Greenland whale. What's more, skate-tails, sea-snails, sunfish-rays, hake bits, Finisterre ray fins, octopus-discs, mermaid's purses, dogfish-bark, stonefish gravel, raw lionfish, great venomous scorpion-fish and such scraps as this and these. And bivalve krogenek slitherers in punnets.

This glistening, chill and unworldly flesh of the sea shivered gelatinously in my plaited-rush basket. I cunningly concealed it beneath my bulky surcoat and returned to the lab for 'feeding time'.....

And what a ghastly and unspeakable feast that turned out to be! As soon as we entered the laboratory, the creature scented the food and started up its anvil-hammering clack, raucous head thrown back in pre-Devonian ecstasy. By now the great woolly chick was soon learning to snatch the flying fishy tidbits out of the air, gulping and hawking them down with fervently unwholesome relish. Rain pattered down on the green-glass carapace windows, running rivulet shadows down across the laboratory. The meal continued, the bellows box-camera of Lazarus capturing grotesque moments – tendrils of stifek squid drooping like vines or veins from its eager ripping beak. Starfish shaken and torn and scattered to supernovae fragments by that vicious, tearing bill. The crawfish crushed, crunched, ground, gutted and gulled down without so much as a 'by your leave'. Krogens cracked – their brittle shells scat, splintered and shattered to shards and smithereens from Saskatchewan to Skibbereen. Winkles picked clean. Bonefish spine of the bullfish stingfish all fine and fair fare for this glaucous speckled downy owlet of primeval parentage and pristine piscine ancestry – heraldry correctly and formally emblazoned on chivalrous family shield with all forms of etiquette pleasant and correct. Serpentine intellect slithered and selected eclectic ecclesiastical eggshell enfolding environs equitably. Now proto-avine, an archaeopterical illusion. It also made fish disappear. Soon no hint, scrap or trace of the watery meal remained and the beast seemed sated and settled into a quiet rest, the bulging barrel of its fat-dog of a body hinting at trouble to come, as its eyes glazed a deep-space-gaze fixed woefully in the barren jelloid moisture of its pupil.

We sat in the reading room as night's shadows fell thick upon the ancient house and chickens pecked morosely outside. The Chinese jades and European works in oils enhanced the cultured calm of the lamplit room. Violet velvet drapes enfolded rich vintage shadows and glows. I took tay with the old one, and, before departing, agreed to return early the following morning to help him tend to that improbable fowl we had penned up there in its makeshift cage of spars and struts. That strutting Spartan departin' scapegrace of sage and shifty shape and voluminous vacancy. That egg-chick of a chick-egg. Half-cracked thing that it be – Easter Island egg – Galapagos lacerta lizard cramming its vile beak with bile-brewing bleak fishy steaks and streaked bakes and fresh flakes of smoked hake. That great brooding hawk-chick of a dodo in its ridiculous furry overcoat, a fluffy kiwi-thing but ravenous and volatile, virulent, instinctive and atavistic, bellicose, mistrustful and mal, a penumbral thing compounded of an unutterably ancient lineage. Ah, for my own peace I must cast that long-legged chicklet from my thoughts!

The Cretan labyrinthos of twisting and tiled alleyways claimed me as it snaked through the Old Quarter and those denizens and teetering tenements that lay between the residences of the goodly Taxon and myself. These archaic streets and Ox-roads never lost their power to fascinate and enthral my minde and I happily gave in to their dizzying influence. Soon sombre slabs and lichenous lintels opened their foggy ways to my home-bound feet. Lanthorn's glow at the street corner a globe of yellow luminescent fluidity – I followed round angular three-sided corners and soon rolled home to my own humble cottage dreaming the forever of a golden day before yesterday came.

And the wind that blew from the sea brought

murmurings of salt and foam and sea-serpent's sarfek moan; of moray and conger eel, sylli Scilly eels that writhe around the Longships, Guava Lake and the Axe Factory where stone-age men shaped liths on a drowned land, watery now under three or four fathoms of aqueous brine. Eternally the damp molecules swelled and slopped and strew and blew around, vapours of the great black mor, the ocean's atmospheric breath, cooling the hot igneous brow of the land of West Kirnowe, a bony and ribby granite growth growanek and encrystalled with sparkling quartz and mica; uplands of gorse's gold and cheerful purple heathland heather with bracken's green and orange majestic tints. And hills bounding upwards, these winds playing around them and shaping the thorn-bushes into embodiments of wind's wild will. Whistling over the checkerboard of ancient fields and farms, of the dark brooding hills, this great free and original wind came o'er the land and washed away the clinging vapours of sleep's leaden Lethe, rinsing dream's fumes and gossamer will o' the wisps into spiralling clouds of ruby and rose carnation sunlight towering mountains. Suffusing the lambent cumulus with a warm rosy, purple and golden hue bright with promise and the upliftment of a new day. Such breezes blew fresh and clean, oxygen threw particular atoms of clean original energy over the scene and the day glowed and brayed the animals in their fields and the beasts and fowls of the farmyard lifted up their voices to the morning. And how rolled and blew this eternal wind? How did its miniature spicules of motion move? What orchestrated its planetary dance? Flapped into fury by the cloak of a Norse God, these breezes could spring from zephyr mellow draughts to raging wolfpacks blasting the sea to a seething whitesquall and grinding galleons to the deep. These draughts of Atlantic dewy air now rustled the ragged curtains of the house of Lazarus Taxon, sending miniature whirlwinds of dancing dust spiralling down the globulous panes of an age-begrimed leaded bay-window. These same zephyrs danced around the angular door of my own goodly, if decaying cottage, blowing and wafting my psyche gently back to Earth and the wakefulness of another day.

Over the next couple of days we worked long hours on

the ornithopter, Lazarus and I. The lace-wing-beetle carapace exoskeletal airframe was duly covered in its swaddles of light-grade canvas sail-cloth, before we painted it with dope all over, to stretch and harden the fabric, and to reduce 'skin-friction', a phenomenon in which too coarse a 'skin', or fabric surface of an aircraft, can over-heat, due to excessive friction from the air. Great pains were taken to properly stress all the bracing-wires that tensioned the 'kite' and basically held it together. All moving parts were meticulously lubricated including control surfaces, suspension on landing-gear and the wing-pivot-joints, that had to withstand the juddering oscillations of our peculiar form of locomotion. The doped surfaces dried to a straw-golden hue and the craft did look fine. We'd modified the box-kite style tail into a much smoother-lined, bird-like monoplane tail, that had an extremely high degree of articulation, allowing for the possibility of near vertical ascensions. The 'nacelle', such as it was, was really just a small, modified canvas screen, demarcating the front of a tiny platform that was to house the aviators and their motor. This new nacelle was in truth little more that a sea-side windbreak, shading the brow of our mechanical bird and affording the 'crew' a little protection from the slipstream.

The machine had an elegant and almost natural look to it. Wings ribbed, bat-like, with protruding spars at the trailing edges, like fingers. The leading edges of the great ribbed wings with their swept-back tips, were also slightly curved back for a better angle of attack. Lazarus showed a stroke of genius when he filled all the hollows in wings, fuselage and tail with specially-made silken bags full of slightly compressed lighter-than-air-gas! Thus he lightened our craft and helped it in its quest to claw aloft into the air. Fuselage broad and strong, to withstand the flapping motion of the jynn-keber petroleum beam-engine. Local ash-wood, strong and light. Struts and spars were varnished and polished, gleaming and glassy. All those mortices and tenons and dovetail-joints and pins and pegs had finally held together in a unified whole, a new and wondrous entity, born merely to soar and swoop, or break-up in the attempt!

After losing ourselves in the work of constructing our aerial-carriage to soar aloft upon the aetherial margins of the sky, I was brought quickly down to damp Kornyshe earth by the realisation that the *thynge* needed feeding – again! The skrawking had set up to a yammerin', and a hollerin' again, fit to bust the ears of a tinnitus-riddled mastodon. Such a foetid and febrile clamour communicated the beast's insatiable lust for scraps of fleshy food, and, as Lazarus was too advanced in years to go running around the countryside procuring meat, the task always devolved upon me. I jumped on the diwros velocipede and cycled forthwith fast and steady up to Unstable-Hobbla, where roosted a goodly chicken-farm whence I secured, scored and procured the freshly slaughtered carcasses of several head of chicken. Having croaked their last they were clucked, plucked and pullulating punnets of poultry-protein for our protean prototype, back in the lab.

A blast of Lapsang Souchong scent in the air and the strains of Satie's 'Ogives' on the phonograph greeted me as I returned to the house that leant on the edge. "How are you getting on with the Nagarjuna – though I don't suppose ye've had time to look at it yet, have ye?" enquired old Lazarus as I deposited the sack of fowls on the floor and took up his offer of a hot dish of tay. "I have to admit I've been neglecting the old book-learnin' a bit recently," I admitted. Lazarus gazed into infinity, space glittering in the moisture of his all-encompassing and vastly deep eye. He was scanning the depths of reality. "Ah yes Elias, when you have time, or rather, when this fledgling grants us leave, Nagarjuna is the one to study. But, time enough, Elias, first we'd better go and take a look at our dear bird."

Once again I followed Lazarus Taxon into the carapace-green-glassed laboratory and, once again, was found beholding a creature changed, transformed, matured, swelled, swollen and expanded. A grown-up, sleeker and more hawkish version of the creature last espied in this very pen, not more than six hours previously, and now, great skittering starfish, by all that howls and gibbers, why *look* – just *look* at the thing!

Standing well over four feet tall, speckled and mottled a

dirty brown-grey dapple on white, head white, beak black – gonys angle sharp to hack, legs stark skinny moribund pink, foot splayed webs of chicken-skin aquatic, eye rimmed in red betraying vacant acute stare of piscatorial vigilance – a great speckled bird, a thing of the aery-sea-skyway – in short – *a gull.*

Scenting the fowl-carcasses that I hauled in my gunnysack, the great Kramvil-hatchling let forth a terrible and nauseating braying, mocking, screaming, laughing call – its ghastly head thrown back now, cackling for all it was worth. Cackling, it seemed, in triumph. Cackling, surely, with a foul, gloating disregard for Humanity and all its fine arts and cultures, all its inventions and past-times, gloating and leering and mocking and a-sneering at all our fine and fancy *human ways,* all we stood for, us and our kin. When that great speckled sea-bird let out that cackling cry, that unutterably vile, dank, foul and eldritch barking and mocking yell, I knew that all was not well.

I hurled it a chicken through the bars. It was rent asunder, yea verily was it devoureth, even as ye beasts that falleth into ye tar-pit. Cracking bones, snapping beak – gone is a chicken, a flap of skin licked greedily up by the braying, feathered beast. Its sickening cry tearing at my eardrums and sickening me to the stomach – foul and yet more foul fell its shrieking decibel syllables on my delicate earlobe extrusions. What a damn rum business this was, and no mistake. A rum old bird and a miss-hatched plot. I threw in a second chicken – only to see it meet the same fate as the first. Ripped, gorged, held down in webbed, almost prehensile claws, to be gouged at and torn apart – broken and reduced by that savage black and broad beak into chunks of gore-dripping and unimaginably unpleasant nutriment. Stabbed, lanced and bayoneted by that beak. Crunched and spattered. Shattered, pulverized and just plain rent and rendered.

I looked into the sack - there were two chickens left. I decided to save them for later and was about to take the sack of provisions away, when the great hatchling showed a savage and violent displeasure. Lunging now with flashing beak it battered the spars of its little enclosed cell with repetitive furious assaults, as if to impress upon Lazarus and I that we could not hold it in there for long….. I caught Taxon's eye then and he seemed oddly amused at what I saw as a situation of spiralling and increasing menace. "I think our little friend considers its dinner to be a matter of unfinished business, old boy." "Do you think he'd like another look at the menu?" I asked, as I hurled the slightly clammy cadaver of a further chicken into the cage and pulled my hand quickly out of the way, and the clacking bill went to work on its meat once more. It occurred to me, as I gazed at the carnage before me, that we were heading for some difficulties with the practical management of the beast. The cage needed cleaning out for one thing – the guano was accumulating like the white cliffs of Dover, and the stench was intensifying all the time, reeling, nauseous, gut-wrenching blet of piscine fodder. The creature needed exercise – it needed space to stretch and flap those spreading wings. Its increasingly frustrated attempts to properly extend and flap its wings were causing it some tension, and this was becoming manifest in its tantrums of shrieking, lunging, cackling, flapping fury – its rage at its captive and subject status – the deprivation of its freedom – and, God knows, an increasing and overwhelming urge to fly!

Chapter 16

Rolling sea, folded crystal-diamond pyroclastic realm of glas-grey salt spray; spawning troops of manta rays, dark beetling Cretaceous lobsters and flotillas of fortuitous and gelatinous floaters and drifters, awash with planktonic myriads. The mist, niwl-dot-vapoured and coagulated in pockets and prairie-plateaus, obscured the seaport towne in blankets and veils – phantom-feathers – rust-red-sails – trawls and skeins, herring-gulls, tar-barrels and waddling whaling-men in oversized oil-skin smocks, fresh in from the Greenland-run.

My familiar seaport home had taken on a sinister aspect of late – perhaps it was just my overwrought nerves, but it seemed to me at this time that a murky quality was subtly at work in the air, enmiring and enmeshing the denizens and villagers in a web of the unknown.

Spiralling sea-birds indicated change, whirling upwards in scatters. Fish rippling the metal-glass of the surface foretell of events hithertofore obscured, unknown and unknowable. Weather builds and the screech of an owl in an ivy-clad ash-tree sends shivers jibbering through jowls and flabby howls shrilled the night's silvery glistening air.

Another fitful night had passed into the dawn and scatterings of rain-pellets raked the window-panes as slate-grey light leaked in and lit my room. The wind flung scraps of kelp in its wake. A feather flew down the street, danced in an eddy of air outside my window for a moment before blowing on down the street.

This instantly had the effect of bringing back to my minde the great speckled bird of ours, that lurked, snapping and clacking and chopping up offal, beaking down fish-meal and swelling cellular and crepuscular/spectacular. That ill-bred hybrid brute brought back brittle slithers of fear's new shoots, surfacing to disturb and darken the day.

But why do I dither, oh gentle reader, why do I not spill the sea-beans and blurt my bloated narrow-boat narrative? Why float I adrift awash amidships away among great myriad millions? Perhaps my very reticence and trepidacious hesitancy stems from the undreamably and shudderingly vast and vile depths of terror, repugnance and disrelish that weave the very thread of my tale. Still, we have journeyed thus far together, thou and I, so let's have it out.

Seized by the grip of urgency, I broke a hunk of bread from the loaf, shoved it into a packet in the pocket of my jacket and sustained my frame on pellets of it as I hot-heeled it through the labyrinthos district of our good porth. Arriving at the aforementioned conjunction of those quiet by-ways I was once again before Taxon's door – and across the moat. Letting myself in, I found the elder experimenteer slumbering lightly on his couch, apparently exhausted – he was not a young man, indeed, I suspected he was an octogenarian and the strain of all our recent 'scientific activities', shall we say, and – he stirred.

A slight noise caught my ear from somewhere in the old, leaning house. Lazarus opened a flashing cataract eye and turned it upon me.

"Elias old fellow – how *are* you this morning? Will you take some coffee?"

I greeted him warmly and as he prepared our refreshment I ate some more morsels and watched drops of leaden moisture trickle and trail down the window's gabled glass.

"I've been observing the hatchling" expostulated Lazarus "and would tentatively say that in its current state of morphohybridism it could virtually merit the binomial nomenclature of *Larus marinus!*"

"No!" I gasped aghast in haggard sparse shuddering revulsion, but knew it to be true. The Great Black-backed Gull is not a homely creature, not a creature to get close to or make a pet of – and we had one – what, four – five feet tall?

Lazarus's eyes gleamed, gleaning and glimpsing far orbiting things.

"The sea of knowledge is vast and largely uncharted. When we set forth as amateur experimenteers, as men of science pursuing a particular line of enquiry, there is no way of fore-knowing the end result of the experiment – the bigger the experiment – the less predictable the result!"

Of course, the eld was right, and a combination of his sound insight and the warmth of his presence (and his coffee) reassured me and rekindled the flickering lamp of my spirit.

"I'll own I'm still struggling to comprehend the sheer explosive rate of cellular growth, the rate of transformation, of evolution…" My voice trailed off in wonderment.

"Aye, Nature has been generous, sharing so many of her secrets and marvels with us," rejoined Lazarus, with a slight smile illuminating the parchment of his ancient visage.

I suspected that Mr Taxon had ventured upon many a voyage of discovery in his many years upon the Earth, accumulating experience, weighing and assaying it but seldom displaying it. His erudition had more branches than seven trees and learning was his leaning– was that a slight noise?

"Indeed Elias, this case poses several rather puzzling questions… each one of which would appear to be as singular as it is perplexing." His jelloid orbs glowed warm living liquid phosphorescence, thrown sharp from an iridescent iris. His brain a vast living net of protoplasmic scintillating fresh genius – his visionary orbs speaking far more than his mere glossal vernacular.

"You have a fine way of reminding me of the priceless academic value of the case, Lazarus – we mustn't let our slight difficulties distract us from our scientific path…"

Thinking of that great gonys *beak* however took my thoughts down quite another turning…

Just about then the noise was there again, only a little louder and more distinct. Lazarus caught my eye. "I think it's coming from the lab" I said.

"We'd better check on the beast," said he, with a calm gravity.

It seemed those gnarled and knotty fowls outside were kicking up a flap, their agitated clucking rose to an access of avine-abandon. That scrawny old chicking that had always reminded me of Taxon – where was it? I cast my eye around and spotted the Taxonomic fowl, lying on the side of the moat, apparently dead. I warded off the vague and unscientific fancy that this was an ill omen, a warning of impending things that would not be relished – things that would leave an acrid, rank and bitter taste upon the tongue of a fly.

I re-entered the house and accompanied Mr Taxon into the laboratory. Great pullulating cuttle-fish, man! I wouldn't wish that sight on anyone! Not the site of that, that *Larus marinus,* great speckled bird of the egg-chick of the snake – primeval lizard-thing, feathered flurry of kleptoparasitic marauding sea-haggard skrawk! Not yet mature enough to have gained its black upper-wing feathers, it was speckled and mottled in intricate patterns of quilted and marbling specks and spicules. The great tail-feathers were dark and the great broad-sword beak already blazing with a flash of yellow. The head and breast now transformed from earlier proto-quills to a whiteness that spoke of cliffs of ice. Its red-ringed greyish yellow tallow eye glassy glistened like congealed candle-fat, gazing, blank, as if far out to sea – searching for the shoals of herring.

The great bird baritone barked its four-note descending

laugh – a great hollow-horned honk that shook the glass. Growth rate still spiralling, the great sea-fowl puffed, flapped and strutted. Splinters on the floor testified to the damage it had done to the makeshift wooden enclosure. Shards and slithers. A lurch of the foot-long breadknife beak had chopped a hole in the side of the structure and it was apparent that it could no longer be relied upon to hold the monstrously-enlarged sea-bird.

And through those great green-tinted carapace windows I saw a spiralling flight of gulls soar and wheel, spinning slowly upwards and all setting up such a clack and a screech. I looked back at the cage in juddering cold horror as the percussive blast of that harsh beak tore into more of its prisoning wall.

"We've got to do something!" I shouted to Lazarus – "I don't think we can *contain* the creature any longer!"

It was the first time I'd ever seen a worried look on Taxon's face. "You're right Elias, we must act – and act fast!"

The Great Black-backed Gull hacked back its beak – it slashed and stabbed at the wood, shattering, splintering and disintegrating it, and all the while croaking a blasphemous and unthinkable hollow and harsh mockery of a bullhorn barking rookery.

Lazarus grabbed an archaic brass crank-handle and began turning it in a socket in the wall which had the effect of gradually opening that great carapace sky-light window, whilst I grabbed a broom-stick with a view to protecting us, should things become awkward. So this was the pass that my 'research', my 'studies' had led me to, I thought, marvelling at the irony of it. All I had wanted was to quietly pursue my obscure and rather dryly academic enquiries into certain aspects of nature and human culture, and here I was, desperately attempting to fend off a giant sea-gull with a house-broom! The squeak of the crank-handle mingled with a groaning noise from the slowly-unfolding carapace-window seemed to further enrage the savage hatchling thing and it rended and rent asunder, smashing, tearing and breaking down its hated, guano-encrusted cage of confining indignation.

"Get back Lazarus, take cover!" I shouted, just before

the great webbed and taloned claw finished what the beak had started.

Fear filled the room – the moon stood black-dark against the sun's day ray. Then horrendum horroridicus – the great bird was out, kicking its way out of the wreckage and lunging, skrawking and barking straight towards us!

I brandished the broom towards its grim face – glimpsing glassy eye, red-ringed – which deterred the beast and seemed to hold it off, as I continued shouting to Lazarus to withdraw to safety.

"This is a two-man job," rejoined the eld archaikos, so saying, he reached for a Javanese parasol that lay furled in a corner, and held it aloft, in defiance of the savage monstrosity he himself had unleashed to wreak wreck and havoc a beak hazard in a blank canvas. The movement of that colourful oriental parasol, however, proved to be Taxon's undoing as it startled the already disturbed bird and, to my great dismay, the great speckled gonys gull lunged forth again, this time connecting with Taxon's chest, making a sickening cracking noise and a stain of deep dark red, as the old scientist crumpled like a coat, dropped heavily to the floor, hitting his head upon the tiles and ceased to move, whilst the *gull* – that fruit of the egg of the tree of evil, the great bird with a mighty bound, leapt to its wings and soared through the open skylight carapace windows to ride the foggy airs o'er old New Lynsmouth towne on wings of doom-blasted salt-splattered *alienage*.

*

I was mesmerised, glued by the eyes to that dark shadowy kite-bat-like form as it winged away and rapidly disappeared – what will it *do* out there? How will it *eat?*

Reeling my gaze back from the skies, to the laboratory in which I stood, I beheld the form of Lazarus Taxon felled upon the floor. I feverishly checked him for signs of life – there were none. No breath, no pulse, no heart-beat – nothing. His ancient and now reposing face wore a subtle look of peace, like that of a man released and gone beyond.

Chapter 17

A grim, bleak and desolate shroud of heavy darkness fell upon me then, clinging and twisting and wrapping itself about me and pulling me down into the quagmire. That great and terrible bird, that *murderous* bird! At liberty in our skies! Free to do to other people what it had just done to Mr Taxon – and I had helped to bring all this about!

The sky seemed to darken and heavy rain-drops were bouncing into the lab – I started to close the great overhead windows, turning the crank, as Lazarus had done. I looked upon him as I worked. His ancient coat stained now with gore. His noble old face looking composed, intelligent – as he was in life. One arm curled in front of him, one arm extended, hand out-flung with finger almost pointing – almost pointing across to the other side of the lab – to the somewhat damaged apparatus from the early stages of our experiment – the magneto-animation device. The *magneto-* why, that's it! A feverish idea gripped my brain – I had to work quickly for there to be any chance of success.

Fumbling through shelves of flasks and tubes and all manner of scientific glassware, I located the special chemical salts with which we had bathed the egg, and started to apply them to the forehead and temples of Lazarus. Then, ripping open his shirt, I applied more of the bluish-grey solution to the ghastly wound in his chest and around his heart and lung-area. I then propped his cooling form against the work-bench, sitting facing the light. A sense of extreme urgency held my natural distress in abeyance, and I was able to focus on the task with startling clarity and lucidity. The lenses next – only one had been damaged – the other mirrors I calibrated and focused on Taxon's heart-area and the orbic apparati was in place. Next I propped the magnetizer against a chair – its support-column was shattered, but, with luck, the machine could still function – as a 'Lab Assistant' with ground-breaking, if brief, experience of the magneto-animation process, surely it was right to try to apply the process to its own inventor! My head reeled with the outré and eldritch nature of this latest experiment – a sudden fanciful dread that the townsfolk would come bursting all of a sudden into the house, to find me performing unspeakably ghastly and fiendish experiments on the freshly killed corpse of a respectable old gentleman!

No! Away with such conceits! I must clarify my minde, cleave to the spirit of science – now, where is that adhesive tape, so I can attach the copper wires to his chest?

Soon all was ready and I applied a cold hand to the dials of the magnetizer, applying just a trickle of electrical fluid. The kommolek massed fleecy clouds then drifted away and the sun's white coinage fell upon our mirrors that were lifted skyward. The sun's kind influence of searing energy rays fell focused and merely bounced through the mirrors and shone their rays on the *deceased's* remains. I very gradually increased the galvanic energy by means of the dials, and an ambient whirring pulse was just discernable over the pounding of my heart, which seemed to fill my ears. Did I hear the wretched skrawking of sea-birds – or was I falling prey to illusions? The mirrors and lenses were glowingly illuminated and lit from within like crystalline phosphorescent honey-combs; pulsing street-light neons; guttering candles, lamps, lanthorns and crystal chandeliers. The light played and bathed upon his old form. The light fell on his face. I turned the dial a little more – with a gasp and a cough, Lazarus Taxon raised up his old head and *looked at me.*

Great shoals of halibut! I froze and near rooted to the spot – overwhelmed by the success of the magneto-animation process.

"Water!" he was asking for water – I lurched to the tap and brought him a cupful – still incredulous at his unexpected return. His eyes swam with the stars and the fishes and time seemed frozen in his dream-sighted orbs.

"What things I have seen," he murmured quietly – I made him comfortable in a chair and put on the kettle, feeling that tay was surely at least half of the answer to all the bizarre assortments of riddles, conundrums and dilemmas that leered large and loomed near…

I stood benumbed in the Taxon kitchen, running my fingers along a row of tay-jars – reminding me of my recent search for the 'elixir-fluid' amongst the glassware flasks in the lab. A thought kept running through my minde – what kind of tay do you give a man who's *just returned from the dead?*

I settled on Lapsang Souchong.

Returning to the scene of so much drama and violence, I found the elder one sitting in a most tranquil repose, almost seeming to emanate a warm glow, a flavour of super-refined minde permeated the air around him and his ancient and cataracted eyes could well be said to glow. Out of respect for his quietness, I silently placed a hot cup of tay before him, then returned with some cheese sandwiches which I likewise placed before him and also a thick heavy quilt which I draped over him and a goose-feather pillow which I insinuated behind the rugged taxonomical cranium.

"Dear friend" said I, "I feel I must try to locate our bird, I'm not sure what I can do, but I must do something – I should at least try to observe and monitor the creature. I implore you to stay at rest – if you move at all, it should be to your bed – I shall return before the day is out." Lazarus nodded his assent, adding that he wanted no doctor – he then fell silent again and I took my leave, accompanied by no little sense of wonderment.

The frequently-haunted ox-bow alleys once again echoed to my phasing footfalls as I hob-nailed it around circuitously, sniffing for a glimpse of a skwark of a skrawik beaked-beast. Flaxen cloak outflung in mottled ruffling slipstream, hat pulled down tight – a shapeless and battered old cap. Villagers gossiping at the well and chattering on down the side-streets, thinking all was just ordinary, not guessing at the hideous and merciless peril that winged soaring aloft somewhere in that deep cloud-flapping sky. How *could* I warn them? How could I approach these stout and goodly folk with the tidings that I had created a monster that was liable to be extremely hostile and vicious to Humankind – perhaps to the point of anthropophagia? No, this seemed an unwise course to pursue at that moment and I settled upon silence. Nerved for action, the streets seemed to go on forever and to wind over more hills than Rome. Thoroughfares spinning and spilling like lava in pyroclastic coils. Crisscrossing the silvery sea-snail

Strand where offerings of finny and broad breams were still left on the sands for the local autochthonous deities, the Buccas. Crates of skate glimpsed by fishing-fleet feet alight on the wing. Creels sagged and oozed fish. Masts creaked and rigging rattled and clacked like epiphytic vines in a jungle of masts and mizzens. These yellow-brick streets had seen Spanish conquistadors and pirates and corsairs of various countries, but then, in the old world, the pre-scientific world, danger had come from the sea, not the air! I hastened on, struggling to weigh events calmly after so much turmoil. The endless streets unravelled beneath my roaming restless feet.

Gradually a niwlek mist descended, seeming to soften the angles, edges and outlines of objects. Hearing herring gulls galled my spleen and I cast a dubious eye into the sky. Restless hawks of the sea – why must they torment and pester me so? Why must they peck and taunt my presence with their ghastly prattling squawks and cackling, hideous, hyena-jackal laughter?

I found myself in the centre of New Lynsmouth and was just passing the pantiled merchant-house when I saw 'Old Ethel', as everyone called the woman who sold the pasties from a little hand-cart that she pushed along from place to place. The green and white stripy awning above her hand-cart fluttered slightly over a golden-brown sea of the hot and tasty pies. Her business was usually brisk. The enticing smell of the pasties could always be relied on to bring forth a gaggle of hungry punters. Sure enough, a handful of fishermen and some fishwives were gathering round Old Ethel. That's when I saw our Kramvil-beast – the great speckled bird! And as I saw it descending, others did too and a most shrill and horrible set of screams from the terror-struck public was greeted by an infinitely more sinister and repulsive braying, hacking cry from the great gulling beast.

The people were scattering like chaff in the wind as the vile and grossly overgrown bird alighted on the striped awning and in a fury of winged raging wrath, kicked the pasty-cart over, sending its load of viands into the cobbled street. Not everyone scattered however, for Ethel remained for a few moments, shaking her umbrella at the bird and shouting fiercely at it in Kornyshe, before wisely taking to her heels. Our hatchling, bigger and sleeker of feather, was to be seen gulping down the pasties, three or four at a time. Scraping and gouging at the cobbles until there was no remaining crumb left of four dozen of the tasty pies. I became aware of a silence and looking around, saw not a soul in the street. Just *Larus marinus* and I, and with a sudden fluster of condor-quilled wing-warping motion, the creature was aloft and gone. Business had been brisk.

*

Who would hazard to hack back at such a gizzard of hapless haphazard buzzard feathers? The brief glimpses of its shoulder-plumage showing increasing patches of black, combined with the yellowing beak, told of the fowl's approaching maturity. Soon, fully-fledged, the great monstrous hawk would talk back with beak and clasping claw, its cold, hungry eye ever-swivelling for food. Aerial mastodon! Relict! Throwback! Mammoth chryselephantine plumed raptor! Pasty-thief! Upsetting the pasty-cart and disturbing the well-earned peace of New Lynsmouth! Egg-chick! Beak-lipped ellipsoid rhomboid yolker- who – *or what* – do you think you are? A sarfek slitherer? A kramvil lacerta sauroid from the Lizard? What is your designation – your patronymic and binomial? What your nom-de-plume, as you ply your quill? You frenzied, Darwinian cellular explosive globule! Gorhengeugh koth! Ancestral gene-pool-shark! Chameleon masquerading as a Canvasback Duck! Malevolent mabyar! Kleptoparasitic archaeopteryx! Shy-talking loud-squawking guano-spattering dartboard dirt-bird! *Rattus aerodynamicus!* Scavenger! Splatterer! Dustbin raider! Pink-legged harbinger of whitesqualls and haddock-shoals! Slime of the ancient milliner! Bad-owl of the billowing surf! Squirming cliff-buzzard with your squid-ink propinquity! Hake-fattened fruit-bat! Water-vulture; sun-hat despoiler; black-backed whitewasher; raucous marauder; screaming beaker-folk-Larus; fell bringer of brouhaha and inestimable gull-duggery; faoilean an cladach; gwylan; gwirionyn; ee glaros; mergus; monstrous; gwrthun; bruidiuil; youthful euthvil; hack-beaked fowl of the seas – in short, gentle reader, an eldritch and utterly ghastly abomination of unspeakable and horrid loathfullness.

*

A running, screaming crowd was pouring down Kyvounder Hill, as overhead swooped and soared the broad wingspan of the aforementioned fowl. Each wing a fathom of feathers. Beak now a bowsprit stout to split and rend and splinter. On ran the mass of people in wide-eyed stampeding frenzy – each face an echo of Munch's 'Scream' – ladies in long skirts and wide-brimmed hats, fishwives with creels on their backs and babes in their arms, men in working clothes, one or two in bowlers and toppers, all running, a screaming mass of terror and dread being driven and goaded and taunted by our great speckled bird.

Its form in the air overhead was reminiscent of some photographs of aeroplanes I'd recently seen in the newspaper. Some of the new German monoplanes had a great ornithological elegance to their swept-back wings and wide, fan-like tails. The bird, however, exceeded any heaver-than-air flying machine in terms of its natural grace in motion – its perfect adaptability for the art of flight. The mabyar gull seemed to have mastered this art with great rapidity (as it did all things!) and I'll own to almost feeling a sneaking admiration for its aerial skills. It seemed to delight in swooping down on particular people, zooming by within inches of their heads – whilst the crowd ran on, sending up its wails and moans, some seeking shelter down side-alleys or running into the open doors of houses.

The pandemonium was contagious, spread by the stampeding crowd like wildfire, through every district that they charged. An air of fear spread its chill vapours throughout our little seaport towne that day, and nothing succeeds like fear.

Elder tendrils cuttled and clutched at the towne, troubling it with a deep and sombre shadow, striking with vicious savagery at the tranquil equipoise of our good village-villa. Fear – casting its shrimp-net over the fisher-folk and sending them running for cover, as a dark shadow swept across the skies. Fear – making the air curiously empty of other birds when that great sea-fowl was in evidence. Fear that sunk into the lichenous and half-rotted beams of the lurching cottages of a district known as the 'Old Quarter'. Fear – that insipid web of tangled thread that snares, trips and thwarts the unwary.

Yea, the shadow sombre clutched and dark splashed the ink down in the deeps of cuttlefish-pool as tendrils elder twitched.

*

The next encounter with the mabyar-fowl took place just outside the seaport, in a tiny hamlet in the hinterland that goes by the name of Unstable-Hobbla. Across the road from the tin smelting-house is the little chicken-farm, where fowls of various breeds run at liberty in a small paddock. It seems that the desperate clucking, honking and squawking of poultry alerted the farmer, who came running out of the old farmhouse to come face to ghastly face with the largest piece of poultry he was ever likely to meet – in the form of *Larus marinus (var. giganticus)*.

What met the incredulous and abstracted eyes of the farmer was a sight of deeply unrelishable carnage and confusion, blood, guts and feathers; heads, feet and wings. The great gull was indiscriminately and frenziedly lashing about and snapping its great beak and grabbing at any of the petrified chickens, ducks, geese, turkeys and guinea-fowl that it could get its beak and claws into. The great braying sea-raptor threw back its head, emitting a gruff, barking, laughing call of raucous rapture, a ribbon of pale intestine dangling from its clacking maw, emerging from the shattered mess of what had just been a goose.

To enhance the sheer howling desolation of this picturesque rustic cameo, half a dozen or more decapitated fowls were flying in circles round the small paddock, spattering rivulets of glutinous sanguinary gore from the stumps of their truncated necks. Flapping, spattering, squawking, rendlng, tearing, crunching, bursting, ripping, feathers flying in cumulus kommolek. A more unrelishable sight had seldom been seen in West Kirnowe. After staring aghast and agape like a dreamer awake, the farmer bolted back to the house, with the single idea of priming his blunderbuss and returning to blast the monster to oblivion. In his excitement, the farmer tripped on entering the house and laid himself out – thereby he probably saved his own life, putting *himself,* temporarily, into a state of oblivion. Meanwhile the farmer's eldest son, an ox-like fellow in his early twenties, came rushing out of the house brandishing a large scythe and rushing impetuously straight towards the Larus Glaros.

The offensive was successful and after a brief barked threat, the great mabyar speckled one took wing, its belly gorged on poultry, a small vestige of intestine still clinging to the osseous proboscis. Once again, business had been brisk. Having thus left its calling-card for the goodly folk of Unstable-Hobbla, the great hatchling turned a feather and stretched a wing and followed the course of the swollen surging river back down to the ancient seaboard towne of New Lynsmouth.

And I regret to have to inform you, oh unfortunate reader, that the return of our sea-going chicken to its roost was not free from more of the reprehensible and utterly bleak occurrences that had become so much a part of life, of late.

The events at Kyvounder House, a home for retired missionary ladies and a most genteel establishment, were of a particularly unpleasant, disturbing and distasteful nature. Once a year, on the anniversary of its founding, the ladies gave a tea-party, attended by a lot of 'society' people, and to this annual celebration it was traditional for Burroughs the baker to bake a special giant pasty, a full four feet long, and deliver it to Kyvounder House as the centre-piece and focus of the event.

There was a marquee in the garden serving cucumber sandwiches, macroons, scones, saffron buns, heavy cake and, of course, the giant pasty. All this would be washed down with copious porcelain cups of Earl Grey tea and perhaps just a little bit of gossip.

Regrettably, on this occasion, etiquette and decorum were somewhat violated by the most unwanted and unwarranted intrusion of a ruffian by the name of *Larus marinus*.

Having parked the wagon outside the pillared portal of the house, the two chefs, in their ceremonial uniforms and wearing overly-tall chef-hats, carried the great platter bearing the over-sized pasty at arms length above their heads and marched slowly and ceremoniously towards the marquee. They were only a few feet from the entrance to the great tent, and the people within were already singing the traditional song of welcome – "We shall come rejoicing, bringing in the sheaves" when chaos and catastrophe struck like the Fury's curse in a Greek drama.

In a moment that struck the watchers like an ice-berg or a sheet of glass, the great speckled Larus swooped lunging at the outsized pie, knocking both chefs to the ground and causing the civic throats to change from hymning to screaming in the wink of an eye. Whilst the horrible fowl was gouging, ripping, gulping and kicking the pasty, tearing and swallowing large steaming chunks of it – inside the marquee pandemonium was breaking loose. Tables were overturned, spilling cucumber sandwiches and iced-buns onto the grassy floor. Gentlefolk elbowed and shoved each other out of the way, trying to escape from the monstrous sight before them. A colonel's widow was in hysterics, her fingers in her gibbering mouth. The Reverend Timothy Kryjyk tried to appeal for calm, but was trampled by the mob. Mrs Fotheringay's Pekinese dog, 'Archie', went whimpering and waddling out of the marquee in a myopic panic, to be skewered by a razor-sharp beak and wolfed down in three bleeding chunks. Porcelain cups and saucers shattered on the ground and were crunched under the desperate shoes of the stampeding gentlefolk. A couple of gouts of dog were shaken from the beak of the ghastly fowl and spattered and trickled down the bright green canvas of the marquee. The

bird was turning its attention within the tent now, as it scented
new food-stuffs. As it stepped within, drawn by the scattered
cakes and sandwiches on the floor, the petrified crowd was
finally organizing its escape, by ducking under the back
wall of the tent, which was being held up by the vicar and
a military-looking chap with big moustaches. A thunderous
and ear-tormenting guttural braying from the brazen beak
further accelerated and encouraged the rapid exodus from the
tea-party. After some intense fear and unseemly pushing and
shoving, it seems that everyone present escaped to the safety
of the house, the reverend vicar sustaining a nasty gash on
his leg – the result of a malevolent claw. A most regrettable
business altogether. A dashed ugly affair….. *dashed* ugly!
Dashed *beastly business!*

After a little more half-hearted scavenging for food,
the gargantuan fowl took wing into the gathering tewlwolow
twilight and feathered its way aloft.

I decided to check on Lazarus and see how he was
doing, after his recent 'reincarnation' or transmogrification
or dethanatization. A matter that seemed to be as singular as
it was perplexing. I wandered down the hill, dwelling on the
astounding events of the day – and the continuing danger and
uncertainty that tomorrow promised. I could see the harbour
and the green sea beyond – wild, rolling water with dancing
white caps mottling like specs and spicules as nautilus turned
and cuttlefish rippled a gelatinous tentacle. Booming surf
fresh rolls in the fog. White foam lingering in gathering dusk.
Crustaceans shuttling about under the billowing diamond
waves. Kelp forests swell and stir, five-fathom ropes drifting
up to the meniscus surface-tension skin of the water's
molecular form. Carragheen swaying, swirling and returning.
Gobies and Lump-Suckers awash in briny haddock-meadows.
Shoals of eels and schools of sprats. Tearing rolling restless
ocean. Restless restless rolling ocean. Squids grasping arms –
carapaces – crustaceans – flotillas – flailing, sarfek sea-snakes
– whirling luminous sea-snails leaving sea-trails. Hollow horn
bullhorn roar. Shells scattered krogenek bladderwrack and
dodder.

*

Stars were whirling in the sky like crystal tears of glass, as I threaded my weary and wandering way back to the Old Quarter.

The stars sparkled, reflected in my jelly-eyes as ere I seemed to see scenes in space displayed and displaced. The realisation of sheer interstellar vastness seemed to sober my minde as I drunk it all in. The stars and chilly, distant, majestic constellations now formed a glittering tiara to crown the illustrious and goodly town wherein we do dwell. Those white twinkling stern stars were reflected also in the oily black cuttlefish-pool glooping waters of the harbour, where herrings fear to tread. They danced upon the brine those stars, shining a scintillating squiggle.

Ducking under an archway, I found my feet gaining ground on Orchard Street, realm of so many wandering turns and adventures. There stood the house of Lazarus Taxon – in all its faded and fly-blown glory, glittering stucco stuck in time like a fly on a gecko's tongue, a mastodon in a tar-pit or a sunken forest. The façade of the archaic manse loomed forth from twixt gleam and gloom, dreaming on that corner, lurching and leaning into time.

These grime and guano-bespattered walls held many a tale and many a wonderful secret of science. The crown-capped chimney-pot seemed as though for ever falling, silhouetted against the ivy-clad bare winter trees on the hill's skyline eye-line brow, clouds scudding and sailing by. The ancient window-shutters were closed and the great house brooded and bided. Amongst the nettles and lank, rank weeds clacked the scrawny little flock of 'chickings' and it was a little singular, somewhat curious and more than a dash perplexing to see the 'Taxon-bird' up on its feet looking sound as a warbler. A mercurial recovery had taken place in the peculiar bird and its vitality seemed fully restored. It picked and pecked amongst the languid and patchy nettles and thistles that rustled and swayed with every breath of night-wind. I let myself into the dreaming house and there I found Mr Taxon sitting in the same chair, having barely touched his repast and sitting peacefully, facing the windows. The aura of quietness and tranquillity which enshrouded him affected me in a subtle and curious way. In resonance with Taxon, something in me seemed to relax and be at ease. This was a novel perception and I had trained myself to observe such phenomena objectively, as a man of Science.

The elder one would seem to have benefited from a species of trance that had taken a burden from his shoulders and the resulting influence upon his features was to make him look considerably *younger* than he had previously appeared to be! The parchment-skin of his face seemed tighter, less creased and time-blasted. His jaws more resolute than ever. His eyes liquid gold warm fire. Deep pools. Hot coals. Those glowing pools of gold flowed in my direction.

I asked after his health and he quietly assured me that he was fine. I then gave him an account of all the outrageous and sanguinary events which I had witnessed. It did not make for a cheerful tale, and I couldn't help noticing a flicker of worry pass like a cloud upon the face of Lazarus Taxon. The screeching of a gull outside startled us both – an echo reminiscent of that hulking, barking *Larus marinus*. Our thoughts were both with our bird, our spectacular hatchling bird-thing as it winged aloft somewhere in feathery ruffling skies.

"You know Elias, we may have to take steps against that bird." I nodded grimly. "I fear you may be right Lazarus." "You'd better be off home to rest" quoth the eld. I looked at him in amazement. "But what about you, Lazarus, after all you've been through today, I should surely stay here to watch over you."

He kindly but firmly dismissed my offer, assuring me that he would indeed be fine, and seeing the state of great tranquillity that was upon him, I also believed that he would be alright. We made our farewells and I stepped out into the misty alleys of the star-splattered night.

Chapter 18

Arose I awoke cloaked in dawn's rosy dew-drenched hue. Dream-echoes and chimeras, feverish and liverish had sweated my night thoughts, haunting my hours of dark rest with an unwholesome presence of mal. Night-vapour's shreds left flapping in the wind like a bat, a crow, an old coat caught on a thorn-bush.

But dawn's liquid luminescent marmalade glow of wakefulness brought not joy, as the events of yesterday instantly reared up before my inward eye, with their augury of further chaos, destruction and danger in the form of that great feathered-hell-bird!

I found the antikwari to be galvanized into a state of animation. When I arrived at the lab, he was busily shovelling up the guano into a sack, and had already dismantled the makeshift wooden 'bird-cage'. But what struck me more than this was that the Taxon I saw before me was a changed specimen. His snowy-white hair was now a steely-grey. He moved with more vigour, more energy. He had discarded his habitual lunettes and his once-cataracted eyes seemed clear, fresh and sparkling. The gnarled 'claw' that once shot forth to grasp my hand, was now as stout as a starfish and as ruddy as a rogue. Great mottled manta-rays! It truly was astounding! I had just offered him my greeting when there was a loud rap at the front door! I glanced at Lazarus apprehensively. "Would you see who that is?" asked Lazarus. I strode to the old pine-planked portal and opened it to reveal the unexpected visages of my friends messers Jack Lane and Paul Hill, esquires, gentlefolk, etc.,etc.. "Hallo Elias! May we have a word – with Mr Taxon – and yourself?" Jack arched a quizzical vulpine brow as he caught my flickering eye a-smile. "Would you show the fellows into the reading room please Elias?" Taxon's voice boomed from within – transformed from its former croaking – now no longer a rasping guttural whispered syllable, but the rich, paw-padded purr of a catamountain aprowl in the Adirondacks.

I did the introductions and Lazarus immediately startled me by asking if they were here about the bird. "We wondered if you might be connected with it in some way…" began Jack searchingly. Lazarus told the thunderstruck pair the essential history of the case and they listened with intense interest. "I think our course now must lie in attempting to subdue or destroy the bird," he concluded.

"We're here to offer our services," put in Paul. "It's a matter of life or death," added Jack, "all for one and one for all!" We shook hands at this and decided to arm ourselves with various clubs, harpoons etc., which we would conceal in our coats and baggage, and patrol the area. We would carry bugles, to communicate any sightings of the creature to each other and raise the alarm. "After all," said Jack, eyeing me archly, "if you *will* insist on unleashing your behemoth beasts on the community, I suppose we'd better help you run the blighters out of town, eh? Ha ha ha."

And with the wind the clouds the morning rainshine. And buffeting winds came in from the rolling sea, bringing the full Atlantic of salt droplets as a fresh breeze in the face. Niwl-damp fogs rolled in, came and went, withering. Morvil hulks wailed awash, waiting in the bay. "How's your wound, Lazarus?" I asked. He opened his shirt and showed his chest. There was barely a mark to be seen at all! This was indeed as singular as it was perplexing. But, in a series of ever-more perplexing days, you can expect explicit perceptive perplexity to perfectly confound and compound complexity, explicated the cataleptic caliph expertly. And blew the cloud-rainshine and thunder-dogs running on as time unfurled. Vigorous though he was, I was still worritted over Mr Taxon's health, and managed to get him to agree to stay in and rest – doing no more than a little tidying up in the laboratory, which he insisted was necessary.

Jack, casting himself as the 'lone-wolf', had gone looping and loping off on the trail of the great mabyar-fowl, reckoning to do his reconnaissance from the hills that overlooked the seaport towne. Paul and I stuck together and wove wandering through skochfordh alleys and quiet dusty by-ways between orchards and little farmsteads, along the tangled, raggy range of the drowsy outskirts.

Caught in Cernyw's granite-lobster-claw, West

Penwithershins, in ye ancient and mythic Countie of Hornwale, blustered a-buffet by surging rollers and salt spray surfs, this claw of horn clutched at the cloaks of those whom here were born. Us players on a stage do be. Flickering shadows who flit and pass through lives as the gleam of a conch. Stirring strings rose and a quartet unwound from a bubble-glass window. An arrangement of Satie's 'Ogives' – I hadn't come across it before, an enchanting piece…

"It's extremely good of you and Jack to help out like this," I spoke. "This whole business came about so suddenly, so unexpectedly…" I trailed off, increasingly overwhelmed by the sheer over-arching tectoral immensity of it all.

"Nobody could foresee a thing like this, my dear fellow," rejoined Paul. "Science is all about exploring the unknown – you've just got a bit out of your depth, that's all." "And helped to create a monster" I added grimly.

Paul looked down, as if seeking inspiration in the shine of his brogues. "From a *biological* standpoint, it's an absolute wonder, a cause célèbre– you should be up for a Nobel prize!" We laughed. Then I remembered the pasty-cart lying on its side, the running, screaming, terrified crowd. "I'm not sure if old Ethel would support my nomination!"

Feeling very *responsible* for the horror being raised, I juddered inwardly, like a gorilla breaking up a piano with a sledge-hammer. We walked on. The ground rose. Clouds flapped the shadows. Somewhere lurked the 'ornapetion' – the 'little-birdie'. Somewhere a taloned claw flap a feather beak. The ground rose, and as it rose the angles dipped and shifted and the brooding hills of the hinterland came leering and looming into view, their towering, twisted and heaped peaks piling up over a plateau of blasted granite, covered over sparsely with a thin scattering of gorse and hawthorns, and riddled through with the adits, shafts, winzes and stopes of countless archaic tin and copper mines.

The 'Ogives' drifted up the hill, contemplative notes of bronze, strung on a gold-wired lyre. Brooding deep-violet velvet folds, a realm of purity. The afternoon peel of celestial bells deeply tolling – blossom – chiming bronze.

"And how about your own scientific work, Paul – how's

that jynn-keber of yours coming along?" His eyes alit at the mention of his engine.

"Well, I've finished the preliminary testing – it's virtually ready to go. If you could let me look at the blueprints for your ornithopter I could make a few calculations for designing the gear system that would connect the engine to the airframe and wings."

It was my turn to smile now. "I can do better than that, Paul, I can show you the completed craft!" "I don't know how you find the time, old man – I mean *monsters, flying-machines,* how on Earth do you *do* it all?" "I work long hours" was my laconic reply.

Something glistened in the road, as if someone had dropped a can of white paint… "Great Haddocks Alive!" expostulated Paul – "It's guano – the beast must be near at hand!"

The vile, spattered mess was steaming in foot-wide gouts before us. "Time to get the weapons out, and for God's sake be careful – remember it nearly killed Mr Taxon." I decided it was best not to mention the bywekheans-tredanek or magneto-animation of that learned antikwari.

The atomic-mosaic of which everything is swam past my eyes in a yellow-flash of brilliance. I became convinced I could 'feel' the presence of the Kramvil, the *feathered-fear.* My skin seethed like a crow on Creeping Lane caught and ruffled. I crept forward with Paul Hill at my side and Mount Mishap at my back. We were approaching the 'Tallcorne', a prominent rock that stood atop a cliff overlooking the river. A reticulated pattern on the upper surface of the carn was locally believed to be the handywork of Beelzebub after a blubbering hullabaloo hubbub from here to Buryan and back.

Planktonic dots vapour niwl aswirl. And there, perched atop the mighty rock was a roc of another kind altogether, a horse of another colour, a villainous monochrome larid abomination – our precious 'hatchling' now fully matured into the devastating, razor-sharp, black and white plumage of *Larus marinus* – the Greater Black-backed Gull – scourge of the North Atlantic's vast thundering sea-scapes! Ice turned to fear turned to rushing water in the veins as adrenalin's artillery went into arterial action. Its densely-quilled, jet-black back was turned to us as it surveyed the coombe below – I glanced at Paul and we silently took cover as best as we could behind some sloe-bushes, keeping the great fowl under close observation.

It seemed to stand as tall as a man – a large man, surely six feet tall on its pink, snake-skin, kigliw-legs. No longer the mottled, speckled thing, the mabyar, the egg-chick; but now a stark and forbidding symphony of slate-black and crisp snow-white. Head rounded. Brow sharp. Eye stern, unfriendly, glaucous fatty yellow-grey ringed in red, reptilian – flung afar. Beak now a brilliant and bright corn-sunflower yellow with that glowing orange-red spot in the gonys-angle of the lower bill. The 'expression' of the face – if such you could call it, was a sour and contemptuous one, as of a haughty disdain for vain Humanity; regal, tyrannical and imperious, resplendent on Tallcorne's lofty throne, Ornitharkos – Ruler of Birds!

Ty goellan hager du! You ugly black gull! Grown so quickly from your egg, little snake, little changeling, saurian-monitor-skink-thynge! Creeping echidna came out in quills, crawling up the evolutionary-ladder. Grown, fledged, feathered and hack-beak razor-bill savage-eyed sharp. Extended mighty wings a black banner of chaos. Slowly the great wings flapped to keep balance as the fearsome beak clacked and chopped. Draped over the carn was a fishing-net, obviously pillaged by the great gull in one of its increasingly bold raids upon the community. Scattered around the ground were a few scraps of skate and dogfish, shreds and slithers of jellyfish, morgowles and morgi. Writhing and flapping in the net was a large conger eel, struggling to avoid that ghastly beak. We'd already agreed that we should attack the bird on sight – Paul had a stout blackthorn bludgeon and I was carrying an antique esquimaux narwhal-ivory-tusk-harpoon. "Ready?" I whispered hoarsely. He nodded. *"NOW!"* I shouted, and we rushed the bird.

With an unwholesome and morbid croaking laugh the great yellow beak was thrown wide open, lunging towards us. Confronted with the screaming, shrill cackling of the flapping, stabbing, wheeling beast, it was all we could do to brandish our weapons towards its face and try to stand our ground. Fortunately for us, the creature was distracted by the conger eel, which it had just succeeded in freeing from its enmeshing net. Grasping the coiling squirming eel in its beak, the terrible new Ornitharkos took wing towards Mount Mishap.

"Great Herrings! That was a close shave!" Paul grinned as he brushed a lock of hair back from his brow. We both burst out laughing then, although there was not the least thing funny in our situation – it was probably the relief of finding ourselves to be still among the living after such a barbarous and unrelishable encounter with so gaunt and savage a beast.

"Let's see if Mr Lane is in the area" I said, and raising my bugle to my lips I called clarion of bronze horn's blow and sounded the brass resonating below. A very faint hint of an answering bugle insinuated down the wind, sounding from a long way off, further into the splintered inland hinterland. Hogweed seeds rattled damp in the mist, the fresh salt sou'westerly grey scudding banks of Atlantic's finest foggy dew. A clacking and shattering noise drifted up from the stone-mill down by the bridge; augmented by sawing from the saw-pits and hammering from the cooperage down in the coombe. An occasional scream, or acute cry of alarm, marked the passage of winged-peril. The river was crashing and roaring, unusually full and fast, a noisy presence in the valley below, darkened with tannin from the leaves of the region's few trees, which found refuge along its banks.

To catch a scattered glance of the vast sea-fowl was a most eldritch feeling indeed and scarce conducive to good digestion. Soaring archaeopteryx atavistic stick-insect thing, its shadow flitted fast across the ground. Great arched wings like one of Lilienthal's gliders. Flash of orange on the beak. Lazy flapping raptor. Aztec sunbird – with your serpent twisting in your dreadful claws.

"What the-" Paul threw out his hand in a quizzical gesture. We both heard it – and instantly divined its meaning. It was a group of screaming women and their barrage of uplifted voices was getting closer, coming down the hill towards us. This would surely be a group of fishwives, whose custom it was to sit on top of Mount Mishap so they could watch for their men-folk returning safely to the harbour, bringing in the fish. Quiet lanes, creeping around the hill, honeysuckle, pennywort and vetch. Campion, cow-parsley, elder and ash. Bullhorn snail's horn eye antenna extended on moist trail. Wild garlic and songbirds abound in the quiet lanes – but not today.

Suddenly the fishwives came tearing round the corner of the lane, they seemed to be in a collective hysteria, like Bachantes. Several were shrieking and they gasped and groaned as they ran. Old and young alike animated by a powerful fear – the great animator.

Wild-eyed, dishevelled, caked in mud and leaves, red-faced, white-faced, rendered haggard, gaunt and aghast, they surged on as a wave. "Run! Run!" several of them screamed. "We're going after it!" I replied – our weapons were still in our hands. "Don't be fools!" One of the women had momentarily stopped and was facing us – it was Scarlet! "You're no match for that – that *monster!* Those weapons are useless – only a canon could bring down a beast like *that.* Run for your lives!" "No Scarlet, we've got to do this," answered Paul. Scarlet glared at us for a split-second, then took to her clacking heels and was gone.

"Your little fellow seems to be creating something of a stir" smiled Paul with suave irony. "Well, my *little fellow* certainly enjoys meeting people," I rejoined, "but I'm afraid his manners lack a certain polish."

We grinned inanely at each other, as men sometimes do when they're about to plunge into perilous waters. I was scared – I don't minde admitting it. I clearly remember a strong and gelatinous presence of cold and sweaty fear. But there were other feelings aflood – wonderment at the beast and its development. Wonderment at the extraordinary reanimation and transfiguration of Lazarus Taxon. Wonderment in the knowledge that if I survived this adventure with this Bedlamite bird, I could look forward to taking Miss Constance Place flying over Penwithershins in a heavier-than-air machine! Ah, the surging thoughts, feelings, waves, so many strange and wonderful discoveries, such amazement – and also fear. Also fear…

Some species of ripples in the galvano-atmospheric aether told my tendrils that we would soon be face to ghastly beak with the unspeakably grim and hideous *rukk!*

A style at the side of the lane led into a field which sloped gently up towards the wooded crown of Mount Mishap. At the top end of the field stood our sea-fowl, out-scaling its surroundings, which added a touch of quaintness and novelty to the unrelishable and nauseous sight of that great Atlantic *hroc,* kicking and stamping in the corner of a Kernyshe field, gulling down the last shattered slither of Conger.

That great bass-horn honk braying laugh, four notes, descending – how unutterably detestable that abominable sound had become to me! How I loathed that hideous, vulgar, repulsive sound with a steady burning intensity. Surely the Halls of Hades could echo with no more unlovely and unrelishable a sound than the voice of that terrible rok of the sea. That brine-rook of guano-spattered doom.

The bird looked at us, rooked at us, and flew straight for us. Tactically, it had not been wise of us to enter a large open field, devoid of cover, and with our adversary occupying the higher ground. Our only real advantage was that we were nerved for action. We ran towards the great feathered roec and it flew towards us, slowly undulating its immense, black-topped wings in fixed transyek hypnosis. And still stood the seconds and everything stood out crystal clear. The wing-beats. The heart-beats. The interval. The distance. The fowl getting bigger, nearer. Soaring over our heads then spinning and wheeling round with gaping razor-beak flailing in fury at human folly. For one of those eternal moments it hovered, flapping and clacking over us – I could see right into its beak and it dawned on me that I could be fated to end up in that nightmarish and osseous proboscis, an outlandishly repugnant prognosis.

In some desperation I hurled the Esquimaux narwhal harpoon up at the beast but it bounced weakly off its beak and probably did little more than annoy the great roek. Just as it was coming in low however, and things were looking decidedly sticky; Paul managed to give it a good crack across the claw with his trusty bludgeon. With a peculiarly distasteful mewing shriek, the grotesque *hruoch* took wing; this time it headed in the direction of Unstable-Hobbla!

This time Paul and I both sounded the bugle-clarion-bird-call and this time the reply seemed a little clearer, a little closer, as if it was somewhere in the region of… Unstable-Hobbla!

'Kleptoparasitic' – the word arose in my minde, with all its unpleasant associations. 'Kleptoparasitic' – the term resounded and repeated like a klephtic lament in the Epirot style. "If that fowl is bound for Unstable-Hobbla it's probably planning another raid on the chicken-farm," I muttered from between tightly clenched jowls. "Yes," agreed Paul, "and it sounds like Jack's in that area – we'd better head down there."

We took to our heels and ran through several fields, working downhill to the river, scrambling over hedges and stumbling breathlessly on, galvanized by dread. Then the hills resounded to an eerie, harsh and blood-chilling sound. A staccato soprano outré larid braying – a most detestable sound! Cursed roek from the very pit of mal! Bad-egg turned foul! Darwinian dirt-bird! Evolutionary interloper! Puffy bird-fish-snake-thing – I know your lizard past, you were the lizard-king, you could do anything! Swaggering saurian air-hog! Lurking fearfully you lurched unleashed and now you peck and rip at the threshold of our peace, making laughing-stock mockery and jocularity of our human angle-clarity.

"Come on!" I hissed and we crossed Pons-Hobbla bridge, pausing to blast the bugle's metal breath. Jack's response came instant and staccato, seeming urgent. We flat-heeled it along the road and could now see the yarji hen-house chicken-ranch. It was altered. Instead of having the free range of the riverside water-meadow, the fowls were now cooped up in a small chicken-wire and wood enclosure in the corner of the field nearest the farmhouse. This pen was supplied with a chicken-wire roof, like an aviary. Into it were crowded the mixed bunch of assorted aforementionables - guineas, chickings, turks, canvasback ducks and honking gustatory geese. The fowls were locked into a cacophonous panic whose unholy clamour blended with the screaming, terror-bray of *Larus marinus* like salt blending with ale. The sight that met our eyes was not genteel or at all refined...

Ghastly, so very ghastly and judderingly repulsive it was. The great sooty-backed brine-rukk stood atop the chicken-run, flapping chaos, feathering its doomy air, *beaking and hacking and ripping* at the chicken-wire and batten roof like a blue-cheeked bee-eater opposing and pursuing a *Upupa epops* mottled hoopoe popster. As the savage gonys orange-spotted beak of the Kramvil-mutable-rhoek gouged and flailed at the roof, the unfortunate poulters below were driven near mad with running, clucking, squawking terror! All was frantic animation alert and adrenalin. There seemed to be people scurrying about – reminding me of busy ants. The old farmer had obviously been expecting more trouble and had got a bit more organized. His burly son and another rustic were brandishing their scythes aloft, trying to reach the goellan's legs. They hacked vainly as the kigliw legs of the beast kept just out of their free range. Two more men were rapidly approaching the scene carrying a ladder. The old farmer was loading his blunderbuss-harquebus. We ran down the lane and scrambled down the hedge and into the field. There was old Jack, pulling a net out of his rukk-sacc, as the ruckus roared and shrieked shattering around him. We heard someone shout to the farmer – "Hold your fire, he's going up!" and Jack was scrambling up the ladder in a wink, the net slung over his shoulder. Events were spinning fast, and what with the dinosaur-funk of the chickings and berds, it all added up to an exploding pandaemonium of unparalleled intensity. "Take it easy, Jacky-Boy!" yelled Paul. We saw Jack pause half way up the ladder, turn towards us, and smile sardonically. "Seagull and chips for tea, anyone?" he quipped, before returning to his assent.

Moments of confusion, of whirling animal fury and blind frenetic turmoil and yea, grette deedys of armys.

But down there in the coombe something strange happened. Down there in that place of typical rustic tranquillity the air rippled with mystery. The river splashed on towards the seaport, a breeze moved through the field slowly. Jack had scaled the ladder and had one foot on the roof, flanked by the vengeful scythes of the farm-folk. Larus was still fixated with trying to rip its way into the roof and was ignoring Jack, who was adjusting his net. This scene hung in my eye a long moment then BLAM! that crazy old farmer let fly a warning salvo with his piece. The effect of this sudden volcanic percussive explosion was to stir the froth of mayhem to a seething dark ocean of catastrophic panic. The goellan-rohk flapped ominously, throwing its head back in a long screaming distress-call – Ahhhk-kri kri kri kri kri kri kri ahhh-harrrrrk! Jack seized his moment and cast the net, in grim parody of a New Lynsmouth fisherman. A great wing brushed the net down, however, and it landed on the grizzly pink feet of our hatchling-bird. It kicked out and struggled, but only succeeded in entangling its vile claws further. The flailing scythes glinted in the air. Jack was tugging and hauling at the net like he was trying to land a hundred cran of the silver darlings. The noise was abominable and the action staccato and rapid. Just as Paul and I reached the chicken-run, the grette fowle barked an eldritch and basso larid skrawk and leaped awing aloft into the air, taking the net with it, and with the net Mr Jack Lane, esquire, gentlefolke etc., etc....... etc...!

*

    Now, I'll admit to being a crazy wild word-whirling lexicon-mosaic merchant, circulating words and pictures like a circus plate-spinner turned phonograph-operator. I've talked up Tallcorne, 'long past Kelmyek and way down to Lamo-Nara, where oriental sages find repose; and I've talked up some wild shoals of words like silver fish scuttling; and I've seen some sights to make a man think twice; but never in my life have I seen a sight like that of Jack Lane, clinging to his mackerel-net as our great feathered brine-hrokr whisked him swiftly over the roof of the farmhouse and into the moist, subtle and insubstantial aery aether.
    Laughing its ugly screeling cry, the black-winged beast soared up over the coombe with Jack now looking very small, caught up in the net like that unfortunate fly in the proverbial

but all-too-real cobweb.

"By Jehosephat!" spat the old farming-man, "come on lads, after 'em!" "We'll go ahead on foot," put in the son. "Father, you saddle the old hack and catch us up!" With that we rushed after the roc, with its Aladdin Lane dangling captive from its claws, flapping lazily up towards the sleepy and charming hamlet of Tread-Our-Toe.

We scrambled desperately up the hill, just in time to see the great fowl swoop down low over 'Dava-Bay', a large duckpond at the lower end of the village-green. Many a time I've sat on the cliffs and watched the quaint sight of a seagull with a starfish in its beak – like an aerial star-nosed mole. Sometimes they drop the pympbys thing into the sea – a curious falling star making a mini-supernova splash as it merges back into the swelling sea-mor.

A falling starfish – that's what it looked like when Jack suddenly dropped, plummeting from the net, with arms and legs spread and slowly flailing; straight into the soft muddy depths of 'Dava-Bay'.

I found good use for the narwhal-harpoon, stretching it out to Jack to aid him back to terra firma, thinking what a lot of *elements* he had experienced in the last few moments…

"Looks like it was nearly 'Human and Chips' for tea, old man," quipped Paul, which had the effect of sending Jack into an access of hilarity. The mirth was contagious and we were all doubling up – as much in relief as anything else. "The best part of it is," chuckled Jack, "I've pipped you to the post, Elias. You thought *you* were the pioneer aviator around here!" More laughter – though the farm-hands looked a little perplexed. Just then the old farmer came along on his old nag, frowning. "What're you lot all laughing at then?"

*

We convened a quick council of war then and decided to head up to the top of the hill, to the sheep-farm from which the village derived its name. The old man lingered at the 'Bay' to let the horse take water. The intense and cacophonous bleating told us that our guess had been well-founded. Y Hen

Ben Dafad – the closely-cropped field occupies a natural plateau, commanding fine views in all directions, both inland and out to Atlantic's rolling swells. Here, once again, a ghastly sight met and infiltrated our globulous jelly-eyes.

Tufts of fleecy wool – flesh – wool – blood on the grass – blood on the wool – entrails – organs – bones – bleating panicking flock – frenzied Larus – flesh-ripping Larus – beak dripping gore – great outstretched wings black, fringed with brilliant white, outstretched, slightly bent and undulating slowly – stampeding flock – thundering hooves – eyes wide in adrenal pounding flight – beak hacks, grabs, stabs, chops, crunches, severs, rends, grinds, shatters, tears, rips, shreds, lances, prods, gores, lunches and bites; rugose eyes fishy and bleared. Bleating sheep – running tumult – hubbub a la gore galore – sheepish jaws clamped in mute animalistic crisis – the bird hurled burly muttons, rams, ewes and lambs, slamming them into the ground in atavistic furious abandon – cramming them into its bill like a pelican – crunching and gulping and gulling them down – going on the lam – drinking the blood and gorging chunks of palpitating warm flesh – decimating and destroying – desolating and bringing ruination unto the land – devastating fowl! Slayer of sheep! Feathery menace! Great blood-speckled bird!

Having observed the scene for a brief harrowing moment, we all agreed to rush the fowl and let fly with all our weapons. At that moment the quixotic figure of the old chicken farmer appeared, astride his old hack, harquebus to hand. He was accompanied by the sheep-farmer, also nuzzling a musket's muzzle and mounted on a cart-horse. As our cavalcade surged into the field, the 'cavalry' took the lead, and soon the enraged farmers were blazing away with their antiquated fire-pieces. No animal likes gun-fire, and the great monstrous gull was no exception. Cramming one last fat ewe into its blazing yellow beak, kicking and bleating in its osseous trap as the *hatchling,* the thynge from the egg in the lab stretched out its sooty black archaeopteryx-wings and, taking rapidly to the air, flew out and over the sheep-farm, over Kyvounder Hill and New Lynsmouth, over the harbour's forest of jostling masts and kept on flying, straight out to the dark and rolling ocean.

We all stood transfixed as the great mal-fowl, the unlovely *brine-rukk* flew straight out to sea.

We said our goodbyes to the farmers, after much discussion of the dramatic events and many jokes about Jack's flight from the chicken farm to the sheep farm. We put away our weapons and headed off down Kyvounder Hill – Jack needed some dry clothes and I needed to check on Mr Taxon and give him the latest ornithological news. We agreed to reconvene at nine in the evening, at my cottage. I bade my two friends farewell and found my way through winding streets of dusk with lanthorns aglow and twirling in the glassy mellow windows of the huddled homes of the fisherfolk of New Lynsmouth towne. Fogbound banks of misty mullet mulled offshore as foghorns honked funereal bullhorn laments. Ship's bells tolled. Eight bells and all's well. Has the bird really *gone?* I hardly dared hope for so much. But the pull of the sea – an atavistic need to patrol the briny realm, to soar o'er empty sea-scapes… The streets were deserted. Lights shone and glimmered through the thickening gloom – mercurial luminosity dancing an ephemeral moment. Tiny droplets of niwl-mizzle-mist now dancing in the air and swirling with the breeze, caught in beams of gaslight's glare. Scatterings of gulls wheeled high above and clouds were blackening and darkling as in a murky looking-glass glimpsed. Brewing breakers and smashing rollers. Great heaving juddering pounding shakers – Atlantic's wrath let loose to roll and rage and rattle Kirnowe's claw.

*

At nine o'clock, my two comrades burst in, seeming very animated by the day's events. The fire blazed brightly in the grate, its flickering snakes of fluctuating flames flung luminous and phosphorescent around the little cottage-room. I poured the tay. "Well," began Paul "in recognition of your pioneering flight from Unstable-Hobbla to Tread-Our-Toe, I humbly confer on you the Honourable Order of the Albatross!" So saying, he produced a yard-long black larid quill and with a ceremonial flourish, tucked it into the buttonhole of Jack Lane's battered tweed jacket. "Bravo birdman!" I cheered as Jack bowed in mock humility.

"What a feather!" he added, casting a quizzically impressed glance at the great avine-fern-aerofoil. The great quill was bigger than the wingspan of many a bird and resembled the relatively flat wing of a heavier-than-air-machine. "A charming souvenir of my little journey," he mused, "and it's a great honour to be a founder-member of the Albatross Society – with any luck you two will be 'getting your wings' too before long – once you get that ornithopter of yours airborne."

"So tell us Jack," rejoined Paul, "what was it like, old man, your flight I mean – how would you describe it?" "Unforgettable!" says Jack. "Terrifying, thrilling, amazing – when I first got whisked up in the net, I really thought that I was about to die, thought the damn bird would drop me from fifty or seventy feet up… and this was coupled with the motion-nausea of being whirled around in the air at high speed – reminded me of once when I was about sixteen I went on a Ferris-wheel after several glasses of ale. Anyway, when I saw how thoroughly tangled round the bird's feet the net was, I thought I'd just hang on for dear life and try and enjoy the ride!" Laughs erupted. "It was wonderful to have an aerial view of the coombe – to look down on the tree-tops and fields and hedges, all looking like little toys. The suddenness of it and the novelty of it had thrown me into quite a state of euphoria and I must say I was a little disappointed when the old bird dropped me off in 'Dava-Bay', still, I s'pose there are worse ways to make your landing!" "Well you certainly stole the limelight," I laughed. "Perhaps, as the experienced aviator, you could give *me* some flying lessons!"

"Incidentally," put in Paul, "how's old Lazarus getting along? I got the impression the hatchling gave him quite a nasty injury." "That's right, it did," I replied. "But Mr Taxon seems to be blessed with truly remarkable powers of recovery." I passed over my own part in his 'recovery'. "Truly remarkable. In fact, he seems to be actually thriving on the stimuli caused by this whole 'egg' business. I could almost swear the old fellow is actually getting younger." Jack arched a questioning brow, an expression of his that I knew well. "I know it sounds improbable Jack, but then I think we've all seen the living embodiment of improbability before our very eyes in the form of that notorious feathered menace, that ill-starred monster-bird we've unleashed." "Well, with any luck, we've seen the last of the creature" said Paul. "Or it may return," countered the laconic Mr Lane. "I think we'd better maintain our vigilance," I concluded "and be ready for anything." We were all in agreement and I felt very fortunate to have such good and loyal companions.

"Crikey!" uttered Jack, momentarily watching his watch. "I'm supposed to be meeting Florence at the Tallcorne in five minutes! Sorry chaps – must fly!" and with a laugh of wild, vulpine abandon Jack was off out of the door and down the lane. "Ask if there's any news from Constance" I called after him. "Will do" he called back.

A vision of Constance rose in my minde, like the rising of a new planet on the horizon. I felt an ethereal, gnossient palpitation of the psyche then, and swam in dizzy depths of silvery light.

"He forgot his feather." Paul's voice brought me back from my reverie and I closed the door and returned to the fireside. Paul was holding the yard-long feather, examining it, moving it through the air to physically *feel* its aerodynamic qualities.

"Oh that reminds me Paul, these are for you," I said, handing him the blueprints of the ornithopter. "And Mr Taxon says you're welcome to pop round in the morning with me, and you can have a look at the kite for yourself." "Splendid! I can't wait! I'll examine these at home – talking of which, I think I'll be getting along – it's been quite a day… Who would have thought it…" He shook his head in wonderment. We said our goodbyes and I was alone again. There was the *feather* – it was lying on top of my newly acquired copy of How To Fly by Claude Graham-White. I picked it up, intrigued by its hidden clues about the nature of flight and the successful development of aerodynamic surfaces. I whirled the great fern-feather through the air and it soared and plunged as I slightly rotated its enormous stem. What a perfect aerofoil! Surely the bird kingdom holds many a secret for the aircraft designer... The feather flashed and glinted – I felt a pang of nausea as I remembered the atrocious scenes of the day. An echo of a deep revulsion and repugnance to that vile *kramvil* thing and all the trouble it had brought in its wake, like a heckling skein of herring-gulls following the boat home, bringing in the fish. I felt the surging rising wave of ornithomania – the 'bird-madness' or 'bird-fever'. I know I must combat this; I must not let the bird get the upper hand.

I sunk exhausted down upon the Egyptian couch and draped the counterpane upon my slumberous form. Leaden limbed, I reclined at ease to muse over this acute and fateful day. There was the case of Lazarus – I'd hardly had a moment to consider it, but he *had* died, he *had* been reanimated, reincarnated into his own body, and his body *had* become biologically younger – of that there was no doubt. Contemplating this gave rise to a strange and giddy feeling, as I wondered whether Lazarus Taxon had perhaps been reanimated *before?* Had he possibly been a student or colleague of the great Galvani? And the whole business of the egg – how could the creature have developed so inordinately rapidly, and also reached such a monstrously gigantic size? Was the giganticism of the bird *inherent* in the egg, or had Taxon's Magneto-Animation Technique, his chemical salts, focused sun and moon-beams and electrical fluids – had this caused the egg to mutate, to develop as it did?

Such questions might well remain unanswered by science, as all our time and energy was now focused on defending the area from the misbegotten results of our ghastly experiment! These puzzles and fascinations shook my minde to the core and gripped my spirit in the gulph of their orbit, as massy forms will draw other and divers celestial forms into their realms. Only the thought of Constance could counter-balance these dread fascinations and bring me a measure of peace. Her image rose up before me as something good and trustable and wholesome, something dark and beautiful. Something...

I must have melted into slumber and there began to

trickle down sleep's tortuous tributaries of ever-increasing and irresistible flow. To sink submerged slowly into deep delicious waters. To relax the worritting everyday minde and dive to deep lagoons of dancing sunlight reflected on the underside of the waves. Forests of coral and glistening krogenek shelfish exotica. White sands, sea-turtles and swaying palms, doctor wind, doctor bird and glittering shoals of flying-fish. High-flying, slow-moving clouds. Drifting in a fleecy slumberdown quilt, owl-feather soft and silent. Drifting with the breeze – a by-the-wind-sailor, gelatinous vagrant, oceanic-voyager. A dreamer adrift in minde's great sea, released and unhindered, fathoming uncharted mountainous depths. What rippling waves of shimmering light can play upon the minde asleep? What dancing dazzling scintilla can run together to form the image, the picture, the vision? This magic-lantern's glimmering display, its thrown-images, its dramas and karmic harbingers played out picturesque on the inner-seeing-vision-eye quixotic, mercurial, shimmering, lucid and reflecting.

So soared I, the dreamer, crossing marine-blue oceans in my caravelle-clipper, slicing through calm turquoise waters in warm latitudes. But aeons passed at night as realms shifted, came and went, revealing myriad scenes, characters and situations. The full moon reflected in a bowl of mercury on a mahogany table at midnight. Bronze sculptures of fauns and nymphs, wet with dew, early one morning in the mist. A French farm scene, a golden warm painting, brushstrokes of golden straw. A formal garden, granite and lichen, a giant chess-board, topiary, cobwebs strung with beads of dew.

A solemn ritual in Ancient Greece, garlanded dancers slowly circling, a sense of *levitation,* of ascension and insubstantiality. Dreams of forgotten cultures, echoes of yesterdays, great voyages and adventures, journeys to unusual places. Illuminating encounters with all sorts of luminary-people. Acquisition of knowledge by para-psychic means. Receipt of knowledge so subtle and refined that it cannot be consciously retained later. Surging, the synaptic sea swells, rises and falls with waves of sparkling energy, the heart fills with joy and visions fill the eye. Sleep's composite insect eye – the leaded glass dome of a cathedral. Sleep's illusory play – running down grassy hills, with patches of woodland, and waving cornfields in the wind, the sun, uniting with the golden land and the silver sun. Fluctuations. Recallibrations. shifts and slides. Tides that rise and fall. Atmospheric disturbances. New scenes come and go, new epochs, realms and strata. Dark wings over the ocean, over the vast and mountainous black, blasted ocean. White-caps from horizon to horizon and not a grain of land in sight. Relentless rolling energy of water in motion, waves of monstrous and dark energy, hiding the dark and terrible depths, the abysses of profound pressure, darkness and gibbering doom. The truly strange, exotic and grotesque life-forms that inhabited these lower depths swam before my eyes in their seemingly infinite variety. And over above the foaming, rolling billows arched the tectonic trajectory of the dark wings, the solitary and poignant wings, wings also menacing, also savage and stark, arched, hunched, stretched and flexed against Atlantic's damp, racing airs. Soar, dark-winged one, to Atlantic's watery realm and all you can find there, wanderer of anti-cyclonic, dark and churning waves. And the sands of time trickled down the hour-glass; and another page was turned.

Footsteps – people running – torches, brooms, scythes – a running, angry mob – dark wings sail overhead. Breaking glass and hoarse, angry shouts. People are swirling through the alleys of the Old Quarter. Flapping wings, flapping feet on the streets and papers blowing down the road. Flapping pages of a book, revealing more pictures, more avenues and possibilities. More forms pass before the mirror and are reflected. More echoes sound. More atmospheres tasted and scented. An eye to the moon, an ear to the harp's sweet lonely melody. The moon in the sea reflected, dancing in liquescent chimerical splattered splinters. Flatfish eye afloat, bloaters mottled moats of grey and glaucous blue, diamond-disc of the sea. Flatfish-eye glassy grips the moon. Moon on the eye of the water. Water the eye of the moon. Moon reflected in oceanic tear. Extrordinaire quixotic excess exotic the masts and mizzens bristled in the brine-dark sea of the squid-ink swirling cuttlefish-pool that went by the name of New Lynsmouth harbour. Diamonds of emerald-solar moonlight danced on dark waters. Silver-mercury ran trickling light through luminous mist aglow in tewlwolow half-light's glare. And like a moon-beam hurtling through space's chasm, so I fell through sleep's epoch deeps. Pools of vision bubbled ephemeral cameos and my psyche wandered noctambulistic. Ancient, modern, primordial, futuristic and ineffable – all realms, ages and strata are represented in the psychic cinematograph. The phonograph is replete with an inexhaustible archive of musical works to weave, craft and augment any conceivable atmosphere. The magic-lantern is lit and the chimeras play. Dawn speckles the dew on starling's wing. Stars dangle and tarry, tangled in webs of fiery gossamer glisten. Gravity pulls our path, lapping in waves of primordial drowsy colour – metallic, autochthonous, spontaneous, a spell-binding play of energy, light, motion and a most quixotic notion. Sliding blue moonlight bars of jade. Mystery moon-clouds. Fleecy scudders. Looming billows of night-neoned wisp. Shadows drifting over pools of water, flickering days.

And if I awoke suddenly startled in the night's silvery dark, it was from a dream of the ghastly larid brine-hruoch spreading its dark wings over the ocean, the monstrous black, seething, unfathomable and utterly arid ocean.

Chapter 19

A few golden days followed and flowed on from here. The shadow had seemed lifted, the nightmare passed – there had been no further sightings of our hellish gull. Since it was last seen flying out to the rolling deep ocean, many thought the beast had taken to its proper element, feasting on squid and cuttles, on far-flung foaming rollers of Atlantic's briny main.

I felt, and fervently hoped, that the great northern ocean was big enough to absorb the gull and give it a home. As each day passed, the sense of relief was becoming more palpable in New Lynsmouth. Even the pasty-trade had returned to normal.

I'd taken Paul round to see Lazarus again, and together we'd inspected the flying-machine. Paul seemed inspired with what he saw, and told us he was heading back to his workshop in the hinterland to get to work on the mechanisms right away. It had been a joy to observe Paul eagerly questioning Taxon on points of aerodynamic knowledge. Their enthusiasm for the topic seemed to lend them wings of golden light. The eyes of Taxon lit globular glowing orbs radioing information to the listener – his face sturdy and refreshed, livelier and more animated, less care-worn; in short – *younger!*

And how fine it had been, to stroll at peace along the sea shore, in roaring wind and sun, beside the bronze-dark white-capped churning sea. Sunshine on the sands picking out patches of sea-holly and samphire flaring in fleshy succulent cachtas green. Tranquil sands, sun-bleached and purified by wind's breathy blast. Friendly sun tingles the heart with joy. Wheeling white forms of gulls at play above. Breakers foaming up the beach, their surging froth rolling the carapace of a sea-urchin over the sands.

Walking the 'Old Road' of cyclopean granite blocks across New Lynsmouth beach – sunken submerged highway of former folk now reclaimed by the restless rannvor sea. Each seeming solid block encrusted with numberless crustaceans, crushed hastily together in adhesive cohabitation. As rollers frothed and spray danced aloft I would walk these ancient elder megalithic slabs as I wandered, took the salt-airs and mulled over all that had happened; hopping rock-pools splashing with the morgroenek blenny and undulating arms of the anemone. Weak winter suns sometimes peeping through rolling grey clouds. The original freshness of the beach was cleansing and revitalizing. Sea-winds can bleach the psyche clean and wash away the worritting cares and burthens of trouble's outrageous load. Winds brushed the backs of surfacing whales, winds that rattled coconuts in far-off warm latitudes, winds now riding Atlantic's slipstream and coming home to West Kirnowe to caress my brow with whispered tales of the sea.

Encased in the carapace of thought's conscious crystallization, I coursed forth upon the caunseway, ahead, alone, adrift, afloat, ahead I walked apace, sustained by grace. Dark and light played on the sand and in the sky swirled cumulus curls. Calcinated shells and exoskeletal relicts snapped and shattered beneath my oscillating feet. These brittle stars of the sea shone red and dark in pools of silver mercury meniscus. Glittering spindrift spicules danced across me toe-heels and the air was split damp with the skirl of a screech-eel. Sea-bats, leather-winged marsupials massed and mashed together, enmeshed in bleary, worldly weather. Pastures of the sea, flat, green and tranquil, haunted by grazing manatees, sea-cows, pinnipeds and flip-sides flopping in finny-'un's wake.

Swirling, churning Keltek mists assailed my nostrillii, fresh vapours of saline drift monolithic swelled and surged in briny effusion. Seething vast marine tides of ocean, surging more, more, an mor again. Hulks rattled and tickled their ribs against each other in Davy Jones' lock-up. Sea-monkeys gibbered and swung from fronds of carragheen and kelp, helpless cuds and cuggers from the curragh of Kildare. The slop of a million billion molecules dropped and dripped together as one.

Yet as I walked and trod this path, my mynde took wing and was cognizant of another, a track through the Western March, seeming to lead to Eden. The mark and stamp of this land was upon my eyes and before my feet. Where will this road now take me, in this unfamiliar countrie? Through a quiet land at eventide, through a land half-perfect, half-empty; under a sky scoured clean by swifts.

I had passed through a village, down a broad way flanked by dwellings of great charm and warmth, and passing the drowsing parish church and the Quercus Rex Ale-House, turned east, and struck into the quiet country-lande. Passing meadows of sweet grass and buttercup clusters, all was hushed and still, not a soul did I meete. Past farm-steads and house-steads and a great slow river, and the side paddocks and meads were deep in the fullness of May. The novelty of this scape of land drew me on, enchanted in a joyful curiosity; as in a dream-journey I ventured. The trees here were numerous and much larger than those of the Shyre. An unexpectedly rich alluvial, glacial soil had fed the roots of innumerable spreading oaks, ashes, sycamores and leafy rowans. Some oaks staghorned stark they writhed octopoid in many-fingered decay, blasted by time. And there came the bleating of many sheep and lambs, as silver dew crystallized on the herbage and moths lepidopteral hovered. No carriage or rider met me on this road and the few cottings I passed were likewise hushed and unlit. Having gone some way thus, I spied a rough lane leading away To The North and turned my toe-heels thither. Now into the deep-country, my heart quickened and the trail was all. I stepped by puddles of fresh-fallen rain and glimpsed a vast sheep-pasture, nibbled short and scattering white-tailed rabbits. The buttercup hay-pastures also rolled and fell off towards a winding stream and a distant manor-house.

Walking the way forth – the lane, the countrie, evening's spell quivering in the air – a stillness. Stinkhorns at dusk – ammonia's sylvan whiff speaks of forest's exuberant fungoid efflorescences, eldritch, foetid and dank. The hour is that of vespertilionidae – things of the night begin and bestir. A style was there on the right, and I saw it opened onto an avenue, dusken, running between two rows of large and ancient hawthorns, their knotted, gnarled and gothy limbs nearly meeting in the middle. This old drove-road stretched out before me, enclosing a zone of obscure shadow and darkling light. It spelled a promise, a fascination, an atmosphere of strange enchantment. A half-formed shadow-figure seemed to loom nigh – a fawn of summer? A chimera or piper at the gates of Eden?

A mere shadow, I expected, and shouldn't pay it any heed, but for a moment-

So I went and I found the past, the shadows of the old drovers, processions of ghost-shepherds in their white smocks and broad hats, driving ghost-flocks along this ancient, twilit way. They seemed to well up and swell about me, as if I were jostled by the great processing flocks and droves.

I emerged into the pasturage, the great sweep of the meadow o'er-arched by the rugose vastness. Blood-red 'n' ruby was the sky, and shattered bars of gold and darkest blue. Rhinolophidus – the horseshoe bat soared circular fly-catching swoops on wings of finest marsupial parchment. The sun fell first forth in the solar way and steam hissed up to Galway.

The reddle-man's run ran rutted and pitted with peat

and mossy bogwort. Brigantes had once passed this way. Chariots and cart-tracks. Hawthorns and oaks. Dew-drenched pasturage a-bleat with the fresh woolly lambs and their tattered old dams. Twilight tracks of crepuscular Albion – Albino – Albingo de lingo. Do you know the way? Then you can walk on by. And by the by, the quiet byways trickle through the land of sleepers, untrod by the somnambulists and penny a farthing trick-cyclists. These dream-roads pick a long way through the countrie of slumber, through night-thoughts and visions, through minde's magic-lantern expression-show. This very path arched o'er and branched with knotty thorns, as darkness creeps in to enclose and encloak, its violet tapestry wrapping shrouds round the shoulders of night's wayfaring strangers. As the air was alive, so I must follow this path. Its secrets palpitated in aery breaths. Trod by the hooves of countless ethereal generations of beasts, the forgotten, muddy avenue unwound like the skein of a dream. I passed as evening closed, I paused cloaked as cold coals caked the cow's cloud. I passed the hawthorn hard, the fleecy lamb so soft, the slumbering land so resilient and still, bat-wing, oak and horned beetle-grub. The sky ached from blazing lava ruby port-wine damask brocade scarlet tapestries of fire. Eventide's curtains of soft purple cloths frayed and melted into clearest ethereal air-molecule fineness. Horseshoes fluttered flung flapping through it in insectivorous secular ecstasy, arcing the circle, tracing airways of fate, fluid and free. Sheep's bleat buffeting the muffled rush roar of a distant locomotive.

Well I walked me on and my cranium swam through crepuscularity and the manifest molecular structures of nature's song of the eve. These hawthorns, hardened by scores of winters, saill éalaigh-tough, gong-like, ringing as bronze rung. The yester-road of the reddle-man opened slightly on one side, facing the emblazoned banner-flags of the ruby port wine of a burst strawberry, a flaming tangerine, impermanently illuminating a cloud of dreams. A trunk of fallen oak welcomed me as a seat from which to cast a gaze over the darkling sheep-pasture, as it ran and rolled gently away towards that distant manse, afar beyond the stream.

I glanced up and was thunderstruck. The trunk to the

front of me offered an awe-abiding and magickal sight. A stark, blasted and moribund oak – pared down to the great stem and one arching branch – together forming the elongated and Dadaist shape of a headless woman with arms raised to heaven – the image of the Winged Victory of Samothrace! The gaunt and gnarled giantess struck me cold with electrical amazement – struck me to the core of my being, an image archetypal and compellingly powerful – a distillation of ancient nature; robust, haggard and blastingly potent.

Inspiring animism. Surviving atavism. Arriving at a vision. Uprising xylem. Arresting totem. Beetle-bored soundboard. Blasted rattled seared rayed gnawed radiated soaked frozen bat-flapped woodpecker-hollowed stark arc arched outstretched arms of headless oaken relict throwback ceremonial Quercus robust or bust bleak quaint bulging nest of Druidic Rhamphoryncus and hall of the noble stag-beetle also woolly coated post of bleaters and fleecers and part-parc-parchment perch of buzzard and tribes feathery and light also deep-rooted plagioclase resilient arch stark gothic dark no bark arms arched to sky one longer one shorter graceful elegant elongated community oblate oblique obelisk old when Napoleon marched through Europe – a sapling fleetingly shadowed by a passing knight on mighty hand-high horse with pennants fluttering.

Starling dark Druidic and startlingly morpheyed into the archetypal and appallingly animated form of an Achaean deity searing you soared loomed and lightning you struck enthralling me most completely.

And before this stark arboreal wonderment rolled the peaceful lamby pastures of an English dusk. And the ruby flared to coral, with cloaks of rich violet velvet flung aloft as rhinolophidae circled gracefully and swifts screeching curves arced paths of aery skyshine.

The light was fading and thickening as Helios' original looming rays bowed around the elsewhere Earth, letting twilight settle tewlwolow till tomorrow's glint. Only with effort could I take my gaze off that orb-inspiring tree-gaunt Samothraki and return to the reddle-man's hawthorn-bordered rustic road, with its dreams of flocks and trods of fleece.

Oakleaves glowed bronze beetlegreen burnish as I herded forth my flowing flock of feet. I shivered a chill and stepped out between the thorn-trees and walked a while through the verdant pasturage. The great open space of this prairie trod meadow; the cool refreshment of the eve-airs; the swifts winging it joyfully – all conglomerated and congealed the very atmospheric rivulets of time's breathing diamond river. And then through a style and into some flat and formal parkland I trailed on. These tree-lined lawns bullfinch rumbling and beloved of prancing lunar unicorns. Parcs empty as dusk fell thicker. Vistas of subtle purple air in pillows of forest-breath-vapour. Through parc after parc and clean sweeping lawns clipped cool. The glint in my eye was from the evening-star as into the darkling forest I plunged.

Swampgrass and muddy the path. Birchwoods and bracken – stinkhorns at dusk emanating an acrid onion-domed odour of sylvan fungoid's sporadic culture. The ferny undergrowth hid garish clusters and globules of toadstools. The forest enclosed me in its own very rich and wonderful atmosphere and happily I strode on, even as the very shadows fell. I breathed an air fresh and different, a bracken, bark and arboreal sweet air. I knew the thrill of unknown ground, terra nova, a twisting path that plunges into the darkling forest as nightfall's solitude gathers in. Enclosed in the starling-scattered wood. Hushed with the hidden fawns of the wood. Alone in the woods where villagers fear to tread as the light melts away to nought and I alone play the wanderer's solo part. My thought was that I must keep to the path, and thus all would be well – were I to lose the path however, knowing not the land, the size of the woods, nor e'en to whither I wander, I could scarce fare worse. Perhaps this solitary and inky ribbon of mud and leaves, weaving through gloaming trees, would deliver me to the village of Lostwetherall – perhaps I would know someone there, perhaps there would be candle-light, warmth and shelter. But were I to lose the path, to lose my way, I could stagger into any and all a great many numbers of perils – not least the cold grip of a roofless night. Branches and twigs to walk into at eye-level; roots on which to stumble and trip; water, swamps, streams and rivers waiting to draw me in; beasts and reptiles; the rain and cold wetnesses.

But I did not lose the path and it unwound before me like a silver-black ribbon, leading me deeper and deeper into that dense and obscure realm of trees. And the balmy airs of summer gave place gradually to the whispered breaths of an owl-down feathery night. And so I rambled on. I found I could barely see the wood for the trees were a blotting cloak of foliage, dense and full. And so I trod the darkling arboreal path. Yet as I walked and trod this path, my minde took wing and was cognizant of another, a mammoth road of cyclopean granite blocks, tracking across a beach in West Kirnowe, seeming to lead to New Lynsmouth towne.

Bronze was the sky as I betrod the barnacles that clung to the ancient caunseway. A wind was blowing in from the sea. Rollers and breakers were bounding up the beach in foaming abandon and the skrawk of sea-fowl stirred strange within me.

I needed to clear my head and collect my thoughts. The sea-airs seemed healthful and vibrant so I decided to stroll around the old fish-market and harbour-pier-area. In truth I wished only to muse on Miss Constance – I should write her another letter – was she still at the field-hospital? These thoughts bubbled up in my minde as the beautiful image of Constance swam looming before my inner eye.

I trod the granite slabs of the old quay, smelling of tar and rope. I watched barges and barques disgorge grunion, bass and haddock. Niwlgorn horns of fog honked the horn hollow as sea-bass sun-beams shot through like pillars of photon-activity. Niwlek misty the fogs hollow shreds driven apart by zephyr's breath. Even in the harbour's helm and arm the sarfek sea-snakes and eels dared to rear, leap and creep, uncoiling and roaming at will amongst hulls, hulks and hauls. And along this rotting and tottering ancient wharf ran that odd assortment of stalls vending all manner of things from the sea. Pympbys pickled starfish in clusters and galaxies – sea-sloths by the barrel or the tub – punnets and platters of krogenek seafood snails and slitherers of all descriptions and colours of carapace – iridaceous mother-of-pearl oyster-shells, shimmering, incandescent shoals. Among these mongers were some who sold fish of all hues, from ferruginous rouge to a yellow-sub-maroon. Bedlamite hags haggled for belemnites and ammonites with meek Mennonite merchants. Business was brisk, as fish-thriving villagers bartered and bid for the aquatic and gelatinous delicacies being hawked beside the old harbour-wall. Species included Flying Gurnards – *Dactylopterus volitans*; *Torpedo marmarata,* the electric ray; alewifes; elder cods; norse cods; mud-skippers; horseshoe crabs; horseshoe bats and sea-horses; sea-hares; sea-snails and sea-slugs on beds of sea-lettuce; sea-cucumber, tangle, oar-weed, kelp, sea-globs, snakelockses, stingrays, mullet, grunion and skate. Barrows lurched and lurked on the quay, displaying the curious and exotic fruit of the sea. Eels and sea-jellies vied with cockles and muscles, stifek squids and carragheen sponge cakes. An air of mist hung about the place.

I thought I should call on old Lazarus later on. His remarkable 'recovery' still perplexed my purple expertise. How could a man…? Oh it was no good trying to figure it out…..! Sometimes we have to accept that very strange things do occasionally happen. Ah, this old market with its creels of haddock and herring, its pie-eyed star-gazey head-crazy larboard-lurching mariners and scatterings of foreigners.

How pleasant it will be, I thought, to return to my studies, the peaceful pursuit of knowledge. The aeronautical experiments naturally preoccupied my minde, but I was also avid to return to the philosophical, anthropological, poetic, archaic, Sinological, botanical and Hellenic.

I wandered on past the seemingly endless row of stalls, mongers and vendors – alewifes, fishwives, waifs, salts, amphibious skippers, strollers and shoppers. The human crowd with its swell and press gave warmth, humour and vitality to an otherwise drab and garish scene. Sea birds were approaching, seemingly all flying the same way – inland. The crowd surged and caps and bonnets thronged and wove around. Urchins ran round shouting, costers repulsing them. More birds – gulls, guillemots, razor-bills and a cormorant.

Ah, the things they sell at this eldritch lurching sea-market! *Aequorea aequorea* – a plate-sized blue dome with four hundred rugose squiggling arms! Hydrozoa!

Cnidaria! Squirming, pulsing things from dim Pre-Cambrian epochs. Things of the sea, things of the deeps. The seaballs of *Posidonia oceania*. Rich green mats of *Verrucaria mucosa*. *Apoglossum ruscifolium,* a liverish, gelatinous branched water-fern. Discoidal holdfasts of the notorious *Dilsea carnosa*. Fronds of the well-favoured and bronzy *Gymnogongrus crenulatus*. Weeds of deep strangeness like the *Calliblepharis ciliata* or the *Bonnemaisonia asparagoides*, or the great worm-like *Nemalion helminthoides*. That people could actually eat such things as these never ceased to amaze me. Noah's ark shells, bearded horse mussels, byssus threads like krogenek dodder, spiny cockles, and the tasty 'heart-shell' – *Glossus humanus*. Ctenophora – the combjellies – glas-grey serrated ribbons and bulbs – orbs and cucumberous membraneous members of little-known phyla. Bulking iridescent and luminous jellies in bags of cellular filmy gossamer. Punters gladly snapping up punnets of snapping prawns, *Alpheus glaber* and the transparent blue nocturnal carapaces of the chameleon prawn, *Hyppolyte varians*. The squat lobster, the shovel-nosed lobster, *Nephrops norvegicus* – the Dublin Bay Norwegian scampering prawn and the common lobster – *Homarus vulgaris*. Also *Eriocheir sinensis* – the Chinese mitten crab with its tufty claws clacking and *Goneplax rhomboides,* that geometrical fellow, the angular crab. The *Pycnogonum littorale* – ovigerous, cephalothoracic and deeply odd. Bristle-tails by the pint or the quart – *Petrobius maritimus*. The crinoids and brittle-stars, cycads of the salt-frothing sea. The goosefoot-star; the starlet or cushion-star – *Asterina gibbosa – who would eat such things?* The sun-star, the purple sun-star and the spiny-star – best chopped fine and fried, so they d'say. Sea-cucumbers, worm-cucumbers and cotton-spinners with the Winsborough Cotton Mill Blues. Hydroids, ascidians, lampreys, hagfish and divers jawless suckers. *Squatina squatina,* Rough hounds and angel sharks. Common or octopus-garden skates – *Raja batis* – King of Baglamas; egg-masses, mermaid's purses and morgis. Lump-suckers, sea-hens, sticklebacks and *Lepadogaster lepadogaster,* that curious succulent Cornubian critter, the Cornish sucker.

The myriad species displayed before my watery and globulous eyes caused me constant astonishment. That such outré and disrelishable fare could sustain and provide sustenance and provender for our humble community was surely witness to the harsh economic circumstances of our times. Indeed, many elder folk around these parts could well remember the terrible days of famine, when the murderous mordros surf would brook no barque and so the sea could not be harvested and bony hunger walked abroad among the villages and coves. The grim laws of necessity had driven people to eat anything that came out of the sea. The ocean was an inexhaustible food-cupboard – both womb and cornucopia, pouring forth fruits myriad and beginningless. This aqueous galactic realm was replete with hallucinatory swarming sparkling stellar masses of teeming life-forms. Truly the clutching claw of Cernyw was widely seen as a Cornubia within a cornucopia. As long as boats could be launched, bloaters could be lanced and lunch could be poached.

But I remember Scarlet once telling me that old man Vagahorn had told her that all the best fish, all the wholesome, presentable and desirable fish goes straight on the steam-train to Billingsgate, and us Kernewek folks are left with the Lepadogasters and leftover tentacles. These severed sea-limbs would be sold by length – a foot of squid or a yard of eel. The kollel-lesa, ochtapas rising with its legacy of sea-legs, jelly-legs, sucker-legs, boneless cuttle-legs, legs that walk not; this leggy embodiment of the Planktonic Form of Eight was best eaten late in October.

Another squadron of sea-birds sailed overhead, over the market, heading inland – was it to be a storm? Lacking the powers of an Ornithoskopos, I could not read the auguries of birds. The study of nature! Natural History – a vast field, in which one could expend countless years of study and research... So I mused as my old shoes traced their leathery way through the stalls, stepping over puddles of squid-ink and pools of cuttlefish colourants.

The vivid thought of Miss Constance was never far from my minde – the sun broke briefly through a curtain of mist. I hoped she would soon be free of the ghastly sights of the field-hospital, and would be able to meet up with me again very soon. I dared not think or hope beyond that, but would be so happy just to be in her presence again. A thunderdog glint of rainbow hue shone from the misty sky and was reflected in miniature on a million fish-scales. For all its gothick quaintness, I was very fond of this place, and relished the prospect of a studious and scientific life here, perhaps with Constance at my side.

Zephyrs seemed to play on the waters, coming in from the Sargasso Sea, whispering tales of the Spice Isles, of drowsy coconut-scented beaches, white sands and tropical flowers.

I thought of the Lyre-Birds and the other Birds of Paradise, with all their gorgeously beautiful plumage and their delicate dances, but on looking aloft, I saw only more sea-birds flying landwards – curlews, cormorants, gulls – what drove them to forsake the waves and haunt instead the firm terrain of Penwithershins?

The sky seemed to darken a little, though the afternoon was yet young. I had reached the furthest end of the market, the most desultory and grotesque of places.

The sky, as I say, had darkened, mist swirled ragged round the rotting, lurching seaport-towne. There was a speck in the sky – another bird. Masts and rigging rattled in the harbour, as a slight breeze stirred around. The speck was coming this way. The exuberant life of the market bustled on around me. A lone bird – dark wings over the ocean. Dark ocean sending a slight chill now, a chill from the vast depths of the ocean. 'What *is* that bird?' I wondered, as I observed it getting closer and bigger. Cold water welling up from the ocean's depths, bringing a profound, rising chill. 'That *bird* – it's very… big! It's…' my minde froze in horror, not wanting to accept what my eyes clearly saw. As it rapidly approached, there could be no doubt about it – I was staring at the ghastly sight of our 'experimental' *Larus marinus* – Great Thundering Herrings Alive! What a vile Hell-beast it had become. Its great outstretched wings were as wide as the pier and as it glided silently towards the market a great screaming rent the misty air, as the sight of the monster met the eyes of the market-folk. People scattered and ran, pell-mell and willy-nilly. The dark form soared aloft, majestic, tyrannical, Ornithaikos – beak-clacking feathery tear, fast, furious, swooping –

Traders and punters dived under the fish stalls to escape the grim brine-rook. Beak clacked and scaly pink webbed feet kicked out, turning stalls onto the cobbles – sending fish flying and eels and squids a-squirming and churning in the cuttlefish pool. Black feathers on white. Terrified pale faces of the village-folk. Splintering wood – ripping canvas. Barrow-wheels spinning – spokes shattered – cockles cracked and lobsters broken on the quay.

That terrible gonys beak – how I loathed the sight of it – would it haunt me forever? Gulling down herrings and pilchards by the cran. Trashing creels and tipping tables crashing and reeling to the ground. Eyes dull – glassy, rimmed in red. Wings flapping for balance, creating strong draughts of wind, sending straw and debris into the air. Again that foul guttural braying laugh rang out, four descending notes, now sunken to a basso profundo bronzen croak. How it contrasted with the shrill screams of the petrified fishwives as they struggled convulsively to flee from the beastly entity. Blood splattered on granite flagstones – a trader clutched his gashed arm to staunch the crimson flow. That murderous beak, wreaking havoc and vile skrawk. Rending, smashing and devouring. Scooping up the scattered sea-food, wolfing down skates, dogfish and congers. Gelatinous writhing cephalopod tentacles hanging from that beak. Sprats, pilchards and kommolek mackerel pillaged from barrels, carts and tables. Steaming, stinking gouts of guano fouling the ground like black snow. People slithering, skidding and falling down in it as they tried vainly to run. Screaming hysterical voices. Barrels rolling. Myriad iridescent filmy silver fish-scales glistening and shimmering on the stones, in the pools and rivulets of water, slime, blood. The foul smell of rotting, clotted fish fell full on my sentient nostrilii – foulness bestirred by a churning beak and tearing web-skinned feet. A foulness of guts and gullets, of gill-slits and swim-bladders seeped out of the littered sea-scraps, betraying their dubious edibility, freshness and provenance. An acrid, retching, foetid, hideous, vast and deeply nauseating stench rolled out in waves, adding to the hellish scene a further dimension of gibbous and gibbering revulsion. Some of this festering mass of marine pulp was already pullulating and flickering with tiny planktonic larvae, which added nothing to its loveliness.

The ghastly *roek* was now lord of the whole harbour and all the stalls that straggled down the Northern pier. It paused, suspended in atavistic kramvil pineal awareness – its head like a great snowy cliff from which blazed a streak of fire – the *beak*. It stood somewhat taller than a man now, fearsome in its maturity – a monstrous egg-chick that should never have been hatched. With a triple of flaps from its pteradactylus wings it soared up two fathoms and swooped aerily and aerodynamically down the pier, alighting on a bleak stall heaped high with filmy transparent sea-jelly domes – morgowles - glopping silver-grey-glas things the size of dustbin lids. The archeopteric density of the hellish mew burst the stall asunder, sending the mucoid smugairles splat, slopping and sliding over the wet granite flags. Braying in ecstasy the black water-bird *drunk* them down like oysters – cackling, crowing and crooning raucous high – a yard-long purple tentacle dangling vile from the larid maw.

The discoidal mor-glops spread and spewed down the pier, changeling its appearance to sarfek serpentine asparagus viridian green – *Crotalus horridus*. The glopping, slopping, *slurping* sound they made, as the panicking crowd stampeded over the jellies was something best forgotten. The outré and outlandish quality of this bizarrerie was further enhanced and exaggerated by the several numbers of townsfolk who slipped and fell into the mass of morek sea-jelly domes, bursting *Aurelia aurita, Rhizostoma pulmo,* and the leafy blue golden-fringed *Cyanea lamarki*... the great chryselephantine *Chrysaora isosceles* and that other nocturnal Pythagorean pelasgian, luminous Alexandrian golowji lighthouse, the *Pelagia noctiluca*. Some of the beasts stung like hot nettles and terrible blotches appeared on the faces of the unfortunate villagers squirming in the jelly-mess. A mere flick of the great sea-fowl's wing tip and a barrel of membranaceous pympbys starfish was thrown into the air, forming an ephemeral galaxy. Skates were skat down in foursquare tessellated terraces and squat-lobsters, scallops and spider-crabs thrown generously around the quayside as the larid monstrosity set about its vile and unholy work. The boats rode and clacked at their moorings, some brave New Lynsmouth fishermen had climbed the mast of their craft and were trying to pelt the grete byrd with gouts of tar. This had the effect of further enraging the frantic creature, which hacked beak and claw in mad, frenzied abandon. Flapping of great wings – a running, screaming crowd – scattered shoals of bonny herring on the market floor – eels asquirm in myriad steel metallic cold blue hues glinting – the beak clacking – a crocodile's jaw – a pair of butcher's knives – krogenek chaos as shellfish are crunched underfoot – more screams – running – a manta-ray is flung to the ground, pecked, gored and savaged – guano adding its fish-reeking patina sheen to the freakish scene – debris, carnage and detritus everywhere – people running and slipping on loose fish and flotsam – halibuts, flatfish – the gaunt, brassy bark of *Larus marinus* – the complete absence of all other birds – the looks of frozen terror on the faces of the crowd, as they surged out of the market area, white, gaunt, haunted – the atavistic fear that a large predator generates – a fear that reeked like gall as it seeped into every soul present – a fearful feathered chaos, harbinger of mayhem, violence and dread – beak hack blood and screams – fish-guts fish-heads fish-scales and fishes – chaos, horror and doom on New Lynsmouth – clacking beak, clash rip and hack.

What an abominable scene to witness – how much more ghastly to feel partly to blame for this chaos, this braeing carnage and wreck. Was there to be no escape from the predations of this unnatural creature? Great Herrings! This really was catastrophic – fish everywhere, costers and punters still floundering and shimmying in the spillage of sea-meats, and presiding over the fear and confusion – *Larus marinus,* bloated, gloating brine-roek.

A lull had settled on the market, the bird was at a distance, preoccupied with a tasty box of kippers. Most of the people had dispersed, some leaping into fishing boats where they could get below decks; others stampeding in Dionysiac frenzy out of the market and into the principal streets of the Old Quarter, spreading fear as they ran. I decided to try and at least keep the sea-fowl under observation, even if I could do little to actually repulse it. I crept closer, ducking under stalls and fish-carts and slipping dangerously on the marine debris once or twice. The guttling guillan had decorated the whole market area with a piscine cold patina, a collage of aqueous species, glittering scales; dead, glassy eyes; fins sagging; lips glaucous, rubbery; gill-slits, cuttles, barbells, breadcrumb sponges, butterfish; bioluminescent entities of mysterious, transparent, bell or sheath or tubular form, lacking colour like tiny glass locusts or dirigibles; products of the oceanic womb. Planktonic, pelagic, mammalian – hydroid, cephalopod, nautilus and morhogh – dolphin – morgath skates and morvil roaming whales; *Dentex dentex,* hornwrack and dactylozooids; polyps, sea-squirts, the *Mercierella enigmatica* worm of the squiggly sea. *Muggiaea atlantica* – tiny swimming jelly-bells – morek *Zeus faber,* old John Dory with his extendable carmudgeon jaw. Rainbow skittering snails in whorls and luminous eerie flotillas, squadrons and flotsams.

Rhamphorhyncus wings suddenly filled the sky as the grete hawk glid swiftly towards the stall I was under, ramming it with all its might and main. Wood split and shattered and fragments burst and scattered. The loathsome maw was gaping and snapping at me – a vile sight which I would rather forget. That vicious beak was lunging and prodding at me and I really thought it was about to rip me apart, when a blast from a fishing-boat's foghorn startled the fowl. The crew had seen my plight and their swift reaction caused the *hrokr* to leap back and cease its attack on me. Ever since that moment, I've always heard a sweetness in the sound of a foghorn. Then, picking and pecking its way through sea-urchins and brine-sturgeons, that haunter of the surfs feasted greedily on dead soles.

Cowering under the wreckage of that filthy costermonger's barrow, slopping around in a sort of *conglomeration* of polyps and medusa, watching a ghoulishly overgrown seagull destroy that market, I started to wonder just what people *saw* in New Lynsmouth. Surrounded by Nature, awash in Nature – my feelings of bucolic joy were at an all time low. Looking at that rogue rook as it wreaked havoc and shook the shore asunder, pillaging, plundering, dung-splattering, guano encrusting, fish-box smashing, hagfish relishing and devouring like a frenetic automaton was an unlovely sight indeed and I railed against the Fates who had sent it my way. The very *peculiarity* of my circumstances struck me most forcefully then, and I could not help being strongly aware of the absurdity and sheer oddness of it, as much as the danger and fear.

Mouth-arms of the jellyfish pulse. Clacking roek splits sack of dog-whelks. Pelagic, thirty-two lobes, sixteen sense-organs. Screaming black-backed pterodactyl attacks fish-traps and blusters down on lobster-pots. Sessile, trumpet-shaped body, attaches onto seaweed with wart-like anchor. The great eye so glaucous, vacant and fatty. Terrible nostrils. Gelatinous, terminal, clustered, filamentous, the rugose branchlets of *Polysiphonia elongata* took the place of terrestrial trees in the outré vignette of grotesqueries. Insatiable hatchling! Experimental hatchling! Elemental predator – hollow-boned water-chicken – morek seamew – moroc sinew and architectonic plenipotentiary of the estuary, gulling your way from Exe to sea and below where the submarine-pasture kelp-forests grow. Eater of rats and attacker of killer-whales and Oregonian/Californian Orcas, dolphins, morhoghs and dogfishdinners! Despised pasti-theif! Bespoiler of gentlefolks' carriages (what ought to know better) and scourge of washday with your whiter than white. Sheep-rustling gannet-thing! Bane of my life and embodiment of momentary folly – how I regretted my decision to become involved with the whole, ill-planned experiment! And now under darkling skies I lurk and watch the birdie do its frightful work – berserk – bellicose and belligerent. Stirring the vile ribbons, shreds and chunks of ripe cephalopod and squid-flesh into a nightmarish paste – webbed-feet flailed and dug. The vapour that was released had started to attract large clouds of bluebottles, greenbottles, houseflies, midges and horseflies, giving a rather 'Egyptian' or 'Biblical' look to our market-scene. Flyblown vignette! Is there no limit to this ugliness?

Apparently not, as there was more to follow. I crept along the pier, ducking from stall to barrow, table to cart, occasionally pulling a distressed fishwife out of the broth of moray eels, sea slimes, green and grey fishes, mixed in with gouts of guano, coins, a shoe, an umbrella, bits of newspaper blowing down bleakly, infamously. I would pull these people out of the polyp-pulp, get them to the relative safety of the stalls, and tell them to creep slowly down the fish-pier, underneath the stalls, and away from danger.

Halfway down the quay was a large and ancient shed that had rotted quietly there for many a tide and many a year. It housed the holding-tanks for arthropods – various species of crabs, lobsters, prawns and the like. A smaller tank was sometimes used to house octopus and squid. The whole structure was rotten through, a mouldering edifice of neglect and decay. The great fowl of the sea threw out its formidable wings and gently flapped them, whilst the sleek head it threw right back – to scream in croaking harsh reptilian voice the Pre-Cambrian sonatas of a demented musicality. It seemed to derive a deep satisfaction out of this animalistic shanty, as if claiming and possessing the territory by filling it with its voice – Ego io io io I I I I I. A breeze was stirring and the sky was darkling yet. My minde, half-numb, clung and hung on to a sense of Science – to observe the animal's behaviour, to be ready to intervene to protect human life, if necessary. Some day these findings must be written up and analysed by eminent zoologists and ornithologists. I certainly had plenty of material to 'record and describe'… The braying Larus was furiously kicking out with its horrible, pink, scaly, snake-skin, kigliw legs, and had soon ripped, beaked and kicked away most of the front of the shed.

The commotion was disturbing the crustaceans, which were swarming and seething with insectivoidal energy. *Corophium volutator, Jassa falcata, Gammarus locusta, Tritaeta gibbosa, Elasmopus rapax, Lucifer acestra, Palaemon serratus, Caprella linearis* – the ghost shrimp, *Crangon crangon* – the common shrimp, *Palinurus elephas* – the spiny lobster, *Munida rugosa, Callianassa subterranea,*

Jaxea nocturna, Calappa granulata, Dromia personata – the 'road-person-crab'. Spider crabs, red spider-crabs, spiny spider crabs, long nosed masked-crabs, edible crabs, inedible crabs, shore crabs, unsure crabs, swimming crabs, velvet crabs, hairy crabs, velvet hairy swimming crabs, sea-spiders, Arthropoda, Arachnida, Pseudoscorpiones, Pycnogonida, the squat, spiny, shovel-nosed, bristle-tailed, telsoned, irascible exoskeletal tribes; the swarming, scuttling carapaced hordes. Tanks and tanks full of them, squirming and scuttling – sensitive antennae gently twitching and probing, on many legs the lobsters, the legsters, the leggiest legest armadillo sea-bed processing scuttlers of sunken armadas and kelp-matted mizzens where cannons corrode away slowly under forty fathoms of brine.

Gwaaa-ow gwaaa-ow gwaaa-ow – the larid bray now a loutish gloating boast – the hatchling stepped into the shed. A hermit crab emerged from its shell and broke its vow of silence by emitting a horrible bubbling, hissing noise. Provoked by the decapod's seething, the eggling lunged with its broadsword beak and rent a great gash in the copper tank. The thick brine came pouring out, and with it a scuttling, wiggling army of Arthropods. Further incensed by this, the great gull ripped out at the other tanks too, sending Niagaras of many-legged exoskeletal scuttlers pouring and bouncing bibyn-bubyn onto the floor and washing out onto the pier.

The Greater Black-backed Gull was scooping up shrimps and gulleting scampering scampi with brine and prawn. The majority of that carapaced crowd were washing onto the pier, however, and forming up into an insectivoidal parody of a quadrille. An unearthly carnival unfolded as fiddler crabs clawed their bows and masked crabs danced like harlequins. Legions of giant spider-crabs, loathsome, spindly abominations, surged into the melee, increasing and bolstering its atmosphere of unwholesome and unspeakable alienage. The clattering and rattling of all those brittle twig-legs set up a calcified staccato percussive rhythm. I was trapped under a stall and that great crawling, swarming brigade of stalk-eyed, antennae-twitching, pincer-claw brandishing sea-life was coming my way! Inching towards me on many-jointed, spidery legs, mouth-parts and feelers and dead, black-olive eyes! My very flesh was crawling in pullulating eldritch repugnance at the ghastly sight. Some of the decapodic hordes had not missed the opportunity to feed on the polyp/medusa mess, and were brandishing the severed blue, white and purple mouth-arms and tentacles of the globose and gelatinous morgowles, sea-jellies, comb-jellies. Some of the squat-lobsters showed a preference for various forms of starfish and sun-stars, and holding these aloft in their great pincers, they seethed and surged forth like a strange new galaxy from Hindu mythology – a hundred thousand suns supported by a plethora of exotic animals. These many-sectioned scurriers were heading towards me like a revolting krogenek stampede – scuttling, rasping and clicking, ghastly claws raised and feelers reverberating and bristling. Feeling, pincing, stalking and clattering on they crept and seethed, exoskeletal sclerotic hordes, bristling with decapodic weaponry, festooned in hydroids, sponges and enigmatic polychaeta.

In my fear-frenzied delirium I thought the scuttling mass reminiscent of stick-insects, praying mantises and rhinoceros-beetles. Yet to flee from them was to risk the attentions of the vile gull that now stalked and strutted, braying, pecking, squelching and crunching its way down the pier. Desperate to flee the swarming mass, I broke cover and ran headlong and footloose through that festering sea-meat before ducking under an eel-barrow, the great ruuk following casually. The bird was distracted however by an abandoned fish-fryer's stall. An enticing smell of fried cod and chips emanated from a large skillet sitting atop a brazier of glowing coals.

Rashly, the great gull gorged on the scalding hot meal. Maddened with pain, it kicked over the brazier of hot coals, which rolled off the quayside and crashed onto the bow of a moored boat – quickly taking hold, amongst the tarry wood, rope and canvas, the fire soon spread from boat to boat. The flame-licked masts, accustomed only to the ethereal flickerings of St.Elmo's Fire, were soon engulfed in the real thing and blazed like a pine-forest in summer. The light from these rising flames was reflected upon myriads of scales, carapaces and glossy surfaces and in many a dead and glassy eye.

Meanwhile under the eel-barrow really harrowing horrors unwrapped their cloaks of darkness. Cregynhyrg shellfish; siorcs; dragonettes and the various fishes of melancholia and choleric malaria floundered and seethed all around me. Bat-stars, butterfly blennies, the eelpout, the dead-man's-fingers, the Goldmans sweetlips – *Plectorhinchus lineatus* and the mighty crown of thorns starfish. Pululating in close proximity were hydroids and cuckoo wrasse, cimwch and gliomach lobsters, chloichean, twyllwr, slefren for, steabhlach, smugairle-roin and smúitiúil aigean crosog mhara. Barrels and boxes spilled over with *Diogenes pugilator* and the ever-silent *Tridacna gigas*. Official sepia images revealed common cuttlefish tentatively tackling incredulous cackling sea-cattle as subtle fishes slipped quietly by. Flies flocked and flickered over the writhe, crystal wings riding the sickening and offensive stench. Not far down the pier swarmed the exoskeletal exodus and a demented, tormented, rhamphorhynchic delirious *Larus marinus* presided over the chaos, a tyrannical Nero skrawking and braying vainly while the flames rose higher and higher.

Lorks a-muzzy! How that desperate, crab-pot despot destroyed and despoiled, wrecked and rooked, wreaked, wrought and rent asunder, pillaging, plundering, burning and looting. Stealing and killing and *gulling!* It galled me to the Gaelic kor to see the coarse and larid lack of courtesy shown by that beaked brute! The damage around me was truly shocking, the broken market-stalls and spoiled goods – the lost earnings of these already impoverished folk – the terror, danger and injury to which they had been exposed. The blame for all these outrages lay firmly at the pink, scaly, webbed feet of the *brine-hrokr!*

There it was – dancing in the flames of its own incendiary and desecrating frenzy – great barking-siorc, black-winged abomination.

It was then that the already damaged and dilapidated eel-barrow caved in on top of me, burying me alive under a nightmare cargo of eels – morays, congers and hagfish – some dead, some living, and instantaneously wrapping and confining me in their cold and powerful coils. I felt as though I were falling through the Earth, so great was my revulsion. Tiny needle teeth were ripping through my clothes and gorging at my flesh. The coils were tightening and yet more eels were falling onto me so I was utterly covered in a seething, living blanket of the sarfek and linear thugs. Like cold, animated ropes they clasped and enshrouded me, hideous hagish faces flashing momentarily before my own. I could see nothing but a jelly of undulating eels, they were blotting out the light and overwhelming me in an eldritch tomb of sea-flesh. Like a flurry of wet jereboas, they were starting to constrict my breathing. Now, at last, the evolutionary advantage of having an exoskeletal carapace was impressed upon my minde. If I only had the hard shell of a fine, strong lobster they couldn't crush me, and with my claws I'd chop and hack at the eels and pull them off me...

I was becoming delirious... lack of air... weight of eels... coils... coils tightening... claws... lobsters... darkness... sleep... heavy... drowsy... e a s i e r t o g o w i t h i t ..... *NO! NO!* This is Death! I must fight! I must LIVE! I struggled convulsively now, as if lit up by an electric eel. I could feel the life-force welling up inside me, the Universal power, the animal power of my own life-will. I know many things flashed through my minde then, but I do not recall them – I only remember thinking of Constance.

In the sharp intensity of my delirium I managed to claw some of the vile beasts off me and rolled out from the wreckage of the stall. The mass of escaped crabs and lobsters was still scuttling en masse down the pier and that's when I got the idea of trying to get them to attack the eels – astakos-style. As I said, I was delirious.

Wrapped in vile congress with the congers and morays, I managed to roll slowly towards the crusty hordes of krogenek crabs, spider-crabs and bustling squat-lobsters. Just as I reached the vanguard of the decapods, I made out two figures, women, picking their way towards me through the carnage, brandishing large knives. "Take it!" One of them thrust a knife into my hand – it was Florence! The other woman was chopping at the eels with two knives – *Scarlet!*

We chopped, sliced, hacked, severed and debodied

enough eels to feed Whitechapel for a week and soon I was freed!

"Thank-" "Not now Elias," broke in Florence, "we'd better get out of here quick!" "NO!" I snapped, "Give me another knife and don't ask questions – *now go!"* Scarlet McAwe looked at Florence Place and Florence Place looked at Scarlet McAwe. "Men!" muttered Scarlet, then they handed me another knife and turned to leave. Some way down the pier Florence stopped and turned. "Don't get yourself killed, Elias," she called out, "Constance will be here in a couple of days!"

I waved my knife in acknowledgment, inspired by this news, and of course by having my life saved from the strangling eels of doom. I felt my powers returning; that I was a living man, not just a decorative bookmark. I found a long spar from a broken cart, and lashing the fish-knife tightly to it, made an improvised bayonette-spear.

Ah, quicksilver wishes and shoals of fishes that silver flash and undulate through flickering coves, quick, exotic, ephemeral. Kernow blistered with action that day, showing itself to be more than just surf and teas. The fish-carnage around me was like a medieval battlefield. Severed tentacles twitched yet and the army of arthropods and crustaceans poured on like Visigoths. I scooped up a sou'wester out of the mess and put it on my head at a nor'easterly tilt.

Next I grabbed an old fish-barrow, and sweeping some scraps of skad off it, I loaded it with my weapons, which now included a dustbin-lid that would do for a shield. I trundled and stumbled through the slithery, fish-mess, my chariot before me, gathering speed as I charged towards the Great Black-Backed Thalassokrator...

Splattering seagoing barrel-jellies into flimsy, film-like slivers of carragheen-gelatine and bursting and crunching the ten-thousand exoskeletal carapaces, I lurched and blustered my isopodic and membraneous way down that fearsome and grotesque pier. I could hear distant voices, shouting, cheering – a small crowd had gathered up in the 'towne' end, above the harbour and they seemed intent on watching my progress towards the vile grete fowl of the sea.

The shattering and hissing got worse as the barrow crashed full-tilt into the army of spider-crabs, squat-lobsters, legest legsters, langoustines, crawfish and crustaceans. Some of those flailing black osseous claws latched onto my clothing and I had to stop and hack back at them with one of the fish-butcher's knives that the girls had given me after they'd rescued me from the eels. I was drenched in the blood of the eels, as well as some of my own, and what with all the polyp-pulp and fish-mess and the *flies* – things were starting to take a slightly grotesque turn.

On through the apocalyptic triptych trash of the mashed market I rushed and barrelled the barrow past bengaljiow bungalow-builds like a deranged Bengal Lancer. There lurked the roek, the rurk, the Beast! The overgrown great quilled kramvil beast! How I loathed it now, how I longed to lunge lance and vanquish, vaunt and vilify the foul, feathery abomination. It was truly terrible to look upon, rearing up vast, wings spread like an eagle of death, hackbeak a cruel executioner's sword. It threw back beak and larid barked and brayed once more, towering over me as I came in close. Seeing its vile, serrated tongue, I hurled my lance between its whirling windmill wings, aiming for the heart.

The beak flashed down and grabbed the lance, but I managed to get a grip on it again and tried to pull it away. Once more I caught the sour expression on that haughty and so feathery a face; rugose orbital ring encasing a greasy yellow reptilian eye. A flashing toccata in black and white plumage – my dread – my nemesis. I struggled vainly with the lance, but the great gull gave a mighty flick of its stark head, flipping the lance and me with it up into the air and down into the chilly waters of New Lynsmouth harbour.

Confound it! I floundered and flummoxed my way up to the surface face-first and fish-like. Gasping with cold, I saw the flames reflected on the waters as the boats burned on. I saw the stout block-work of the pier looming above me, and in the murky tewlwolow gloom of an evening sky, I saw the Great Predator Gull, taking wing, over the 'gaps', over the piers and away out to sea again.

I didn't relish the idea of wading through that revolting,

fly-blown tide of flesh again, so I swum over to the South Pier and thus was able to make my way home unobstructed and unhindered.

Chapter 20

The night jarred my shattered nerves with its incessant whirling trill of night-birds and whip-poor-wills, its murmurings, hints and night-thoughts.

I awoke to a washed-out, dreary dawn, the sky leaden, heavy and oppressive. There, next to the rococo divan, lay my pile of books, representing to me all the highest aspirations of science, culture and philosophy. And there, right next to my beloved books, lay that enormous feather – representing the nightmarish *fruit* of those aspirations! The hustling hand of urgency pushed me on. Stale bread and cold tay made my meal and I was soon out of my door, and on my way to Jack Lane.

A drear had settled down upon the Old Quarter again, rendering it cold, huddled, frightened. The few people I did pass seemed ill-at-ease, preoccupied and distracted. The usual cheery greetings were not offered, but rather mere furtive grunts and mumblings. I wove from alley to byway like a snail threading through grass. Yellow stucco flaking and rotting off the walls. Granite lintels and decaying porches, dim, greasy tallow-light flickering within. The sky seemed to get darker rather than lighter. Whirling fog-particles niwlek dripped and congealed, then wisped away. A tapping noise approached – *the blind man* – and I think he saw me! His figure, wrapped in canvas cloak and claret-rotted ruff, breeches, gaiters and country boots, filled me with an inexplicably perplexing species of nausea.

"Alms, brother!" His very tone seemed to mock and jeer, to hint at the unwholesome. I nervously deposited three groats and two ha'pence farthing into his little tin cup, which he then rattled, as if weighing and assaying the contribution, before tipping it into his gnarled hand, which in turn shrunk back into the folds of his cloak, as if to bury his treasure.

"Thank 'e master, and how go the studies?" What was it

in his manner that inspired my dread? "Quite well thank you," I muttered and made to stride on. The dead orbs bored into me like ship-worms, the seer saw deep. I was ruffled and away would creep; but his glassed gaze unseeing held me and my minde did sweepe.

"Counting your chickens, I'll warrant!" blurted the wretch, his marmaroglypheion visage cracked stark like a lightning-raked peak.

"What – what are you saying man?" I wheezed aghast at his bluster, the tobaccular snuffbox temerity of his utterance. "Let me pass, man!" I seethed 'tween gritted teeth.

His bone-leathery claw shot forth, grasping my arm in a revolting grip. "Home to roost, *master,* home to roost!"

"Enough of your riddling!" I babbled, "let go of me and be gone!"

The wretch shuffled off at last, laughing quietly to himself in a most unpleasant fashion, and not without flinging back a final "home to roost, I say!"

I was glad to see the canvas-back of him, as it seemed he saw too much. His hints and aphorisms had unsettled me. His repellent presence seemed to bode ill-fortune – by Jehosephat! Had I not troubles enough?

The alleys unwound once more as my feet flowed forth. Earthly airs of moss and damp, wind-raked ash-trees, coated in a gloss of ivy green, swirling, fresh. Earth's woody richness blending with saline breezes – a wind was coming in from the sea. Winds lifted, stirring leaves; gusts puffed, buffeting people unawares. The wind coming in from the sea had a brittle, hard, pinching feel to it, bringing a hint of Atlantic's vast basin of cool waters. Aye, the wind was coming in from over France-Water too; swirling kommolek cloudy skies pouring in from Armorica, Breten Vyghan, Biscay and the great briny deeps. A handful of crows glided overhead, riding the wind sideways – a shrieking and cackling mob. Absently adrift, my thoughts returned to our experimental ornithopter, and I wondered if it would prove sturdy enough to ride the winds like the crows did with such an insouciant sashay. Tottering chimneys leaned over the alleys, stark against the rushing, scudding clouds.

When I got to Jack's cottage there was an excitable urchin waiting outside. "Mr Gillpitter, squire?" he enquired "I am Gillpington," I replied and he thrust a folded scrap of paper into my hand. It simply read 'Gone to L.T.'s. See you there. Jack.' I gave the young fellow a shilling and he flew off in the general direction of the sweetmeat shoppe. Such are the ephemeral joys of childhood. Such simple things stood in stark splintered contrast to my current situation. The shadow was well and truly on New Lynsmouth now – dark wings that blotted out the light and stirred up primal fears – the shade fell fast and festered in the form of our terrible hawk of the sea. I took solace in the knowledge that I had good allies to rely on, in the form of Jack and Lazarus, and uplifted by this, I hurried on through those twisting Cretan byways, towards the fabled and sepia-toned corner of Iron-Foundary Way and Orchard Street.

All was as before. The stunted, twisted thorn-bushes and lank, stringy nettles in front of the centuried and worm-ridden house. The same, scraggy chickens pecked and croaked, stamped and scratched around the little 'moat' and the curtains hung bat-wing-ragged in the bubble-glass blistered windows. The shuttered rooms gave out no light. The old house seemed to be leaning more, sagging and sinking into the ground, entombed under its own weight. The wind stirred and trees creaked ominously. Kommolek grey banners of rain-cloud unfurled imperiously above in aethereal molecular splendour. A wind was coming in from the sea, planktonic and pelagian, things were stirring, wings were whirring.

The door opened to reveal Taxon – a man revitalized and truly recharged; living proof of the success of his 'Bywekheans Tredanek' or 'Magneto-Animation' technique. The cataracted whiteness of his eye was now replaced by a streaming glow of sharp awareness; his ebony voice dark and pure. "Come in dear Elias," he resonated. "Mr Lane's been telling me about your adventures at the fish-market."

"You're looking well, Lazarus," I spoke as he closed and bolted the door. "How is that wound of yours coming on?"

For a passing moment he looked puzzled. "Wound? Oh yes, that's quite better now. Let's go through to the reading-room."

The sidereal bronze-black harp-toning notes of Satie's 'Ogives' unwound from Taxon's Victrola. The house, so bleak from the outside, with its sagging gables, frowning shutters and time-battered stain of antiquity was redolent inside with an air of sagacity, intellectual endeavour and cultivation. Those timeless Chinese wood-block prints, showing Taoist anchorites, blissfully happy in their far-off mountain caves. The vases showing pagodas and cherry blossom. Views of classical antiquity. Tomes and scrolls and volumes, dictionaries, texts and chronicles. And sitting there, surrounded by all that erudition, was Mr Jack Lane, old *'Vulpes vulpes'*.

"Hallo, Birdman," I sayeth and grasped his hand. "Hallo Lancelot!" he smiled, "I heard you were feeling a little *eel* last night… News travels fast in New Lynsmouth!" "Ha ha – yes Jack, I did have a spot of bother, but thanks to Florence, and Scarlet, well, eel's well…"

Lazarus returned with a large pot of tay and started filling up the cups. A globule of rain burst against the greenish glass of the leaded window-pane. It trickled down, and was followed by another. Timelessness hung in the air. Tay poured into a cup. Calm descended and settled. A clock tocked softly from another room. Atmosphere moistening in glaw globose raw rococo rain-shatter, pattering patterns on the drumskin of glass. The sky darkened palpably and *hwyth* – a blast of wind barged the beams of the roof.

"I feel we must renew our vigilance," I started.

"Absolutely! We must continue our armed patrols," agreed Jack with enthusiasm. "And this time I will join you," added Lazarus. I caught Jack's eye. We both knew there was no point in trying to dissuade him…

"It's agreed then," concluded Lazarus. "We'll get out there and try to intercept the beast – but not until we've had a decent lunch. I'm going to put the pasties in the oven!" And he pottered off to the kitchen, as Jack arched an amused and vulpine eye-brow.

On Lazarus's return we discussed strategy. "So far we've simply lacked effective weaponry," began Jack. "I've got a couple of pals who work up at Tingaling Mine, they can get me some dynamite and…"

"I agree we need more fire-power, Jack," I expostulated, "but dynamite's risky stuff, particularly for town-use."

"Hmmm, true," arose Lazarus, "but I suppose we could always try and bait the bird with dynamite-filled-salmon – ha ha ha."

"If we could get hold of an explosive-harpoon…" I mused, "but it would need to be mobile, and the weight would require a carriage, so it's not very practical really…"

"Well, funnily enough," sayeth Jack, "I know some of the whalers who sail from here. I'll ask them for advice on portable harpoon technology – they might be able to help."

"We must try any and all possibilities," put Lazarus, "but in the meantime, what have we got? The old harpoons, bludgeons and bugles."

"Well," said Jack, casting a lugubrious eye on the steadily increasing rain, "I suggest we wear oilskins and sou'westers too – that way we'll just blend in with the wandering pyskadors and we won't draw unwelcomed attention to ourselves."

Finding ourselves in agreement, we settled down to enjoy the *kroust* of pasties and tay. The rain peppered down.

If e'er the air were where mere molecules briny mixed met and merged it was then, as cumulus dark drifted and spilled its moistureous dripping waters; moistening, wetting, hydrating and glibly saturating the towne.

The kroust soon gave us strength. Encased in the crusts were many good things grown from Gernuak soil.

"Lazarus showed me your flying-machine earlier," spake Jack. "It certainly *looked* impressive. Do you reckon it'll get off the ground?"

"Well," I said, "that partly depends on the ingenuity of Mr Hill, our Kernuak Beam-Engineer. If he's managed to successfully overcome the old power/weight-ratio conundrum then we're in with a good chance."

"The other day, Paul was mentioning some ultra-fine tin-steel alloys he had been developing. He seemed to think these held the key to the whole project," added Lazarus.

"In the opinion of this humble troglodyte, the boy will go far," said Jack, who was actually a well-known and respected mine-surveyor.

"He's possessed of a very perceptive and enquiring minde," added Lazarus. "His jynn-keber design brilliantly marries our traditional Kernewek industrial design to the aerial-carriage of the future! That shows both scientific rigour and creative imagination – a depth and breadth of abilities that constitute true cultivation."

"Your own studies seem to take in quite a range of subjects," said Jack, indicating the vast bookshelves with a sweep of the hand.

"Much preparation have I done," responded the eld, "but my greatest experiment has gone horribly wrong in the most unforeseeable manner."

"But you couldn't have known!" broke in Jack. "Discovery and danger often go hand in hand. Who could possibly foresee the *culmination* of such an experiment?"

The rain was tapping softly on the windows as it trickled in its liquid transparency, softly darkening the room. There was a faraway look in the eye of Lazarus Taxon, but a slight smile played upon his lips.

"I've always thought it was better to venture into unknown territory than not to venture at all. An element of risk is inherent in the pursuit of discovery and progress. My early studies had given me some insight into electrical fluidity and magnetism. Years later, I found myself on a plant-collecting mission to China. During some periods of spare time, I brushed up on the language and started travelling in the interior, getting acquainted with some of the hermits and mystics who dwell in the solitude of the mountain fastnesses. These followers after Lao Tsu and Chuang Tsu I found to be men of great virtue and erudition. There were women-hermits also, though fewer in number. The wilderness magnetized these people and nurtured their self-cultivation. When the botanical mission was completed, I decided to stay on in China and study the hermit-culture in more depth. For a few brief months I turned my back on the 'world of dust' and immersed myself in the 'way', as it is known. I was lodging in the simple hut of a Taoist known as 'Chirping Bird'. They all change their names when they retire to the mountains. Chirping Bird was a most gracious host and teacher, always modest and attentive. I learned a lot from him and spent countless hours basking in a kind of tranquillity in those beautiful and remote mountains. Eventually Chirping Bird said the time had come for him to take me to see *his* teacher, an exceedingly old and elusive fellow who went by the name of Lightning. We stayed in his cave for three days and nights. Not a lot happened at first. Old 'Lightning' looked about a hundred and twenty years old and seemed to spend most of his time wrapped up in a blanket, dozing on the sunny mountainside, or else drinking copious amounts of tay and laughing a lot. On the third night however, he conducted a long and intricate ceremony in the cave – it seemed to go on for most of the night. I'm not supposed to say too much about it, but I can say it gave me an insight into the body's vital energy flows. It was only years later that I started to realize the connection between these experiences, and my earlier research into the electrical flow. A synthesis of these diverse elements, with certain modifications, gave rise to my system of Magneto-Animation."

As he said these words, a flash of lightning lit the sky, ripping through clouds; it was followed by a long and ominous roll of thunder. The rain was raining harder now, gushing, running and splashing, it showered the house with its watery drops.

"Well," concluded Taxon, "I suppose it's time we got those oilskins and harpoons. The *hatchling* could return at any time."

We decided to patrol separately, relying on the bugles for communicating the alarm. Once more the alleys, vounders and lanes unfurled before me, seen through a pewter-translucent curtain of fabled rain. Huddled in my sea-going surcoat and sou'wester, narwhal-tusk harpoon to hand, I felt like a proper New Bedford whalerman, about to ship-out for a two and a half-year voyage around the World in pursuit of Herman Morvil. Where *was* that great feathered menace? How much more time would I have to spend hunting this quilled-lizard?

The rain got steadily stronger, streaming through the various quarters and deepening the already-swollen river.

As the downpour worsened, I scuttled and slunk like a great crested newt from alley to alley, to vounder, to side-street. Cutting across little squares and cobbled courtyards I turned a wary eye skyward, watching out for the stark, sharp-hacked, sly, unsettling silhouette of larid pterodactyl form. Glistening cobblestones. Rain of emeralds, phosphorescent. Raindrops bouncing in miniature coronas. Under my oilskin-carapace, my nerves tingled as I tried to sense the presence of the great water-fowl. We had to assume that it would reappear, and it could do so at any moment. The thought chilled me, despite the warming effects of the pasty and tay. Where *was* that gull – it must be around here somewhere… It surely was *quiet* around New Lynsmouth that afternoon. But appearances could be deceptive – at any moment I might join a thin-living, stern seagull.

The needle-teethed eel bites had weakened my constitution with their hagfish parasitic feasting on my precious ichor, those precocious ichthyosaurs! I begrudged the coiling monsters those precious mouthfuls of my life-blood, the squirming mor-sarf sea-serpents! I leant against a wall for support, feeling rather dizzy. The rain dripped and splashed and a fog-horn honked funereal in the cloudy vast distance. I felt momentarily as if I was spinning and floating, soaring in the air. Then I lurched and reeled on my boot-heels, as images of that hideous *geometry,* that ghastly *automatic calligraphy* swam up before my gloss globular eye, egging again an atavistic, chill and primal horror. A revulsion wretched, rank and utter. A harrowing, horrifying, gut-wrenching spasm of nauseous and hateful *mal* rippled and pulsed throughout my being, tingling my over-wrought nerves and flapping my soul like a flatfish. Those outré *diagrams,* that *script* why did they revolt me so? What could it all possibly mean? In extremis I found myself driven into an almost philosophical sense of detachment. The pressures I had been subjected to seemed to enhance and concentrate my curiosity and yearning for truth. I had the strong presentiment that if I could only resolve the situation with this outlandish seagull, I could then devote a peaceful and useful life to the pursuit of knowledge. These were the thoughts that flashed vividly through my minde as I lurched against that dripping wet wall. As to those outré geometric patterns and symbols, I felt I would have to be patient, and hope that the future would shed light on their meaning. The clear Celtic air revived me, as it always did, and through the rain-washed streets I trod.

The rich aroma of wet earth hung in the air – who would be digging in this rain, I wondered. Great Herrings! It was indeed a strange World. The vounders and alleys of the ghetto seemed to writhe and shimmer like a plate of spaghetti in an earthquake. I waddled on, wrapped in my whaler's guise from herring-hat head to sea-booted foot and stealthily brandishing narwhal-tusk harpoon in canvas cover – an experimental aeronaut armed with a stone-age weapon! Notched narwhal Arctic ivory totemic shamanic Esquimaux harpoon with Greenland patina and sheen of the midnight sun.

Up Verboase Street I heard the fishwives a chatterin' and clackin' on. "Oh that *bird!*" "Oh 'tis *dreadful!*" "Dreadful!" "And I just came up by Tallcorne way, and the river's getting awful deep. 'Tis nearly up to the bridge!"

There was much consternation at this piece of news. "My dear life, whatever shall become of we?" "And tonight's full moon bringing a high spring tide!" "And the southerly wind, pushing the sea against the mouth of the river." "Oh my dear Lord!"

They were right of course – the combination of those weather conditions could prove utterly devastating to the decaying and half-rotten dwellings of the Old Quarter and the Tallcorne districts of New Lynsmouth.

I pressed on, leaving the womenfolk to their lamentations – I could only hope that conditions would not worsen, so perhaps the towne would get off lightly.

Soon after that I saw a cart full of sand standing outside the pantiled merchant house in the pouring rain. A group of men in heavy coats and workman's caps were shovelling the sand into sand-bags, which were being laid in front of the doorways along the street. A cat wailed somewhere close, and hwyths and squalls of rain blasted into the storm-torn towne.

The merchants and shop-keepers in this low-lying part of towne were preparing for the worst, even though the river had not flooded in living memory. Personally, I quite liked being flooded in living memory, but this was no time for retrospection. Silver, mercury and pewter rivulets running rich in sylvan memory's power, run, flow in flux, run, come back another hour, another day.

Dripping, lurching, reeling I stumbled on, into a warren of narrow alleys. The place exuded a shabby and run-down air of desolation. In bright sunlight it might at best look grim – in this intensifying rain and gloom it gave off all the charm of a Dantean pit. An unimaginably dank, mouldering, wet, earthy smell seemed to pervade the airs hereabouts, until its vapours were dispersed by a ubiquitous stencharoma of greasy cabbage soup. An ugly thought was beginning to form at the back of my minde. Turning a corner I beheld the unrelishable sight of a large gout of what was obviously fresh guano. About four feet across, the calcinous piscine filth was dissolving in the pouring rain, emitting a gut-wrenching cloud of malodorous maritime stench into the damp and chilly air. Great rattling carapaces! This did not bode well! At the rate the stuff was dissolving, it could not have been there more than five minutes! I raised my bugle to my lips and blasted out a hollow, brass-throated clarion call. It reverberated around the narrow backstreets and died in the rain. The streets seemed to get progressively more squalid and pestilent as I proceeded. Then it dawned on me – surely this must be the ill-famed Ynkleudhva district – that vile and villainous ghetto that sprawls around the periphery of an ancient and lichenous cemetery. I tended to avoid the place usually, but since the *hatchling* seemed to be in the area I decided to patrol round the local streets, hoping meanwhile for my 'reinforcements' to turn up. I could smell roses and loam and frankincense. For all its poverty and deprivation, the inhabitants of this quarter seemed to be peculiarly well-dressed. I kept seeing ladies in lace and satin gowns and bonnets and the menfolk in their Sunday-best, with flowers in their button-holes. Perhaps they were off to celebrate a wedding, or some such happy event – they all seemed to be going in the same direction. The solemn tolling of a church bell seemed to confirm the idea. Its deep, sonorous and mellow clanging reminded me of the melancholy tones of a bell-buoy, riding the rocking waves above a jagged and treacherous reef where eels haggard dwell, hager du. The shreds, scraps, shapes, shards and scrapings of niwlek fog that swirled and abounded here only added to the strange sensation of being lost at sea – adrift – marooned – shanghaied and salted. I could *smell* the tide; I could *smell* the waves coming in – something was afoot and I'll warrant the foot was webbed.

"Going to the funeral, young sir?" an old woman addressed me in a time-worn voice. "Funeral?" I echoed vaguely. "Why yes, 'tis the burial of young John Teythyogyon, only twenty-one years old, the poor dear cheeld-vean!" "But what happened to him?" I asked, looking into the pools of her shiny eyes. "He'd gone up Windrawn way, got a job down a mine over there, Wheal Triggans. Terribly crushed he was, poor boy. Load of atal c'llapsed on 'im from a rotten platform – something to do with a powder-explosion – poor dear boy!" Off she tottered, leaving me to digest this terrible information. Naturally it reminded me of Constance and her work with the injured miners of that area. I was cheered to recall that Florence had said Constance would be here in a day or so. Then with dread I realised that she could be in danger from the hatchling! Nobody was safe as long as that monster was at large – it really must be dispatched – but *how?*

Picking my way through the heaps of festering rubbish which so characterized this dismal quarter, I drifted with the pelagian tide of stooped, black-clad mourners shuffling through the torrential rain, the crowd was thickening as it reached the Ynkleudhva – the old cemetery.

Aghast and blasted by time's wearying wind, hunched, huddled and brooding, stark, bleak and dark – the Ynkleudhva! A few Victorian mausoleums – onyx, obsidian and marble black. A gaunt obelisk – askew. Tombs and sepulchres, yawning and gaping, sunken graves. Humble graves, simple granite slabs – lichenous. Leaning stones, ancestral epitaphs. Tangled thickets of crosses, leaning, lurching, tumbling. This harrowing scene of interment and mourning, of funereal bleak, black mystery was soaked and slaked by rods of driving relentless rain. Robbed of their umbrella of flesh, even the long-buried bones of the village-dead got a soaking – tibias, fibias and ribias washed by trickling rivulets. The ground hereabouts seemed to keep sinking and settling – perhaps one day the whole bone-yard would open up like a vile and monstrous hungry maw that would swallow down the ancient towne and hurl it into the pit.

The black-clad mourners were congregating in the ancient chapel – crowding together in the tiny building to see off the soul of John Teythyogyon. I would remain outside – vigilant, eager to protect the still-embodied souls of the village from the real physical peril that swooped from above to devour and despoil. I wandered alone down the sodden pathways of black marble chips, between rows of cavernous sepulchres and sunken graves. An angel embossed on a slab, a dove, an anchor. Rest in Peace. Sacred to the Memory. Sleeping with the Lord. Called to Heaven. Departed this life. Resting. Resting. Waiting. So many nautical men sunk here, and so many miners working their final lode. So many mothers of so many, many children – and so many poor dear children taken from us so young. My thoughts turned to the world of science, all the new vaccines and the great progress in medicine and hygiene. Surely in the near future, scientific medicine will prevent many of these tragic infant-deaths. Surely science will improve and uplift mankind, making these grotesque and overcrowded burying-grounds a thing of the past.

A quaintly archaic social hierarchy seemed to prevail here among the dead. I had left the grandiose structures of polished black marble, the ostentatious sepulchres and monuments behind. I had passed through a zone of sturdy granite slabs, cumbrous and bulky, past the narrower and more humble slate headstones and had now reached a most unpretentious realm of small wooden crosses and simple unadorned graves – the resting-place of the parish-poor, the humble, the desperate; those whose end was quickened by the harrowing cold wind of Poverty. Many of the little wooden crosses were disintegrating and rotting away, leaving no trace of the departed soul, other than a name, dimly passed down the generations. Such gloomy thoughts held my attention briefly, but the knowledge that that monstrous bird was in the area overshadowed all other trains of thought.

Walking a little further through the puddling rain, I came upon a freshly dug grave. A heap of earth was piled up next to it, and next to that a rough trestle-table on which to rest the coffin. Poor John, I thought, dying so young; young and strong and killed – killed because circumstances had driven him to earn his bread in a dangerous industry, an industry that crushes men, and sends them 'up-top' to be buried a mere fathom deep. Such a common, everyday, heartbreaking tragedy.

There is much progress needed in our mines. People like Jack were constantly pushing for higher safety standards and better conditions for the men – but he seemed to be up against the dead weight of the traditional attitude of the mine-owning class. These people, with some notable exceptions, seemed usually much more concerned with the state of their personal fortunes than with the well-being of the workforce. There would always be more men to fill the places of those like John who died trying to make a living. I'll never forget one story Jack had told me. He'd been doing some survey-work down Wheal Tewlwolow and had noticed that a section of ladder on level three was dangerously rotten and dilapidated. When he'd mentioned it to the Mine-Captain, he in turn informed the owners who said they'd repair it "when it broke." Jack said he'd had to argue till he was blue in the face and threatened to abandon the survey before they'd finally spent a few shillings to replace the ladder. That sort of thing was common-place. These mine-owners! You'd think they had fangs!

I looked into the grave, like looking through a door into another world. An inch or so of muddy water was accumulating within. Scudding grey clouds were reflected in the water, making me feel that I could fall into the sky. Tiny brown rivulets were running off the heap of earth and merging into the grass like miniature deltas. I looked more closely at the trestle-table. What were those curious marks on it? Was it a natural pattern, or some oriental script, or…..?

A rising nausea welled up within me, my body and head felt light, weightless. I clutched the table for support as those strange and unsettling images swam before me. It was those same outré patterns and configurations that I had recently scribbled in my sleep! That hateful and loathsome 'automatic writing' or autochthonous geometry. Those alien diagrammatic forms, scripts and abstractions that haunted my feverish dreams and somehow encapsulated for me all that was fell, mal, eldritch and foul. A profound alienage, shifting, disturbing and morbidly inhuman, that writhed, slithered and cackled in the margins of the phenomenal universe.

These sinuous and angular jagged lines spoke to me of all that was unrelishable, all that was repellent, horridus and deeply hostile. It spoke of our kramvil-changeling thing and its mocking 'development' from serpent-sarf to crawling pedrevan-lizard to posturing archaeopteryx to sleek-feathered monstrous Grotte Mantelmew – quilled nemesis of New Lynsmouth!

It spoke of those stark, blasted hills of the hinterland, some of which revolt me so with their inexplicably sinister atmospherics and air of ill-concealed malevolence. And somehow, this bizarre geometric tablature also brought to minde the blind man – as if he would be the only one who could read it!

I rubbed my eyes and the searing visions seemed to fade and lose their burning intensity. I breathed deep and lifted my face to the rain – determined to maintain alertness and not sink ineffectively into a morass of chimeras. A throng of dark-clothed people was making its way towards me through the blades and prongs of rain. Others had already joined me at the grave-side. I stepped back a little way to make room for the family and friends. Numerous villagers were gathering round, some still in work-clothes, but bareheaded in the rain. The cortège was approaching, headed by six pallbearers carrying aloft the earthly remains of John Teythyogyon, 1890 – 1911. Hwyth blew the ill-wished wind, soughing, sighing and surging, sending sparkling watery droplets sailing and crystal sandy spicules spinning round the shiny black shoes and hobnail boots of the greft and boroft family.

The people plodded forwards, slowly approaching the grave. The Reverend Kryjyk led the way, limping slightly from the nasty gash of the gull gone septic. His white surplice against all the dark suits struck a note of purity. Bareheaded, he clutched the crosier with a hand firm in faith. Oh bearers, bearers, put him down – they laid him on the table-oh… The scene before my visual eyes was archetypal, rain-slaked and bleak, with the coffin now resting on that trestle-table where I had once again encountered that fantastic 'automatic script.' Each glistening raindrop seemed to reflect the whole World, the vastness of Space. They danced together, shimmering, and the atoms fell out in perfect symmetry. The people shuffled uneasily, waiting for the ceremony. A parishioner, an elder, was fumbling with an umbrella to shield the priest from the merciless weather. The cold iron hands of the clock seemed to hold stillness. The sound of rain falling into the grave was joined by the weeping of a woman. The vicar then started fumbling with his spectacles, the weeping was spreading. Darkness fell thick over the scene. Sobs turned to shrieks. Everyone was looking up, hands were raised, pointing aloft, or shielding faces in horror. The unthinkable. The detestable. The terrible black-backed beast. The kelenken kramvil was circling low over our heads, in a sky of dark, ragged clouds.

Fear rippled through the crowd like wind through the barley. The powerful and frightful wings of the great thallasokrator flapped furiously as it descended into the petrified throng, the wing-wind flinging hats, handkerchiefs and flower petals spinning into the air. People were scrambling and scattering and clambering over each other in a frenzy of gut-fear. Pan's panic fluted lighting ran searing through the seething madding crowd. Black feathers against white. Screams. Webbed feet flash flesh pink. Stampeding mourners slithering in mud. Eye ringed in red, glassy, cold, fatty and terrible to behold. Rain slaking down vertical. Villagers eyes rolled back in fear, showing whites. Frenzy, mud and panic. Then a brittle hyena hollow cackle blasted from beak and raked the wet air harsh. The monstrously overgrown kramvil-bird landed with its claws clutching the Teythyogyon coffin and perched there in obscene triumph, braying and skrawking, head thrown back in avine atavistic ecstasy. Then, with that savage hack of a jackhammer yellow beak it pecked, and thrust at the coffin-lid, splintering its flimsy timbers in sharp scintillating slivers. The ghastly way it chopped, cleaved and hammered at the coffin reminded me of a thrush trying to break open the bullhorn shell of a snail. An access of great frenzy seized the brute kramvil and it kicked the coffin to the ground where it shattered and burst open, revealing the chilled white lifeless face and the mortal remains of John Teythyogyon the miner.

Eldritch wails and screams rent the damp air and waves of revulsion shuddered through many a heart. The ghastly roek grabbed a cold white hand, and *yanked* on it, just as it would a starfish or a scrap of mackerel. Stamping down a pink snakeskin prehistoric foot on the hand, the grette fowle plunged its vicious, blazing, yellow, orange-spotted *beak* into the innards of John Teythyogyon, and like a blackbird pulling a worm up out of the ground, it drew forth a fathom of greyish-red intestine. The smell that came with it was not to be dwelt on. The monstrous bird was gulling down its latest meal with relish, slurping and lunging as more of the dead man's innards spilled out. This was too much for the vicar, the Reverend Timothy Kryjyk, who held the crosier defiantly aloft, shouting "Be gone! Foul denizen of Hell! Be gone I say!" The brine-rook deftly flipped a black wing-tip, sending the vicar sprawling into the wet pile of earth beside the grave's yawning mouth. The foul kramvil brine-rook threw back its gaunt cliff-head once more to croak and roar and scream unendurable shrieks, its upper beak forming a straight line with its back and tail, a loathsome shred of human intestine dangling and swinging from that beak.

The sexton had picked up the long-handled Cornish shovel and stepped forward to protect the prostrate form of the Reverend Kryjyk. Two or three others were also approaching with rakes, brooms and a sickle. I seized the moment and aimed my Esquimaux narwhal-tusk harpoon at that stern reptilian eye and hurled it as hard as I could. I watched its bone-yellow barbed archaic flight through the few rainy feet of air, as if glued to a magic-lantern show. A white-fringed, sooty-black aerofoil was raised, and the harpoon struck this, dislodging a couple of yard-long black feathers before it fell to the ground beside the outstretched hand of the dead man.

The lurid larid hatchling then turned suddenly towards me, gaping, skwawking bill, wings up and flapping irregularly, it's unspeakably vile serrated tongue reeking of its macabre meal of corpse-flesh. Its guttural dog-like grunts and shrill gibbering chatter were hurled into my horrified face. How I loathed and abhorred every element of this ill-hatched behemoth with a detestation that seared and burnt me. Having no weapon remaining, I instinctively stepped back as the monster-thinge reared over me in screaming, primal predatory rage. I saw deep into that glyb and gelatinous eye-ball, and I saw hatred, malice, rage and doom.

And then I felt the solid ground no more for I was falling, plunging headlong into a cold, dark and grim chasm. It was the grave of poor John Teythyogyon into which I fell, and striking my head in falling, I knew no more.

*

Autochthonous, awake and alive, I stirred to consciousness but my leaden limbs would not respond. I instantly recalled the nightmarish sequence of events that had led to my premature entombment. I had no way of knowing how much sand had trickled through the hour-glass, whilst I lay in my watery grave, but the tumultuous events that preceded my *fall* were still being played out. I was lying in muddy water, my clothes were soaked through and a savage chill had crept into my bones from the unwholesome and pestilential *soyle,* that sandy-clay/loam dark and acrid *erth,* the very stuff of the Ynkleudhva. I was benumbed and immobilized and could only stare at an oblong of racing grey cloud and rain, whilst listening to the tumultuous and cacophonous hubbub going on above.

"It could return at any minute – we must arm ourselves!"

"I will not leave brother John unburied, in this frightful condition and I intend to complete his rites as soon as possible."

"Weapons!" "Aye, save the living first, then we'll worry about the dead."

"A Christian burial, as is right and proper."

"I'm going for me cutlass." "And I'll get me fowling-piece!" "Don't be a fool, man, that piece was last fired in 1868 – it'll probably blow up on you!"

"Arm yourselves by all means, but I'd like the sexton and two volunteers – strong men, minde, for this is no work for women!"

"We'll help you get brother John into a new box and lower 'im down, won't us Jim?"

"'Course we will, y'r reverence, but after that we're going bird-hunting!"

"Good men, thank you. We'll need a tarpaulin – to cover the remains. George, would you go directly round to Mr Voltor the undertaker and tell him we need a new coffin right away? He's got the measurements."

"Leave it to me, your reverence."

"We'll be back to pay our last respects after we've seen off this, 'scuse me vicar, but, this *bird of Hell!"*

"I quite agree, men, it is our duty to protect our families. God speed you, and may He make you victorious!"

"Yes, we must arm ourselves, but this situation also calls for a little *strategy."*

"Taxon! What are *you* doing here?

"I'm here to fight and kill that monstrous *bird,* the same as the rest of you, I'm just saying it would be better to coordinate our efforts and agree on a logical plan."

"Oh, *logic* is it, *master* Taxon? Was it logic to raise a beast like that?" "What are you talking about man, I'm here to *fight* the creature!"

Voices were mumbling in the rain.

"I may be blind, *master* Taxon, but I see's plenty!"

I could hear voices murmuring darkly – I don't know *what,* or *how* he knew, but if the blind man convinced the

248

villagers that Lazarus was responsible for the appearance of the monstrosity that had done such foul damage to this community, well, I don't think his life would be safe – which didn't put me in a very good position either…

Lying injured and immobilized in a pool of icy rainwater in a death-pit didn't feel like a very good position to be in either. Is *this* where our science had led us to? *Me* languishing in the grave, whilst Lazarus teeters on the brink of it…? I heard Lazarus's voice ring out like a Chinese bronze gong:

"This is not the time for quibbling, we should be pursuing the beast!"

I heard murmurs of ascent at this, perhaps Taxon could yet win over the sympathy of the people.

"Quibbling you say, *Mr* Taxon, *Mr* scientist, quibbling, you say? Why even when we were boys at school your experiments always went too far. Then you got yourself thrown out of that fine and fancy London College of Science, or Anatomy or whatever it was, didn't you *Mr* Taxon, sir?"

"That's not true man, the allegations against me were trumped up. It was a clear case of professional jealousy – I was discovering elements and species whilst my teachers were dozing over their outdated textbooks…"

"Call yourself a scientist, do 'e master? More of a *sorcerer* I'd say! Tampering and tinkering where Man weren't meant to go – studying that which weren't meant to be a-studied! Hatching things-"

"Enough man! Hold your tongue and cease your babble! This is getting us nowhere!"

Things were turning ugly – other, harsher voices broke in to the dialogue…

"Are you saying he's behind these gull attacks?"

"…tampering with nature!"

"…meddling scientists and atheists spoiling the World…"

"Maybe we should take him prisoner and find out if he knows anything!"

"YES – seize him!"

"No! We shouldn't take the law into our own hands –

why don't we call a constable?"

"A constable? That could take hours! We'd better make our *own* justice!"

"Meddling sorcerer! We should *burn* him!"

Lazarus Taxon was definitely in danger now and I struggled and fought to regain some power of movement in my limbs. Exerting, as it seemed, every last atom of my will-power, I dragged myself slowly to my feet and started trying to climb out of the grave.

Have you ever tried to claw your way out of a sodden, crumbling grave-pit, gentle reader? Have you ever fought and struggled to free yourself from the fatalistic pit of living *DEATH,* dear reader? If so, you will know it is no light task. Galvanised as I was by fear for Taxon's safety, I somehow found the strength, and, with the help of a little basic rock-climbing technique, I was soon emerging from the grave.

The effect I produced was electrifying. Grown men took to their heels and high-tailed it out of there. Others looked pale and faint, staring with unbelieving eyes as I rose up out of the ground.

"Necromancy!" shrilled the blind man, backing away through the headstones, "necromancy and demonology! They're both in it – *master and student* – *black, black arts* – raising things what ain't ought to be raised!"

The villagers were falling back from the grave-side, but not without some ugly and dark murmurings about 'sorcerers' and 'mad scientists'. I found myself alone with Taxon. "You chose a good moment to rise from the grave," said Taxon as he patted me on the shoulder "and I thought *I* was supposed to be Lazarus... Well, I think you'll be needing some dry clothes and perhaps a wee tiny totty of brandy – we'd better try to get to the Old Quarter without running into any angry mobs, eh?"

His good humour was infectious and we were soon on our way out of the most harrowing Ynkleudhva district and its ancient and terrible burying-ground.

*

It had been raining most of the afternoon and as dusk's tewlwolow gloom sunk the day, the worsening rain helped wash the towns into night. I was already saturated from my spell in the grave but Taxon at least was protected from this monsoon by his whalerman's coat and sou'wester. We walked in silence. The moon was rising full and fat like a Spanish doubloon thrown into the sky. Its silver-white light was reflected everywhere from myriad glyb and glossy wet surfaces. The rain in the runnels held strings of moon. The splashing puddles flickered fracturing diamond flashing moonlets. Slabs, gutters and gullies were overlaid with a fine patina lunar sheen. Racing ragged kommolek cumulus clouds roared by, drawing dark curtains before the moon, only to tear them away and reveal the fat, silver doubloon. The moon in a hundred thousand liquid rain-drops fell; and shattered moon-dust molecules into the luminous rain. Surging barrages of gwynjak zephyr winds breathed blasting breath to scatter the dancing drops of mineral rain. Dusk was fattening. Eels were whispering. The day was spluttering out. Dusk roamed like a fell, tusked beast through the dripping streets, lit tentatively and furtively by the feeble, spluttering glow of a few fogbowed pewter lanthorns and the tepid, greasy light of tallow candles, leaking through steamy grey-green bubble-glass windows. The storm seemed to come with the failing light and the rising moon, stirring the wind to a Valhalla blast and throwing down the rains in Gangetic abundance.

Turning a corner onto Coombe Road, we were amazed to see the swollen river rushing down from the flood-flashing hinterland had burst its banks and was flowing down the road with great vigour. The doors of the cottages and krowjis along the road had all been sand-bagged, but at some doors the moon-glistening waters were already lapping and licking. There was nothing else for it – Taxon and I started wading our way down the street.

We encountered all kinds of strange flotsam drifting down the street. A sheaf of barley, followed by a scythe and an empty cider-jug; various newspapers and periodicals; clogs; umbrellas; underclothes; hats; twigs and branches; arthropod carapaces; pages ripped from Cotton Mather's

'Wonders of the Invisible World'; a rag-doll; a corn-dolly; a corncrake; penny-dreadfuls; broadsheets and handbills; more twigs, pine-cones and sheets of bark; leaves and straw; an old boot... A small shoal of eels swam up the street, taking the place of horses and carts and bicycles.

As we approached the towne's centre, the waters deepened – we were now knee-deep in the swirling, black, moon-spattered flood. I stumbled on, benumbed and frozen, drawing psychic strength from Taxon – and the promise of warmth, dry clothes and cognac to restore my vital-warmth.

Across the street, or rather, the river, as they were now one and the same, figures were prowling around – some armed with various ad hoc weapons such as pitchforks, poles, agricultural implements and *saill éalaighs*. They seemed to be giving us suspicious glances – we pressed on. The fat moon drew the rolling tide to its zenith and the howling banshee wind kept piling up the great angry waves and throwing them at the shore. Just as another armed group were looking our way, the sea came rushing up the river-mouth, bursting over the old hump-backed bridge and surging into the already deluged main street. This spectacular and elemental event served to divert attention away from us, though Lazarus and I found ourselves wading virtually chest-deep at one point, with surging sea-waves now rippling up the river-swollen street. The cruel blasting wind smote the churning dark waters and frothed them into a whitecapped, whitesquall fury, a miniature boiling, tumbling ocean which rolled and danced along the sunken street. Passing the Marlin tavern, we took Iron-Foundary Way and found ourselves free of the floods and back on terra firma. Scraps of bladder-wrack, wrasse and spindrift lined the high-water mark in the alley.

After we'd refreshed ourselves and put on some dry clothes, Lazarus filled a vial with a special ointment for the Reverend Kryjyk to put on his leg-wound; then went round to a neighbour's house to arrange for it to be delivered to the vicarage as soon as the floods subsided.

After that Lazarus and I took some hot tay and set out once again to patrol the rain-raked streets of New Lynsmouth. Guttering lanthorns swung and creaked in the gale, sending

dim pools of light onto the rain-slashed cobbles and ancient
flagstones. Slithering scuttlers lurked and lurched pattering
away on tiny claws. Flatfish flopped in the cuttlefish pool
and burned-out boats rode at rusty anchor. The fish-market
was trashed, the pasty-trade in a downward spiral and now
the locals were turning from villagers into vigilantes. All
these catastrophes, as well as numerous other outrages, could
be laid squarely at the vile, pink, kleptoparasitic, corpse-
trampling feet of our *little friend – Larus marinus*... Truly it
had brought the shadow upon New Lynsmouth, and only its
utter destruction and annihilation could lift that shadow from
our lives.

Chapter 21

Lugubrious indeed were the events of that unspeakable night,
a night which lives on in the memory, luminous and strange,
vivid and hallucinatory as a mirage seen once in a dreaming
night. These moon-shred rippling clouds that curtain our
night-rich inner theatre; they flicker and rip apart to reveal the
drama that played out in that little fishing-port. Like a flocking
herd of gaunt flapping dromaeosaurs the charcoal-black and
silvery-white-edged clouds would drift apart to reveal the
glistening lunar disc, then close in, coagulating into fantastical
shapes before wringing out fresh deluges of scattering rain-
pellets. Just a mad poem of the night, I thought, seeing the
old towne clinging to its hills and glistening like an oyster-
shell. A net of phosphorescent pinpoints, blasted by elements,
primeval, savage and unpredictable. A towne, hacked, pecked
and harried – desecrated, violated and mauled. A towne
awash and aflood – inundated by river and salt-blasting sea.
As if to enhance and exaggerate the troubled and dramatic
atmospherics, a dark barrel of thunder rolled slowly across the
restless sky. Vast and deep-toned gongs of darkly burnished
Ching-Dynasty bronze resounded in reverb suspended. An
elephantine granite ball was rolling slowly across an immense
and massy pewter plate. The autochthonous ancestor-giants
from the bleakly *hills* had resumed their ridiculously ancient
and bellicose game of hurling rocks at each other, shaking the

bones of West Kirnowe and shivering its gaunt craggy form.

The mood was ugly as sullen lurkers slunk furtively through thoroughfares shady and armed groups were glimpsed as murky, slinking haunters of the gloom.

The rains fell on the towne and the rains fell on the harbour, with its market area, its piers and the remnant of the fishing-fleet that the blaze of yesterday had left intact. The rain also fell on the unspeakable remains of that detestable maritime offal, that seething and thoroughly *rotten* polyp-pulp and sea-flesh; dead, congealed eels; all manner of gelatinous, exoskeletal and fishy remains. The rain dispersed apocalyptic cumulus clouds of dark flies into the airs, released seething multitudes of wriggling maggots and grubs, and also dispersed an acutely hideous and overwhelming retching reek of carnage and decay.

As Taxon and I spun our sinuous, noctambulatory route through the narrow streets overlooking the harbour we could see the rolling black sea bucking before us as a rodeo herd of bone-backed bison bucks. Splashing, rolling and wallowing in the tewlwolow halfling half-light, those monstrous Atlantek billowing waves could well be a great sea-battle between flotillas and fleets of whales, walruses, narwhals, leopard-seals, orcas and ubiquitous piscine briny species. This churning, twitching, dancing, *burning* mass of watery damp seethed and raged out of control. The cyclopean waves burst against the pier and poured over it, washing the decaying sea-flesh into the harbour and splattering it against the stark blackened ribs of the ghost-fleet. The dark waves surged on, megatheriums head-butting the pier and plesiosaurs leaping its headlong length.

The overarching ragged sky was darkening, lit only by some faint flashes of lightning, muffled and swaddled in the fleecy and massy cloudscape. Gloom thickened. Dim smears of light were twinkling. The sound of running feet. A battering wind. Shouts. More running feet – which way were they going? Where was the *kramvil?* Uneasy thoughts flickered through my minde – Lazarus appeared calm and alert. We plodded on, grimly determined and focused on our grisly task. The ceaseless rain muffled all sounds and covered them with its hissing, splashing, pattering music; and the wind crowed merry. Howling, snarling and prowling around, like a great snuffling snouted beast, the gwynjak blasting withering wind ripped and kicked at the old towne. Only desperation could drive people outdoors on such a cataclysmic night, but considering what the people had been through in the last few days, they were certainly now in a state of desperation. The mood, as I mentioned before, was ugly – very ugly. Like sheer glyptodon hyphae, fine resilient filaments of raw *fear* spread searching tendrils across the darkling night.

From a side-alley a group of about ten men suddenly burst upon us, brandishing a couple of flaming torches, a scythe, boat-hooks, sharpened poles, an old halberd and an arquebus. They milled around us, flinging out questions.

"Seen the *bird,* 'ave 'e?"

"What are you up to then?"

"Let's get a look at 'em!"

A course kwallok of a fella thrust a guttering torch of blazing tar dangerously close to Taxon and I and instantly a cry went out – "It's *them* – the *alchemists! – the necromancers – GET 'EM!"*

Lazarus and I took flight instantly and fear lent us wings. Pterosaur's membraneous wings of rudimentary soaring terror they were as searing we tore through alleys and courtyards, trying frantically to lose our hound-like pursuers. Have you ever been chased and hunted by a baying, snarling, slavering mob of armed men on a stormy and terrible night, dear reader? If so, perhaps you will recall the most powerful and malevolent sense of animal-terror, that blindly claws at your viscera and stomach, your nerves and your bones, lacerating your very *soul* with a savage and maniacal intensity. You will recall the pounding of your heart as it churned and frothed in a cyclonic ocean of adrenalin; your lungs screaming in fatigue as they battled and struggled for breath; the hot and cold clammy rivulets of chilly perspiration that seeped through clothes and dripped from brows, but primarily you will vividly recall the sense of bestial, gibbering, vile, animalistic fear that all but washed you away and blasted you asunder.

We ran, Taxon and I, like foxes from the hounds, and

like hunted beasts, we sought to go to ground. We had gained a little distance from them and, rounding a corner, we found ourselves in a quiet little street with cottages on one side and warehouses on the other. The street ran steeply upwards and water was pouring down it several inches deep. "Quick – up here!" gasped Taxon, pointing to a metal fire-escape on the side of an old wooden net-loft. We swiftly scaled the rusty ladders and climbed up onto the gently sloping roof of the building. We lay in the running rain, hearts pounding and ears straining to hear any sounds from below. The sounds came soon enough – running feet in heavy boots, coarse grunts and exclamations, oaths and imprecations.

"They've got to be round here somewhere…"

"Meddling *scientists!*"

"Lost my boat thanks to *them!*"

"We need to comb the whole area till we find 'em, and then, why…."

"We need more men, reinforcements. Let's get down to the Marlin and see who'll join us."

"Yes, good plan!"

Perhaps there was something in the 'Marlin Tavern' part of the plan that had an uncanny appeal for these men, and to our great relief they all suddenly went running off in the other direction. The fact that the pub was under half a fathom of water didn't seem to trouble them too much…

For a minute or two neither of us moved, but stayed still, listening, waiting and watching – the coast seemed to be clear.

I caught Lazarus's eye. He seemed to be listening intently, straining that musically trained ear of his, that super-refined sense-channel that had already heard so much and dwelt in Minde as Sound. The ghost of a frown knitted his brow. "We'd better get down." he hissed.

Then like an *Archeopteryx lithographica* the angular dark quilled sinister sinuous wings of the vile egg-chick were printed on the sky above us – an indelible image of berserk animalistic darkness incarnate.

Even as the shock was registering, the grette fowle was spinning, swooping sniping down on dark, archaic wings. In this instantaneous mayhem I had not a moment to unsheathe

the harpoon but I instinctively raised it anyway. The hackbeak lightning lunged at me but adrenalin leant me speed and I rolled aside – not quite quick enough as the harsh proboscis grazed the side of my rib-cage, ripping some of my rib-flesh. Being savaged by a large wild animal is a fear archetypally embedded in our consciousness, the very stuff of childhood nightmare, but in those harrowing moments pain and fear seemed strangely remote. There was only action and reaction. A curious lucidity can pervade the minde in such moments of crisis.

The terrible snowy-white head was pulling back for another cruel strike. Again I was looking into the cavernous and all-devouring maw of the beast, as at Fate. I could only roll another couple of feet before I was at the roof's edge. Death by falling? Or death from a gluttonous and vulgar vulture? Just when existence seemed to narrow down to these two horrific possibilities there was a blinding flash of pinkish-white light which sent the hellish kelenken bird flapping, screaming and cackling away into the niwlek night air. Taxon was standing there holding a smoking hod of photographic flash-powder.

"That was brilliant, Lazarus," I enthused, "thank you!"

"Quick" replied the eld, passing me a small vial, "pour that over your wound to kill the bacteria."

The liquid felt strangely hot and cold. The wound was not troubling me at that point, and the departure of the monstrous grotte mantelmew precipitated an onrush of well-being that bordered on euphoria. A stout, earthy feeling about the heart; a sunny, earthy, easeful and *expansive* wave lifted me up and raised me up. Thus bolster did myne soule soothynge seeke and yea dyde fynde a grette pes ande tranquillitie.

We climbed back down the fire-escape and melted into the alleys.

We covered the various quarters of the port, Taxon and I, through leaden emerald rain, racing rags of fog and the werewolf-moaning wind. Through twisting districts of distinct elicit distilleries and carapaced capillary villainy – sinuous. Through rolling vistas and vignettes of a huddled and vilified village. Down streets of sleeping slumbering dreamers, all oblivious to the storm. Back to the broken-down and inundated harbour-district, Ox Road, Cat Alley and the shops, taverns, work-places and markets. Past Tremillions the estate-agents and Peter O'Liam's Garage; past Hugh Morris's Joke Shop and past Vagahorn's Stores – that fly-blown and dilapidated establishment that had actually supplied the egg in the first place!

A little further along, by the Golowji Tea-House, the road was under water, the churning, flotsam-carrying, dark, briny waters of a madly writhing black and white sea... Seeing no sign of our *experimental* bird, and not wishing to get soaked again unnecessarily, we headed back towards the web of condensed streets that seethe above the harbour and straggle up Guava Hill.

Lazarus and I looked down over the inundated and storm-battered porth. Before our astonished eyes, the great sea-tempest was punching holes in the granite walls of the promenade and ripping away many tons of earth from the Green. Monochrome furious salt-blasting sea was in grim destroying mood, as before, when the restless waters had gradually taken the towans around Wheal Weary, and then the old cricket field and the old road, whose cyclopean blocks are still to be seen at low tide, like the sunken walls of Cuzco. This process of Kirnowe's oceanic erosion had been going on for geological epochs, shaving several miles off the coastline – but to see it happening before your very eyes was shocking, disturbing – thrilling. The Shyre was being washed away, slewed into the sea, our ground felt infirma; terrifyingly impermanent! Cernyw's four hundred and forty four minerals were being pulverized, reduced to dust and rinsed out to sea again as chemical solutions; perhaps to lay down sediments and some day form the bones of a *new* Kirnowe, a *new* land of Horn-Whale, inhabited by an entirely new species of Hornwhalian... Meantime the withering blasts of Atlantek sea salt-storm kicked, barged and broke over our towne, brokering destruction, bifurcating structures and beggaring belief. Whyths and dashes – spray-foam-clouts clots and clods – rocks, pebbles and stones of various grades hurled onto the prom, with seaweed, sand, adriftwood, flotsam, wreckage and shattered carapace fragments – krogenek molluscs stranded on land – stacks and drifts of bladder-wrack piling up on the path and spilling into rain-shattered streets – roaring surf – waves like grapnels slung ashore by mor-sarf marauders – thundering booming roaring mordros surf – surf hissing back, rolling myriad singular shingles, the voice of ten thousand nagas, cobra-kings, water-dwellers and saurian aquatic entities – surf – spindrift and spray – brinefroth – foamclots flying and kelp thrown splatter at windows – windows put in, with edible crabs landing on kitchen tables and a message in a beer-bottle smashing through the post-office window – soft the boast of the sea was uttered and chattered through mordros muttering waves, hwyths and blasts as it revelled in bleak power and subjugated the terrestrial realm. Feet were running – voices shouting – lights flickering – disturbing and uneasy the rain-splattered night – cobbles glistening as feeble lamplight shimmers and flashes in the rain.

"I think the mob's getting nearer," spake Lazarus "we'd better become inconspicuous!"

We flitted down a long and shadowy alley, overhung with lofts and fishermen's tottering krowjis and cottages. An armed group was heading towards us with lanthorns, billhooks and poles – we doubled back but they gave chase. Suddenly they seemed to be everywhere, these vengeful, desperate and highly dangerous villagers, many of whom were nigh pickled in rum and jars of cheap stout and ale. The night was turning uglier. Again we took to our heels, closely pursued by that swarming seethe of vigilantes. Ugly cries went up – "There they are! It's they two meddling physicists!"

"Doing the Devil's work – they must pay for their crimes!"

"'ere! Come back you two – we want a *word* with you!"

Taxon and I both proved to be excellent runners – there was something in the manner of those fellows that lent us swiftness in our flight through the madly echoing and storm-blasted alleys of that excruciating and eldritch night of which I write.

The storm blasted on and the floods worsened.

Lightning's tredanek rattling electric flash lit the lurid scene intermittent-pink-white – crackling with raging voltage. The pursuing angry crowd swelled and grew, as people surged out of their cottages en masse, to merge into the madding melee, grabbing lamps, brooms, boat-hooks, anything that came to hand. Lazarus and I were running for our very lives now, and mine at least had never felt more vulnerable as we hared it through the night. Running along the road that follows the cliff-top above the harbour, we caught glimpses of the burned-out ghost-fleet rattling grimly at the wharf, like an elephant's graveyard of brittle manatees and skeletal sea-cows. The moon's neon disc broke through a cloud, throwing a vast scintillating gleam onto the sea – a myriad million dancing white diamonds in a heaving meniscoid sea-quake splendour. The glister – a shimmering, glittering field of pure luminosity gracing the relentless black sea.

And across this sparkling white sea of light, compounded of luminous foaming, moonlit breakers, a pterodactyl form appeared – a dark form, ghastly, stark and harsh, wings outstretched and riding the storm with bleak horrific strength – *Larus marinus!* Our bird-beast – our Kramvil, distant but unmistakable in its atavistic lineaments, its monstrous scale, its swift and harrowingly beautiful flight – our bird was back and it was coming our way.....!

The enraged swarm of villagers was almost on our heels as Taxon and I headed down the slope that leads to the Southern Pier of New Lynsmouth harbour. This was the moment that the crowd became aware of the monstrous and dreaded *gull* coming in over the harbour at great speed. There was a moment when time seemed to congeal and stumble as a brief stillness descended. The terrible rook of the sea was pinned against a moonlit backlit cloud like a museum specimen pinned to a board. The moon's flinty shine brought out the brilliant edges of the fowl's wings. The black upper surfaces seemed glazed in a varnish of powdered moon-crystal which shimmered and glowed exultant. The awfully familiar angles and lines of the head and bill were etched again in memory's mnemonic corollary. The bird was suspended and then the bird lurched forward and the crowd let out a dreadful wail and the mad stampede turned mayhem hack-beak terror and carnage…

The foul braying cry croaked harsh and painful on the ear – a most detestable and unlovely sound, a mocking, cruel and morbid sound, how it haunts me still! Panic rippled through the half-delirious villagers and fisherfolk hapless slithered helter-skelter down rain-slicked slipway slopes and creels were spilled and oaths and eels were flung. Aureliferous rainshine scattered arcs and puddles – clattering boot-heels and sea-boots – the beak – the blood – the bone-shattering blows of osseous golden beak on frail, gentle human flesh, the ripping, the chilling screams and cries, the beak, always the beak – flashing, hacking, bleeding, gushing, pouring, goring, ripping and battering and pouring it on like rain as people swirled hither and surged thither in mute nostril agony.

Weapons were raised, only to be dashed from hands, or have their owners kicked or beaked into the black waters of the harbour. The melee spilled down onto the Southern Pier, a horrible medieval battle scene played out between a desperate mob with flaming torches, scythes and rakes, against the kind of unspeakable behemoth that could only crawl forth from the nefarious nightmare of a tormented and feverish twelfth-century serf, raving and fighting demons, having eaten of bad bread.

Taxon however seemed strangely calm amidst all the panic, chaos and terror. He grasped my shoulder and the steely strength of his jelly-glass eye shone through bright.

"Bugles, then weapons," was all he said, and we both gave our best bronze-noted baroque fanfares and toccatas ablaze on those old copper horns before going for our weapons. Wherever was Jack? I hoped he hadn't already fallen prey to the *hrokr* – nothing was impossible with this feathery leviathan….

Again and again the frenzied crowd would try to hack and lunge at the moa-morek, only to be repulsed, decimated, injured and thrown to the ground. Wounds ran blood and fear ran riot. Taxon and I joined in with these sallies and jabs at the beast and looked deep, once again into those gaunt, cold and red-rimmed reptilian eyes as we struggled desperately to destroy the harrowing result of our most *regrettable and unfortunate experiment*.....

Black archaeopteryx wings unfurled ceremonial aflap with sinuous quills. The gaunt and gulling brine-hroc threw back its thalassokrator head and barked obscene avine wails and sounds unspeakably vocalized. Defiant and tyrannous it strutted, a monochrome turkey, vain, cackling cockerel of the rolling breakers, loathsome, repellent and bellicose, beak raised stark against the cloud-sailing lurid moon.

As if to survey the carnage and gloat over the groaning and injured people lying scattered on the flagstones, the great sea-fowl flapped once more those mountainous wings and landed its scaly kigliw feet atop the seaward wall of the pier.

"Quick!" shouted Lazarus, "we need to remove the wounded from the area!"

I went to his aid, as did several others, and we quickly carried away the injured. It was no pleasant task, what with the stark evidence of their intense pains – those who were still conscious; and the shocking nature of some of the injuries. Whilst doing this work, we eyed the gull with great trepidation. It seemed content with its braying, honking and barking display, strutting like a dictator, or a capricious Ancient-World-God, amused to watch us puny mortals scurrying about, following our insignificant little destinies, to be tolerated or annihilated according to whim.

The wind whistled, moaned and bayed, tearing at our clothing and driving the dark rolling sea unto the brink of madness. The full moon pulled at the waters, drawing and tugging at them with its non-linear gravity-waves – the telluric meniscus bowed out towards the orbiting lunar globe – the tide was still rising.

The gwynjak withering blasted wind sent that dark rolling sea battering Penhwyth and chucking seething spray over the top of the pier. Some of the men were regrouping with their weapons, eager to fight on, relentless as Spartans. They seemed to have forgotten that a few minutes ago they were hunting us! Taxon and I stood with harpoons ready, with the others; there was a moment of stillness, as if we were all waiting for the signal that would initiate our unified attack on the monstrosity of a meeuw that had plagued our lives for too long now.

Time seemed to stand still. Splintered mosaic of moonlight on water and twinkling lights in the distance. The main mass of villagers were retreating up the slope, carrying the wounded. A trickle of armed men was still adding to our numbers, as we stood a little way down the Southern Pier, watching and waiting, many a sea-jelly-eye turned upon the Greater Black-backed Gull of the Sea. There must have been twenty or more of us, closely packed together, all brandishing weapons aloft like an army of medieval peasants. For the first time, there was a feeling of some confidence, a bolstering of spirits – a sense that together we were a potential match for the bird.

The moonlight picked out brilliant sparkling facets of crystal in the harbour-wall. The sky was a hypnotic veil of glittering stardust, obscured and revealed by flotillas of jelly-fish-clouds drifting and coagulating in clotted silver Knossos mosaic. Towering over us, the hatchling, the black-wing, terrible of eye; terrible and terrible of eye.....

KAAAARRK! KRI KRI KRI KRI KRI KRI KRI! The utterly chilling and revolting cry rent the night-storm-air once more. An apocalyptic blast rocked the pier as a vast black towering wave swelled spilling and welling up over the sea-wall.

That great bulge of water swelled and frothed in the moonlight, and as it rose up like a mountain range arising, a form emerged out of it, looming over the Kramvil-gull-bird, dwarfing it with its four fathoms of glistening blue-black exoskeletal carapace from telson tail to tip of claw – *Legest Meur – the giant lobster from the downvor deep caverns of the sea!*

A startling vision of spiny-legged decapodic horror, bristling pincers, claws, antennae – lunging with the fearful, nine-foot long right-claw, it grasped the kramvil-bird around the neck, dragged it into the waves, and sheared off its head in an instant.

Black frothing blood gushed and black wings flapped in convulsive reaction. For a moment, the mighty Legest Meur seemed to sit atop the Southern Pier, the vast claw raised as if in arthropodic salutation; snapping open and shut, open and shut. In the next moment, the whole picture dissolved as the lobster vanished back under the waves, dragging its prey with it, back to the downvor depths from which it had come. With the exception of a small quantity of gigantic feathers which washed ashore on the beach, no sign was ever seen of the Legest Meur or the Kramvil-Beast again.

*

Swirling confusion swept through the tempestuous night like a poisoned legacy from that terrible bird. Some of the whalermen and fishermen were cheering with jubilation, others shouting out warnings about more 'monsters' attacking. Screams, groans and weeping were mixed with the cheers of the villagers 'up top' on the harbour-cliff, witnesses to the extraordinary and shocking turn of events. Half the crowd were cheering the demise of the great sea-fowl, the other half screaming in terror at the eldritch glimpse of the elephantine, gliomach lobster.

There was a bustle of movement through the crowd, some whalers were approaching, pushing a little cart. As they careered down the slope I recognized some of them – Bob, Peter, Barney and was it? Yes! Jack Lane himself! The cart was carrying a large, almost military-looking projectile.

"The explosive harpoon! Told you I'd get one! Now where's that monster-bird hiding out?"

Jack looked about him, a faint air of disappointment in his eye.

I patted him on the shoulder. "Well done for coming up with the hardware old boy, but you're too late! The Kramvil-Beast is dead."

The vulpine brows traced an unspoken question.

"It was most astounding, Jack. The Legest Meur rose up – a gigantic lobster, easily twenty-five feet long! Hacked its head clean off with one snip – like garden shears dead-heading a rose!"

"Well I'll be- you mean, you mean a giant- a giant

lobster you say? But that's- that's-"

"Even stranger than a giant seagull?" I put in, trying to help him give words to his dilemma.

"Yes, that's it…" murmured Jack thoughtfully, "stranger and stranger yet… where will it all end?"

The general air of confusion, fuelled and enhanced by rum and pale ale, seemed to spiral like the hypnogogic dreams of an anaesthetised nautilus. Everybody seemed to be shouting and nobody seemed to be listening. Some villagers got it into their heads that "the whalers killed the monster-gull" and the great goddess Rumour ran flapping through the streets and vounders, spreading seeds and setting flames wherever she ran. I managed to tell Jack that Lazarus and I were returning home and hoped to meet up with him the following day. The next minute, the 'whalers', still protesting, were carried shoulder-high through the streets and into the saloon-bar of the 'Red Sea Lion', where ale flowed free like the Liffey.

*

Taxon and I were determined to get as far from the madcap, laughing, shouting, roaring crowd as possible. The people we passed in the street didn't give us any trouble. Perhaps they were too drunk to care, or perhaps since Taxon and I had been seen in the thick of the fight, we were considered as 'fighters', rather than the tenuous, nebulous and tenebrous charge of being 'scientists.'

So whilst the goodlie villagers and fisherfolk revelled and sang and danced to express their joy at the passing of that great shadow that had so haunted, oppressed and tormented the towne of New Lynsmouth, the atmosphere too seemed to undergo a gradual metamorphosis.

The tide turned and the waters started to recede, inch by beetling inch. The wild banshee wind dropped from tempestuous to angry to cross and even the rain lightened a tiny bit. The streets seemed suddenly still and subtly hushed as flushed thrushes sashayed through bushes, thoroughly chuffed. The familiar glistening cobbles of the niwlek misty night, the dear old alleys, vounders and side-streets, washed fresh by the storm – and free! Free from the peril that came from the skies.

The rolling kommolek cloudscape was breaking up now into quilts of mackerel and islands of light and dark, the radiant cool lunar luminescence diffused in dialogue with the scudding sailing silver cumulus. The very sky seemed fresh and clean. Venus become visible and many other stars were sprinkled as diamonds in a fountain between the cloud-pillows. The rain had passed and the wither-wind was down to a healthy blow. A new sound met our ears. A whispering, rustling, whirring, quiet commotion. The air seemed charged, alive and whispering – what on *earth* could it be? Stretching my hand to grasp the moon-drenched sky I merely felt the mizzle-mist. And then, rushing over the roofs and over our heads came a few birds, oyster-catchers and curved, numinous, clear-throated curlews, heading out to sea. Then more birds, an mor again. Avocets, kittiwakes and Sabine's gulls; guillemots and razor-bills, cormorants and gannets, wave upon wave of them against the wonderful monochromatic sky, hypnotically beautiful, prodigiously graceful as they flocked overhead in mesmeric formation. Many species of gulls also went wheeling, mewing and skrawking by – black-headed gulls, Bonaparte's gulls, Caspian gulls, herring gulls, common gulls, yellow-legged gulls, Armenian gulls, ring-billed gulls, slender-billed gulls, lesser black-backed gulls, and, of course, greater black-backed gulls – *Larus marinus*. These now seemed but ornapetions – little birdies… On and on they thronged, a nebulous, elephantine constellation of fowls of the foaming sea. Cloud of fowls. Fruit of a hundred thousand eggs. Egg of a thousand chicks. Flap of a myriad wings. Flight of a billion feathers. Glistening jewels of the air, catching the moonlight and scattering sailing shadows over the dazzling lunar gleam on the dancing meniscus downvor deeps. As the great bird-cloud passed, it left the sky washed clean. The shadow was lifted, and the birds were restored to the waters of the sea.

Chapter 22

I became conscious of a fresh, vibrant, clear breeze, blowing a new day down from the North and rippling as it did the silken fabric of time's continuum-flux. Full well-rounded stout hearty and venturesome rolled the hour in which I rose, minde rising like the Sun, a spreading blaze of awareness.

In the next quatrain of a second arose the thought of Taxon, his wound - and then the realisation that the *hatchling* was no more – that the darkness had at last been dissipated and expelled forever. But what now, I mused? What would be the consequences, the after effect of all these devastating and frightful occurrences? Even this foreboding, however, could not diminish the great sense of lightness and relief in knowing that at last the Kramvil-Beast was dead!

I stepped out into the alley and unwound my peripatetic and preposterous pedal-extremities down rose-petal cobbles with copious dexterity under a blue-white cloud-fleecy sky. Through the old Nagdarf; the For' Ojyon - the Ox-Road; the Keel Alley and Wandering Way; the Downvounder and the Little Kyvounder; past High Mountains and Bottomless Chasms and divers picturesque, latent, lambent and lurking by-ways.

The folk seemed bright, calling out their greetings cheerily, as of yore. Carts clattered by and horses stamped, puffed and clopped. Barrows of fish were trundled up alleys to be salted or smoked in cavernous granite tenements and warehouses. Women hung washing and chatted...

"Snipped off 'is 'ead with 'is fore-claw 'e did, then went clicking and clacking back to the downvor deeps, 'e did!"

"Aye, cheeld-vyghan, 'twas the Legest Meur what did 'un!"

"S'not what I 'eard! 'Twas our jolly whaling boys what did it, wi' our Jack Lane as Chief Harpooneer!"

I smiled to myself as I caught their fragments of conversation in passing by. The controversy surrounding the events of last night had seemingly not diminished, and had had the curious effect of turning Jack Lane into a popular local hero! They'll be building a statue of him next, I chuckled.

I walked on down the gallery of antient places, seeing faces familiar, Keltek and bright. Sun-speckled shadow did play and creep across a sky of softest blue.

But as I ambled along gambrelled and time-rotted Orchard Street, that lurching, teetering, lurking and chittering footway of medieval provenance, a falling and darkling air seemed to descend upon the Quarter. Opposite the Taxon house was an old 'peeth', or well, which was in regular use. As I made my way up the street I glimpsed a furtive and dark figure by the well, and that figure seemed to glimpse me – but whether I had been seen was another matter. The dark figure then turned a canvas-cloaked back and ducked down the alleyway acting surreptitiously, scuttling rodentially down Iron-Foundary Way towards the Marlin Tavern. Something about this sliding, scuttling, sideways slitherer aroused a mild antipathy in my breast and I'll own to a vague and nebulous sense of dread, of unease, of *mal*.

I found myself at the Dreaming Corner, the intersection of memory and futurity, the mystical crossroads whereon lurches that epoch-bespattered and utterly forbidding manse that had dreamed and drowsed on that sun-drenched and weather-beaten corner since the days when square-rigged ships filled the harbour and rum and baccy were spirited into the land.

The chickings were kicking up a devil of a row, what with their inane cluckings and cawings; their screechings and skwawkings – something seemed to have spooked the little critters – or were they also rejoicing, knowing in their hollow, air-filled avine wish-fulfilling *bones* that the great roek of the brine was no more aflap?

Then a curious thing happened, one of those silly little incidents that add colour and humour to the day. I noticed the old chicken that had always reminded me of Taxon – it was very animated and would not cease its cooing and flapping. As I watched it in mild amusement and curiosity, it suddenly flapped its old wings in a violent flurry of effort and, flapping cumbersomely into the air, it landed on my shoulder and let out a long series of clucking, cooing, buck-bucking vocalizations before taking off again. It flapped around Orchard Street a little before returning to the 'moat' where it caused further excitement amongst the flock of feathery and scrawny-gizzarded fowls.

I knocked and Taxon immediately ushered me in, locking and bolting the door again, as was customary.

"You look remarkably well Lazarus," I said, shaking him by the hand. He did indeed emanate a vital glow, an elan, eclat, et cetera etc..

"You look a lot better yourself, Elias, how are those *ribs* of yours doing?"

His question shook me a little as I'd quite forgotten my injury of last night, which had seemed fairly serious at the time.

"I'll take a look." I said, opening my shirt, but was amazed to see that the healing process was extremely well advanced, as if I had received the wound two or three weeks ago, rather than mere hours ago. I looked at Lazarus, there was a knowing twinkle in his eye.

"Cup of tay?" he enquired, rhetorically, and we proceeded to the kitchen.

"I've been pursuing a little chemical-research work this morning," spoke Lazarus, once we were settled in the reading room, our tay before us on a small Chinese lacquer-work table.

"I'm following up a few hints from one of Humphry Davy's notebooks, the preliminary results are most promising. It's somewhat similar to the work I've been doing on the crystal-animation-salts, but with a more nuanced emphasis on poly-metabolic enhancement at a sub-molecular level – it's pretty dry stuff really."

"Not at all, Lazarus, it sounds fascinating," I enthused, "unfortunately, my own understanding of that branch of science is pitifully limited, but I'm impressed! Most people would have taken a day off, after the events of the last few days, but you've already started a new research-project! I don't know where you get the energy!"

We both smiled at this, as most of Lazarus Taxon's long scientific career had been focused on the enquiry into the fundamental nature of energy. Time seemed to stand still, suspended and quiet, like a hover-fly in a sun-beam. Again the dizzying depths of his learning staggered me like staring into the heart of the eye of the pin-wheel cosmos.

"I must admit to a great sense of relief, now that the *kramvil-hatchling* has gone, though I fear that there may still be *repercussions,*" I brooded.

"Yes, the beast wrought untold damage, injury and offence – it wouldn't be pleasant if our role in the proceedings was publicly known."

"Not at all," I agreed.

"I've taken the precaution of cleaning the lab of anything linking us to the *Larus marinus giganticus;* I put the photographic plates into storage, so there's no evidence remaining here."

"Good work, Lazarus. I suppose if our names get linked to the monster-gull, it would be wise to leave the area for a while, just until things blow over and settle down a bit..."

Our conversation soon turned towards aeronautical matters, as we enthused over some of our favourites among recent designs in aircraft. I was an ardent admirer of Horatio Barber's machine – the Valkyrie, liking it for the bold, minimal eccentricity of its lines, whilst admitting it had serious problems with stability and handling, due, in part to its rudimentary wing-warping approach to navigation. It was notoriously prone to side-slips, I had to admit, but what a strange, beautiful bat it was...

Lazarus, for his part, was more taken with the graceful, trailing-winged monoplane, the Handley-Page Bluebird – a far more sleek and sophisticated 'kite', I'll own... We shared an enthusiasm for certain types of machine, such as the new De Havilland Biplane, the A.V.Roe Triplane that got airborne on nine horse-power, the Antoinette monoplane, the Farman-Gnome, and of course, the wonderful Blériot monoplanes – we both agreed the French had come up with something special with the Blériot...

"Oh that reminds me," said Lazarus, "I wanted to show you a letter I received a couple of years ago from Octave Chanute, expressing interest in ornithopter research; now where did I put it?"

He got up to search for the letter. I was very keen to see it... Mr Chanute had been studying aerodynamics since before most of today's aviators were born. He corresponded with scores of aircraft-designers around the world and had encouraged and mentored many of the great pioneers, including the Wright brothers. The interest of such an eminent and venerated figure in aviation was extremely exciting and encouraging – I was most keen to see the letter, but in the next moment there was a knock at the door.

It was one of those eel-shriek moments of crawling flesh, fluttering heart and sudden clamminess. Who could it be? I was surprised by my exaggerated state of apprehension; the last few days must have taken their toll on my nerves.

Lazarus drew back the heavy iron bolts and unlocked the door – it was Florence!

Standing there in her long skirt and a little green velvet jacket, her chestnut hair swept back over her intelligent brows, her eyes sparkled and there was something in her fresh, natural beauty that reminded me a little of her cousin, the dark and lovely Constance.

Florence was confident by nature, a staunch advocate of the Votes For Women movement and not at all hesitant to speak her minde; at this moment, however, she looked worried.

"I'm sorry to bother you Mr Taxon," she said, gazing from Lazarus to me, "but you and Elias, you're both in danger and I wanted to warn you about the situation."

"Please sit down, my dear, I'll pour you a cup of tay and you can tell us about it."

"Just a quick cup, thanks, it's really rather urgent – in short, there is much gossip and clack in the towne, much rumouring, debate and speculation, concerning the recent series of ghastly and inexplicable events – the *gull!*"

"We heard some strange talk yesterday and at one point we were chased by a mob," I replied, as I recalled the harrowing, withering, clawing fear of pursuit.

"One of the rumours going around is that you both raised the bird and then released it – another tale has you unleashing a giant, experimental lobster to kill the gull – surely *this* can't be true?"

Florence looked searchingly at us, as if no longer sure *what* to believe.

"The lobster was nothing to do with us" said Lazarus flatly. "We hatched an egg – not knowing what we were *bringing forth!* Not realizing what unrelishable consequences would also hatch and grow!"

"Well tongues are wagging now," continued Florence gravely, "more and more people are connecting your names to this whole *bird-business* and I fear the people are in an ugly mood – vengeful, retributive and bitter. I think the blind man is going around fanning the flames of hatred and I'm not sure it's safe for you to remain here."

"We were thinking along these lines ourselves," I agreed.

"The other day, Paul said we were always welcome up at Chy-an-Brae, the Hill's family house. Perhaps we should head up there for a spell?"

"Yes Mr Taxon," replied Florence earnestly, "I think that's an excellent idea – I think you should leave without delay – please *I implore you* – go quickly – for your own safety!"

"Thank you for coming here, Florence," I told her, "it was good of you to warn us."

Florence rose to go, then an enigmatic smile played over her face. She extended her left hand, showing a golden ring upon her finger. "I met Jack on New Lynsmouth bridge last night," she went on confidentially, "he proposed to me and gave me this ring. It's Cornish gold, from Bal West. We need to keep you safe so you can be Jack's Best Man!"

"Florence, that's wonderful news! I'm very happy for you both!" We gave her our congratulations and agreed to meet up, with Jack too, at Chy-an-Brae; and Florence took her leave.

Though gladdened at the news of Florence and Jack's betrothal, her *other* news had a more disturbing effect. I began to feel the rapidly increasing influence of an unlovely and luxuriant mal, an uliginous and tenebrous cluster of sclerotic hyphae were weaving tenuous filaments of ghastly, rich-rotted and fungoid nightmare around the core of my minde and somewhere a raven clawed at my name, written in blood upon the Book of ye Fates. I passed a palsied pympbys hand across my seeping brow, a jaundiced starfish limping over a slippery rock at low tide. Perspiration clammed and clung wet dripping and weren't the arcane whip-poor-wills more frenzied and atonal than was healthy at this hour?

"We ought to leave soon," said Lazarus, breaking me out of my dark reverie, "but first there's something I'd like to show you in the lab – don't worry; it's not another egg!" He smiled.

We walked through and into that airy and spacious chamber, with its carapace-green sky-light windows and its gleaming mahogany work benches; the sketches of aircraft pinned to the wall, next to the iridaceous collection of Rhinoceros-Beetles. Blue vials, beakers, vases and flasks were ranged linear on spotless shelves – all spoke of *rigour, intelligence, progress;* nothing whatsoever remained to hint at the incubating or hatching of *elephantine larid monstrosities* or such of similar ilk. Taxon's laboratory exuded an air of refined intellectual enquiry, of a systematic search for the truths of the physical world.

"These are the lobose cycads from which I extracted certain unusual fungoid hyphae." He indicated what looked like some shrivelled brownish plant-material lying in a glass dish, next to an antiquated set of apothecary's scales.

"And here," he continued, gesturing eagerly towards a test-tube partly filled with a fumaginous, powdery substance, "here we have a specimen of cryoplankton from the south face of Mount Erebus. Now the funny thing is, once you start mixing distillations of these two with a little bit of *this,"* and here he pointed to a test-tube of purplish glasrudh *froth...* "which is essentially an extract of hypertrophied scotophyte from the Schizostegiales Order – well, we end up with a substance that displays some singularly curious and perplexing phenomena..."

The jelly-eye of eld lit sparkled again with sprite-like glee, as enthusiasmos's sacred flames were kindled once again in his luminous awareness. How many times I had seen that look, as the sacred flame of Olymbos flickered and danced across his ancient brow. Before I could find words to comment, he was off again, following his scintillating daemon aloft to the snowy peaks of inspiration... "Beyond this point it gets a little technical; you see the cycad-hyphae globules become super-saturated with flocculent humicolous diatoms, which in turn release statoliths, which, having been centrifuged and mixed with the periplasmodium obtained from the Antarctic cryoplasm, led to a fundamental mutarotation occurring at the sub-molecular interface. Now, as you can imagine- *what?!"*

The brittle music of disintegrating glass shattered Taxon's discourse and sent a rolling wave of fear through the laboratory.

"Sounds like trouble!" I opined.

Entering the vestibule we saw a rock lying on the carpet, in a glittering jewel-heap of glass-shard fragmentary diamonds. One of the panes of the ancient fan-light above the Chilean pine-plank door had been put in, and through it's broken stalactite maw ugly voices leached into the house.

"Meddling physicists!"

"Gorthkryjyans – *heresy* I say, *heresy!"*

"Darwinist blighters – is *this* their hide-out? Let's warm 'em up with a nice little fire shall we?!"

"Quick," called Lazarus, "the shutters!" and we both raced to close the heavy wooden screens across the windows, even as glass shattered and splintered around us. Having succeeded in securing the windows, we dragged a weighty oak table across the room and used it to buttress the door. Guttural grunts and hoarse, muffled outbursts continued to reach our ears, coupled with the din of a ferocious and demoniac percussive *battering* on the door, which flailed and clawed at my palpitating viscera, hurling me into a churning cauldron of pullulating loathsomeness.

"It'll take them a couple of minutes to get through the door – we have to be quick! Listen, Elias, you go and open up the old stable and pull the ornithopter out into the courtyard. I'm going to get something from the lab – see you down there in a moment, now *go!"*

Taxon's words galvanized me into action and in less than half a long minute I was trundling our wonderful mechanical dragonfly creation across the yard, where it sat, poised in readiness under a sky of scudding, high-sailing kommolek cloudscapes and a fresh Northerly breeze setting the sky in motion.

Taxon reappeared seconds later, his arms full of mirrors and lenses and in each of his hands a test-tube of turquoise-grey effervescing sludge.

"Now quickly – prop these tubes up against the wall there, that's it," he spoke rapidly, "now, help me set up the lenses and mirrors, focus them all on the metal spot there."

It was only then that I noticed a discoid plate of fine tin, about five feet across, embedded in the centre of the courtyard...

Working together, we soon had all the mirrors and especial lenses made ready and finely focused, so that from their various angles of configuration they contrived to capture all the available beams of light, and bring them to play, sharply and brightly upon the metal disc, which was emitting a soft preternatural light, suffusing the yard with a lambent and yearning glow.

"Now the aircraft," uttered the antikwari, "let's get it in the middle of the tin-disc, pointing North!"

We briskly swung the craft round and adjusted its position according to Lazarus's instructions.

The noise from the streets was getting louder and more chaotic – in short, the mob was baying for blood – *our blood!*

"Grave-robbers!" "Necromancers!" "Boat-burners! – Let's get them!"

A flaming torch came flying over the roof and landed next to the ornithopter – Lazarus nonchalantly kicked it out of the way. I was most curious about just what *was* his plan of escape, but, handing me one of the test tubes and holding the other to his own lips, he bade me "drink!"

The mucilaginous fluid tasted extraordinary; and not very nice. The shouting continued, with smashing of glass and a rather disturbing chant of "Burn them! Burn them!"

A stray cobblestone suddenly found its way into the yard,

luckily doing no damage. That rock offended me though, to think of the mindlessness of being killed by a flying stone, thrown by an unseen hand. A wave of anger seemed to blow through me, I could feel my strength increasing and the anger melting into a calm excitement. Lazarus grasped my wrist and looked at his pocket-watch, as if taking my pulse.

"I think the Erebus Compound is taking effect," he murmured thoughtfully, "we'd better get on board..."

We scrambled into the tiny nacelle of the aircraft, which suddenly seemed a very frail contraption of canvas and sticks. I turned to Taxon in dismay.

"But the *engine!*" I protested, "we haven't got an *engine!*"

He calmly held up a hand to silence me, then his globular glance fell upon the banks of mirrors, lenses, reflectors, looking-glasses and magnifying glasses; and the lambent glow swelled and bloomed. Next, he laid his hands on the connecting spar, designed to join the movable wing to the oscillating beam-engine, and motioned to me to grasp the handle on *my* side of the fuselage.

Surely he didn't think... but even as my *head* was grasping his purpose, and rejecting it as madness; simultaneously with this, I felt a gradual but profound up-welling of physical energy, of strength and exuberance rising in my blood, and somehow my *body* seemed to know that it could be done.

"Now, it's vital to keep in rhythm, particularly at the first stage, so I'll count to eight, and on the ninth beat, start flapping that wing!"

I thought I saw a look of extreme exaltation flash momentarily across the visage of the revivified Taxon; a wild look, vivid, ebullient and inspired.

"Breathe deeply!" called the old scientist, then slowly, rhythmically, he started counting from one to eight....

"One." A deep inbreath sent subtle tongues of cool fire licking through my musculature, my blood seemed to glow with a stream of oxygen. The air swelled my lungs and filled my chest. It smelled pure, clean. More shouting and crashing around outside. "Two." I see Taxon breathing slowly, calmly

– the compound must be affecting him too; he seems steady, reflective – the living antithesis of that howling, irrational and murderous pack of ochlocratic hot-heads just a few yards from us... "Three." My shoulders flexed and rippled with a new-found biologic force. I remember feeling like a great ox that longs to try its strength against various burdens or obstacles, like an elephant pushing down a tree. "Four." Some fool's lobbing all kinds of rubbish into the yard – there goes a beer-bottle. That front door'll surely give way any minute now – they'll come back with axes and bars and... "Five." I wished he'd count faster, the seconds seemed to stretch out like melting toffee. Must slow down, keep my port-wing synchronized with his starboard one. "Six." Breathe slowly – that's it – *shrapnel* – *breaking glass* – cover face, that's it, safe. Breathe slowly. "Seven." This is madness – mirrors – reflectors – hand-powered aeroplanes – Polar fungus potions – oh well, all in a day's work... Deep breath now, that's it...

There was a terrible rending and splintering noise – surely that was the front door going, or maybe they'd smashed their way through one of the windows? Great Jehosephat, I mused, I'd been through so much since I first made the acquaintance of Lazarus Taxon, antikwari! Ever since the other day – could it really be just a few days ago? Ever since coming across the wonderful selection of rare and learned tomes offered up for sale in that drowsy and slumberous backstreet, ever since meeting the old man – well he had *seemed* old when I met him – and getting involved with a certain *biological* project, my life had been a cyclonic vortex of adventure, struggle, danger, misfortune and *mal;* an unpredictable toboggan-ride through a land not recognizable to my eyes; a land of strange, inexplicable and dark singularities – a land of marvels and shadows, shifting shadows that can never be still. So many thoughts seemed to pass, or rather to hang suspended in my minde, reeling and spinning with the events of the previous few days. The whole egg-kramvil-hatchling experiment and all its many, many ghastly consequences; my deep infatuation and admiration for the lovely Miss Constance Place – who should, incidentally, be expected in this area imminently; our construction of the ornithopter.... the extraordinary Legest Meur which destroyed the Kramvil-hruoch; the mob, the baying, howling, cursing mob – they're getting nearer... I hear them... The great kommolek cumulus cloudscape opened out and the great Sun-disc was revealed in a fresh sky of soft light blue. The vibrant photonic sunbeams streamed into the series of mirrors and lenses and the glow of the disc below the craft intensified noticeably. A gull skrawked. A drunken voice roared a blurred string of oaths. "Eight," shouted Lazarus, "aaand, *down!*" We depressed the levers with ease... "And up," he called, maintaining the rhythm.

The light, rhamphorhynchus wings gently started to flap, slowly at first, but making a strong draft of air in the little yard. The blazes of light in the mirrors were small white suns, beaming their energy into the metallic spot beneath the undercarriage. The light blazed strong and, due to some cryptic process that Lazarus was exploiting, the aircraft seemed to become proportionately *lighter* as the sun blazed brighter.

Riding a current of this curious new strength, it was a relatively easy matter for Taxon and I to set the wings into a good, strong, steady rhythm, and, as the tin-disc continued to blaze with light below us, I noticed that we were a foot or so above the ground!

To rise aloft, afloat on a beam of light! Working the fragile pterodactyl wings like slow, syncopated oarsmen and slowly gaining 'lift', as the aerofoils gracefully sliced through the very air and fluttered up. The calm, glowing yet vigorous effects of the Erebus Compound were allowing us to metabolize considerably more oxygen than usual, and as Taxon and I worked the ornithopter's levers together, we seemed transformed into the animated muscularity of a great man-made bird awoken and brought to life. Steadily we flapped the levers up and down and the graceful wings cleaved upwards, aided and enhanced by that ethereal and otherworldly glow of sheer-photon-hue-light-stream, blazing bright through the taught 'skin' of the little craft and causing it to shine golden bright. With every foot of height gained, a quiet euphoria, a nebulous evdaemonia loomed large afore me. Soon we were level with the gutter of the stable – I shot a fleet glance at the laboratory – time seemed slower – I saw, through those great green-grey-bubble-glass windows the awestruck faces of some of the vengeful mob, who were frozen, transfixed in hypnotic, fascinated wonderment – all thoughts of murder and mayhem slayed and confounded. They seemed almost like a figment from the past – no longer to be feared – since stepping forth into the aery realms, we had taken a great leap into a new dimension, the earthbound seemed now so many *Pan troglodytes,* gibbering and pointing bones and hairy fingers at the sky. We flapped on up and soon found ourselves at roof-level. A great hubbub and hullabaloo went out from below as the crowd in the streets caught its first glimpse of our extraordinary craft. I think I could hear the words 'Necromancy!' and 'Sorcery!' and the crowd seemed to scatter in fright, having had more than its fair share of monstrous, outlandish and inexplicably unnatural events in recent days... As the little aeroplane rose above roof-level, we could immediately feel the North wind under our wings, and we knew the feelings of old-time mariners when they leave harbour and feel the wind filling the sails and bringing life and motion to them.

    As we were heading straight into the prevailing breeze, our lift increased dramatically and we soared upwards over the roofs of the Old Quarter, with seemingly very little effort. We performed a great sweeping arc in the sky and swung, looming forty feet above the Marlin Tavern and the pantiled merchant house.

    "Can you manage both wings?" shouted Lazarus, "I'd better grab the controls!"

    "Alright Lazarus – just say when."

    Lazarus gave the signal and we managed the switch-over without lurching too badly. I now sat like a rower, an 'oar' in each hand, a golden lepidopteral wing; whilst Lazarus sat forward in the nacelle, his hands on the 'joy-stick' that not only controlled the elevators on the tail-plane, for soaring and diving; but, together with the rudder-bar, controlled lateral mobility via our experimental technique of 'wing-warping'. As Lazarus got a feel for the 'helm' my work became easier.

He quickly learnt how to constantly steer the craft into the wind currents, to *ride* the wind so we could afford to flap the wings considerably slower, just like rowing a boat on a drowsy summer's day.

I heard occasional screams and shouts from below, as we were spotted. A dog was barking, running along below, as we flew over the coombe, its floodwaters receded now, but flotsam and debris were still scattered around like toys. And that was it! We were flying! Truly flying, and in an airframe of our own devising! The great rock of Tallcorne passed under us, the river was a silvery sarfek ribbon, or the pewter-grey back of an eel. There, maybe sixty feet below us lay Unstable-Hobbla, where we'd had all the yarji-bhaji up at the hen-coop poultry-farm... there were the patchwork fields of variegated mossy and emerald fresh green. We flew, swooped, soared, loomed and glid, at one with our great tykki-Dyw flitting frittilary butter-flye. Sheepish clouds in a luminous lapis lazuli sky, an oceanic and expanded sky, a sky that rolled on for ever.

I threw a glossy-eyed glance back over my shoulder and caught the momentary sight of New Lynsmouth's warves and jetties, its ancient harbour, a dark forest of masts; the Old Quarter with its richly rotting, lurching and tottering gambrelled tenements and writhing labyrinthine Cretan alleys and vounders. A cluster of gulls swirled and skwawked above old New Lynsmouth towne and the vision was gone and I saw the old towne no more.

We were ascending steadily into the lambent and fleecy-clouded kommolek accumulations of aetherial and winged elation. It seemed we flew not on wings of sail-cloth and wood, but rather wings of joy, wings of blinding light sprouting straight from the Soul. I'll own to an elevated sense of blissful sheer *life;* of a primal and universal euphoria that blossomed in the joy of flight.

"Take a break, Elias," called Taxon, "conditions are excellent, I think we can *glide.* We seem to be entering some large pockets of warmish air, and of course the light-beam from the tin-plate will have expanded the molecules of gas in the hollows in the wings and fuselage, which should, according to my reckonings, make the aircraft approximately ten per cent lighter. Then there is the head-wind which is ideal for gaining altitude, and the fact that this machine seems to display the characteristic signs of 'inherent stability', so even if I relinquish my grip on the controls..." and he did just that... "the machine automatically returns to the optimum angle of incidence and simply levels out!"

"A tribute to your thoroughly-researched design, Lazarus," I answered, "it's a *marvellous* creation, truly amazing!"

"Well, old Chanute helped me with some suggestions that proved very insightful, and you also made a major contribution; particularly with the improved mono-plane tail." He added. "And, of course, there *is* the metabolic compound... I thought that if I could find something that would increase fat and oxygen metabolism, *without* perceptibly increasing heart-rate and blood pressure, it would be not only safe, but extremely useful in certain serious conditions... Escaping from that angry mob and getting this kite off the ground proved to be an ideal field-trial for the compound and, so far, I'm very pleased with the results," observed the eld.

The strange craft flew on, stretching sweet wheatstraw golden wings to the zephyr wafts of aery Kernewek vapours.

Tiny shrouds and veils of lacy cloud wisped, hwythed and whispered by, rippling flecks of cloud mallow-pillows and downy undulating puffs. The air was quiet, apart from some little creaking sounds as Lazarus adjusted the lateral controls and the wings warped like the roof of the Tallcorne Inn... The wings flexed and hunched, morphing and freely changing angle of tip... wind whistled shrilly through the bracing wires as we soared forward and the bright tapestry of the Brythonic territory unrolled below us. To see the land as only an *aviator* can see it, from a new dimension, a realm of molecular air – what a wonderful bright feeling it was, at once ultra-modern and primordial. To be riding on a high and windy day, deep in the heart of Kernweal, gently gloring and soaring, rising and looming up on aery puffs and sloughs of soughing keltek breath, the vapours of the Atlantek, the breath of seals, water-wallrustics and kelpies; to rise, to soar, to lift aloft and *flugh*. Little fields and miniature roads and farms slip scudding under our undercarriage's undertow. Toy houses and fields of galloping ant-cows and a beetle-wagon pulling in to a toy-town village. The land is a counterpane, embroidered with pictures, reminding me of childhood dreams and long-forgotten visions. The sighing in the rigging wove an Aeolian breath of harmony, glinting colours of rainbowdog sound.

"Well, here we are, Lazarus," I laughed, "riding our wood and cloth bird through the sky – it's been quite a week!"

"Yes! Isn't it *beautiful?*" laughed old Taxon, as he warped the wing-tips like a buzzard and made a wide, graceful, swooping turn, "Handles like a true thoroughbred! I pored over a lot of Lilienthal's designs when I started my aeronautical studies and his influence is vast and fundamental. This kite reminds me of some of his later gliders, and if she flies this well on two *man-power*, imagine what she'll do on twelve and a half *horse-power!*"

"This could be the first ornithopter to win the Gordon Bennett Cup!" I mused.

We soared on, heading generally towards Chy-an-Brae, the Hill's ancestral manse, which lay on a small green plateau between the craggy, rugged and ragged rocks of the ill-hinted batholithic upland hinterland of Penwithershins. But of that kommolek and cloud-fleeced afternoon, that mystic day of aery sky, that patch-work quilted, ravelling land and vaporous aetheric firmament, of rolling and tumbling kommol wisp nebulae, glowing, diffuse... The whispering meadows of the sky where cleaving feathers leave no wake, where dragon-flyes and moths come out to play and mortals formerly feared to fulsome tread. The *freshness* of the sky, the *freedom* and boundless openness it offered had kindled a warm evdaemonia within me, I felt like an Olympian, with vision and inspiration running over like streams of phosphorescent silver-mercury. All around me was vital and charged. The land seemed resplendent, as if blessed and basking in Truth. Our craft seemed to emanate a nobility and grace, representing and embodying a victory for the world of science, of rationality and applied knowledge. In my eyes, the aircraft looked beautiful – I couldn't see it any other way...

To ride the skies, skimming clouds like Aladdin clinging to the back of his Roc, letting vision sweep the land, lighting aloft to rarefied realms of free-streaming molecular air...

"Why don't you have a go at the helm?" called Lazarus.

"I'd love to!" I called back, and we gingerly swapped places, in the manner of people in a punt. The machine demonstrated its 'inherent stability' once more as we shuffled into place and I settled into the very snout of the craft. Now there was nothing before me but the sky and the land. I held the controls and could instantly feel them responding to the swirls, eddies and ripples in the ocean of air. I felt at ease. It felt *right* to be flying. I became aware of a humorous upwelling of fondness for the aeroplane, its dragon-flye fluting spindling spars, its superstructure box-girder skeletal airframe; it was our Chinese wind-up toy – I could imagine it being powered by a giant rubber band! I could imagine it skiing down a snowy mountain and taking off over a glacier – or swapping the undercart for floats and landing it on the sea!

We were flying over the hinterland now, those rocky uplands of undulating gorse and bracken, those *hills* – they almost looked serene from this novel point of view, granite whales, stranded in a sea of gorse. Here lay those isolated and bestial hamlets of such atavistic ill-repute. The stark upland pastures on steep, stony slopes with thin, bitter and acidic soil; the bellows of beasts of the barnyard, braying madly at the butcher's block; the foaming pitchers of warm, fresh gore – *what do they do with them?* What goring, gouging, kornek, horned howling hunch-shuffling insane squirming hybrid beast-creatures are kept concealed in their dark, dusty and archaic granite barns? The sight of those dark almost medieval and forbidding farmsteads on these moors always did have a slightly *unsettling* effect upon me, it's the way they wallowed in time, never developing, always clinging to old rites and superstitions; forebodings and suspicions. Largely Puritan by tradition, these isolated rustic zealots had only recently stopped wearing the stove-pipe hat and square collar... These dour and reclusive throwbacks ever clung to their benighted and archaic handful of scattered hamlets, scorning their more gregarious neighbours in the 'low-country', as they dubbed the rest of Kirnowe. The land itself seemed huddled, hunched, brooding and blasted. The few trees that languished here were stunted parodies or gnarled grotesqueries – life was sparse, hard and harsh here and the innumerable granite boulders rendered the area largely desolate.

The presence of several jynnjyow or engine-houses added little comfort – only two of the chimneys were actually smoking; the others were stark, ivy-smothered ruins round which rooks clacked, quaked, quivered, quilled, feathered, mine-shaft dark and ivy damp dripping. The industry was caving in, abandoned shafts and workings were filling up with cold dark water – a world was disappearing. The people were thrown back on farming – those that didn't leave for a new life in the colonies. Those who stayed in these barren hills eked out a living of sorts, scratching up a few thin crops, raising whatever fatstock they could, and a little poaching and foraging. This was the hinterland and the place had a singularity about it that was every bit as perplexing as it was bewildering...

Our lepidopteral rhinolophidus leapt and flopped, ornithopterally looming aloft on wings graceful, spindular, spiky. Trailing edges like the grasping ferruginous hack-talons of the rhamphorhynchus – somewhat also fish-like, piscine, like the great grey ray that flutters and undulates along on the wings of a fish.

The haggard aeon-shattered granite hills sent out their unspeakably vast and primordial batholithic influence into this realm of heathers, sundews, bracken, furze, and gwynjak thorns. Shrunken, misshapen, almost *prostrate* specimens of elder trees grew here; their dead-bone barkless branches festooned in the mountains of the moon and epiphytic gelatinous pendulous and globular mycelia pullulating in tremulous atavisms. It was said of this quaint region that the very *rocks and stones* emitted a subtle but noxious vapour, that crept into your bones like the ague and slowly laid you down, to be included among the dead.

As we flew on over small paddocks, the hedges were increasingly made of dry-stone walls, leaving the more verdant and bushy Kernouac hedges behind in the 'low-lands'. The weather was changing, the hills were distorting the very *atmosphere* and churning it into packets and pockets of rising and swirling turbulence. I was having a rapid education in the art of wing-warping – a hybrid activity, combining the skills of a sailor with those of a musician.

"I'll give us a bit more lift," called Lazarus, gradually increasing the motion of the aerofoils, "we should be there very soon, *wind permitting..."*

"It's blowing up a bit isn't it?" I rejoined. "Still, once we're over that ridge we just follow the valley up to the plateau and then we should be able to see Chy-an-Brae."

Old Taxon was plying his 'oars' like he was in the Oxford to Cambridge boat-race.

"That's it, nearly there – steady as she goes, Mr Gillpington!"

My piloting skills were being tested now, as buffets, crumpets, crumhorns and hornbills, bill-posters and poster-paints and paint-brushes and hair-brushes and air brushes the undercart of the fragile pterodactyl craft, bill-horning and hooking it, prodding and a-pawing at it like a porcupine playing with an eel. It was those *hills* – they broke the weather up into currents and hurled them like broken biscuits at our juddering rhamphorhynchus craft. I gripped the controls more tightly, I could feel the machine pulling back and vying for control. I was learning to fly – and I hadn't even read the *book* yet! In fact, it was around that time that I started to realize just how important it was to balance book-learning with hands-on, experiential learning, as I fought to control our home-made experimental aeroplane in those eddies and *hwyths* of blistering gwynjak wind. Now pallid electrons of niwlek coagulating withering mist were sweeping in in shreds and shrouds. A crow flew flapping sideways by, cawking and karking at us telluric interlopers. Intruders in an aery realm. Tricksters in a paper bird. Sorcerers and dabblers, going beyond the bownds.

Through ripped ragged curtains of mizzle and fog I caught glimpses of the small fields that clung to the sides of the undulating hills. A herd of thin cattle, lanky and angular, had stampeded at the sight of our machine and we could clearly hear the pounding of their cloven hooves on the turves as they ran riot in the rocky enclosure. At this point we were only about forty or fifty feet up, the weather was becoming inclement, the light was failing and the ubiquitous aqueous moisture was coagulating and condensing on the surfaces of the aeroplane, adding to its weight and also inhibiting the action of the special gas-pockets that were built into the wings, tail and fuselage. The area over which we flew showed many traces of the Beaker Folk and other tribes of Ancient Britons. The mighty granite walls of their cyclopean circular houses were scattered in the bracken, with sometimes a lone menhir, an old Celtic finger pointing at the sky; or sometimes on a hilltop, a strange and eerie circle of standing stones, leaning and gaping like an old man's teeth. The sombre scene was further augmented by the vague and muffled *animalistic* sounds that came up from that murk-myred realm of lost and bewildered valleys and huddled, brooding, *leering* hills.... The distant baying of hound-dogs, regressing into howls and pitiful whimpering. The hollow lowing and brazen braying of the decadent breed of cattle scattered on the trackless acres of bracken. The plaintive bleating of a few head of upland sheep, of an ill-kempt and derelict flock. Occasionally the raucous tones of a rooster drifted up to us, evoking a world little changed since the Iron Age had metamorphosed into the Age of Steam. Somewhere a farmer was chopping wood and somewhere else a beast bellowed, stamped and snorted, wild-eyed, frothy-mouthed and quivering like a pail of curds and whey.

Soaring over this dew-drenched and gorsey land, minde sharp and clear like the light on an Antarctic glacier; glimpsing more of the Bronze Age dwellings, I imagined those ancestral folk peeping out of their smoky, thatched huts to gaze in hypnotic awe on the great yellow bat with two men riding on its back.... Brythonics dissolve back into time's misty past and the vision is gone – swallowed like the land in thickening fog. Orn we thopt hopping and rearing up as we rode the aery rollers and breakers, skimming and bouncing along on air's chubby and succulent cushion. Nuddens and gouts of mirk and niwlek fog-pools glanced off our butter-flye fluttering wing-tips like toads jumping into the pol kroenogow toad-pool. Splashes of rain were starting to trickle down my face and the flying-machine was becoming noticeably more sluggish and less responsive. I wondered if Lazarus was beginning to feel fatigued.

"Are you alright there Lazarus?" I called back to him, "would you like to swap places?"

"I'm fine," he replied, "you keep the helm, you're doing well. A wee tiny totty more *altitude* wouldn't go amiss though." he added laconically.

"Going *up!*" I pulled back on the controls and Lazarus plied the wing-levers with new vigour.

We sailed low over another of those isolated and dilapidated farmsteads that had drowsed here since well before the Norman Conquest. A sudden flash of dripping wet grey slate roofs, an outhouse with slates missing and beams exposed – a dim light within and much straw and cattle. The farmhouse itself somehow bleak and forbidding, cheered by no flowers but groundsel and camomile, curtains ragged in dark windows, rusting implements and buckets lying around. The farmyard over which we silently flew was a rolling, pitching sea of cow-dung, through which plodded an old farmer, his raincoat fastened with binder-twine, leading a great hog by a string in his right hand – in his left he clutched a hatchet. A dog, mis-bred and belligerent, was barking and snarling, staring up at us, but the farmer didn't even look up as we loomed over, our tail-skid missing the farmhouse weathercock by less than a foot.

A series of shrill and eldritch piping squeals were cut short with a terrible gurgling *roar* and the hound howled on in demented frenzy, fading away in the gathering twilight, the fog of tewlwolow.

We struggled to gain height, but the withering wind was throwing us around the sky, and with the light fading fast, our position was starting to look a little perilous. A wind had sprung up over Iceland-Water, a restless and wandering wind, a wind that swirled and prowled all down Atlantek's briny pathways until it hit the Shyre – West Kirnowe – Penwithershins – it blasted and blustered and hurled our little craft into the dark and ominous clouds. Dark brown, bronze and swirling they were, and cast from finest pewter. The great wind from the North was making our machine swing and veer wildly in great arcs – we were in danger of falling off, not having foreseen the need for a safety-harness. As we swung across the sky like fate's pendulum, a 'jynnji', an old engine-house, with its great granite chimney topped with red-brick loomed up straight in front of us! I threw my weight against the controls, and simultaneously Lazarus held the starboard wing in the raised position. We missed the lichenous and ivy-smothered smoke-stack by the narrowest of margins, and as we skimmed by, a party of crows came rooking and clacking out of the old jynnji, swarming around the aeroplane like hounds round a boar. Rookbeaked squawkers, they called, cawed and cackled, before melting evasively back into the plagioclase mist.

Rain and darkness enveloped us and at times we could see nothing at all. I was losing my sense of the horizontal and fervently hoped I was not steering us off our course. I was getting very wet with the rain, but somehow the coldness didn't seem to bother me, perhaps this was due to a side-effect of the curious potion that we'd partaken of. *No* potion could cure the giddy and nauseous feelings of *dread* and *disorientation* caused by this virtually blindfold flying in stormy weather though; we seemed to have lost control of our destiny, like a rudderless ship in a tempest. We were in a very dark place – a very dark place indeed. Lost in the sky. Sailing along at a good rate of knots, with no idea of our altitude, or what might lie ahead, looming into our path with no warning.

We were at the mercy of the air now, that most fluid and mercurial of elements; ungraspable, insubstantial and mighty. It began to seem like sheer *hubris* to think that we could arrogantly *conquer* a primordial and all-powerful element such as this. It crossed my minde, fleetingly, as I wrestled with the aero-controls, that this was just like the Kramvil Experiment – we had gone too far, strayed way out of our depth, and had little power to put matters right. It would be ironic indeed if the WORLD'S FIRST SUCCESSFUL MAN-POWERED ORNITHOPTER FLIGHT ended up as an AERONAUTICAL DISASTER – TWO MEN KILLED! We would be a footnote in history, remembered as much for our folly as our achievement, and ornithopter research would probably become another extinct branch of scientific investigation. The noble ornithopter – not just our one, but the whole genus– would be regarded humorously as a 'white-elephant', a 'red-herring', a mere 'rugose crinoid', to be snickered over by future generations of morons *who'd never designed an aircraft in their lives!*

It's amazing what passes through the minde, when the fate of the body dangles by a gossamer thread. I began musing over the evolution of the heavier-than-air flying machine, and speculated on the sleek and high-powered machines that we might expect to see in a few more years of progress. I was conscious that the machines of yesterday and today would come to be regarded as so many picturesque obsolescences; moschopses, baluchitheriums, glyptodons and yea, e'en *mega*theriums; the crude and elephantine precursors of today's graceful, aesthetic and efficient quadrupeds. Such were my ruminations on the gramnivorous, the aerodynamic, the linear progression, the Darwinian, the Euclidian and the charming megafauna of ages past. And the thought of all those many extinct species of animals brought back the juddering realisation that Lazarus and I might be about to join the fossils of beasts gone by.

"I think we need to get down, Lazarus, this blind-flying seems a bit suicidal, don't you think?"

"Exactly," he rejoined, "let's look out for a light, to show us where the ground is, then we'll just have to make the best landing we can."

"Yes, if we don't land soon we'll be out over the sea... I'll try and swoop a bit lower, see if I can see anything."

"Easy does it," added the elder. I eased the stick forward a little, straining my jelloid orbital eyes for a glimpse of land, like an ancient mariner. The thrill of flight had metamorphosed into a mere craving to survive the experience. Rain splashed and soaked us. The wires creaked and sung. Darkness was consuming and digesting us – soon there would be nothing left. We are creatures of *light* and without its illumination we cannot thrive, cannot survive. The darkness squirmed and coiled round us like eels; yes, like eels crushing, strangling and smothering; gnawing, gashing, subjugating all and pulping their shattered bodies. The eels of darkness were closing in, clogging and cloying like vile hagfish or monstrous, ghastly *morays*... I raged inside against the darkness. I raged against the leering skull, the ensnaring doom that would crush my life. Then I thought of Constance and my heart yearned for life like a flame blazing up and I felt strength renewed.

We flapped on through the gloom. A faint glimmering materialized almost in front of me, bleary and indistinct like a Van Gogh.

"Can you see that, Lazarus?" I called back, "I'd better try for a landing."

"Try not to scratch the paintwork," he replied, "I'll slowly decrease the lift!"

I could almost *feel* the ground swelling and rising beneath our skis, waiting gravitatiously to claim us as its own. Dark earth of Kernow – don't be in a hurry to swallow your sons. I glimpsed what must have been a tree-top rushing below us, then more darkness. The darkness yawned and pitted, it could be infinite. It seemed to stretch in all directions, and yet it was nothing, had no dimension, no extension, no existence. I hungered for the light with all my soul. The ornithopter flew gracefully on, flapping slowly now, like a honey-hunched buzzard, ready to swoop down and claw at the land.

For a few more seconds, our sprightly féileacán, our Cornwealas glöyn byw butterfliege flew, fluttering like a tremulous psyche, a pyskie impetuously leading us witherfore on the high and withering moors of old Penwithershins.

I was just a-trimmin' me wing-tips with the Laconic Wing-Warping Apparatus, straining towards the dim lights in the murk ahead of me when a form loomed forth suddenly, mere yards ahead – a form loathly and repulsive, inexplicably *eldritch* in its harrowing familiarity! A form, I say, two fathoms high and looming large, proud, haughty and malevolent, those rounded outlines and angles *I knew so well...* that towering glacial head with savage red-rimmed eye! That abominable, rapacious, gonys *beak! The Kramvil! THE KRAMVIL!*

Fighting the rising cyclone of sub-polar ice that rose in my blood, I pushed the joy-stick hard to port and swung the rudder-bar round – but the starboard wing-tip was caught firm in the nightmarish *beak* of the creature, and with the sound of splintering wood and ripping sail-cloth in our ears, Lazarus and I were flung back to Earth where darkness whelmed us over.

Chapter 23

Shimmering beams of sunlight filled the air, mingling with the sweet music of song-birds. Even without opening my eyes I could see the blazing golden radiance and I could feel its warmth on my face. A breath of fresh breeze stirred around, bringing flavours of gorse, damp earth, hedgerows and heather-crowned hillsides – the original smells of the land and the country. I felt I had been floating a long time in a warm and drowsy ocean, an amniotic oceanic Lethe, fresh gurgling clear deep crystalline aqua placid waters of Pacific's far lagoons, where the all-knowing tuatara basks on his last remaining vestigial rock of Gondwana-Land. I must have drifted with the crinoids and feasted upon cycads, circling the planetary oceans, a globose and footloose medusa, a pelagian planktonic drifter, riding the Great Sargasso Sea, the Grand Banks of Newfoundland where cod and herring fatten; drifting on, picking up the Gulph Streame and catching a westerly wave.

I was an *Elasmotherium sibiricus* that had tumbled its great kornek way into a glacier in Chukchi-Land and had flowed with that Pleistocene glass river, half an inch a year, for untold aeons of Earthly time; lately to emerge, to thaw out, to feel the warm, loving sunshine and walk again, horn held proudly aloft.

The oceanic feelings of bliss welled up and I felt I'd been an albatross, skimming the waves from pole to pole, feathery migrant voyager of the great watery globe. Long solo journeys content in nature, afloat in luminous waves of frothy light, an ebullient being, joyfully on the wing. Winging through clouds of light.

Opening my orbital eyes of sight a tiny fraction initiated an initial photon-bombardment of staggering proportions, the light flared and blazed wildly and whitely – my eyes must have been closed a long time to acquire such an acute sensitivity to the light of day… How long had I lain, and where? And oh, my body ached, my ribs burned, my skin seemed punctured and perforated. My head slumped and lumped lollygagging back on the fat pluvak pillow, coagulating back into Lethe's slumberous dark stream.

*

The next time I awoke the atmosphere had changed – the former brilliant blazing radiance was now softened and mellowed into a honey-rich golden phosphorescence, the golow of a pleasant glass beehive. I ventured to open my eyes of seeing, and seeing light I reflected in my minde on the goodness of light. Seeing and knowing, the eye holds the World. Holding the World, the minde knows light. I opened my eyes and the light flowed in like a tide. As my orbs adjusted I betook my first glympse of the chamber wherein I lay. Generously proportioned and furnished in a style of archaic and rustic simplicity, the place was obviously no mean hovel or poor-folk's dwelling but seemed more like the home of a minor country-squire or prosperous farmer. A couple of oil paintings of men in top-hats, holding long-legged thoroughbreds confirmed the impression. A pair of stout, brass candlesticks glimmered in the sunshine that streamed ebulliently in at the window. Coals glowed rugose 'n' homely in focus. A bookcase across the room was stuffed with volumes. I couldn't make out the titles from where I reclined, but I could see that this was no den of illiteracy. Even the rugs on the floor looked like they could have been woven in Persepolis or Bactria. Their richly intricate patterns wove sinuous crenellations and tessellations across the multi-hued floor. Deep burgundy red, lapis lazuli blue, coral, saffron, ginger and bronze. I felt a strange contentment, mingled with a rising curiosity as to where I was. As soon as I tried to move however, my body ached in numerous places.

A door opened beside my bedside and in walked quite a large, middle-aged lady, dressed in a long skirt, blouse and shawl. Her face showed a noble character, tinged by warmth and humour.

"Ah! So you've decided to wake up, have you? Well, I s'pose you've had a nice long rest."

"Uh... have I? How long have I been asleep?"

"Oh, just the five days!"

"FIVE DAYS?!"

"And nights."

My minde was whirling now, trying mechanically to make sense of my experience. The woman seemed to read me.

"You've been in a coma my fine fellow. Concussed in a flying-machine accident. Now don't excite yourself, everything will be explained to you later, what you need now is to take your medicine and get some more rest."

"And my companion, Mr Ta-" "Mr Taxon is making a good recovery. You can see him later on. Now, swallow this tablet. Here's some water." I swallowed the medicament and washed it down with some cool, fresh water.

"My name is June, June Hill," she clasped my hand gently, "and this is Chy-an-Brae. I live here with my husband Paul, or 'Old Paul'. I believe you are a friend of our son, 'young Paul'," she said with a smile.

"And I am Elias-" "Gillpington. Yes, I've heard quite a lot about you already Elias; you aviators attract quite a lot of attention you know!"

"And you've been looking after me all this time! I am deeply indebted to you."

"Oh I haven't done much," she smiled her wise and humane smile, "most of the nursing was done by Miss Constance – she's hardly left your side!"

"Constance! But where *is* she?"

"She's gone down to the village to get some groceries. You'll be able to see her later. *After you've had some more rest."*

And with that she was gone.

*

I was coming back from far away – I'd been floating again, drifting with minde's high tide around a world of luminous dreams and realms beyond dream's reach. I was surrounded by rich ruby-red light, with bars and blazes of orange and gold. I was in a rarefied place, a subtle and aetherial zone of quiet bliss, slowed down to eternity. Someone was speaking my name, quietly calling to me. Everything was perfect.

I felt the presence of a pure being – my soul flowed out.

Suspended in transyek warm light, beyond the grasp of Kronos, another being was flowing to me and I was flowing to the other. This was more familiar, more *real,* more true.

Gradually though memories of another world trickled back – a world of solid physical *things;* a world where you must use your voice to be heard and use your feet if you want to move. A world of gravity, temporality and entropy. A clumsy, blundering world, where people make mistakes and misunderstand each other, where people are subjects of hunger, of loss, of the elements and all the ailments of the flesh that blooms and withers, blooms and withers.

The picture shifted – a hand took mine – I was awakening and a golden-red phosphorescence was flooding the chamber.

"Elias." It was the voice from before, still trailing subtle tendrils of *beyond.*

"Oh Elias, are you really back?"

It was Miss Constance! It could be no other. I struggled to the surface of a golden pool of light, blinking my eyes open and gasping in awe at the beautiful face before me."Constance!"

She was surrounded by the lambent rays of the red old sun, her dark hair and eyes aglow. I instinctively tried to sit up, but as I did so, a wave of pain and nausea sent my head crashing back upon the soft pluvak pillow, swooning back into the lake of deep forgetfulness.

*

Then, fast in my slumber, I seemed to roam the land, teeming forth with the great transhumance, crossing *all* lands and transmigrating across the continents and nations of the Earth. This *danse gothique* took me along with the early medieval pilgrimages and the equestrian conquests of Ghengis Khan. I flowed forth from the cradle of Africa, I trampled the Sibirisk tundra in pursuit of the mastodon and other juddering megafauna. I went walkabout in the outback where the sugarbags swarm and the kookaburras cackle in the jacarandas while *Jaculus jaculus* jumps for joy. From Kamchatka I swarmed with my people through Chukchi-Land and the Aleutian land-bridge into Alaska and Great Turtle Island, scattering into Inuit, Aztec, Cherokee, Toltec, Comanchee, Hopi and Sioux. I trekked for months on camels in great caravans that trod the Cathay road of shimmering silk, following the trails of Alexander and his Macedonians. Krakow and Warsaw and Petersburg loomed before me, as did Chicago, New York, Detroit, St.Louis, Pittsburgh and San Francisco. I travelled the roads and the rails and I tramped and meandered and stood on the highway with my thumb out in rain, snow and hail. And the miles piled up, and I circled this globe again and again, circumambulating endlessly, and always heading home. And I became the carefree wanderer, the gentleman of the road, the footloose drifter you saw on the edge of town the other day – always movin' on, pushin' on, never stopping, never settin' or a-settlin' down, but trav'lin' trav'lin' trav'lin' on through and headin' for yonder blue horizon out *there* somewhere…

Finally I was flung out into the stars, cast adrift and raftless in the vast glittering spatial firmament, a realm of immeasurable and terrifying beauty.

I was surfacing again, dizzy from dreams and wearily opening my eyes. I instantly remembered Constance and was moved at heart. My gaze took in the glowing coals in the grate, and through the window a star-splattered diamond sky.

The door opened quietly and a dark figure walked into the room. I heard the rattle and scratch of a matchbox and a candle was kindled. The figure turned and approached me.

"Elias, old man! It's wonderful to see you back amongst the living! We were starting to get a little worried, you know."

"Paul! It's good to see *you* again – it seems such a long time," I struggled for coherency, "there's a few things I don't understand, for example-" "Now listen here old man," he butted in, "Mum's made you some soup and doctor's orders are that you've got to drink it before engaging in any conversation. Sorry pal, but it should be quite tasty – watercress, I think it is…"

He propped me up on some pillows and I felt the warm and rich broth flow into me like life itself. For days I had fasted, bedridden and cataleptic, a cocooned and vlewek caterpillar building a voracious hunger. And before that there had been the exertion of flying the autochthonous ornithopter, the clockwork tickydew flutterer. The influx of nourishment settled and clarified my minde, helping me recall my former sense of equilibrium and lucidity.

The small bowl of broth might have been a veritable Jacobean banquet in terms of the fortitude and vigour it gave me.

"Your mother told me I've been lying here for *five days,* Paul, since the crash, since…"

Some murky and misshapen form was looming up through the fog of diffuse memory, casting a malevolent and unsettling shadow over me. Then it flew in my face – *THE KRAMVIL!! The Kramvil had attacked us and brought down the ornithopter!*

But it made no sense – we had clearly seen the Kramvil decapitated by the Legest Meur at New Lynsmouth harbour, and yet –

"The *Kramvil,* Paul – is it dead? I don't understand!

"Calm yourself, dear chap, the Kramvil is definitely dead, you need have no fear of that."

The wave of relief that flowed through me was profoundly pleasant.

"Old 'Moss-Chops' isn't too pleased with you though," continued Paul, with a glint of humour in his eye.

"What, Old Paul Hill? What have I done to offend him?"

I wondered.

"Well, you only chose his beloved giant topiary chough to crash-land your flying-machine into! He's been cultivating that thing since I was a little nipper, won't even let old Mr Delenn the gardener touch it! For some reason old Moss-Chops seems to reckon it looked better *with* a head... ha ha ha."

"Crikey! A chough you say – *Pyrrhocorax pyrrhocorax* – and I could have *sworn* it was *Larus marinus!*"

Suddenly the abject absurdity of it absorbed us hill-lair-iously and we both burst into laughter.

"Well, the old man isn't too *paloresed* about it, but I suppose it should grow back quite *priskly*," quipped Paul. "Anyway, it's hardly surprising you mistook it for the Kramvil – what with the darkness and fog, coupled with your recent, rather harrowing and intense experiences with that monstrous gull – these things leave an impression on the minde, you know."

The candle-light mixed and mingled with the rugose fire-light and through the window a glittering, shattering array of diamond stars sprinkled their twinkling dust through a cool black velvet universe of night. Out there in the Great Nebulae it was always winter. Out there in the stars it was perpetual sunrise – Howldrehevel!

"Yes, the hatchling has been rather dominating my thoughts recently," I agreed laconically.

"Sometimes when you were in the coma you would shout about the Kramvil. The doctor wanted to give you morphia, but Mr Taxon wouldn't allow it, he prescribed some remedy of his own devising and it had an obvious calming effect on you."

"And how is Lazarus now?" I asked.

"He sustained bruises and cuts and seemed fine after a day in bed."

"Good! He does have remarkable powers of re... restoration." I nearly said *revivification*.

"There is one thing though," said Paul, a slight frown of puzzlement flickering across his usually jovial face, "when we picked you out of the wreckage, we all noticed that you both looked, well, *changed.* Much thinner, and *younger* than before."

Paul placed a brass oil-lamp on the bedside table and lit it. Then he passed me a looking-glass – I was shocked at what I saw. My cheek-bones stood out, giving me an oriental look, whilst my eyes glittered with youthful fire and vigour. Looking closer I could see no trace of a wrinkle or blemish on my face whatsoever.

"According to my, admittedly rather approximate calculations," declared Paul, by way of explanation, "Mr Taxon and yourself must have been working at a minimum of five horsepower each, to get that much weight off the ground; even if you were largely riding the air-currents once you were up topside – it's hardly surprising you lost a few pounds in weight, yet from a *physiological* point of view it should take *weeks* to metabolize that much body-weight…"

"Ah well, that's due to another of Mr Taxon's scientific marvels," I explained plainly, "namely the Erebus Compound, a sort of metabolism-enhancing *gruel* that he cooked up in the lab from some sort of polar *lichen* or something."

"Great Herrings!" exfoliated Paul in wondrys amaze, "truly our Mr Taxon is the Da Vinci of Penwithershins!"

"Ha! He is that!" I greedily assented. "The compound is no mere 'accelerating syrup', as sold by the snake-oil merchants and likely to make your heart pop! This stuff is the product of a radically different and infinitely more subtle paradigm. The initial inspiration came from the writings of Davy himself! Due to the extraordinarily subtle laws of nature that are being harnessed, oxygen consumption is increased dramatically, leading to a hyper-efficient metabolisation of the surplus bodily fats. Hence the weight loss. You said Lazarus was looking thin too, didn't you?"

"That's right. Slim, lithe and *young!* How old *is* he? I always thought of him as an *old* geezer, but now he looks about thirty! And *you* Elias, you've still got the body of a twenty-five year old, but your *complexion* makes you look about nineteen!"

We both laughed at this and my body grumbled in pain. Paul must have seen me grimace.

"How are the wounds doing, dear chap?"

"Uhhnnghh! Me rib-flesh feels a bit funny and me back is a bit tender – it's these damn *eel-bites!* They've started to itch like billy-o!"

"Shall I get the eel-tincture for you?"

"No, stay a while Paul, it'll pass. I'm enjoying our chat."

"Alright old fella, as long as you're not getting too tired."

I smiled at this, feeling the vigorous eternal Chi flowing through me like the breath of a silver dragon.

"How about if I just rest for a while and you tell me all about the crash and what's been happening since I've been off with Pysky?"

"Of course, you relax and I'll talk."

Paul wandered over and looked out of the window at the stars for a moment before pulling a chair up beside the bed.

"I was in the workshop at the time, but it seems that old 'Blue', Dad's old hound started howling and moaning – this was on the Tuesday evening, a little after five. Blue slipped out of the kitchen door and proceeded to yowling and crooning all around the gardens. Well, the next minute Old Delenn goes out with a lanthorn to look for Blue but he came running back a couple of minutes later, shouting and raising a right old hubbub and a hubberdigullion altogether, I even heard it from the workshop. Delenn was babbling about 'wrecked craft' and 'machines' and 'dead men all over the shop'. So we ran back out there with him – me and the old man, closely followed by me mother, Mrs Kegyner the cook and 'Red', the other dog."

"You paint a very dramatic tableaux, Mr Hill," I observed laconically.

"Oh yes, it was certainly a moment of high drama," smiled Paul.

"When Delenn took us to the scene, we found you and Lazarus on the ground – Lazarus was knocked senseless but he arose within a few minutes – but in *your* case, we couldn't manage to awaken you. The aircraft sustained some *fairly* serious structural damage but could obviously be rebuilt. I noticed some scraps of sail-cloth entangled and dangling from the heraldic chough-hedge. Then I couldn't help seeing the funny side of it. Old Moss-Chops always says 'The Chough stands proud,' as if it symbolized everything that is dear in his world. But the chough stood so proud that *you went and flew into it!* Ha ha ha." I laughed with him and me eel-bites hurt again.

"Anyway," continued Paul, "we picked you both up and brought you into the house. After that Dr Heskenn came and examined you both. He found Lazarus virtually unharmed, apart from a little bruising. He recommended a couple of days of bed-rest and stout rations – Lazarus lasted a day in bed and the following day was strolling in the hills and setting up what he calls his 'miniature laboratory' in a corner of the workshop. The man's indefatigable! In your case though, old Doc Heskenn was a lot more concerned. Because of your continuing state of unconsciousness he made several return visits. What really puzzled him though was the eel-bites. He couldn't make head nor tail of them and couldn't decide whether you'd sustained them during the accident or beforehand. I tried to fob him off by saying that you did a lot of hunting with ferrets, by way of a pastime, and it was probably just the result of an old sporting accident. I'm not sure he bought it though, as he went away muttering to himself," here Paul pulled a grotesque face and mimicked the doctor's voice... "Most peculiar.... Hmmm... perplexing... and somewhat singular... hmmm... *never seen anything like it in all me born days!* Ah-*HA HA HAA!*

Well, the following day, old Delenn and I put the remains of your lovely kite onto a hay-cart and trundled it over to the workshop. We'd just finished unloading the old cabbage-crate and I'd put the kettle on the stove for a nice drop of tay to wet our whistles. Delenn was plying me with questions about 'these 'ere flying-machines then' – he'd been converted overnight into an aeronautics-maniac and wanted me to tell him everything there was to know on the subject. I was just trying to explain to him that that might take quite a while, when old Red and Blue started up a yammering again and a carriage arrived – it was Miss Florence and Miss Constance, hot-foot from New Lynsmouth and the strange goings-on down there. They expected to find you here and as my mother has known both the girls' families for many years, she invited them to stay at the house. Constance's nursing skills became immediately obvious and your care has been largely in her hands." He caught my eye. "I think it was my mother and Mrs Kegyner who bathed you the other day though, ah-*HA HA HA!*"

It was funny to think of being washed in my sleep – like a great catfish being scrubbed by the fish-monger. In unconsciousness we all relapse into proto-therapsid primal ecstasies as we float in a rich, fermenting stew of impressions, concepts and images, our bodies left conveniently behind on the shores of Terrafirma.

"Miss Florence, or should I say 'the future *Mrs Lane'?*" he grinned, "has also made herself indispensable about the place – everything from helping Mrs Kegyner prepare the meals, to keeping father busily engaged in debate on such topics as 'Women's Suffrage' and 'the future of Ireland' – I get the impression they both love a good lively argument and wouldn't have *half* so much fun if they saw eye to eye!"

I could see the two fiery souls fighting it out – one for tradition, one for progress – one for entrenched stability, one for youth's winged adventure and daring deeds. I hadn't met Old Paul Hill, or 'Moss-Chops', as his son preposterously dubbed him, but everything I'd heard seemed to describe a man of panache, tenacity and a flaring blaze of individualism.

"In the meantime, and with the approval of Lazarus, I've been dismantling the damaged parts of the machine, removing torn areas of 'skin' and all the broken and tangled wiring. We decided not to start the reconstruction until you were able to be involved."

"Thanks Paul, I appreciate that."

"Well anyway, Lazarus has spent a lot of time pursuing what look like *chemical* experiments over in his corner, when he's not doing his exercises or walking in the hills, that is! Yesterday he even took one of the horses out for the afternoon – I think he's enjoying his… convalescence – or should I say *rejuvenation?* He really is like a man re-born!

Delenn has started taking his numerous krousts and

'little drops of tay' in the workshop and is building up a good rudimentary knowledge of applied aerodynamics."

"Well you know Paul," I vociferated, "we've always been brilliant engineers here in the Shyre, perhaps if the mining is in decline, then our local innovators will take to the air – sounds better than burrowing around underground if you ask me – ha ha ha…"

"Hmmm, I'm not sure if Jack would agree with your sentiments, even though he is a true *pioneer-aviator himself!*"

We laughed again at the memory of him dangling from a net in the claws of the Kramvil, flying over Unstable-Hobbla.

"How is Jack anyway?" I asked.

"He's fine. He was here a couple of days ago and I think we're expecting him back tomorrow, if I remember rightly."

Paul paused in his narrative to stoke the fire and add some more coal and a couple of hawthorn logs. The fire crackled noisily before blazing up in a fountain of golden-ruby warmth and radiant glow. The room shone with the little chough's beaks of red flame – the fire-crow! The fire-crow! Richly glowed the chamber, every shade of amber, coral, claret, honey, balsam, stained-glass and mahogany; violet velvet and chestnut myrrh. My body glowed with energy from the bowl of soup, the quilts and blankets seemed luxuriant and resplendent with ease and contentment. Paul's discourse had also relaxed me. It was good to hear news of people and the great onward flow of life and unceasing activity. I had slept like Rip Van Winkle, but, as the profound cliche has it, 'life goes on'.

"As far as the local news goes," continued Paul, "one or two of the uplanders must have spotted the ornithopter coursing through the foggy dusk, as when Mrs Kegyner was up at Gwynjak Wartha she heard some wild talk of giant birds or bats invading the area – there seemed to be a lively debate going on as to just what form the *behemoth* took! By now, rumours of the events in and around New Lynsmouth will also have filtered into these parts, so no doubt people will be avidly on the lookout for monstrosities, crustaceans and misshapen and misbegotten creations in general… With any luck this climate of fear and unease will at least keep people close to their own hearths and deter them from snooping around here whilst we're trying to conduct scientific work."

An owl hooted in the chilly crisp air of the plateau of night, the feathery voice of nature, ancient and wild.

"Well, old fella," Paul concluded, "I really must cease my clack and leave you in peace again – I was cautioned not to tire you out. Miss Constance is most protective of you Elias, in fact, I suspect she might be a wee tiny bit *fond* of you, if I'm not mistaken…"

"I expect you are Paul," I rejoined flatly and we both laughed again.

"Well, I'll be off, but first is there anything you need?"

"No, thanks a lot but no. You've all been very kind to me."

"Well, we like it when people drop in unexpectedly!"

He extinguished the oil-lamp and candle and left me to slumber. I felt fortunate to have such reliable friends as these. Nestled in warmth, I gazed out into the wintry sky where myriad stars were flung far and phosphorescent, like a shimmering fire-fly herd.

I felt better after talking with Paul. It was good to know that the Kramvil was definitely dead. It was thrilling to think of Constance being here, and that I would finally be able to spend some time with her. After the maelström of recent events, it seemed almost miraculous to be able to spend some peaceful time with a lovely girl. This thought filled me with dizzy warmth and I rested my head content in a pillow of dreamy bliss.

Dozing, skimming along the surface meniscus of sleep's brimming beaker, sinking briefly into dream, then soaring up to wakefulness, thus I rested and mused, and another thought rose slowly in my minde. The flight… we had succeeded… we had flown! Lazarus and I could now be counted among the ranks of the pioneer-aviators. We had built a craft to our own design and successfully flown it over several miles of open country. We had flown without an engine and we had flown at night – these things simply *weren't done!* I felt very enthusiastic about rebuilding the ornithopter and trying out Paul's engine. It went beyond enthusiasm – to build and fly your own aircraft seemed like the finest thing in the World and to be living in the Age of Flight was an incredibly fortunate occurrence – surely the aeroplane is at least as great a breakthrough for humanity as the discovery of fire, or the invention of the wheel or the printing press... Of all the people who had ever lived upon the Earth, to be among the tiny handful who had ridden the air in a flying-machine felt like we were making history, contributing to the advancement of human culture. Then there was another thing – flying was fun, flying was extremely exhilarating and flying gave you an undreamed-of sense of freedom – I couldn't *wait* to go up again...

The glowing coals in the grate were dimmer now, greying over with ashes. The owl hooted again from out in the winter night and the stars sang their notes of light against a dark ground. I was flying *between* the stars now, I had left my body behind and found myself flung free from my fleshy envelope, tracing the trajectories of comets, asteroids, galactic-clusters...

Then the whirring of wings, many wings and the chirping of myriad beaks was heard. Feathers fluttered and the air was a-stir. Highways opened in the air as vast flocks of migratory wanderers swarmed across the globe, driven by forces ancient and collective, inherited from Seymouria and the ancestral Cotylosauria.

The great solitary condor floated over mountain-peaks whilst the wren flitted through the rambling hedgerow. All wings were a-stir and all birds were a-wing. Wings whirled up new winds which went wisping hwyth with withering whistling squalls hurled around the World. Blusters blew battering barns abroad, bundling bales of billows bowling blithely skyward. Wings rode the winds and claws clew the clouds.

These dark and towering accumulations of cloudy moisture carved ephemeral continents displaying ceaseless originality and invention – a realm of appearance without form. These wispy mountains of the World's steamy breath stretched out in an open and rolling topography that seemed to undulate and spread its reach to the far corners of space.

Glas yw an ebrenn. Blue is the sky. Y ouranos. The sky… The sky shadow a Gothic skuggwa – cloud-mirror of archaic rune-riddled Awld Nawz skuggi – the sky – Open wide the vault of heaven… this and similar phrases echoed through my dew-drenched and richly rippling psyche; divine consciousness, riding the breath like a buttorfleoge arisen from the slumbering kuchuan of the causal chatapelose. Sleep. Minde hanging nowhere in space. Minde like sky. Mentis skiuja. The skio – the sceo; the scuwo. Skimming linguistic labyrinthine layers of memory's archaic mnemonic archives; body floating off down the Lethe, riverrun down to merge with the Liffey at the polyglot confluence of many an aled-time babbling tongue, glossy and hospitably spitting glossaries at the horsepittal. Neigh! Aye! An' all in the name of the eye-blue sky. Caelestis sparkles with phthallo-blue, and blue is the sky – glas yw an ebrenn. And we threw our gaze upon a grette glassy heaven, and we knew that it was *good.*

The insubstantial swirling world of clowdes unfurling through ringing radiant galleries of blissful *goodness.* Echoing bronze chimes down aery halls, agoras and stoas; fish-flecking mackerel skies spreading flocks of woolly-pelted cloud-scheepe of the skye scattered on hills of pluvek plough (pluff) and buffeting hwyths of Chywoone's juddering chough. The wonderful jynn-ebrenn. The aeroplane. Sailing over the Shyre in our jynn-edhen – ornithopteral heaven! Blue is the sky deep-lit with summer's brilliance extending to infinity – this clear immaculate cluudscape. Molecules of lapis lazuli mosaic dancing in dazzling space. Blue is the sky. The sky is blue.

*

The hooting of a feather-festooned ulchabhan oulys, gwdihw in ivy-trees silvery, holding on with claws clutching chilly twigs – idhyowek, occasionally punctuating my misty smúitiúil dreamings with the purple wild cry of its rhynchus beak and secret fluty throat. I founde myself to be flying over scapes of the rustic nocturne, woods, hills and fields and streams glinting with the marmaroglypheion phosphorescent glaze from the rays of the rising moon. The lands o'er which

I magically flew were wrapped in restful sleep, hushed silent still emptied and pure. I followed my daemon and wilfully travelled wither whetherfore wherever I wished to go. This form of flight was full of ease – I knew it to be my true condition – I felt I had recovered a buried secret gift. The mother-of-pearl landscape unfurled its cloak before me in shades of blue, silver, pewter and grey whilst a subtle breeze stirred the trees to gently sough and shimmer brittle lacy twigs. Forests, woods and fields, unfamiliar lands of beauty and charm were given to my eye. Waxwings pecked at hawthorn berries and the churring of the red-necked churranos nightjar rippled up in fronds of cloud-mirror night-time. A land held fast in dreaming. A sky galactic and kommolek, in mackerel scattered flecks immaculate and slowly moving, to accentuate its grace. More stars than clouds really, and more moonglow light than starlight as the chipped white disc rolled slowly up the sky. The constellations were standing sharp in cold wintry air. Fields of endless beauty and variety, painted in silver, in pewter, in blue-white lunar sheen…

The churring night furls, rolling rich rugs and tapestries of bucolic topography. The land. The land. The Holy Old Land. Dripping rich in history, its ghostly players strut a batholithic stage. The land a mere island, a mere finger sticking out of the sea – most of the land is drowned over and turned to the dominion of the fishes, making Cerniu so small and precious – gem-like. This rich sliver of land, bubbling up with metaliferous treasure and crusted and dusted in a loam-layer of dorek soil, from which untold throngs of country-folk had drawn a Spartan living. Under the hush of night, a curtain of tranquillity was drawn over this land, and in muted greys and blues, with pools of dark hollows and patches of looming tewlwolow, the dorean land gave freely of its solid-earth-lucidity. Mute adoration filled the dewy valleys, wisps and hwyths of ethereal mists slowly spun subtle spindrift plumes for the moon to lume with silver light and each pond and puddle was ablaze in diamond cassiterite scintillating blazing glory.

I felt the tide of my soul flow out, the cloudy luminescence quietly brightened into a rising glow – I felt a presence approaching me – I felt I *knew* this being.

Gradually this weightless sense of knowing and communing faded away and I could feel my aching body and I wonderingly opened my eyes.

The moon had crept into the room, painting its silver sheen and rarefied glow-worm shine all around. Its broken coin was peeping in through the window-pane, throwing its light on a vision of deep and rare beauty – Miss Constance!

She was sitting in a chair beside the bed, wearing a long skirt of dark maroon velvet with a matching jacket. Her luxuriant dark mahogany hair cascading over her strong, young shoulders. Her eyes gleamed, yet her face exuded kindness and concern. To me she was a vision of the perfect woman, a goddess in the flesh. I couldn't feel ordinary in her presence. We looked at each other for some moments.

"You look a little better, Elias," she said quietly, in a voice mellifluous and warm. She shyly took my hand and squeezed it gently.

"I *feel* so much better, *now,*" I replied, and we held each other's hands tightly for a moment, before both withdrawing in shyness, and an electric silence.

We had been raised under a rigid code of propriety and formal etiquette. Even though she *was* a nurse doing her duty and I *was* a legitimate patient recovering from a serious accident; still, she was also a *woman* and I was a *man,* in bed…

Then again… it was 1911 and we were both adults, who, though young, had already faced life and death – me as a scientist and aeronaut and Constance in her work with the horrifically injured and dying miners of Parc Hellis.

The tension between form and feeling was becoming too much for Constance, added to the shock of what she had seen at the field hospital, and then several days of sitting by my bedside, wondering if *I* would ever wake up, her feelings welled up and overflowed. I noticed she was quietly weeping. I glimpsed a falling tear glint in a moonbeam.

"Constance! What *is* it?" I asked, shocked by her outburst. But she leant forward, holding me by my shoulders and let herself be carried away by a rolling tide of weeping, dripping her salty tears on my face like a divine dewfall. I held her in my arms and tried to calm her, feeling, as I did so, an arising glow of tenderness rising up like the Sun.

"Oh Elias! Sometimes I thought you'd never wake up from your coma. Or I thought maybe you would awake, but be *damaged* somehow, that you might never recover your memory, or your ability to function or, or, *that you might just die! When you have so much to offer the world, with the flying-machine, and... and...*"

As another wave of sobs washed through her I held Constance tight in my arms and she soon became still. A calm, still, natural woman. After some moments she looked up and caught my eye – she looked transformed, as if she had returned from an epic voyage, almost a rite of initiation, of experience.

"Constance." I said her name as if it were a magical cypher that held the secrets of eternal truth, of inexplicable layers of mystery. "I couldn't have died – I haven't taken you flying yet!"

We both laughed at this and it lifted and lightened the atmosphere. Constance sat up, wiping her eyes, and smiling – I couldn't get used to her beauty. Footsteps were approaching down the corridor. We looked at each other, both knowing that the new world that was tentatively growing up between us was about to be intruded upon by someone else. A last brief gaze into the deep-space of her eyes and the door quietly opened.

It was Mrs June Hill, carrying a small tray containing a lighted candle, a glass of water and a lozenge.

She smiled serenely and put the little tray on the bedside table and without a word, handed me the lozenge and the water – being a man to take a hint, I swallowed both. She then turned towards Constance.

"And how is our patient getting along Constance?" asked June with a kindly smile.

"Oh I believe he's starting to recover, Miss June," answered Constance in a voice that revealed a depth of feeling.

"Thanks to you both!" I put in, "without your kindness I

don't know where I'd be, I really don't!"

"Still tangled up in my husband's beloved *hedge* presumably!" said June with a smile and we all laughed. She was an understanding woman and seemed to intuit the emotion between Constance and I.

"Well my dears," she concluded, "It's three twenty a.m. and I think it's time we all got some rest." She paused just a second. "I'll leave you two to say goodnight." With that she was gone.

I sunk my weary happy head back on the pillows. There she was! She looked on me tenderly, glowing in dark feminine radiance. For an instant her lips brushed my forehead, then she blew out the candle and slipped out of the door. The moon was setting and even the owl was still.

*

The origin of Chy-an-Brae, like the origin of phenomenal reality, is lost in the sacred darkness of Tewlyjyon. A Hill family legend claims that when the Normans sent a man to the Hinterland to survey the resources of the local area, for what was to be the Domesday Book, back in '86, a remote ancestor of the family, one Gorhengeugh Brayye, had entertained the tax-collector at his Manor; plied him generously with mead and sent him back to Exeter sitting backwards on a donkey. When he got there, the poor fellow had no recollection of where he had been, and hence very little tax was ever collected from the Hinterland, a tradition that had hardly altered right up to the present time. Since the area had escaped official intrusion, it was very much left to minde its own affairs. The brooding isolation of the surrounding hills had cocooned the central plateau in a distinct and discreet screen of secrecy.

Chy-an-Brae, in various forms and incarnations, various rebuildings and versions, had stood resplendent at the heart of this central plateau since at least the Bronze Age, if not the Neolithic. Continuous occupation of strategic sites was the norm here, in this wild upland country, just as it was everywhere else in Penwithershins. Epochs had drifted past the eaves of the old manse. The same stones had been raised up to form the house, many times over, separated by the gulphs of many sunny and dust-dancing centuries. The generous deposits of tin in the surrounding hills had been worked by local tinners for four thousand years. There was a most resilient continuity of culture in this region, and somehow the old house came to embody the ongoing spirit of that culture.

Country-people hereabouts still carry folk-memories from the dark ages, and many uplanders are familiar with the twilight tale of a grette and terrible pestilence that fell on the Shyre, bringing a morbid and premature end to above one third of the populace. This was a time of great migrations and peoples on the move. To escape the plague, large numbers of Kornyshe folk fled the Shyre and sailed across France-Water to start a new life in Armorica. This flow of souls from Kernow to Europe had originally been encouraged by the Romans, who were busily pushing the Gauls back from the Armorican Peninsula. This vast new influx of Ancient Brythonic Kernouac immigrants, happy to escape both the vile pestilence and the increasing Saxon threat to Dumnonia, made their new country a little version of the Britain they had left behind and named it Breten Vyghan, or Brittany. Many of those left behind in Cerniu were not so fortunate and many villages were plagued. Graveyards were running out of space to include any more corpses and the *plague-pit* came into being. When tidings of such eldritch nature started reaching the ears of the hill-dwellers and upland-folk, they effectively cordoned off their entire locality of scattered farms and hamlets and sealed their borders to all outside contact. This was done with such zeal, and so effectively, that many, many years after the pestilence had left the land, the *hills* remained cut off in their lofty isolation, a closed kingdom, a miniature Tibet.

Chy-an-Brae had always been thought of as something of a sanctuary and some people associate the locality with monks or hermits – on what evidence I know not. One thing is certain though – the old house had stood dreaming away, its slate roofs dripping in the good, niwlek, mizzly, Cornysh mist for numerous very long and eventful centuries. Many a Hill had been raised here and many a Hill levelled flat.

Thus in this storied and ancient house it was that I awoke to find the chamber flooded in bright and cheerful sunshine. I felt well rested and happily content, energized and curious to explore my surroundings – *and find something to eat.*

I sat up, feeling only slightly dizzy, then gingerly stood up. I immediately had the curious sensation of being a species of weightless jelly-fish; a sort of floating head. At most a torso. A disembodied, insubstantial, polymolecular torso, floating along on a river of syrup. I floated over to the dresser and was fascinated to see my 'new' face, younger and thinner – verging on the gaunt. I needed *food!* I found my clothes all laundered and folded up and with some effort, managed to put them on. Finally I left the chamber where I had reclined for so many days and nights, lost to the World, and set out to have a look around.

Feeling like a feather in the breeze, I glided down a long and wide corridor, a geometric corridor, punctuated by many stout oaken doors and between the doors were various dark and antiquated portraits of this ancient family; for around these parts there were not many families that were as old as the Hills. The portraits, even at a glance, spoke of pugnacious and independent people. One particular character caught my eye as I continued my plagioclase flow down the landing – a mid-eighteenth century gent-fellow in preposterous powdered wig of rolling curls and coat of multi-hued paisley silk. His cravat was an outrageous and extravagant efflorescence of finest Kernish lace, his jaws swaddled and coddled in fluffy puffs of prodigious mutton-chop excrescences. I remember wondering how such an ugly specimen could sire a line that would manifest itself in the form of my goodly colleague Paul Hill (the younger) who, after all, was really not at *all* hideous to look upon.

I walked on down the hall, feeling a little bit more substantial and embodied. The staircase was eight feet wide. I followed its grand sweep as it twisted down into a spacious hallway. Luxuriant leafy plants and ferns stood around in pots. Here and there an ancient and rusty pair of swords, an antiquated arquebus, a long-barrelled gun of the sea, a pair of duelling 'barkers', and a shield embossed in Keltek curly-work. Everything in this ante-chamber seemed to gleam with vibrant sunlight, including a small chandelier that broke the light into vivid prismatic lyws and hues. My eye followed the vivacious sun-beams to a window, through which I beheld a garden of great beauty and charm. Without hesitation I opened the door and stepped outside.

The sunlight burst upon my orbitals in howlyek streaming polychromatic photon-bombardment. My lids squinted and my pupils contracted, retinas reflected and optic nerves connected. Light streaming and languorously pulsating. The luming light had a curative and awakening effect, ushering in health and vitality after my time of darkness, when I had floated in pelagic suspension like a jellygraph image of a comb-jelly.

As the wisps of light cleared from my eyes, I could see that I was in an extremely large and formally laid out garden of great charm and allure. I felt like a chess-piece moving into a new game. Checkers and squares of paving-stones ran in sweeping geometric lines; gravel drives curved gracefully around; avenues of divers trees – columnar cypresses, yews, beeches; rearing up here and there were monkey-puzzles, round which clacked rooks flocking a-flap. There were balustrades and gate-posts topped with enormous globes of granite; herb-gardens, ponds and pools of various sizes; vegetable plots; greenhouses and hot-houses and meadows, little patches of woods and many decorative flower-beds and shrubberies, interlaced by sinuous meandering paths with secluded arbours and bowers. There was a rose-garden and a stoa festooned in wisteria and passion-flower. There were many areas of open green lawn with rustic seats and benches scattered around, and there was the derelict ruin of an archaic building known as the Magor. Near the southern perimeter of this quiet and idyllic realm was the topiary-hedge that we'd crashed into.

The day was drenched in sunlight and wandering around this vast and beautiful garden, after so many days of dark isolation, filled me with a euphoria that bordered on trance.

This garden, or rather I should say 'these gardens', as they really were manifold, myriad and divers; offered endless charming surprises, views and juxtapositions of epiphytic genera.

Ambulating slowly and languorously through, I looked forth into a mesozoic jungle – a miniature valley totally filled with tree-ferns, their archetypal and atavistic fronds reaching down to me with finger-tips of freshest new green. Well could I visage a herd of ancestral, morek, drenek, spiny, green, mottled, air-lunged, pedreven pelicosaurs foraging here, in this forest of early trees. Diametrically opposite the geometric zig-zag wandering path, with its daphnis, chloe and rhododendron, here where terror soared on leathery membranes, scaly feet trampled the dust of trilobites and dimetrodon leers large, looming after the inexplicable edaphosaurus.

These proto-plants were built in sinews of symmetrical whorls and bracts, arching off and interlacing each other into intricate and graceful compositions. Innumerable beads of dew clung to the tree-fern fronds, blazing tiny dazzling flashes of deep violet, crimson, scarlet, viridian, lapis lazuli, azure, topaz, orange, citron and vivid purple. This enhanced and transformed this therapsid paradise into a subtle, glittering piskie-land of miniature multicoloured glints of myriad lyw and hue.

I walked on through this glistening primordial forest and found myself on a path, running between low and neatly clipped box hedges. To my left lay a highly cultivated vegetable garden, richly composted and awaiting spring-planting. To my right lay a small and secluded lawn, encircled with apple and pear trees with, in the far corner, a granite bench in a little 'grotto', a folly of rough-hewn blocks, constructed by one of the more energetic ancestors, no doubt.

As I continued, I could hear the gurgling and splash of running water and I soon came to a small but lively stream and crossed it by an ancient bridge of a great granite slab. The gardens opened out into parkland, with meadows, fine chestnut and beech trees, and feathery strands of mist drifting over the lake where cows waded the muddy shoreline and dragon-flyes manoeuvred and spun on the wing, hunting the winged arthropoda. Suddenly I felt ravenously hungry and the gelatinous, disembodied feelings of spinning, weightless dizziness returned. I thought I should go back to the house and seek nourishment there. The gardens were indeed vast and rambling, as I discovered when I tried to leave them... I roamed from parkland to woodland and from there to far-flung shrubbery. I floated through formal herb-gardens, walled-gardens and leafy quiet arbors and bowers of soughing silence. Though nine times gnawed by hunger's howling claws, yet was I so fascinated and entranced with the endless variety and natural beauty before my thirsty eyes that I was most happy to wander, to ramble and roam, lost in a sort of paradise. Eventually I tripstumbled upon a paved courtyard with stables and workshops on three sides of it. I peered through a dusty window but saw only some horse-stalls, hay and tackle – obviously a working stable. The waft of sweet hay added to my light-headedness with its overpoweringly intoxicating fragrance. I leant against the sunny red-brick wall to steady myself, I really did need to eat – something very large; very soon...

I opened another door and lurched within. Something went flying past my head – a giant dragonfly? No, it was a tiny model aircraft with noisily flapping wings driven by a rubber band! The toy bounced off the wall near my head and landed on the floor, where it buzzed and flapped convulsively.

"Gillpington! What are *you* doing here? The search party's been looking for you all over the shop!"

The oil-streaked visage of Paul Hill grinned at me good-naturedly; behind him, a figure approached from across the spacious workshop – it was Lazarus Taxon!

"Wonderful to see you again Elias," he said, grasping my hand warmly, "you've been away for quite some time, you know..." I was searching his face, he looked *different,* younger again and slimmer, just as Paul had said... "It's good to be back, Lazarus," I replied with a smile, "when are we going to start rebuilding the kite?"

"Now slow down, old man," put in Paul, "for one thing, you're supposed to be recuperating from the crash; and for another thing, we haven't had kroust yet!"

"Did you say *kroust?*" I must have betrayed a certain zealous enthusiasm – they were both laughing and Paul produced a large box of cheese and pickle sandwiches.

I can honestly say that I've never feasted on more wonderful fare in my entire life – the sandwiches melted away under my velociraptor grinding and guzzling jaws like they'd never existed. Paul brewed some tay on a little stove, then he and Lazarus sat in a couple of deck-chairs, while insisting that I reclined on an old couch and referring to me amongst themselves as 'the patient'.

It was a soporific pleasure to recline in rococo style and listen to the aerudite discussion of 'wing-morphing', drag-reduction and the loose torque of aerial beam-engines. The heavy bread was dragging me to the brink of the abyss of sleep – I wasn't fighting back. I felt a deep solidarity with the scientific endeavours of my two colleagues, and being witness to the interplay of their clear, vivacious and powerful mindes was rich food for the intellect......

"It's the eel-bites, I think they're at the itchy stage." Lazarus was explaining to Florence, who was listening earnestly.

"He should not have gone wandering around like that! We were getting concerned. Mrs Kegyner's been in a flap all day and Constance has been strangely quiet..."

I opened a groggy eye or two. I was drenched in sweat and the eel-tooth-needle-wounds were giving me level three gyp! My rib-flesh groaned in renewed complaint and I felt like a low-down dog who drunk dirty water and slept in an ol' holler lawg...

"Sorry Florence – itchy feet – hope I haven't caused too much upset..."

"You men and your *science!* Couldn't you at least recover from your last wild adventure before hurling yourself into the next one?" Her frown became a smile and she walked over and gave me a kiss.

"It's good to see you again Elias," she said warmly, "how are you feeling now, after all you've been through?"

"Sweaty and itchy, Florence, I think 'the patient' needs a

bath!"

"Well, Chy-an-Brae happens to contain a bathroom," she hinted, "if we can extract you from the clutches of your fellow mad-professors for five minutes!"

Paul looked at Lazarus. "I think we'll have to let him go, Mr T!"

"Looks that way," returned the eld laconically, "better take this 'snake-oil' to put on the bites after the bath."

I took the proffered vial of scintillating juice, thanked him and went with Florence back to that sprawling, centuried manse set in its archaic realm of mystery, at the heart of the hinterland-plateau.

*

"Father, this is my dear friend Elias Gillpington!" Paul spake unto Paul and I found myself gazing upon the legendary 'Moss-Chops' at last – Old Paul Hill!

"It's a great pleasure to meet you at last, Mr Hill," I said, taking the hand he offered.

"Nice to have you *drop* in on us, Mr Gillpington. I trust you are making a good recovery?"

"I am, thanks to the great kindness of everyone here."

"Good! Good! Glad to hear it," he said heartily, "now, tell me, what exactly do you have against the noble art of topiary?"

His blunt and woolly face loomed towards mine, above a bulbous eye-globe a brow arched in Lacadaemonian humorous irony. His chops were indeed mossy with a snowy exuberance of abundant, whiskery hirsutelage. His calfish visage, domed pate, furious white hair, laughterous eye and port-stained lips minded me of one of the ancestral portraits upstairs. Not a tall man, he was muscled as an ox and had enormous shoulders and a barrel-chest that made him look like a guardsman standing to attention when he was reclining in an arm-chair. He looked like he was constantly rearing up like a horse that's trodden on a snake. The scarlet jacket he preferred to wear only added to the outré and idiosyncratic flavour of his character. His eye glowed with soul, a-glint with therapsid and protean intelligence as it met my gaze.

I was mentally trying to frame an apology, as I knew that the Chough-Hedge meant a lot to the old duffer, but he surprised me by bursting into loud laughter.

"Well, it needed a trim, I suppose – but, damn it all; *let's eat!*" His chops quivered with mirth's shivering outburst and with that, the three of us went through into the dining-room to join the others.

The spacious chamber exuded an air of solidity rather than ostentation. More like the architecture of Tibetans or Minoans than the timid neo-classical you would expect to find in such a house as this. A purposeful fire bloomed bright in an inglenook that could sit half a dozen large rustics. Myriad candles and oil-lamps pooled their glow and a photoprismatic chandelier split and mixed the light anew. There was a fine painting of the Sphinx of Egypt, one of a clipper-ship in a tempest and a third showing a large man in a long coat and truncated top-hat holding an astronomically vast bull by a rope. In a corner of the room stood a fathom-high and antiquated concert harp, its bas-relief angelic figurehead embodying the Parnassian Muse. Finding myself somehow to be sitting opposite Miss Constance, I wondered if I'd be able to take my eyes off her and join in the general conversation... She was wearing a regency-style dress with her hair swept back, something like a vision of a Kouri from the Akropolis of Athens. Her modest smile let me know I was forgiven for going 'walkabout'.

As soon as Mrs Hill had mumbled a hasty 'grace', Old Paul stood up, picked up the carving knife and started grinding it rapidly against a steel. This was obviously a pre-arranged signal as no sooner had he started, than a door flew open and in trooped Mrs Kegyner and Mr Delenn, each carrying a platter bearing a roast chicken. These they placed on the table and withdrew, soon to return with various vegetables and sauces. I felt a strange aversion to eating the birds, and pleading a light appetite, settled for some vegetables and potatoes. When all the plates were heaped up Old Paul tapped his glass with a knife.

"I'd like to propose a toast," he announced, leaning

forwards in his chair, his scarlet elbows on the table, his robin-redbreast sternum stuck out in sympathy with his pugnacious jaw. There was a moment of silence, then he continued.... "to Lazarus Taxon and Elias Gillpington and their successful flight from New Lynsmouth to Chy-an-Brae."

To the amazement of Lazarus and I, they all started clapping and cheering us as if we were some kind of homecoming Homeric heroes back from Troy! I looked at the faces around the table, stunned. There was old Moss-Chops, implausibly leading the chorus of applause, his face now taking on the hue of his lucid jacket. Red and Blue sat at his feet, a habit that annoyed his wife, who considered it 'medieval'. The hounds now bayed us be silent. The younger Paul sat next to his father, face lit with enthusiasm, then Constance, looking happy and possibly proud of our strange flight. There was Lazarus, his eye aglow with contented intelligence. Next to me sat June Hill, clapping vigorously and looking from side to side, smiling at everybody as if to say "They flew! They *flew!* On my other side was Florence, looking euphoric. Lazarus Taxon bowed his head and held up his hands for a silence that took a while to arrive.

"Dear friends," he started, "we could not have flown to a better place! Since we blundered our way into your home, you have tended our wounds, mopped our fevered brows and shown us the greatest possible kindness. We will never forget that. Flying here, to Chy-an-Brae, was what we scientists call a successful experiment. As you know, our previous experiment, the case of the gull, was a terrible disaster that brought incalculable harm upon New Lynsmouth and thus, by way of recompense, I plan to donate the ownership of several of my patents to a trust I am setting up. This will accumulate monies and, as soon as is possible, set up an engineering works in the port to employ local labour, skilled and apprentice, and pay them Union rates. The profits, after all costs are paid out, will go towards repairing the fishing boats and paying medical bills and other damages and expenses incurred by the terrible bird."

This met with warm approval from the gathering. I was moved by Lazarus's plan.

"You know Lazarus, I'd be very happy to relinquish any credit for the tail design on the ornithopter patent, if you were thinking-" "Yes, I was thinking of donating the ornithopter patent, if you are in agreement."

"Well," put in June "the patent to your 'man-made bird' must be worth a king's ransom! I should think it could pave the streets of New Lynsmouth with gold!"

Paul looked up, a bright look in his eye. "You can have the beam-engine too. Put the patent towards the fund."

This caused another explosion of feeling. Old Paul patted his son proudly on the shoulder.

"Well done, boy! You'll never be rich, but you will get to heaven!" Then he filled two glasses with wine and insisted that Mrs Kegyner and Mr Delenn join us in a toast, "to the future!"

The jangling of a distant bell set old Red 'n' Blue a-howlin' and a hollerin' again, and Mr Delenn disappeared and came back with none other than the lanky and laconic Jack Lane.

"I would have got here sooner," he paused dramatically, "but I haven't got an *aeroplane!* Ha ha ha!"

Jack pulled up a chair between June and I and was given food and drink. He pursued his plate of chicken with vulpine relish, like a fox raiding the hen-house.

Old Palores Paul, the Chough of Chy-an-Brae puffed out his great rugose Palaeozoic chest and ambled into a vocal outburst. "Dear friends," he rumbled, "let us drink another toast, to Jack and Florence, the future Mr and Mrs Lane – may they have every happiness!"

"And may the lanes of New Lynsmouth echo with the patter of many little feet!" blurted out June, in a moment of inspiration that was met with mirth and warmth. I hesitated to catch Constance's eye, but when I did she met my gaze with a wise and knowing smile.

The candles glinted in magical marmareegy glittering light, the air was as if compressed by the wings of fruit-bats, whip-poor-wills and goatsuckers – compressed, that is, into blocks, chunks, bricks and ingots of extremely rarefied and mystically charged atmosphere in which we basked resplendent.

June Hill was most curious to know all about the flying-machine and started plying Lazarus with questions, to which I noticed Mr Delenn paying close attention.

"Well, you see, a *conventional* aeroplane, whether biplane or monoplane, gains its 'lift', or upward motion by the rapid propulsion of aerofoils through the air," began Lazarus, "whereas *our* kind of aircraft, an *ornithopter*, attacks the air in a much more vertical fashion, more in the manner of a bird."

"A bird, yes." agreed June excitedly.

"Unlike a typical 'fixed-wing' machine," he continued, "the ornithopter actually *flaps* its wings."

"Extra-*ordinary!*" spluttered the woolly jowls of the scarlet patriarch, a saturnine therapsid satrap rattling rasps of theoretical rhapsody.

"Not only that," flowed the eld, "but each time the wings are raised, they fold along two lateral axes and diminish the surface-area opposing the air. Then, on the down-stroke, the wing widens out as it unfolds, thus pushing against the air and raising the machine."

"Utterly extra-ordinary!" repeated Moss-Chops.

"Indeed so," concurred Taxon "and whilst all this is going on, the wing-tips are also being warped up or down, to facilitate a 'banked' turn." He demonstrated the movement with a sweep of his hand.

"You'll be able to see for yourself soon enough, Mum," added Paul, "as soon as we've rebuilt the old kite and stuck the new engine in we'll be doing test-flights around the area!"

This brought further excitement – the idea of an *aeroplane* flying around the place suddenly struck everyone as an extremely wonderful thing to see.

"Great bats o' the Moon!" thundered Moss-Chops, "I hope you'll be watching out for me ruddy hedges, ya young *dare-divils!*"

"Don't worry father," rejoined his ebullient namesake, "we'll leave the hedge-clipping up to you, eh Mr Delenn?" and he leaned back and clinked his glass with that of the old gardener, who also doubled as butler, coachman etc., etc....

"And whilst we're on the subject of *hedges,*" postulated Taxon, "I've been conducting a few minor experiments in the workshop, and I believe I have produced a compound that I very much hope, Mr Hill," he said, addressing himself to Moss-Chops, "will restore your heraldic topiary chough to its former glory with great rapidity. I could start the treatment tomorrow, if you are in agreement..."

"Why yes, by Jupiter!" blurted our rugose host, "it's about time we had a bit more *science* around the old place, what? Please carry on, Mr Taxon, and let's see what your compound can do!"

"Excellent!" replied the eld, "I'll start the treatment in the morning and when that's done perhaps we can get to work on the flying machine?"

He looked round at Paul and me. Paul assented immediately.

"I reckon I'll be up to it Lazarus," I said, "if my nurses permit it?"

"We'll see how you get on, keep an eye on you, won't we?" Mrs Hill secured the agreement of Mrs Kegyner, Florence and Constance. I felt slightly that the whole female race would be monitoring my activities, but after all, what could I say? Besides, I was rather fond of all of them, after all we'd been through.

"Oh father," asked Paul, "since there's not much to do in the garden at this time of year, perhaps you wouldn't minde too much if we employed Mr Delenn in the engine-shed, we could do with some extra-hands in the reconstruction."

"Well I'm blowed!" puffed Old Paul, "so you're an aircraft-engineer now, are you Robbie?" his pop-eye scrutinized the elderly gardener, "well, so be it! So be it! Can't stand in the way of progress, and all that sort of malarkey, what? Carry on, Robbie, you can be the first Kornyshe gardener to help build a flying-machine!"

"Thank 'e Mr 'ill!"

"And no doubt you've been teaching Mrs Kegyner all about the suffragettes and the socialists, priming her for the imminent uprising, eh Miss Place?"

"I'm sure I don't know what you mean, Mr Hill," said Florence, affecting the utmost coyness.

"Oh yes you do!" jested the mutton-chopped gentle-squire, " a few more of your propaganda sessions and Mrs Kegyner will be slitting our throats in the night and turning this place into a revolutionary peasant's commune – ah Ha ha ha!"

"Oooohh Mr Hill," shrieked Mrs Kegyner, "the very idea!"

"Really Paul!" chided his wife; but we could all see she was laughing too. I noticed that from time to time, Old Paul would surreptitiously spirit a potato off his own plate and pass it under the table, always meticulously dividing it equally between his brace of longhounds, Red 'n' Blue. This operation was performed with the consummate stealth and skill of a master-thief. I saw Constance observe the rugose one's ruse herself, and we silently shared the joke between us. Her dark eyes flashed and gleamed with lively humour and her beautiful mouth curved into a subtle smile. I was becoming magnetized again, falling into her eyes. The candle-light seemed to dance and blur all around us, countless twinkling little flames aglow golow brightly shined around us and food and drink, warmth, hospitality and good company unravelled its laughter, conversation, banter and conviviality through the evening air.

"And how are things down in New Lynsmouth Jack?" asked June. The question galvanized all of our attention.

"Well," returned Jack, "I suppose things are starting to return to normal – well, as normal as they ever are *in New Lynsmouth!* Ha ha ha. The other day I was strolling along the road up above the harbour in the direction of Porthmouse. It was just dusk, and as I approached the top of the slipway going down to Southern Pier, there was this great procession of women and children, hundreds of 'em all dressed in white, and all carrying these Chinese paper lanterns with candles inside, so it was like a river of light flowing up the pier, past the spot where the Kramvil was finally vanquished by the Legest Meur and on up around the harbour towards the church – it was a memorable sight, rather, er, beautiful!"

"Oh Jack," said Florence in an access of emotion, "what a poetic image you weave!"

"Well yes," he went on, "it seems the parade was

celebrating the end of the dreaded *gull* – it was led by the Reverend Kryjyk, who later performed a thanks-giving service which, it seems, was extremely well attended." Jack raised a quizzical and Lacadaemonian eye-brow at this. Though of a rather sceptical, perhaps somewhat *atheistic* temperament himself, he was urbane enough to avoid offending the beliefs of others and so the raised eyebrow represented the furthest extent of his protestation against the shackles of dogmatism.

"The other news isn't so good," he continued, "there was a mysterious fire at the pantiled merchant house, the whole shop was gutted, the fire almost engulfed the Marlin too, but we set up a chain of water-buckets and doused the roof of the pub – it was quite a drama. Anyway, a great deal of valuable food was destroyed in the fire and we are now left without our most important shop!"

"Those poor fisherfolk," murmured June, "now they'll have to troop all the way into 'town' for all their supplies, the poor dear beauties!"

"Or they could always go to one of the other grocery shops in New Lynsmouth," pointed out Paul with his infuriatingly accurate logic, as, at that time, there were numerous small shops in New Lynsmouth, supplying a multitude of various provenders.

"Well, the devil of it is, if you'll excuse me saying so Mrs Hill, is that people are putting the blame for the fire on 'they physicists'! The fact that you were both out of towne when it happened doesn't seem to have crossed anybody's minde – it's probably best if you two stay well clear of New Lynsmouth for the time being, the mood is still rather ugly..."

I caught Lazarus's eye – he didn't look too worritted.

"Well as far as I'm concerned, you two fellas can stay on here for the duration," announced Old Paul Hill, "we could do with a bit of company round the old place, couldn't we June?"

"Of course dear, of course; you stay as long as you like."

She beamed at us, her kindness showing through her eyes. We both thanked the Hills profusely but our thanks were brushed aside modestly. "Tell you what," said Old Paul, "since your house has been under attack, Lazarus, and since you'll both be needing your books and equipment, how about if we send a cart down there and bring everything from your two houses back up here to Chy-an-Brae?"

"That would be extremely kind and helpful to us." I agreed.

"Perhaps I could do that," said Jack, "and I could board up the broken windows and salvage any laboratory equipment that might be still intact."

It was agreed that Mr Delenn would go with Jack to the old seaporte towne the next day with the horse and cart. This was a great kindness to Lazarus and I, as our property was no longer safe in our own houses, owing to the unfortunate sequence of events previously alluded to. These events, ghastly, loathsome and deeply perplexing as they were, had now receded a little and seemed worlds away from the simple warmth of Chy-an-Brae, our oasis. Being wary of wine, especially in my 'convalescence', I took only a few light sips but I did notice bottles and decanters going round and crystal goblets being refilled and clinked again. And also I noticed how the servants were always offered wine and food too, but were much more abstemious in their habits than the others, particularly Mrs Kegyner, who hardly took more than three small glasses.

After apple-pies and cakes had been brought in for desert, Mr Delenn brought in a Victrola and a stack of shellac wax platters. Gleaming black discs, ten inches wide and weighing half a pound each. They came in gaudy modern jackets and boasted of Foxtrots, Rags, Cake-Walks, Polkas, Waltzes, Marches, Shuffles and Shimmies. Old Delenn cranked up the machine and dropped the ferocious 'Ferox' needle onto a lively disc of Tarrantella dances from Magna Graecia. The piquant, lively and melancholy dance unwound its exotic tale in glimmering notes of glass. The glittering diamond web was spun with dewdrops and the dance was done. Ancient Muses were weaving their age-old spell. Delenn set the machine to rewind – 'Fishwalk' was the next tune, an old favourite of everyone's; even old Moss-Chops seemed to enjoy the music, even though it was shockingly modern, arrhythmic and atonal.

Suddenly Old Paul said to his son "The party's not complete. Why don't you go and get Papynjay?"

"Oh you and your pets!" objected June in mock-resignation.

The next moment Paul returned with a cage on a tall stand, covered with a green velvet cloth which he whisked away ceremoniously. "His nom-de-plume is Papynjay; isn't it Papynjay-boy?"

The many-hued lugubrious luxurious beakster fluffed and pluffed up its iridaceous pluvak plumage and plum-coloured bloomage before making a series of clicking, clacking noises and whistling like a steam boat.

Constance was addressing June – "Your gardens, they're so lovely, so varied, they must bring you a lot of happiness, a lot of peace."

"Well yes dear, we're very lucky, very lucky. The gardens are very restorative, very beneficial to recovery. You must see that 'the patient' takes lots of walks and gets his fresh air."

"Oh, I will," said Constance, smiling and looking down, perhaps with a very slight blush – perhaps that was just the wine.

"A lot of the gardens were laid out by Squire Greenhorn Hill, back in the sixteenth century, although the herb-garden is meant to be pre-Norman, so it's a bit of a mixture really. The Victorian generations expanded the gardens considerably and put in a lot of green-houses and summer-houses and things all over the place. Personally I like the rose-garden best – have you seen it yet Constance?"

"No, not yet," replied she, "but I am very fond of roses."

"Then I shall take you there tomorrow," enthused June, "and we shall bring Elias too, for his recuperative fresh air – if we can prize him away from his flying-machine, that is!"

"Oh I should love to come along," I answered, "I've always been interested in roses." And for some reason everybody was laughing.

*

For decaying gentlefolk marooned in the fastness of the igneous granitic extinct batholithic *uplands,* seemingly isolated from the benign rays of civilization and surrounded by a virtually medieval culture, Old Paul Hill somehow contrived to keep a surprisingly well-stocked wine-cellar. This may have had something to do with 'free trade' or 'fair game' or deals struck at shingly coves by moonlight, with galleons and gallons and illicit fiascos of flasks, casks and clipper-ships at night. Nobody could be too sure, but one thing was certain – Old Paul was well known in the district as a generous host who loved nothing better than feasting his guests and sipping a glass of wine.

Many cakes had been eaten and many glasses drained out and mysteriously filled again. Mrs Kegyner had brought jugs of coffee and water with a bowl of fruit. Candles flashed and spattered – some had burned out, leaving strange lunar mountains of congealed tallow. June was talking of her 'camellia walk' which incorporated nearly two dozen varieties and how beautiful it looked after rain, when silver droplets bejeweled the glossy dark green foliage. Lazarus started talking about *Camellia sinensis* – the tea-bush, and from there we got onto the culture of China, a subject on which he waxed enthusiastic, and one which old Moss-Chops seemed to find more and more extra-*ordinary.*

Papynjay, who had been surprisingly quiet until then, started echoing his master's voice, and muscling in with his grotesque avine accent – *"EXTRA*-ORDINARY! *EXTRA-*ORDINARY!" and whenever *that* happened it was usually followed by June Hill saying "oh, *that bird!"* and Jenny Kegyner bursting into a fit of giggles.

"Dostoyevsky doesn't just portray the *people,"* insisted Florence, "he portrays the innermost psyche of the people, the *soul* of the people!" For a minute I thought she was going to bang her fist on the table.

"I read this yarn once, about a chap that was washed up on a desert island..." started Paul, but by now the two cousins were off on their Russian theme, and English writers tended to be brushed aside with a wave of the hand.

"After I first read The Overcoat," said Constance,

"whenever I saw someone in a big coat with a fur collar, it would remind me of the story and I'd find it hard not to burst out laughing!"

"I've got a coat like that!" ebulliated Moss-Chops, amidst more laughter. Since the girls didn't want to talk about Robinson Crusoe, young Paul ended up having a rather technical but nonetheless highly animated conversation with Robbie Delenn on general points of aerodynamics and the specific structural problems inherent in the ornithopter.

"Well, I left the village-school when I was twelve," said Mr Delenn, "and I was apprenticed to a coach-builder down in New Lynsmouth, so I learned quite a bit about how vibrations and fatigues can weaken your carriage-frame if you don't put 'n' together proper in the first place."

"I know the feeling," quipped the woolly-jawed patriarch, "me old back's been givin' me right gyp lately, ah ha HA HA!"

Who could imagine the solidity and squat, squamous bulk of Moss-Chops ever suffering an infirmity? The man radiated brute vitality and bucolic vigour, he looked like he could, and would, knock an oak-tree down with his forehead; he looked also as if he could shoulder a great boulder and send it tumbling and trundling afar; like one puff from his legendary and lichenous chops could shatter a glass-winder or rip its way through canvas.

"Right gyp! *EXTRA*-ORDINARY RIGHT GYP!" observed Papynjay. He had a succinctness I lacked. Red and Blue howled a very unusual chord together in response to the parrot and Chaos threatened to reign supreme until Mr Delenn had the presence of minde to leap over to the phonograph and put on a copy of Sub-Carpathian Snake-Skin Shoes, a well-known foxtrot of the day.

"Chrysanthemums, now *they're* flowers for you!" exclaimed June with fervour.

"Oh I *love* them!" agreed Constance.

Old Paul was passing his hounds stealthy morsels of plum-cake, half for Red, half for Blue – that should keep them quiet, he thought.

"You *feel* like Raskolnikov! You feel as though *you*

yourself had committed the murder!" asserted Florence with some conviction.

"Sounds frightfully..." Paul was searching for the right word, "frightfully... well, frightful really!"

Jack burst out laughing at this, knowing Florence's passion for Russian books was almost a religious impulse. He decided Paul might be happier talking about engines. "All that trouble you took designing your aero-engine, and these jesters make you redundant by flying all round Penwithershins *with no engine at all! Ha ha ha!"*

"Hhmmm," frowned Paul, "well, at least they were civilized enough to use an aeroplane – they didn't just hitch a free ride with a *seagull!* Ha ha ha!" Laughs all round and clinks of glasses and baying of hounds stirred the mellow tallow-lighted air of the rustic chamber and firelight flickered and faces glew. The night waxed on, but I was waning, suddenly wearied by sopor's leaden breath upon my brow. I bade a fond goodnight to One and All, as we say in the Shyre, and made my tottering, noctambulatory way back to my chamber. The fire was still aglow and I felt deeply relaxed as I reclined in bed. Through the window a chilly sky was etched in dark velvet blue and stark moonlit cloud-white. The restless wind stirred and moaned as it sailed up to Gwynjak Wartha. Ivy rustled stark and frosty in the leafless tracery of trees and far off hooted a solitary owl of the night.

Chapter 24

Sunset – Sunrise. The stages of motion are naturally accomplished. From the great darkness arises the young light and from stillness arises flow.

The quotidian mysterious victory of light over darkness ushered in a hushed new day into the Shyre and the house of Hill, trading tewlyjyon's mystic inky cloak for a glowing mantle of marmareos glittering radiance. Softened by rain and ruffled slightly by a South Westerly wind, the light fell in particular waves that washed the World anew. Flickering fell the rising light on the claw of Kernow and on the gardens of Chy-an-Brae, in veils of mist, in trails of mystery wisped in vaporous fogdrops. The course of nature arises spontaneously and follows its own way.

West Kirnowe shone resplendent under the perfect glassy light of a winter morning's moist, refracting particles. The rain was easing, the fog was lifting, air shifting and wafting and little clouds of sunlight flitted by. From somewhere in the depths of the time-mellowed walls of Chy-an-Brae wafted the opening notes of Ogives, quiet at first, followed by a mysterious dignified peal of tuned gongs and bronze gamelan splendours recalling the turn o' stars in the heavens. The music arched up in mellow gothic swirls, chimes and blazes – slow, contemplative and permeated with an otherworldly and ennobling sense of awe.

The music faded away like the night and its dreaming lands. I finished my breakfast and applied the eel-tincture. The bites were less troublesome today and me rib-flesh had also improved considerably. I smiled to recall Paul's implausibly tall tale of carnivorous ferrets – I bet old Dr Heskenn was still puzzling that one over.

I walked through the old house; mahogany, aspidistras, framed prints of birds, leaded windows peeping at leaden skies with pewter eyes, decorative tiles, flake-mosaic sections, polished parquet, Papynjay's erratic didactics, vellum volumes encased in rosewood bookcases, rambling potted cacti – relicts and curiosities composed the molecular chattels and earthly goods of this good earthly family. The place exuded stability, antiquity and quiet, a quality that inspired me.

I stepped out through the front door and there was June – and Constance.

"How are you Elias?" she asked.

"A lot better today thank you Constance – and yourself?"

"Oh I am very well, Elias, very well."

"You do look a lot better Elias," added June, "I expect the food has done you good, so now for your next prescription – *fresh air!* Come, I will show you around the gardens," she smiled, "now, where shall we start?"

June led the way and we were soon wandering down dew-drenched spider-paths, through sunken gardens and water-gardens, and ways that wound and meandered. Miss Constance was looking fluorescent and radiant in her long skirt of tight green velveteen, her little matching jacket with the Chinese buttons and a large maroon Tam O'Shanter that held her hair, all but one lock which danced and bobbed around her neck and shoulders. Her garments were the colour of rich, forest moss, and like moss to a tree they clung to her body. June was pointing out different shrubs and rare trees – an interest in botany was something we all shared and took pleasure in. The first flowers were already adding their sweet notes of colour to the garden, even in this raw and early season, and soon we came upon the camellia walk which was a fiesta of countless blooms – whites, reds and all possible hues and chromas between the two. Glistening jewels of rain-drops festooned and glistered the blooms and sprinkled looming scintilla on voluminous shimmering petals of camellias from Bactria.

The generous efflorescence of the Camellia Walk wove its spell on us and we drank deeply of its rain-dusted beauty. To my eye there was one special flower that I kept wanting to look at again and again... June was pointing out a lovely rich burgundy flower-bush and Constance was just leaning forward to smell the fragrant, fragile petals. How graceful she looked, lithe and womanly. My minde was distracted and excitable and I was not really feeling up to a coherent conversation, but luckily June kept up a steady chatter about the different bushes and their characteristics. Surrounded by flowers, their swelling buds aching with yearning and joy, I felt like a buzzing bee, dusted with golden pollen, alighting on an enchanted flower of bliss.

"Oh yes," June was positively shining, "so many varieties... *Camellia japonica, Camellia hongkongensis, Camellia yunnanensis, Camellia kissii,*" she glanced at Constance and I, *"Camellia connata, rusticana, vietnamensis* and of course, *Camellia sinensis,* the Chinese tea-bush. How did Mr Taxon call it in the Chinese tongue, do you recall, Elias?"

"Funnily enough, I believe I do; they call them cha-hua, which means 'tea-flower'. The word 'cha' is related to words such as chai, tsai, tsa, tay and tea."

"Tea-flower" repeated June, "what a lovely name! I shall always think of them as the 'tea-flowers' now.

A figure was approaching – it was Mrs Kegyner.

"Oh, Mrs Hill, the vegetable-man is here and I couldn't for the life of me find the vegetable-list and I thought I'd better check with you and see, and…"

"Yes, alright Jenny, and I *do* wish you'd drop the 'Mrs Hill', and just call me 'June' like everybody else does!"

Jenny looked vaguely uncomfortable, then smiled. "Yes, Mrs H- June!"

"Come on," urged June, "we'd better go and talk to the vegetable-man and sort things out. If you two carry straight on past the first orchard, as far as the oak-grove, then follow the path down to the right, you'll come to the rose-garden. There won't be anything flowering yet, but there's a wonderful view of the lake… and Constance-" she looked inquisitively at June… "make sure 'the patient' gets plenty of air."

And with that, June Hill walked off with Jenny Kegyner, discussing matters of the larder, and leaving me alone with Constance.

"Did she say past the first orchard and turn right at the oak-grove…?" I asked, almost scared to let silence build between us.

"Yes, I think so," smiled Constance, "come on!"

I was relieved at her light-hearted tone and felt more at ease as we strolled together past carpets of snowy milkflowers, those 'timely flowring Bulbus violets'; and outbursts of delicious, amrita-rich, mauve clusters of *Daphne odora*. My head was spinning in the warm joy of confused euphoria. We passed a mossy and venerable orchard, lichenous and dripping with mist. The scenery opened out into a meadow surrounded by lofty beeches, elegant and startlingly delicate.

"Oh, isn't it beautiful here!" exclaimed Constance, looking about her in wonder.

"I've never seen a more beautiful sight." I said, looking at her steadily. She smiled and we walked on.

The Cornish mist hung heavy in the air, shrouding,

softening and mellowing the gardens into an aetherial dreamscape of wisps, veils and billows. Trees and shrubs loomed, then disappeared, swallowed by the niwlek ocean of vapour.

The oak-grove was a gnarled, knotty, twisted writhe of ancient and rock-hard dwarf-trees, dripping moisture, hushed, hunched and brooding – a Druidic clump hiding in its summit and centre a great upstanding menhir. This pointing finger of stone stretched up two fathoms of the stars's gulph and seemed to indicate infinity and vitality simultaneously. In this fog and dew the old trees loomed up and melted away, the great stone melted away and the known-world was a far-away place. We followed the furrowing path down yards and furlongs and wound through mist-softened country. The dream-shrouded gardens were weaving their spell on us, cocooning us in their rarefied and subtle atmosphere. We didn't feel the need to talk. The path curved down, through a patch of heather and dodder into a snug little valley that seemed to welcome and nestle us, its warm and sheltered sides nurturing many varieties of early-flowering herbs and plants, pussy-willow catkins bloomed soft to stroke and snowdrops carpeted the groundly earth with their pure and frosty whiteness.

Leaving this charming russet rustling rusticity behind us we encountered a gateway of towering granite posts topped with great globospheres – we stepped through – it was the rose-garden.

Even in its dormant season, the rose-garden was still exquisitely alluring and beautiful to behold. There was an archaic, Magna Graecian geometric perfection in the aesthetic and kinetic layout of it. Paths swept off spectacular angular and trellises trailed innumerable tendrils of roseate species. Banks of scented herbs and rosemaries exuded sweetness and the quiet, formal beauty of the place enfolded us in its secret.

The paths led round the grids of rose-beds and herb-beds, creating that familiar effect of a Cretan maze that minded me momentarily of the old towne; or of a great chess-board, upon which would soon begin a new game.

We walked side by side until we reached an open area,

bordered on one side by a marble balustrade overlooking a stand of magnolias, festooned in pink and white blooms on their leafless twigs. Beyond the magnolias, the ground ran gently down to the lake, where the cows waded and lowed contentedly in the mist-dusted waters. Owing to the density of the vapours, the scene had no apparent limit, and seemed to simply blend into a white voidness. Looking over the balcony, we took in the scene in quiet wonderment.

After a few moments, a watery sun peeped through the pewter cumulus clouds and threw a quiver-full of Olympian javelins of light into the lake, which glowed ephemeral lit. Then a blossom of colour caught my earthly eye.

"Look Constance, it's a thunder-dog!" I pointed up at the little vivid rainbow-hued blotch in the sky.

"Oh!" gasped Constance, "it's so beautiful! What *is* it?" She turned her inquisitive wide-open, dark-eyed gaze into my eyes.

"Well, it's the play of the light, it's a rare thing; rare, fine and very beautiful…" her face gazed up at mine, her lips slightly parted, her eyes sprinkled with wonder…. I felt sick with love for her then, like a madman standing on the edge of a thousand-foot cliff. I was melting and losing conscious control, the feeling was possessing me – I adored her…. "like *you,* Constance." I said quietly, as we stared into each other's eyes and then mysteriously our lips met and the tips of our tongues gently met and I was holding her tightly in my arms and we seemed to be flying together, into a brand new sky.

The gardens melted away. There was only Constance and me – not even *us,* just bliss. I held her head in my hands and gazed on her in wonder – "Will you be mine, Constance, always?"

As I spoke the words, I realised how intense and impetuous they must sound, how *mad!* She met my gaze "Yes Elias, *always."* She said it with such solemnity that I knew her to be true and I wrapped my arms around her and could not let go. Eternity came to Earth that day and our destinies seemed to flow into each other as two rivers that meet and join together as one.

My Constance! I looked at her and felt that I had been

reborn in that moment, I was now a new kind of creature, showered with heavenly blessings I walked beside this gorgeous woman and felt a new completeness. Then a slight shadow passed over my minde.

"You know, Constance, because of all the trouble in New Lynsmouth, I will probably need to leave the country for a while, possibly for a long while." I wondered what effect these words would have, but Constance simply said "I will go with you."

Some force within me kept pushing me forwards, lending me boldness. I took Constance's two hands in mine.

"Constance… will you come with me as my wife?"

"Oh Elias," she smiled, "of *course* I will!"

I picked a sprig of the richly-scented daphne and gave it to Constance and we kissed again, slowly, passionately and lost in the far nebulae of love manifesting as awe.

*

Wings of the tikki-Dyw spread wide before me, skeletal structures, fragments, mechanisms, crates, packages, blueprints and the reek of aeroplane-dope. Initially the wreckage of the craft had resembled a caterpillar – a squat hunched bulb of withered wheaten canvas, piled up on the flagstone floor. Now swarming and seething around the great khukuan buzzed Paul Hill – beam-engineer, and Lazarus Taxon – antikwari, sinologist and polymath. 'The patient' was reclining on the couch, watching the arthropodic scuttling activity around the aeronautical relict. My repose was interpreted as part of the 'convalescence', but in truth it had a lot more to do with my incredible adventure with Constance in the morning. I was so filled with her that I could barely keep my minde on the business of engineering at all. To go through all those hellish and bizarre experiences in New Lynsmouth, the extraordinary flight of the ornithopter, the lost depths of the batholithic coma and then to win the love and devotion of a fine and beautiful being like Constance – I could hardly take it all in, and what with the after-effects of the Erebus Compound I felt a genuine need to lie down.

I was happy to recline, observe and be consulted, for now, I would be a 'sleeping partner' in the operation, while Paul and Lazarus worked out the finer points of attaching the jynn-keber, or petroleum beam-engine to the airframe.

"Talking of airframes," asked Paul, "how did you get on with old Choughie this morning, Lazarus?"

"Oh I think it went quite well," replied the eld, youthfully. "I collected up some large fragments of hedgebush and dipped them in the, er, Chough-Compound and then bound them in place with strips of linen. It will soon be obvious if the operation was successful – I know it means a lot to your father and I hope we can restore it to its former glory."

"Oh yes, the Chough shall rise again!" said Paul with mock-solemnity.

"And so shall the ornithopter!" I added, insouciantly addled by love's maddening nectar. Lazarus and Paul got into an extremely long conversation about bearings, connecting rods, stress-points and such matters, I found my minde was elsewhere....

I languorously drowsed in and out of wakefulness whilst Taxon and Hill, esquires, laboriously pored over the plans, pausing to consult an abacus and a slide-rule.

Later that afternoon Mr Delenn and Jack Lane rattled into the yard with a large cart covered in a tarpaulin. We unloaded our gear into the workshop. I noticed that Lazarus seemed particularly pleased by the relatively good condition of the *animating apparatus*. Also among the cargo were a couple of large rolls of fine sailcloth, a quantity of ash-wood spars and some rolls of aero-grade wire. We were well supplied for rebuilding the fluttering flying thing.

"Well, I'd love to stick around with the aeronautical fraternity," smiled Jack, "but Florence wants to show me round the gardens – some sort of 'Lobelia Walk' or something.... Better not keep the lady waiting I suppose. I'll pop back in a day or two and see how the old 'cabbage-crate' is progressing – cheerio!"

With Mr Delenn's enthusiastic help, the jynn-keber was soon bolted to the fuselage, after which he and I started reconstructing the wings, whilst Lazarus and Paul started connecting the engine to a complex array of rods and levers

As we discussed," spoke Paul, "because the wings don't merely flap up and down, but rather push forward whilst rising and trailing slightly back during the downstroke, I've devised a gear-mechanism whereby the motion is accomplished in six stages and the seventh brings return."

"I see the cranes flying over the lake," murmured Taxon, in one of his obscure sinological reveries.

The work progressed well, but it would be several days before this bird could fly.

*

The next day strolling so wind-blown and happy down a rolling country lane with my Muse, my goddess, my Constance. The upland scenery unfurled before our feet as we walked hand in hand, absorbed in our fresh young world of love.

The attraction between us seemed to charge the air with mesmeric waves of magnetic fluid. Wrapped up in an ankle-length cloak of deep violet hue and a broad-brimmed maroon felt hat tied on with a scarf, her dark locks stirring in the breeze, she embodied all the charm and charisma of womankind.

"I've always loved these hills," she was saying as we crested a granite ridge and a vista of rolling topography opened itself before us, "they're so *wild and free!*"

"You see everything in such a good light, such a *pure* light. I've always found the hinterland a little bleak, even a bit *sinister*, whereas *you* see it as wild and free – you have such a beautiful *minde,* Constance."

"Oh, is it my minde you love me for now, is it Elias?" She tried to pout, but you can't pout and smile at the same time.

"Not only your minde!" I said as I wrapped my arms around her and held her warm, soft, young woman's body pressed tightly against my own awakening flesh.

We embraced tightly and kissed gently as our passion

smouldered and smoked, spreading like a slow wild-fire. Eventually she broke away like a wild colt and ran off down the lane shouting "Can't catch me!" and I gave chase, following the flowing folds of her magic cloak as it swirled around the curve of her hips, a joyous elasmotherium, chasing down its mate.

The land was sparsely quilted with small fields between rugged areas of heather and gorse, studded with those ubiquitous granitic boulders and carns, whittled and rounded by vast pre-Cambrian epochs of eternity into a gallery of weird and fantastical bizarreries. A buzzard's thin cry. Distant lowing of cattle. The trickle of a tiny rivulet beside a country-road. Dappled light, dabbed and daubed on the wild upland heaths as great kommolek billows and vapour-nebulae sailed slowly over the land. We walked down the road together hand in hand and the first drops of rain started to fall.

"Oh Elias, you're only wearing a light jacket, and with all that weight you've lost, you mustn't risk catching a chill. Here, come on."

She unfastened her voluminous cloak and threw it over my shoulders, so it swaddled us both around in its warm folds. Through her silken blouse I could feel her warm body gently rubbing against me and I could smell her subtle, sweet feminine scent.

"You certainly know how to look after 'the patient'," I said to her.

She looked at me with a quizzical glint. "Well, somebody has to do it, don't they?"

"Only you, Constance."

The rain-pellets were scattering harder and the sky was throwing on its cloak of darkest black. We passed a clump of thorns, where a crow clacked and cawed darkly and the wind moved up the scales. A signpost, dilapidated and leaning like a drunk proclaimed Gwynjak Vean one and a half miles, Trewither two miles. The road was deteriorating and the rain was rattling worse, but with my arm around Constance's waist, and our thighs sometimes just gently brushing against each other's, we were lost in our own world.

After a while we saw a very humble-looking cottage by

the road and just as we were walking past, the door opened to reveal the figure of an old woman in archaic bonnet and shawl.

"Come in, my dears, come in and drink tay by the fire 'till the rain passes."

"Thank you! You're very kind and your offer is most welcome," I answered as we approached the door. The woman at the threshold appeared to be around ninety years of age, her wizened parchment face lit with a beatific smile.

"Come in, my children," she urged, "what's this? Just the one cloak between ye? Ha ha ha! Come in now and get warm."

The dwelling seemed to be just one room, with a brass bed-stead in one corner and a little kitchen in the other. Strings of onions and herbs dangled from the rough-hewn rafters and a hen clucked, bucked and fluttered around the floor.

Before shutting the door, the old one threw a glance out at the swelling downpour.

"We need the rain. The crops need it and the meadows need it – it's nature's way."

She ushered us over to a wooden settle by the kitchen range, an oasis of warmth and comfort.

"Give me the cloak, cheeld-vean, I'll hang it over this chair, to dry by the fire."

"Thank you, but what is your name?" asked Constance.

"Agnes" replied the old woman and we told her our names. She toasted some saffron buns on the range, and spread them with butter and gave them to us with hot tay.

"A little morsel always helps, doesn't it now, me dears?" She chuckled good-naturedly to herself, in the way of the old who have seen many things and lived down many troubles.

"My dear life!" she exclaimed, grasping a handful of the material of Constance's long skirt, "But it's soaked through! Take it off now girl, and I'll dry it by the fire."

I was shocked. Could the old woman not *see* right? Did she think we were *children?* After a suspended second's pause, Miss Constance coolly caught my eye, then started unbuttoning her ankle-length skirt. The fabric flowed over her legs like a theatre-curtain opening. She handed the wet skirt to the old dame and sat back down on the settle in her white silky drawers and buttoned-up boots. The curve of her legs burnt into me like a white-hot meteorite coursing through space – I thought I would faint with desire.

I looked at her face. She was blushing and casting down her eyes in sudden humility, wavering on the borderline between mature womanhood and the shyness of a girl. I couldn't bear to see her in any discomfort, it tore at me, and turned my raging hunger into tender concern.

"You're beautiful, Constance," I whispered into her ear, the scent of her hair filling me with sweetness. Then I took my jacket, which was barely damp, and spread it over her gorgeous silky thighs. She shivered, and smiled in gratitude, "thanks Elias," she said warmly, squeezing my hand. Everything made me love her more.

Old Agnes bustled about, refilling the tay-pot and stirring a large pot on the stove.

"I've got me hens and I sell a few eggs, see? I've got three hogs, twenty-eight sheep and a donkey. I look after them and they look after me – 'tis nature's way, see? Now! Let's take some more tay together."

"It was good of you to ask us in," said Constance, "that sudden squall quiet took us by surprise, didn't it dear?"

"Yes indeed!" I spluttered, reeling with delirious joy – I was aware of feeling *younger*, euphoric and excitable, volatile like a youth. I think the Erebus Compound played a part in this.

"Well I d' like a little bit o' company once in a while. We don't see many strangers up in the *hills* you know. Now, you'll have some cake. Go on, take *more* than you want!"

Her curious turns of speech were amusing to us and her warm humour made us relax. The tay was hot and refreshing and the saffron cake was very tasty.

"What delicious cake!" pronounced Constance warmly, "is it easy to make, Agnes?"

"Why goodness me, dear cheeld! You'll never wife till ye can bake a cake! Now listen and I'll tell ye how 'tis done. First you d'take 'zactly three or four cups of good flour and some nice eggs, see…."

She launched into an intricate and rambling description of the baker's art while I stared at Constance's pretty calves and tried not to.

"…and after 'zactly thirty or forty minutes 'tis ready to take out of the oven, see? Then you let n' cool down and then you cut a great slice and give it to your man, see? And that keeps 'im 'appy, see? Tis nature's way! I should know, I've 'ad four of 'em. One 'usband and three sons – all gone! All gone! There we are."

Agnes stirred the big pot on the range.

"I'm sorry, Agnes," I ventured, "you must miss them."

"I'm used to it now dear!" she returned. "I've still got a couple of grandchildren up Gwynjak Wartha, and great-grandchildren too! Time is the healer… My husband fell off a ladder coming up the mine-shaft at the end of his shift. It had been raining and the ladders get slippery. Twenty fathoms he fell. Our boy Robert died in the Indian Mutiny; Samuel died of the yellow fever, down in Jamaicee and Arthur went to South Australia and we never heard from him again."

"How terrible!" exclaimed Constance, "I am sorry for your sufferings, you strike me as a very courageous woman!"

"Thank 'ee m' dear. Life is hard but I keep the faith. The small-holding keeps me busy and provides my needs."

Her piety and simplicity touched us both – she shone with an unworldly purity. I started to realize then that I had misjudged these *hills* and the hillfolk, for any region that could produce a woman such as Agnes obviously had a lot of good in it. Granite – the rock produced the soil and the soil produced the people. Thunder in the Earth. The people go on. The generations spin. The cycles repeat… The old woman's voice called me back – "And may you be blessed with strong children!"

*

Later we walked hand in hand back through the upland hinterland hills. The rain had flown and the breezes swirled patches of mist. Gaunt thorns and haggard wind-warped dodder-drenched gorses adorned this haunt of furze and heather. Somehow our conversation had come round to China and I had been telling Constance about Chuang Tzu's Dream of the Butterfly.

"I feel they had a very subtle understanding of life, these old Chinese poets," she said, "a butterfly is such a delicate and ephemeral creature, isn't it? The soul is a butterfly, fluttering in the blue summer sky of the heart."

"The sky of the heart – I *like* that! You're a poetess, Constance, you speak like a bard!"

"Oh, it's – I just like *words!"* she giggled; but I knew from then on that she had the gift of poetry.

"But butterflies are fragile, ephemeral things of great beauty, aren't they, so they've always inspired people, or at least, anyone who's sensitive to beauty," I enthused, "always inspired the most rarefied feelings of- what's *that?"*

"I don't *know,"* answered Constance. The steep lane down which we walked was an old holloway with high hedges on either side so we could not see into the fields through which it ran, but coming from over the hedge we could hear the most eldritch braying, grunting and bellowing, as if two great beasts were fighting it out to the death.

Constance looked at me in curiosity. "Whatever could it *be,* Elias?"

"I don't know, it sounds so wild and strange, look, there's a gate, we might be able to see what it is."

We walked over to the little rustic gate, set in the lichen-encrusted granite dry-stone wall; and there in the field in front of us was a massive black bull mounting a Frisian cow and ramming his loins into her hind-quarters like life depended on it.

My Victorian upbringing threw me into a species of moral-panic at this point and my first thought was to protect Miss Constance from such a barbaric, primitive and unwholesome display of animalistic vulgarity. I raised my hand to cover her eyes.

"Look away, dear, it's too horrible for a young lady to see!" I implored her, but she laughingly pushed my hand away. "Oh Elias!" she twinkled mischievously, "don't be such a silly boy – *'tis nature's way!"*

*

Something in the *lab,* something in the workshop, stirring and filling out in stark skeletal glory. Embryonic relict – skinning up the sailcloth – spars and grids – aerofoils, tailplanes, undercarriage – Mr Delenn, working away with tenon-saw and sandpaper – showers of rain, mugs of tay – the rattle of hail on the windows – Paul stoking and coaling-up the stove – coils of wire, wood-shavings and engine oil – Lazarus consulting the blueprints and doing mathematical calculus equations on old scraps of paper – the precision of the sliding joints which allowed the wings to change shape – brass fittings, polished wood and the steel-gleam of the engine – I was becoming habituated to the atmosphere of a small aircraft assembly-shop, with the ongoing discussions of aeronautical repercussions and ramifications and the intense interest in aviation shared between The Engineer, The Polymath, The Gardener and The Scholar. The re-assembly process had allowed us to incorporate some syncopated improvements to the design of the original ornithopter. We slightly improved the nacelle, so it would offer more shelter. With the engine doing all the work, there should be no reason for the crew to exert themselves, so keeping warm was one of our concerns. Lazarus had the wonderful idea of feeding the engine exhaust pipes through the floor of the nacelle, to act as an ariel hypocaust and warm the craft. The precise configuration of this masterpiece of airborne plumbing was the subject of further debate….

The image of Constance flowed into me and flooded my minde and all of me. What a girl – so lively, wise, playful, intelligent and *lovely* – I felt deep-whelmed in good fortune, incredulous with wonder. I'd always imagined that 'bookworms' like me were not very attractive to women, but curiously it was my bibliomania that led me to Taxon, and that's when all my wild adventures began, and somehow Constance came along and wanted to fly with me, so maybe it was a case of 'action brings good fortune.' Whatever the mysterious and unfathomable cause, born from a seed at the birth of the Universe, Constance and I were together now and our spirits shone bright in union.

".... and then we'd surround the whole thing in a perforated cowling, to dissipate the heat and protect the crew against burns…"

They were *still* talking about the exhaust pipes! That's the funny thing about being in love. I felt like I'd got the Secret of the Universe, I was seeing from a new and much greater perspective and the 'ordinary' world became slightly remote and irrelevant.

Nifwl! A great nebulaeic gelatinous fog danced and swirled and a ghost-dance of acrid and pullulating phenomena beflitted by me as I drowsed a cysglyd oneiro dream; a cocooned and encarapaced catyrpel encased in chryselephantine phantom chrysalis of luminous bliss. Lobsters cimwch a-scuttle – waves pound crash and roar, rolling spindrift smoking seas and northerly forties – test-tubes beakers and flasks, precious myrrh and drops of golden liquid fire in glass flasks agolow in bioluminous numinosity in the laboratory – cycling to Porthmouse for the meat! The viands! The outrageous development and career of the eggsnakelizardquilledgullthynge – such times to live through…. and the patter of rain on grey slate roofs far away, and windows – wind blows chimney pots like flutes, crown-pots, leaning stacks, crumbling eaves and tottering and lurching tenements, the Old Quarter, feet chasing down Cretan twisting streets – torches flaming, bricks hurling – gut-wrenching *bird* ripping at the miner's corpse in the korflann boneyard – such times, such times – amser, amser, time! Aimsir –

"Now, how's that famous mechanical *bird* coming along then, eh?"

It was the rotund and jocular-spectacularity known locally as 'Moss-Chops' who snapped me out of my musing tumbling thoughts as his fleshly envelope loomed large in the doorway.

"Good to see you Mr Hill. Come on in and I'll show you

the craft."

But he motioned me back to the rococo couch with a wave of his hand.

"You relax old fella – let yourself heal up – I'm sure these gents can show me the ropes, eh?"

He poured himself forth into the room, like claret being poured into a glass, his personality splashing and rebounding off the four walls like spray.

"Ah, Mr Taxon – how are you, Lazarus? How's the old kite coming along, eh?"

"I'm very well, Paul, thanks to your hospitality, now would you have a look at this? Your son is a master-engineer, a true heir of Trevithick! Why, just look at this fine and compact little jynn-keber he's concocted, and, as you see, we've already got it installed in the fuselage."

"Extra-*ordinary!*" boomed the maroon, bewhiskered, mutton-chop Mossy, looking on with incredulous, therapsid, globular opticals.

Genau-Mwswgl – Old Moss-Mouth stared in pelicosaurian absorption at the diametrically connected wing-drive rods and the intricate assemblage of gearing for the jynn-keber, obviously impressed with his son's work.

"And when do you expect this steam-powered *chicken* to flap its jolly old wings then, eh?"

A quizzical quiver ran through his juddering jowls as a grin lit his chin.

"Probably another day or so Dad," answered Paul the younger, "why, do you fancy going flying?"

The carragheen quiver turned to a jowl-shaking shiver as the scarlet patriarch seemed to rear up, leaning forward on his fore-limbs in bold blunt blundering oblique saurian wonderment, as if about to catch a fly with his tongue.

"Thought I might give it a try, yes, keep abreast of the new science and all that – but I wouldn't mention it to your mother just yet…"

He tapped his nose conspiratorially like an arch-sneak at a secret meeting of clandestine and top-secret sneaks.

Bryophytic, Brythonic, a genius in his own genus, Old Paul Hill walked around the body of the incomplete ornithopter, as it lay supported by trestles, wings alongside, disconnected; undercarriage and tail-section similarly detached and in pieces. He examined the anatomy of the aircraft with scrupulous and avid attention, scanning every detail with his great Permian eye.

"Perhaps I was a little unfair calling this wonderful creation a *'chicken'*, why it's really more of a… more of a… what do *you* think it's like, Robbie?"

He consulted the old gardener whose face lit up.

"She's a Ticky-Dew, if you ask me, Mr 'ill, a butterfly's what she is!"

"Hhmmm… 'Ticky-Dew', I like it," mused Lazarus, "I think you're right Mr Delenn, a fluttering butterfly…"

"A fine name!" blasted out Moss-Chops, "dashed fine name!"

"I vote we adopt it as the name of the aeroplane," I suggested. We were all in accord, so the name stuck and the 'Tykki-Dyw' it was - with various theories on how to spell it!

*

Constance and I stepped out through the kitchen door into the looming silvery light of the waning moon

"The house is blest where snails do rest!" she quoted the ancient Cornwealas motto of the Hill family, and the rambling krogenek chitonic hive that is Chy-an-Brae. A moluscoid *bullhorn* was slithering its idiosyncratic way across the path, heading towards the house.

"There's a fellow who's always got somewhere to live, no matter what," I postulated. "He's always secure, always sheltered from the weather…"

Constance took my hand as we entered the gardens, a smile lit her face.

"I do believe you're jealous of a *snail*, Elias!" she teased.

"Hhmmm… I suppose it looks that way!" I laughed. "What I meant was, that snail has more security than *I* can give *you* – I'm practically on the run – I don't know where we might live or what the future might bring, or-"

Constance halted my monologue by planting a kiss on

my lips.

"Wherever it might be," she said, looking into my eyes, "I'll go with you."

We ran on deeper into the gardens, light of stars and moon sprinkling a dust of sparkling scintilla over the drowsy, slumbering acres of deserted topography.

"Oh Constance, it's a wonderland, isn't it?"

We ran past a lily-pool reflecting the moon in its still waters.

"Yes Elias, and it's *our* wonderland, *our* moonlight!"

She was right, of course.

Chymonanthus praecox sweetened the young winter night with its Chinese incense scent reminiscent of a leaf, torn from The Book of The Yellow Emperor and flung into the air. The small light of the moon and stars enchanted the noctambulation and the gardens became less solid; occasional swathes and wraithlike plumes of mist wove a nimbus round this niwlog Arupaloka – foggi ffwrmless werlde – gossamer glistening nightworld – gorhan void voodoo hudoo hudel mysteriodis nichtwerlden – a shadowy world of sparkling vivid mystery where nature's intricate tracery spun lace-wing apparitions and rustling visitations. Scurryings in the leaves. Rattlings in the twigs. Owlings on the hoot. Howlhounds of the baying cloud night. Cloudhorns of the chalky hills. Herb gardens of the dewdripping bay. Footprints of the nightwalking pair. Handhold a-link. Souls entwined. Leafless trees o'ertowering, fingertwigs sweeping to grasp the shadows, carving statues out of mist. Words of love between man and woman and whispering a windblown glistening hwystra. Through ancient mossy gardens, down winding twisting pathways, my lady of the moonlight, beside me as I drifted, down avenues and arbours, past rolling sheepy meadows, and formal cultivations, through blizzard tides of snowdrops, forming oceans in the moonlight, and ever on we wandered, myself beside my soul-mate, and no-one else was with us, 'cause the night was made for lovers, and our fingers wove together, as we listened to each other, and the clouds were scudding over, and the moondrop hung suspended, and the owlings in the dark wood, and the branches that are swaying, and the crocuses are glowing, as we follow in the valley, and the stars stood out as witness, and the skies shone out in glory-

We walked through a moonlit meadow, Constance and I, watching the long grass undulate in oceanic ripples. Silver glimmering sheen gave a moonglow patina of iridescent dust to the nightworld and its mysteries. Corncrakes clattered and crarked as the odd bittern would sometimes boom and even the worldly and churlish churra-nos nightjars, goat-suckers, whip-poor-wills and other, more obscure nightbirds were oddly loquacious and babbling forth generously with their bird-like burblings. The air was thick with their feathery flutings. The meadows rippled like ocean-tides, we were adrift in a sea of love, mystery, destiny....

On a slight rise stood an odd circle of trees, twisted oaks and sycamores woven by the Atlantek winds into an unusual basket-work fence. We walked round the perimeter until we found a path allowing us to enter. Inside the dense circle of trees was a spacious clearing, the summit of the gentle hill. At the top of this rise stood the gaunt and archaic ruin of an ivy-clad building.

"The Magor!" I pointed to the hushed and fallen-in structure before us. "Doesn't it look ancient and mysterious?"

"You don't think there are any *bats* in there, do you Elias?"

I'd never seen Constance worried about anything like that before, her vulnerability worked a charm on me, just as much as her usual confidence did.

"Don't worry, Constance," I told her, "I'm the battiest thing you're going to encounter tonight!"

She smiled and seemed to relax – I think she liked my honesty.

"Come on." I took her hand and we approached the time-blasted structure, the old old ruin in the circle of trees on the hill-top. Our footsteps rustled through ivy and scraps of dry bracken. The rooking, churring, roaring of the nightbirds was increasing in volume as we approached the Magor. Were these feathered songsters trying to *warn* us? Were they trying desperately to ward us back from a fate at once ghastly and unthinkable, monstrous, inhuman, gibbering, writhing and reeking of an utterly eldritch and foul alienage? Or were the little golden birdies actually welcoming Constance and me to their woodland home, perhaps those warble-beaked flutterers had winged words for the trained-ear of an eminent ornithoskopos? They were re-acquiring their status as spirit-messengers, as portents, as go-betweens carrying messages between the various realms. Their wings speckled the night sky, flitting through star-clouds and slicing up the moon.

The Magor stood stark like a blasted archaic staghorn oak, its broken carcass bleak-hunched and tendrilled round with twisting ivy. The empty shell of the rough-hewn granite building was around fifteen feet long, the width being about half that. At one end of the crumbled and lichenous structure, an ancient stone tower rose up about twelve feet – the relict of a once-greater tower. The spiral staircase had long-since fallen, leaving the stack unclimbable. The roofless husk of the old ruin was paved with a floor of massive flagstones and little stone benches were set in alcoves around the walls. A massive, table-like stone at one end of the Magor was suggestive of an altar or ritual-podium of some kind. The whole place had an air of rarefied antiquity that was both singular and perplexing. Moonlight glinted in myriad quartz crystals embedded in the granitic walls, somewhere far off an owl hooted. Cool white luminescence seemed to flood into the Magor, as if it held the light of the moon and the stars in the glittering marmareos surfaces of its krogenek shell.

We stood in the centre of the Magor, Constance and I, entwined in each other's arms and I held her tight as the clouds scudded past the moon.

"Constance," I said her name softly between kisses, "I think we should get married as soon as possible."

"Yes." Her eyes said more.

"Then I'll go into Pensanskrit and make the arrangements. It might have to be quite a simple affair, I'm sorry, it's just the circumstances, being a fugitive and all…"

"It's alright Elias, I understand how it is. Let's just keep it simple, why don't we? Who needs all the fuss anyway?"

"Oh Constance, are you sure you're not just saying that

so I don't feel bad about it?"

"Don't be silly now Elias – let's just get married and then… go wherever fate takes us!"

"That's why you're my Goddess, Constance – 'cause you've got the wings to fly!"

We held each other tightly for a long time. More nightbirds took up their trilling and spirited vigil. The smell of Constance's hair was a dizzying intoxicant to me, swooning me and looming o'er me. Our bodies pressed together and I could hear her heartbeat. Her firm breasts were pushing against my chest and her powerful legs were quivering. I went to kiss her beautiful lips, but she threw her head back in sudden abandon, as if possessed by a species of trance; her eyes stared open wide and from her parted lips came a long-drawn-out groan of ecstasy – Miss Constance seemed to be in a visionary or mystical condition – I had no idea her religious sensibilities ran so deep… She gasped, breathing irregularly and with great force; she clutched me with an unknown strength and she quivered and shuddered, trembling like a fawn lost in a thunder storm. I held her tight until the strange phenomenon had passed, after which time she seemed acutely *relaxed and tranquil,* as if her visions had brought her a deep sense of satisfaction. What an extraordinary young woman she was, capable of such intense outbreaks of spirituality one moment, and light-hearted and jovial the next – would I ever fathom the full mystery of this celestial woman? I felt she had much to teach me. She sighed heavily and kissed me tenderly on the forehead.

"Yes Elias, let's get married as soon as possible," she whispered softly to me.

"Leave it to me, darling," I said, "shall we head back to the house now?"

"You know I'll follow you anywhere," said Constance with a mischievous twinkle in her dark and beauteous eye.

*

The following morning I had left the fellows in the workshop to carry on with the reconstruction, whilst I set

out by velocipede for Pensanskrit. I'd taken the precaution
of dressing as a humble poor man, and neglecting to shave,
which, coupled with the curious rejuvenating affect of the
Erebus Compound would, I hoped, make me much harder
to recognize. In a small town like Pensanskrit one is always
bumping into acquaintances and meddling blighters when
all you want is a bit of peace and quiet.... The place was
uncomfortably close to New Lynsmouth and dark tales of
the 'pesky scientists' were probably circulating all round the
district by now.

Dew rose as steam in the air as I cycled out of the great
globose gateposts of Chy-an-Brae. My route was virtually
down hill all the way, so I could relax and enjoy the fresh
crispness of the air and the bright, late-winter sunshine as it
glossed its glow over the rolling hinterland of Penwithershins.
Once in towne, I conducted my business briskly, secured the
marriage-license and bought two rings for Constance at the
jewelers shop. An engagement ring of pure tin, set with an
emerald glas stone; the other a simple band of Kernouac gold.

I was soon back on the bicycle and glad to be away from
that bustling little towne. The return journey was a bit more
strenuous, but I felt curiously light and dynamic – youthful.
With the rings in my pocket, I felt that I was symbolically
carrying my future and this time, as I approached the rolling,
hills of the hinterland, they had lost their sinister aspect, they
had come to seem almost like home.

Eventually the central plateau opened up before me and
then I passed through the cyclopean gates and was following a
broad and winding drive up through the varied and extensive
gardens of the House of Hill.

I halted the bicycle outside the Minoan-style pillars
which fronted the ancient manor – a pheasant on the great
front lawn honked, squarked and flapped noisily away. I saw
through the front windows – they were taking tay inside.
Then I remembered my ragged clothes and decided to go
upstairs and change before joining the others. Walking past
the ancestral portraits upstairs my globose globular optical
was particularly taken by the likeness of Sir William Hornbill
Hill, resplendent in breastplate, cloak and plumed tricorn hat.

In the background a galleon rode at anchor, stuffed to the brim with gold and treasures stolen from the Spanish main. Old Hornbill Hill had sailed the seven seas and conquered them all and now, in the twentieth century, his descendent Paul Hill the younger was helping to advance man's conquest of the air.

I wandered downstairs and found Mrs Kegyner bustling around in the kitchen.

"Oh Elias, would you do me a favour, dear? I've got a batch of saffron buns in the oven – could you just keep an eye on 'em whilst I go and get the tay-pot to make a fresh brew?"

She clattered her crinkled crinolined way off down the passages of Chy-an-Brae leaving me alone in her realm of steam. I opened the oven and had a quick look – the buns looked *raw* to me.

"Oh Elias! All your skills and you can *cook* as well!"

Constance had walked into the kitchen with a tray of empty cake-platters. I started to protest my culinary ignorance but she just laughed and gave me a kiss.

"It's alright darling," she smiled at me, "don't look so worried. You can build the flying-machines and I'll make the food – *for now*. Who knows how things may be in the future? Florence was saying that with more young women going off to university these days, more young men are having to look after themselves – well, those who can't afford servants anyway!"

"I wouldn't minde if you wanted to study – I can see you doing literature, or possibly higher medicine – but you might have to teach me how to make a pasty first!"

"Well, it's a bit more simple than making a flying-machine!" she retorted and we both laughed.

We held each other tight in the dusky light of the steamy kitchen. I kissed her tenderly and she clung to me like ivy.

"How did you get on in towne?" she whispered shyly into my ear.

"Well, I have the license, and also, shut your eyes Constance."

I took the tin and emerald ring from my pocket and quietly knelt before my Goddess. I took her hand and put the ring on her finger.

351

"Constance," I asked, suddenly feeling tearful, "will you be my wife?"

"Oh *yes* Elias, you know I will! You *know* I will!"

We kissed again and again, tenderly and with the awareness that we were sealing our union.

An acrid smell was creeping into the room.

"Oh no!" I exclaimed, "I think it's the cakes!"

I dived over to the oven. Black smoke poured from the oven door and the cakes were carbonized ash. The kitchen was filling with smoke.

"Quick, open the kitchen door, Constance."

She flung it open and the pure Kornyshe air rushed in. Mrs Kegyner also rushed in with June Hill and pandaemonium broke out, with cries of 'King Alfred' and everyone coughing and laughing in the smoke – and then Jenny Kegyner noticed Constance's engagement ring and so the news came out and with it more pandaemonium which brought the rest of the household crowding into the kitchen to find out what was going on; and everybody congratulating Constance and I – the women, even Florence, tearfully – the men heartily. We decided to return to the drawing-room and have tay – and champagne and enjoy a little party. We'd only just sat down, when the engineers came in to join us, adding their voices to the cheery hubbub. The room was a bee-buzzin' hive, tremulous with excitement, humour and companionship.

Moss-Chops reared up on his back-legs, face flushed with rapid therapsid stimuli.

"I'd like to propose a toast," he reverberated, "to Constance and Elias – may they have every happiness together!"

Glasses raised clinked emptied filled raised. Tay also circulated and I stuck mainly to this as these days alcohol seemed to make my head spin like the Gnome Rotary Engine.

"I reckon you'll be the first couple in the World to go on your 'oneymoon in a flying-machine, won't you?" laughed Jenny Kegyner.

"Aye, there's many a true word said in jest…" I replied, fully aware that our 'honeymoon' might be more of a desperate escape from the consequences of the *kramvil-kaos.*

"Will it be a long engagement dear?" asked June.

"Oh, two or three days, probably," I returned nonchalantly. Everyone seemed to find this hilariously funny – they must have took it for a wry jest, as if I'd stoop or swoop to the level of *Jynx torquilla,* the Eurasian wryneck.

"Why wait around, eh? Get on with it, that's what I say!" opined the flossy-chopped head of the Hill-clan.

"We didn't wait around, did we dear?" he offered, to the slight encrimsonation of June, "how long was *our* engagement dear?"

"It was about two and a half years, Paul." answered she.

"Hhhhhrrrrummmmmphphphph! Was it really? *EGAD!*" thundered the fluctuating epiglottis of the atavistic and bovine host, his clownish puffs of white hair standing out sideways in neat kommolek amazement.

"GET ON WITH IT! Hhhhhrrrrummmmphphphph! EGAD!" observed Papynjay with laconic accuracy and Sokratik succinctness. I noticed Constance and Florence catching each other's eye – they seemed to be trying to suppress a collective fit of girlish giggling.

"And what about *you* dear?" June asked Florence, "how long is your engagement to Jack going to be?"

"Do you know, June, we haven't actually talked about it yet, but I don't imagine it will be an overly long period of time."

Florence looked as if she would explode with mirth.

"GET ON WITH IT! EGAD! GET ON WITH IT!" It was the bird who spoke, albeit somewhat parrot-fashion.

"Really Paul!" expostulated June to her antediluvian husband. "It's getting nigh on impossible to have a proper conversation in this house without *that bird* making a mockery of it! I do wish you'd cover him up!"

"Nonsense dear!" salvoed the rugose host, "he plays a valuable role in the house, provides, what's it called – *social commentary."*

"Social commentary?" echoed his spouse aghast, "Social commentary? I've heard better 'social commentary' from the village idiot!"

"SOCIAL commentary – SOCIAL commentary!" reiterated the plumed repeater.

"Oh really!" exasperated June, "where *is* the parrot-cloth?"

She wandered about the room, looking in vain for the avine-inhibitor.

"Well," said Jenny "perhaps I'd better go and rustle up another batch of buns – only *this* time, I'll keep an eye on them myself!"

She winked a mischievous eye at me and headed for the kitchen. Lazarus started a monologue on the betrothal customs of various classical far eastern lands.... I looked over at Constance who was sitting next to me on the sofa. Suddenly the background activity seemed to fade away and a sort of *beam* or wave or cloud of strong golden light glowed between us. The light was powerful and induced immediate feelings of deep well-being, peace and a heightened feeling of awareness or intelligence. Golau aur. A glowing aura. Solas orga. A light made of gold. We were in the light of knowing. Golow owrek. Suffused and illuminated, drenched through with luminous phosphorescence. Krysous phos. The golden golow glow of ten thousand gleaming beeswax candles, beacons beaming bright, luminous Alexandrian golowji houses of light. Gylden leoht. Goud licht. Lux, lumen, leukos, the glow waxed buzzing bright and pure, then faded like a cloud and was no more.

"….. you see, as the keber rocks back and forth, it doesn't turn a wheel, like a normal beam-engine – in fact it's got a cylinder on each side of the beam, and by firing these alternately, the beam simply powers an axle which drives one wing, while the other is on an adjacent axle, driven by cogs."

"I always knew you'd be a mad professor! Tell me, son, what makes the old 'Butterfly' flap its wings then?"

"Petrol, Dad, good old petroleum, so we don't need to carry any coal or water! Ha ha ha!"

"By Jehosephat! You watch out for that hedge, minde, ya flash young *flyboys,* eh?" He patted Lazarus on the back.

"The transmission system is based on a seven-part cycle of-" Paul was cut short by the scarlet-coated patriarch –

"What's that? A cycle?"

"Never minde the boring details Dad, we think it'll fly, that's the main thing!"

"Fly? The 'main thing'? Yes! That's it! Flying! All the rage these days – soon everyone will be doing it. But as usual it's we Kornyshe lads that lead the way!"

Moss-Chops certainly did seem enthusiastic about the future of aviation and if he exaggerated the role of the Kornyshe in the *development* of aviation let's just put it down to paternal pride.

"Perhaps you'd like to fly into these," quipped the verdant Mr Delenn, offering round a tray filled with glasses of champagne.

The terrapin twinkle in his eye seemed to say 'it's no good trying to say no, now is it?'

"I will if you will, Robbie," wobbled the woolly and juddering jowls of the megalognomon gentlesquire, "after all, you're one of these *fly-boys* now, aren't you, eh?"

He clinked glasses with the old gardener and roared with benevolent laughter, a batholithic basilisk basking in casques of raki; cones of powder; cubes of nostalgia; elephantine slabs of peppermint candy; a physique that made Bob Fitzsimmons look *un*fit; lord over acres of dodder and furze, bracken and carns, Old Paul was in his element.

Mrs Kegyner returned with a large dish of buns, to everyone's amusement. Young Paul cranked up the Victrola and put on Dance of the Dodekanese, a 78 of 7/8 shuffles, shimmies and struts. The night flowed on, starry and mysterious. June had heard enough about aeroplanes and steered the conversation round from canvas to silk wedding dresses most skillfully. The winter chills blew wild outside. Inside the candles and lanthorns were blazing and the log-fire was flaming. Since the women were talking about clothes, I jestfully asked Moss-Chops what he got married in. His answer, declaimed with therapsid hand on heart was "Love, dear boy! Love and me best suit! Ha ha ha!"

"A fair answer, Paul," I assuaged, "that's it! All you need is love - and your best suit – I'll remember that!"

"Well, we can't talk about silk," began Lazarus, in

another attempted tangent, "without considering the Silk Road from China to the West – one of the most important cultural conduits in Human history…"

"Ooh Mr Taxon," beamed June, you really do have the most *encyclopaedic* knowledge of far-away places and long-ago things. Why, if I'm not very much mistaken, you must be *Kirnowe's foremost Sinologist!"*

"Well, it's a sadly neglected field," he explained, "and so there aren't many others around."

"Elias was telling me that you've actually spent some time in China," Constance said to the 'eld'.

"Yes, that's right," he replied, "I spent an extended stay there, and became familiar with some aspects of the culture. I have also pursued much further research and study back in the Shyre; it's something that's always interested me."

"By the Herring!" exploded Moss-Chops suddenly and without warning, "an afternoon's shopping in Pensanskrit's like a trip to China to me! As soon as I leave Chy-an-Brae I feel like I'm on foreign soil, don't feel quite right, what?"

"I don't blame you, Paul!" added Florence with feeling. "Why would you want to wander far from such a beautiful place?"

"I think that's what Jack says about *you* Florence!" I jested.

"Besides," put in the younger Paul, "your garden's nearly as big as China anyway, isn't it Dad?"

We all laughed at this, as it had to be said that the gardens of Chy-an-Brae were indeed vast, commodious and huge.

The light of the day was long gone and the myriad nebulous stars stood out in late-night individual precision and luminous glory – glittering – stark – hard. The stars cast their sprinkle on the land and lights twinkled in the houses. Thunder rumbled under the Earth and the young light was born again. A speck amongst the stars, the World turned. Twinkling as it spun, catching and losing and chasing and catching the rays of the sun – Sunrise – Sunset – Sunrise – Sunset….

Chapter 25

We ploughed the fields of time and the hours fell like bronzen leaves from the trees of Life's sacred grove. Wrens peeped and cheeped, flickering into the ivy – shadows crept across the lawns – mists of silver shimmering mizzles condensed cool and dripped from the statue of a faughan. Happily passed the time and hwytha friska wisped a whisker as fresh whirled the zephyr's breath, whistling up to Gwynjak Wartha.

Vast but perfectly formless, ceo druidechta, a shining cloud of Keltek mist spread forth into the unforeseeable past.

The mist cleared as the morning blazed on – the sun hot howlak licking up the moist vapours with tiny tongues of fire. A buzzing started to fill out the air as billowing insects rattled carapaces, wing-cases, polypod feet – bare to the breeze – and antennae seemin' to sense. All a-whirl and a-buzz, whirring to pulse and pullulate with life.

Flickering images dance in silvery splennyjyon llewyrch phosphorescence in the looking-glass. All that is came from all that wasn't.

*

Paul and I rolled back the double doors of the workshop and guided by Delenn and Taxon, the spectacular Ticky-Dew flapper emerged from its krogenek cocoon, out, into the light of day. A wondrys fine sight it was. Aerofoil ridges arcing through the canbhas sailcloth skin now doped to a deep Brythonek racing green. Nacelle nozzling forth to sniff the Northern breeze. Tail-planes and fin piscine, ribbed, edges trailing. The great wings, outstretched and slightly elevated, brought to minde another pair of dark wings, whose shadow cast such a foetid and abysmal blight over the quaint and ancient Prydeinig towne of New Lynsmouth. The gleaming keber, pistons and rods of the Hill Aeronautical Motor added a hint of *power* and a dash of modernity to the wonderful lepidopteral ornithopter.

We trundled the craft round to the grand front-lawn for take-off. The rest of the household were visiting Ysgwier

Kentrevak and his family at Chy-Hwytha that day. We thought it best to conduct the preliminary flight-trials when they were out, just in case of a crash – we didn't want them to witness anything too ghastly.

How strange it would have looked to an observer, as the aeroplane roared into life and started slowly undulating those great green gwyr wings. Paul and I exchanged a grin and I increased the power. The noise was terrific – we inched forwards, gaining speed as the wings flapped more air. The far-forward rush of oncoming air – the accelerating progress of the machine as it rolled along on its spidery wheels – all gave rise to a euphoric rapture that rose like the sun in my breast. A golden, joyous rapture, one that I must not become lost in. I cleared my minde and focused on piloting the craft.

Like a stone skimmed across the water, we suddenly left the Earth behind and took to the air. The airframe lurched, strained and soared – we were riding the frothy and diffuse molecules of a gas! Outrageously we flapped over the Grand Lawn, gaining altitude. I banked to port and went into a great circuitous lap around the stolid and archaic bulk of Chy-an-Brae. The difference the engine made was phenomenal. Flight was now powered, controllable and effortless! I turned the nose towards the lawn and we got down without too much of a bump when we returned, laughing, to Earth. Cheering, laughing, shaking hands – Delenn and Taxon greeted us with delight – as did Jack Lane, who suddenly seemed to appear out of nowhere, like a fox emerging from its burrow. He was clutching a yard-long, black and white feather, which he offered to Paul.

"Well done, old fella, and please accept this feather, in token of your initiation into the Honorable Order of the Albatross! Now, are you going to take me up in that kite of yours?"

Thus, in the course of that golden blazing unforgettable afternoon, Paul took Jack for a circuit round the grounds; after which Lazarus piloted Mr Delenn for a memorable flight that took them out around the wider hinterland.

After the spiny bird had returned to its roost we had our tay on the lawn and enthused over our successful flights.

Delenn was in a state of some amazement. The sudden chance to fly like a bird, over his native land, at his age, had impressed him profoundly.

"I never would have thought it! Never in a million years…!"

"I think you've earned this," said Jack, passing him a monstrously etiolated quill of jet black larid plumage, "welcome to the Order Mr Delenn."

"It's a great honour and a great joy to me, Mr Lane, and, I, I can't believe it! Flying like the birds! Just like the birds! I can't believe it, I really can't!"

The old gardener shook his head in the euphoria of amazement.

Something had been puzzling me.

"By the way, Jack," I bespoke, "where did you get the *Kramvil*-feathers from?"

A rye smile rippled over the stubble-field of his face. "For several days after the destruction of the Kramvil by that inexplicable decapodic leviathan, large feathers were washing ashore and being collected off the beach by the enterprising local children who sell them as souvenirs! The going-rate is usually half-a-crown for a decent plume, but they only charge me a tanner! Ha ha ha! Little blighters!"

"By Jehosephat! What an enigmatic and ephemeral aberration that great carapaced scuttling brine-beast *was!*" I rasped through chattering jowls at the thought of the briefly-glimpsed, but never to be forgotten sight of the Legest Meur.

"Hmmm, curiouser and yet more inexplicable…" murmured Lazarus thoughtfully.

"Strange times indeed," added the gardener.

"Perplexing epiphanies… biological anomalies… provocative irregularities…" mumbled Jack in debonair exegesis.

"Aye, we're all fly-boys now…" I droned, "what a difference twelve and a half horse-power make! Your engine's a work of genius, Paul! Goes like a sewing-machine, true genius!"

"Only when combined with the Tikky-Dyw airframe!" elucidated Paul – a point we all acknowledged in the gleam of an ocular.

Sunbeam's splendour cylindrically lit 'n' enriched the crystalline cellular crescendo of the day's sepia nostalgic rapture. Experimental aviators exchanging aerudite theories and enthusiastic theses on these breezes gwynjak aflap. With newly-sprouted wings we tried the air and found it to be good. In very truth we flew the flugh, fought gravity's drag and flying forth we soared on clouds cobalt, sky grainy blue and fresh Atlantek breath Kernowac.

In raptured sunlight fell the day and subtle blue the breath – all golowyjyon in the gwynk of an eye, an eye... Gloywder shone splendid mellow luminosity, yea, even on the insignificant trychfil insect, carapaced scuttling rustler crackling through billowing blooms of dodder. The sunny air we'd flown through now quivered gelatinous between us, quixotic bird-men and autochthonous aeronauts of West Cornwall, in the year 1911.

The heady air of modernity was shattered by the archaic sounds of barking hooves and galloping dogs – Red 'n' Blue in hue 'n' cry, hollerin' an' follerin' the clip-clopping hoofs of a mighty steed, seated bestride said steed being none other than himself, Old Paul Hill, therapsid thane of the rocky hills and rain.

"Whoa there, Buxtehude! Ease up now girl!"

Moss-Chops reigned-in his horse and reared up in his saddle, looming forth like the forward surge of evolution itself. Temples glistening with sweat, his jowls ululated slowly up and down in nullifying bemusement.

As Mr Delenn led old Buxtehude back to the stable, followed by Red 'n' Blue, Moss-Chops greeted the company and gazed curiously at the aircraft.

"You fellas got this thing off the ground yet?"

"Oh yes, several times," his namesake assured him, "are you ready for a flight, Dad?"

The looming bulk of his face was lit with a knowing smile. "Well, that's it, y' see?" he enthused, "that's why I galloped back from Ysgwier Kentrevak's house on old Buxtehude – had a hunch you fellas might be flying today, so I though I'd come and have a go – while there's no-one here to *stop* me, if you know what I mean...."

While Paul and Jack refuelled the machine and checked it over, Lazarus and I took a moment to look at the totemic topiary chough – *Pyrrhocorax pyrrhocorax* – with Old Paul.

"Great Haddocks!" thundered Mossy, "it's flourishing with *inordinate* vigour! Excellent work Mr Taxon! Ober da!"

The graft had indeed taken well and the foliage entwined in flowing tendrils of vital green shoots – they were already forming a bosky and healthy mass, which could soon be trimmed and snipped into shape and the noble chough would once again sport its sleek corvid profile to the withering mists of the hinterland plateau – *Fire-crow! Fire-crow!*

Temporary moments later, the two Hills, father and son, boarded the Ticky-Dyw and made a successful ascent into the realm of air. We watched the take-off from the Grand Lawn; Lazarus, Jack and I – it flapped swiftly aloft like a pteropus flying fox on a tropical fruit-bat flight. We resumed the discussion of our flying experiences and some technical aspects of the aircraft. My minde, formless and without size, was more cognizant of the *romantic* possibilities of flight and my promise to take Constance for a ride in the Heavier-Than-Air-Machine.

"There were a couple of times during *our* flight," was Jack speaking, "when I felt that the centre of gravity could do with being lowered a little, to enhance the stability when wing-warping into a turn..."

"Yes... I had a hunch that weight-distribution might become problematical once we fitted the engine," agreed the Taxonomic eld.

Mr Delenn wandered back from the stables, still elated by his promotion to the Bird-Realm. His battered hat backed on to the top of his marmareegos, glittering, verdant head.

"I've been thinking," he began, putting out the budding shoots of an idea, "all this talk of Albatrosses made me think that a bird that can rest on the water, well, it can go a long way, can't it? It can go anywhere it likes! But a land-bird now, can only land on the *land,* now, can't it? See what I mean?"

Jack's brow arched in recognition like a rainbow over Mount's Bay. "You mean put *floats* on the old kite instead of wheels?"

"That's very much what I'm thinking, Mr Lane; only the floats could have miniature wheels mounted inside 'em!"

"Most ingenious!" spat Lazarus, "and the extra weight and air-resistance would also have the favourable result of lowering the centre of gravity! Most serendipitous! I think your apprenticeship in the carriage-builder's shop is proving very useful Mr Delenn!"

Then it was my turn to be inspired… "You know, if we ran a drive-shaft from the jynn-keber down into the floats, we could have a little ship's propeller on the back of each float, so we could have the option of nautical propulsion!"

"Excellent idea!" enthused Jack, "but what about in the event of engine-trouble? Perhaps you could incorporate a means of manual-propulsion…"

I was having visions of my recent *manually*-powered wing-flapping escapade all over again…..

"I think it's a first-rate idea," chirped Lazarus, "and I reckon a set of bicycle-pedals and a couple of chains should do the trick!"

We were all extremely excited from our recent flights and the ideas seemed to be fizzing like a bucket of yeast on a sunny day.

There thence began a lugubrious braying – the loud-throated and sleek-pawed hounds were baying a-howl – ol' Red 'n' Blue – something was up; *rough hounds of the sea!* Something was going down, be not mistaken. Niwllaw swirls and flurries of smúitiúil vaporous tendrils crept through the sky of glass. Evening was descending with a damp. The hounds howled forth again however, harthing and barqueing both dulcet, muscular *and* crepuscular. Some figures were approaching across the great *steppe* of the lawn. It was June Hill, with Florence and Constance!

Eternity squared out and became each sleek and shimmering footfall of the lady Constance – for in my eyes I beheld only her, though I saw them all. Lithely she flowed forth towards me, a luminous creature of Parnassos or the banks of the Voidomatis. She advanced across the chess-board lawn, Queen of my Heart, looming to take me and check-mate

362

me, whilst I, the King, dreamed on, immobile and entranced, watching her flow in like the tide.

We all exchanged fond greetings and the Danse Gothique of conversation spooled and spieled like silk. It suddenly crossed my minde that June might not take too kindly to the idea of Old Paul being chauffeured around the cloudscapes of old Penwithershins by their son, on the back of a man-made flap. I think it had occurred to the others too, as Jack did his best to engage her interest in non-aeronautical topics, asking her all about old Squire Kentrevak and the latest news from Chy-Hwytha. Jenny Kegyner appeared, bearing a large tray of tay and buns, with a small selection of macroons. I gazed into Miss Constance's eyes and chewed macroon. The precise combination of her radiant beauty and the coconutty crunch of a really well-baked macroon was enough to swoon a stray swain.

Lazarus sipped his Lapsang Souchong, in preference to Oolong-oolong. Inwardly, he sketched out an improved gear-system for the Tickee-Dywe-flyer whilst wrestling with the riddle of Rongo-rongo. Delenn rustled and fluttered around, looking like he wanted to leave. He nibbled nervously at his choice of pastry, which in his case was the gooseberry *roulade* – tangy, yet undeniably crunchy – contrasted with a smooth yet grainy inner pulp. Florence, ever-lively and fireish, warm as the auburn spitfire, was enjoying the brittle solidity of a ginger biscuit. Now Jack was asking if the ysgwier still had the same old butler, the one with the glass eye… Constance's perfect and graceful hand was reaching for the plate of sweetmeats – what would she *pick?* Could it be…. could it….? By Jehosephat! Yes indeed! She's chosen the *macroon!* This was too good to be true, I hadn't dared hope for *this!* Our eyes met….

"And does anyone know where my *husband* might be?" enquired June, rather loudly I thought, as if she perhaps sensed our evasion.

"I think he's, er, that is to say, *popped upstairs,"* blustered Jack, "would you like to see how the topiary is recovering?"

But June seemed oddly uninterested in heraldic hedge-birds at that moment. Blue set up a moan and Red came back with a dirge, head thrown back to the sky – the darkening sky. I involuntarily looked up – was that the sonorous, fizzing drone of a jynn-keber? The ghostly and fragile flutter of subtle paper wings? The rustle of a bat or the mere moan of a wandering and restless wind, racing over the darkening moorlands and boulders, carns and dewy dodder-meadows and pastures of gorse, thistle and thorn, that grace the gripping horn of Cernyw's gritty granite claw?

We peered through the dusk shades of tewlwolow, the Kernewek particular mist that muffles mine-stack 'n' mizzen-mast alike – a speck was approaching in the sky – it was emanating a peculiar noise, a puttering, airy drone.

"Merciful Heavens!" juddered June with autonomic abandon, "what on *earth* is that thing in the sky?"

Florence Place caught Lazarus Taxon's eye knowingly, "we'd better step to the side of the lawn," put he, "I think it's coming in for a landing."

We started to withdraw to safety, but Jenny Kegyner was stooping down for the tray of refreshments.

"You'd better leave them, Mrs K!" called Jack, grabbing her arm and leading her briskly after the others.

From the vast, crenellated edge of the Grand Lawn we watched the approach of the bat – the bird – the motor – the machine – an jynn-ebrenn – an jynn-*edhen* – an engine of heaven – a bird-engine; aerial-carriage; heavier-than-air-*flapper:* fruit-bat of Borneo's tropic latitudes – sinuous undulating pterodactyl – green carapace-shell of canvas, stretched sail-cloth and wickerwork beehive of spindly spars, wired together like a *Stegosaurus stenops* – in short, it was our own home-made Tycky-Diw ornithopter that we saw languorously flapping it's way back through the tewlwolow dusks of the hinterland, coming back in to land.

The wings hunched and buckled, held high like a honey-buzzard, reminiscent of the gothique lineaments of Mr Ader's 'Eole', that audacious tendril of the Steam-Age, issuing through a mechanistic fissure into the Age of Flight.

There were gasps of amazement as the aeroplane swooped steadily down, flapping gracefully towards the lawn.

Another gasp followed as June Hill recognized her husband and son sailing blithely in to land upon this great mechanical flutterer.

With a short series of hops and bumps, the aeronauts returned to Earth, scattering fragments of macroon-shrapnel across the dewy grass.

Paul Hill the younger cut the engine and for a long moment silence reigned – only to be broken by his irate mother, June Hill….

"Wait till I get my hands on you, you old fool, flitting off in a flying machine like that, at your age too! And you Paul," her wrath briefly rested upon her son, "you shouldn't have let him into that contraption of yours, you really shouldn't!"

"Sorry Mum," murmured young Paul, "but you know what Dad's like, he wouldn't take 'no' for an answer…" he smiled.

"Oh I know what he's like alright…."

The aviators climbed down from the craft and joined us.

"Now that really *was* extra-ordinary!" sputtered Moss-Chops jubilantly as he embraced his wife, who soon abandoned the pretence of protest and laughed with the rest of us as he spun her round in his mighty arms. Truly he was a krogen-headed tower of tapinocephalidaeic power, surging forth boldly and breasting the flow of time's tide.

"*Extra*-ordinary! Life is truly *Extra*-ordinary!" he announced and I suddenly felt deeply moved. We all cheered and applauded and joviality rose like the warm sun and everybody started talking at once. We decided to trundle the aircraft back to the workshop then prepare for the evening's feast. Constance caught my eye as we were about to leave. I sensed a pensive quality, as if she was yearning for something.

"Don't worry darling," I told her, "we'll fly tomorrow – I haven't forgotten!"

Her face was lit with a beautiful smile and a shaft of light seared into my heart.

I caught up with the companions, the rapidly-growing flock of 'Albatrosses' rolling the little machine back to its shed in atmospheric elation. Once the flying-machine was safely put away, everyone headed back to the house – except for Lazarus Taxon and me, Elias Gillpington.

*

A few drops of rain pattered against the workshop windows, the wind was rising and the sky was darkening. Uchelfryd, the learned Taxon sprinkled Pre-Cambrian coals into the fire with a steady hand, transformed from the archaic, clutching claw of yore.

"Well, Mr Gillpington, a very successful day for science," he beamed, a golowji of enthusiasmos, "the twelve and a half horsepower petroleum beam-engine ornithopter has exceeded our wildest hopes and proved itself a thoroughly air-worthy machine!"

"It's certainly easy-going compared to the *muscle*-powered version!" I jested.

"Yes, and old Delenn's idea about converting the Ticky-Dyw into an amphibian makes a great deal of sense, particularly as we are surrounded by the sea here so there will likely be a strong demand for these kinds of craft, and also," he caught my eye meaningfully, "it gives you the possibility of escape over the sea, if need be."

"Yes, amphibious craft are wonderfully versatile," I agreed, "and I suppose we may indeed have to go on the run if the whole *Kramvil* business catches up with us…"

"I've been thinking about all that," began the elder scholar as his orbs scanned the margins of Time, "the craft will only carry two – I think that if it's no longer safe for us in the Shyre, then you should take the Ticky-Dyw – the *proto-*type that is, and perhaps you'd be taking Miss Constance as well?"

"Well, I wouldn't want to leave without her of course, but what about *you* Lazarus? What would you do? How would you escape?"

"Well, I'm not sure I *would escape,* geographically, that is – I thought I might stick around actually," the physicist murmured with a cool ironic relish.

"But you have to think of your safety Lazarus," I objected, "you know as well as I do that you'd be about as popular in New Lynsmouth now as an arsonist in the British Library."

"Yes, I quite agree," countered he "but any vengeful locals would be looking for an *old man* named Lazarus Taxon…" he glanced over to the magneto-animation equipment arranged in his laboratory corner, "not for, shall we say, a twenty-year-old engineering student, recently arrived from overseas, perhaps with a name like…. Erasmus Jackson!"

"But- how- how-" I was spiralling in inexplicable dizziness – recalling Lazarus's 'reincarnation' with the help of that magneto-animation gear, after that monstrous fowl *killed* him. "Erebus Compound!" I mumbled the phrase in gradual comprehension. There was no doubt it had made us both years younger in terms of physiology.

"Yes, Erebus Compound," he continued calmly, "combined with the chemical animation salts and magneto-animation treatments – then I would have to practice my accent and learn to play a new role, rather like an actor…"

I stared at him, amazed, but saw that he was serious. He seemed to play with time like clay.

"So you would simply replace your *old* self with a young and ostensibly *different* self? A most original ruse, combining all the advantages of running away *and* sticking around!"

"That's it exactly," agreed the eld. "The *old* 'me' goes away and a new – and different 'me' returns to carry on building aircraft, setting up a factory, making New Lynsmouth famous for her heavier-than-air amphibious flying machines and bringing some prosperity to the village!"

"It's an audacious plan," I mused, amused at his mystical simplicity, "but I see you mean to go through with it Lazarus and I admire your vision."

The simple temerity of his hypothesis teemed and fizzed with myriad brilliant scintilla. He hacked a track through time and faithfully followed his daemon. If I'd learned one thing from being in his presence it was to never under-estimate the possibilities of a situation. The stark, strange truth of it was that Lazarus Taxon was already well on the way back to being a young man, so there was no rational reason why he could not go *further* – become *younger!*

"I don't imagine a physical organism can be kept in a state of *indefinite* animation," began Taxon, "but, with repeated treatments, the cellular activity could be prolonged to many times its current normal span... perhaps several centuries. I shall of course be recording all my data and findings with scrupulous rigour..."

"You speak of a rigour that transcends mortis!" I gasped aghast at the ghost of his atemporal genius.

"Renewed vigour brings new rigour," he smiled. "I've lived a long life and accumulated a lot of learning. By turning back the mortal clock of age, I shall buy precious years with which I can use my knowledge to contribute to science, to uplift people's mindes and advance the great tide of progress!"

"And to bring it all to fruition by building flying-boats in New Lynsmouth – why, it's absolutely brilliant, Lazarus, dazzlingly brilliant!"

I was moved by the boldness and depth of his visionary plan, and in awe of his courageous exploratory work in the new field of magneto-animation. The man seemed to inhabit a realm of almost pure minde – it seemed right that he should live on. Why should the World be deprived of such a brilliant minde? Tell me *that,* oh arbiters of Reality, oh limiters of possibility! Tell me *that!*

Rain spattered and shattered drops popping and bursting on glazed and liquid glass, leaden, pewter, piscine, glaucous, glistening, glinting, running in silver rivulets, vaporous juice of Atlantek's main, coming home to roost on rustic rooves. A thousand rain-drops pattering and battering on glass – the sound of Cornwall.

The wind was whirling its cloak to the sky and the brittle rattling tracery of twigs creaked and shook in the ivy-clad trees that huddled hither and thither in shimmering groves. Winter rode the night.

*

After a bright and cheerful meal, I excused myself from the company, bade a fond goodnight to the lovely Miss Constance and retired early to my warm and comfortable room. Many things were on my minde as I stared into the glowing red coals in the grate and listened to the wind and rain outside. There blew breezes that blasted Chy-an-Brae to blue blazes and rain rattled the gutters and splattered the galoshes with aqueous watery washes. I thought of the lovely Constance of the glossy dark hair, the shy, knowing look, the earnest beauty of her gleaming eye and her vigorous radiance. Rain pattered and wind sighed. I thought of Lazarus swimming back against the Stream of Time – was this not a hazardous and experimental venture into dangerously new ground, just as the whole Kramvil adventure had been? Or would Taxon's audacity pay off again, as it had done with the aircraft-project? The wind moaned low and the rain laid siege to the window. There were occasional puffs of smoke as a down-blast played around the chimney. In my minde's eye I beheld the gleaming pistons and churning keber of the Ticky-Dyw, whistling wires in wing-warped tension and the land unfurled beneath the undercarriage like an ancient Celtic tapestry. I recalled the rising euphoria, the rapture of flight, induced by even a short flap around the house – I reminded myself to be vigilant and not to succumb to 'aero-rapture', as I dubbed it. Dubbed it. Rapturous delight. A syndrome characterized by an inordinate access of joy. Glee. Glaw. Glutinous rain poured down dowr and dampening, moistening the night and scattering jags of wetness. This glyb mineral backdrop stirred my thoughts and helped them flow and flux and flesh out my ideas. The eel-bites had healed well, as had that vicious beak-gash on my ribs. When I thought of old Lazarus recovering from a *death*-wound from that same ghastly, squawking, ravenous, hack black beak, my minde was once again filled with wonder.

    A whitesquall of battering hail punctuated my reverie with its icy bullets. I thought of the Kramvil and the horror it had visited upon New Lynsmouth. The unspeakable outrage, misery and desecration. The dread. A dread now transmuted to a deep calm relief, with the sure knowledge of the beast's destruction.

    I was slipping into slumber, like an ice-berg calving from a vast, creeping glacier and plunging into the sea. I was being subsumed in an ocean of impressions, images and feelings and blissful thoughts of Constance that rose like bubbles in my drowsy minde. Sleet shot the sky with watery ravens – erghlaw gouts of freezing fog-wets and Kernouac grey mists, wind whistling wild 'n' high, roaring like the beast from the pit. Tearing, rending, grinding and jabbering, gwynjak twisting wind unwhirled.

*

    Well it's a still wind that blows nobody good and it's a wild wind that whistled and roared and pelted the old house and its upland environs in rain and sleet for three days. Flying was out of the question whilst this tempest raged, so Constance was obliged to wait stoically for her maiden voyage in the Tikki-Dew.

    The rainy interlude did however provide an opportunity to carry out the improvements to the aircraft that we had discussed. The work was virtually all done by Paul and Mr Delenn, with Lazarus mostly dabbling away in his own laboratory-corner, but somewhat overseeing the work, and myself mostly leaving things in my companions' capable hands, whilst I spent time with Miss Constance or delved sporadically into old Paul's fine library, which contained works in all of the dozen native tongues of these islands, as well as many in Greek, Latin, Hebrew, Aramaic, Arabic, Persian and Sanskrit; not to mention French, German, Italian, Spanish, Dutch, Russian and Polish. Curious what you find in these old country houses. Cultural trails leading off all over the place – an atmospheric backdrop to my romance with Constance. It was a busy house, at times a bustling one, yet the two of us managed to find quiet moments together to bathe and bask in each others presence like co-practitioners of a strange new religion. The old house became an enchanted realm for us, just as its great gardens were, and we enjoyed many simple yet unforgettable moments together in that magical and archaic place. Taking tay together in the conservatory whilst the rain skittered over the roof and the afternoon sky darkened, holding hands and laughing, we drank the days down like the sweetest wine.

*

The following day, like an exploding slice of prismatic simultaneity, everything seemed to happen at once.

It all started at breakfast-time, I'd just finished my porridge and was washing it down with a hot cup of Chinese Breakfast Tay, when Mrs Kegyner came in with the morning paper for Old Paul – the Penwithershins Gazette. This particular local fish-wrapper had always struck me as frankly rather dull, with its endless preoccupation with pasti-suppers, Young Farmer's Club meetings and inconsequential and inaccurate tittle-tattle of miniscule import. This morning however, it seemed to have a rather electrifying effect on old Moss-Chops, who spluttered, gasped and puffed in pelicosaurian baffling amazement.

"Great Hawks of the North!" he exonerated, "rum doings in New Lynsmouth, and *no* mistake!"

The crimson krogen of his great head leaned forward atavistically, great shoulders and paws hunched, bunched and looming forth in crescendo of flesh.

"What is it, dear?" asked June, giving voice to the question that was ominously forming in the mindes of all present.

"Well, listen to this," began Mossy, grasping the cheaply-produced broadsheet between truculent and beefy fingers and inflecting his voice with a slight tone of the orator. 'NEAR-RIOT IN NEW LYNSMOUTH! The local constabulary had to be called in last night to quell a disturbance in the Old Quarter of New Lynsmouth that was threatening to get out of hand. Scuffles broke out as a riotous group of men attacked a house in Orchard Street, pelting it with stones, daubing it with slogans such as 'Woe to the sorcerers' and attempting to set fire to the building. Neighbours from Orchard Street joined the fray, fearing that a fire might spread to their own dwellings. Sergeant Penndegys of Pensanskrit police station said that he'd come within an inch of reading the Riot Act, but in the end, had managed to restore order by threatening to arrest the next man who threw a stone. When he asked the crowd the reason for the disturbance he was met with some rather baffling answers which seemed to allude to an alleged incident involving a giant gull that the villagers believed to have been reared by local scientists and released to wreak havoc on the local population. They blamed the monstrous sea-fowl for various recent outrages in the area, including sheep-worrying, poultry-pilfering, destroying the fish-market and the burning of fishing-boats as well as grave-robbery, upsetting the pasty-cart and the eating of a small dog.

It was noticed that a lot of the belligerents smelled strongly of rum and ale and our more sceptical readers might wonder if these liquids contributed to the rather colourful nature of the accusations. One of the more senior members of the angry mob for instance claimed that the giant bird was in fact a *mechanical* bird and that it was killed in a sea-battle with a giant mechanical lobster!

Well, dear readers, far be it from me to accuse the good people of New Lynsmouth of a tendency towards exaggeration, but let's just say they've always been good story-tellers!

After Sgt. Penndegys had dispersed the mob I asked him whether he would be taking any further action in the 'case of the giant seagull'. He informed me that he would make his report on the incident and await further orders.

Any readers with information on the whereabouts of any giant seagulls, monsters, sea-serpents etc., etc., please contact the Penwithershins Gazette, 13 Voundervour Lane, Pensanskrit.'

There was a moment of stunned and brooding silence. We looked at each other in dismay. It was Paul – the younger – who spoke first.

"Talk about adding insult to injury," he lamented indignantly, "after all that those people have been through, that self-satisfied reporter was virtually laughing in their faces! He made a mockery of the whole idea of the gull!"

"First they are violated and terrorised by a monster," it was Jack who spoke back, "then they are publicly ridiculed in the press for mentioning it – people's blood must be positively *boiling!"*

"Add to that all the public speculation and discussion of the gull that the article will generate and the unwelcome attention that focuses on us *and* a possible police-investigation…" added Lazarus.

Florence seemed very concerned – "I'm not sure it's safe for you and Mr Taxon to remain in the Shyre." she sighed pensively, looking from me to Lazarus to Constance. "Have you given any thought to your escape-plans?"

Old Blue suddenly moaned and whimpered lugubriously, adding to the air of languid gothic melancholia that was seeming to pervade and possess the old house, creeping in like a chilling, killing cold.

"Oh those *dratted* newspapers!" muttered June Hill in an access of indignation, "always stirring up trouble when it's not wanted!"

Paul was on the verge of asking his mother when trouble *was* wanted, but then thought better of it.

"As a matter of fact," ventured Lazarus, "I'm planning to leave today, for London, and possibly on to the continent after that. I shall be travelling incognito of course."

He looked around the table – I think we were all a bit shocked.

"I can't thank you enough for your kind hospitality," he said, addressing Old Paul and June Hill, "I shan't forget my stay here. Perhaps you could use my scientific equipment in the aeronautical workshop, Paul, and I'll arrange for the other things to be put into storage for the duration. And if I meet any budding aeronautical engineers on my travels I might send 'em down to you to help develop the latest model 'Ticky-Dew'!"

"You're welcome back any time, Mr Taxon," said June "and don't worry about storing your stuff," added Moss-Chops considerately, "we've got bags of room here so you can both leave your bits and pieces here while you go on the run – and I hope the blighters don't catch you!" he added with feeling.

"I can only echo Mr Taxon's heartfelt thanks," I began, but Mossy waved the subject away. "Never minde all that, old boy, you know you're always welcome here at Chy-an-Brae, but dash it – what are you going to do?" he eyed me with genial, pugnacious concern.

"Well, I'll be flying off in the old Ticky-Dyw with Miss Constance, if she'll do me the honour…?"

"Oh Elias, you know I will!" she smiled radiantly.

"But first, we'll be needing a clergyman." A slight gasp was heard around the table.

"Well you're in luck there," announced Moss-Chops in florid jubilation, "the Reverend Kryjyk always visits his relations up at Trewither House on a Thursday. If we could get a message over to him, I'm sure he'd come round, especially if it's *official* business…" he winked jovially at Constance and I.

"Well, since the weather seems to have cleared, and since the aircraft will need a test of the new undercarriage before a major voyage, why don't I fly over to Trewither House and drop off an aerial-telegram? Paul – fancy a spin before Elias flies off with our beautiful prototype Ticky-Dyw?"

Moments later the petroleum beam engine roared into life and Lazarus Taxon and Paul Hill were trundling across the Grand Lawn with gradually increasing speed as canvas wings amazingly flapped and grappled the air aloft. The 'take-off' went well – the floats apparently having no impeding effect with their slight addition of weight. It always made a deep impression on me, seeing that frail, spindly machine fight its way into the air with slow rhythmic undulations like a turkey-vulture. A strange, sombre, futuristic, gleeful, glittering sight for the eye of the minde, vast void volatile voluptuous and cultural – the ascent of the ornithopter was richly symbolic of Man's struggle to conquer new realms with science – it felt *historic, glorious* and slightly disturbing.

Birds flew flocks in auguries – passerine birds of passage – Bran the Crow and *Corvus corax,* the Raven.

A wind was blowing across the fluttering, dancing pages of an open book, an ancient book – the book of tales, the tale of fates, the fates of lives – myriad teeming lives. Different birds and fowls of the air were alighting on the pages of the book, as they flapped and shuffled, opening and closing, showing flashes of Destiny.

On some pages a cheerful rudhek robin would land, on some a sweet melodious blackbird would pour forth song, or a chuckling jay or nightjar would churra and flute forth feathery throat-notes. Other pages were ripped and despoiled by the scratching claws and beaks, the harsh carks and honks of gaunt ravens, rooks and crow-bran-buzzards, honey-buzzards, vultures, bitterns with their chicks and baby-boomers, egg-rattlers, throaty squawkers and avine tribes various. Our fates in the feathery wings of the air. Destinies whirling round like blazing star-sparks. I wondered of the fates of Constance Place and Elias Gillpington then – on what page they were writ and what manner of feathery visitor would sing our tale and so illuminate our page in the ancient fluttering book.

Chy-an-Brae hummed, buzzed and throbbed with activity that morning, like a great bee-keeper's skeep, a droning hive of wasps. The news of an imminent marriage was met with much emotion, and naturally the women wanted to plan a feast and dress up and all, but I had to remind them that the whole reason for haste was that we were fugitives and had to flee from danger, so, if the Reverend Kryjyk materialized, it would be a quick ceremony and straight off in the aeroplane.

"But what about your wedding-feast? And your journey – you'll need food for that too – oh what should we do?" pleaded Jenny Kegyner with an air of rising panic. An unceremonious wedding was something quite new to her and alien to her soul.

"Dear Jenny," I answered her, "perhaps a batch of pasties would be the best thing. We could take some on the flight with us. We won't have time to feast, as we'll need all the available hours of daylight for visibility."

"Very sensible old chap!" boomed Mossy, "Don't want those Luddite blighters catching up with you and wrecking the kite in a fit of rage, do you?"

"That's right Mr Hill," I agreed, "the essence of time is unknowable but haste we must make ourselves!"

"But where will you *get* married?" asked June duly and quixotically.

"I thought the Magor would make an ideal chapel, it looks like it used to be one anyway."

Everyone assented warmly to this idea, particularly Constance, who smiled happily when I said the word *Magor*. Jenny went off to create a batch of pasties, taking June, Florence and Constance with her. We were ordered not to disturb them – I think it was some kind of woman-business.

I dashed upstairs and started putting on all the clothes I had. Even with a centrally-heated nacelle, flying was still a draughty and chilly experience. I had my set of oil-skins and Jack had kindly donated a set to Constance and we each had motor-cycle goggles and leather gauntlets. The Hills had also given us various woolly jumpers, socks and scarves.

Carrying a sheepskin bundle of swaddles and clothings I left the peaceful room of my five-day coma and walked once more the ancestral portrait corridor. Each archaic face set and embedded in its own time, its own history, destiny – Character etched in intrinsically characteristic flesh – Human dramas caught on canvas. Old Gorhengeugh Hill, remote ancestor and progenitor; Old Cybele Hill, Great Granddam and tribal Grand-Mother – the faces of epochs flitted by, catching my orbital eye as I walked past glimpsing aspidistras, harquebuses – oddly objective, feeling cool and detached, though I was about to embark on the double-voyage of marriage to Constance and a daring, long-distance flight in the Tikki-Dyw.

To float and fly in bardhonieth, versing and singing the tides of my times, lyricising with lute and lyre, singing and chanting and reciting in groves, in robes, in droves of doves and cedars such forth I seek to sing, aspiring to inspire divine fire. Walking down the corridor of fate I swelled and surged with tonnek oceanic upswirls, my ancient universal psyche unfolded glittering depths in preparation for trial by air and water. And so, oh quixotic and numinous reader, in recording these events, sensations and phenomena, in writing of my experiences and times, in this most lugubrious and foetid journal, this Jeremiad; *here'S my chance,* I thought, to sing to the winds and stars and shine a little light onto a time of darkness, turbulence, struggle and mystery. And a time of love, I felt most strongly, as the image of Miss Constance again loomed, blossomed and glowed before my inner eye, my inner heart.

As I meandered through the knotty Knossos of dog-trots and passage-ways that riddled the old house like the aqueous borings of ship-worms, I walked past the closed kitchen door and caught a sound-wave of laughter – or was it sobbing? *Something* was going on in there. Once more I drifted through the halls of the house, afloat in thought and reminiscence, moving by a form of polyp-friction. Surfing the *vritis,* riding the thought-waves was a tekter tonic for my bywek psyche, y psykie mou, and following the thoughtstream as I tap-toed through the old house, I found myself beached in the drawing-room with Jack Lane and Old Paul Hill.

"Hallo Elias," grinned Jack, "you look like a blinking *yeti!"*

"Yes, I think I'd better shed a few layers before I pass out," I quoth.

"Where are you heading to, old boy, *ICELAND?"* rumbled the bryophytic and autochthonous host.

"Hmmmm…" I mused… "Change the C for an R and you have it."

"BY THUNDER! The Emerald Isle, is it? Excellent idea! Good place to lie low for a while!"

"Absolutely", smiled Jack, "I believe the green hills of Eirinn have given shelter to many a brave soul in the past!"

"Well, we enlarged the fuel-tank", I explained, "so Lazarus reckons it'll hold enough juice to get us over the waters – all I have to do is bear north-west and I can't really miss!"

"You make it sound so simple!" observed Jack, "like crossing the road!"

"Well, I s'pose it's just a very large and watery road," I volunteered.

"Well, flying over *land* is one thing," expostulated the chops of moss, "but water now, that's slippery stuff, a treacherous medium, do you see? I hope you're well-prepared for this voyage of yours." Mossy leaned forward, turning a glassy and speculative eye my way, eyeing and weighing me.

"I'm planning to avoid the water as much as possible," I ululated, "but I'm taking me bugle, so if we do have to land in the drink I'll just toot out the Morse code for S O S and if the worst comes to the worst, I can always *pedal* the old kite over to Blarney, can't I?"

"Ha ha ha –" Mossy obviously loved this idea. "You'll go down in history as the first man to cross the Irish sea by bicycle!"

Awyr – ayr – aer – air – vibrating – pulsing – carrying sounds – compressing – pulsating tingling aether carrying messages – pullulating – ululating air – carrying the dull warp and throb of an aerial-beam-engine.

We rushed to the French windows and were just in time to glimpse a great green slow-flapping heron, a heron-gull, a purple swamphen trychfil hweskerenn insect aflap above the lawn, our spindly and graceful creation coming home to roost. Moments later, Taxon and Hill, polymath and jynn-keberist were standing before us, calmly elated by their flight.

"Mission accomplished!" beamed Paul. "When we flew round Trewither House, they came swarming out like ants! We had the note for the Reverend Kryjyk all ready in a canvas bag, which I lobbed over the side, once we'd got their attention – they *definitely* got the message alright!"

"That's wonderful!" I infused, "and how about the craft? How did she *handle?* How did she *feel?*"

It was the turn of the elder to speak, but an *elder* he was no longer, having already started the mytho-poetic rejuvenation process, he now stood firm of form before us as a dark-haired, strong-jawed, *athletic* type of fellow, bursting with vigour, photon-clouds illuminated by the sharp flavour of his very presence. Those eyes, once elliptically caked and carapaced in cataracted and dim senescence, now gleamed with the fire of youth. The time-bespattered and decrepit relict of a scholar who sold various divers, antiquated, quaint and curious volumes from a ragged trestle-table in the quiet back-alleys of old New Lynsmouth was turning back the Sun and Moon and walking the path back to youth…

"She handles like a dream, Elias, flies like a bird!" He shone like a luminous light thing.

Much activity followed, as the Tikki-Dyw needed topping up with fuel and water, as well as some basic supplies. Jenny Kegyner came and announced that she and June Hill were off to prepare the Magor for the ceremony, in the hopes that the reverend vicar would indeed show up. Mr Delenn went along with them, to put up a bell-tent as a 'changing-room' for the ladies. Constance and Florence remained in seclusion, no doubt engaged in a heart to heart talk before the wheel of events started to spin and hurl out the episodes of destiny's manifestation.

Thus, spinning like the pyroclastic dust of the sun, the shimmering veil of causality, mother of the ten thousand things.

Howl hounds and harth, the glasrudh blended bark of Red 'n' Blue, those howlak hounds of the Sun. It was the vicar, and that meant the marriage was on!

"It was good of you to answer our request, Father Timothy, especially after all the trouble we've caused you…" I began. "How is your leg healing up?"

"Well," smiled the priest benignly, "I could hardly ignore a summons from *heaven,* could I?" he chuckled, "and the leg has healed remarkably well, thanks to Mr Taxon's unique medicament; a *remarkably* rapid recovery…. And so I'm here to discharge my duty and perform the ceremony of marriage – I believe the aerial letter mentioned utilizing the *Magor* for the purpose…"

The Reverend Kryjyk chattered on in good-natured vein, it seemed he'd genuinely forgiven us for the outrages he'd suffered at Kyvounder House and the Ynkleudhva.

And so we left the old house and we trod the lawns Trelawny trod, dew-drops brilliant strung upon the cobweb on the statue of the dancing faun – ancient hedges framing secluded walkways and the bosky chough bursting forth with fresh, strong new growth – the sap was rising.

As if seen through a jewel, the Magor seemed to glisten and ripple in a kind of light.

Glittering granite glagolitic, the formerly gaunt Magor had been graced with bunches of snow-drops and white camellia in crystal vases – the batholithic floor had been strewn with sweet *Daphne odora* – blue rippled the wintry air, stillness descending – the company assembled – my minde a-whirl and my heart a-pounding – and there was Constance.

And beauty filled my eye and I had no doubts – I felt as if we were already married, that our union was rooted in the whirling wheels of time and space, the infinite pastures of the soul. It almost made marriage seem *superfluous,* whilst at the same time illuminating and sanctifying it. Dearly Beloved. My Goddess was standing before me, a warm gentle honey-amber glow deep in her eyes. We are gathered. Fugitives, desperadoes preparing for fledgling flight, surrounded by our little group of friends. Here together. A tear in Jenny Kegyner's eye. Magor's archaic granitic sparkle. In the sight of God. The Reverend Kryjyk's head slowly tilting back as he looks to the heavens – watching for flying-machines perhaps? To join these two. The gleaming white of Constance's dress – the dark rivers of her rolling hair – the stillness of the people in the hushed old relict of a chapel – an old crow, inky flapsterhude winging an oily feathered beak down the ragged ivy-branch-rattling wind. In holy matrimony... Silvery rivers running together in splendourous moonlight. Clouds of fleece in a soft blue sky, puffed like smoke from a dragon's nostril. Do you Elias... Cloud's flickering shadows flittering nebulous over the roofless rack of the ruin – inside stillness hung between each word. And do you, Constance... Monastic relict of time-encrusted and lichenous liths lilts listening in time's still eternity rippling. I do said Constance and the Reverend Timothy Kryjyk pronounced us man and wife. And like a gleaming gold band, the moment was sealed in time's amber resinous flow. I kissed my bride and our eyes focused in on each other. I knew we would not part, death or no death. Though there was much congratulating, tears, kisses, handshakes and good wishes, it was all as if a little distant, and my gaze rested like a beam of luminosity on Constance, unceasingly sensing her radiant presence.

With his evergreen glow, Mr Delenn handed round the glasses of champagne and we feasted on some crocus-yellow saffron buns.

"Dear friends," I chimed, "I wish to thank you all for everything you have done for us, for helping to arrange this rapturous and spontaneous wedding. Marrying my dear Constance has completed my happiness and the only poignant note to the day, is that we must now bid you all goodbye. You have all been such true friends in these times of mystery and turbulence, that it is not easy to part from you but I fear we must – after all, it's a long way to Ireland! I very much hope that we will all meet again, in auspicious circumstances."

Through tears that welled I saw the scene and time's silver mirror flickered and clouded with mnemonic scattered scintilla in shimmering pieces froides and white like snowflakes. Constance, my new bride, had gone to the tent with her ladies in waiting, to get changed into her flight-clothes.

"We've had a compass installed," sayeth old Delenn, "and a Davy lamp, in case you need it on your way over the waters."

The old man looked close to tears himself.

"Bless you Mr Delenn," uttered I, "you've made a great contribution to aviation, turning our old bird into a water-fowl!"

I shook the hand that had tended ten thousand green things and thought of his unlikely new role as an aircraft-designer. Strange what can happen in the mystical Cornique hinterland when the right causes and conditions come together and the right seeds are sown.

"Well, old man," smiled the vulpine and lowarnek Mr Jack Lane, "don't forget to send us a postcard when you get there, let us know you've made it safely."

"I'll do that Jack," I assured him, "anyway, it should be safer than trying to catch a free ride with a giant *gull,* like some of us, eh?" We laughed at the memory and clinked glasses merrily one last time.

I swaddled myself up in the oilskins, woollies, etc., etc.,

the open air already issuing tugging tendrils, urging me to wing-it aloft and grasp the empty sky.

"Come on, ya bloomin' old *yeti,*" rumbled and mumbled Moss-Chops in burly bucolic abandon, flaring and raring with sheer therapsid joy, "we'd better start loading the pasties 'n' tay aboard that magnificent *kite* of yours. You might get a trifle peckish on your way to Tír na nÓg; or Tipperary!" His humours welled and surged like the currents of the restless sea – jocosity was his rugose philosophy. A blazing yellow molecular Keltek flow, showing me back home to whom I am. Constance and the other ladies emerged from the tent – my young wife now garbed in the futuristic dress of an aerial explorer and pioneer. We walked hand in hand towards the Grand Lawn, where the Tikky-Dyw crouched like a grasshopper, ready to spring. I felt a levity, a lightness and strength coming to me from being united with Constance. We stole glances at each other as we walked and chatted to our friends.

"There's eight pasties in that parcel, minde," informed Jenny, "and they're proper-sized, minde – oh *do* be careful up there in that machine of yours!"

"Don't you worry Jenny," sayeth Florence to comfort her, "Constance is a brave lass and Elias is a very good flyer – aren't you Elias?" Florence eyed me, questioningly.

"Oh, er, yes," I mumbled, "a *very* good flyer!" And I suppose for someone with a couple of hours experience, I *was* pretty good....

"You've been very kind Jenny," I jested, "I think we could get to *America* on that many pasties!"

"If you need to jettison any ballast on the way," hinted Mossy with an archly raised brow, "start with the pasties – they must weigh a good five pounds each, eh?"

"Oh Paul, really!" chided June in mock-despair and nudging the walrustic bulk of himself in the ribs. Himself grinned knowingly, as did his son himself. The Hills were a happy tribe – 'Young Paul' also beamed like the Golowji of Alexandria. "It's been splann, er, splendid working on the jynnweyth, the engineering side of things with you Elias old man," he sputtered, holding out his hand, "now you'd better take Constance safely over the water for a while but be sure you both come back to us as soon as it's safe – we've got some aeroplanes to build, eh?"

"That's right Paul, there'll be wings over New Lynsmouth again, only *this* time they'll be bringing progress instead of chaos. I certainly hope we can work together again before too long."

"Well," he answered, "fare ye well, and the best of Brythonek luck to the both of you!"

A good friend was Paul, and a *fine* scientist, I felt sure his name would bring fame to New Lynsmouth and the Shyre.

In the late morning sunshine the gardens were aglow with living light. The chirruping of the first few song-birds could be heard warbling and trilling away in atavistic majesty, scenting the air with song. The land oozed sweet leafy nostalgia – a place of solidity and mellow security, a robust realm of form and structure. The sea was deep and wide, the air subtle, ungraspable and insubstantial. The path we had chosen led away from the known – I looked at her – our fates were fused together now, it was as one that we would venture into dangerous skies – and as one that we would live or die. Our wings were truly wings of fate and young wings can fly higher than you know. Wings of words aflap as printed pages catch a roaming breeze and lexicons spill out their contents. Dizzying gulphs and chasms seemed to yawn before my minde's eye as I contemplated that great oceanic wash that slopped and rocked from here to Blarney and the Blaskets – after all our outré adventures, it seemed that once again I was going to have to put my faith in science to see me through – Dark wings over the ocean…

A hearty pympbys hand, stout as a starfish patted me on the shoulder. The alert and vitally intelligent gaze of Lazarus Taxon met my jelly-orb eye – Lazarus Taxon? Or should I say *Erasmus Jackson?* For in very truth he was well on the way to a new identity – barely recognizable as the shuffling, rasping, half-blind creature with skin like savoy cabbage and eyes like frozen puddles who had sold me some rare books on the fabled street-corner where time slumbers in mellow dreams.

"It's a long road, Elias," sayeth he, "all our adventures

– past, present, future – a long road and I feel certain we will meet again. You have passed through many trials and kept a cool head under adversity, never wavering in your scientific rigour. You have earned my respect as a scientist and I would like to work with you again, in the future, in one form or another."

"You're very kind Lazarus, and do you know, I haven't had a moment's boredom since I first met you. Why, if I hadn't got involved with your magneto-animation and aeronautical projects I'd probably be sitting in Pensanskrit library, studying Latin grammar by candle-light! Now, thanks to you, I see that many things are possible…" I trailed off, minde benumbed by wonderment at the thought of Lazarus's vast contributions to science; his learning, erudition and transformative potential, his sheer power of minde.

The eyes of wisdom met mine once more – a kind of golowyjyon phosphorescence was being spectrally exuded, in gossamer waves of grace. "Best not delay," he hinted gently, "fly now, and take your Queen over the water."

Constance was looking tearful as Lazarus took her hands in his. "Good luck my dear, you will be safe in Elias's hands." He paused, and reaching into his coat pocket, he pulled out a couple of crystal vials with a greyish-blue tint.

"This is for emergency use, there's one each – *Erebus Compound!*"

We bade our final 'Goodbyes', embracing everyone and shaking hands tearfully.

"Bless you both and may the heavens protect you!" June Hill nearly crushed the two of us in her arms.

Florence took us by the hands and stared into our eyes for a moment. "Don't stay over there too long – come back soon! We need you back in the Shyre!" Then she threw her arms around her cousin and wept a bit, then kissed us both and that was it! Constance and I were getting aboard the Tykky-Dyw and everyone else was retiring to a safe distance for our departure.

I buckled up Constance's safety-belt and gave her a kiss. "Don't worry darling." I said. She looked at me with warmth and wisdom. "As long as I'm with *you* I'll be safe!"

I took my place in the bows of the generously-wide nacelle and switched on the engine.

*

A roar–a flap – beam rocking – a final wave and we were trundling forward, gaining velocity, gwyr pteranodon wings working in pulsing rhythmic warp – lurching forward, we took to the ayr. Ascending rapidly, we were swimming into the ocean of aer on the back of a manta-ray. The jynn-keber's cyclopean voice filled our ears and made conversation impossible. I glanced at the compass as we sailed airily over the several quaint gables of Chy-an-Brae – a slight adjustment to the rudder, a warp of the wings and we were on course, headed due North-West.

We passed over the sparse, granite-hedged fields of that rugged and austere corner of the Hinterland – twisted thorn-trees bowing to the wind – narrow, winding lanes, cart-tracks and holloways – gorse – bracken – heather – dodder – boulders and logan-stones – thin cattle and tumble-down old farmsteads, rusting, dreaming, growing lichen and stonecrop, groundsel swallowing up the farmyards and nettles running and bursting wild – the hinterland – *the Hills* – the batholithic backbone of the Shyre – An korf eskern Kernouac yw – jynnjyow idhyowek – the ivy-festooned fingers of the now-derelict engine-houses, pointing up into the highways of the air, the Continental Drift, the Great Vowel Shift and the Long-Shyre Drift. Aero-euphoria rising quietly within as our wings ply molecules diffuse and fine – breathe deeply, keep an eye on the compass – rhythmic unfoldment and *flap* of the wings taking us steadily up into realms aethereal and vaporous – little dragon-puffs of cloud in a blue sky – glas yw an ebrenn – a fox running across the moors, high-tailing it over the hills and far away – cattle stampeding below us like swarming insects – tiny green fields with grey hedges round them – gorse – bracken – dodder and pinks and suddenly the land was fractured and it fell away, sheer and broken, into the sea – goodbye to the Shyre! Dyw genough why Kernow! The land fallen away and gone, just as if it had never come into existence in the first place and we were catapulted into new elements, realms and aggregates of ephemeral aqueous evaporations and vast kommolek sea-fog mysteries awaited us.

A flash of white down below was the frothy Atlantek bursting its billowing waves on the krogenek and embarnacled boulders of Penwithershins' granite seaboard and then there were only waves, sky, clouds and air.

I reached behind me and Constance and I briefly squeezed hands – our journey was truly underway now, with only the waters below us and an unknown future ahead.

Flying my Queen over the water. Ireland-Water, shimmering like miroirs, rippling billows, far across the foam – trasna na dtonnta. Briny splash a moisture desert. A-prey to propinquity; thought-waves and brine-storms. Now only the *flooded* land lay below us – the vloed, the floundering fluot, vast gothique flodus, rolling in flatfish splendour to the ends of the Earth. Airy puffs of light, clouds and clufts and tufts of vapour sailed by. Our heron-gull wings undulating slow hypnotic flap punctuated the dracului monotone drone of the jynn. Light raced over the surface of the water – a liquid Antarctica heaving in tonnek surges of energy – moisture as landscape. Morvran dips below the surface – cormorant emerges. But what else lurketh below the turbot waters, beneath the swirling ripples and pools of inky deeps where cuttle-fish fear to tread? Grasping its vastness, my heart sung now of the glory of the great molecular meniscus – realm of the slithering deeps. And in these myriad dark and fathomless abysses under the dancing waves the *land* runs on, hidden, sunken and drowned, but land for all that. And these fish-riddled realms beneath the sea are replete with hills, valleys and towering mountains; forests of kelp and carragheen, oarweed, Irish-moss and sargasso-wrack. And following the wracken-forest's full-flown fathomed furlong ever downwards, the Batholithic realm awaits, unfurling an immeasurable tapestry of shadow-cast tewlwolow gloom, eldritch in its immensity, hopeless in its inchoate and hypogeal darkness and *mal* in its ghastly and unutterable *alienage*. This lair of luminous and gelatinous animalculae sparkles and abounds in the outré, with various divers species of lugern-bysk – lantern bearing fishes with the faces of uthek dragons and terrible *buccas*. Here they swarm and gnash their viperous fangs, prongs, proto-claws and vast and bulbous eyes, e'er agape for any stray photon that occasionally penetrated these night-like shades of the deep.

These *weird* and abysmal predators hover like the hawks of a world-made-water, soaring high over the channels of ice-age glaciated river-beds and ice-chiselled mountain-ranges, and over plains of softest subtle silt, many fathoms deep – the sea-ground dust of myriad kotis of krogens, fish-bones, cuttles, exoskeletons, carapaces, cowries, seal-bones, whale-stones, walrus-jaws, dog-fish-eggs, langoustine membranes, corals, polyps, pelagian protean wayfarers and enhanced water-things. This continental silt ran amok in all directions, actually covering more of the Earth's surface than is covered by grass. Blanketing and enshrouding the bed of the ocean, this second sea, this sea of silt soon swallows and consumes new arrivals – morvughow, dolphins, amoeba, haddock, mullet, mackerel, men 'o' war...

And sinking, plunging, being sucked down into this silt, below its deepest layer, where fossilization is already taking place; the bedrock, the great igneous crust of the World. *Conceived* in fiery chaos, thousands of millions of years ago; the seething, caking, laval crust of a white-hot World, an incandescent blob of lava spat from the mouth of the Sun – fated to hang in space, to spin, to mother the ten thousand things, to unleash the chain of being, pour forth the pitcher of life and cultivate the seed of humanity. Whose seed are ye, whose seed am I.

Down through the titanic rocks, layer by layer through the swirling marmareegy molten flux of pyroclastic granitic *form*. The rocks warming now, basking in the geo-therm, the heat of the Earth. But even these great drowned and flooded aboriginal rocks are not as solid as they seem, for bold Kernow has extended searching tendrils and tunnels under the ocean, seeking for minerals and hidden wealth and suddenly the solid world of rock opens to reveal a candle-lit scene of labouring men – Old Janner and his mates from Chyannor, breaking new ground and opening up another level. Beneath their hobnail-booted feet, the rocks gradually become warmer and hotter, approaching the moon-sized globe of molten metal – the core of the Earth – the *true* sea bed. Over this sea of molten laval chaos swirls our familiar sea of brine, An Mor Keltek – An Mhuir Cheilteach. Down yw an mor – deep is the sea – to invoke it is to smell brine and hear gulls – being beyond the sight of land, the sea takes on a whole new significance – in a flash its mighty power is realised – it's rolling prairie could swallow you up in a minute! Its seething crowd of dancing waves stretched out to infinity, the waves darkening a little now, as the day was no longer young.

We were maintaining a good altitude, probably around a thousand feet, though it is hard to judge when flying over water. I passed a pasty back to Constance and the touch of her hand filled me with warmth. I started gnawing at a pasty myself, they were extremely good and brought back the atmosphere of Chy-an-Brae and all the times we'd had there. The pies had a restorative effect and the nacelle was tolerably warm thanks to the exhaust/hypocaust system. The sea stretched on and on without end and the engine roared like the apocalypse. Our great wings unfurled and undulated in mesmeric hexagonal cycles, canbhas gwyr, green, doped, Brythonek and taut. We rode the air like a Chinese dragon in an ancient fable. The oscillating tonnhys dance of the waves at play, fête des belles eaux, a wobbling, atmospheric mass. The great haddock-prairie glinted beneath the undercarriage of the muireitlean Ticee-Dyoo machine as it lurched forward like a chicken-of-the-sea. Once, as we winged forth o'er ocean's billowing, newsprint, spell-binding main, we passed over a trawler and could see the kipper-coloured oilskinned men scurrying on the deck, awestruck at the 'edhen-meur', the great bird that roared at them from out of a mackerel-sky. An angular 'aerostat' automaton appearing *alien,* an Atlantek zygodactyl. We flew on, riding the ephemeral mellow reverie of psyche's winged flight. Sunlight glinting on sepia-grass-green sailcloth fuselage. Wawe waves wagian waze glintering sea silver, siolfor, silobar, silbir, slopping, sloping slung as spray splashed skywards and pewter tonnek mountains of moisture swelled from glassy blue to stark slate-grey.

Y thalassa eine vathys–dark wings undulating over waves darker and deeper – endless tundra of water, cool water, watar, wazzar, voda, watins, wezzern and waterich, gewaeterian and watering the orb of the Earth. Down yw an mor – deep is the sea, wide, wild and wet, the great planetary meniscus shivers and shakes and the canvas wings fly on, trasna na dtonnta. And fast fell the cloak of dark, muting mackerel brilliant orange skies, through tones of purple and chill grey to a uniform, squid-ink black.

Between rhinolophidae fflapio of our canvas-feathered wings Constance and I would sometimes briefly hold hands, stealing moments of warmth and joy, gliding a motorbat, through the night airy skies of the Keltek Sea, on this, our wedding-night.

Marbled, mottled and bletted, kommolek puffs extended out in all directions. The jynn-keber's drone was modulating into a grand and sombre tonality and light-clouds drifted flickering by. All aether and awe, atmospheric activity assumed an acute aura. The music blazed brighter, intensely shining, drawing me on to zones luminous and subtle. And I saw in the sky a road of rugged clouds, swirling and churning; and along that road of clouds was a great row of luminous orbs, the size of boulders, and seated on each golowyjyon glowing globe was a Muse in the form of a beautiful woman playing upon a lyre – but though they played a music of indescribable beauty and enchantment, but yet they were blindfolded, and saw not other than the music. The silvery play of the musical lyres captivated me and I wished strongly to stay there and give myself over entirely into the music, but I was compelled to ask one of the Muses – Why do you not remove your blindfolds? The sybil turned her countenance towards me – Then why do ye not look behind ye? She sayeth to me most mysterious and suddenly I was back in the aeroplane.

I felt chilled, a creeping, seeping cold had leached in and the dark wings of a shadow of doubt, of dismay and afright seemed to fflap and agitate my soul. I remembered the words of the lyre-player and looked behind me – frozen horror blasted my minde to spattered pulp – *Constance was gone! She must have fallen out of the 'plane!*

I awoke with a sudden start – must have nodded off at the controls, that was *dangerous*... I craned my neck round to glance at Constance – there she was, thank *Jehosephat!* I could see here eyes glinting in her aero-goggles, she momentarily took the scarf off her mouth and smiled at me. We squeezed hands again. I felt a delirious form of happiness then, the vile stag, the unrelishable and abominable nightmare had only served to sharpen and quicken my love for Constance. Her safety had to be my only concern and I had to be a latter-day, indeed a twentieth-century knight-errant, dedicated to his divine Lady. I also felt a strong wish to *talk* to Constance, and I thought of a way we could manage it. I eased back the controls and gradually gained more altitude, reckoning that if we were high enough up, I could risk cutting the engine for a brief minute – as long as we glided with reasonable *stability,* and we could have a moment to speak to each other. Y nikterida, dark-flapping bat-thing of the night, the ruffled puff-winds of the sea, and gwynjak yw an mor. Up we rose through dark-mackerelled cockerel skies of scattered matter, dark matter and molecular vapours, through all the cumulus cloud-towers and fog-hollowed gulches we soared, fleogan, vliegen, fljuga – we flew.

Up above the cloudlands at last, we were atop a vast Himalayan range of insubstantial mists, drenched in the light of the full moon. A soft, phosphorescent luminosity bathed the cloud-carpet in its milky, mercurial light. This exquisite realm was for us alone, spread like the carpet of Zeus.

I took a deep breath and cut the engine.

"Don't worry," I called back to Constance, "we can glide for a minute – I just wanted to see how you were – I love you Constance!"

"Oh Elias, you do make me laugh! I love you too! Did you turn off the engine just to tell me you loved me?"

"Yes I did, I suppose I did – 'n' yes I *do!"*

"Oh... it's so *beautiful* here, it's like a whole *country* made of clouds – a magical land, isn't it Elias?"

"Yes, my darling, a magical realm, an enchanted cloud-country specially made for the delight of young lovers eloping in flying-machines!"

"It's the most beautiful thing I've ever seen… it's wonderful."

We were moved by the radiant scene. There was a moment of silence, the craft seemed to hang in the air on stilled wings, a butterflye holding its breath.

Eternity loomed.

Radiance everywhere.

Riding the skies with my beloved.

I glanced back at her, and she at me.

I made myself focus on practical matters. "Are you warm enough Constance?"

"I am getting a little chilled now," she admitted.

"I think fatigue is starting to set in," I thought it best not to mention my momentary sleep-episode, didn't want to scare her, "we'd better each have another pasty, and then perhaps share a vial of the Erebus Compound, it'll keep us warm and alert and banish the lethargy that cold can bring."

"Yes my darling, we need to stay warm and lively – do you think it's far to Ireland now?"

"It can't be much further now – you know, your courage during all this is a real inspiration to me – I'd better turn on the engine again now."

We exchanged a brief glance and touched hands, before I turned the key to ignite the jynn-keber. Monochrome and gelatinous seconds ticked by–I turned the key again, heart now pounding in nocturnal dread surge of mal unease as again the jynn failed to awaken and come to our aid! Finally I succeeded and all twelve and a half of the plucky little horses that powered the engine came rearing, stamping, running and a kickin' back to life with the roar of a thousand assorted wild beasts of various orders, proclaiming their autochthonous, unorthodox and aboriginal right to roam and roar.

Having restored powered-flight, we ate the aforementioned pasties that Mrs Kegyner had so kindly baked and then I opened one of the glass vials. The familiar, strangely rank *bouquet* of the Erebus Compound tickled my nostrils as I gulped down half of the sludge-like blue-grey *gruel* with a shudder and passed the rest of the vial back to Constance.

Streams of living blue luminosity flickered through my veins, my cells glowed rich in oxygen, I felt keen, sharp, very conscious. *Now* I won't be nodding off at the controls, I thought with a smile.

The lugern glew and the compass drew us to the North-West, the 'Hill Aero Motor' droned steadily on and we swept through the air with the grace of a bat. The deeper fell the tenebral gloom of night and all sight of sapphire sea now dissolved into the gothick pit of velvet gloomy shades.

I was flying quite blind, seeing only the compass and a small section of the nacelle. The apocalyptic roar of the jynn deafened me to any other sound and left us flapping over a dark ocean, at an unknown altitude and with a limited amount of fuel left in the tank. Hurling through the screaming black void, I felt strangely at home, oddly content... perhaps it was the pasty...

Or was it simply that the myriad dubious, unlikely and outrageous experiences I'd had, since that fateful meeting at the corner of Orchard Street and Iron-Foundary Way, had prepared me for almost anything? I did think it would be a cruel irony though, to fly all this way over the sea at night, only to fly straight into a cliff!

I coaxed the craft upwards, but the bronco was beginning to buck like a hulking Buxtehude – the air was becoming choppy and I had to really work the controls to achieve any altitude. Whitesqualls and black, boomed, blasted and hacked at the fragile clockwork toy, gwynjak blasts and hwyths started to buffet and rock our little ship. Lightning suddenly flashed – tintreach – flash – lughesenn – crash and the keser rattling pelt of hail-bullets fusillading on wings and fuselage, mercilessly pelting and harrowing us. I think the compound was keeping us immune to the weather – I felt not cold nor damp, only a glowing and aerated awareness, keen as a raven riding out a storm. The dark sea's immeasurably vast, deep, saline and alien wilderness raged, shattered and trembled beneath us and all around us.

This rolling, gloopy, dark *brine-realm* teemed and

seethed with the archaic and atavistic, the protean and pelagian, the gelatinous, exoskeletal, the quixotic and the ephemeral. Here the lobster scuttled and here the mussel clung. Starfish shone radiant in dark depths, things unknown to man stirred and tottered on multiple, spindly, jointed legs and blubberous and fatty fish puffed lethargically through strata of salt-water brines and oceanic currents. The whale lurks and the sunfish rises. Here where the gannet flies, the krill swarm and the morhogh noses purposefully on through mats of knotted twisted kelp. Mermaid's purses and sea-eggs, strange flotsam abounds. The froth churns in Atlantek's swell and the dark sea smokes in anger. Black spattered white are the waves, and deep is the sea – down yw an mor.

And as the storm blasted it threw our little ornithopter around the sky, tearing and grasping at our brittle Ticky-Dyw with hands of aerial-tendril fingers. Lightning's white flashes – split-second illuminations – I could see no sea, only the searing universal splendour of vast white light, briefly filling all directions. Flash! And darkness returned. But a darkness of howling, ripping winds and bursts of torrential rain. The swirling black cyclonic watery night engulfed our tiny 'plane', as it warped forth, an archaic aerial-carriage aloft Atlantic's airs. Buffeted. Barged. Barraged by the wind – wings sometimes being twisted by the wind, misshapen and tested to the upmost. Withering tempests racked the black rolling ocean's continental swill as meniscoid scuttlers rattled segmented carapaces and antennae felt tentatively around. A watery turmoil below the surface and an airy chaos above. Thunderbolts crackled and the sky blinked a pink-white electric blaze.

No nightjars nibbled pouting pecks of spindrift spicules now, nor whip-poor-wills churring warbles sounded melodious sweet; this wilderness was the field of auks, razor-bills, gannets and gulls, the harsh, hardy, squamous and bleak fowls of the brine. The tempest flapped mad and the wires sung and screamed in desperate harmony with the wind's elemental chant. The machine was creaking and straining, I thought the sudden changes of air-pressure and wind direction might crush the craft like a matchbox under the foot of a corpulent and drunken kwallok.

From the void of unknown and unforeseeable possibility a form was flying into my tiny lugern globe of light, a form both intimately familiar, yet strangely miniaturized – the terrible white-edged jet-black wings and ice-berg head, glaucous, red-rimmed eye, harsh spike of a red-spotted, gonys beak – a *Larus marinus* – pinned and transfixed for an instant in the light – wings spread in harsh broken gothic arch – the broadsword beak gaped wide and spat some dark thing at me and the visionary beast was gone – completely gone, leaving only a shudder of revulsion to course through my bones. I looked down at my feet. There, just behind the rudder-bar was the object dropped by the greater black-backed brine-rhoek. I picked it up in my gauntleted hand and held it under the Davy lamp. It was the size of a finger, bulbous, also tapered, festooned in writhing papillae that extended and shrunk back in ceaseless, tonnek, undulatory motion – in short, a starfish-arm! My minde leaped to the land. Seagulls collect starfish from *rock-pools* at low-tide – we must be near the shore! The convulsive, rhythmic, waving and extending of the pympbys papillae sung to me of *life!*

The miniature fingers coating the severed limb, stretched up, searching and probing, waving, extending, *feeling* for life, expressing the restless, searching *energy* of life – this atavistic scrap of radiata, pulsed, squirmed and throbbed with energy, motion, *life!* Even separated from its body, like a ship far from its home-port, the scrap of ancient flesh just emanated essential vitality. I placed it under the lamp, where I could glance at its talismanic undulations and draw inspiration from it.

Ylektrismos – brittle crackles of leictreachas wattage discharged through atmospheric moisture tredannek, snapping with brilliant energy. Violet aethereal tongues of luminous electric flame streamed forth from the papilionaceous airframe – these glowing blue jets of light-flame sprouted from the tip of the nacelle, the floats, wing-tips and tail, as well as from various projecting parts like the compass and lanthorn. These mysterious streaming lights were canwyll yr ysbryd – spirit-candles, a spectral display of energy. I twisted round – I could see Constance laughing with wonderment. How celestial and pure she looked, a sky-Goddess, haloed in dancing violet rays. A sight I'll never forget as long as I live. Perhaps it would be my last sight. If the lightning struck we'd melt like a moth in a campfire. I remembered when I was a boy, some of the older country-folk in Penwithershins used to say that moths were really the souls of the dead – they used to call them pyskies; which reminded me in that lucid instant, of psyche, a Greek word that encompassed both 'butterfly' and 'soul'. Quaint what goes through your minde as you fly into a lightning-storm at sea... Suchlike thoughts flashed through *my* psyche as lightning lughes splashed through black, churning skies, whirling skiuja gwynjak skio. I fought for altitude, chasing the black clouds of tewlwolow du like a night herring galloping after ephemeral chimerical sheep of the lapis lazuli void. The pympbys papillae finger writhed atavistic, pulsing universal Chi – the moon-disc blazed between rays of cloud. The finger pointed onwards, North-West, imitating the magnetic finger of the compass.

Thunder rolled away in basso operatic waves, deep as Dolcoath. The lightning passed but a mist descended – a newlak, smúitiúil vapour – y omikli – niwlog mizzle-moist particles – *Keltek myst!* This stuff had crept up on many an unwary personage and marooned them in the Arupaloka – the *Formless* Realm. I felt we were on an ynfydrwydd flight of fancy, winging like a cloud of starlings through gzugs med pa'i khams – ffoedigaeth ynfydrwydd...

The density of dark and massy fog had melted into a more luminous and lunar numinosity, a celtchair dhichlethi cloak of raven-gloom gave way to the generous splennyjyon of ceo druidechta – the Druid's fog....

Moon-bathed now in pale white light, the papillae on the starfish-arm continued to extrude and retreat, undulating and surging with ever-fresh vigour; insisting on existence. Sometimes I thought I caught the ragged echo of a lyre or a harp calling through the luminous mist – perhaps it was just some overtones in the beam-engine's song.

Basilisk gigantomachy was the restless war of meteoros winds and the harsh rain was thrown in our faces. Piloting the ornithopter in these conditions was like to buck the bronc of a rodeo showdown on a radio hoe-down. Lugubrious fronts of air-pressure shoved and creaked the craft, buffeting and shaking it convulsively. I was just wondering how much more of this treatment the old Tykki-Dyw could take, when the engine coughed a couple of times, then stopped dead. Suddenly I could hear the wind in the rigging and the percussion of rain on the 'skin' of the aircraft. In the same moment I noticed that the pympbys finger, still rippling and scintillating in papillae, had turned around and was now pointing South. I tried to fire up the engine again, but we were out of fuel and that was that.

"Hold tight!" I called to Constance, "we're going to land!"

Down through the darkness we dropped, gliding blindly on still wings. Blind-flying is one thing, but a blind *landing?* Surely we were jumping the jaw of the beast and leaping into a cauldron of frothing, seething woes. A blind landing? Sheer madness! But we had no choice. The jynn-keber had performed marvellously well but now it was merely ballast. At least we were making a steady descent, the machine was displaying its inherent stability – I thought it a good job that Mr Taxon had made such a thorough study of Herr Lilienthal's biplane-gliders. It was also fortunate that the wings had stopped moving during the fifth phase of their cycle, offering an increased surface area which gives more 'lift' when landing. The gwynjak singing wires of the kite keened and wailed like desolate spirits in the empty places of the Earth. Clouds flecked in moonlight – cloud-rags sailing – the moondisc revealing – crepuscular cumulus heaped high around – the skrawk of a gull – I thought I could smell the ocean – wings warping – raindrops streaming through the lugern glow of the lamp – showers of diamonds – visceral swooping motion – the rush of the machine – a dot in an elemental storm-cauldron – a speck in the eye of a clacking storm-raven – a straw in the wind – riding the hwyths, squalls and blasts – clouds shifting, revealing, then hiding the moon.

The light shifted, the mists parted and there was the gleaming white glistering moon surface of the sea, rising steadily to meet us! We were descending into an ocean of light, rippling, dazzling, scintillating light. This great sea of light seemed to rush towards us in an all-encompassing blaze, absorbing and swallowing us... I eased back on the controls and the floats kissed the waters, we taxied a few yards then stopped, little waves lapping around the undercarriage and a light breeze stirring the milky moon fog. I felt Constance's arms wrap around me and her voice in my ear. "You *did it,* Elias! You got us down safely!" We laughed for sheer joy, for sheer life.

"It was a close thing, more luck than skill," I confessed.

"Nonsense darling! You're a pioneer-aviator – the first ornithopter-flight to Ireland! You'll go down in history!" She seemed determined to see me in a heroic light and I can't honestly say that bothered me.

"Well, I suppose we'd better switch to manual propulsion – perhaps we will be *cycling to Ireland* after all!" I adjusted the mechanism and lowered the pedals into place.

"But you're soaked through, Elias, and you've been flying all night, are you sure you'll be alright? Maybe you should take some more of Mr Taxon's medicine."

"Good idea, Constance, but you seem to be pretty well soaked too, maybe you should have a little drop yourself."

"Alright darling, but you have most of it, and let's share a pasty and some tay to wash it down!"

So once more we quaffed of the potent taxonomic potion and once more we chewed the crusts of one of Mrs Kegyner's finest pies. The calm blue fire trickled through my veins, flooding me with oxygen – I started pedalling, the Ticky-Dyw crept forward like a dragon-flye on the water. What a happy, dreamlike reverie crept stealing over me – what a great relief to get down from that dark, blind, brutal and lonely sky – even if we were still out at sea.... Anyway, I mused, we could not be far from land – there was our living proof, the starfish-arm! I glanced down, it was still rippling with animation.... The wind had dropped and moonlight dappled and painted the foggy airs, there was an ethereal calm, a quietness that shone through the smúitiúil mist and lightened the night.

"Look!" gasped Constance in wonderment. A great halo

encircled the moon, arcing gracefully through the night-fog.

"It's a fog-bow," I murmured, stunned by its celestial hypnotic beauty. I cycled on and we drifted through quiet realms of moondrenched vapours.

"The sea's so calm, so still," she said.

"Yes, I think the storm has passed," I agreed. We were lost in the beauty of the moment, the calm of a lunar mist.

Baaaaaaa! We looked at each other in amazement. *Baaaaaaa!* There was no mistaking it.

"A *sheep!*" we both said together, then burst into hysterical laughter again.

"Well, sheep don't live in the ocean," I opined, "we must be within a few yards of the shore!"

The next minute a bump went through the machine and we had apparently grounded on terra firma.

"Land-ho!" I called. "I'll moor the kite and we'll have a look around."

"Be careful Elias," she said, as I grabbed the Davy lamp and the mooring-rope and scrambled out of the nacelle and into the waist-deep water. As I waded ashore I was amazed to see swamp-grass growing at the water's edge – I thought swamp-grass only grew next to *fresh* water… I found a little blackthorn tree and passing the rope round it, I pulled the Tick'ee D'you ashore and made it fast and then lifted Constance down out of the nacelle. I carried her ashore in my arms.

"Welcome to Ireland, my darling bride!" I kissed my new wife and set her feet down on Irish soil.

*

We stood holding each other tight, melting into the embrace of bliss. Little waves were lapping at the shore. No more noise, danger, fear and uncertainty, only peace and safety with my Constance at last.

Baaaaaaa! We looked at each other and started laughing again.

"Oh Elias! We're alive! I thought we were going to drown in the dark sea together, but we're alive! Safe!"

"I thought we were going to be struck by lightning!" I laughed.

"We're *alive!*" sung my Queen and I sung it back to her, and back and forth we sang it. "We're alive! We're alive! We're alive!"

*

Solas na gealai, leoht of the silobar mune lyghtede th' bilowys of clowdys, silibir mercury lume. The londe was chayngyd and transfigured. Holding hands we danced and spun, laughing and singing together as sailing kommolek skies mottled and flickered slowly by, infused with a subtle luminosity.

"But *Elias,*" she looked intensely at me, "you really are soaked through, like a lion drenched in rain – aren't you cold?"

"It's the *Erebus Compound,* it raises the molecular transpiration-rate – even in a *lion!*"

We laughed together deliriously.

"Yes, I feel pretty warm too, though a lot of that *horizontal* rain got in through my oilskins – that potion really works!"

"True, but still, the potion will wear-off – we should try to look for some shelter and warmth."

"Well, there must be a *farm* around here somewhere or a *pub* or something," she smiled.

"Well, we are in *Ireland!*" I agreed, "let's see what we can find!"

Niwlek mist eclipsed the gloywder drithligh moone, scattering shimmering splennyjyon splashes of light, seliniakos across the scintillating syzygy night. We held hands and walked.

Glittering crystal starlight brought forth the dews and miniature diamonds and jewels were threaded on the rippling cobwebs. Uisciuil droplets, caught, split, refracted the light and glistened the glyb grass with subtle hues and liws. We wandered through the foggy dew, enchanted by the beauty of the scene. Celestial pools of luming light emerged between the over-flying clouds. We were walking uphill on soft, springy turf – and as we climbed that hill, the dappled mackerel skies opened up above us and the view opened all around us, marmaroglypheion white and spectrally pure.

"Oh – *LOOK!*" gasped Constance in amazement, one hand in the air, eloquent digits extended.

We found ourselves on top of a ridge, before us stood a little *bothy*, a mellifluous bee-hive-hut of ancient stone construction. The land fell away on all sides.

"An *island!*" I half-murmured in loerek, moon-fueled folly, "we're on an *island!*"

"Yes," she smiled, "an island in a *lake! A land-locked lake!*"

"A land-locked-lake?" I echoed in a surge of absurd mirth, "a *land*-locked-lake?"

We stared around us in wonder. The steep little island was about as long as a street and as wide as a field, set in a lake of calm waters, about a quarter of a mile long. We were encircled by the green hills of Ireland, cast adrift in our own realm, an ethereal isle that seemed to us a paradise, and we the very Gods that dwelt within it. Little waves were lapping at the shore and the mist flickered in will-o-the-wisp whimsical hwyths, ephemeral, molecular, ceremonious.

Looking down, we could see the tiny form of the Tikky-Dyw perched below, like a true insect, the spindly ephemeron that had carried us over the water. Above us the glittering vault of scattered crystal stars span slow in rapid rapturous eternities.

"I feel like I'm still flying!" laughed Constance as we walked along the narrow ridge towards the bothan. The lake's silver mirror blazed back brilliant moonlight scintilla all around us. The venerable bee-hive-honey-hut dripped lichen from its ancient stones, a moondusted Keltek relict, shepherd's croft and winter-shelter.

"We'll go to the Gaeltacht and lose ourselves in the language…" I murmured, abstracted.

"Yes," enthused Constance, "we could *fly* there, couldn't we Elias!"

"Either that or we could trade the ornithopter for a

donkey and cart and go the old-fashioned way... Let's have a look at the old bothog."

The solid and rustic door swung open to reveal a small but cosy space within – circular, consisting of flat stones sealed with peat, a couple of tiny windows and a fire-place. A generous pile of wood and peat stood next to the hearth and there were plenty of candles. Apart from that, there were no furnishings whatsoever. The bare minimum was provided, but to us, this Spartan domicile was as welcome as a palace.

"Well," I said, "it ain't the Ritz, but at least we can get warm – I'll get the fire going."

"And I'll light the candles," said my beautiful Constance, "and then we can dry our clothes in front of the fire. There's a blanket in my bag, we could spread that out on the oilskins..."

I prepared the fire and little flames were soon crackling, as smoke rose from the kindling and the larger wood started to catch. The firelight danced in many forms on the beehive bothy walls – Minoan – Cyclopean – Glagolitic – the heat soon filled the tiny room and ruby flames threw out their myriad golow mirages on the archaic walls of the dome, causing the stones to sway and shimmer, to come to life again, as in their laval past.

I added some peat to the fire, my minde a-whirl with the events of the day – our marriage – the flight – the roar of the jynn-keber and the endless hours of flapping through darkness, over that great and terrible sea – and now we were safe, the dark wings had passed over the ocean and the dream-dappled Shyre lay far behind us. After all we'd been through, it seemed inexplicable and full of joyful mystery to finally be safe, to be together and even *married!* Only a couple of hours ago I thought the sea would be closing over our mortal remains and pulling them down, deeper and deeper – down yw an mor – down into the tenebrous hagfish-realms of tewlwolow gloom, where moray eels and clingfish scitter and eldritch tentacles squirm and slither. Aqueous meadows of twilight scuttling crustaceans and exoskeletal decapods, browsing through corals, anemones and limitless watery pastures of undulating carragheen, dulse, wrack and kelp.

But instead…. I looked round. Constance was looking at me curiously, flashes of firelight dancing in her hair and in her eyes.

"Hey there, Dreamy-Head," she said quietly, "how about helping me get undressed?"

POEMS

These Days And Those Days

Those days with the wind swaying in the trees
those grey misty days of swirling leaves,
of tumbling autumn days falling into water -
the sea lapping around the legs of the pier,
watching days, days curled up and crinkled...
do you remember that day, when-

Evenings firelit – rain rattling on slate -
wind howlubub hubbing at the tiles above -
rain spatters the window's hollow green glass.
These days and those days –
rose from above the zenith
soaring time's track.

Cool evening air between beech-tree groves
where leaves flutter down to fascinate the wanderer,
nature's miniature moves a thrilling Muse to eye of joy
and woodsmoke's incense curling and diffusing...

Golden days, silver days of rain's glistening tracery -
moons, crunching paths a-wander through furlongs fresh,
harvest globes aglow,
rippling pewter mirror of mackerel scatter
newt-tracks – crinkling the zenith

Sandstone ruins rooked by clacking crowbodies -
beaks – feathers blueblack
and beaks that clack – clutching claws cold
days of rooks a-flight in fluttering glassy nights
and dew-drenched hedgerows of bramble
by the gypsy's canvas hut.

Days on the move, horses shunting at the collar,
hooves a-clatter, sparking on roads of night -
past bramble miles and brackens
braking hills adrift with pink clouds glowing,
slows in the hedge, cobwebs, moss and sedge.

Faded brown photographs of days
in dreamy sunlight – kept in mahogany box -
monoplanes whir,
their wires taut, strings of improbable Chinese guitars
of the Butterfly brand -
sealed with ambergris – turquoise -
wax flocks in flux of beeswax bucks -
days like these flood by in flocks.

14 or 15

I am a wild bird, caged in a human body,
I am infinity wrapped in meat

My Home Land

Fresh cloudy heaven
blue/grey/green rags blow away
ghost-blanket
and flying-carpet for the crow

wet grass
as a little furry caterpillar creeps
in carapace overcoat

The Caterpillar

"Who are you?" asked the caterpillar
but I didn't know – so what could I say?

I thought about it for a bit
but realised there was no answer
and this was not a problem

Old Crow

Old crow
your eyelids are grey
rapidly blinking
some small loose feathers fluttering
on your neck and tail.
Don't fly away
I want to de-scribe you
I want to tell them
what colour you are

Jackdaw

A jackdaw
at the back door
with a hacksaw
in his black claw
made my back sore
what was that for?

Remember When We Were Free?

Remember, my friends, when we were free?
Remember the white sunlight on the hot dusty streets?
Remember when songs were sung without looking over our shoulders?
When poems were spoken out loud, in cafes? In the street?
When laughter knew no check, no nervous glance?
Yes my friend, I know you do, even if you can't
look me in the eye.

Once we danced around a fire – we spoke of whatever came into our minds -
I know you know this, inside yourself, I know you keep it,
deep inside your secret chest. Under your grey
and inconspicuous coat.

I know you all yearn for the return of a past mode.
But it will take years, war, a revolution -
and then, us survivors will be old.

Yes, we will be old, those of us who live.
Those of us who are not broken by those who wear the black.
Perhaps we'll run together into the evening sun,
stir the ashes of an old song
and look for life in it.

Hollowed

You hollowed out my poem
and stuck your
(adverts)
into it

this made me feel pretty strange
because-
Do we share our dreams
so you can (advert) cinema tickets?
(advert)
shoes handbags jewellery glasses
(adverts)
corporating insidious (adverts)
into our dreams
into our dreams
into our dreams

Ghostmoney

Ghostmoney -
It'll hauntya -
But what is ghostmoney, you ask -
Ghostmoney is the dream
of the value
of the money you spent
it all long ago.

Ghostmoney is foreign currency
that we all use -

Ghostmoney is currently collected
by the customs and exorcise -

This chilling private-value-system
haunts vaults
vaunts and flaunts fiscal
risks, faults, fails, falls
into a Great Depression.
Haunting stark for the gaunt poor -
Ghostmoney dreams flapped
from the wings
of a mammoth Mammon mastodon.

A Short Story

Once upon a time-
AAAAGGHH!!!
The End.

Greenhornhood

Greenhornhood heavy hung however wholly haloing halfling's holy head. Thinking through these thick thoughts thoroughly though therefore that's thought's threnody thus through and through. Greenhorn gores dirigible though, punctiliously and pitiably deflating the gasbag envelope. Avidly attempting to avoid responsibility though he attempts to involve the antelope in culpability. However heavy though hung the halo halflight around Greenhornhood's head.

Lorekeet Laureatte

Lorekeet Laureatte
You'll peck those words,
Motormouth motivatin'
Berries, cherries,
Pickin's rich in birds

Wingin' it, wordin' it,
Wearing whirring wings
Absurd i'n'it?
Spreadin' the word in it
Fly like a bird in it -
Land in the laurel,
singing
Lyre-Bird!
Now for your lyrics laurels
Are conferred on you!
And subjects once taboo
You blew so open wide
Now the people see
Inside of things
So spread those wings
Lauretta Poetta
Give those words
Some peacock feathers,
Aye?!

Inveterate Invertebrate

Inveterate invertebrate
embrace a vertical rockface
facade of veterinary race
inverted, braced, a molecule's pace
mollycoddled mollusc lusting
for the last bus,
in a flap
in a fuss
roaring full-born
dew-drop bull-horn

Tide swirling your
side twirling ripples
slithering in rivulets
letters ripped from catalogues
log-jams, lumbering word-jams,
verbose invertebrate
syllables coagulate
veering off a typeface
tentacles scrabbling for limp
pictorial hieroglyphs
glyphics mystic and molten cliffs
larva slips – hatching
in lunar eclipse
graphics grappled – coming to grips
inveterate invertebrate -
must it come to this?

Dubstep Hubcap

Detached, loosed, struck off on The Strand,
Dubstep Hubcap rolling and tumbling cross the land,
losing the race with th car what shedya,
spinning, turning, trundlin' so graceful long th Strand,
scatterinya blessin's all the way from Lhasa
past piers of fish, asphalt avenues, iron-mongers,
ale-mongers, monks, friends – you Holy dish -
set alight the street you did,
set alight the Strand

"Stuck behind a rubbish-collection-bus"
"Don't you mean a dustcart?"
Trash wagon, a flash flagon of flim-flam filth -
OVERTOOK the hubcap,
gazed directly into the Heart of the whirling Blessing Deity -
Dubstep Hubcap of spinning spontaneity

A Paltry Nugget

The egg is empty
The chicken born of form
Morphs to an ovoid
Devoid ov I.D.
Chick-hen devoid of dentistry
Can't get it's teeth into
Concepts of solid identity
Just clucks, pecks, struts and glides
Singing for joy, freely speaketh the beak

Summer Subpoema

Granite snowman
growanek growth of gold
lichen licks your old head -
your grass-skirt and blessed
pointed head to the sky.

Sweet birds of summer
come to swoop by you,
fly-past swiftly African aircraft
swallowing midges a-wing -
sing simple songs flung
over dungmellow flatfields -
summer a-come.

Licking breezes cool
wrapped around old stone spool,
then a stillness
in the cloverdotted pathcrossed field,
stone holy to ancients
with oceanic view,
glimpse the stars
Look! Old is new

Jack Kerouac's Typewriter Rhythm Unrolls

Jacaranda jaculus – jaculus Caractacus
Caraway immaculus.
Hacking haikus home from travelling the page.
Merrimac memory-babe, clacking keys
on your portable machine
writing the epic paperback roadflick
lickin' up ink, highways, lush-nights
and scenes of your time, your 50's
w e s t e r n d r e a m i n g

Lost, mocked, most honoured scribe
scribbling in endless notebooks
with your
c h e a p w i n e
sharing-it-with-anybody -
YOU didn't mind –
you knew we all sprung from the same meatwheel,
the same karmic revolving circus -
from Mary's drunken Buddha-Heart.

In fellaheen earth
in tents
in Mexico
in automobiles
in neon city night-lights
in sagebrush coyote deserts
in doldrum drinking blues
in ships of the oily dark sea
loving the tragic world

loving the magic words – keys clack
ribbon spins and whirls
unravelling on your cheap solitary desk
tales of ten thousand miles
to bless the dream-soaked youth
an' flying souls to the sun

Mind Knowing Light

Clean as Light in Space
Photons stream pure – no room for neurotic thought
Photons stream pure – bouncing off illusory matter, silently

Photons clean in space travelling -
Colour to the eye, eye to the mind -
Mind knowing light

Light in time sagging -
Distorting by gravity's lure -
Stars unborn seen first -
Unborn Mind seeing light between atoms dancing

Moonbeams, friendly white neon-glow
Luminous - clean, no room for stale ideas -
Throw your radiance onto the sea of the earth

Sun on earth, arriving pure – steam rising from damp earth -
Green shoots rising – young teeth and beaks nibbling -
Lizard-eye blinks, glazes, gazes at the sun

Clean as light in space -
Photons stream pure -
Prismatic split spews radiant colour vision in jelly-eye -
No room for darkness here

DREAM MANIFESTO

(BEING A MANIFESTO OF DREAMERS, DREAM AND DREAMING.)

WE THE DREAMERS do hereby affirm and assert the Right to Dream whensoever and howsoever We, The Dreamers, do see fit. We claim unto our multifaceted non-selves the Right to choose the expression of our own Dreams in a manner we find fit, fulsome and worthy. To cling to the clock is not to tock away our time in sorrowful lost and low lacklustre states, chronically and chronologically dependent on the pendulum of proprietous punctuality. Slewing away and forever forsaking the dead realms of misery's unlovely maw, we will uphold our psyche's flights, glimmering and joyful, like a new dawn. We will not surrender our Dreams. We will not sell out our Dreams. We will not compromise, cheapen or misrepresent our Dreams. We hold these Dreams to be the self-evident, self-luminous display of the slumberous mind. We view these Dreams to be not empty of reason, teaching, knowledge, example, illustration, narrative, psychodynamism, drama and humour. We acknowledge the fact that not all Dreams are pleasant. We acknowledge the view that all Dreams are the manifestation of Consciousness itself, and therefore are not without value. Not for naught have these Dreams been seen, felt, lived and, on occasion, broadcast afar to share with other Dreamers. We honour and uphold the Democracy of Dreaming, wherein all peoples are stripped of their worldly baubles and launched down slumber's slipway, onto that great, common ocean of unconsciousness, imagery and subtle psychic balancing and adjustment. Upon this great, rich and deep sea sail all souls and unto all souls do we honour do.

Further to our stated aims, is the glorious struggle to bring Dream into life, into the waking worldly World of Dust, into the minds, habits, culture, consciousness, mass media of all classes, lexicon, vocabulary, priorities, prerequisites, propensities, tendencies, fashions, myths, rumours, graffiti, glossolalia, sandhyabasha, samadhis, graces, insights, ephemera, epiphanies, warmths, enthusiasms, passions, fascinations, folk-ways, behavioural patterns, thought-forms and downright fundamental FACE of Humanity.

To this aim we shall wage and conduct a ceaseless and unremitting campaign of subterfuge, subversion, blending-in and contaminating the false-purity of the everyday mind and its rational assumptions. We shall secretly sow the seeds of subtlety upon a snoozing nation, a drowsy planet. We shall walk among the wakeful and instil a sense of serenity. We shall be found on all street corners, hangin' out, seeming to ride the breeze, secretly transmitting from pocket-swaddled miniature hand-held transmission units. We will spread our vision. We will spread our vision. We will spread our vision. And we shall spread it far and wide, upon virulent zephyrs of trembling breath. Having furrowed and enriched the ground, we shall sow many seeds of high things, things of vision, things of Humanity's great gleaming future. And the Dream that we sow, being essentially good, wholesome, an inherent and integral component of the Vast Human Psyche, shall be seen to be good through and through. To the dreary forces of gloom, false vision and stag, we shall at all times practice forbearance, for it is only necessary to Show one glimpse of the Vision for it to be recognized, loved, understood and aspired to by all whomsoever enjoy exposure to it. Thus we shall step up and double our efforts as nightly dusk falls twilight upon the silvery globe and our people betake themselves to slumber. At the setting of the Sun we shall send out our transmission into the One-Psyche. Our nocturnal clarion shall sound and resound, uniting our Brethren and Sistren in the Unity of I and I.

Having stormed the castle of cold grey conformity and stabilized our great action, we shall transmute all Earthly institutions into those that reflect and manifest our floating essential Divinity. We shall declare the ethereal and honour the misty breath. We shall unfurl the great banner of visions, the picture-tapestry of the contents, illusions, states and truths of the mind humane. We Dreamers shall leave no soul unturned in our quest for Oneness. We shall overlook no sleeper, from the humblest to the most high. Tirelessly in our ultimate mission we shall surge forth, yea, as a deep and mighty river surges forth in spate, in spring, in thaw; carrying before us the smiles of all souls. We shall carry away the Hearts of all as a tide that washes upon the shore, and, reaching unto all places at once, we shall shimmer as the ocean shimmers, throwing off scintilla and dancing dazzles of mind's crazy and ever-fruiting inventory of invention. Bathing in the mystery, the Dreamer declares a state of Bliss and deep understanding to be the norm, and actively wishes and promotes this norm upon all souls, sleeping and otherwise. In promotion of crystalline clarity of vision, stability and knowing, the various cells of Dreamers will zealously forward the work of the great vision. Displaying signs, leaving stone tablets, songs, poems, paintings, novels, movies and mystery-plays in phone-boxes and other such mundane locations in the Human Loka, all such Dream-Activists will do untold good to the common cause of large general upliftment.

Luminous Dreaming. Dreams of Light. Dreams lit from within. Dream-episodes suffused with alba-gollow, glow white, glow wise. Such as are in this category are a class of experience apart. To this possibility we wish to point the mind of man that he may moan no longer alone.

The members of each local Dream-Cell shall come to the rescue of anyone whomsoever that cometh within their reach, if in distress. The group-antennae being ever a-twitch for signals of traumatized Dreamers. Upon location of such an one, all cell-members shall beam their light upon the sufferer, thus raising said being out of the fogs of that which is ill, and bringing them into the clear and shining radiance of the true. However intriguing the individual Dream of the Dreamer be, it shall be dropped in an instant to come to the aid of a victim of the dread stag. Such will be the priority of said wistful Dreamers when dealing with their troubled fellow-souls. Thus shall be the level raised. Thusly will tranquillity be firmly established. This in itself will be seen to be good.

The 'Dream That Is More Than A Dream' is a highly special category of experience encompassing the Visionary Dream and suchlike extraordinary nocturnal phenomena. This realm, strata, sphere, zone, this thing in all its manifestations shall be given oxygen, honour, ink and air.

For the furtherance of Dream-Literature in all its forms, competitions, prizes, publication, and enrichment will be given to contributors who further fertilize the rich native soil of the mind owned by all. Thus fecund abundant funds will support the artists of the nightly nictiplanctus whose wanderings live on to inspire the wearying group mind and refresh its sparkling shine.

These truths we take to be the illusory flickerings of a night moth's shadow on a page of the manuscript by moonlight and ivy-flower.

This Manifesto, rather than being a solid thing of the nature of a kerb-stone, suit of armour, ice-berg, iconoclast, fossil, tabernacle or impediment, shall be but a fluid and Brythonic changeling, going from one to one and being but echo's remembered shadow-form reflected upside down in the hat-pin mirror of a long-gone smiling lady. Thus may it morph, melt and surge. And to you all a very good night.

GHOST-HULK OF A PHANTOM

Oh lapping phantom, oh ghastly hulk that dogs me round the poles of a spinning world, dogs and hounds me, chasing and pursuing, pursuing and a follerin' me, a whale of a dog, a staghound of the night, a gaunt mammalian cordate mandible thing comin' fer to swaller me up. How did it start? How did it come to this, that I find myself pursued from time immemorial by the bloated and haggard carcass of a Morvilean sea-beast, a beast that won't live, yet will neither die a decent death; a beast ethereal and spectral – gaunt, ghast and creepin'? *Get it off me! Oh please just get it off me!* Get the vile, bass stench of its cadaverous breath from out my nostrils and the embarnacled bloat of its darkly grandiose presence from without the halo of my being. I thought I'd laid the ghost at last and least thought to see it swim into harbour and make fast. Ne'er thought to see the beast lurch and slither obscenely through the streets and *fin my door down* with one unlovely flick 'fore baleening me into a thousand fragments – yeah, just call me *fishmeal.*

*

Fittingly enough, the hulk first started to show itself in the very nations that most ardently pursued the whalerman's bloodclat way of life – Norway and Japan. First in the North-Land the phantom wraithed up like mist, knitting molecular structure from abstract ideation and mere conceptuality. This plastic dub-plate echo of an ectoplasmic literary whalfisch manifested itself right near the boat of some fishermen who had put out from the small fishing-village of Bokus, up near the Arctic circle. Wreathed in threads and swirls of foggy mist the apparition loomed suddenly before them like pure Apeiron. Struck by mystic wonder, those who tried to clutch at it found that they held mere puffs of air but nothing of more substance than that. Those who looked for its trail upon the ocean saw nought but froth, moisture and billows. Of baleen there was none to be seen. Perhaps a slight slick of ink with a hint of a

Keltek accent on it, but definitely nothing more. When fazed and bemused the fisherfolk spun their yarn of *den horned hval* to the bland-blubbers ashore it was met with mute hoots of mutual laughing-stock mockery. Dead men might walk, but do *dead fish swim?* Do dead books talk? Skeletal ravens skwawk? The idea was really not handsome. The reaction of the villagers was enough to stop the men talking about what they had seen, but they knew what they'd seen – they knew. And as the wind blew howling at night and the Northern Lights lit up the icy moonscape of snow, the great chimera would loom again in the ocean of their thoughts.

The Japanese experience was not dissimilar. This time however it was witnessed by a great many more people. *Tsuno no aru kujira* formed like a heavenly cloud of light-mist before the incredulous eyes of scores of peasants who lined the shore – the sea-dragon rose like an octopus, shimmying and fluttering in the sea-haze like a painted fan. Kaiju! Monster! Sakana no yurei! Ghost of a fish! This mythical ichthys gored the very air with unique Cornique protuberances, gored, clawed, humped and finned the salt swirl of breath and planktonic Asiatic watery realms. This unquiet anamniote, this fish of the sea of the mind now swum into the poems of some crazy Zen scribotypes who took it to heart as a legendary theme of their own. Like the most subtle themes of poetry, this was a fish which refused to be caught, a chimeric beast, easily blown away by the winds and waves of restless and turbulent thought. The more the writers tried to pin down and portray the apparition, the quicker it seemed to simply melt away, like the memory of childhood snow on a sunny day long ago or the pink cherry-blossom that soon falls and fades from mind's eye.

*

Arthur Buxtereide swallowed a final mouthful of tea, reached under the table for a drab and battered cardboard folder and removed the large rubber-band that held it together. Inside the first folder was a second, which he opened and carefully placed the contents on the table before him. It was a manuscript – well, a typescript to be more accurate – but anyway it was a project Arthur had been working on for some three or four years now. Over that time he'd patiently pieced his beloved manuscript together, his magnum opus, and the focus of so many hopes. As autumn's breezes wafted through the streets he had completed the ink drawings that would illustrate and illuminate his fictional outpourings. Again and again he'd completed his 'final edit' of the piece. Constantly learning new and deeper levels of refinement in punctuation, layout, spelling, and such matters as structure and thematic-development. The years of work stretched out behind him like a vast beach and he sometimes felt like a tiny crab, making faint, oblique and easily erased marks upon the numberless sands of words, commas and dots. He looked back to the previous summer when he had sat in his lawn-chair in a field, scribbling down chunks of his story into a notebook, to be typed-up later at home. Then it had seemed to be merely a question of finishing the book. It should be plain sailing after that, or so he thought.

*

The haunted husk of a hollow hulk, derelict, desolate, haggard and ruined; afloat on an inky ocean of words, adrift in the worldmind, bobbing up like a water-logged cabin from a sinking ship – the entity was getting away from me and self-animating with a ghostly dream-light that flickered with subtle glare within. The dreams were getting worse. The night-sweats more frequent. By day I worked on single-mindedly, ever spinning the threads of my tale, keyboard clacking as I edged towards the conclusion. And by night the hagfish and morays returned to feast upon my soul with their wanton cruel jaws. I took to walking in the neighbouring countryside to refresh my constitution and focus myself upon the all-consuming task of completing the *book,* that weighty and massy burthen that I ever carried upon my shoulders like Sisyphus of olde. And returning from those shattered moorlands and blasted heaths, egged-on by the beauty of this wild and hardy country, I would sink wearily into my decrepit old chair and pick up quill to write; the harsh rooking of crow-beaks still ringing in my ears.

I won't dwell on my hardships – nothing of value was ever created without struggle and writing fiction is no different from cleaning a floor or unloading a truck. Suffice it to say that after four years of writing, combined with the yellow-jaundice and malaria I'd contracted out east, I was but a shade of my former youthman. The work had, with time, progressed well however, and I was pleased to have woven a world and spawned a flock of little fictitious people (and animals). The all-consuming nature of this work, satisfying though it was, created an ever-present urge to advance the progress of it and only publication would finally bring ease and release to me. I'll admit to hoping to impress a few people as well, and, of course, to the desperate need to make some *money!* Since I'd given up my steady job as a penniless artist in the fire-escape trade to become an author I'd used up most of the cash I'd salted away. I knew I would start earning money from the book as soon as it was published – I'd staked everything on it, by Jehosephat! I had no doubt I could start selling decent numbers right away. Having finally nailed a deal with a major publishing house, I could use that fact to generate my own publicity locally and further afield. Nothing could stop me now.

*

So perhaps you are wondering how it was that our friend Mr Buxtereide was transformed so very quickly from an enthusiastic and optimistic novelist into the shattered and battered relict of a wraith-like will-o-the-wisp. Well, hold back, reader, take time and ensloth thyself. Let us not prod at the poor fellow too much just yet. Let him enjoy the illusion of his ambition. Let him count his imaginary money and read his imaginary reviews – after all – dreams are free, aren't they?

If we were to lift the roof off his house, like a doll's house, and peer within, we would see Arthur inside, diligently working away at his calculating-engine, working away at his very special manuscript. He keeps it under the table, yet he's constantly paranoid that a cup of tea will somehow get spilled all over it and ruin it! Why doesn't he organize himself properly? Why does he live in this chaos? Where is his basic sense of Order? These artists, ya know, they abstract themselves out of everyday reality! They really do live to an utterly different paradigm, a different template altogether. They get so lost in 'creativity' that they forget that what the world cares about is money. We've all met them, 'specially round here... Arthur Buxtereide is just such an one as this – head in the clouds and clouds in the head. Still, the world needs stories, to entertain it during breaks between bouts of making money, so Arthur figured his product might be of value to a scattering of people out there somewhere. It might bring a smile to a weary, drooling, droopy lip somewhere or perhaps a glint to an eye glaucous, glassy, glazed, gazing in fixed stare like that of a tuatara.

The writer put down his pen and stood up. A malarial malaise sent him spinning to the melody of mal. Beadlets of sweat conglomerated on his brow. The ocean of the floor surged in great rolling waves and the darkness of ten thousand bats blotted out the sun from the moon of his starry eyes. His head spun. His body rotated. His world stood still.

*

I was in a strange town, strange, yet not entirely unfamiliar. It was in some northern realm, remote and austere. Or was it my home town? I seemed to recognize a lot of people. I was strolling along down the middle of the road, throwing out copies of my book 'Whale of a Beast' to passers-by, who were catching them and applauding me like I was some kind of star. Finally I was getting the recognition I craved and had worked so hard for. Modesty was evaporating and I felt elated to be out in 'the world' getting my message out to people. This was great, attractive women were giving me admiring looks, academics and great writers were throwing laurels and flowers to me, I was on top of the world. I was pulling a rope that was attached to a little barrow full of the copies of the book and this barrow was clanking along merrily after me. After a while though, I noticed a subtle difference in the crowd's reaction. Some of them were frowning at me and some gesticulating in a strange way. Others turned their backs or simply walked away. This was most disconcerting to me. Was the public so very fickle? Had they gone off the book already? Changed their minds so soon? The looks I was getting were becoming more and more hostile now and disapproval was turning to disgust. I knew something was wrong when a respectable looking man in a suit vomited vigorously at the sight of me. Now they were shouting. Now they were making threatening gestures and starting to throw things… I looked behind me to see that the little barrow full of my wares was no longer to be seen and in its place was the bloated, discoloured and malodorous carcass of a whale. I was struck through with frozen horror, yet for some reason I thought it was *my* whale and therefore I had better just keep on dragging it through the streets, public-outrage or no public-outrage. After all, why should the odd gargantuan decaying mammalian cadaver or two in the street bother any open-minded citizen?

With such questions as these to entertain me, I stoically plodded on down the street of that little remote town, dragging as I did so, that great foul and ghastly entity to which I now seemed yoked, as if by the dictates of fate. The great beast did not feel particularly heavy, the only thing that really disturbed me about it all was the most eldritch and revolting effect I was having on the collective psyche of the good townsfolk. They wore expressions of the inexpressible. Masks of enhanced revulsion. Moaning and ranting. Fingers pointing. More vomiting as the stench of months-old blubber hit unsuspecting nostrils. I was hoping all this was not going to affect sales…

Perhaps it would be wise to quicken my pace, try and slip out of town without attracting any more attention, I thought. I did what I could to affect an air of nonchalance and inconspicuousness, but I think the *whale* was having a compromising effect on it. Damn these fickle, superficial villagers! Can they only see the rotting whale? Can they not see the sensitive artist who *drags* the rotting whale? Are they so shallow and lacking in human-understanding as to think that I really *enjoy* lugging this unspeakably foul hunk of rank death through their precious boulevards?

I strode on through the quaint streets, determined to get out of town in one piece. The sea-mammal was bouncing along merrily on the end of my rope, tongue lolling like a double-bed and dead, dinner-plate eyes spooking out the eyes of the living. The next thing I knew the streets seemed to be deserted. I had made it to a quiet, outer-district. The whale had mysteriously disappeared. I felt cold though, a nasty deep cold had snaked up on me and I quickened my pace. After a while I saw a fire in the distance and as I approached I could see a small group of people gathered around it. They called out to me in a friendly manner and I drew close to the fire. The villagers could only speak a few words of my language but they made me understand that I was welcome and I was soon enjoying the warm glow of the fire and their friendship. I was trying to explain to them that I thought some of my ancestors had come from this part of the world and they seemed very interested. The fire was burning down a little and one of them called out for more fuel. Two men in long winter coats came up to the fire with arms full of stuff to burn. What had they got there? Were they some kind of solid fuel brickettes or something? They weren't the right shape for logs, more sort of cubic, box-like, or like books, yes, like books. The men came closer and I could plainly see what they were carrying. Each man had a generous arm-load of copies of Whale of a Beast – I'd know that cover anywhere, it took me three days to draw it! The men started hurling the books willy-nilly into the fire as ugly chuckles and sniggers were heard. One of the villagers held up a copy and pointed to my picture on the back cover. The next moment they were lunging and snarling at me like braying and ravenous wolves and I was running, running, running blind in panic and sweat was running malarial down my pulse-bursting brows.

*

There he goes again, lost in the minutiae of his own individual consciousness, chasing false-pictures that he projects upon the clouds. Meanwhile a distant rattling sound echoed throughout chateau Buxtereide – Frau Buxtereide was furiously bleaching the curtains. CLANG!

*

Must get some more quinine lozenges from the pharmacopeia – must- what was that noise? Oh probably nothing. I dragged myself out of the twisted, sweaty sheets and decided to take a stroll into town. The air did me good. I soon found myself in the main street, I felt light. I paused in front of a window, it was the Edge of Oblivion, a trendy book shop and cafe. Thinking I might meet an acquaintance, I walked in.

And through my feeling form swept a strange tide of nausea, an icy and bleak mal. I was looking at the advertising display for a new book. A book that featured a whale on the cover. The giant cardboard cut-out reared up over me like a tsunami of chill dread. Yellow lettering on a blue background: Deep Leviathan by Nathan William Haswell! Great Scott! The pretentious bastard would have to have *three names, wouldn't* he? That's *my* cover! That's- how *could* he? He's out-*whaled* me! Just when I was only weeks away from publishing! Just when I was going to bring out the great *whale* book, *I* was going to be the heir of Melville, not this fly by night interloper, this triple-barrelled ponce, this- this-

"NO!" A splenetic bellow of universal despair roared from my vast and vascular lungs as my eyes darkened and the room spun again. I clutched as I fell, and down came the display, the great pasteboard-cetacean, and fifty-one copies of Deep Leviathan by Nathan William Haswell, crashing onto my head and shoulders as I sprawled prostrate at the edge of oblivion.

*

Like a Victorian etching from a penny-dreadful, the hulk reared through the shrouds of sea-fog that beclouded the tiny island of Stagadon. Krawks of gulls scrinkled the briny air. Exhaling breath of baleen, salty lungs, the great fish snorted a steam of misty spray that startled the two melancholy fishers who had put out from the Armorican port of Aber Wrac'h. "Morvil!" whispered the living lips of the old man – a whale! They stopped rowing the little lobster-boat and a clump of bladder-wrack drifted slowly past in poignant display of time and nature. All was hushed. These men had seen many things in their years at sea and one or two things on land as well. They were not fools and no more superstitious than anyone else; however, the tales they told when they returned to the quayside of Aber Wrac'h were enough to raise more than one eyebrow on a weather-beaten Keltek face. The creature, the animal, so they said, was not quite solid, or had something slightly, how do you say, insubstantial about it, almost as if it was not quite properly there. Also it glittered very subtly, coruscated with pastel glimmering hues among the darker tones of its hide. The dark waters lapped at it so beguilingly hypnotic, it drew their eyes like a loadstone. Dark horns soared bisonic over its cavernous cuboid of a head and rather than displacing any water, it seemed rather to interpenetrate the water like a magic lantern picture thrown upon a pool. The whale-fish edentulous left the fishers well incredulous. Encrusted in luminous planktonic micro-organisms of bio-luminescence, or so it seemed, the soft glow melted into mystic mysticeti mist and the appearance was no more. Only old Stagadon threw itself gaunt from out the water's lap.

*

As these cetaceous events and marine apparitions continued unfolding in various locations around the world, Arthur diligently continued his preparations for the publishing and publicity side of his project. Soon the great day would draw near, and, after many a struggle and many a day, he would unleash his great work upon an avid world.

Arthur's publisher told him he had sent off for his book-catalogue number to the official book numbering institute and sure enough, shortly afterwards he received a proof-copy of the book, complete with his own artwork and the thirteen-digit number on the back – all very official looking, like a 'real' book. How satisfying it was to see the project nearing fruition. He had gone on a long voyage indeed to get the thing off the ground and it had cost him dear, but he'd do anything for the precious book, because, after all, what this world really needs is a Whale of a Beast.

The publishing-house informed Arthur that when his book was published, one of the things they do is to inform the book-distribution industry, in advance, of all new releases. His book would be advertised via a vast and complex network of distributors and their subsidiary agents. They needed to finalise the publication-date, and after careful consideration decided that two more months would more than wrap up the project and agreed on October 18th as the day of publication.

Acquaintances and friends would always ask "how's the book coming along?" and Buxtereide would either moan, carp and witter about the difficulties or, when things were going well, go into rather too much detail on just how well it was all going. He got used to seeing eyes start to glaze over or wander off into the distance.

*

As soon as it's out there in the world, I thought to myself with relish and tenacity, everything will start to turn around. A steady trickle of sales, gradually increasing to a reasonably good flowing river of cash. The pleasure of getting away from desk and type-writer to go out and hustle my 'product' – I was looking forward to that. Financial stability, artistic recognition, maybe even a 'serious' publishing-deal and some grown-up money, who knows? I would gulp down another quinine lozenge, grit my teeth, and surge onwards like a tide. Nothing was going to stop me now. No siree.

*

One evening I was enjoying a quiet pint in The Hagfish, when I just couldn't seem to help over-hearing a conversation between two rather arty ladies sitting at a nearby table.

"Wasn't it sad about that dead whale on Tremarazephron beach, did you hear about it?"

"Oh yes, poor thing, it's so sad, isn't it?"

"Ooh that reminds me, I've just finished reading this really brilliant book about whales, and the ocean. It's by this chap Nathan William Haswell, he's *such* a sensitive writer. Yes, it's called 'Deep Leviathan' and it's a really good title, 'cause, you know, he does go *really* deeply into the subject of whales and all that, you know."

Round about this time, had a physician been present, he might have diagnosed me as starting to show symptoms of headache, disorientation and an increasingly acute wave of nausea.

"Sounds really interesting Imogen."

"Yes, I really feel that I've almost literally, in a visceral and gritty way, *swum* with the whales!"

"Really Imogen, it sounds like a *wonderful* book!"

"Yes, you *must* read it when I've finished, Magnolia, you'd learn so much from it! For instance, did you know that a whale can hold its breath for an hour! I mean that's amazing, isn't it? Actually it might be half an hour, but it's a bloody long time anyway, so you get my point, don't you?"

The two ladies were joined by a 'male-friend', Matthew, who worked at a local gallery.

"Oh, are you talking about Deep Leviathan by Nathan William Haswell, it's absolutely *brilliant* isn't it? Such insight and profundity, mixed with wry humour and an eclectic approach to content. He's written the last word on whales alright!"

"That's what I was just telling Magnolia," retorted Imogen "that's the thing about Nathan William Haswell, he's so thorough in his research. For instance, did you know that whale-blubber can be up to a *foot* thick? I mean, that's incredible, isn't it?"

"No, I think it can be up to two and a half feet thick, I think that's what Nathan said," objected Matthew, with a slight air of one defending a righteous hero from foul and infamous accusations.

"Well, however thick it is, it's *bloody* thick!" retorted Imogen as she dashed off her last mouthful of gin and tonic.

Oh it's Nathan William Haswell this and it's Nathan William precious little Haswell that! I seethed silently to myself over my bitter, bitter ale. *That affected little triple-barrelled middle-class pampered little rich-boy! What does he know about his subject, eh? Oh! A whale has blubber! Oh! A whale can hold its breath! Oh! Oh! Look at me everybody! I'm the one who knows all about whales! Look at me, everybody, I'm Nathan William smug little wise-guy Haswell, AREN'T I? Jesus Christ he makes me sick – I've got to get out of this dive!*

"Well then," announced Matthew dramatically, "you'll no doubt be glad to know that he'll soon be our new neighbour! He said in the paper he wants to buy a nice place in West Cornwall so he can saturate his creativity with an authentic Celtic mysticism – when he's not in London and New York, that is."

"How wonderful to have such a talented and important writer moving into the area" enthused Magnolia.

"Yes, I read a deeply moving interview with Nathan William Haswell in the New Literary Nation Review of Books and Magazines in Britain Today Now, it was taut, pithy journalism, straight to the point-stuff! The poor man has just been through another dreadful divorce, he just wants to rebuild his life and he's looking at properties in West Cornwall – can you be*lieve* it? Wants to make a fresh start in a rural and authentic place, he said, and Cornwall fits the bill!"

"Divorced, you say?" cooed Imogen smokily, "hmmm, that's interesting. Not a bad-looking famous rich-man, if I remember rightly!" she gushed.

"Hey, why don't you see if you could interview him for your arts column in the Penwithershins Gazette?" suggested Magnolia archly. "That way you could meet him under the guise of business *and* get to check him out and spend time with him, oh my God Imogen, you should do it! You could end up being the new Mrs Nathan William Haswell!"

I went to get up to go, but a sudden pain coursed down my back. The residual effects of being buried by 51 copies of Deep Leviathan, thank you very much Mr Nathan William Haswell! With gritted teeth and icy resolve I forced my pain-racked form into an upright state and tottered towards the door in cold rage. As I passed their table, I heard Matthew declaring earnestly "at *last* we have an author who truly understands the *spirituality* of the whale in all its nuances-"

And at that point I lost control of my temper, spun round and blurted out wildly "Spirituality? *Spirituality?* He's washed up, he's nothing, I tell you, *nothing!"*

"Oy, sling yer 'ook!" shouted the barman menacingly and my hook I slung.

*

To anyone observing the bustling human traffic on Cheapside, in the City of London, the figure of Dexter Jonas would not in any way have stood out as the least bit remarkable. A middle-aged man of average height, slightly portly and lacking any particular distinguishing features – he looked healthy enough, and focused on his business as he hurried down the pavement towards his next meeting. Little-known outside the hermetic world of publishing, this was the man who had offered Arthur Buxtereide a contract to publish Whale of a Beast. This was the man Arthur revered as some kind of messiah – his deliverer from the biblical deserts of artistic obscurity and poverty, into the promised land of plenty. To Arthur Buxtereide, this chubby, forty-eightish nonentity was viewed quite literally as a saviour.

Not that Jonas had had an easy time convincing the top brass at Reid, Warbler that Whale of a Beast was a good investment. They'd objected that it was too obscure and irrational for the typical reader, that it was bloated, waffling and incomprehensible, that it was, in short, little different to a steaming hill of dung masquerading as 'art'. After much persuasion he'd talked them round however, and there appeared to be no further obstacles to publication going ahead. Still, the Head of Fiction had tried to impose various annoying and humiliating conditions and caveats to the contract, as if to hinder its progress, it seemed. He had insisted that the author be responsible for the local publicity in Penwithershins for instance, and had haggled and quibbled over the national promotional budget – shaving off a thousand here, a couple of thousand there. Still, even with these minor glitches, Buxtereide's magnum opus looked well on course for its projected publication date of 18th October.

Arthur meanwhile had focused on the local publicity. In fact, he had focused on it with such blistering zeal as to invest almost his last farthing in an advertising campaign whose grandiosity was matched only by its rampant braggadocio. There were full-page ads in all the local papers presumptuously telling the public to 'Indulge in a literary feast – it's a Whale of a Beast!' There were the forty thousand leaflets that he had paid a local printer to produce – these Arthur intended to personally deliver to every home in Penwithershins. There were the posters, the coasters and the souvenir ballpoint pens.

Financially speaking, Arthur Buxtereide had extended himself to the very limits, like the tendril of a great marine-mollusc searching avidly for food, like an unwise primate going too far along a fragile branch, or perhaps like a harpooneer of old in his tiny boat, hitched up to a fish that's destined to drag him down to the black depths of a watery hell. His precious book was everything to him and he would follow it where'er it led, superstitiously imbuing the 'object' with 'anima'.

The last few weeks leading up to October 18th was a period of intense activity in the psyche of Arthur Buxtereide. The constant concentration on the minutiae of his manuscript was not conducive to health. The poring over obscure and little-used diacritic marks and other matters of such infinitesimal relevance, by the insufficient light of the poor-quality ear-candles that economy had forced him to rely on – all this was drawing on his vitality and energy. There was a powerful force sustaining him however, and that was the anticipation of publication. Until October 18th he would be known to the world merely as an ex-fire-escape-salesman. From thence forth, he would be known as an author, an artist, somebody who had written a book. He relished the opportunity of showing everyone that they had misjudged him – they had thought him a mere drifter, and now he would be vindicated, applauded, lauded and pawed-at. He would emerge from his obscurity and enter society as an 'exotic', a figure of fascination and charisma. He would charm women and flabbergast men. He would stun animals and hypnotise anamniotes. Small children would grow old and tell their grandchildren of the day they once caught a glimpse of the legendary Arthur Buxtereide himself walking down the street! Was there no end to the glories that should soon befall our heroic writer, our man of belles lettres? Which newspaper would be the first to feature him prominently in their Culture section? (Probably on the front page!) Which media-outlet would be the first to offer him an interview? Which famous person would be the first to come out publicly in support of his great work? Who would first proclaim its genius to a fascination-hungry world? Like a great gelatinado he floated and basked in the warm sea of his fantasies, following the labyrinthine and relentless current of his thoughts. The trumpets played a regal fanfare at the entry of the distinguished author – Fantasia para un Gelatinado… He bowed solemnly to the panel of international judges. A footman advanced towards him bearing a purple velvet cushion on which glittered a noble decoration. The president of the society graciously bestowed the Order of Merit, for his major contribution to Arts and Literature, on that universally revered genius from Great Britain, MR ARTHUR BUXTEREIDE!

Then of course he'd be asked to appear on Culture Today Now and he'd get to meet the lovely presenter, Sheila Hotston, a woman nationally revered as much for her piercing intellect and sharp humour, as for her beautiful smile and unforgettable body. She'd probably want to continue the conversation outside the limitations of the telly-programme and who knows where it could all end up? Arthur remembered seeing her ages ago on Culture Today Now interviewing an Irish writer whom Arthur had thought was total hogwash.

She'd been awfully sympathetic to him though, saying that she was fascinated by Celtic culture and by the sea, and that he'd brought these themes to life with great beauty and simplicity! If she thought 'I Sing To The Sea' by Joey McGee was the real deal, just wait till she gets a-hold of my Whale of a Beast, dreamed Arthur, then we'll see who's the new Celtic Poet-boy to bamboozle the Brit Lits and blow them all away with hwyths of shimmering Keltek mist... It's a well-known fact in the book-trade that every two and a half generations the industry will feast on the presence of a 'Celtic poet/genius'. Market-research has proven that periodically, the unstoppable river of English literature must be challenged, teased and beautified by an influx of the Celtic. There are deep historical reasons why this happens in Britain – it is partly the acknowledgment of our Celtic roots, our Ancient British past – and it is partly the deep need for an industrialized and media-dominated society to re-assert its creative, irrational and endlessly poetic tradition. The Druid and the Bard are not yet dead in Britain – they live on in our writers, poets, singers, musicians... When the British look for songs and stories, they look to the Kelts, as they always have. To this very day the Keltic Bard is still revered in Britain – be it as rock 'n' roll singer or poet. So why shouldn't this reverence come to Arthur Buxtereide? Why should not he, rather than Joey McGee be the new Dylan O'Joyce? What had McGee ever done? Spent most of his time as an academician, hanging out at American campuses, making elephant-loads of money. For all his 'authenticity', he had never stepped outside his middle-class bubble and had to tough it out in the world of unskilled labour, never had to face down the spectre of poverty or the ghoulish mediocrity of a hand-to-mouth existence. He'd learned most of his Celtic mythology at Harvard, rather than in the Gaeltacht, as he would have his punters believe. Those yanks'll buy anything with a shamrock on it thought Buxtereide bitterly, as he schemed to promote the pysky over the leprechaun and the pasty over the, the, whatever they eat in Ireland!

Somehow Buxtereide never let his central European ancestry get in the way of his intense Celtic patriotism and artistic conceit. He had briefly toyed with the idea of Kernicising his name into Trebuxtereide, but somehow it didn't quite sound authentic. Besides, most of Europe had been Celtic in the good old days before the spoil-sport Romans came along and ruined everything, so he felt he had some right to his tribal claim. Anyway, he could explain all that to Sheila Hotston on their first date, he was sure she would find his genealogy every bit as fascinating as his art, his dreams, his fantasies.

*

I was yanked back to reality by a persistent knocking on the door. It was the postman with a letter that needed singing for. It was from the tax department and it seemed they required the sum of four hundred and seventy four pounds and sixty three new pence. Well, we all 'require' things, I thought, as I crumpled up the letter and dropped it into the coal-hod. We all require things, don't we, hmmm? Fame, success, recognition, *royalties, oh yes, royalties!* That's what I require, some fat royalties and a frog-hop out of this derned ol' poverty-game! No more scrimping by on squid-ink and rice-paper! Writing with those stupid eye-brow pencils by the light of those inane ear-candles, no siree! Four hundred and seventy something pounds indeed – *who did they think they were?*

*

Koot-hulu! Koot-hulu! The rasping croak, the warble, nay, the very rattle of the nightjars had woken Arthur from his sleep and now he lay there with their irascible and insatiable hooting pullulating through his bejangled nervous system – was there no peace to be found in this world? Was man merely put here to be pecked at by the unthinkably vast carrion birds of doom? Picked, pecked and tormented; gouged, gored and gulled down by forces greater, and grosser, than himself? Alone in the dead of night sometimes he couldn't help wondering if all mankind were dwarfed by entities great and terrible, ancient beyond fathomable belief, lurking and abiding in the spaces outside and between ordinary space and time, emitting a foul carnal stench, squirming in the margins of reality, rearing forth into dimensions beyond conception with powers ungraspable to the tiny minds of mankind. Seething, bubbling, gibbering in demented eternal frenzy, these great and terrible entities required the assistance of certain humans to initiate their 'breaking-through' into this world. What was before, shall be so again; and what has long slept shall yet awaken... With a grinding and roaring, the void shall fill with vast, leathery wings, with tendrils and tentacles, suckers and trunks, spines and bristles, mouths, eyes and fangs, terrible fangs. Hacking and devouring, they swallow worlds and stars, they drink time down like mead and a flap of their raven wing would send a dark ripple through reality's elastic tapestry. The jangling croak of the doom-pecked birds, insatiable, pullulating – the rasping croak of the night-jars – *Koot-hulu! Koot-hulu!*

*

Ye Gods! What vile dreams I've been having of late – like something out of an H.B.Lunchcraft novel – unspeakably ghastly and eldritch! Disrelishable to all but the most loathsome and unwholesome of entities! Talking of lunch-carts, what was there to eat in this gaff, I wondered? The fridge resembled a cornucopia that could no longer cope. Rations were thin and tack was hard. Oatcakes with a scrape of marge again... one day... one day... I poured a sprinkling of oatmeal into a bowl, turned on the cold tap and let the water play over the oats. Low-fat milk was my sardonic name for this nutritious liquid, and in truth, it really didn't taste any different to the real thing – once you got used to it. I didn't mind making these little sacrifices for the sake of the *book*. It's like tea-bags – most people think they are for making just one cup of tea. They don't realise that if you save three or four of them, you can then re-boil them and get a perfectly good cup of tea for free! I soon gave up trying to tell people about this when I saw the derisive sneers on their sleek, consumerist jowls turn to leers of vehement heinous contempt. From a Yugoslavian I learned the trick of splitting matchsticks down the middle with a razor-blade, thus doubling the amount of matches in a box! (As long as you didn't break the flimsy little slivers.) I'd been given a copy of Food For Free for free and found it full of food for thought. I started experimenting with nettle-broth and limpet-roulade... I soon found that nature is remarkably well-stocked with edibles and comestibles and that the price-tag is refreshingly low. Thus I frequently eked out my outlandish fresh feed from the land. The farthings and ha'pence I so stoically saved were put towards the spiralling cost of biros. Also, of course, for the local promotional campaign, or LPC, as I'd annoyingly dubbed it. This damned LPC was soaking up money like a dipsomaniac soaks up beer on a hot day. I'd decided to go for the glossy posters, no point in compromising with a *matt* finish, not after all that blood I sweated to write the damn thing. No sir, *this* Whale's gonna shine like a shiny-thing! No point in being modest, muttering quietly to the world that you think your product might not be all that bad. Oh no, you've got to get out there and scream it into their chubby and vacant faces. You've got to take your message out there and declare it boldly from the mountain-top, as Moses did. Well – at least from the rooftop. You've got to sell, sell, sell. You've got to hustle people, hassle people and shake them down. You've got to say 'look world, I tried to do this the nice way but you wouldn't listen so now I'm gonna ram it into your lousy fat face', ya know, *sell,* like they do in Amerika. Chase people down the street, lassoing them if necessary, or using a bolus or other applicable device to merely slow them down long enough for you to get at them and *make a sale!* I mean, *how hard can it be?* Just how hard can it be to patrol the high-street, select a victim, pursue and lasso, and then simply pour on the sales-pitch once you've got them on the ground? I mean, come on, they're gonna buy, aren't they? They're not going to say no after you've demonstrated such incredible fortitude and originality in your marketing strategy, are they?

Note to Self: Start eating properly.

*

"Awright Art, 'ow are ya doin' mate?"

"Oh hallo Sidney, I'm alright, how are you these days?"

"Awright Art, can't complain, ya know, business is booming. Matter o' fact I might be on the telly!"

"You're joking Sidney! Are they giving you your own comedy show?"

"Nah mate, they're doin' this document'ry, ain't they? Removal Men it's called. Sorta fly-on-the-wall type malarkey i'n' it? I'm on the short list for the starring role, ain't I? All they do is folla ya rahnd with a bleedin' cam'ra all day while you do a couple of 'ouses, then ya get a fat cheque at the end of the day, don't ya?"

"Bloody hell Sidney, they're gonna make you a star! You'll have housewives ripping your clothes off when you go to the Co-Op!"

"That's right mate, and once I'm famous I'll be able to raise me rates for the removals, won't I?"

"Yeah, if you're not too busy doing press interviews and hanging out with the rich and famous!"

"That's right mate, next stop the Asura Loka! Ha ha ha! What are you up to these days – still writin' that book of yours?"

"It's coming out on October 18th! *Whale of a Beast*, published by Reid, Warbler, available at all good retailers!"

"No kidding! That's brilliant news mate! Put me down for a free copy, ha ha ha! By the way, if you need a bi' of casual work, I sometimes need an extra pair of 'ands – just the odd day like when Jimmy can't make it. Ten quid an hour, mind! I know you don't like to leave that desk of yours but it'd be good for ya!"

"Well, I could do with a bit of cash. Give me a ring if a job comes up, Sidney, I might well be interested."

"Awright Art. Oh talkin' of books, you know Brian's fishing book is coming out soon don't ya?"

"You're joking, aren't you? *Brian!* You mean Brian has written a book! I can't believe it! I mean, I knew he was into fishing in a big way and all that, but, *a book – Brian?* It hardly seems possible! I mean, Brian of all people!"

"I know what you mean, mate, but he's got 'imself together these days. Got off the booze and all that. Apparently 'e's one of Britain's foremost authorities on the rainbow trout nowadays!"

"Well, there you go – everyone's a celebrity these days, aren't they?"

"Seems that way, don't it Art? Thought I might write a little memoir of my days in the removal business meself actually. Thought I might call it 'A Moving Experience', whadaya think?"

"Ha ha ha! I like it Sidney-boy! You should go for it – everyone else is. We're all stars today, aren't we?"

"Nice to see you Art. I'll look out for your book!"

"And I'll look out for you on the telly, mate, ha ha ha!"

*

If you could part the curtain of the clouds and look down from the sky, you would see a tiny dot slowly making its way up the hill, carrying something large on its back, just as an ant does. This was no termite, mind you, but rather what you might term a man of mighty temerity. A man struggling against gravity with his burden, as all men do in their way. The figure slowly snailed its way forth, making little detours to approach every door along the way. Unlike the typical conch though, which leaves a trail of slime, this particular specimen was leaving a trail of self-promotional literature – the notorious LPC.

Sweat stood out as beadlets before trickling in mountainstreams down the palsied and jaundiced brow of Buxtereide as he beetled forth about his whale of a task. With vigour, verve and zeal he pursued the goal that his mind projected out before him, eagerly planting his leaflets, the seeds of his future good fortune, into the receptive slots of many a door. Satisfying work indeed, sowing the seed of his ideation, the fruit of his imagination in the mind-womb of the people. All those little characters he'd dreampt-up – they could truly come to life now, make themselves at home in the psyche of the readers. Those 'readers' he hoped to catch were regarded rather like a beautiful woman – he would need to woo them and try to seduce them, win them over to his side. He hardly dared hope to succeed, but then again, he had pinned everything on this venture and there was no going back, hence the LPC... He seemed to be energized by his work and even his normally shattered health was better. The doctor had recently told him that the malaria in his system was now attacking the jaundice and they were slugging it out to see which one would take control of him. A most unusual development, the doctor had to admit, but, these things do happen.

Most people were out when he delivered the leaflets, but occasionally he encountered people at home. Often they were bemused, or seemed not to understand what he was doing, though he clearly told them he was advertising a book. A few seemed genuinely interested and one or two seemed oddly hostile or perhaps resentful, as if he was hustling or punting dodgy goods or something. Maybe they thought the leaflets were just a cover and really he was just casing the joint to come back later and rob it. After all, some people don't take too kindly to a stranger at the door.

"What's all this then?"

"Oh hallo. Would you like a leaflet? I'm advertising my new book – it's fiction – set locally..."

"I'm not interested."

"Fair enough." *(Slam!)*

Undaunted, the quixotic crusader pressed on to the next house.

And after many and many a house, the crusader still surged forth, like Johnny Apple-Seed, only more Johnny Sperm-Whale-Seed. The soles of his boots were eroding. The load on his back was lightening. The beads on his brow were a drippin'. The word he was gradually spreading. A Whale of a Beast was a-comin'. And people you'd better be ready. A beast of a book was among us. A brawny and battering ram-goat. A horn of the splattering sea-tide. Ha tonnek meur lemmyn an mor yw. A tale of the flickering side-streets. Where boot-heels go noisily clacking. And things are not quite what they should be. New Lynsmouth is smothered in darkness. And things coming out of the future. A world in a book in a new hand. The reader creating the story. Perception phenomenal matter. Time is the consciousness spaces. A beast was a wailing and roaring. A roar was all wailing and beastly. A tale of a feast of illusion. A Whale of a Beast was a-comin'.

At another house the door was opened by a lady who seemed nice.

"Oh! You've written your own book! That's so wonderful! I've always wanted to write a book! What's it about?"

Buxtereide proudly handed her a leaflet and started to explain the romantic and mysterious nature of his work when he was interrupted.

"Wait a minute! I think I've heard about this. You're famous, aren't you? No – don't tell me, I know, it'll come to me in a minute! Yes! You're that Nathan William Haswell, aren't you?"

But there was no-one there to answer her question.

Later in the day, as Buxtereide tramped across the windy desolation of Pigmoor, he came upon an isolated farmstead that had lurked there since the dark ages. He'd picked his way across the dung-bespattered farm-yard, his ears filled with the ominous lowing, braying and bleating of unseen beasts. Curiously, the snorting and guttural grunting of hogs was absent from this cacophony – perhaps they had all been turned out on the moor to forage for dodder and sundews for fodder. He made a point of going out of his way to deliver leaflets to these remote farms and rustic cottages. He would bring the light of culture, poetry and imagination to places where it was least expected! He was a nineteenth century revolutionary spreading his inflammatory and liberating propaganda. He was an evangelist singing the joy of the gospel. He was a sooth-sayer, wandering bard and droll. A peller, story-teller and snake-oil-merchant all rolled into one.

Having posted his precious message through the farm-house door, Buxtereide noticed that the babble of animalistic jabber had quietened down, only to be replaced by a furious mewling noise. And as if from nowhere, a pair of extremely large stripy cats came whirling like furry dervishes, descending upon Bux. (As we might sometimes call him, for the sake of brevity.)

These unprecedented moggies soon had our man on the run, high-tailing it out of there like a human-mouse. Terrible beasts, these cats can be, especially up Pigmoor way, or so they d' say. Alas, Bux did not get away quite unscathed – to this day he carries the mark of a livid gash on his starboard shoulder-blade; a stigmatic manifestation of the crusader's sublime willingness to risk his all in the quest for poetic expression. The Local Publicity Campaign had cost a fortune. It had cost Bux some blood, sweat and a few tears in his clothing. As for toil, the toll of that till was tall oil. Tall tales of edentulous whales, awash in an ocean of words.

*

Dexter Jonas had always had a yearning to see the Moss Gardens of Kyoto. His interest in Japanese culture can be traced back to his art-school days, when he'd admired some of the same graceful prints that had inspired Van Gogh and Gauguin back in the nineteenth century. These startling images were evocative enough to bind with his memory and create a permanent impression of beauty and simplicity. Later on, when he was a mere rookie in the book-trade, Jonas had come across the poets of Zazen and from that moment on was transformed into a genuine devotee of Japanese culture and all the riches it had to offer. He'd read some of their modern writers too of course, and some of them he found fascinating, but it was those stark and enigmatic medieval aphorisms that he would always return to. In more recent years, as he worked his way up the echelons of the publishing game – first at Opaquenheimers, then at Reid, Warbler – he would often relax in the evening by uncorking the sake, putting a cassette of koto music into the tape-player and pondering with delight over the words of Hakuin, Ryokan or Basho. These unworldly sages took him to a place unique. The subtle power of their words brought a clarity previously unknown to him and left him feeling refreshed and very much part of nature.

One of the things Dexter liked best about his promotion to Associate Editor at Reid, Warbler was the foreign travel that went with the job. He'd enjoyed his jaunts to Chicago and San Francisco, Berlin, Barcelona and Moscow. These trips came up every few months and usually involved a lot of good meals and conversations in fancy hotels with editors, authors and contract-lawyers. A little business was naturally involved, but there was always plenty of time to explore these locations in a bit more depth.

When he was asked if he'd like to go to Osaka to talk to a Mr Kajimoto about a contract for a Japanese edition of I Sing To The Sea by Joey McGee, Dexter Jonas got a taste of *satori.* Suddenly he felt blissfully happy, as if he was finally going home. By combining the business trip with a bit of holiday time, he'd be able to travel up to Kyoto and visit the object of an obscure life-long yearning – the Moss Gardens.

*

In the 2nd October issue of The Penwithershins Gazette was an interview with Arthur Buxtereide, conducted by Ripley Porter, Arts Editor:

RP: Arthur, without giving too much away, would you like to tell us about your new book, which is titled Whale of a Beast?

AB: Certainly Rip. It concerns some monstrous goings-on in West Cornwall, some years back. The sea plays a large part in it. It's a mystery/romance, written as a non-linear adventure in linguistics.

RP: Sounds intriguing! Any car-chases in it?

AB: Sadly not, but the book's not out for three weeks, I could put one in if you like.

RP: That's very considerate of you, Arthur, but I'm sure the book is better without any input from me! So it's out in three weeks, you say?

AB: Yes. October 18th. Published by Reid, Warbler.

RP: And is it your first book?

AB: That's right, my first. Before becoming an author I used to install and inspect fire-escapes, mostly commercial premises, but occasionally somewhere really unusual. In fact, it was when I was installing a fire-escape on a lighthouse that I first got the idea to start writing. It was the sea, being around it on a daily basis, I found it naturally inspired me to start stringing words together, so it started from there.

RP: Quite a journey – from commercial fire-security solutions to Dadaist novel/poems, isn't it?

AB: These things happen Ripley.

RP: Have you always lived in Cornwall?

AB: My childhood and youth I spent here. I studied philosophy at the Camborne School of Minds. During the fire-escape years I was based in Dulwich. I felt I was wasting time though, I needed a more fulfilling life, a way of, I know it's a cliche, but a way of expressing myself.

RP: So you moved back to the west-country to become a writer?

AB: That's it exactly.

RP: Now I have to say that I've read the book Arthur, and it's not exactly an easy read, is it? I mean, it's studded with foreign words, Cornish words, a lot of apparently made-up words, long passages of free-floating word-association and stream-of-consciousness surrealism, dream-imagery... I mean, let's be honest, the average punter is going to be totally flummoxed by this, don't you think?

AB: Well, sure, it's not for everybody perhaps, but I think it'll have its audience, given time. Also, I think it's good for readers to stretch themselves, challenge themselves a bit sometimes. There's always a fundamental choice for any writer, any artist in any media – are you going to be yourself or are you going to pander to fashion and shape your product according to a populist concept of how a book should be, or how a film or song or pair of trousers should be? Anyway, my book's not really all *that* surreal. It's got plenty of romance for the girls and adventure for the boys, even if it hasn't got a car-chase!

RP: Why did you decide to sprinkle the text with Cornish words?

AB: Because Kernewek or the Cornish language is the key to a much deeper poetic understanding of the place and the people. I regard it as a magical touchstone, the door to another realm, a cultural missing link that is loaded with information. Poetically, it has a unique sound and resonance, and to me, certain words of Cornish have a talismanic power, a power to enchant.

RP: Should I ask which ones?

AB: Let's just say they're in the book!

RP: Well, thank you very much Arthur Buxtereide for talking to me today. It's always a pleasure to meet a local celebrity, a local success-story. I hope the book's a best-seller! Available October 18th, published by Reid, Warbler, it's Whale of a Beast by Arthur Buxtereide.

*

After giving that interview I was nervous as a house-cat, pacing back and forth with the now all-too-familiar beadlets of gritty perspiration sliming down my beetle-crusted brow. Punter-flummoxing dream-imagery indeed! What did *he* know, that hack Rip Porter? Smugly pronouncing the book unreadable then wishing it every success! How insincere can you *get?* Probably just jealous. Stuck behind his desk at the stupid little Penwithershins Gazette, that contemptible rag, that wearisome throwback to a former age of boredom. Still, now I'm in the paper, I may as well redouble my efforts with the local publicity campaign – the LPC – *why do I call it that?* I've got to stop calling it that, it sounds like some self-satisfied little inter-departmental office acronym – how tedious. Anyway, I'll redouble my efforts on the LP- the local publicity campaign – that's what I'll do… I'll concentrate on getting the posters up in all the local towns, that's the best follow-up to all the leaflets that I've already put out – damn! Shoulder's playing up again – *pesky cats!* I think the jaundice seems to be colouring my view of the world, I'd better go and see Doctor Billy Rubin, he's known as the west-country's foremost practitioner of tropical and exotic medicine. At least the old croaker can write me a script for Ian Quinn the pharmacist – *I'm nearly out of lozenges, damn it!*

*

Ah yes, observe Mr Bux, scurrying around, pursuing his destiny, chasing soap-bubbles and thistle-down, seeking for fame and fortune when all the time the birds are singing as the world spins doggedly round and the stars sing out their song of eternal amazement.

There he goes, beetling up hill and down dale, plastering the vicinity with his glossy posters. Sticking them on billboards, bus-shelters, back-alleys and main-streets, he doesn't care – he's out to push his product, to ram his genius into the soft and pleasant face of humanity, as it were. The fact that humanity might not actually *require* his product had never once blown through that well-aerated mind of his. Don't be fooled by the air of modesty and detachment he put on for that newspaper hack, that's just a little trick he pulls to cover up his slavering and desperate craving for recognition, for literary validation, for *stardom*. It's not even the money so much, not that he'd mind it, though he's well-accustomed to poverty after all these years. No, it's more about the 'glory', the 'statement', the 'aesthetic resonance' – all the hogwash that goes with the word-industry. And with what great industry he goes about gluing up his Whale of a Beast posters. Soon his fingers are caked and flaked with squamous, flapping scraps of dried glue – it looks as if his hands are suffering from a ghastly malady of the epidermis. When he picks up his glue-brush it sticks to his hand. The poster also adheres to his gelatinous claw like a fish-flake in a rattling lobster mandible-jaw. He ends up with little bits of torn poster stuck to his coat. Fragments of his own name stuck to his elbow and 'Beast' stuck to his haunch. He didn't know it was there until some young wise-guys started calling out "Hey Beast! Hey! Beast-Ass!" in a most annoying manner. Then when he tried to remove the offending word, it kept sticking to his hand and he was close to getting into a fairly rancid mood over the whole affair until he was saved by an exceptionally heavy downpour of rain which soaked him to the skin, thus making the piece of paper considerably easier to remove.

In St.Truborne he had more luck. He got chatting to the

owner of an alternative type book-shop who not only agreed to putting up a poster in the shop, but booked him to come and do a reading and book-signing event! That was more like it! While he was talking to the owner, he noticed two rather nice looking ladies seemed to be listening in. As he was about to leave, the brunette with the glasses and beret approached him – her face radiated eager anticipation, her eyes shone and her moistened lips smiled, before parting to pose a question. "Hey, sorry to bother you, but didn't you write I Sing To The Sea? I think it's a *wonderful* book!"

"Er no. That wasn't me, actually. My book's called Whale of-"

"Oh yeah, that's right, it was Joey McGoo, wasn't it? He's a *wonderful* writer, don't you think?"

"Er, its McGee, I think. I haven't read him myself."

"You really should, you know. Well, it was nice to meet you, Mr Boosterinder."

"Buxtereide."

But by now the two women were retreating out of the shop in a fit of giggles. Will no-one take Bux seriously? Exhausted, soaked-through and riddled with tropical maladies, the protagonist headed for home, grimly satisfied with the day's progress.

*

Bread and marge again – I didn't care, soon I'd be slurping down the finer things of life, as soon as, you know – as soon as the *book* comes out. I had been getting a bit thin lately, I must admit, but then, hey, who wants to be fat? It's a fact that most people eat far too much food. It's simply not good for you. Food is a vulgarity to be tolerated only with extreme restraint, or so I managed to convince myself. Of course, I had been a little more rotund in the days when Mrs Buxtereide was still around to cook the meals. Before she ran off with that estate-agent bastard, shortly after I quit the fire-escape game, that is! Told me she didn't fancy starving in rustic obscurity and relocated to Chiswick she did. Funny thing is, sometimes it seems like I can still hear her bustling around the house. Just my nerves I expect. Just my nerves.

I thought I'd relax with a cup of tea and read the paper for a while, just to calm down a bit. Leafing through to the literature section, I came upon an interview with Allan Ffordd, a Welsh poet who I thought was over-rated. He was waffling on about his new collection of poetry, Rhonda's On My Mind – Recollections of a South Wales Idyll. Thinks he's so original, so way out, when really he's just a copy-typist, aping his deity – following in the zig-zag mackerel footprints of that curly-haired, boozy ruffian who bragged in the pubs about a young fella long gone ghost echo faded away and forgotten. Nobody can equal Zimmerman Thomas, the bard of our age – it's vulgar hubris to even try. I mean really, just listen to this… "My work has been informed by the landscape and inspired by the urban scene. Sometimes, when I'm walking, patrolling my hills alone, I almost seem to forget where I end and the hills begin – I feel as if I *am* the landscape, the spirit of the land. It has entered into me and inspired me. It has purified me and showed me who I am. I feel the spirits of our warrior ancestors stirring in the hills, telling me to be their voice, to sing their song, to be their truth…" There's more, but I really think I might projectile-vomit in a minute… I'll just make some more tea… What's this? Oh no, this is really intolerable, this just shouldn't happen… "Next Tuesday night I've been invited to appear on Culture Today Now, so I'm very much looking forward to exploring my work and discussing my ideas with Sheila Hotston. I feel she is a woman who has an intuitive understanding of my work, a really remarkable woman. It should be a memorable meeting of minds…" Oh he'd like to have a memorable meeting with Sheila alright, and not just of minds either, the sneaky little chiseller… Oh! My work is informed by being a pompous windbag! Oh! I feel the ancestor-spirits bestowing the gift of a silver-tongue upon me! Oh! The ancestors are advising me on a portfolio of investment opportunities! Oh! I'm such a wild Kelt, I'll just drive my four by four back to my double-glazed, centrally-heated, ostentatious great stinking pile of vulgarity! Oh! Look at me everybody, I'm a wild and woolly minstrel from the hills. Check out my avant-garde haircut, my avant-garde trousers and my avant-garde poetry – that's right everybody – *I avant-garde a clue!*

*

The day in the Moss Garden was one which Dexter Jonas knew he would remember for the rest of his life. For seven hundred years the visionary gardeners of Kyoto had quietly cultivated this bryophytic paradise. Innumerable books and treatises have been written on the tranquil joys of meditation, but only in Japan do you find wisdom and subtle insight manifested within the form of a garden. In this place of unspeakable beauty, Dexter Jonas came to know a peace both unimaginable and intimately familiar, the peace of the soul coming home to nature, to itself.

Masanori Hayakawa switched on the windscreen-wipers of his truck – it *would* have to start drizzling now, when he only had one more delivery to make. Now the traffic would slow up again as the fog descended. He was hoping to finish work early that day, looking forward to seeing his family. Oh well, he thought, such is life. His truck slid gracefully down the road, past pines and people with umbrellas. It was a very large truck. On the side of it was a huge logo: Hamamoto Whale-Meat Company.

Fog and rain and a whale of a load. Masanori Hayakawa had been driving for years, he knew the roads well and was a pretty good driver but he just didn't have time to stop. Dexter Jonas appeared to simply step off the curb without looking. In an instant the vehicle struck him and in an instant he was dead.

*

In a final and fund-fluttering, fund-withering, wuthering wind-thundering flurry of ostentatious and self-inflationary bombast, Bux blew his last bucks renting out the local Nutshell Theatre for a gala launch-party on the night of the 18th. He certainly was out to launch, and out to launch in style. He hired three local bands of varying musical subgenres; stilt-walkers, jugglers, fire-eaters, dancing-girls and a bloke in a gorilla suit. The last item was a mistake. He hadn't ordered a gorilla-man from the agency but one appeared and he was duly billed for the services of a rather unconvincing and strangely beer-thirsty ape-man – such is art.

Bux was feeling pretty good about himself. He felt a little bit like a great general, confidently contemplating his strategy on the eve of a great campaign – perhaps like Napoleon himself. His phone was ringing a lot more often now, suddenly people wanted to talk to him. The best of it was when he was asked to do a brief interview for a local television arts programme. Although it would only be seen in the Shyre, still, it was great exposure and contributed significantly to the spiralling sense of self-aggrandisement that Bux started manifesting during those days of anticipatory delirium.

People seemed to see him in a different light. He walked taller, his charisma emanating forth all around him like a Druidic fog. Finally, with everything in place for the book-launch, he allowed himself the illusory luxury of fantasizing about his future success. The interviews he would give – the interviews he would turn down. The fellow-writers and poets he would get to hang out with – now he would be not just admitted, but positively *welcomed* into the inner circle, the heart of the clique of the art-set chic, obliquely leakin' lucre.

Bux's euphoria was quickly turned to sadness when he learned of the death of Dexter Jonas. The publishing house had informed him of the sad news, and although Buxtereide had only met Jonas once, he had liked him and was shocked by his sudden demise. Over the next couple of days he got out into the countryside, tramping many a muddy mile in deep fog and passing curtains of shattering rain. The tendrils of watery vapour wreathed around his ankles as he walked. He walked home and slept like a heavy clod of rain-soaked clay, only vaguely disturbed by dim hulking spectres of the unquiet night.

*

On the 14th of October Arthur received the following letter:

Dear Mr Buxtereide,

Re: Contract between Reid, Warbler / A.Buxtereide

Regrettably I must inform you that the above contract is no longer binding in law.

The reason for this eventuality is essentially that in accordance with sub-clause 37b – Substantiation of Compound Residuals in Significant Territories – all territories must be contractually secured before the agreement is considered to be binding.

Pete D'Ante, Head of Fiction, Reid, Warbler, has brought it to our attention that certain documents of contractual details have not been signed by the agent in Japan and that furthermore the agreed time period for so-doing elapsed yesterday.

It is therefore the position of Reid, Warbler that no contractual relationship exists between themselves and yourself in any form whatsoever. All previous agreements dependent upon the aforementioned contract are therefore to be viewed as null and void.

Yours faithfully,
Piers Hellbetch, Senior Partner,
Suckblode, Hellbetch and Feand,
174 Darke Place, LONDON W1 1FU.

*

The rainbow turned to grey for Arthur Buxtereide then and the swelling buds of his fresh blooming flowers seethed and pullulated with ten thousand head of foul white maggots. Numb disbelief alternated with searing rage and desolate sorrow – a morbid broth of foetid humours coursed through his jangling nervous system. He read the letter over and over again, nausea rising in his innards – one thing was now abundantly clear to him – his book had been dropped – with the untimely death of Dexter Jonas, Whale of a Beast was now also doomed, condemned. Already his precious whale was a bloated cadaver, sinking down, slowly, deeper and deeper into the lightless chasms of grim and crushing obscurity – *the grave-yard of unwanted books!*

Bux racked his brains for any possible solution to this nightmare and in a moment of lucidity, decided to show the letter to Ricky Hahsler, a law-practitioner who'd recently set-up in town, and who's rates were relatively cheap – for some reason. He managed to make an appointment for the 17th, and left the letter from Suckblode, Hellbetch and Feand with the receptionist, for the urgent attention of Mr Ricky Hahsler. As Bux walked home his shoes felt uncomfortable, his tongue felt dry and his shoulders hunched into a mountainous ridge of acute muscular tension. The traffic was too loud, the sea-weed stunk as he walked along the promenade and some teenagers walked past him with a radio which was blaring out a deeply grotesque little pop-tone which then lodged in his mind like the fixed idea of a stuck record and jingled his jangling nerves to Blighty and back.

The next couple of days passed in a blur of misery. Bux did his best to maintain his storm-blasted spirit, but, alas…

Perhaps it is best if we draw a veil over those days and leave Bux to lick his wounds in peace. Sometimes, when a wild creature becomes wounded or sickened, it must find shelter in the woods somewhere. It must cover itself with leaves and huddle and sleep, as the wind prowls and moans around the wintry land.

On the 17th he went to the meeting with the practitioner of law.

*

He's got this brass plate outside with his name on it and all these letters after his name, but when I first saw Ricky Hahsler up close, with his pencil-moustache and slicked-back hair, I thought he should be wearing a pork-pie hat and sheepskin jacket, punting whelks and eels off a barrow in Whitechapel.

"The news is not good, Mr Buxtereide, not good at all." He spoke with a slow deliberation, in a hollow and nasal voice and stared into my eyes with an exaggerated look of woe frozen upon his face, in his raised, Chaplinesque eyebrows and pouting, downturned mouth. What grotesque reptiles people can be!

"Well I was under the impression that I'd entered into a legal contract with Reid, Warbler to publish my book. I don't see how they can worm out of it on this ridiculous technicality about Japanese royalties. It makes no sense – surely this can't be right, I mean, I thought the contract was binding!"

I noticed Hahsler staring at me in a most disconcerting manner.

"Well, I tried phoning Reid, Warbler direct, but nobody there would take my calls, so I then phoned Suckblode, Hellbetch and Feand and managed to have a little chat with Piers Hellbetch who informed me that since our friend Mr D'Ante became Head of Fiction at Reid, Warbler, all new author-contracts have included sub-clause 37b and that this is not the first time that the clause has been used to drop a book at the last minute.

He informed me quite cordially that you wouldn't stand a chance in hell with a breach of contract action, even if you could afford to proceed with one and, bitter truth, he's almost certainly right, Mr Buxtereide."

He rubbed his hands slowly together like a fly, knitted his brows into a frown and pouted his thin lips under his thinner moustache.

"Well, how much would such an action be likely to cost?" I enquired of him.

He chewed on his pencil thoughtfully for a long moment, gazing abstractedly off into an incalculably remote source of gravitational waves, gnawing like a beaver, before suddenly blurting out "at least sixty thousand just to get started – after things hot up, who knows? A hundred thousand, two hundred thousand – how much have you got?" He suddenly leaned forward, eyes boring into mine.

"Never mind," I returned briskly, "I can't afford that kind of justice!"

"Precisely Mr Buxtereide, precisely" reiterated the legal one, "you *can't* afford that kind of justice, can you?" He looked at me with a puzzled, aquiline countenance.

"Therefore, in practical terms, Mr Buxtereide, you have no case!"

"Then I have no book!" I rasped in the full futility of exasperation.

"How much do I owe you, Mr Hahsler?" I asked wearily.

"Thirty six guineas, squire," he said archly, "but since you didn't get much of a result we'll just call it twenty quid, shall we?"

"Thanks for trying" I said, thrusting a bank-note into his hand and heading for the door.

As I shuffled grimly home like a condemned man going to his fate, I was haunted by a repeating stanza from the letter from Suckblode, Hellbetch and Feand; therefore to be viewed as null and void, therefore to be viewed as null and void, as null and void, null and void, null and void, null and void.....

*

Heavy were the lids on the eyes of Arthur Buxtereide as the 18th of October dawned dull; heavy they were, and strangely unwilling to open. Why would they want to? Why would those eyes want to gaze on the still-burning wreckage of his dreams? Why would they wish to see the day his sacred harvest, the fruit of all his work, was riddled with mould, turned to dust and scattered to oblivion? Why would they want to look upon the day his glorious triumph was cruelly replaced with catastrophe and ruination?

And as he ruminated bitterly on the rejection, the cancellation and nullification of his book, it suddenly struck him that it was far worse than just that. It was the ultra-public, high-profile nature of the disaster that made it seem infinitely worse to the deflated ego of Bux. The LPC had aggressively imposed its message on his area and focused a lot of expectant attention onto him. Now, when people asked him about the book they would laugh in his face. Yes, openly laugh and ridicule him.

Then there was the TV interview scheduled for the next day and the launch-party all set for that very evening! Bux felt like a lost-soul, a headless chicken. A rising sense of nausea and disgust asserted its presence in his oesophagus and the beadlets of sweat had returned to his icy brow once more.

Great God! This is an awful fate! The thought reverberated and ricocheted through his psyche as he grappled to comprehend the depths of mal abomination into which he had so suddenly and unexpectedly been cast. Desperately searching for any scrap of anything with which to counteract the swirling vortex of unloveliness that threatened to swallow his life like a gluttonous ogre, Bux clung grimly to a thought that swelled his breast with pride: *At least I never sank to the level of writing in the continuous present tense like Joey McGee and Nathan William Haswell do the whole bloody time!*

*

Perhaps we can forgive the poor *artiste* these outbursts of petty rancour – he had, after all, been through a lot and, let's face it – there's only so much a man can take! What a good thing he didn't turn immediately to the bottle to drown his sorrows, as so many would have done in his situation. Not Arthur Buxtereide! He may have his faults, but he was not one to habitually evade his troubles by recourse to alcohol – in fact he hardly ever touched the stuff and consequently had an unusually low tolerance to it. Arthur sensibly decided that the best thing to do would be to take a walk to clear his head. He thought he'd probably phone the Nutshell Theatre and tell the staff that he was unwell so would not be attending his launch-party – for now he couldn't face telling anyone the real reason for his indisposition. No. A sensible country walk and on the way home he could pop into the butchers and get a nice fat steak for his tea, or maybe a juicy cut of fish. Who could blame him? He only wanted to forget that damned *book* and try to carry on with his life, his humble existence of obscurity. Maybe he would go for devilled kidneys, offal always made him feel secure. Then he mused on the joys of the poulterer's diet and all the nourishment that can be plucked from it. He considered the evolution of chickens, then birds in general, fluttering mentally between rustic husbandry and elementary taxonomy. He filled his head with all sorts of ephemera, anything other than the topic of books, literature, publishing, contemporary fiction, etc., etc.. Still the sweat trickled down his brow and still the beadlets crept.

Coming out of the fishmongers with a haddock of plaice filleted away in his inside pocket inside its packet, Bux was about to head home when he ran into a casual acquaintance and soon found himself mysteriously transported to the saloon-bar of The Hagfish, a pint of strong bitter before him on the table. There's an unexplained, yet commonly acknowledged law of physics that states that one pint of beer can easily turn into two, three, four, or any multiple of one, up to quite a few. Bux met several acquaintances in the pub, both casual and serious. He also met several drinks, both ale and cognac. Conversation was a lively blur, with Arthur's book being the main topic. Many mysteries have their roots in that night and perhaps much will remain untold. One thing is clear. During the early hours of the evening of the 18th, Bux underwent a complete reversal of his former opinion on the launch-party. Instead of dreading it as the living epitome of embarrassment, he had realised with sudden clarity that he should put a brave face on it, see the funny side and go to the party anyway! After all, it was *his* party, wasn't it?

The Nutshell was stuffed full of people. Friends, friends of friends, media people, arts people, all kinds of people, and all there because of Mr Arthur Buxtereide and his fictional talent. What an elaborate fiction life is – fiction upon fiction…..

When Arthur walked in, the country and western band were still on stage so he headed straight to the bar, where he soon found out he wouldn't need to pay for any drinks, as everyone insisted on getting him one to congratulate him – the results didn't do much for his sobriety, or his refinement. He started talking loudly to a large group of people, holding forth on his theories of 'the writer's art' and all kinds of similar twaddle. The pompous phase wasn't so bad, it was when he started verbally attacking other writers that things started to show signs of turning just a little unpleasant. His voice was coarsening, slurring a little. His utterances were becoming labyrinthine and senseless, mere noise. It livened up when someone asked him if he'd been very much influenced by Nathan William Haswell.

"No, not very much, not at all, in fact. Not none whatsoever, he's an illiterate berk, that's what *he* is!" asserted Bux with total moral authority. "Why the hell would I want to be influenced by an illiterate berk?" One or two shocked glances were exchanged, along with one or two knowing grins.

"He couldn't write to save his fat ass, stupid overblown windbag, he wants *editing* he does, *permanently!*"

A woman with red hair got up and left the group hurriedly. Others were frowning. Arthur didn't notice, he was just getting into his theme. "Bunch of pretentious charlatans, the lot of 'em!" he declared vaguely. "Not one of 'em has any feeling for words, for their *rhythm,* their *flow*... Look at McGee! What a chancer! How does he get away with it? Why do they bother printing that dross, that dung, that damn *candyfloss* he spins by the yard! Fobbing off the rich intellectual yanks with that leprechaun bullshit – what does he know, eh, tell me that? Bunch of spoiled little….. Allan Ffordd, he's another one – goes out of his way to be so *cosmic,* so *deep and mysterious,* but in reality he's just a prosaic bore, a spewer of tedium, humdrum flimflam and dross, just dross! Oh sorry, was that me?" Arthur's dramatic gesticulations had brought down a pint of beer flooding across the table like a malted tsunami. Ladies shrieked as their dresses were drenched in lukewarm ale and men let out gasps of indignant horror.

"Come on Art, I think you could do with a breath of fresh air, mate" said Sidney, grabbing the author's bicep and marching him none-too-subtly towards the exit.

Moments later Arthur was seen to flow back into the building like the tide coming in, inevitable, relentless and lacking in reason. Sidney was still making valiant efforts to keep the *artiste* in a civilized state, but deep down he knew it was a lost cause. For some reason he decided that this would be a good moment to introduce Bux to Rowena Trelevysian, the woman scheduled to interview him for local TV the following day. The conversation started worse and became more so.

"I've just finished your book, Arthur, and I must say, it's original, dense, colourful and plotty. Who are your *influences?*" This innocent question triggered instant resentment with its possible implication of his very un-originality!

"Janet and John! Biggles! Noddy and Big-Ears! Anything and everything other than that pseudo-poetic bilge from the likes of Joey McGee, Patrick Thistle, Allan Ffordd and that arch-garbage-merchant Nathan William Haswell – what a sorry bunch of self-inflating, vacuous, pretentious *hacks* they are! Not one of 'em could write a *parking ticket* much less a work of integrity, a work of depth, of meaning, of-" "Oh, that's a surprise" interjected Rowena. "I found *your* work to be very derivative of the 'New Tribe' movement – I thought it had Haswell, Mcgee and Ffordd stamped all over it!"

"I'd like to stamp all over Has-Smell, Mcgee and Ffordd!" roared Bux in an access of dumb, belligerent fury. Rowena looked a little stunned and deeply offended. She had expected to meet a man of culture, not a drunken egomaniac hell-bent on insulting everyone in sight. There is nothing in the least bit attractive in a ranting, slurring, incoherent drunkard, especially as he descends into hostility.

"I've always been a staunch supporter of those authors, particularly Ffordd and McGee. I personally happen to believe that 'I Sing To The Sea' deserved nominating for a Pullitsir prize! How dare you talk that way about men of genuine sensitivity, you, you drunken fool, look at you, you're a mess, that's what you are, a damn mess!"

"Yeah, well at least I haven't sold my soul to the Corporation – sucking up to these minor poets to build your own career as some kind of arbiter of culture! Who do you think you are?"

"Well, I certainly won't be arbitrating over your *so-called culture,* Mr Wiseguy Buxtereide, because *I wouldn't interview you on my show if my career depended on it!* You can just *forget it!"*

Rowena Trelevysian turned abruptly and walked away from Arthur Buxtereide – taking his chance of a TV appearance with her as she did.

Bux leaned back leisurely against the wall and wet his whistle with a pint of strong imported lager. Alcohol was transforming him into an epiphyte. He was instinctively seeking support from vertical surfaces, like ivy. Around him spun a lively gathering under the balloons, the coloured streamers and the special extra-large Whale of a Beast posters. A generous sea-food buffet was spread resplendent for the guests, its centre-piece was a whale made of blue jelly that was the size of a bath-tub. Around this exquisitely gelatinous cetacean radiated a carapacious cluster of lobster; concentrically surrounded and encircled by expanding circles of crab, eel, bloater and shrimp. A variety of fondues and roulades were also available. Suddenly there was a bizarre, feral and unpleasant yelping sound – A Wom Bom a Lupa – A Wom Bom Bam Rooti Tooti! *"Jesus! What the hell was that?"* slurred Bux loudly. How was he to know the Elvis impersonator he'd booked had sprained his ankle playing euchre so the agency sent the Little Richard impersonator instead? The Little Richard impersonator lived in a state of constant clinical paranoia that the *real* Little Richard would get to hear of his act and sue him, so, as a precaution, he always 'subtly' changed the lyrics to the songs – thus rendering his hero's world-famous and beloved gibberish lyrics into the disturbing syllabic speech of the ultra-isolated. But hey – let's be honest – when you live in Pensanskrit, you can't be too fussy about entertainment!

To the alcohol-besieged brain of Arthur Buxtereide, the whole room was taking on the homogenized quality of a painting, or perhaps a soup. A sea of faces familiar and unfamiliar, swum before his goggling eyes. People dancing to the pseudo-fifties music, doing the Mashed Potato, the Hully Gully, the Watusi and the Camel Walk. People in fancy dress costumes – clowns and jugglers, dancing-girls in their oriental gear, fire-eaters sending out clouds of livid flame, harlequins, mannequins and cowboys from the band all swirling round and round the room, jivin' and twistin' the night away.

Someone had even shown up dressed in a giant cardboard whale-suit.

At one excruciating point in the proceedings, Arthur jumped up on stage and shared the microphone with the Little Richard impersonator. His inarticulate attempts to sing Good Golly Miss Molly and The Girl Can't Help It were a genuine and terrible nadir in the realm of amateur music-making. He kept stumbling over the mic-lead repeatedly and being caught and held up by the impersonator, who could be clearly heard telling Bux "that's enough now, I'll take it from here…" but to no avail. The impersonator was sporting an elaborate 'conk', the kind of greased and piled-up hair-do that had not been seen in public since 1959. This always took him a good hour to prepare and was his pride and joy. For some reason, Bux felt the urge to give this amazing hair a friendly ruffle with his hand and the whole thing collapsed like a paper-plate of eels at a rainy garden-party, spilling greasy locks around his trembling and sequined shoulders. Richard stormed off in a huff, with Arthur bawling after him "you don't sound nothing like Elvis – and you don't look nothing like James Brown either, mate!"

Have you ever noticed how a microphone has the same effect on a drunk that a candle has on a moth? Seeing the mic there on its stand, all in the spotlight, Arthur teetered up to it, spontaneously deciding that this would be a good moment to make a speech. Sadly, Richard had flicked off the power-switch as he'd sashayed past on his way to his dressing-room – the mic was dead and no-one could hear him. "Hallo ladies and gents – *readers*. Hallo. Can I have your attention please? HALLO? *Oh fugthalodaya!"* he mumbled darkly, tasting the welling rage of the ignored.

Everyone seemed to be clustering around some figure who'd just walked into the gathering, a small man in a camel-hair coat and glasses. People seemed to be hanging intently on his every word, and laughing appreciatively at his constant stream of witticisms. Teeth fixed in a sneer, Arthur lurched towards the newcomer. Who was this overdressed fop? Who was this charismatic dwarf? thought Bux sarcastically. The next moment his friend Phillip was introducing Bux to

Patrick Thistle himself. Accounts vary as to what happened next, but seemingly a discussion of literary technique soon turned extremely ugly and the *artistes* moved very rapidly from deconstructing the genre, to threatening to deconstruct each other. The breaking-point came when Patrick Thistle suggested that Arthur Buxtereide should have stayed in the *fire-extinguisher trade!* If there was one thing that was always guaranteed to make Bux see red, it was when ignorant fools confused the fire-*escape*-trade with the fire-*extinguisher*-trade, I mean, my God, how could people make such an *elementary* mistake? Thistle had rubbed Bux up the wrong way now and in the throes of apoplexy Bux clutched at his heart. His hand felt something soft and fleshy as it went into his pocket and in a moment of inspired frenzy the up and coming novelist was seen to repeatedly slap the Scottish poet and man of letters around the face with a damp and fragrant haddock.

Around this time, the pubs had been closing and a lot of the town's drinkers had drifted into the 'Nutshell', in hopes of getting a late drink. Things quickly descended into mayhem. People seemed to be hyped up for a brawl, as if the evening's belligerent atmosphere was contagious. There's nothing more volatile in this world than a room full of arty people and a copious supply of alcohol and it was only a matter of time before Ol' Man Trouble came a knockin' at the door…

Bux was leaning around at the buffet, pontificating at anyone who'd listen. A girl in a low-cut flowery dress seemed amused at the author's antics and was encouraging his outbursts. Bux immediately assumed she was in love with him and yearning to mate with him. Just as he was lustfully fixating on the young lady an outlandish figure approached. Dressed in expensive tweeds of an archaic cut, slicked-back silver hair, cravat, monocle and moustache! The old duffer looked at least seventy seven and had an air of assumed authority about him that instantly caused offence. "Now then Buxtereide – it's all very well playing the drunken bohemian poet you know, but I came here for a book-signing! Now – *where are the books?"* This abrupt intrusion, this outrageous figure, this brusque manner of speech, all combined to hurl Arthur into a cold and inhuman rage. What was worse, other people, hearing the outburst, joined in the hue and cry "where is the book? Where is the book?" The mocking chant echoed throughout the capacious rafters of the Nutshell Theatre. Just then the 'Hawaiian' band came to the end of a song. It was time for their break. The chant was now taken up by more and more people. *Even by the entertainers Bux was paying for!* The monocled gaffer in the cravat leaned towards Buxtereide with mocking contempt written all over his smug countenance. "Yes old boy" he drawled, "where *is* the book? Where *is* this whale of yours, hmm?"

We have already noted that a man can only take so much and this, regrettably, was too much for Arthur Buxtereide to take. He eyed the monocled intruder with the cold eye of a reptile about to devour a fly. "Oh, it's a *whale* you want, is it?" he rasped darkly from between clenched molars as his hands gripped the finely-tailored lapels of the infuriating tweed jacket. "How's *this* for a whale, you insensitive *monster?"* snarled Buxtereide as he hurled the Editor in Chief of the New Literary Nation Review of Books and Magazines in Britain Today Now into the great blue jelly whale, which burst into scores of glops of gelatinous slime that soon turned the dance-floor into a hellish skating-rink. The crawfish fiesta was shattered and carapaces scattered into a chaotic mulch. People were slipping and slithering in the detritus, it was becoming biblical, apocalyptic, messy and ugly. Bux found himself surrounded by a menacing ring of people that included his friends, some of the circus performers, members of the cowboy-band, the gorilla-man and the person in the whale-suit. He could hear their indignant and angry voices all about him. "We've had enough of this, let's get him out of here!" "Yeah! Run him out of town!" "Calls himself an *author?* Drunken *fraud* more like!" "Let's run him out of town on a rail!"

Arthur lurched towards the exit, hunted and despised like an animal. The mood was ugly – mob-justice was in the air and Bux could smell danger. It's never dignifying to run pell-mell down the streets of your own home-town, pursued by a seething clutch of your associates, particularly when their ranks are swelled with a colourful sprinkling of 'exotics' –

jugglers and clowns, mimes running silently in white-face, cowboys, dancing girls, fire-eaters brandishing their flaming torches, a cardboard whale and a man in a gorilla suit. When poor Bux heard the mob baying the hackneyed phrase "Get him!" he finally knew what it was to be sought-after, what it meant to be in demand by the public. Somehow he stayed one step ahead of the furious mob of art-enthusiasts and after a couple of narrow escapes, he dived into a skip, where he spent the rest of the drizzly night, curled up under a scrap of piss-stained old tarpaulin, hoping to God those slavering beasts didn't get their hands on him. Lying there reflectively amongst the concrete-rubble, wood-shavings and old paint cans, Bux gradually slipped into a death-like stupor, wondering as his head spun like a dervish, how it was that Tuesday the 18th could have turned so catastrophically into Friday the 13th?

*

The dreams started around that time, the dreams and the apparitions. Blubbery things of the sea seemed to rear up from the ocean of his mind and occupy his nightly thoughts, filling them with images of the disrelishable. Fins flapped and blow-holes sighed. Great lungfish of the rolling ocean loomed. Cetacean carcases drifted, pecked at by gargantuan clouds of scavenging gulls, their cries echoing down the corridors of the sleep of the night of the mind. Timbers creaked and ropes were hauled on. The faint echo of nautical commands and scraps of old shanties could be discerned through the roar of the brine-meadows, the surge of the swirling main. The spyglass of Bux's mind was fixed now upon the sea, the deep cold sea and its denizens, its seething life, its floating death. Like a man embarking from New Bedford on a two and a half year voyage around the watery parts of the globe, Bux seemed to sail into new and turbulent waters, leaving the terra firma of his old life behind him. The old life, after all, had been built on artistic ambition and he had just witnessed the public crucifixion of all those kind of dreams. He didn't feel able to face the whole sorry mess of it and hence he lost his purpose and became as a rudderless ship upon the high seas. And like a hulk he drifted, abandoned, unwanted, derelict and without purpose. Take away a man's purpose and you've taken away the man.

*

I was walking along Gwynjak Towans on the way to Tremarazephron. It was a sunny day with a fresh breeze coming in from the sea. I was feeling a rising evdaemonia as I looked on the bright sunlight sparkling silver on the sea. Then I saw a form, a dark and vast form show its back among the foamy waves. Though it was still some distance off, the sheer bulk of the thing struck a note of awe into my soul. It gradually swam nearer and I knew it to be *my* whale, the one I'd so patiently reared over the last few years. I'd know that beast anywhere – it was, in a very literal sense, part of me! If anyone should know that great dark, barnacled air-fish it was me. From the stalactite baleen of its jawbones to the tips of its juddering horns, I knew that beast like no other. It seemed to have matured, it had just reached the stage of independence and liberty when a whale can swim free in the oceans of the world. I was thrilled as it approached the shore, communing with me in a high-frequency Whalesh language of bleeps and squeaks. Then joy turned to horror. The creature had become beached on the shore and some figures were wading into the surf towards it. I recognized Rowena Trelevysian and there was also a man in a tweed suit and a woman with red hair. As they reached the whale, these critics pulled out gigantic butcher's knives and started hacking and chopping at it with harrowing effect. Streams of gore gushed from its tormented body as they mercilessly tore away great strips and hunks of blubber. The beast writhed and thrashed its tail, but was no match for the cruel cold steel blades of this ravenous species of creature. The critics will have their pound of flesh. Soon more people started to turn up. They were all the servants of those three butchers. They aped them in dress and mannerism, as if they hoped to curry favour and gain promotion in the world of literary criticism. I recognized Pete D'Ante there as well, egging them on with their work of cutting and gutting

– occasionally pausing to enjoy a cynical joke with Piers Hellbetch. Soon this magnificent creature, to which I felt such a deep connection, had been butchered and rendered lifeless. Now they were engaged in carting off great chunks of fresh blubber in little hand-carts. They were taking it to Tremarazephron market to sell to the villagers! Later I found that I too had gone into the whale-meat trade and had set up a little stall in the market selling deep-fried whale and chips. I was doing a pretty good trade and was popular with the locals but one day a new establishment opened up right across the street from my stall and it immediately started killing my trade. Everyone started talking about the new place – 'The Big Four' it called itself. Someone gave me one of their advertising leaflets and I noticed that all their food was presented in a very down-market sort of way. Whale-burgers, low-calorie blubber shakes, krill-fries, ambergris-cola, that sort of thing. They obviously added loads of saccharine, cornflower and general froth to all their products….. Not like my pure organic offering, the product that suddenly no-one seemed to want anymore. I glanced disdainfully at the leaflet again, sneering at its picture of glossy opulence and dubious nutrition – its misrepresentation of what a whale-feast could be. Its superficial approach combined with its phenomenal popularity ignited an indignant repugnance within me. Even the lettering of the advert looked ostentatious. My eye read on. "….so next time you want the best seafood in town, remember, come on down to The Big Four –come and try our Fast Sea-Food restaurant in Tremarazephron, with beautiful views of the bay! That's The Big Four, folks, *Haswell, Thistle, Ffordd and Mcgee!"*

Ah-ha! So that's what those scoundrels are up to, I thought! Trying to undercut me with their homogenized, mechanically rendered pap! They may fool the public, but they don't fool me with that ersatz hogwash, that over-processed sludge they sell as whale-meat. My indignation was short-lived though, for my customer-base was dwindling by the hour and my supplies of blubber and whale-steak suddenly started going off. I couldn't give the stuff away, it was starting to reek and nothing reeks like rotting whale-blubber, I can tell you that for sure, my laddie. Blotches and blets of livid blue mould were erupting on the blubber-cuts and rendering them foul, unspeakable and unsaleable. Flies were gathering. Potential punters were holding their noses as they walked past my stall and my 'regulars' were blanking me. By contrast, the establishment across the road was doing an obscenely healthy trade. Quite often a queue could actually be seen forming outside the door of The Big Four, as the undiscriminating public flocked to their temple of populist pap. The final nail in the coffin was when the food hygiene inspectors came to check my stall. They were very officious and pompous and wore a uniform of smart tweed, I think they worked for the old man... After a barrage of sarcasm and sneering mockery at the expense of my business operation and the vehicle of all my dreams, they summarily closed down my stall and festooned it in bright yellow bio-hazard tape. I was just about keeping my dignity and holding down my temper until I happened to glance across the road and see the leering mugs of messers Haswell, Thistle, Ffordd and McGee peering out of their window at me, looking like a line of grinning baboons done up in collars and ties. A great wounded feral bellow welled forth from my lungs and I awoke drenched in malarial sweat, shivering.

*

Around this time, it dawned on Arthur Buxtereide that there may be other publishers who would be interested in Whale of a Beast. He'd been so derailed by the launch-fiasco that this idea only occurred to him a couple of days later. What about Opaquenheimers? They were the only other publishing house of note who had an interest in the kind of Keltek surrealist narratives that suddenly started popping up in Britain in those days. Most publishers shunned the 'New Tribe', as these writers became known, but Opaquenheimers had a reputation for backing the underdog, the outsider. It suddenly seemed screamingly obvious to Bux that they would be his best bet, in fact his only bet, for finally publishing Whale of a Beast and reclaiming his reputation as a serious artist.

This thought saved him from the pits of depression and gave him fresh hope. He shared his new scheme with his pals Sidney and Phillip as they strolled along the windy promenade. Phillip looked at Arthur with an intense gaze. "It's a great idea, Bux, except for one thing." "Oh yeah, what's that?" asked the man of letters. "Well, it's like this. During your highjynks at the Nutshell the other night you managed to cause varying levels of offence to a number of people…" "Did I?" asked Arthur vaguely. "It wasn't a pretty sight, mate, I can tell you" confirmed Sid. "Well," continued Phillip, "one of the people who took particular offence to your comments on some of 'her' writers, was Ruth Opaquenheimer – Ruth Opaquenheimer of Opaquenheimer Books, that is. You might remember her. Pretty woman – quite tall – red hair." "Damn!" muttered Bux. "Yeah, and you remember that fella you threw into the jelly?" asked Sid. Bux looked blank, uncomprehending. "Well anyway, you chucked Huntley Beal, Editor in Chief of the New Literary Nation Review of Books and Magazines in Britain Today Now into an oversized ornamen'al jelly. That man's been in the book business for over sixty years and e' knows absolutely everybody of any influence in the trade, 'e does. After what you did to 'im, you can be sure that 'e'll use all his considerable power to make sure that you never get published in this country, or anywhere else in the known world for that matter. You really couldn'ta picked a worse bloke to throw into a jelly!" "Damn! *DAMN!*" hissed a spluttering and deflating Bux, as he started to realize what he'd done. "I'd say you're damn lucky old Beal isn't suing you for assault," added Phillip. "Yep, you well and truly pissed on ya chips there mate!" laughed Sid, summing up the situation in a nutshell.

*

Things slid rapidly downwards from that point. Arthur Buxtereide, so recently teetering on the very brink of greatness, now began to feel like a stigma with a person attached to it. He was, for all his follies and faults, a sensitive being – the first time he'd had to kill off one of his own characters he'd felt like handing himself over to the police. The drunken charade the other night had been quite out of character for him and he felt terrible about it – not that he could remember much about it, just a few scattered and disturbing images of people slipping and falling all over a food-encrusted dance-floor, and a bellowing gorilla threatening to rip him apart as he ran in a mad panic through the darkened streets of Pensanskrit. Still, it was abundantly clear from what his mates had said, that no-one was going to touch his precious book with a long pole, barge or otherwise. As this fact sank in, Bux too seemed to sink, to drift into an oceanic fog, to become lost and at sea like a ghost-ship that drifts abandoned around the poles of the maritime world. This claggy, dense, yellow-grey fog coloured Arthur's view of everything. He'd even dragged himself in to see Dr Billy Rubin again, but he'd merely said that he thought the jaundice was getting the upper hand. Not that the malaria was diminishing, in fact it seemed to gather strength from the challenge and come out fighting, determined to finish off both the jaundice and Arthur in one fell swoop. Night sweats. Night thoughts. Night gaunts. Haunted, shattered and bitter were the thoughts of Bux as he contemplated the full extent of his undoing. And still the beadlets crept.

*

And whilst I slept the spine-bleeds started, and I awoke to find myself dangerously enervated and drenched in maroon gore – damn! Another trial, another burden – I cursed my ill-stared fortune and wondered what the heavens would send me next. Like a great Druidic cloud of starlings, my psyche writhed and swirled and underwent a constant shifting of shape under this new onslaught upon my already well-harrowed constitution. These were not easy days for me. I was living on offal and kale, in an attempt to improve my strength, and after several more days in bed, with one or two more spine-bleeds, I thought I'd try to drag my pale form along the cliffs for some good rejuvenating Kernewek air. I hurried past the last dwellings and struck out for the coastal footpath. Icy rivulets of perspiration chilled my temples and I paused frequently to rest. I was at that stage of malaise where the slightest effort, even talking, is almost painfully taxing but I was determined that the curative benefits of the walk would outdo the discomfort of it and sure enough, I soon felt the invigorating and purifying effects of the ozone-rich Atlantek airs. How wild and silky writhed the great ocean below the 'cleeves', how natural and free it seemed when compared to all of mankind's self-important dreams and projects. I suppose I was trying to forget about that beast of a book of mine, that bloated monster I'd created. As I walked through Porthmouse however I saw one of my own posters, that I'd tacked up in a warm burst of enthusiasm. Was that really me? How different things are now. I walked on grimly, musing on the quixotic nature of our human realm and the fates of its denizens. I'd promised myself not to dwell on my problems, but I could hardly escape the LPC when its evidence was everywhere, courtesy of my authorial and entrepreneurial frenzy. Why did I have to go and brag to the whole district about that stupid book? Why did I have to make such a song and dance about it, before it was even out in print? Never mind, life must go on, somehow I have to survive, like anyone else. I suppose there's always the fire-escape trade – I could move back to Dulwich, I *know* Harry would hire me again, he was broken-hearted when I left. I chewed over all kinds of topics as I wandered through the ancient cow-pastures above the sea where little herds of docile cattle chewed on the clover and grass.

After a while it started to drizzle, a mist descended, as it so often does along that seaboard, and visibility was diminished. Cows loomed up out of the fog and ancient standing-stones took on a haunted, powerful quality. The lichen growing on them was older than many of the new cities of China. A jynnji – the derelict engine-house of an old mine pointed a stark finger into grey obscurity. I felt like a jellyfish floating in a sea of misty forgetfulness, a drifting thing at one with its dense, glaucous element. As I neared the tiny village of Lamonara I gazed once more on the ocean and I saw a sight to chill my blood, split my hairs and curdle my brains.

It just seemed to form up out of the mist, a dark vastness, a brooding, hulking bulk. It scintillated and flickered in and out of clear perception, it reared up and loomed and disappeared. Dark, glimmering, and frighteningly huge – it was the back of a whale. That massy form struck a chill into me, a chill not unmixed with fascination. Who could fail to be captivated by such a magnificent animal? Who would not be strangely moved at such a sight? But of course, to me, the sight was a particularly loaded one, also a spectral and haunting one, as if it lacked proper substance, proper corporeality. Nausea swooned at me like a flapping shroud. Could I even believe my own senses? The whole experience was marked by an otherworldly sense of enchantment, of the illusory, of the phantasm. I searched the foamy waves with my spyglass-eye but could see the beast no more. Had it dived to the depths, or simply burst like the bubbles of a hot-air baleen? Had it been there at all? I didn't like the feeling of being tricked by my own eyes….. This would prove a most difficult mysticeti to solve. This new crisis rushed in upon my shivering psyche and I dissolved unto inconspicuousness, sprawling out among the wet grass and cow-parsley as darkness came upon me.

*

Over the next few days Bux was constantly bombarded by letters and telephone calls asking him about the book and where people could get hold of a copy of it. He soon wrenched the phone out of the wall and took to ignoring most letters – at least the unofficial-looking ones. He happened to open one from the tax department – up to their old tricks again… wouldn't they ever leave a man alone? Now he'd poured all his money into that ridiculous and overblown 'local publicity campaign' of his, the bane of his life, he found himself in serious financial difficulties. He was used to scrimping, but there is only so far you can stretch things, only so many cups of tea you can get out of the same tea-bag….. In desperation, Bux went down to the local phone-box, dialled Sidney's number and asked him if he could offer him any work.

"You're in luck mate, I've got a big job up on the north coast next week and Jimmy's off sick again so I could do with an extra pair of 'ands. I've gotta rush now, I'll pick you up on Monday mornin', alright? Seeya."

Wracked, wrecked and weakened by fever, Arthur was sorely requiring to rake in a fiver or two, and if that meant moving heavy objects up staircases, so be it. He had the whole weekend to favour his recovery and build up his strength. At least the spine-bleeds had apparently stopped. Perhaps they were just an abominable and gothic manifestation of the creeping sense of mal that had stealed into his world of late.

On Monday morning Sidney picked him up as promised and they headed north in the van. It turned out they were heading for a spectacular destination – 'The Bustard's Roost' perched on the dizzy summit of a bleak granite outcrop that towered over the countryside between the village of Zazennor and the fishing port of Chives. It had changed hands recently and there had been a certain amount of local speculation on the identity of the new inmate, or rather, owner. A certain faded air of notoriety hung about the place – the area had been associated in the past with the secret life of Lawrence and other colourful figures. It certainly would make a great home for a writer, thought Bux, in a moment of self-indulgent fantasy. He instantly dismissed the thought though – he was there to do physical labour – not to torture himself with the old dreams of literature and culture. Oh no, by Jehosephat! All that bookish balderdash had got him precisely nowhere, had made him into a penniless and ridiculous pariah. Far better to work for Sidney, fetching and carrying for his ultra-rich customers. After all, most men had to humble themselves to earn their bread in the day to day world. Why should he, Arthur Buxtereide be so exempt from the common lot as to reside in the refined splendour of some literary I 'fore E tower?

"So who's the new owner then Sidney?" Bux asked as the van drew up to the Roost. Sid looked archly at him. "I'm not really supposed to say, mate. What's the difference anyway, it's just some rich geezer with money to burn, who fancied a sea-view, in'it?" "Yep, I s'pose you're right!"

conceded Bux and they set to work unloading the large van. Sid had the keys to the house, the owner was expected later. He'd drawn out a little plan of where to put the furniture so they could have it ready for his return. The two of them laboured away like ants, gradually carrying and trolleying all the large, expensive items of furniture into the Bustard's Roost. It was a curious assemblage of antiquities and futurist monoliths, sixties egg-chairs and rococo gilt kitsch. There were a couple of massive Jacobean elm bookcases and many tea-chests marked 'books'. Bux wondered hungrily what tomes these might be. The house itself was truly spectacular and anyone would have found it an inspiring place to live. Bux's feelings were split between admiration and jealousy. How remote for him was the possibility of ever owning a gaff like that, how profoundly alien to his experience of life and its struggles against capricious fate and fortune. Imagine seeing a house like that and simply saying to yourself 'that looks nice, I think I'll have it,' as if it was a pair of shoes or a new cup. What different worlds people live in...

After several hours of proper physical work all the heavy and expensive objects had been moved from Sidney's van into the large, beautiful and stunningly-situated Roost of the Bustard. The movers of heavy objects had had their kroust and Bux was just folding up some blankets in the back of the van when he heard a car pull up on the gravel. Being near exhaustion and riddled with ailments (but concealing it from Sid), he ignored the car and kept on with the blankets. Sid was right anyway —what did it matter to them who it was who bought the place as long as they paid up? Most people are far too nosy about each other's business anyway, he thought with superiority, as he started to wonder vaguely who this prosperous acquisitor might be. Unfortunately Buxtereide had forgotten to take any quinine lozenges to work with him and by this point he was feeling light-headed, nauseous and weary. Shortly afterwards he vaguely heard another car pull up. All he wanted to do was get his hard-earned money, go home and collapse into bed. It was only desperation that drove him into working for Sid anyway. He'd hoped to be recouping some royalties by this stage and living from his pen, not hiring himself out as a human donkey at his age. Bux had been through a lot, but give him his credit, he was fighting against the rising chaos, not simply giving in to it. Girding his malarial, jaundiced, *spine-bleeding* and artistically disappointed body into the rigours of manual labour had been a superhuman feat for him and he had endured it with stoic grit.

Sidney poked his head round the back of the van. "The owner's well pleased with everything, Art, but 'e just wondered if we could unload a couple of suitcases out of his girlfriend's car – 'e 'inted at some kind of tip. What the 'ell!" "Sure mate," replied Bux, working hard to falsify a sense of easy-going cheer whilst shuffling his malarial carcass down the van where he slithered off the tailgate. Buxtereide was, let's face it, a little otherworldly and knew nothing about motor cars, but even he could tell at a glance that the little Italian sports car that now roosted at the Bustard's did not come cheap. Look at the number-plate – HOT 1 – ha ha ha, I bet she is, thought Bux bleakly. How did the woman get so many suitcases into such a small car, he wondered? Sid had prised out a couple of valises and was marching ahead. Bux was feebly wrestling with a case that was lodged into the foot-well behind the seats. Like a very old and hungry sloth that's been given rum and barbiturates, he grappled vaguely and ineffectively at it. He was getting annoyed. Instead of signing his own books, building his reputation as an author, meeting beautiful, cultured women, getting quietly wealthy and generally thriving, he found himself becoming a freestyle porter, who could be worked to exhaustion, carrying the rich-man's treasures for him, then asked to carry the guest's bags in like some bleedin' bell-boy! A rosy mist fogged the mind of Bux and he grappled at the suitcase with renewed vigour. He lost his balance as the case became dislodged and they both tumbled onto the ground, the case bursting open and scattering on the ground a random collection of expensive, black, silk lingerie of a rather interesting looking nature. Bux took a moment to pick himself up off his back, then after momentarily glimpsing the panties and stockings fluttering in the breeze, decided he'd better put them back in the case before they blew away. On hands and knees, almost swooning from exhaustion, Bux had just scooped up a silk stocking in one hand and an almost non-existently small thong in the other when he heard the crunch of footsteps on the gravel approaching. A nauseatingly thin voice rang out behind him. "Perhaps when you've finished *trying them all on* you wouldn't mind bringing the clothes *into the house like you were told to!*" White light exploded in Bux's brain as this final insult bit into the relict of his pride. "What the-" he spun round just as a pair of lacy French knickers blew into his face. As he pulled them clear of his eyes he was greeted by a sight that knocked him cold – the hideous, leering presence before him was none other than Mr Nathan William Haswell and his lady friend was the universally admired and desired Miss Sheila Hotston!

*

When they let Mr Buxtereide out of the local hospital the following day he had at least benefited from a couple of reasonable meals and a check-over. He also found an envelope of money in his coat pocket. £130 – not bad for a day's sweat, he thought dryly. There was something about that figure though, something disrelishable and mocking in it. It smelled of betrayal, of a sell-out. Then the penny dropped – take the one off and you are left with thirty – *thirty pieces of silver!* Damn Haswell's gall! He must have known – *he's a symbolist-poet, for God's sake!* A nasty, cold and murderous rage welled forth in the breast of the Bux like mercury rising up the thermometer when you put it in a cup of tea. And the thought of that vile lizard getting his clutching little claws into the heavenly Sheila Hotston – that was a torment no man should ever be made to bear. It simply could not be borne. Still, it *must* be borne. It *had* to be borne! What choice *was there?*

*

Things hadn't been going so well for me of late, I must admit. You see, I'd wanted to put this book out... did I tell you about my book? Did I? Oh yes! *Sure.* You know all about *that,* don't you? Smug little... *Any*way, I'm putting all that bookish stuff behind me now, waste of bloody time that was. Soon as I've got my health back I'm applying for a job at the St.Truborne fire-escape foundry – they're bound to have something going in the office sooner or later, and with my experience in the industry, I should be a real Jonah- *Jonas*- I mean *bonus* to the company... time for a rest, I don't feel too good. Probably just my nerves, probably.

*

The £130 melted away to pay bills instantly, leaving Arthur Buxtereide feeling no richer. Seeing the approaching twilight of poverty, he racked his brains for an idea. There must be some way he could raise a few bob. He had stopped thinking about erudite topics these days and mainly just wondered how he would feed himself, but as anyone who has actually been hungry will tell you, it's not so easy to think clearly on an empty stomach. His mind kept wandering off to all kinds of colourful topics, like a bee shopping for pollen among a garden of flowers. Who would not do the same in his situation? Then he got annoyed with himself for failing to concentrate on finding a solution to his problems. Finally dejection set in and his head lolled despondently forwards in slumber, drool trickling from his lip. When he awoke a couple of minutes later with a cricked neck, the same thoughts instantly preoccupied him. He stared at the carpet – the Persian carpet. *That's it! I'll sell the carpet!* he thought, in a sudden realisation that it was probably worth a couple of hundred pounds. Down he jumped to examine the rug, it was so familiar to him that he took it for granted, but he'd always known it was a decent piece. Yes, it should fetch a good sum, but it would be heavy to carry in to town, especially for one so weakened by tropical ails.

Just how heavy *was* it, he wondered? Bux started to roll up the rug, but then stopped. He'd noticed something odd, something he hadn't noticed before. One of the floorboards had been sawn through and fitted with a tiny handle – Bux was sure he hadn't seen it when they'd first moved into the house. He grasped the little handle and lifted. Up came a piece of floorboard and Bux was amazed at what he saw revealed. The little compartment was chock full of a weird assortment of luxury preserved foods, the culinary equivalent of the Comstock lode! Jars of olive-paste, caviar, artichoke-hearts, smoked-salmon in olive-oil, sun-dried tomatoes, pickled walnuts, haloumi, tins of baby squid, anchovies and more salmon; nut-pastes and rare organic coco-blends, Hymetos honey, hand-rolled sweetmeats and candied tropical fruits in little boxes; all these tasty delicacies and a couple of letters from that worm in Chiswick..... *very* sneaky, thought Bux – all that time we were toughing it out on cabbage soup and bread and marge and she was secretly hogging down the goodies! A wave of resentment surged through him and dispersed with surprising rapidity. Soon he was laughing out loud at the thought of her stealth and secrecy, he couldn't help seeing the funny side. When the Chiswick chiseller had given her the green light to move in with him, she must have forgotten about her stash in her excitement to plan the big escape. Anyway, he now had enough food to last him about six weeks and that changed everything.

Buxtereide enjoyed a sumptuous banquet of deluxe Mediterranean treats and soaked up every last drop of olive oil with his coarse black bread. He nearly wiped his mouth with the back of his hand, but then, realizing that this would waste calories, he meticulously licked his quivering lips instead. Ah, that was better! After a short doze, he decided that some fresh air would be a positive thing. He was soon striding out for the coast at a brisk pace. After the privations he'd been through, the food went to his head. The rush of such rich nourishment to a nutrition-starved brain can cause side-effects of euphoria and excitement. Bux was vibrant with unfamiliar energy and unwisely decided on a seriously long hike. He took a great swing through the countryside before emerging onto the low cliffs near Payennuthnow.

*

The door closed and a car drove off towards the west. The driver had been tolerant and civil, but eventually had had enough and simply walked out. She had not liked his callous treatment of the removal men. She had not liked his giving it out that she was 'his girlfriend', when it was simply not true – he had merely invited her to stay as his guest at The Bustard's Roost. They were two friends with a professional interest – certainly not a romantic one. At least that had been *her* understanding of things.

Still, having driven from London, she was tired and decided to make the best of it. He was, after all, a fascinating, if slightly egocentric character. He could certainly cook, she'd say that for Nathan. He was a good talker too, as you might expect from one in the word-industry. But for all his unique and poetic ways of seeing things and all his encyclopaedic knowledge about just about everything, Sheila Hotston was beginning to find his increasingly drunken, increasingly lecherous and decreasingly subtle outpourings very tedious indeed. The last straw had been when he'd laid his clammy hand on her thigh. Having reached the limits of tolerance she got up and left the Bustard alone in his Roost.

The Italian motor was soon winding its way down into Zazennor where Sheila stopped to make a phone call. She'd known Jenny since school and had stayed with her in Pendoom once before. They always got on well. Putting down the phone with a smile, Sheila started the motor and pointed the nose of her car towards the slaty little mining village of Pendoom in the far west of Penwithershins.

*

Arthur scrambled down the rough track and onto the shore. His feet crunched along in the sand and when he looked back he saw a long line of prints, reminding him of poor Robinson and his lonely wanderings on a far-away beach of white sand under a blazing azure sky. Here in Cornovaglia the skies were a softer blue, a greyer blue, or just grey. The inrush of food had made the sky a little brighter to Arthur, had lifted some of the darkness off his soul. It had also inspired him to walk for many miles when already weakened by his multifarious ails and diseases. Seeing a little rocky headland sticking out from under the cliffs, he decided it would make a perfect place for a rest. Arthur scrambled over the tiny outcrop of limpets and winkles until he'd found the right spot. He curled up with his back against a great rock, his gaze falling upon a rock-pool that seemed a microcosm of life. In his younger days he'd had an interest in testaceous malacology and he would always regard the humble krogens and sea-snails as mighty and noble beasts. Pleasant thoughts of a long-past conchological field-trip lulled his mind like honey. A ray of gentle sun and a puff of dreamy breeze were enough to waft Arthur gently over into the other side. Soon his quiet snores blended with the murmuring zephyrs and the breaking and plashing of wave after wave.

An unearthly whine, or hum, seemed to pass through Bux and alert him of the presence of the creature. The atmosphere had undergone a subtle change, the normal solidity and grossness of the world was very slightly diminished. Shapes ethereal flitted, unknown things were in the air, the krogens crept and something was afoot. The sound came again, the sound of a unique instrument, the sound of a voice, a voice not human or earthly, a voice that spoke of realms not dry. The voice was vast, searing and shrill; calling out in falling tones of a profound melancholy depth. It was singing out its language, calling out its message, its cry of life. Bux listened in fascinated dread. He knew the beast was coming for him. He knew what to expect. He knew it would come to this. He had created the beast and given it life, only to deny it the destiny for which it was given birth. Now the beast hovered between the worlds, neither fully living, nor yet fully dying, and that is a terrible condition to be in. Through the flickering falling fog Bux could hear the thing breathing, just as he breathed. And through the dancing waves it came, sombre and inevitable, rising up like a black cliff, the head of the great whale. Buxtereide knew what the beast was up to. It wanted his life. Not his death but his life. Only by absorbing the total energy of its creator could the beast hope to take on a full life of its own. This creature was desperate and would throw everything it had into the struggle. Bux looked around him for an escape route as the titanic head loomed up out of the darkening waters. He soon realised that he was stuck on a tiny rocky island and escape was impossible. The island was steep and treacherous, covered with slimy seaweed and pools of chilly water. Bux felt trapped. The head was coming out of the water again and its curtain of baleen was dripping iridescent plankton. It shone yellowish-white like water-ivory and gnashed and gurgled. Vast rasping sighs spoke of its breath – yet did it breathe air or aether?

Bux tried to claw his way onto the higher rocks, hoping for safety. The breath of the thing struck fear into him. The reek of baleen sickened his stomach. The shrilling, moaning sea-horn of its spectral voice unnerved him. The vast darkness of its hulking bulk threatened his stability. The atavistic glint in its eye impaled his heart and made him cold. The froth-churning flap of its barnacled flippers wrought horror upon him. The mad, churning twists of its back threw hypnotic glazes into his eyes. The prongs of its terrible horns bisonic and barbarous looming. A-clawing at slippery granite. And barnacles scratching and grazing. He whirled like a man under motion. Motor-function the essence of movement. A dark form is lashing the ocean. A man is pursued and tormented. A beast was let loose in the seaways. Released and set free into motion. And now the creator is fleeing. The beast is a thing of his being. Art-forms autonomous life-forms. Thought-forms embodied as aether. Either the man or the whale. One thing will certainly perish. Clawing at slippery granite. The whale looming near in the waters. Bux tried to elude the dread presence but he kept slipping. The tide seemed to be rising. The whale opened its vast, cavernous mouth and its mighty tongue emerged, ready to grab Arthur Buxtereide and roll him straight in and swallow him down. As Arthur attempted to get up a large, sloping rock, he lost his grip and started sliding down, down towards the great baleen mouth. It towered up over him like a leering grimace of watery death. For a second he was electrified by stark terror, staring into the eye of it, then he felt his feet slipping slowly into the cold sea of wet, universal death.

*

"That was absolutely delicious, Jenny" said Sheila, "I've always loved your lasagne, and that chianti is lovely too, you've really spoiled me tonight!" "Here, have some more", offered Jenny, passing the bottle, "and tell me more about what you're up to these days. The world of arts/media seems pretty exotic when you live in Pendoom and sell watercolours for a living you know!" "Sounds pretty idyllic to me," smiled Sheila, "a little calmer than being in the media-game, but that sounds rather appealing, to a city-dweller like me. You know Jenny, I sometimes wonder what it's all about, all this chasing after these exotic 'creatives', these purveyors of fascination, you know. We build them up to such a mythical status and then turn against them when they turn out to be ordinary human beings after all." "I know what you mean Sheila, it's a bit sort of, *fickle,* the star-making machinery, a bit fickle and superficial – *superfickle!"* The two women started giggling. The wine was relaxing them and they shared the sort of intimacy that comes when you've known someone from childhood.

"So who are the 'culture-stars' you've most enjoyed meeting then?" asked Jenny. "Well, Joey McGee was an interesting guy to talk to. Very eloquent. Good looking too – *married!"* They both laughed. Jenny refilled the glasses. "Alan Ffordd struck me as a naturally poetic writer, but rather self-absorbed – I mean, all writers are, I suppose, but some of them manage to retain a sense of humour…" "I know what you mean, but it's all relative, isn't it? At least he doesn't sound as bad as the dreaded Mr Haswell, ha ha ha!" They both laughed at this, as Jenny had already been told the full story of Sheila's grim evening in the presence of Britain's current best-selling fiction author. "He can certainly write" continued Sheila, "but his behaviour needs editing! Oh, that reminds me, Jenny, I was going to tell you. I went to the funeral of a friend of mine recently – Dexter Jonas – he was an editor at Reid, Warbler." "I'm sorry Sheila – did you know him well?" "That's the funny thing, I'd probably only met him eight or nine times but we always got on really well, we had amazingly similar tastes in our reading matter. He was a lovely guy, brilliant mind. Yes, it's a real pity. But anyway Jenny, before he went to Japan, which is where he died, he'd given me a proof copy of a novel to read and I remember him mentioning that the author lived in Pensanskrit. I'm very excited about the novel, it's a work of rare brilliance and I'm hoping to track down the author while I'm down in Penwithershins." "Sounds like a mysterious quest!" said Jenny archly, "I told you you lived an exotic life, didn't I?" she laughed. "Well, I suppose I can't complain!" smiled Sheila to her friend. The firelight cast a warm and comforting glow around the room. Vivaldi added a mellow dynamic to the air and the two ginger cats dozed in front of the fire as the women chatted, laughed and shared their experiences of life in the World.

*

The wave splashing on my feet woke me up with a sudden start – I shouted out in alarm – those damn dreams again – that damn *beast,* that beastly whale, it dogs me through my sleep! I must have dozed off in the sun. The walk wore me out, I was foolish to drag myself over the countryside for miles like that. I looked about me with a gnawing sense of doubt. The sea that now splashed around my feet had changed the look of the little rocky headland I was on – suddenly there was very little of it left to be seen! Never mind, I thought, I would simply get back onto the beach and head for home. I started making my way along the ridge of the rocky promontory, the sea was much choppier than before I went to sleep, I took care not to lose my footing. My heart sank as I saw through the failing light that the beach was now totally under water on both sides of the outcrop and that where it joined the cliffs, they were vertical, so there was no possible chance of escape that way. I was trapped on the rocks! Cut-off and stranded with a rising tide and night falling! Suddenly the damp and eldritch tendrils of the great cephalopod of fear itself came tapping me on the back, nudging me towards the black, churning waters. What if the tide totally covered the rocks? I could drown! I'd have to do something – I must keep calm. I suddenly thought I might be about to die and I didn't like the idea one little bit. All I'd wanted to do was to get my book published and become a moderately well-known writer who wouldn't have to sell fire-escapes again and now look at me, trapped like a ship's rat in a barrel of rum! My heart was beating fast and sweat ran trickling down my brow. Then it started raining hard and the rocks became even more treacherous to walk over – what was I to do? I could either take my chances sitting it out there on the rocks, in the rain, or I could try and swim round to the nearest bit of beach above the tide-line. If I jumped into the sea I might get thrown against a rock or carried out with a current. But if I sat it out on the rocks I could die of exposure or be drowned by the incoming tide. It didn't seem like a choice to relish and I relished it not. I was bleeding all over from barnacle-gashes – when you brush against them they hack at you like demons. The sea was angry now and was throwing hunks of kelp into my face, along with the occasional starfish – those things never taste too good. My clothes were drenched in rain, spray and malarial-terror-sweats. Gulls were descending in squawking droves to torment me with their harsh screams. I inched along the rocky ridge like a green basilisk lizard, or marine-iguana, until I reached the point where it joined the overhanging cliffs, and dived into the dark, churning waters.

Aahhh! Black and grim cold were those waters, cold as old man Death comin' for to call. He wears a fedora hat at a cheeky angle on his bleached dome, a snappy black suit with boot-lace tie, white, ghastly skeletal finger-tips gesticulate dextrously, almost effeminately (but don't tell him that I said that) he beckons laconically, stretches forth a horribly osseous hand lackadaisically, flicks the ash off his cigar discriminately, adjusts his white bow-tie scrupulously, scrutineering his albumen complexion in a fragmentary sea-shell mirror. Oh thin white duke that everyone dreads, why are you ripping my soul to shreds? Why do you stalk through the waters of night, clutching at mortals to put out our light? Old Boney Jones, still strippin' the bodies off souls, still recycling your cosmic debris, still breaking down the elements, same old game eh? Well it's nice to meet you but I've got to be going now, got an appointment up top, over on the other side, ya know – *life!* Swim, you fool, I told myself, and managed to drive the thralldom of dark visions from out my mind and fight for my life.

My sides seared with pain, as if I'd been skewered and grilled. It was my lungs in crisis. My muscles were becoming spasmodic – cramp can kill in situations like this – in terror, darkness and considerable pain I struggled upwards towards air and life. With each agonizing movement of my limbs I was rising towards the air, I thought it was getting lighter above. In another long second or two I could clearly see the surface above me. I stretched forth my hand and felt the cold wind blowing on it. Ecstatically I threw my body upwards - horrifically something clutched my ankle and thwarted my progress. Screaming for air, my head was boiling in pain, my whole body was cramping up and in terror I grappled at my ankle to free the grim white skellyboned hand from it. Just a piece of kelp and the next moment it was off and my head was back in the life-air of happy mammalia. All I could do was breathe and breathe as I slowly trod water and rejoiced in the bliss of conscious existence. If you've ever been deprived of air for any period of time, you will appreciate what I went through and just how sweet that Cornish foggy sea-air tasted to me at that moment. I took a good long few lung-fulls, taking it down deep and re-oxygenating me cells thoroughly before setting off to swim back to the shore. Gull's thin cries serenaded my struggles, foamy waves burst into my face, froth of bubbles was bursting around, limbs still aching but grimly functioning, fear still poisoning the wind but not quite choking me, sprays bursting in spires about my incredulous ears, ruffles and puffles of water dancing everywhere, a soup of ten billion fish and I was one of them. We were all swimming together, all manner of squamous anamniotes and me, swimming cross the Atlantek and up the Ausable River to spawn with the salmon. All the young gloops followed in my wake, cuttlefish clusters in fizzy flotillas. Doomy tendrils tried in vain to clutch and drag me down. Dulse flutters flew still into my face, enriching my lips with micro-proteins – it all helps! I shared the sea with myriad teeming life-forms and we swum as one fish, as one sole. Down yw an mor – deep is the sea. I ploughed on through the frothy brine like a water-locomotive – the beach was my Waterloo and I fought for every blessed fathom of it. After a while I felt different, though still struggling and wracked with pain and fear, I no longer identified with those aquatic flotillas and now I yearned to move amongst the beasts of the land, the furry, mammalian, land-lubbing critters of which I was very much one. In short, the delirium of cold-water shock was receding as I neared the shore and I was regaining my 'equilibrium' – such as it was. I forced myself on, feeling weaker and weaker but my mind was forcing my body to keep going. When my foot brushed the sea-bed I could have wept for joy. Moments later I was staggering up the beach on boneless octopus legs.

After a few paces I sunk to my knees then sprawled full out in the sand. I lay there for a long moment, enjoying the sensation of stillness and calm after the eldritch goings-on in the sea. But coldness fell upon me like an elemental tyrant and I knew that I had to drag myself up and start moving again. I tottered along uncertainly, feeling like I was still swimming in the sea, or just floating without volition. I saw my feet shuffling forwards like the feet of another. I soon found the same rough track that I'd used before and was making for the village of Payennuthnow. I knew someone who lived there and with a bit of luck they could lend me some clothes. I felt in my pocket and pulled out a couple of dripping wet ten pound notes. Unfortunately, the friend proved to be out so I reluctantly went into the pub to phone for a taxi home. How they stared, those well-dressed punters eating their seafood dinners when I walked in dripping wet and haggard. I phoned a cab and ordered a large brandy. Noticing the water dripping out of my sleeve onto the bar, coupled with my wet hair, and my wet money, the normally unobservant barman was prompted to ask "Is everything alright sir?" I nearly started to tell my tale, but was too weary to start. "Fine thanks. I don't suppose there's a blanket in the house is there?" "A blanket sir?" asked the barman with a bovine look to the eye. I was using my last calories of power just being patient with this oaf. "Yes, a blanket if you have such a thing please – I've just fallen into the sea." "The sea sir?" lowed the calf-like visage. "Yes, *the sea – and it was very cold!* Now have you please got a blanket?" At that moment the landlady intervened and produced a blanket right away. It was all I could do to stop her phoning an ambulance, but I assured her that I was fine and just wanted to get home. The next moment the cabby turned up and the landlady kindly said I could keep the blanket and I was on my way home in the back of the cab with the heat turned up full, wrapped in the warm woolly blanket and still holding the double brandy in my hand – I felt like a God!

*

When Buxtereide got home he had a warm bath and went to bed. He'd prepared a hot-water bottle and put extra blankets on, but still the shivers came a-sneaking up on him like a lizard in the night. He remembered when his foot touched the sea-bed and how grateful he had felt just to be alive, not to be dying. Less than three hours later Bux's elation was fading and he found himself wondering just what he was living *for*. Though he was grateful for *life,* for *living,* it was just his own unique individual life that seemed to have no value. Sure, he could probably nail some lowly office-job and pursue a humdrum and unchallenging existence, but where was the joy in that, compared to the dizzy freedom that a writer claims for his realm? And now the writing career was shattered and destroyed, worse than that, it lived on, luridly transformed into a living public humiliation, thanks to his own over-zealous efforts with that little old 'local publicity campaign' – and his monstrous ethylated exhibition at The Nutshell. How we mortals do fill our foolish days with folly.

Arthur Buxtereide sank into sombre soporific slumber like a dead cetacean sinking into a deep ocean ravine off the coast of Japan – sinking down and down into fathomless obscurity to be devoured by the terrible, clutching and uthek jaws of the deep-sea sharks, his soul floated free in a world of his own psychic imagery and language. He saw himself walking out of his office at the end of the day. He had work to do at home, lots of it. For this reason he carried not just one briefcase, but at least four or five, all stuffed with highly important papers that must be worked on that night. Stoically he strolled along the seafront for a breath of salt air on the way home, but a strangely familiar form struck a note of nauseous repugnance and abomination into his seaside stroll. Would the beast never leave him alone? "I work in an office now!" he bellowed in desperate self-justification. Surely the whale must know that the old days are over now, that it's not like before? It *must* know! It's no fool, that fish. He cast an imploring gaze out to sea but the ethereal sea-mammal replied by lunging bisonically its great stark curved horns at Bux and impaling one of his briefcases on each one. Apparently it meant business. He turned and ran, like a man in a fifties black and white horror movie, but the worst of it was that the beast was still coming after him, waddling and finning its way down the streets with surprising rapidity. As he ran through the crazy, jagged, *angular* streets of the town he glimpsed news-stands and billboards with headlines screaming at him – POD OF DEAD WHALES WASHED ASHORE IN DENMARK – MORE LOCAL WHALE SIGHTINGS – 'GHOST-WHALE' SEEN OFF CORNISH COAST – so, other people can see the beast too, he thought with spirally fear. He shot a glance over his shoulder and still it was flapping, flippering and waddling along just behind him, its ghastly baleen breath choking him with gut-quivering nausea, the lone, sad sea-horn of its unearthly voice booming and ringing in his pulse-hungry skull. Scraps of newspaper were blowing down the streets as he ran, newspaper and bits of posters and flyers – the words 'whale' and 'beast' kept occurring in this fragmentary literature. Some of the bits of paper looked quite old and weathered, faded by time and the sun, as if they were already well on their way to disintegration, forgottenness and oblivion. He grieved to see the symbols of all his hard work and all his dreams crumbling like so much street-dirt. They reminded him of one of the great stone heads of Anatolia, taller than a man, once a mighty ruler, now forgotten and forlorn in the lonesome desert. So crumble the works of man – but it hurts a bit when it's your own works, specially when they haven't even seen the light of day! Still the whale-fish flubbered after him on blubbery protuberances, a shrill-skreeling, krill-reeking, head-breathing sea-stag, haunting his nights away, swimming constantly through the sea of his days. On it came, it's breath surging like bellows in the wind, its blubbery form slapping down onto the road with every crude lurch of its prehensile fins. This nauseous psychic torment dragged on through most of the jaundiced and pale night. A sweet mal clammy layer of malarial sweat beadlets clung to the sheets of his bed. Drips of liquid salt rivullated his head and he murmured and stirred restlessly all through the night, like a man who can find no comfort, nor shelter from wind and rain.

*

Bux awoke feeling decidedly uneasy. He thought he'd heard *Mrs* Buxtereide prowling round the house again and slamming the toilet lid open with military precision. No, just the nerves again, no doubt. He was alone, alone and washed up, like a dead you-know-what. No-one in the house but Bux and Bux was not good company for himself on that bleak morning. Trouble was on the man like a giant spider-crab clinging to his back. Conflicting urges pulled at him. He felt trapped at home, yet the thought of going out didn't appeal either. He'd either meet someone who'd moronically – but quite reasonably – ask him *how the book was going,* or else, if he tried to find solace by the seashore, that damn *beast* was likely to surface and harry him. What choice does a man really have? He felt trapped on the horns of a beast of his own making. Poor Bux, grimly he brooded on the absurdity of his life. After a moderately successful career selling fire-escapes and marriage to Mrs B, he'd turned to literature, figuring he was good at selling escapism, and returned to his rustic roots. He'd poured his soul, blood and guts into that book, nailed – or so he thought – a decent publishing deal, and gone crowing about it from the rooftops like a demented chicken. And where, precisely, had it got him? Exactly! That's right – nowhere! He might as well have got a job sealing the lids onto tins of peas – at least that would have had some social value, however miniscule and bogus. Why bother trying to be a writer, a poet, a bard o' being even, just to have it all destroyed in front of your eyes and flicked back into your face, bit by agonising bit? He could hear the rhythmic slamming of many doors – it was the doors of opportunity clanging shut in his face, one by one, in endless rapid succession. His life felt like it was an old car with its wheels taken off, its axles sitting on a couple of breeze blocks. He couldn't bear the thought of meeting anyone he knew. The eldritch fiasco of The Nutshell was still a pullulating and acute wound. His battered pride stuck out like a sore thumb. How could he face his colleagues and associates again? He was shattered like a lobster, carapace cracked open to reveal the tender, vulnerable innards. At least a lobster had claws, thought Bux bitterly, feeling suddenly clawless and without any kind of a carapace. Even a humble decapod has some protection, some means of fending off life's vicissitudes – why not a man? Why must we be torn apart like krill? Sucked in by the baleen-filter mandible jaws of the whale-fish of eternal doom? Tell me why!

Arthur sighed heavily and wearily dragged his cadaverous form into the kitchen. He put the kettle on for tea and forced down a light breakfast of stale bread with Kalamata olive paste and a pickled walnut. Without this mana from underground he wouldn't even have anything to eat! Blessed is the underworld, he mused, realm of the gorgeous Goddess Ishtar the Fruitful. The olive-oil soaked into the dry bread and reinvigorated it, giving it a second lease of life. To a starving man it seemed almost mystical. New life springs autochthonous out of the Earth, thought Bux, wallowing in the bitter irony of the situation. He had no milk for his tea though and that was enough to plunge him back into despair like a no-brand tea-bag in a cracked mug of boiling water. The air seemed to carry a whiff of rancid blubber, as if the specksioneers and fat-cutters had been at their greasy and lugubrious work. The sky was clouding over and a salvo of rain rattled against the window-panes. As it trickled down the glass, it was mirrored by the tiny streams of clammy malarial perspiration that started to run down the brow of Bux as he contemplated the long, lonesome, empty and frankly unwanted day in front of him.

*

Sheila Hotston stepped out of the shower and wrapped a burgundy towel around her perfect loins and another around her exquisite shoulders. She opened the window and let the cool, fresh Cornish air play over her naked body as she slowly dried herself. Then she looked in her suitcase for something to wear, pulling on a black thong – but the sight of her lingerie only brought back the memory of that painful incident with the removal man. The poor guy had been more than humiliated, he'd been traumatized! He'd been hospitalized! She'd felt terrible about it, but somehow Nathan had brushed the incident aside as if it was of no significance – the callous, bombastic fool! How could she have been so dazzled by that pompous wind-bag as to have overlooked the needs of that poor man, just trying to do his job and being mocked and sneered at like that – why had she not made a fuss when it had happened? Sheila was a conscientious woman, and now she was feeling that she'd let herself down, lowered her moral standards by failing to defend that poor workman from that reptilian writer. She arranged her perfect breasts in her bra and clipped it up, making a vague vow to herself to always defend the underdog, to stand up for the right in any situation. She was a good-hearted woman and found it hard to forgive herself any breach of her personal code, however unintentional. She even thought about trying to contact the removal man, to pass on a letter or something, perhaps just a card hoping that he'd made a good recovery. But then that would mean going through that slug Haswell again and the thought of more contact with *him* left her cold. It was funny, but she'd noticed that after meeting Nathan William Haswell and finding out what he was really like, his book seemed suddenly pretentious and forced, *shallow* even, when she tried to read it again. By contrast, she'd spent more and more time reading and re-reading that proof copy of Whale of a Beast by Arthur Buxtereide. The mere thought of the title sent her mind spinning and her heart racing. The book was like a galaxy of twinkling stars, it oozed brilliance, wit and insight – *humanity* – that's what it had, humanity – not like the slick, clever but ultimately cold outpourings of Mr 'Deep Leviathan' Haswell…

Sheila pulled her mini-skirt up around her perfect bottom and did up the little zip on the side, then pulled on her long, black, high-heeled boots. Who *was* this Buxtereide fellow anyway? How had a vivid work of incredible, stark and poetic writing like that gone unpublished? What had Dexter been planning? Surely not to side-line it, pass it over for the usual predictable pap from the big names? Who *was* this man-of-words who could steal away souls with the spell he cast? This enchanter of minds, spinner of worlds, this latter-day bard, she wondered. And the more she wondered, the more she wondered. Having met and interviewed most of the great writers, and indeed painters, film-makers, musicians and other artists of our time, Sheila had learned to tell sincerity from contrivance, reality from ostentation. Over the last couple of days, when she wasn't strolling on the adit-riddled cliffs or country lanes with Jenny, she'd mostly been engrossed in the writings of Arthur Buxtereide, and it had dawned on her with uncanny certainty that here, at last, she had found a writer who, she strongly felt, deserved a place in the canon, a writer who would be read in future centuries, *not* just a clever pen-pusher who could imitate the fashionable style of the day. This was a thrilling discovery and she'd resolved to track him down, which, thanks to the phone book, took her about twenty five seconds. When she'd nervously tried to phone him she'd got a dead-tone, as if the phone was permanently disconnected – she'd just have to go round to the address in the phone book and hope to catch him in.

*

Bux wiped the icy sweat off his jaundiced brow with the sleeve of his shirt. He noticed the elbow was just on the point of disintegration, it could probably do with a wash too. He looked at his jeans, faded, yet slightly begrimed. His trainers were dilapidated and broken down like a pair of old horses. Glancing dejectedly out of the window to the street below, he saw a couple of attractive young women walking by, the wind playing at their skirts. Simultaneously with a little pang of desire came the painful realisation that those sexy young girls would shrink back in horror from a scruffy, wild-eyed, middle-aged, crazy-man like him. He realised that his youth had slipped by, he was getting grey and wrinkled and women very seldom gave him the eye. Even when they did, it was almost always an eye that he did not desire to look into. Poor Bux had never felt less attractive in his life. He didn't even know how to approach women any more, all those years with Mrs B had taken the romantic out of him, left him disconnected and alienated from the world of women. With a snort of free-floating anger, Bux drew the curtain closed and blocked out the street. His little scheme to unleash himself upon the world as a blazing star in the sky of literature had fallen flat, and with it any chance to push himself forward as a charismatic, mystical and otherworldly object of fascination and desire. Have you ever lost a dream, dear reader? Seen one shrivel up and die in front of your very eyes? I'm sorry if you have, but you will at least know how Arthur was feeling at that point. You will at least know the dark, sinking, falling feeling of pointlessness and oblivion, of a deep, creeping sense of why bother.

    The sweat coursed down his back. His temperature seemed to be rising. His thoughts were scattered and fragmentary like Babylonian pot-sherds. The jaundice was staging a major offensive against the malaria and Bux was starting to wonder if a third army had joined the internal war. Ever since one of those whirling ginger unearthlies had clawed his shoulder-blade he'd had a subtle but increasing sensation of burning heat around the area. Perhaps he'd contracted the nefarious Cat Scratch Fever... should he go straight back to Dr Billy Rubin, or make a feline for the nearest *vets?* Just another whiskery dilemma for brain-boggling Bux to unpick at his ill-relished leisure.

He felt ragged, eroded and blasted by time, fate, the elements, life, and all manner of everything. Frazzled, worn-down, *bled.* Enervated, disempowered and uninspired. Sluggish, heavy and gross. In short, he felt the onrush of a fountain of self-loathing, never something pretty to behold. And worse than all this, he was beginning to feel decidedly *old* and that's not always what people want to feel. Even if I manage to worm my way back into the fire-escape game, he mused pityingly, I'd be an anachronism, no, an *atavism* more like! It's not even called the fire-escape trade any more, it's called the 'pyro-logistic security sector' or some-such overblown crap! I'd just be the office-throwback, the Cro-Mag they keep on the pay-roll out of kindness. What's the point? *WHAT'S THE POINT?* he screamed inwardly – which is the worst kind of scream of all. Then he started framing the question not as rhetoric, but as a real question – what is the point of my life? Put as blankly as that, he found it very hard to come up with an answer for himself, and that is not a good feeling either.

*

Perhaps I just need my medicine, thought Arthur in a moment of lucidity, if the fever drops I'll be able to think things through more clearly. He rooted around for his quinine lozenges and put the jar on the table. Then he thought he'd see what else he could find in the medicine cabinet and produced a half-bottle of cognac, a packet and a half of opiate pain-killers and an old bottle of kaolin and morphine. These he lined up on the table, morbidly realizing that there was enough poison in front of him to kill a horse – or a failed writer.

*

After a delicious vegan fry-up at the Radiant Radish café in Pendoom, Sheila embraced Jenny warmly and said goodbye. Sitting in her little car like a pert Goddess on her golden throne, Sheila enwheeled for Pensanskrit, hoping to discover a major living writer. As she wound the skein of country roads under her purring tyres, she gradually descended from the foggy, craggy and bleak hinterland, down to the lusher area of the bay. Shafts of celestial light broke through the grey clouds like the spears of the Olympian Gods, striking the sea around the Mount in stark elemental beauty. Sheila felt an expansive mood sweep through her. As she neared the town however, the traffic slowed to a crawl. This was annoying – it certainly wasn't holiday season or anything like that….. After several more frustrating minutes she could see that the road was closed at the next junction and the traffic was being diverted. As the cars crept along at less than walking pace, she wound down her window and caught the attention of a policeman. (Catching the attention of any man was not a difficult thing for Sheila Hotston to do.) "Morning sergeant," she called out. Policemen were always 'sergeant' to Sheila. She figured a quick promotion usually made them even more sympathetic to her when necessary. "Could you tell me what's going on please?" The 'sergeant' looked round with alacrity and smiled at Sheila. "Certainly miss, I'm afraid we've had to close this section of the B31, there was a collision between an ice-cream van and a pasty-lorry, and then a charabanc full of Hungarian tourists skidded in all the ice-cream and ploughed into a fish-truck *and* a minibus full of mining-heritage enthusiasts – thankfully there were no fatalities. It could only happen here, couldn't it miss? Now if you wouldn't mind turning left at the diversion sign…." "Thank you, sergeant," said the lovely lady and down went the perfect high-heeled foot on the Italian accelerator.

Forty-eight minutes later, a little car was to be seen pulling out of the village of Nancegoliath and *this time* turning west, in its third or fourth attempt to break out of that picturesque but bloody frustrating maze of little meandering lanes and get to the town of Pensanskrit. When the driver had paused to look at her road-atlas she'd noticed a message on her phone from Nathan William Haswell:

Dear Lady, may I tempt you to a delicious dinner and wine at The Bustard's Roost? Don't say No. Your worshiper, Nathan.
Jesus, what a slimy creep! She shuddered and deleted the message before hitting the road again. In her mind, Haswell now represented only falsehood, false-life, decadence. She yearned for something *real* in life, something that lived free of the shackles of money-making. She was looking for the living source of creativity, nothing less. Somehow, this searching, yearning part of her, that had been slowly developing throughout her life, had now become fascinated and fixated on the idea that this original source, this stream of creative mind, could perhaps be found embodied in the living form of Mr Arthur Buxtereide.

Sheila didn't think anything of it when she was overtaken by a speeding ambulance, siren wailing and lights flashing. She assumed it must be on its way to that traffic accident the sergeant was talking about.

*

Arthur was slumped in a chair, looking extremely pale. His pulse had retreated and slowed to a mere murmur. His breath, once so vital, inspired and full of life was now reduced to the tiniest whisper, the fluttering of the breath of a dormouse. His head throbbed painfully and a thick, black darkness was descending over him as his body seemed to melt away, become lighter and start to dissolve from particle to wave. Rather than resisting this downward river of extinction, Buxtereide seemed to enjoy letting go, giving up the great struggle and slipping away into the warm stream….. He felt cosily numb to all the pains now, he drowsily wondered why he'd ever let anything bother him at all, when it was possible to feel so warm and cosy, so drowsy and comfy, so light, subtle and woozy….. Bux felt as if he were on a great roller-coaster, he was being pinned back in his seat by the gravity, overwhelmed by the titanic and unthinkable forces of nature, he was dizzy, light-headed, he was an atom being spat out of the sun, he felt the power of the universe surging and pulsing through him and blasting him apart and he felt that he was flying through space, flying through the universe on some new journey somewhere else.

*

Sheila Hotston shuddered involuntarily. She suddenly felt a little vulnerable and sad, sort of pensive and poignant and she didn't really know why. Just then a bright sun-beam burst its way out of the dark cloud-head and transformed the scene into a glimpse of heaven. Her heart felt lightened, as if somehow she could trust to nature and stop worrying. Who was she, after all, to try to fathom the hidden fates of mortals? Do we not all hold our own destiny in our hands? You can try to help another person, but in the end, if they don't want to be helped, what can you do? A philosophical calm permeated her thoughts as she cruised through Tremarazephron and headed towards the outskirts of Pensanskrit. The traffic was slowing up again, must be the residual effects of that ice-cream/pasty incident mused the Goddess to herself as she patiently guided her luminous chariot through the throng of metal boxes that crept and crawled towards the small Cornish town like an invading horde of night-gibbering death-watch beetles. This entomological throng was either going somewhere very, very slowly or it was going nowhere fast. Why did Penwithershins in general and Pensanskrit in particular always attract this kind of arthropodic and distinctly insectivorous slow-motion tide of conchological *freaks?* There is no answer to a question like this and besides, these things were certainly of no concern whatsoever to Sheila Hotston, for her mind was elsewhere.

*

Arthur Buxtereide felt icy cold, chilled to the very bone. He was floating like a water-logged log or a half-drowned anteater. He kept bobbing up against little chunks of floating ice, pancake-ice, bumping his head against these miniature bergs, but he did not mind – he really couldn't feel a thing anymore. There was a most curious, subtle and intriguing high-pitched sound in the air, like the soft ringing of a great bronze gong or bell of deepest pewter. Floating in the water were lots of little scraps of seaweed – no, it wasn't seaweed, it was paper. Bits of torn-up paper. Some of them had writing on. He kept seeing the words 'Whale' and 'Beast' on them. He felt no particular connection to these symbols any more – in fact when he saw the words, they might as well have been in Arabic or Chinese, they no longer formed part of his world. He was much more interested in the incredibly beautiful play of the light on the water as it danced and sparkled around in a myriad of infinitely changing and ever fresh brilliance. He felt he was melting into these dancing, dazzling little lights, that the difference between him and the lights was fading away and he was merging into them. He felt a great upwelling of peaceful and natural euphoria. His soul was rising and his universal mind was drenched in startling visions. It was a joyful thing to let yourself melt into the light, to go with the vision, to float off into a new ocean.

The subtle, almost angelic tones that filled the air underwent many modulations, unfolding numberless curtains of a sound-world of inexpressible clarity and beauty. Bux felt that he was at one with the music, he *was* the music, and would be forever. But this passed, for gradually the sound changed again, modulating down into a thicker, throatier and more melancholy sound – a sound that instantly hit Buxtereide like a bucket of warm squid in the chops – it was *the whale, it could be no other!* The iridescent spectral structure loomed up dark and terrible from out of the icy waters and sent dread into the heart of Bux. Desperately he looked around him for a means of escape, but all he could see was tiny ice-bergs, no bigger than a kitchen-table, bobbing around in an endless sea of icy and deserted waters, brooded over by an oppressive bank of terrible, black, cyclonic clouds. The albatross screamed out its terrible scream and Bux groaned aloud in bleak despair. The churning waters were threatening to suck him down to water-hell even before the terrible ghost-fish could consume and devour him! The unforgiving gouts of ice were threatening to crush him between them like a grain of barley between two grinding-stones. The abominable descending cadence of the whale's fog-horn groan of a voice sat on the waters like a slick of refined blubber, or worse, like blood. Bux grappled with hungry fingers at the hostile and hateful ice – he could get no purchase on its alien surface and weakly he slithered again and again into the harrowingly cold waves of the dark, rolling sea. He could hear the great bellows-breath now, and see clouds of vapour where the beast vented angrily through its blow-hole. Ice cracked and shattered, splitting and cracking apart under the cruel blows of the beasts flailing fore-fins. Bux stared mutely in cold dread – the eye of the great whale was upon him and he could not wrench his puny human orb away from its command. It seemed to be talking to him. Why did you give me life, it said? Why did you start the job if you weren't going to finish it, it said? Bux could give no answer – neither could he avert his eye – neither could he bear the agony for another second. In utter howling desperation he managed to claw his way up onto one of the miniature little ice-bergs and stood shakily on top of it, feeling about as safe as a rabbit when it sees the shadow of a buzzard descending on it.

  The sea was swirling now into a great chalice of storms, sending the ice-bergs clanging against each other with an ethereal chiming sound. Buxtereide was finding it harder and harder to stay atop the tiny berg as it rocked around madly in the oceanic broth. He was so cold he could barely react at all, his mind, nerves and limbs were benumbed with the chilling, killing cold that had crept like a leech unbidden into his soul. He knew the jig was up now and he was fighting for his existence. He knew the chips were down and the fish was out of the water. A surge of the rolling main sent Bux off his feet and crashing down onto the ice, feverishly clawing at it with disembodied, feeble, sponge-like hands. He could see a generous splash of what must have been his own blood there on the ice, but was too numb to feel where it might have come from. Also, his fear-blasted consciousness was too busy trying to focus on survival to care too much about the odd splash of blood. Bux clung to the ice-berg on his belly and looked around him – the whale seemed to have disappeared. He lay there shivering and shuddering in mute, nostril agnosticism for a long painful moment, not knowing what to believe. The waves came on like water-hills, but where was the whale? Where was the beast? There was only the infinite, dark, howling, lonely and bleak cyclonic ocean with its endless array of clinking ice-islands and frothing, churning waves, stretching out to the black and hopeless horizon. Oh that ghastly beast, how it does dog me and hound me, how it hides merely to torment me and prolong my sufferings, how I abhor its unspeakably ghastly presence with every last molecule of my psyche! Poor Bux raged alone in his mind then, alone, on an ice-berg in a deep and icy-cold sea of troubles.

And then, at last, the beast showed itself again, or rather, I should say, it showed *what was left of itself,* for before Buxtereide's fear-flecked and petrified-white eyes, the flesh, blubber and guts all peeled and fell away from the bones in vastly accelerated seconds, to reveal, within a stench-cloud of blubber-fumes, the gaunt and ivory-white skeleton of the whale-beast – but still it swam on, creaking and snapping like an osseous filigree fish-thing. Bux was losing what was left of his self-control, he was groaning involuntarily and shaking with abject terror. A wave rocked his ice-berg again, this time with enough force to send Bux tumbling into the icy sea, where he came up a moment later, gasping for breath as the eldritch baleen jaws of the skeletal sea-beast gaped open and lunged right at him, comin' fer to swaller 'im up. Arthur Buxtereide stared into the slavering jaws of death and screamed. He could hear the vile ghastly jaws of the whale knocking together in rhythmic salvo. He screamed again. Knock knock knock. *"Get away from me you monster! Get away from me I say! Get it off me! Oh great God please just get it off me!"*

*

"Mr Buxtereide! Mr Buxtereide! Are you alright in there?" Knock knock. "Mr Buxtereide! Please open the door! Open the door, will you?" *Knock Knock KNOCK!*

Something told Arthur that he was no longer drowning in the Arctic Ocean, being eaten by a dead whale, but was now required to answer the door. He felt a strange sense of relief. *"Mr Buxtereide! Arthur! Are you alright in there?"* It was a *woman's* voice, and she sounded extremely concerned about me, thought Arthur as he groggily lurched to the door and flung it open.

When their eyes met, Arthur and Sheila both uttered the word "You!" at the same time and gazed on each other with the deepest amazement. They were both in profound shock, but it hit Arthur the hardest and he found that he was shaking uncontrollably and the tears were running down his face. "Arthur!" said Sheila tenderly as her eyes drunk in the scene, "It's *you! It's you!"* Poor Buxtereide's spirit was now blasted by a great tempest of love that swept him away and he fell headlong into a swoon. It was all Sheila Hotston could do to drag his slumbering form into the house and lay him out on the floor with a cushion under his head. Luckily she was a big, strong girl.

Sheila was a worldly and experienced woman and knew how to deal with a tight situation. She closed the door and put on the light, with the curtains closed she hadn't been able to see much before then. Oh my God! She saw the table, the brandy bottle, the various tablet-sachets scattered around, the quinine-jar and that ugly old bottle labelled Kaolin and Morphine – this did not look good. How could she tell if he'd taken an overdose or not? How could she tell? There did seem to be quite a few pills left, maybe he hadn't taken a load of them – how could you tell? Suddenly she got a sensible idea. Check him for vital signs, pulse, things like that. First she grabbed his wrist, it felt frighteningly cold, and, no, she could not seem to find a pulse! With rising fear she felt around his neck, searching for where she thought vaguely the jugular was supposed to be. Again, no apparent pulse, only the cold clammy flesh of a fish, *a dead fish.* Trying not to panic, but starting to sob with fear, she leaned over him to see if she could detect any sign of breathing. She placed her face right up close to his mouth and nose, desperately hoping to feel a tiny puff of breath, anything, any sign of *life, oh for God's sake don't let him die!* She could feel nothing. She paused for an agonizing half-second, then, once again clarity came upon her mind and she realised that she should try mouth to mouth resuscitation. Hitching up her skirt, she got down and straddled the unconscious Buxtereide, pressing her sweet mouth against his pale ghost lips and blowing her life-sustaining air deep into his lungs. Her mind was racing and her heart was pounding in anticipation – her whole system was flooded with adrenalin as her animal instincts told her what to do. Would he live? Oh God, would he live? She blew her air into him again and again as she squeezed his hands, her body squirming against his in the animalistic fight for survival. If only he would show some sign of life, some sign of vitality, she thought in frenzied angst. What else could she do? She tried so hard to think clearly. That's it, she thought, loosen his clothing, you're always meant to loosen people's clothing when they pass out. Without hesitation she opened the first few buttons of his shirt and pulled off both his shoes. She looked at him. He still wasn't moving. Quickly she undid his belt and pulled his jeans down a little way. Oh God, Oh God, he's gonna die! She rushed into the kitchen, grabbed a glass of water and splashed it in his face. Most of it missed and went on the floor. She climbed back onto him and pressed her lips against his – if only he would show some sign of life! Her heart pounded and she shuddered and shook like a leaf on a tree. Suddenly she got a strong intuition that he *was* still alive after all – something hot was pressing against her labia, something hot and very full of life. Over the next few minutes Sheila and Arthur were very much alive – alive like the first woman and the first man were alive on their very first night together under the crystal stars.

GERLYVRYNN KERNOUAC / CORNISH GLOSSARY

amser – time, **an** – the, **antikwari** – antiquary, **atal** – mine-spoils, rubble, **Atlantek** – Atlantic, **a-vorow** – tomorrow, **ayr** – air, **bal** – mine, **bardhonieth** – poetry, **bengaljiow** – bungalows, **bibyn-bubyn** – shrimp, **boba** – small calf, **bounds** – tin-bounds, territory claimed by a miner for mineral extraction, **Breten Vyghan** – 'Little Britain', Brittany, **Brythonek** – Brittonic Celtic, British, **bucca** – autochthonous deity, **bullhorn** – snail, **bywek** – lively, **bywekheans-tredanek** – magneto-animation, **bywnans** – life, **carn** – tor, **cheeld** – (dialect) child, **churra-nos** – nightjar, **da** – good, **diwros** – bicycle, **dorek** – earthy, **down** – deep, **downvor** – deep sea, **dowr** – water, **drenek** – thorny, **du** – black, **Dyw genough why** – God be with you, **ebrenn** – sky, **edhen** – bird, **eglos** – church, **elowek** – elm-grove, **elowenn** – elm-trees, **erghlaw** – sleet, **eskern** – bones, **eur** – hour, **euthvil** – monster, **eyles** – sundew, a carnivorous plant, **fougou** – an ancient Cornish subterranean stone structure, **Gernuak** – Cornish, **glas** – green, blue, grey, **glasrudh** – purple, **glaw** – rain, **glyb** – wet, **goelann** – gull, **golow** – light, **golowji** – lighthouse, **golowyjyon** – radiance, **gorhan** – enchantment, **gorhengeugh** – distant ancestor, **gorthkryjyans** – heresy, **growanek** – granitic, granite outcrop, **guillan** – gull, **gwighenn** – periwinkle, **gwin** – wine, **gwydh** – trees, **gwynjak** – windy, **gwynk** – wink, **gwyr** – green, **ha** – and, **hager** – ugly, **hal** – moor, **harth** – bark, woof, **howl** – sun, **howlak** – sunny, **howldrehevel** – sunrise, **howlsedhes** – sunset, **howlyek** – sunny, **hudel** – magical, illusory, **hunros** – dream, vision, **hweskerenn** – insects, **hwystra** – whisper, **hwyth** – a blast of wind or puff of breath, **hwytha** – to puff or blast, **idhyowek** – coated in ivy, **jynn** – engine, **jynn-amontya** – computer, **jynn-ebrenn** – aeroplane, **jynn-edhen** – bird-machine, **jynnji** – engine-house, **,jynnjyow** – engine-houses, **jynn-keber** – beam-engine, **jynn-skrifa** – typewriter, **jynnweyth**

– engineering, **karrak** – ship, **karrek** – stone, **Keltek** – Celtic, **Kernewek** – Cornish, **Kernewes** – Cornish woman, **Kernow** – Cornwall, Cornishman, **Kernuak** – Cornish, **keser** – hail, **keynvor** – ocean, **kigliw** – flesh-coloured, **kober** – copper, **kollel-lesa** – octopus, **komol** – cloud, **kommolek** – cloudy, **korev** – beer, **korf** – body, **korf eskern** – skeleton, **korflann** – burying-ground, **kornek** – horned, **koth** – old, ancient, **kramvil** – reptile, **krogen** – shell, **krogenek** – shell-bearing, encarapaced, **krowji** – one-roomed cottage, **kruskynn** – beer-jug, **kwallok** – large personage, **kwilkyn** – frog, **ky** – dog, **kysten** – box, **legest** – lobster, **lemmyn** – now, **liwyow** – paints, **loerek** – moonstruck, **losowegi** – vegetable-garden, **lowarnek** – foxy, **lugern** – lantern, **lughes** – lightning, **lughesenn** – flash of lightning, **lugern-bysk** – luminous fish, deep-sea angler, **lynn** – lake, pond, **lyw** – colour, **mabyar** – chick, **magor** – a ruin, **medhow** – drunk, **melek** – honeyed, **meynek** – rocky, **mengleudh** – quarry, **meur** – great, **mis** – month, **moenek** – mineral, **an mor** – the sea, **mor** – sea, **mordros** – sound of the surf, **mordryk** – low tide, **morek** – maritime, **morgath** – skate, **morgi** – dogfish, **morgowles, morgowlenn** – jellyfish, **morgroenek** – blenny, **morhogh** – dolphin, porpoise, **morrab** – sea-board, **morsarf** – seasnake, **morvil** – whale, **morvran** – cormorant, **morvugh** – walrus, **newlak** – foggy, misty, **niwl** – mist, fog, **niwllaw** – mizzle, **niwlek** – misty, foggy, **niwlenn** – fog-bank, **niwlgorn** – foghorn, **ober** – work, **ober da** – good work, **ojyon** – ox, **oll** – all, **oulys** – owl, **owrek** – golden, **palores** – chough, **parc** – field, **pasti** – pasty, **pedrevan** – lizard, **peeth** – well (for water), **pen** – head, headland etc., **pigell** – pickaxe, turf-hoe, **pinenn** – pine, **piskie** – one of the little people, **pluvak** – pillow, **pluvek** – pillow, **pol** – pool, pit, **pol kroenogow** – toad-pool, **pons** – bridge, **porth** – port, **prysk** – bush, **pympbys** – starfish, **pyskador** – fisherman, **pysky** – the little fella, **pyw** – who, **rabmen** – gravel of decayed granite, **rannvor** – an area of sea, **rudhek** – robin, **sans** – sacred, holy, **sarf** – snake, **sarfek** – serpentine, **skawennow-gwragh** – sycamore trees, **skeulyow** – ladders, **skeusek** – shadowy, **skochfordh** –

alley, **skovenn** – tin-rich ground, **skrawik** – black-headed gull, **skrifer** – writer, author, **skubyon** – sweepings, **slynk** – slippery, **Sowsnek** – English, **splennyjyon** – brightness, luminosity, **spriggan** – a mischievous mythological figure, **sten** – tin, **stennor** – tinner, miner, **stifek** – squid, **sylli** – eel, **tay** – tea, **tekka** – more beautiful, finer, **tekter** – beauty, **tewlwolow** – twilight, dusk, **tewlyjyon** – darkness, **tir** – land, country, territory, **tonnek** – wavy, turbulent, **tonnhys** – wavelength, **transyek** – ecstatic, **tredanek** – electric, **tren** – train, **ty** – you, **tykki-Dyw** – butterfly, **uthek** – eldritch, monstrous, **vean** – little, **visgey** – pick, **vlewek** – hairy, **vyghan** – little, **vounder** also **bownder** – lane, **wartha** – higher, **wheal** – mine, **wondrys** – wondrous, **yarji** – hen-house, **ynkleudhva** – graveyard, **yw** – is.

A Word About Cornish

The Cornish language or *Kernewek* has evolved from the Brythonic Celtic tongue spoken in these islands long before the Romans came. There are four extant forms of Kernewek in use, reflecting different chronological phases in its development. In earlier forms certain words ended in 'ek', corresponding to the suffix 'ic' in English. In Late Cornish the 'ek' became 'ak'. I have used both, as my interest in the language is more poetic than formal.

Cornish is a language of mutants. You will find initial K's mutating into G's, depending on the final consonant of the preceding word. B's and M's can also turn into V's. There are several other such mutations at work. My aim here, in peppering the text with occasional words of Cornish, has been to share my delight in their archaic, venerable and Druidic beauty.

INTERNATIONAL GLOSSARY

(Includes archaic forms of English)

Abbreviations for languages used in the glossary:

AG. – Ancient Greek, AN. – Anglo-Norman, Arab. – Arabic, Ch. – Chinese, Du. – Dutch, Egy. – Egyptian, F. – French, G. – German, Goth. – Gothic, Gk. – Greek, Ir. – Irish, It. – Italian, Jam. – Jamaican Patois, Jap. – Japanese, L. – Latin, MDu. – Middle Dutch, ME. – Middle English, Me. – Melanesian, MHG. – Middle High German, MLG. – Middle Low German, Nor. – Norwegian, OE. – Old English, OF. – Old French, OHG. – Old High German, ON. – Old Norse, OS. – Old Saxon, OSl. – Old Slavonic, Pers. – Persian, Pl. – Polish, Pt. – Portuguese, Ro. – Romanian, Rus. – Russian, Skt. – Sanskrit, Sp. – Spanish, Tib. – Tibetan, W. – Welsh.

aer – Ir. air, **aigéan** – Ir. ocean, **aimsir** – Ir. time, अमृत – **amrita** – Skt. nectar of immortality, Ἀγγλικός – **Anglikos** – Gk. English, **anguis** – L. snake, ανθρωποφάγια – **anthropophagia** – AG. the eating of human flesh, απειρον – **apeiron** – AG. the fundamental substance from which all appearances arise, अरूपलोक – **Arupa Loka** – Skt. the Formless Realm, ἀστακός – **astakos** – Gk. lobster, αστραλόγοι – **astralogoi** – AG. tin ingots, असुरलोक – **Asura Loka** – Skt. Realm of the Jealous Gods, **aur** – W. gold, αὔριον – **avrion** – Gk. tomorrow, **awyr** – W. air, **bloodclat** – Jam. blood cloth, **bolb** – Ir. caterpillar, **bothán** – Ir. hut, **bothóg** – Ir. hut, **brúidiúil** – Ir. brutal, **butterfliege** – G. butterfly, **buttorflëoge** – OE. butterfly, **cachtas** – Ir. cactus, **caelestis** – L. of the sky, heavenly, **canbhás** – Ir. canvas, **canwyll yr ysbryd** – W. spirit-candles, St.Elmo's fire, **carraigín** – Ir. moss, **catyrpel** – AN. caterpillar, **celtchair dhichlethi** – Ir. cloak of darkness or fog, **ceo druidechta** – Ir. druid's fog, 茶花 – **chahua** – Ch. tea-flower, **chatapelose** – OF. caterpillar, 氣 – **chi** – Ch. life-force, **chloicheán** – Ir. prawn, χρυσοῦς –

chrysous – Gk. golden, **cimwch** – W. lobster, **Cornovaglia** – It. Cornwall, **Cornwealas** – OE. the Cornish people, κόσμος – **cosmos** – Gk. world, people, **cregynbysg** – W. shellfish, **crosóg mhara** – Ir. starfish, **cysglyd** – W. sleepy, **deedys** – ME. deeds, **den horned hval** – Nor. the horned whale, **dracului** – Ro. devil, **drithligh** – Ir. gleam, glint, glow, **druid** – Ir. starling, ευχαριστήριον – **efcaristirion** – AG. thank-offering, ἐκκλησία – **ekklisia** – Gk. church, εἴδωλον – **eidolon** – Gk. idol, ενθουσιασμός – **enthousiasmos** – Gk. enthusiasm, ευδαιμονία – **evdaemonia** – Gk. in good spirits, **faoileán an cladach** – Ir. gull of the shore, **féileacán** – Ir. butterfly, **fête de belles eaux** – F. play of beautiful waters, **fflap** – W. flap, **fflapio** – W. flapping, **fföedigaeth** – W. flight, **flēogan** – OE. fly, **fljúga** – ON. fly, **flōdus** – Goth. flood, **fluot** – OHG. flood, **Gaeltacht** – Ir. a predominantly Irish-speaking district, **genau** – W. mouth, **gewæterian** – OE. to water, η γλάρος – **y glaros** – Gk. gull, **gliomach** – Ir. lobster, **glöyn byw** – W. butterfly, live coal, **gloywder** – W. brightness, **gofalu** – W. mind, **golau** – W. light, **goud** – Du. gold, **grette** – ME. great, **grotte mantelmew** – Du. greater black-backed gull, **gwdihŵ** – W. owl, **gwirionyn** – W. greenhorn, **gwrthun** – W. repugnant, **gwylan** – W. seagull, **gylden** – OE. golden, གཟུགས་མེད་པའི་ཁམས་ – **gzugs med pa'i khams** – Tib. the Formless Realm, **Y Hen Ben Dafad** – W. Old Sheep's Head, **horrēsco** – L. to dread, **horrendum** – L. horrible, **Horus** – Egy. god of light, **hröc** – OE. rook, **hrókr** – ON. rook, **hruoch** – OHG. rook, 怪獣 – **kaiju** – Jap. strange beast, κασσίτερος – **kassiteros** – AG. tin, **kastam** – Me. custom, tradition, κεφάλη – **kefali** – Gk. head, κύον – **kion** – AG. dog, कोटि – **koti** – Skt. a vast number, Κρόνος – **Kronos** – AG. father of Zeus, κρύσταλλον – **krystallon** – Gk. crystal, λαβύρινθος – **labyrinthos** – Gk. labyrinth, **lacerta** – L. lizard, a sea-fish, **leictreachas** – Ir. electricity, **lēoht** – OE. light, Λέθε – **Lethe** – Gk. the river of forgetfulness, λευκό – **levko** – Gk. white, **licht** – Du., G. light, **llewyrch** – W. brightness, radiance, **llithro** – W. slip, slide, glide, **lūmen** – L. light, **lūx** – L. light, μαρμαρύγη – **marmareegy** – AG. glittering, twinkling, **μαρμαρεος – marmareos** – AG. shining like marble, **μαρμαρογληφειον – marmaroglypheion** – AG. marble workshop, **meeuw** – Du. gull, **μεγαλογνομον – megalognomon** – AG. noble-minded, **μεις** – meis – AG. (Æolic dialect) month, **mentis** – L. mind, **mergus** – L. diver, **μετέορος – meteoros** – Gk. up in the air, **μεθώ – metho** – Gk. to get drunk, **An Mhuir Cheilteach** – Ir. The Celtic Sea, **miroirs** – F. mirrors, **muireitleán** – Ir. seaplane, **μουσική – musikee** – Gk. music, **mwswgl** – W. moss, **μυστηριώδης – mysteriodis** – Gk. mysterious, dark, नाग **– naga** – Skt. snake-deity, **nebuloso** – Pt. cloudy, **η νυκτερίδα – y nichterida** – Gk. bat, **nifwl** – W. mist, fog, nebula, **niwlog** – W. foggy, misty, **nudden** – W. mist, fog, **ochtapas** – Ir. octopus, **όλος – olos** – Gk. all, **η ομίχλη – y omichly** – Gk. fog, mist, **η όνειρο – y oneiro** – Gk. dream, vision, **η ώρα – y ora** – Gk. hour, **órga** – Ir. golden, **ορναπετιον – ornapetion** – AG. little bird, **ορνιθαρκος – ornitharkos** – AG. ruler of birds, **ορνιθομανια – ornithomania** – AG. bird-madness, extravagant fondness for birds, **ορνιθοσκοπος – ornithoskopos** – AG. an observer of birds, augur, **η ουρανός – y ouranos** – Gk. sky, **perhorridus** – L. horrid, **Φλεγέθων – Phlegethon** – AG. mythological river of fire in the underworld, **phrenēticus** – L. delirious, **φώς – phos** – Gk. light, **Prydeinig** – W. Brittanic, British, **η ψυχή μου – y psychy mou** – Gk. my mind, my soul, **ποίος – poios** – Gk. who, **roec** – MDu. rook, **roek** – Du. rook, **rök** – MLG. rook, **rukk** – Arab.– Pers. rook, **saill éalaigh – shillelagh** – Ir. a blackthorn bludgeon, 幽霊 **– sakana** – Jap. fish, **sandhyabasha** – Skt. the paradoxical 'twilight language' of yogis, **Sasanach** – Ir. English, 悟り **– Satori** – Jap. sudden Enlightenment, **sčëo** – OE. sky, **scuwo** – OHG. sky, **σεληνιάκος – selyniakos** – AG. from the moon, **serpere** – L. creep, crawl, **serpiente** – Sp. snake, **Set** – Egy. god associated with darkness, **silbir** – OHG. silver, **silobar** – OS. silver, **siolfor** – OE. silver, **siorc** – Ir. shark, **skio** – OS. sky, **skiuja** – ON. sky, cloud, **σκουπίζω – skoupeezo** – Gk. to sweep, **skuggwa** – Goth. mirror, **skuggi** – ON. shadow, **slefren fôr** – W. jelly-fish, **sliogán** – Ir. shell, **smugairle–róin** – Ir. jelly-

fish, **smúitiúil** – Ir. gloomy, overcast, **solas** – Ir. light,
solas na gealaí – Ir. moonlight, **specksioneer** – Du. chief-
harpooneer, fat-cutter, στερεά – **sterea** – Gk. mainland,
道 – **tao** – Ch. the way of nature, ἡ τέχνη –**y techny** – Gk.
art, skill, τενεκές – **tenekes** – Gk. tin, Ἡ θάλασσα εἶναι
βαθύς – **Y thalassa einai vathys** – Gk. the sea is deep,
θαλασσοκράτωρ – **thalassokrator** – AG. ruler of the seas,
tintreach – Ir. lightning, **Tír na nÓg** – Ir. blessed isle of
eternal youth, **trasna na dtonnta** – Ir. across the waves,
trychfil – W. insect, つの の ある くじら – **tsuno no aru
kujira** – Jap. the horned whale, **twyllwr** – W. deceiver,
animalcule, **uchelfryd** – W. high-minded, **uisciúil** – Ir.
watery, **ulchabhán** – Ir. owl, **vespertilionidae** – L. a large
taxonomic family of insectivorous bats, βίος – **vios** – Gk.
life, **vliegen** – Du. fly, **vloed** – Du. flood, Вода́ – **voda** –
Rus., OSl. water, **vriti** – Skt. thought-wave, **wagian** – OE.
wave, **walfisch** – G. whale, **watar** – OS. water, **waterich**
– MLG. watery, **watins** – Goth. water, **wawe** – ME. wave,
wąż – Pl. snake, **waze** – ME. wave, **wazzar** – OHG. water,
wezzern – MHG. water, ἠλεκτρισμός – **ylektrismos** – Gk.
electrism, ἥλιος – **ylios** – AG., Gk. sun, **ynfydrwydd** – W.
folly, **ysgwïer** – W. squire, 幽霊 – **yūrei** – Jap. ghost, 座
禅 – **zazen** – Jap. meditation, ζωγράφος – **zografos** – Gk.
artist, painter of life.

Further Reading

DEPARTMENT OF CORRUPTION
Darren Rainey: The Untold Story.
By Harold Hempstead
2019 – Crusader Publishing.

Printed in Great Britain
by Amazon